Sri Lanka

Joe Cummings

Teresa Cannon, Mark Elliott, Ryan Ver Berkmoes

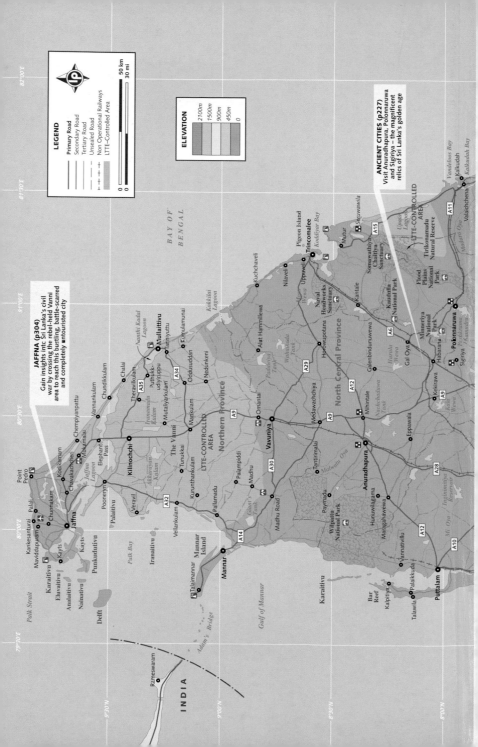

LEGEND

- Primary Road
- Secondary Road
- Tertiary Road
- Unsealed Road
- Non Operational Railways
- LTTE-Controlled Area

50 km
30 mi

ELEVATION

- 2100m
- 1500m
- 900m
- 450m
- 0

JAFFNA (p304)
Gain insights into Sri Lanka's civil war by crossing the rebel-held Vanni area to reach this bustling, battle-scarred and completely untouristed city

ANCIENT CITIES (p227)
Visit Anuradhapura, Polonnaruwa and Sigiriya – the magnificent relics of Sri Lanka's golden age

BAY OF BENGAL

Point Pedro
Kankesanturai
Palali
Chunnakam
Jaffna
Kayts
Karaitivu
Eluvaitivu
Analativu
Nainativu
Delft
Punkudutivu
Kankesanturai
Mavittapuram
Chavakachcheri
Kodikamam
Nilaveli
Elephant Pass
Pooneryn
Palativu
Veravil
Vellankulam
Iranaitivu
Talaimannar
Mannar Island
Mannar
Palaikkuda
Talawila
Kalpitiya
Bar Reef
Puttalam
Vannativillu
Karaitivu
Paymadu
Wilpattu National Park
Madhu Road
Palampiddi
Madhu
Pallamadu
Kurunthankulam
Tunukkai
Kilinochchi
Chempiyanpattu
Vannarkulam
Chundikulam
Chalai
Theravilkulam
Puthukkudiyiruppu
Mutaliyarkulam
Mullaittivu
Vattapalai
Kokkulamunai
Nedunkeni
Oddusuddan
Matkulam
Omantai
Vavuniya
Tantirimalai
Anuradhapura
Hunuwilagama
Maragahawewa
Kekirawa
Kalkudah
Kokkilai Lagoon
Kuchchaveli
Trincomalee
Uppuveli
Pigeon Island
Mutur
Sampur
Sampalawila
Somawathiya Chaitiya Sanctuary
Naval Headworks Sanctuary
Kantale
Kaudulla National Park
Kandulla
Minneriya National Park
Habarana
Sigiriya
Polonnaruwa
Gal Oya
Galenbindunuwewa
Mihintale
Medawachchiya
Horowpotana
Alat Hammillewa
Kantale
Flood Plains National Park
Tirikonamadu Natural Reserve
Valaichchenai
Eppawala

North Central Province
Northern Province
The Vanni
LTTE-CONTROLLED AREA
LTTE-CONTROLLED AREA

BAY OF BENGAL
Jaffna Lagoon
Nandi Kadal Lagoon
Chalai Lagoon
Palk Strait
Polk Bay
Gulf of Mannar
Adam's Bridge
Rameswaram

INDIA

A9
A32
A14
A35
A34
A30
A29
A12
A9
A6
A11
A15
A9
A28
A10
A12

Kodiyar Bay
Vandeloos Bay
Kalkudah Bay
Upaar Lagoon

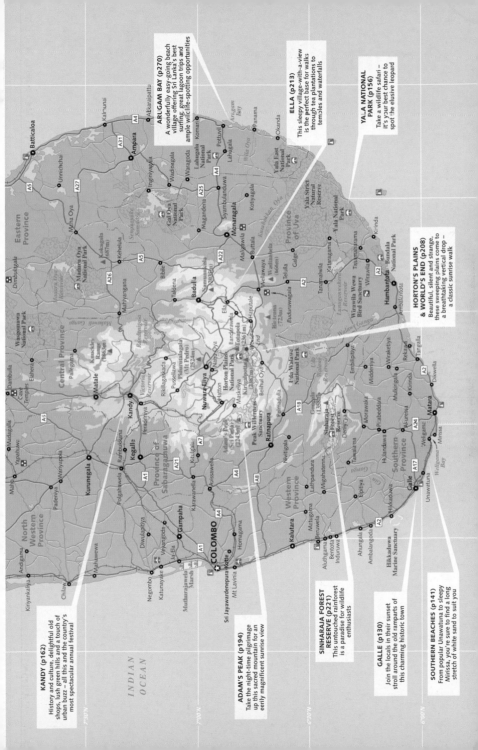

KANDY (p162)
History and culture, delightful old shops, lush green hills and a touch of urban buzz – all this and the country's most spectacular annual festival

ARUGAM BAY (p270)
A wonderfully easy-going beach village offering Sri Lanka's best surfing, great lagoon trips and ample wildlife-spotting opportunities

ELLA (p213)
This sleepy village-with-a-view is the perfect base for walks through tea plantations to temples and waterfalls

YALA NATIONAL PARK (p156)
Take a wildlife safari – it's your best chance to spot the elusive leopard

HORTON'S PLAINS & WORLD'S END (p208)
Beautiful, silent and strange, these sweeping plains come to a breathtaking vertical drop – a classic sunrise walk

ADAM'S PEAK (p194)
Take the night-time pilgrimage up this sacred mountain for an eerily magnificent sunrise view

SINHARAJA FOREST RESERVE (p221)
This untouched rainforest is a paradise for wildlife enthusiasts

GALLE (p130)
Join the locals in their sunset stroll around the old ramparts of this charming historic town

SOUTHERN BEACHES (p141)
From popular Unawatuna to sleepy Mirissa, you're sure to find a long stretch of white sand to suit you

Destination Sri Lanka

Long before Marco Polo declared Sri Lanka the finest island of its size, this beautiful country found its way into Greek, Egyptian and Indian literature, where it was known as Taprobane, Serendib or Lanka.

The Sri Lanka mystique perseveres, unfurling before the senses as soon you arrive: the heavy warm air, the rich green foliage, the luxuriant swirls of the Sinhalese alphabet, the multicoloured Buddhist flags, and the kaleidoscope of saris, fruits, jewellery and spices on display in the markets.

For a small island, Sri Lanka offers a truly amazing variety of attractions. The coasts are studded with palm-lined beaches, some with world-class surf breaks. The Kandyan dances, elephant-led festival processions or any temple on *poya* (full moon) days will delight culture hounds, as will viewing the stone-cut Buddhist art and towering dagobas (stupas) of the ancient capitals of Anuradhapura and Polonnaruwa. Head into the Hill Country and the heat of the plains will fade away to reveal rolling green hills carpeted with tea plantations. Or take a 4WD trek through well-preserved national parks inhabited by elephants, leopards, monkeys, crocodiles and rare birdlife.

These pleasures come with welcoming people, good food, lovely places to stay and reasonably low costs – all wrapped up in a compact, easy-to-navigate package.

A Tamil-Sinhalese truce in 2001 spurred an unprecedented growth in tourism that was nearly halted by the December 2004 Indian Ocean tsunami. As resilient Sri Lanka bounces back from the tragedy, tourism is recovering quickly – so now is the time to go.

ANDERS BLOMQVIST

Festivals & Celebrations

Make the pilgrimage up illuminated pathways to the summit of Adam's Peak (Sri Pada; p194)

Marvel at the spectacle of the Kandy Esala Perahera (p167)

Admire Kandyan dance (p50), considered to be Sri Lanka's national dance

OTHER HIGHLIGHTS

- Join the celebrations as pilgrims complete their 45-day cross-island trek in time for the Kataragama festival (p159)
- Observe the massive, elephant procession of Colombo's Navam Perahera (p93)
- Experience Vel (p93), a festival celebrating the Hindu war god Murugan (Skanda), in Colombo

Ancient Cities

Pay your respects at Mihintale (p255), the birth-place of Buddhism in Sri Lanka

Admire the intricately carved guardstones at the ruins of Polonnnaruwa (p237)

Weave through the prayer flags surrounding Anuradhapura's Sri Maha Bodhi (p250)

OTHER HIGHLIGHTS

- Ascend the rock fortress of Sigiriya (p233), admiring the gardens, frescoes and mirror wall as you climb
- Gaze at the beautiful Gal Vihara Buddha images (p241) at Polonnaruwa

Explore the Unesco World Heritage–listed
cave temples at Dambulla (p231)

Wander around Anuradhapura's
Thuparama Dagoba (p250)

Study the reclining Buddha statues at Dambulla (p231)

Beaches

DALLAS STRIBLEY

Bargain with fruit sellers on Hikkaduwa beach (p123)

OTHER HIGHLIGHTS

■ Chill out in laid-back Arugam Bay (p270), on Sri Lanka's east coast

■ Find your own hidden patch of paradise in the many coves and beaches between Galle (p130) and Tangalla (p149)

■ Surf the powerful left-hand break at uncrowded Midigama (p142)

Contemplate the totems on the beach at Unawatuna (p138)

ANDERS BLOMQVIST

Dive, body-surf or just relax in Unawatuna's lovely surrounds (p138)

DALLAS STRIBLEY

Catch a glimpse of local life on the beach at Hikkaduwa (p123)

Let your worries fade away in idyllic Tangalla (p149)

Admire the sunset from one of Hikkaduwa's beachside cafés (p123)

Hill Country

Visit the dagoba at Adam's Peak (Sri Pada; p194) after making the predawn ascent

Join the pilgrims at the Temple of the Sacred Tooth Relic (p166) in Kandy

OTHER HIGHLIGHTS

- Hike or cycle between dagobas, waterfalls and tea estates in the lush countryside around Ella (p216)
- Live the life of a colonial tea planter in a luxurious tea-estate bungalow near Dikoya (p196)

Enjoy the stunning views in the hills around Nuwara Eliya (p199)

Nature & Adventure

Come face to face with inquisitive elephants in
Uda Walawe National Park (p220)

Stare down wild buffalo in Yala
National Park (p156)

Hike to World's End in Horton Plains
National Park (p205)

OTHER HIGHLIGHTS

- Explore Unesco World Heritage–listed wilderness at Sinharaja Forest Reserve (p221)
- Shoot the rapids on a white-water rafting trip down the Kelaniya Ganga (p197), near Kitulgala
- Add to your bird-spotting tally at Bundala National Park (p152)

Shopping

ANDREW BURKE

Browse Colombo's (p102) galleries-cum-handicraft-shops for covetable collectables

CHRISTINE NIVEN

Admire the craftsmanship of the mask carvers in Ambalangoda (p122)

Splurge in one (or several) of the gem showrooms in Ratnapura (p224)

MICHAEL AW

OTHER HIGHLIGHTS

- Wander through the antique shops in Galle's colonial Fort district (p137)
- Plan a new wardrobe with Sri Lanka's beautiful hand-woven textiles; try Colombo (p102) for a wide range of shops

Contents

Regional Map Contents

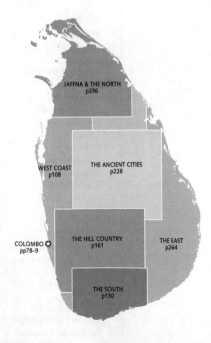

JAFFNA & THE NORTH
p296

WEST COAST
p108

THE ANCIENT CITIES
p228

COLOMBO
pp78–9

THE HILL COUNTRY
p161

THE EAST
p264

THE SOUTH
p130

The Authors

JOE CUMMINGS
Coordinating Author, Colombo, The Hill Country, The Ancient Cities

Born to a military family in New Orleans, Joe was raised in many different locations. Shortly after earning a master's degree in South and Southeast Asian studies, he began updating Lonely Planet's Asia guides. Joe first travelled to Sri Lanka in the 1990s to research dagobas (stupas) for Lonely Planet's *Buddhist Stupas in Asia: The Shape of Perfection*. When he's not on the road, Joe lives next to the ruins of a 15th-century stupa in Chiang Mai.

Joe also wrote the Destination Sri Lanka, Getting Started, Itineraries, Environment, Directory and Transport chapters for this book.

My Favourite Trip

I'm happiest wandering around the Hill Country, talking to tea-factory managers about the local teas, and hiking in the hills around Dikoya (p196) and Hatton (p196). When driving from Colombo I'll stop off in Kitulgala (p197) for a swim in the Kelaniya Ganga (Kelaniya River) and lunch at Plantation Hotel. For another perspective on the local geography I'll hop on a train from Nanu Oya, the train station for Nuwara Eliya (p199), to Badulla (p217), with a side trip to Ella (p213) or Haputale (p208), my favourite towns for kicking back and catching up on some reading. If I have enough time I'll make a longer detour from Ella to indulge my passion for Buddhist art at the undervisited Budurwagala (p219), where Sri Lanka's tallest Buddha was carved into solid rock over a thousand years ago.

MARK ELLIOTT
The East, Jaffna & the North

When Mark first visited Sri Lanka in 1987, the country was racked by violence: a bus station had been bombed and the JVP was running amok. However, meditation retreats, cycling through tea estates, and the ever-welcoming population created a contrasting sense of calm. Fascinated ever since by this troubled paradise, Mark jumped at the chance to visit the 'other Ceylon' – the Tamil and Muslim areas that had been effectively off limits for decades.

Between researching travel guides on places that range from Iran to Indonesia to Greenland, Mark lives in blissfully quiet suburban Belgium with his beloved wife Danielle, who found him at a Turkmenistan camel market.

RYAN VER BERKMOES
West Coast, The South

Ryan was first beguiled by Sri Lanka when he read Paul Theroux' *The Great Railway Bazaar* as a teenager. Visiting after the tsunami he was overwhelmed by the devastation, even after a long career covering wars, disasters and other calamities. Ryan was happy to return to Sri Lanka to research this book as it allowed him to catch up with many people he'd met months earlier.

Born in the beach town of Santa Cruz, California, Ryan worked as journalist for many years before turning his attentions to Lonely Planet. He's written scores of guidebooks on places ranging from the Arctic to the equator. He definitely prefers sand between his toes to ice.

CONTRIBUTING AUTHORS

Teresa Cannon had been stuck for too many years in a suffocating bureaucracy when she felt compelled to escape to the rarefied environment of the Himalayas. There she trekked within century-old rhododendron forests and traversed the peaks and passes of the western moonscape region. She succumbed to the gentle and continuing welcome of 'Namaste', which flowed like a mantra throughout the landscape. She wanted to stay. But visas run out and bank balances diminish.

Her love of travel led her overseas several times, especially to Asia. She has written numerous nonfiction works about Sri Lanka, and this is her sixth project for Lonely Planet. For this book she wrote the Snapshot, History, Culture and Food & Drink chapters.

Dr Trish Batchelor is a general practitioner and travel medicine specialist who works at the CIWEC Clinic in Kathmandu, Nepal, as well as being a Medical Advisor to the Travel Doctor New Zealand clinics. Trish teaches travel medicine through the University of Otago, and is interested in underwater and high-altitude medicine, and in the impact of tourism on host countries. She has travelled extensively through Southeast and East Asia and particularly loves high-altitude trekking in the Himalayas.

Getting Started

While Sri Lanka is arguably the easiest place in which to travel in all of South Asia, a little advance knowledge and planning will go a long way towards making your trip more fulfilling, hassle-free and fun.

For the most part you'll find that larger towns – and even smaller towns with a highly developed tourism infrastructure – cater to all travel budgets. In places more off the beaten track, especially those in the Hill Country and in the North, luxury accommodation and high-standard dining are relatively hard to find, but the offerings are usually sufficient for all but the most finicky travellers.

The 12 August 2005 assassination of then foreign minister Lakshman Kadirgamar by a suspected Tiger sniper heightened political tensions and security concerns, and violence again broke out in April 2006. Added caution may therefore be needed when travelling in the North and Northeast; check the situation before leaving.

WHEN TO GO

Climatically speaking, the driest (and best) seasons in Sri Lanka are from December to March for the west coast, the south coast and the Hill Country, and from April to September for the ancient cities region and the east coast.

December through March are also the months when most foreign tourists visit, the majority of them escaping the European winter. During the Christmas to New Year holiday season, in particular, accommodation anywhere on the island can be tight due to the huge influx of foreign visitors.

See Climate Charts (p322) for more information.

July/August is the time of the Kandy Esala Perahera, the 10-day festival honouring the sacred tooth relic of the Buddha, and also the time for the Kataragama festival in the South. In both towns accommodation just before, during and immediately after the festivals is very difficult to come by, and rates usually double or treble. Be sure to book rooms well in advance.

Sri Lanka's climate means that it is always the 'right' beach season somewhere on the coast. The weather doesn't follow strict rules, though – it often seems to be raining where it should be sunny, and sunny where it should be raining. Rainfall tends to be emphatic – streets can become flooded in what seems like only minutes.

Out-of-season travel has its advantages – not only do the crowds go away but many air fares and accommodation prices drop right down. Nor does it rain *all* the time during the low season.

DON'T LEAVE HOME WITHOUT...

- Packing a light suitcase – clothes can be readily bought in Colombo, Galle and Kandy.
- Bringing along a windbreaker, parka or jumper for cool nights in the Hill Country.
- Checking with a Sri Lankan embassy or consulate to see whether you need a visa (p333).
- Confirming what medicines or inoculations you need (p344).
- Checking government travel advisories for general security issues (p323).
- Building up your chilli tolerance.

TOP FIVES

Our Favourite Festivals

Virtually every week of the calendar there's a festival somewhere in Sri Lanka. The following list is our pick of the ones worth seeking out, but see p326 and throughout the book for other festivities and events.

- Navam Perahera, Colombo, February (p93)
- Vesak Poya, throughout Sri Lanka, May (p326)
- Kandy Esala Perahera, Kandy, July/August (p167)
- Kataragama, Kataragama, July/August (p159)
- Vel, Colombo and Jaffna, July/August (p93 and p327)

Best National Parks

With over a dozen national parks and forest reserves in Sri Lanka, you could spend months exploring them all. To help you prioritise, here's our list of favourites based on accessibility, scenic beauty and presence of wildlife.

- Yala National Park (p156)
- Uda Walawe National Park (p220)
- Minneriya National Park (p245)
- Sinharaja Forest Reserve (p221)
- Wilpattu National Park (p109)

Lie-Back-&-Relax Beaches

Sri Lanka's east, south and lower west coasts are lined with bays, coves and beaches. Most structures along these coastlines experienced at least some damage during the 2004 tsunami, and many buildings were completely destroyed. The beaches themselves suffered least of all, although some are still being cleaned of rubble. Here are our favourite sand-and-sea getaways.

- Kalkudah Bay Beach (p284)
- Nilaveli (**p292**)
- Unawatuna (**p138**)
- Mirissa (**p144**)
- Induruwa (**p118**)

Hill Country Scenery

Sri Lanka's Hill Country covers a huge chunk of the island and almost all of it could be classed as 'scenic'. For truly dramatic views, however, these are the top five.

- Adam's Peak (p194)
- Ella (p213)
- Horton Plains National Park (p205)
- Knuckles Range (p194)
- Haputale (p208)

COSTS & MONEY

Sri Lanka is more expensive than South Asia or India, but costs are still reasonable. Double rooms with bathroom, mosquito net and fan cost about Rs 500 to 1000, while an international-class hotel room may run to Rs 10,000 or more. Most high-end hotels quote room rates in US dollars but accept either dollars or rupees; some also quote in euros.

The cost of accommodation in the touristy areas drops considerably out of season. Expect to pay triple the usual accommodation price in Kandy during the Kandy Esala Perahera and in Nuwara Eliya during the April high season. Because of the lack of tourism infrastructure following long years of war, room rates are also much higher than the norm in Jaffna.

Local food is reasonably priced, though it's about three times more expensive in guesthouses than in local restaurants; it's around Rs 300 to

---

FOREIGNER PRICE

There's no way to put this diplomatically: many Sri Lankans try to overcharge tourists for anything from a bus fare to a gemstone necklace. Most hotels have one price for foreigners and another for Sri Lankans, and government departments continue to arbitrarily ramp up foreigners' entry fees, which are often 10 or 20 times higher those paid by locals.

---

450 at a guesthouse, or as little as Rs 100 at a local restaurant. Dinner at the country's better restaurants costs around Rs 2000 per person.

At national parks, entry fees plus (often mandatory) 4WD hire and other extras add up to something between Rs 2000 and 5100.

Public transport is cheap. Hiring a car (or van) and driver for a day costs Rs 2500 to 4500 depending on the condition of the vehicle.

TRAVEL LITERATURE

Considering what a colourful and culturally rich destination Sri Lanka is, it's surprising that more writers haven't left a trail of ink chronicling their experiences here.

Running in the Family, by Michael Ondaatje, recounts a return to Sri Lanka in the 1970s after growing up here in the '40s and '50s, and captures many of the little oddities that make up life in Sri Lanka.

RL Brohier records his travels around Sri Lanka as a British surveyor in the first half of the 20th century in *Seeing Ceylon* and *Discovering Ceylon.* Both books capture lots of intriguing historical titbits that are hard to find elsewhere (even if they're not 100% accurate, on occasion).

A Village in the Jungle, by Leonard Woolf, is a rather depressing account of local life in Hambantota. First published in 1913, it is in the same vein as George Orwell's *Burmese Days.*

An engaging, insightful story, *July,* by Karen Roberts, tells of two neighbours – one Sinhalese, one Tamil – growing up together.

Elmo Jayawardena picked up literary prizes with *Sam's Story*, the tale of an illiterate village boy working in Colombo. It's a simple, often light-hearted read that deftly deals with the wider problems of society.

INTERNET RESOURCES

Ever since the World Wide Web grew out of the old US military Arpanet it has become a rich resource for travellers. You can research your trip, hunt down bargain air fares, book hotels, check weather conditions or chat with locals and other travellers about the best places to visit (or avoid!).

A good place to start your explorations is the Lonely Planet website (www.lonelyplanet.com). Here you'll find everything from the Thorn Tree Forum, where you can ask questions and dispense advice, to World-Guide, which provides useful predeparture information.

Other good websites:

Art Sri Lanka (www.artsrilanka.org) A gateway to Sri Lankan high culture, this site covers art history, contemporary art and religious art from various traditions.

Crazy Lanka (www.crazylanka.com) A cheerfully silly website with lots of parodies of current news events. There are lots of in-jokes but some amusing gems nonetheless.

InfoLanka (www.infolanka.com) This has links to recipes, chat lines, news, organisations, nature, entertainment and more.

Sri Lanka Tourist Board (www.srilankatourism.org) The official tourism site, with tons of information. It's a good starting point.

Sri Lanka Web Server (www.lanka.net) This has lots of links to Sri Lankan newspaper and magazine websites.

HOW MUCH?

Air-con bus Colombo–Anuradhapura Rs 210

2nd-class train Ella–Badulla Rs 12

Lunch packet (fish) Rs 75

Cultural Triangle round ticket Rs 4120

Guesthouse double room (Kandy) Rs 1800

See also the Lonely Planet Index, inside front cover.

Itineraries

CLASSIC ROUTES

CAPITAL, COAST & HILLS
Three to Four Weeks

Start with a few days in **Colombo** (p77), sampling some of Sri Lanka's finest cuisine and becoming acquainted with the city's vibrant Buddhist temples. Then hug the coast south, stopping off in **Bentota** (p118) and **Hikkaduwa** (p123) to relax on palm-lined stretches of sand. Next comes **Galle** (p130) and its 17th-century Dutch city-within-a-fort – a must-see if you're interested in the island's colonial history.

From here head inland to **Horton Plains National Park** (p205). Make a side trip to the 240m-high **Bambarakanda Falls** (p208), Sri Lanka's tallest waterfall, and spend a night or two in the misty ex–colonial hill station of **Nuwara Eliya** (p199), which earns another superlative as the island's highest city.

Continue north to Kandy, stopping off for a tour and tea tasting at **Labookellie Tea Factory** (p198) and, if you haven't had enough waterfall action, **Ramboda Falls** (p198). **Kandy** (p162), Sri Lanka's main cultural centre, will delight you with its mild climate, colonial architecture, frequent festivals and sumptuous Buddhist temples. From Kandy it's a relatively easy ride back to Colombo.

This 547km route takes you through Sri Lanka's highlights in under a month. Lie on palm-fringed beaches, check out colonial architecture and stare at stunning Hill Country views. Just watch out for the traffic on the Colombo–Galle road.

NEGOMBO & ANCIENT CITIES   Two to Three Weeks

As the seaside city of **Negombo** (p111) is closer than Colombo to Bandara-naike International Airport, it's easy enough to kick off your trip here and skip the capital altogether. Whether or not you decide to spend a night or more in the historic city, Negombo is worth a stop to see the historic remains of the Dutch fort, charming Catholic churches, bustling fish markets and the rich marshlands of **Muthurajawela** (p116).

From Negombo head northeast to North Central Province and into the Cultural Triangle, so-called because it contains three of the country's most significant historical sites; it's also a centre for handicrafts. Your first stop should be **Dambulla** (p231), a series of cave shrines painted with vivid Buddhist murals. From here it's a short jaunt to **Sigiriya** (p233), a 200m-tall rock outcrop that was once either a palace or a monastery (depending on whom you believe) and is truly one of the island's most amazing sights.

Further northeast the former royal capital of **Polonnaruwa** (p237) offers an inspiring collection of Buddhist sculptures and monastery ruins dating back nearly a thousand years. In the vicinity, **Minneriya National Park** (p245) is well worth a visit to view the largest herds of wild elephants in Sri Lanka, along with plenty of other wildlife.

Next head northwest to **Anuradhapura** (p247), an even older ex-royal capital with an extensive, well-preserved historical park containing the ruins of monasteries, palaces and dagobas (stupas). Stop off in **Mihintale** (p255), just 13km east of Anuradhapura, to view its small yet impressive collection of monastic ruins and dagobas, and the remains of an ancient Ayurvedic hospital.

This 347km trip through Sri Lanka's ancient cities region takes in centuries-old dagobas (stupas), monasteries, sculptures and palaces as it rolls across hilly green plains and farming valleys and meanders through arid, East Africa–like topography.

ROADS LESS TRAVELLED

EAST BY NORTH   Three Weeks

The North and East region feels like a different country. And in some places, controlled by the Liberation Tigers of Tamil Eelam (LTTE), it effectively is. Just check the security situation before starting the trip.

Start off in the delightfully laid-back surf beach of **Arugam Bay** (p270), then head to **Ampara** (p276) to see elephants parade past the Peace Pagoda as though timetabled. Having peeked into dramatic **Gal Oya National Park** (p278) from atop Inginyagala Dam, continue north to the intriguing city of **Batticaloa** (p281) and have a splash at the deserted beach at **Kalkudah** (p284).

Get your first taste of Tamil Tiger territory by taking the post bus on to **Mutur** (p286), from where ferries cross Koddiyar Bay into **Trincomalee** (p286), arguably the world's finest deep-water harbour. Recover from the bumpy trip with an agreeably restorative stay at the beaches of **Uppuveli** (p290) or **Nilaveli** (p292), and do a little diving at **Pigeon Island** (p292).

Then, cut inland to **Vavuniya** (p298) to prepare for an eye-opening journey to Jaffna. This takes you through what the locals call Tamil Eelam (Tamil Precious Land), the unrecognised but de facto country run by the Tamil Tigers, complete with its own police force, banks and even a kind of visa (available at the border). You'll eventually arrive in **Jaffna** (p304), an intriguing city of contradictions: officially government controlled yet loyal to the Tigers, welcoming and friendly but with a heavy military presence, lushly comfortable in its suburbs despite a bombed-out centre.

Rumble through humid coastal plains, relax on deserted beaches and transit Tamil Eelam, Sri Lanka's country-within-a-country – this 553km route promises a trip that's as thought-provoking as it is attractive.

TEA, TREKS & TEMPLES   Two to Three Weeks

Start your trip across the heart of Sri Lanka in **Kitulgala** (p197), a gateway for rafting and canoeing the Kelaniya Ganga (Kelaniya River) as well as for jungle hikes. From here it's a relatively short hop to misty **Hatton**, **Dikoya** and **Maskeliya** (p196), three small towns centred on one of the top tea-growing regions in Sri Lanka. Aside from getting to taste incredibly fragrant single-estate teas in arguably the most scenic part of the Hill Country, you can bed down in luxurious ex–colonial tea planters' bungalows, explore winding, village-to-village trails or make the strenuous predawn climb up Adam's Peak (Sri Pada).

Head across to **Ella** (p213) and **Haputale** (p208), on the Hill Country's precipitous eastern side, for more hiking, stupendous views and small-town ambience. If an encounter with Buddhism is on your agenda, head northeast to **Bibile** (p279) and attend a meditation retreat at Nagala Viharaya. Then, travel southeast to **Monaragala** (p267), the jumping-off point for one of Sri Lanka's most atmospheric ancient Buddhist sites, **Maligawila** (p266), which is home to an 11m-tall standing Buddha that's at least a thousand years old.

Cut back west to Wellawaya to take in **Buduruwagala** (p219), a set of seven colossal figures – including the tallest Buddha in the country – carved into the side of a rock cliff.

From Wellawaya descend to the coastal plains of **Kataragama** (p157), the terminus of the Pada Yatra, a pilgrimage that begins at the other end of the island. One of Sri Lanka's oldest and most venerated dagobas can be found in nearby **Tissamaharama** (p153), which is also a convenient entry point for forays into **Yala National Park** (p156).

Expect hairpin curves and breathtaking views for much of this 304km outing; hike, taste some of Sri Lanka's tea and view ancient Buddhist sites before dropping down to the coastal plains.

TAILORED TRIPS

UNESCO WORLD HERITAGE SITES

Anuradhapura (p247) The remains of monasteries, palaces and other monuments that belonged to a royal capital that flourished for 1300 years.

Dambulla Cave Temples (p231) A pilgrimage site for over 2000 years, the five caves here contain important Buddhist murals and statuary.

Galle (p130) Founded by the Portuguese in the 16th century, this is the most well-preserved example of a fortified colonial city in South Asia.

Kandy (p162) This city served as the last capital of the Sinhala kings before Sri Lanka's occupation by the British. The Temple of the Sacred Tooth Relic (Sri Dalada Maligawa) is one of the world's most famous Buddhist pilgrimage sites.

Polonnaruwa (p237) The compact ruins of Sri Lanka's second royal capital include both Buddhist and Brahmanic monuments, along with the impressive 12th-century city works created by King Parakramabahu I.

Sigiriya (p233) The remains of King Kassapa's palace (or possibly a monastery) grace the slopes and summit of a 370m granite outcrop.

Sinharaja Forest Reserve (p221) Sri Lanka's most famous protected area harbours its last major tropical rainforest.

OUTDOORS & WILDLIFE

Adam's Peak (Sri Pada; p194) Sacred to Christians, Muslims, Hindus and Buddhists, this mountain rewards a predawn climb with far-reaching views and a glimpse of the peak's triangular shadow on the clouds below.

Arugam Bay (p270) The bay and nearby beaches and mangroves provide ample opportunities for surfing, cycling, hiking and nature-watching.

Gal Oya National Park (p278) Explore the rolling grasslands and evergreen forests surrounding Senanayake Samudra, a large tank (artificial lake) frequented by elephants and other wildlife.

Horton Plains National Park (p205) Precipitous views, mossy stunted forests, unique plant and animal life, and a cool climate guarantee an especially good romp in the outdoors.

Minneriya National Park (p245) Minneriya is renowned for its large herds of wild elephants, but there's plenty of other wildlife roaming the park as well, including toque macaques, sambar deer, cormorants and painted storks.

Sinharaja Forest Reserve (p221) This Unesco World Heritage Site is home to over half of the island's endemic species of mammals and butterflies; there's also a high number of endemic birds and many rare insects and amphibians.

Wilpattu National Park (p109) This park, famous for its jungle, leopards, sloth bears and birds, reopened in 2003 after years of war.

Yala East National Park (p275) This park contains the Kumana mangrove swamp and birdlife in spectacular numbers.

LUSH LIFE

Amanwella (Mawella; p149) This is perhaps the island's ultimate romantic beach getaway – you'll never want to leave your oceanfront suite, with its private swimming pool and terrace.

Galle Face Regency (Colombo; p95) Stay in the Royal Oceanic Grand Spa suite and bubble your troubles away in either of the two Jacuzzis – one inside the mammoth bathroom, the other on the ocean-facing teak veranda.

Galle Fort Hotel (Galle; p135) Whether or not you overnight in one of the rooms in the thick-walled former 17th-century Dutch merchant's home, do treat yourself to the stellar Asian fusion cuisine served here.

Taprobane Island (Weligama; p144) You can't get much more lush than renting your own stunning island, complete with six staff, an infinity pool and an open-air, five-bedroom five-bathroom villa that was built by Count de Mauny-Talvande in 1922, and later owned by writer Paul Bowles.

Tea Trails (Dikoya; p197) Live a tea-estate manager's life – without the accounting problems – in your choice of four colonial bungalows dating from the late 19th and early 20th centuries. The house chef cooks perfect Sri Lankan and Western dishes and, since the place is owned by the Dilmah tea company, you'll drink nothing but the best teas in the Hill Country.

BEACH OUT

Aluthgama, Bentota & Induruwa (p118) These great beaches come with lively markets, a turtle hatchery, and the placid waters of the Bentota Ganga.

Arugam Bay (p270) The island's surf mecca has a laid-back, friendly village and a mellow party scene.

Hikkaduwa (p123) Take scuba-diving lessons, body-surf the gentle waves or simply do what most visitors do – wander from one beach café to the next while the sun sets over the Indian Ocean.

Kalkudah Bay (p284) You'll probably share this long, palm-lined beach with only an occasional fishing crew.

Midigama (p142) If you brave the coral and rocks, you and your board will love the powerful left break.

Mirissa (p144) If sleepy is what you want, Mirissa can oblige, but there's also excellent snorkelling and surfing.

Tangalla (p149) The pretty bays and long stretches of white sand offer a private corner for everyone. Medaketiya Beach is beautiful, but watch the currents.

Unawatuna (p138) The South's most popular beach has it all: good swimming, creamy white sands, a dearth of traffic, and laid-back beach cafés.

Uppuveli & Nilaveli ((p290 & p292) Whale- and dolphin-watching tours and dive trips to nearby islets are the main activities here, along with relaxing and frolicking in the turquoise waters.

Snapshot

When the noted scientist and writer Sir Arthur C Clarke made his home in Sri Lanka in 1956, he did so claiming that Sri Lanka was the best place in the world from which to view the universe. Looking out from Sri Lanka to the universe is a fascinating activity; looking within Sri Lanka, one finds a universe in itself.

Sri Lanka may be tiny but it defies a tiny definition. It is, as the travel brochures proclaim, a resplendent paradise. It is jungle, green and fertile. It is also desert, red and arid. Just as its landscape is diverse, so too are its people and its stories – stories overlaid with centuries of varied narrative and meaning.

Sri Lankans love their country and have a strong desire for others to love their country as well. They'll besiege you with talk of Sri Lanka's beauty, history and scenic sites. It's a delight to hear and is one of the quickest ways of gleaning the lowdown on places to see and stay. Mind you, the yarn and the reality may be hugely different, but you'll no doubt experience something you'd not intended. Living up to the country's name (the word serendipity is derived from its earlier title, Serendib), Sri Lanka is a happy series of unexpected discoveries, whether it's people or places, old or new.

Relationships and connections are important to Sri Lankans. Men will reminisce for hours about the old school tie, the fallout from the 1981 South African cricket tour or the last mass elephant capture in the 1950s. If they weren't there, they've heard the stories and are capable of passing them on as if they'd had a prime part in the action. And while recollecting their own schooldays, plans for the next generation's schooling are determined with much deliberation. Education is highly regarded in Sri Lanka.

Rice and hoppers (bowl-shaped pancakes) are not just food for feast; they're also food for thought. According to many, today's commercial rice has shrunk in taste and variety – all the more reason to have a paddy of one's own.

'Peace' is a catchword here, but in practice it's never quite caught on. Most Sri Lankans wish for a country where harmony reigns, life is secure and prosperity flourishes. But the country has a long history of conflict, and the majority Sinhalese and minority Tamils have been involved in an on-and-off civil war for 25 years (p35). As Norwegian negotiators attempt to bring the parties together in some semblance of a peace process (p37), old questions repeat themselves. Will there ever be peace? How and when will it come? Is the cost of compromise too high? Is the cost of no compromise too high?

Between talk of peace and cricket comes talk of prices – rising too much and too quickly.

For the moneyed, there's the problem of servants: the difficulties in hiring good ones, compounded by the monthly holidays on *poya* (full moon) days, when there are no servants at all. And the wealthy still find the veranda a haven for slow drinks and happy chatter, but this can be easily disrupted by a guest – perhaps a factory manager – trying to keep staff in line by yelling directions down his mobile phone.

For the less moneyed, it's life much as their ancestors knew it. Some are servants to the wealthy while others cultivate the land or fish the sea. Some leave the conviviality of the village to toil at the factory, hoping to

FAST FACTS

Population: 19.9 million

Population density per sq km: Colombo 2500 people, dry zone less than 50.

Life expectancy: female 75, male 70

Adult literacy: female 90%, male 95%

Year women received the right to vote: 1931

Tsunami 2004: 30,000 lives lost, over 1 million people left homeless

Emigration due to civil unrest: 1 million people since 1983

Internally displaced people: Almost 1 million (362,000 due to civil unrest, 555,000 due to the tsunami)

GDP per capita: US$4300 (USA: US$41,800)

improve the economic circumstances of their families back home. Others serve and clean in the tourist industry. And a few beset the traveller with 'worthy' schemes (aka scams) to enhance their meagre earnings.

Like many other countries, Sri Lanka has a range of views on its original people, now known as the Veddahs (p43). Some historical texts describe them as spirit people who could morph from human to animal, at will – a 'useful' assessment of nonexistence and therefore a nonconcern. Today, only few people identify as indigenous. Their actual numbers are not known but they are certainly diminishing, perhaps because they have assimilated into the majority groups, perhaps because the struggle for land and identity are just too much.

Of all Sri Lankans, Kandyans retain a special status, borne of centuries of resistance to invading powers (p31). Even non-Kandyans can be noble for a day – at many a wedding the bridal party don Kandyan ceremonial garb and drummers in traditional dress beat ancient rhythms.

Perhaps it's the *peraheras* (processions) that best embody the complexities of this small nation. Drummers, fire walkers, dancers and elaborately adorned elephants parade in a fusion of ancient and modern. Like the nation itself, the *perahera* is intricate, fragile and contradictory. Where else will you see a sequin-adorned elephant carrying relics of the Buddha along a white cloth that is ceremoniously laid before it, followed by a truck with a generator to power the neon sponsorship signs on the elephant's back? This is current-day Sri Lanka.

Arthur C Clarke is right, of course. Sri Lanka is a fine place from which to view the universe. For the traveller, making even the smallest sense of the universe that is Sri Lanka is indeed a privilege and an adventure – one guaranteed to include many serendipitous encounters.

History

PREHISTORY

Legend and history are deeply intertwined in the early accounts of Sri Lanka: did the Buddha leave his footprint on Adam's Peak (Sri Pada) while visiting the island that lay halfway to paradise? Or was it Adam who left his footprint embedded in the rock while taking a last look at Eden? Was the chain of islands linking Sri Lanka to India the same chain that Rama crossed to rescue his wife Sita from the clutches of Rawana, king of Lanka, in the epic Ramayana?

It is probable that the Ramayana has some fragile basis in reality, for Sri Lanka's history recounts many invasions from southern India. Perhaps some early invasion provided the elements of the story of Rama and Sita, recounted throughout Asia.

Whatever the legends, the reality is that Sri Lanka's original inhabitants, the Veddahs (Wanniyala-aetto), were hunter-gatherers who subsisted on the island's natural bounty. Much about their origins is unclear. However, anthropologists generally believe that Sri Lanka's original inhabitants are descendants from the people of the late Stone Age and may have existed on the island since 16,000 BC. The first Sinhalese, originally from North India, arrived in Sri Lanka around the 5th or 6th century BC. Traders and fisherfolk from South India who visited Sri Lanka during the late centuries BC also made the island their permanent home. The intermingling of the new arrivals produced a harmonious multicultural society – a state that, unfortunately, did not continue in the centuries that followed.

The early Sinhalese are credited with the invention of the pit valve, an ingenious irrigation device that contributed to their successful early settlement in Sri Lanka.

THE RISE & FALL OF ANURADHAPURA

According to Sinhalese accounts it was crime and banishment that led to their settlement in Sri Lanka in the 5th or 6th century BC. Vijaya, son of a North Indian king, was ousted from his title and kingdom due to his acts of assault and robbery. With a contingent of 700 men, the *sinha* (lion) prince was set adrift on the high seas in dilapidated ships, to face his destiny – punishment by death. But destiny took a different turn and as they travelled south, Vijaya and his men were blessed by the

---

WHAT'S IN A NAME?

Changing the country's name from Ceylon to Sri Lanka in 1972 caused considerable confusion for foreigners. However, for the Sinhalese it has always been known as Lanka and, for the Tamils as Ilankai; the Ramayana, too, describes the abduction of Sita by the king of Lanka. But the island has been known by many other names. The Romans knew the island as Taprobane and Muslim traders talked of Serendib, which means 'Island of Jewels'. The word Serendib became the root of the word 'serendipity' – the art of making happy and unexpected discoveries. The Portuguese somehow twisted Sinhala-dvipa (Island of the Sinhalese) into Ceilão. In turn, the Dutch altered this to Ceylan and the British to Ceylon. In 1972 'Lanka' was restored, with the addition of 'Sri', a respectful title. In the 1980s pedants pushed for the spelling of 'Shri Lanka', but 'Sri Lanka' now seems entrenched.

TIMELINE

Prior to 6th century BC	6th–5th century BC
Island is inhabited by the Veddahs (Wanniyala-aetto)	Sinhalese come from northern India to settle in Sri Lanka

Buddha and (as accounts would have it) came to land on the west coast of Sri Lanka on the very day that the Buddha attained enlightenment. Vijaya and his men settled around Anuradhapura, forming the basis of a Sinhalese kingdom that developed there in the 4th century BC. Later, the Sinhalese kingdom of Ruhunu was established in the southwest but Anuradhapura remained the stronger kingdom. Early settlement took place mainly along rivers, as the aridity of the north was not conducive to human settlement and the cultivation of crops. No doubt banishment and the need for survival can be great motivators: Vijaya and his descendants demonstrated impressive resourcefulness. To overcome the challenges of climate they constructed water channels and reservoirs (known locally as tanks) – great feats of engineering and mathematics. Such inventiveness enabled the early settlements to develop and prosper.

The bodhi tree in Anuradhapura has a 2000-year history of human care and custody, making it the world's oldest tree of this kind.

In the 3rd century BC the Indian emperor Ashoka sent his son Mahinda and his daughter Sangamitta to the island to spread the Buddha's teachings. Mahinda soon converted the Anuradhapuran king Devanampiyatissa, an event that is tremendously significant to the Sinhalese as it deeply influenced their customs, created a sense of national identity and, by developing scriptures and commentary, instituted a literary tradition. The mountain at Mihintale (p255) marks the spot where the conversion is said to have occurred. Today 1840 steps lead up the mountain to the site – it's a popular pilgrimage place, especially on the June *poya* (full moon), the reputed anniversary of the king's conversion.

Sangamitta brought to Sri Lanka a cutting of the Bodhi Tree under which the Buddha attained enlightenment. She planted this in Anuradhapura, where it still survives today, garlanded with prayer flags and lights (p250). Other bodhi trees, grown from cuttings of the Anuradhapuran tree, now spread their branches beside many of the island's temples.

With the conversion of the king to Buddhism strong ties were established between Sri Lankan royalty and Buddhist religious orders. Later, these ties strengthened as kings, grateful for monastic support, provided living quarters, tanks and produce to the monasteries. A symbiotic political economy between religion and state became consolidated. When the Sinhalese king Valagambahu fled from South Indian invaders he was given safe haven by monks who resided in the cave structures at Dambulla. When he regained his position in about 90 BC he expressed his gratitude by developing a huge cave-temple complex (p231). Since that time it has been a centre of Buddhist practice.

www.lankalibrary.com is broad in scope but sometimes short on facts! Read it in conjunction with other material to form your own view on anything Sri Lankan.

Buddhism underwent a major development when the teachings, previously conveyed orally, were documented in writing. Sri Lankan monks played a significant role in the documentation process, when, at the Aluvihara monastery (p229) in the 1st century BC, they began in-depth commentaries on the teachings. Their work forms the major part of the classical literature of the Theravada (doctrine of the elders) school of Buddhism (p44). It was in Sri Lanka that the Theravada school developed, later spreading to Buddhist countries in Southeast Asia. Even today, Buddhists of the Theravada school in Myanmar, Thailand and other countries look to Sri Lanka for spiritual leadership and interpretation of the scriptures.

Another event that served to intensify Buddhism in Sri Lanka was the arrival of the tooth relic (of the Buddha) at Anuradhapura in AD 371 (see

4th century BC	Late centuries BC
The kingdom of Anuradhapura is formed	South Indians make Sri Lanka their permanent home

p166). It gained prominence not only as a religious symbol but also as a symbol of sovereignty – it was believed that whoever held custody of the relic had the right to rule the island. Modern-day presidents, prime ministers and governments see it as their duty to protect the relic and the rituals that surround it. It now lies in the Temple of the Sacred Tooth Relic (Sri Dalada Maligawa) in Kandy.

For a controversial account of Sigiriya, see former archaeologist Raja De Silva's *Sigiriya and its Significance*, which argues against earlier views about the site.

In AD 473, King Kasyapa assumed the throne by engineering the death of his father and the exile of his elder brother, Mugalan. Kasyapa's skills were not limited to eliminating relatives – he also recognised a good piece of real estate and was a dab hand at property development. His reign saw the construction of the spectacular rock fortress of Sigiriya (p233), with its intricate water systems, ornate gardens and frescoed palaces. However, the exiled Mugalan, incensed by his ousting, returned to Sri Lanka with an army of Indian mercenaries. Mugalan defeated Kasyapa and reclaimed the throne, but he established a perilous precedent. To retain power, future Sinhalese kings found themselves beholden to Indian mercenaries. Centuries of interference and disorder followed with repeated invasions and takeovers of Anuradhapura by South Indian kingdoms, and self-defeating entanglements in South Indian affairs by Anuradhapura's rulers.

Anuradhapura was pummelled many times but rebuilding was possible through *rajakariya*, the system of free labour for the king. This free labour provided the resources to restore buildings, tanks and irrigation systems, as well as to plant, cultivate and harvest crops.

Finally in 11th century AD, Vijayabahu I, weary of the continual cycle of conflict, destruction and renovation, abandoned Anuradhapura to make Polonnaruwa, further southeast, his capital.

THE KINGDOM OF POLONNARUWA

Polonnaruwa (p237) survived as a Sinhalese capital for more than two centuries – a period that provided a further two kings of note. Parakramabahu I (r 1153–86), nephew of Vijayabahu I, was not content simply to expel the South Indian Tamil Chola empire from Sri Lanka, but carried the fight to South India and even made a raid on Myanmar. Domestically he indulged in an orgy of building in the capital, and constructed many new tanks around the country. But his warring and architectural extravagances wore down the country's resources, and probably shortened Polonnaruwa's lifespan.

His successor, Nissanka Malla (r 1187–96), was the last king of Polonnaruwa to show interest in the wellbeing of the people and in the construction and maintenance of buildings and irrigation systems.

He was followed by a series of weak rulers who allowed the city to fall into disrepair. With the decay of the irrigation system, disease spread and, like Anuradhapura before it, Polonnaruwa was abandoned. The jungle reclaimed it within a few decades.

TAMIL KINGDOMS

During Polonnaruwa's decline the first Tamil kingdom established itself in Jaffna. Movements of people between India and Sri Lanka had been happening for centuries but from the 5th and 6th centuries AD resurgent Hindu Tamil empires such as the Chola, Pallava and Pandya repeatedly threatened the Buddhist Sinhalese rulers.

3rd century BC	4th century AD
Buddhism arrives in Sri Lanka	The tooth relic of the Buddha arrives in Sri Lanka

With the decline of the Sinhalese northern capitals and the ensuing Sinhalese migration south, a wide jungle buffer zone separated the northern, mostly coastal Tamil settlements and the southern, interior Sinhalese settlements. This jungle zone, called the Vanni, was sparsely inhabited by mixed Tamil-Sinhalese clans called the Vanniyars.

Initially the 'rulers' of Jaffna were possibly diplomatic missions from the early South Indian kingdoms. At other times Jaffna came under the sovereignty of the major South Indian centres of Madurai and Thanjavur. However, developing rivalry between Indian empires allowed Jaffna to gain autonomy. It became a trade centre, especially in spices and elephants from the Vanni region, and established weaving, dyeing and pearl-fishing industries. An important centre for art and literature developed at Nallur (near Jaffna) in the 15th century, and studies combining astrology and medicine provided health services to the population. But things changed with the arrival of the Portuguese in 1505.

EARLY MUSLIM LINKS

Muslim settlement in Sri Lanka developed from centuries of Arab trade. In Arabic the island was called Serendib, from *seren* (jewel) and *dwip* (island). Gems were a valued item of commerce, as were cinnamon, ivory and elephants. With the advent of Islam in the 7th century AD Arab traders arrived with their new faith. Some stayed and settled on the island and many Sri Lankan Muslims are proud that their ancestry can be dated from the time of the Prophet.

Muslim traders found favour with Sri Lankan kings, and relations were generally cordial. Early Muslim settlements took hold in the north at Jaffna and southwest at Galle, as well as on the eastern side of the island. However, with the arrival of the Portuguese many Muslims fled inland to flee persecution.

THE PORTUGUESE PERIOD

After Polonnaruwa, the centre of Sinhalese power shifted to the southwest of the island, and between 1253 and 1400 there were five different Sinhalese capitals. During this period Sri Lanka suffered attacks by Chinese and Malayans, as well as periodic incursions from South India. Finally, the Portuguese arrived in 1505.

By this time Sri Lanka had three main kingdoms: the Tamil kingdom of Jaffna, and Sinhalese kingdoms in Kandy and Kotte (near Colombo). Of the two Sinhalese kingdoms, Kotte was the more powerful. When Portuguese Lorenço de Almeida arrived in Colombo, he established friendly relations with King Bhuvanekabahu of Kotte and gained a Portuguese monopoly on the spice trade, which soon became very important in Europe.

Tamil-Portuguese relations were less cordial, especially when the colonial missionaries attempted to convert the local population to Catholicism. Infuriated by this, the Tamil king Sangily organised a massacre of the missionaries and their converts.

The different responses to the Portuguese – alliance from Kotte and hostility from Jaffna – made no difference to the end result: Portugal took over the entire coastal belt. However, the Portuguese were unable to

Want to understand more about people's names in Sri Lanka? It's all revealed at http://asiarecipe.com /srinames.html.

5th century AD	7th century AD
King Kasyapa constructs the fortress of Sigiriya	Muslim traders begin to settle in Sri Lanka

conquer the central highlands, and the kingdom at Kandy resisted several later Portuguese attempts at capture.

With the Portuguese came religious orders such as the Dominicans and Jesuits. Many of the Karava fishing communities on the west coast converted, but reluctance to assume the new faith was often met with massacres and the destruction of local temples. Buddhist priests and others fled to Kandy, whose role as a stronghold and haven endowed it with a special status on the island – one that was consolidated by later colonial failures to capture it. This status is still cherished today by many Sri Lankans, especially those from the high country.

The Portuguese tried to entice their compatriots to settle in Sri Lanka. Some did, intermarrying with locals, and their descendants form part of the small group known as European Burghers. The Portuguese also brought slaves from Africa who are today almost totally assimilated. Known as the Kaffirs, their contribution to Sri Lankan culture is evident in the *bailas* – folk tunes based on African rhythms.

THE DUTCH PERIOD

In 1602 the first Dutch ships arrived in Sri Lanka. Like the Arabs and Portuguese, the Dutch were keen to acquire trade, and they vied with the Portuguese for the lucrative Indian Ocean spices. For the Kandyan king, Rajasinha II, the Dutch presence provided an opportunity to rid Sri Lanka of the Portuguese. A treaty was duly signed, giving the Dutch a monopoly on the spice trade in return for Sri Lankan autonomy. This, however, only succeeded in substituting one European power for another. By 1658, 153 years after the first Portuguese contact, the Dutch had taken control of the coastal areas of the island. During their 140-year rule, the Dutch, like the Portuguese, made repeated unsuccessful attempts to bring Kandy under their control. And, just as the Portuguese had done, the Dutch encouraged their fellow citizens to reside in Sri Lanka. Their descendants, the Dutch Burghers, comprise a minority group in Sri Lanka today.

The Dutch were much more interested in trade and profits than were the Portuguese, and developed a canal system along the west coast to transport cinnamon and other crops. Roman-Dutch law, the legal system of the Dutch era, still forms part of Sri Lanka's legal canon.

THE BRITISH PERIOD

The British, concerned that they may be defeated in conflicts with the French in South India, and requiring a safe port in the area, began to consider the eastern Sri Lankan harbour of Trincomalee. The British ejected the Dutch in 1796, and in 1802 Sri Lanka became a crown colony. In 1815 the British won control of Kandy, thus becoming the first European power to rule the whole island. Three years later a unified administration for the island was set up.

The British conquest deeply unsettled many Sinhalese, who had long held the view that only the tooth relic custodians had the right to rule the land. Their apprehension was somewhat relieved when a senior monk removed the tooth relic from the Temple of the Sacred Tooth Relic (p166), thereby securing it (and the island's symbolic sovereignty) for the Sinhalese people.

During the British administration, Major Thomas Rogers is reputed to have killed 1400 elephants.

10th century AD

1505

In 1832 sweeping changes in property laws opened the doors to British settlers – at the expense of the Sinhalese, who in the eyes of the British did not have title to the land. Coffee was the main cash crop but when leaf blight virtually wiped it out in the 1870s the plantations were quickly switched over to tea or rubber.

The British, unable to persuade the Sinhalese to labour on the plantations, imported large numbers of Tamil workers from South India. Today these workers' descendants, totalling about 850,000 people (5% of the population), form the larger of the two main Tamil communities. About 700,000 of them still live and work on the estates.

The British influence lingers: the elite private schools with cricket grounds, the army cantonments and train stations, and the tea-estate bungalows, not to mention the English language. English was demoted from being the official language after independence, but the requirements of a globalised economy have helped bring it back into vogue.

Sir James Emerson Tennent's affable nature shines through in his honest and descriptive writing about 19th-century Sri Lanka, now serialised at www.lanka web.com/news/features /ceylon.html.

INDEPENDENCE

In the wake of Indian independence, Sri Lanka, or Ceylon as it was then known, became an independent member of the British Commonwealth in February 1948. The first independent government was formed by the United National Party (UNP), led by DS Senanayake. His main opponents were the northern and plantation Tamil parties, and the communists.

At first everything went smoothly. The economy remained strong and the government concentrated on strengthening social services and weakening the opposition. It certainly achieved the latter, as it disenfranchised the Hill Country Tamils by depriving them of citizenship. Eventually, deals in the 1960s and 1980s between Sri Lanka and India allowed some of the Hill Country Tamils to be 'repatriated' to India, while others were granted Sri Lankan citizenship.

DS Senanayake died in 1952 and was succeeded by his son, Dudley. An attempt a year later to raise the price of rice led to mass riots and Dudley's resignation. Sir John Kotelawala, his uncle, replaced him, and the UNP earned the nickname 'Uncle Nephew Party'. The UNP was easily defeated in the 1956 general election by the Mahajana Eksath Peramuna coalition, led by SWRD Bandaranaike.

THE BANDARANAIKES

The Bandaranaikes were a family of noble Kandyan descent who had converted to Anglicanism for a time in the 19th century, but who had returned to the Buddhist fold. The 1956 election coincided with the 2500th anniversary of the Buddha's enlightenment and an upsurge in Sinhalese pride, and SWRD Bandaranaike defeated the UNP primarily on nationalistic issues.

Nearly 10 years after independence, English remained the national language and the country continued to be ruled by an English-speaking, mainly Christian, elite. Many Sinhalese thought the elevation of their language to 'official' status would increase their power and job prospects.

Caught in the middle of this disagreement (English versus Sinhala, and Christian versus Buddhist) were the Tamils, whose mother tongue is

1658 | **1796**

Dutch colonial period begins | The British take over Sri Lanka's rule from the Dutch

Tamil. When Bandaranaike enacted the 'Sinhala only' law, Tamil protests were followed by violence and deaths on both sides.

The contemporary Sinhalese-Tamil difficulties date from this time. From the mid-1950s, when the economy slowed, competition for wealth and work – intensified by the expectations created by Sri Lanka's fine education system – exacerbated Sinhalese-Tamil jealousies. The main political parties, particularly when in opposition, played on the Sinhalese paranoia that their religion, language and culture could be swamped by Indians, who were thought to be the natural allies of the Tamils in Sri Lanka. The Tamils began to see themselves as a threatened minority, and pressed for a federal system of government with greater local autonomy in the North and the East, the main Tamil-populated areas.

William McGowan's *Only Man is Vile* is an incisive, unrelenting account of ethnic violence in Sri Lanka, penetrating deeply into its complexities.

Despite coming to power on Sinhalese chauvinism, Bandaranaike later began negotiating with Tamil leaders for a kind of federation – a decision that resulted in his assassination by a Buddhist monk in 1959. Despite this, Bandaranaike is still seen by many as a national hero who brought the government back to the common people.

In the 1960 general election the Sri Lanka Freedom Party (SLFP), led by SWRD Bandaranaike's widow, Sirimavo, swept to power. She was the first female prime minister in the world. Sirimavo pressed on with her husband's nationalisation policies, souring relations with the USA by taking over the Sri Lankan oil companies. Most of the remaining British tea planters left during this time. The economy weakened, and in the 1965 election Dudley Senanayake and the UNP scraped back into power. However, Senanyake's reluctance to turn back the clock on the SLFP's nationalisation program lost him much support and the UNP was massively defeated by the SLFP in the 1970 elections.

Soon after, Sirimavo Bandaranaike took the reins for the second time, a wave of unrest swept the Sinhalese heartland, feeding on a population boom and a generation of disaffected young men facing unemployment. In 1971 a Sinhalese Marxist insurrection broke out, led by a dropout from Moscow's Lumumba University, Rohana Wijeweera, under the banner of the Janatha Vimukthi Peramuna (JVP; People's Liberation Army). Its members, mostly students and young men, were quickly and ruthlessly eradicated by the army. Around 25,000 people died, but the JVP was later to regroup.

The revolt allowed the government to make sweeping changes, write a new constitution and create a new name for the country – Sri Lanka. The bureaucracy became politicised, and some say corruption became entrenched. Meanwhile, the economy continued to deteriorate and in the 1977 elections Sirimavo Bandaranaike and the SLFP (in its new guise as the United Left Front) went down in a stunning defeat at the hands of the UNP.

TAMIL UNREST

Meanwhile, two pieces of legislation increased Tamil concern. The first piece, passed in 1970, cut Tamil numbers in universities; previously, Tamils had won a relatively high proportion of university places. The second was the constitutional declaration that Buddhism had 'foremost place' in Sri Lanka and that it was the state's duty to 'protect and foster' Buddhism.

1815	1948
The British conquer Kandy, the first European colonial power to do so	Sri Lanka becomes an independent nation

Unrest grew among northern Tamils, and a state of emergency was imposed on their home regions for several years from 1971. The police and army that enforced the state of emergency included few Tamils (partly because of the 'Sinhala only' law) and therefore came to be seen by the Tamils as an enemy force.

In the mid-1970s some young Tamils began fighting for an independent Tamil state called Eelam (Precious Land). They included Velupillai Prabhakaran, who founded and still leads the Liberation Tigers of Tamil Eelam (LTTE), often referred to as the Tamil Tigers.

OPEN ECONOMY

Elected in 1977, the new UNP prime minister, JR Jayawardene, made an all-out effort to lure back foreign investment. He attempted to emulate Singapore's successful 'open economy', and his policies yielded some successes: unemployment was halved by 1983, Sri Lanka became self-sufficient in rice production in 1985, and expat Sri Lankans and tourists began bringing in foreign currency.

Jayawardene introduced a new constitution – Sri Lanka's third – in 1978, which conferred greatest power on the new post of president, to which he was elected by parliament.

In 1982 he was re-elected president in national polls (after amending his own constitution to bring the voting forward by two years) and then, in the same year, won a referendum to bypass the 1983 general election and leave the existing parliament in office until 1989. As usual there were allegations of electoral skulduggery.

ETHNIC VIOLENCE

Jayawardene promoted Tamil to the status of 'national language' for official work, but only in Tamil-majority areas. Clashes between Tamils and security forces developed into a pattern of killings, reprisals, reprisals for reprisals and so on. All too often the victims were civilians. The powder keg finally exploded in 1983, when an army patrol in the Jaffna region was ambushed and massacred by militant Tamils. For several days after, mobs of enraged Sinhalese set about killing Tamils and destroying their property. Between 400 and 2000 Tamils were killed and some areas with large Tamil populations – such as Colombo's Pettah district – were virtually levelled.

The government, the police and the army were either unable or unwilling to stop the violence. There had been small-scale ethnic riots in 1958, 1977 and 1981, but this was the worst and for many it marked the point of no return. Tens of thousands of Tamils fled to safer, Tamil-majority areas, while others left the country altogether; many Sinhalese moved from Jaffna and other Tamil-dominated areas.

Revenge and counter-revenge attacks grew into atrocities and large-scale massacres. The government was condemned for disappearances and acts of torture.

The area claimed by the Tamil militants for the independent state of Eelam covered Sri Lanka's Northern and Eastern Provinces – equal to about one-third of Sri Lanka's land area. Tamils comprised the majority in the Northern Province, but in eastern Sri Lanka Muslims, Sinhalese and Tamils were nearly equal in numbers.

Not an easy read but an important one, *When Memory Dies*, by A Sivanandan, is a tale of the ethnic crisis and its impact on one family over three generations.

1956	1970s
Protests and conflict break out after the 'Sinhala only' language law is passed	Formation of the Liberation Tigers of Tamil Eelam (LTTE)

The violence cost the economy dearly. Tourism slumped, the government spent crippling amounts on the defence forces, and foreign and local investment dried up.

INDIAN INTERVENTION

In 1987 government forces pushed the LTTE back into Jaffna. In an attempt to disarm the Tamil rebels and keep the peace in northern and eastern Sri Lanka, Jayawardene struck a deal with India for an Indian Peace Keeping Force (IPKF). A single provincial council would be elected to govern the region with substantial autonomy for a trial period.

Soon it became clear that the deal suited no-one. The LTTE complied initially before the Indians tried to isolate it by promoting and arming other Tamil rebel groups. Opposition to the Indians also came from the Sinhalese, the reviving JVP (below) and sections of the Sangha (the community of Buddhist monks). This led to sometimes-violent demonstrations.

Jayawardene was replaced as leader of the UNP by Ranasinghe Premadasa, the first leader from a common background. He promised to remove the Indian peacekeepers; when they withdrew in March 1990, they had lost more than 1000 lives in just three years. In June, however, the war between the LTTE and the Sri Lankan government began again. By the end of 1990, the LTTE held Jaffna and much of the North, although the East was largely back under government control.

RETURN OF THE JVP

The presence of the IPKF pushed the mood of young Sinhalese past boiling point. In 1987 the JVP launched its revolution with political murders and strikes, which were enforced through the use of death threats. With 16 years to study the failed 1971 revolt, the JVP, still led by Rohana Wijeweera, had prepared brilliantly. They were tightly organised, with recruits from students, monks, the unemployed, the police and the army. It attempted a Khmer Rouge–style takeover, aiming to capture the countryside and then isolate and pick off the cities.

By late 1988 the country was terrorised, the economy crippled and the government paralysed. The army struck back with a ruthless counter-insurgency campaign that still scars the country. Shadowy militias and army groups matched the JVP's underground warfare in brutality. They tracked down the JVP leadership one by one until Rohana Wijeweera was killed in November 1989. The rebellion subsided, but 30,000 to 60,000 people had died in the three-year insurrection.

Within a few years a new leadership brought the JVP into the political mainstream, and it now has seats in parliament and supports the current government and the president, Mahinda Rajapaske.

Anil's Ghost, by Booker Prize–winner Michael Ondaatje, is a haunting novel about turmoil and disappearances of late-20th-century Sri Lanka. The book has received much international commendation and some local condemnation.

WAR IN THE 1990s

In May 1991 Rajiv Gandhi was assassinated by an LTTE suicide bomber. It was generally assumed that Gandhi's assassination was in retaliation for his consent to Jayawardene's 1987 request for the IPKF. Soon after this, war between the Tamils and the Sinhalese intensified.

Although a high proportion of Tamils and Sinhalese longed for peace, extremists on both sides pressed on with war. President Premadasa was

1983	1987
Conflict and riots between Sinhalese and Tamils intensify	Indian Peace Keeping Force (IPKF) attempts to establish stability

assassinated at a May Day rally in 1993; the LTTE was suspected, but never claimed responsibility.

The following year, the People's Alliance (PA), a coalition of the main opposition SLFP and smaller parties, won the parliamentary elections. Its leader, Chandrika Bandaranaike Kumaratunga, the daughter of former leader Sirimavo Bandaranaike, won the presidential election and appointed her mother prime minister.

Although the PA had promised to end the civil war, the conflict continued in earnest, and Kumaratunga was targeted by a suicide bomber just days before the December 1999 presidential election. She was injured, losing sight in her right eye, but won the election. Curiously enough, the economy was showing signs of life during this period. Garment exports grew, growth ticked along at 5% to 6% a year between 1995 and 2000, and the ongoing war partly solved unemployment in the rural south.

In the October 2000 parliamentary elections President Kumaratunga's PA won a narrow victory. Sirimavo Bandaranaike, the president's mother and three-time prime minister of Sri Lanka, died shortly after casting her vote.

> At least one million land mines were laid during 1990s Sri Lankan hostilities. Efforts to clear the mines have meant that thousands of displaced people have been resettled.

ELUSIVE PEACE

In 2000 a Norwegian peace mission, led by Erik Solheim, brought the LTTE and the government to the negotiating table, but a cease-fire had to wait until after the elections of December 2001 – won by the UNP after the collapse of the short-lived PA government.

Ranil Wickremasinghe became prime minister. He and President Kumaratunga (both from different parties) circled each other warily. Under Wickremasinghe economic growth was strong at 6% per annum and peace talks appeared to progress. But in late 2003, while Wickremasinghe was in Washington meeting with George W Bush, Kumaratunga dissolved parliament (although it had a mandate to govern until 2007) and called for elections. By combining with the JVP, Kumaratunga formed a new party, the United People's Freedom Alliance, and in the subsequent elections defeated Wickremasinghe and his UNP.

Peace talks stumbled. Time and talk passed, and the situation became ever more fraught. Accusations of bias and injustice were hurled from all sides. In October 2003, the US listed the LTTE as a Foreign Terrorist Organisation (FTO). Some believed this to be a positive move; others saw it as an action that would isolate the LTTE, thereby causing further strain and conflict. In early 2004 a split in LTTE ranks pitched a new dynamic into the mix. Among killings, insecurity, accusations and ambiguities, the Norwegians went home in September 2004.

Almost all of Sri Lanka, including most of the Jaffna Peninsula, is now controlled by the Sri Lankan government. The LTTE controls a small area south of the peninsula and pockets in the east, but it still has claims on land in the Jaffna Peninsula and in the northwest and northeast of the island.

> John Richardson applies his long experience in international resources and relationships to produce his huge tome *Paradise Poisoned*. Important and timely, it investigates terrorism in Sri Lanka, with recommendations that can be applied globally.

TSUNAMI & BEYOND

An event beyond all predictions struck the island on 26 December 2004, affecting not only the peace process but the entire social fabric of Sri Lanka. As people celebrated the monthly *poya* festivities, the mighty

1987–90	2000
Janatha Vimukthi Peramuna (JVP) creates a rebellion in which 30,000 to 60,000 people die	Norwegian peace mission initiates peace talks between the government and the LTTE

waves of the tsunami cast their fury, killing 30,000 people and leaving many more injured, homeless and orphaned. Initially there was optimism that the nation would come together in the face of catastrophe, but the optimism soon faded into argument over aid distribution, reconstruction, and land tenure and ownership.

Meanwhile Kumaratunga, seeking to extend her presidential term, sought to have the constitution altered. However, her plans were thwarted by a Supreme Court ruling, which directed that presidential elections occur in 2005. Among the numerous contenders, two candidates were the most likely victors – the then prime minister, Mahinda Rajapaske, and the opposition leader, Ranil Wickremasinghe. With an LTTE boycott on voting, Rajapaske, supported by the JVP and the Jathika Hela Urumaya (a party of Buddhist monks), won by a narrow margin. The LTTE's motives for the boycott were unclear but their actions cost Wickremasinghe an expected 180,000 votes and the presidency, and, perhaps, the country a better chance at peace.

As president, Rajapaske pledged to replace the Norwegian peace negotiators with those from the UN and India; to renegotiate a cease-fire with the LTTE; to reject Tamil autonomy; and to refuse to share tsunami aid with the LTTE. Such policies did not auger well for future peace. Meanwhile, LTTE leader Prabhakaran insisted on a political settlement during 2006, and threatened to 'intensify' action if this did not occur. Within days of coming to power, Rajapaske reneged on his first undertaking and invited the Norwegians to continue their negotiations. But tensions were high and once again Sri Lanka was perched on a precipice. Killings, assaults, kidnappings and disappearances occurred on both sides, and commentators predicted the worst. As the first anniversary of the tsunami approached, world leaders, aid agencies and the global community pleaded with the government and the LTTE to stop the violence and return to the peace talks. Both parties agreed, and in February 2006 the Norwegians were able to help negotiate a statement that included commitments to a cease-fire and to further talks.

Tensions eased, and the country returned to the intricate process of creating peace. Yet in April 2006, interethnic violence once again threw Sri Lanka's future into doubt. For the sake of the island, its peoples and cultures, one hopes that the peace process can continue.

A candidate for the 2005 presidential elections sought to impress the electorate with a promise to import Indian cows to Sri Lanka.

2002	2004
Cease-fire begins	The waves of a tsunami hit Sri Lanka, taking 30,000 lives and leaving many more homeless

The Culture

THE NATIONAL PSYCHE

Visitors to Sri Lanka notice first the gentleness of the land and people. Life is leisurely. Time moves at a different pace. Rivers make an unhurried journey to the coast. And at the coast, waves gently lap the sands. Inland, white-domed dagobas (stupas) send their slim spires high into the skies. Wattle-and-daub homes and large mansions settle easily within the natural environment. People wander with flowers to temples. And throughout the island, people greet visitors with warmth and hospitality.

Markets may bustle. Bus stations may hustle. Yet the sway of sarong, sari or skirt preserves a pace that is slower and more refined. And the heat and humidity insist upon it.

Every so often, things are less gentle. Rivers swell, inundating the land and snatching lives. Tides rise, destroying everything in their path. Ethnic violence engulfs the people and more lives are lost and shattered.

Yet somehow Sri Lankans continue to overlay this chaos with gentleness. They exude a charismatic charm that is immediately alluring. For the visitor there is still the warmth of welcome. There is the waiter, barefoot and composed, delivering the king coconut to the traveller by the pool. There is the hand of assistance up the steep steps of Adam's Peak (Sri Pada) or Sigiriya. There is the invitation to share home-prepared rice and curry, or to attend a relative's monastic initiation.

This island nation has welcomed those from afar for millennia. Different faiths and ethnicities have mixed and married, yet clear distinctions exist. Each is proud, and rightly so, of its heritage. Yet in a nation where a single statement about an ancient event can shatter the harmony, history can have an electrifying currency.

Poverty exists beside luxury here, where servants tend their masters as they have done for centuries. The modern exists beside the ancient as the young park their 4WDs near rickshaw drivers, whose transport may be their only home.

But gentleness, especially for the visitor, persists.

Culture Shock! Sri Lanka by Robert Barlas and Nanda P Wanasundera gives travellers a confidence boost by offering a glimpse into the unknown and unfamiliar.

LIFESTYLE

Daily life for Sri Lankans depends very much on their position in society. Monks rise early to chant or meditate. Devotees make an early morning visit to the temple. Other Sri Lankans walk on the Galle Face Green or visit the gym. Tea pickers don their colourful clothes and hurry to the leaves. Servants prepare breakfast for the family. Stockbrokers and engineers are chauffeured to the office, farmers cultivate their land and stall holders arrange their *kadé* (street-side huts) with fruit and goodies.

Spice exports from Sri Lanka create Rs 5700 million (US$56 million) in revenue annually.

Sri Lankan Life

Traditional life in Sri Lanka centred on the *gamma* (village). This was a highly organised hub of activity, where each knew their role and how to fulfil it. Agriculture was the mainstay, with rice paddies dotting the landscape around the village. Buffalo, a source of rich curd, wallowed in ponds while poultry strutted their stuff beneath jackfruit, mango, banana and papaya trees. Some villages focused on particular products such as pots or masks, and still today you'll pass 'car-tyre-gamma' and 'cane-furniture-gamma', as well as delicious Cadjugama (Cashew-Nut Village), where you'll be hard pressed to resist the cashew sellers.

Modern Sri Lanka, on the other hand, is a fusion of old and new. Twin towers – tributes to trade – soar above shanty huts. Computers record stock-market results and machines cultivate land and cut timber. Yet, in some areas, only 3% of homes have water on tap and only half have electricity. Many people still live the traditional village life, albeit with a TV or motorbike.

The belief that Sri Lanka would become another Singapore has not eventuated. Modern buildings emerge, but their construction on marshland has the inevitable consequences of sewage blockages, flooding, and transport and pollution problems.

Each year the 800,000 Sri Lankans who work overseas (mainly in the Middle East) boost the economy by sending home US$1 billion.

Employment

Aid organisations advise potential volunteers that the Sri Lankan work ethic is different – it is unhurried. Yet this belies the fact that most Sri Lankans work long, hard hours.

Villagers traditionally had a strong sense of duty to family, community, monarch and monk. The *rajakariya* (labour for the king) ensured the achievement of massive projects such as temple building and tank construction. When a task was vast, such as harvesting the crops or threshing rice, it became a community task. Some people had agricultural or home duties, while others had more specific roles, such as astrologer, medicine man or toddy tapper. No doubt if astrological or medical counsel failed the toddy tapper came in handy! This idea of working for the common good persisted well into the 20th century, and even now public servants talk of performing *rajakariya* (although they do get paid).

There is no minimum wage in Sri Lanka. Instead, 38 boards determine basic wages for each industry.

Today graduates and teachers earning between Rs 3000 and 5000 per month bemoan the fact that garment workers may earn more than them, but at Rs 114 per day, garment workers need to work long hours to achieve such an income. Sri Lanka's strong jewellery trade and the high profits associated with it mean that jewellery cutters and polishers can receive from Rs 6000 to 10,000 per month.

It's clear that improved economic conditions have mostly benefited 20% of the population, who tend to reside around Colombo. The remaining 80% have seen little benefit, and income inequality is increasing. Almost 25% of Sri Lankans live below the poverty line and, while unemployment is estimated at 8%, it is generally agreed that many workers, even those working long hours, do not earn a liveable wage.

The minimum age for employment is 14 unless the child is working for a parent. In 2002 over 200,000 children were working and not attending school. Also, the Liberation Tigers of Tamil Eelam (LTTE) recruits children as young as 13 into its army.

Although bonded labour is illegal in Sri Lanka, some children are bonded as servants to pay off family debts.

Society & Attitudes

While Sri Lanka may seem to be a conservative society, it displays, as it has for centuries, a range of attitudes and behaviours.

Traditionally, marriages in Sri Lanka were arranged. Although young people may now choose their own partners, horoscopes, caste and parental approval are still important factors.

Homosexuality is illegal, although the law is rarely enforced. That said, discretion is advised – it's probably best to avoid a 12-year jail term. Censors are strict – the play *Bed of Nettles,* by Gratiaen Prize–winner Visakesa Chandrasekaram, was banned because of its homosexual themes. However, the gay community is becoming ever more vocal.

The eldery are respected in Sri Lanka, and old age brings increased security. Elders usually remain an integral part of the extended family.

The caste system has traditionally played an important role for Sri Lankans, but it now has minimal influence. Although Buddhism discourages distinctions based on caste, a caste system operates among Sinhalese. About 50% of Sinhalese belong to the highest caste, the Govigama (descendants of landowners and cultivators). Traditionally Govigama were royal dignitaries and aristocracy. Today they are still the people of power – politicians and corporate flyers. Lower down the scale come the Karava (fisherfolk), Hakurus (makers of jaggery sweets), Berawaya (drummers), Paduvua (palanquin bearers), Radhu (washerfolk) and the Rodiya (beggars and itinerant entertainers). Today, these distinctions are virtually irrelevant (indeed, the one place it has any influence is in the marriage market, particularly in partner-seeking advertisements, where caste is still one of the many desirable 'qualities'), and you're more likely to hear tut-tutting about Kandyans and low-country Sinhalese (depending on the speaker).

For Hindus, caste has been more important. The Brahmin (priests) is the highest caste, and other high castes include the Vellalas (landlords akin to the Govigama), Karaiya (fisherfolk, similar to Karava) and Chetti (involved in commerce). Artisans and labourers come next, followed by those involved with butchery and cleaning. The lowest castes, traditionally known as Untouchables, were once forbidden to enter temples and own land. The Jaffna Tamils, mainly of the Vellala caste, used education and employment in prestigious positions to increase their influence throughout the last century. However, the Hill Country Tamils, who pick the tea, mainly come from lower castes. Some caste customs are still practised and social problems caused by caste inequity persist. However, legislation and equality-based social welfare are causing caste distinctions to fade and many people go about their daily lives happily ignoring caste and the disparities it may bring.

For gay information and contacts, visit the promising www.sricon nection.net, or the more accessible www.utopia -asia.com/spec/sripride .htm. For lesbians, there's www.wsglanka.com.

Ritual & Ceremony

Traditionally, rites of passage, often celebrated with elaborate rituals, brought families and villagers together. These connections were sealed with beliefs that linked nature with the supernatural; the land, rivers, trees and sky were all seen as life-givers and therefore land was tilled with respect and its produce was received with gratitude and ceremony. Every village had a protector deity (or several), usually associated with aspects of nature.

Tradition still has an important role at times of life transition. A newborn child may be named according to an auspicious time and letters, indicated by the astrologers. The child's first solid food is *kiri bath* (coconut-milk rice), the traditional food of ritual and celebration. It's common for children to receive a *pancha uda* (necklace of five weapons), containing small charms of a sword, bow, arrow, conch and trident – all symbols of protection.

The divorce rate in Sri Lanka is one of the lowest in the world, with just over one divorce per 10,000 people per year.

A custom still practised by some families, especially in villages, is the daughter's coming-of-age. During her first period she is separated, usually in a room of her own. Female family members keep her company and feed her special foods. At a time determined by the astrologer, she is bathed and later celebrated with gifts of jewellery and clothes.

The wedding ceremony depends on the religion of the couple, although it's usual for mixed-faith couples to marry with customs from both religions. Buddhist weddings usually take place on a *poruwa* (square platform) decorated with flowers. Religious stanzas are chanted in Sinhala and Pali (a dialect of Sanskrit), and the bride and groom pass betel leaves to their parents as an expression of thanks. The bride's little finger on her right hand is tied with thread to the little finger of the groom's left hand, the end of the thread is lit and, as it burns towards their hands, water is poured, extinguishing the light and symbolising their union. The couple cut the *kiri bath*, sign the register and join the feast.

Hindu weddings are religious affairs that occur in the temple. The Hindu wedding takes place around a fire that symbolises Brahman, the supreme being. As with most new ventures, prayers are offered to Ganesh, the elephant-headed deity. Sacred texts are recited and the end of the bride's sari is tied to outer clothing of the groom. They circle the fire seven times, a symbol of commitment and union. After exchanging rings they are usually showered with rice and flowers.

The *nikaah* (Muslim marriage) is usually a simple affair. There is no religious ceremony, just an agreement by the couple. Celebrations and gift-giving depend upon the orthodoxy of the couple – the greater the orthodoxy, the simpler the event.

At funerals mourners invariably wear white, and white flags are strung along fences, providing a guided path to the place of cremation.

POPULATION

Unlike other countries, Sri Lankans have not made a marked exodus from country to city. Twenty-five percent of the population lives in the city and many of these city dwellers retain close attachments to village life through family and continued land ownership.

Now with a population of 19.9 million, Sri Lanka's population doubled from seven million in the 30 years following the departure of the British in 1948, somewhat giving credence to the old adage, 'No sex please, we're British'.

The social policies of most governments since independence have given Sri Lanka a creditable literacy and health record. Sinhala and Tamil are both national languages, with English described as a link language. Most Sri Lankans are bilingual, even trilingual. See p351 for useful words and phrases.

Sri Lanka's ethnic groups have formed around language and religion. Throughout history, relations among the groups been marked by integration and cooperation, as well as tension and conflict.

Sinhalese

The Sinhalese constitute about 74% of the population, speak Sinhala and are predominantly Buddhist. Their forebears came from northern India in about the 6th century BC.

Sinhalese sometimes divide themselves into 'low country' or 'high country' (ie Kandyan). The Kandyan Sinhalese are famously proud, stemming from the time when the Hill Country was the last bastion of Sinhalese rule. Today, for Sinhalese Buddhists, Kandy is the spiritual capital of the island.

Computer literacy in Sri Lanka ranges from 3% in some rural areas to 20% in the Colombo area.

For an interesting and humorous read see *The Postcolonial Identity of Sri Lankan English* by English scholar Manique Gunesekera. Then you'll know what's happening if you're called a *bittaree*!

IN CASE YOU MISSED IT

'But that's a case of koheeda yannee mallee pol, no?'

This is actually a case of Singlish – a combination of Sinhala/Tamil and English. Some Sri Lankans bemoan this development, claiming it is a breakdown of their home culture or an abuse of the English language. Radio broadcasters have even been criticised over the inclusion of English words in their programmes. Yet it continues – not usually in print, but certainly in speech.

And what does the above statement mean?

It means '[But that's a case of]...they got the wrong end of the stick.'

Phrase quoted from The Postcolonial Identity of Sri Lankan English by Manique Gunesekera.

Tamils

The Tamils constitute 18% of the population, are predominantly Hindu and speak Tamil. About 60 million more Tamils live across the Palk Strait in India. While connections exist between Sri Lankan and Indian Tamils, especially for religious rituals and pilgrimages, they generally see each other as discrete racial groups.

There are two distinct groups of Tamils in Sri Lanka, separated by geography, history and caste. The Jaffna Tamils are descendants of the South Indians who settled in northern Sri Lanka during the late centuries BC. Most still live in the North and some reside with communities of Sinhalese and Muslims along the northeast coast.

The other Tamils are the 'Hill Country' or 'plantation' Tamils. Their ancestors were brought by the British from India in the 19th century to work on tea plantations.

Muslims

About 9% of the population is Muslim. Most are the so-called Sri Lanka Moors, who are the descendants of Arab or Indian traders, and whose presence goes back at least 1000 years. Escaping persecution from the Portuguese, many moved into the hilly interior, and you'll still come across enclaves of Muslims as you travel around the hill towns. They are also scattered all over the island, perhaps more thinly in the South and North.

Muslims have largely steered clear of the Sinhalese-Tamil troubles, though there has been some conflict in the East.

The Malays are a smaller group of Muslims; their ancestors came with the Dutch from Java. They still speak Malay and mostly live around Hambantota. Another small group, the 'Indian Moors', are more recent arrivals from India and Pakistan.

Veddahs

The Veddahs (Hunters), also called the Wanniyala-aetto (People of the Forest), are the original inhabitants of the country. Like so many other indigenous groups, the Veddahs have fared badly. Each wave of migration seized more land, leaving the Veddahs with less forest on which to subsist. Today their numbers are highly disputed, with estimates ranging from 200 to thousands. Some people contest Veddah existence, claiming they long ago integrated into the majority cultures. Only a small (and diminishing) number of people identify themselves as Veddah and retain a semblance of their old culture, which emphasised a hunting lifestyle with close relationships to nature and their ancestors.

When the Dutch arrived in Sri Lanka there were Veddah communities as far north as Jaffna. Today there are two groups: Kele Weddo (jungle-dwelling Veddahs) and Can Weddo (village-dwelling Veddahs), living mainly in the area between Badulla, Batticaloa and Polonnaruwa.

While Sinhalese legends claim the Veddahs were descended from evil spirits (a view that has certain political uses), it seems they are related to the Vedas of Kerala, India. Like some traditional Keralan groups, they have a matrilineal society.

Central to the issues of Veddah identity and land rights are the traditional hunting grounds of the Veddah in the Maduru Oya National Park, which was created in 1983 as a refuge for wildlife displaced by the Mahaweli irrigation scheme. Sri Lankan law prohibits hunting and gathering in national parks and Veddahs have been arrested for such activities. As they continue to work for the right to follow their customs, the official line may be softening – due, perhaps, to UN support for the

For an absorbing insight into historical and contemporary Veddah life and customs see the comprehensive website http://vedda .org/index.htm.

Veddah cause and the growing recognition that Veddah knowledge is vital to forest protection.

Other Ethnic Groups

The Burghers are Eurasian, primarily descendants of the Portuguese, Dutch and British. Even after independence, Burghers had a disproportionate influence over political and business life, but as growing Sinhalese nationalism reduced their role in Sri Lankan life, many Burghers emigrated to Australia and Canada. It's estimated that about 34,000 remain in Sri Lanka. Nevertheless, names such as Fernando, de Silva and Perera are still common.

There are also small Chinese and European communities, as well as a few downtrodden South Indians, who perform mostly menial tasks.

RELIGION

Buddhism is the belief system of the Sinhalese, and it is followed by 70% of the population. It plays a significant role in the country, spiritually, culturally and politically, and Sri Lanka's literature, art and architecture are, to a large extent, a product of its Buddhism. About 15% of the population, mainly Tamil, is Hindu. Muslims account for about 9% of the population and Christians about 6%; they include both Sinhalese and Tamil converts.

There is much mixing among religious groups. Buddhists, Hindus, Muslims and Christians all venture to some of the same pilgrimage sites – Adam's Peak and Kataragama in particular. And a Catholic may well feel the need to pay respects to the Hindu god Ganesh to ensure that no obstacles impede a prospective venture. As one Sri Lankan commented, 'I praise Lord Buddha, I praise Lord Hindu and I praise Lord Catholic.'

The Sri Lankan government, while seeing Buddhism as the island's foremost religion, established ministries representing each of the major faiths of the island. However, on election in 2005, President Rajapaske combined these into a ministry for religious affairs. Concerned for its Buddhist heritage, the primarily Sinhalese government is opposed to proselytising by other religions, particularly Christianity. This has caused some tension as Christian groups endeavour to spread their faith.

Buddhism

Strictly speaking, Buddhism is not a religion but a philosophy and moral code espoused by the Buddha. Born Prince Siddhartha Gautama, on the border of Nepal and India around 563 BC, the Buddha left his royal background and developed philosophies and disciplines for understanding and overcoming life's challenges.

The Buddha taught that suffering is inescapable, and that everyone will experience suffering as long as they are attached to the sensual and material aspects of life. Freedom from suffering comes from developing a higher consciousness, mostly by training the mind through meditation and by living by a moral code. This is an evolution through many rebirths and many states of spiritual development until nirvana (enlightenment) is reached, bringing freedom from the cycle of birth and death.

Central to the doctrine of rebirth is karma; each rebirth results from the actions one has committed, maybe in a previous life.

In his lifetime the Buddha organised a community of celibate monks, the Sangha, to spread his dharma (teachings).

The conversion of the Sinhalese king to Buddhism in the 3rd century BC (p29) ensured that Buddhism became firmly implanted in Sri Lanka.

Translating the Buddhist scriptures receives government support in Sri Lanka.

Each year in May, the anniversary of the Buddha's enlightenment (Buddha Jayanthi) is cause for huge celebration in Sri Lanka. This was particularly so in 2006, when the 2550th anniversary occurred.

A Concise Encyclopaedia of Buddhism, by John Powers, attempts a nearly impossible comprehensiveness, and covers everything from Anuradhapura's Abhayagiri monastery to the Tibetan Lama Tupden Zopa.

POYA DAYS

Poya days fall on each full moon. On these days, devout Buddhists visit a temple, fast after noon and abstain from entertainment and luxury. At their temple they make offerings, attend teachings and meditate. These days, which are public holidays in Sri Lanka, have been observed since ancient times. Each *poya* day is associated with a particular Buddhist ritual. Some notable days:

Vesak (May) Celebrates the birth and enlightenment of the Buddha.
Poson (June) Commemorates Buddhism's arrival in Sri Lanka.
Esala (July/August) Sees the huge Kandy festival, which commemorates, among other things, Buddha's first sermon.
Unduwap (December) Celebrates the visit of Sangamitta, who brought the bodhi tree sapling to Anuradhapura.
Durutu (January) Marks the first visit of the Buddha to the island.

A strong relationship developed between Sri Lanka's kings and the Buddhist clergy, creating a Buddhist theocracy.

Worldwide there are two major schools of Buddhism – Theravada and Mahayana. They have much in common, but Theravada (*thera* means 'learned elder') scriptures are in Pali (the language of the Buddha's time), while Mahayana (Large Vehicle) scriptures are in Sanskrit. Theravada is seen by some as more academic, Mahayana as more universal. The Mahayana school claims to have extended Theravada teachings.

Theravada Buddhism, by Richard Gombrich, details the context, history and practice of Buddhism in Sri Lanka.

While Mahayana Buddhism is practised and studied in Sri Lanka, it is the Theravada school that has been widely adopted. There are several factors that have consolidated the significance of Buddhism (especially the Theravada stream) in Sri Lanka. Firstly, Sinhalese Buddhists attach vital meaning to the words of the Mahavamsa (Great Chronicle; one of their sacred texts), in which the Buddha designates them as the protectors of the Buddhist teachings. The commitment emanating from this was fuelled by centuries of conflict between the Sinhalese (mainly Buddhist) and Tamils (mainly Hindu). For some Sinhalese, Mahayana Buddhism resembled Hinduism, and therefore defence of the Theravada stream was crucial. Also, the destruction of many Indian Buddhist sites in the 10th century AD heightened Sinhalese anxiety – it provided further impetus for preservation of Buddhism.

Sri Lankan monks took Theravada Buddhism to other Asian countries, and over the centuries there has been much interaction between the various Buddhist schools. Thai and Burmese *theras* have lived in Sri Lanka to revive higher ordinations that had lapsed; the order of Buddhist nuns (the Bhikkuni) was re-established as recently as 1996.

In *Buddhism: Beliefs and Practices in Sri Lanka*, Lynn de Silva combines lucid writing, fascinating information and a scholarly (but never inaccessible) approach that casts light on much that can appear incomprehensible.

Since the late 19th century an influential strand of 'militant' Buddhism has developed in Sri Lanka, centred on the belief that the Buddha charged the Sinhalese people with making the island a citadel of Buddhism in its purest form. It sees threats to Sinhalese Buddhist culture in European Christianity and Tamil Hinduism.

Sri Lankan Buddhism, historically intertwined with politics, can and does exert great pressure on politicians. Indeed, it was a Buddhist monk who, dissatisfied with Prime Minister SWRD Bandaranaike's 'drift' from a Sinhala-Buddhist focus, assassinated him in 1959 (p33). Today, some Buddhist monks oppose compromise with the Tamils and not all follow a virtuous path. On the other hand, many monks are dedicated to the spirit of Buddhism and are committed to the welfare of devotees.

Besides the festivals and the numerous ways that Buddhism permeates people's daily lives, Buddhists gather at temples on *poya* (full moon) days to make *puja* (prayers and offerings) and to hear the ancient truths from the Sangha.

SYMBOLS OF SRI LANKA

In Sri Lanka, symbols are everywhere. Some are subtle, quiet and unnoticed. Others demand attention. These symbols are the keys to the stories and the ideas that have woven their way through Sri Lankan culture from ancient times. Interpretations of the symbols vary from person to person, and from place to place, and may range from the practical to the profound. The list here is not exhaustive but it provides an entrée into the meaning of the symbols and their cultural significance. However, always ask if you want more information. And ask again. The different interpretations you receive will provide for rich reflection.

Astamangala

Since ancient times the Astamangala (Eight Auspicious Symbols) have been seen to bring good luck and happiness. They were often placed at the base of temples and dagobas (stupas), and were worn by kings and nobles for luck and protection. Today the symbols still have meaning: for the 50th anniversary of independence, the Central Bank in Sri Lanka released a coin with the Astamangala. Buddhist groups differ on the composition of the Astamangala, but in Sri Lanka the following generally constitute the eight.

Ankus (elephant goad) The ankus disciplines and directs the elephant. Likewise, the teachings of the Buddha discipline the mind and direct the individual to the right path.

Bhadrapitha (throne) The portrayal of royalty here is clear. However, the throne also represents the attainment of enlightenment, somewhat akin to royal or noble status in the spiritual realm.

Camara (fly whisk) The whisk is a gentle deterrent. Devotees, too, must be gentle with intrusions or impediments that may obstruct them their path.

Matsya-yugala (pair of fish) Because fish breed prolifically, this symbol represents fertility and life. Originally the two fishes denoted the two great rivers, the Ganges and the Yamuna, symbolic in themselves of the sun and moon, and male and female. And because fish swim freely, they also symbolise the notion that

devotees will not become submerged in life's difficulties but will be buoyed by the Buddha's teachings.

Nandyavaria (swastika) This is a symbol of peace, of luck and, sometimes, of the Buddha's heart.

Purna-kalasa (vase) The vase is considered to encompass wealth and prosperity.

Sankha (conch shell) The sound of the conch pierces the atmosphere and continues to reverberate. Similarly, the Buddha's teachings reach out to all and continue to resound.

Srivasta (goddess Lakshmi) This goddess is a symbol of fertility, life and prosperity.

Bodhi Tree

Trees are important symbols in Sri Lanka but the bodhi tree (also known as *pipal*, or *Ficus religiosa*) is all-important. It was beneath a bodhi tree that the Buddha achieved enlightenment – *bodhi* actually means 'enlightenment' – and a cutting from that sacred tree still grows at the ancient city of Anuradhapura (p250). Bodhi trees grace the courtyards of many Sri Lankan temples, and the incense and lamps burning beneath the branches of these trees are offerings that symbolise the light of wisdom.

Dagoba (Stupa)

You'll see dagobas everywhere throughout Sri Lanka (p56). Domed structures with fine spires rising high into the sky, they hold the relics of a sacred person and are the destination of many a pilgrimage. Some people say they represent the body of the Buddha, while others equate them to the five elements, with earth represented at the bottom, and water, fire, air and nothingness rising to the sky.

Elephant

In Hindu mythology elephants were linked with clouds and, therefore, with rain. As such they are seen as symbols of water, life and fortune. They are also seen as noble and gentle, the qualities achieved when one lives a good life. In Sri Lanka, only the elephant gets to parade with the sacred Buddhist relics and

Hinduism

Tamil kings and their followers from South India brought Hinduism to northern Sri Lanka. Today there are Hindu communities in Colombo, Kandy, the tea plantation areas, the North and the East.

Hinduism often appears to be a complex mix of beliefs and gods. Essentially, all Hindus believe in Brahman, the One who is uncreated and infinite.

Hindu statues. A little white elephant Is associated with Saman, the deity of Adam's Peak (Sri Pada).

Footprint
The footprint symbolises a place visited by a holy person – hence the pilgrimage site at Adam's Peak, also known as Sri Pada (Holy Footprint). Each faith sees the site as sacred; Buddhists believe it was visited by Buddha; Christians and Muslims believe it was Adam who visited; and Hindus hold that it is the abode of Shiva.

Lamp
Lamps are lit to represent the light that dispels ignorance and evil. They are particularly evident at the Vesak festival, celebrating the Buddha's enlightenment (usually in May) and Deepavali, celebrating the triumph of good over evil (usually in October). Any important event in Sri Lanka begins with the lighting of the Garuda-headed lamp; Garuda, half human, half bird, symbolises the banishment of all evil.

Lion
Seen as a forceful creature, the king of the jungle and the protector of the clan, the lion represents the knowledgeable beings who protect the sacred teachings and places. Lion statues are often seen at the entrance to temples.

Lotus
Rooted in mud, the lotus grows through water and blossoms in the light above. It symbolises the human path from the depth of difficulties through the fluidity of life's concerns to the glow of knowledge and enlightenment.

Moonstone (Sandakadapahana)
The moonstone is the semicircular first step in a flight of steps leading to a sacred site. Ornate sculptures follow the arced shape of the stone, and each arc symbolises another step on the path from human life (the outer arcs) to enlightenment (the inner semicircle). The flowers of the outer arc depict human life, while the arc of animals (elephant, lion, horse and bull) represent life's challenges: birth, disease, old age and death. The vine that weaves among these elements depicts the entanglements in which humans get caught as they are lured away from an upright path, and the swans signify the saints and ancestors that may assist along this path. The vine near the centre represents the cosmic/heavenly spheres and, finally, the centre with the lotus petals is nirvana (enlightenment).

Parasol
The parasol signifies protection from cruelty. It also indicates royalty and is often seen above the image of a deity.

Peacock
The peacock is believed to be capable of eating poison yet surviving. As such, it is symbolic of great beings who take on the suffering of others, transmuting it into knowledge and understanding. The peacock symbolises the path through challenge to liberation. When depicted in pairs it represents the duality that exists in life – good/evil, sickness/health, black/white. The peacock is the vehicle of the favoured deity of Kataragama, also known as Murugan and Skanda.

Sun & Moon
This is the twin representation of truth – the truth of earthly life and the truth that exists beyond comprehension.

Vel
Generally associated with Kataragama (Murugan), the vel, with its spearlike point, signifies warrior strength, as well as the piercing of ignorance and the creation of an opening for knowledge. There are Vel festivals in honour of Murugan in Jaffna and Colombo around July/August.

The myriad deities are simply manifestations of this formless being, where one may come to understand life and all its facets. Although beliefs and practices may vary, there are several unifying factors. These include beliefs in ahimsa (nonviolence), samsara (the recurring cycle of births and deaths until one reaches a pure state and is reunited with Brahman), karma (the law of cause and effect) and dharma (teachings about laws for living).

Hindus believe that living a life according to dharma enhances the chance of being born into better circumstances. Going the other way, rebirth may take animal form, but it's only as a human that one may gain sufficient self-knowledge to escape the cycle of reincarnation and achieve moksha (liberation).

For ordinary Hindus, fulfilling one's ritual and social duties is the main aim of worldly life. The Hindu text Bhagavad Gita is clear about this; doing your duty is more important than asserting your individuality.

For more information on Hinduism, avoid the hype and glitz and go to www.bbc.co.uk/religion /religions/hinduism.

Hindu worship takes many forms, but has a particular connection to *darshan,* the act of seeing and being seen by the deity present in a shrine.

GODS & GODDESSES

The Hindu pantheon is prolific; some estimates put the number of deities at 330 million. Brahman is often described as having three facets, known as the Trimurti: the three deities of Brahma, Vishnu and Shiva. Tamil Hindus usually revere Vishnu or Shiva but they also pay respect to the many gods and goddesses of the harvest, the arts and prosperity. Gods are usually associated with a goddess, who represents *shakti,* the female force that gives life to creation.

Brahma & Saraswati

Brahma created the universe. His essence infuses the cosmos, continuing its creation. His consort, Saraswati, is the goddess of learning, wisdom and music.

Vishnu & Lakshmi

Known as the preserver, Vishnu is lawful and devout. He is usually depicted with four arms, which hold a lotus (symbolising the unfolding of the universe), a conch shell (symbolising the cosmic vibration from which all existence emanates), a discus (symbolising the mind) and a mace (symbolising power). Vishnu has 22 incarnations, including Rama (of the Ramayana) and Krishna, who depicted in blue and is known for his dalliances with *gopis* (milkmaids) and his love affair with Radha.

Vishnu's consort is Lakshmi, goddess of beauty and fortune.

Shiva & Parvati

The destroyer of ignorance and evil, Shiva is often symbolised by the *lingam,* a phallic symbol. With 1008 names, Shiva takes many forms. As Nataraja, lord of the *tandava* (dance), his graceful movements begin the creation of the cosmos.

Shiva's consort, Parvati, is capable of taking many forms, from the universal mother to the ferocious and destructive Kali. Known as the 'black one', Kali is the most fearsome of the Hindu deities. She manifests power to destroy life. Kali is often depicted garlanded with human heads, dancing on a corpse. An odd sect of ascetics propitiates the goddess with mortifying acts of necromancy – it's supposed to be a short cut to ego death, but there's a high dropout rate into madness. You may come across Kali shrines in Sri Lanka's Hill Country.

Other Gods

The elephant-headed Ganesh, chubby, wise and kind, is held in great affection. The elder son of Shiva and Parvati, he is the lord of beginnings, remover of obstacles and patron of scribes – he used his broken tusk to write the Mahabharata.

Murugan (Skanda), the Kataragama deity and the god of war, is the younger brother of Ganesh. His devotees offer crimson garlands when they visit his shrine. Under the name Skanda he is viewed as a protective deity by Buddhists.

Hanuman, the monkey deity, embodies bhakti (devotion). A hero of the Ramayana and the loyal ally of Rama, it was Hanuman who discovered where the King of Lanka, Rawana, was hiding Sita. There is a cave at Ella (p216) that is claimed to be the site of her captivity.

The goddess Pattini has been popular with Sri Lankan Buddhists and Hindus. Elaborate rituals were undertaken in her honour, particularly when requesting her help to eradicate disease. Pattini's main shrine, in Navagamuwa, some 20km south of Colombo, is now somewhat eclipsed by a Buddhist site. Her devotees are mainly pregnant women seeking blessings for a safe and healthy birth. There's a small shrine in Kandy and a large *kovil* (Hindu temple) at Vattappalai, near Mullaittivu.

The guardian deity of the popular pilgrimage site Adam's Peak is Saman, who is associated with a little white elephant. You'll see shrines to Saman as you approach Adam's Peak. Pilgrims of all religious persuasions seek his assistance as they make the long climb to the top.

Myths of the Hindus and Buddhists by Ananda K Coomaraswamy and Sister Nivedita converts the 'bibles' of Sri Lanka – the Mahavamsa and the Ramayana – into accessible stories that provide insight into Sri Lankan beliefs.

Islam

There are 1.8 million Sri Lankan Muslims, descendants of Arab traders who settled on the island from the 8th century.

Islam was founded in the 7th century in present-day Saudi Arabia by the Prophet Mohammed. The Arabic term *islam* means 'to surrender': believers undertake to surrender to the will of Allah (God), revealed to Mohammed through the angel Jibreel and recorded in the poetic scriptures of the Quran.

Islam is monotheistic, and believes that everything has been created by Allah. The purpose of all living things is to submit to divine will. Humankind's weaknesses are its pride and its sense of independence.

After Mohammed's death a dispute over succession split the movement into two main branches – the Sunnis and the Shiites. Sunnis emphasise following and imitating the words and acts of the Prophet, interpreted by different schools of Islamic law (Maliki, Hanifi, Sha'fi and Hambali). They look to tradition and the views of the majority of the community. Shiites believe that only imams (exemplary leaders) are able to reveal the meaning of the Quran. Most of Sri Lanka's Muslims are Sunnis, although small communities of Shiites have migrated more recently from India.

All Muslims believe in the five pillars of Islam: the shahada (declaration of faith: 'there is no God but Allah; Mohammed is his prophet'); prayer (ideally five times a day); the zakat (tax, which today is usually a donation to charity); fasting during the month of Ramadan; and the haj (pilgrimage) to Mecca.

Christianity

Some Sri Lankan Christians believe that their faith arrived with the Apostle Thomas in the 1st century AD. Certainly, during the early centuries AD small numbers of Christians established settlements along the coast.

With the Portuguese in 16th century, Christianity, specifically Roman Catholicism, arrived in force and many fisherfolk converted. Today Catholicism remains strong among western coastal communities. The Dutch brought Protestantism and the Dutch Reformed Church, which mostly has a presence in Colombo. Evidence of the British Christian denominations, such as Protestantism and Anglicanism, can be seen in the

Hill Country, where quaint stone churches dot the landscape. Christian communities have decreased in numbers in the last 25 years, but Our Lady of Madhu Church (p301), near Mannar, remains popular, with up to 300,000 pilgrims visiting every 15 August.

WOMEN IN SRI LANKA

As you travel throughout Sri Lanka you'll see women participating in most aspects of Sri Lankan life.

Neloufer de Mel's *Women and the Nation's Narrative* probes Sri Lankan 20th-century history from a women's perspective. It's an important work that confronts conventional views about caste, colonialism, guerrilla warfare and morality.

Sri Lanka became the first country in the world to have a female prime minister when Sirimavo Bandaranaike was elected to office in 1960. In 1994 her daughter Chandrika Bandaranaike Kumaratunga became president. This, however, should be viewed more as a continuation of dynasty than an indicator of gender equality; mother and daughter attained office in the absence of their husbands, both of whom had been assassinated. Today, 5% of parliamentary members are women and their representation in local councils is much less.

Given the importance placed on education in Sri Lanka, girls have opportunities to move into all occupational areas. However, the situation for women depends very much on their position in society. In general they are responsible for the home – a role that is viewed with respect. A professional woman may have servants to whom she can delegate such duties, while poorer women undertake home duties and may also work in the fields.

The ethnic conflict has had catastrophic effects on women. One in five Sri Lankan households is now headed by women, and human rights agencies warn that with fewer men and boys for combat, women, and even young girls, are forcefully enlisted.

For some women, widowhood still remains a stigma. Other women avoid widows, fearful that they too may suffer the 'curse' of solo status. The practice of a man taking another wife, while not common, is also not unheard of. This can have distressing effects on the first wife who, restricted by finance and the potential stigma, remains in an unhappy marriage. But as more women pursue higher education, careers and greater freedom, they are less subject to these restrictions.

At www.onlinewomen inpolitics.org/lk/lkorgs .htm you'll find listings of, and links to, women's organisations. Although sometimes out of date, the sites provide valuable insight into women's issues in Sri Lanka.

Sri Lanka's vibrant feminist movement acts as an umbrella organisation for several groups that focus on issues to do with peace, missing relatives, racism, agricultural and factory workers, and refugees from ethnic conflict.

No matter the status, the education or the position of a woman, in social situations she is usually demure. Men do most of the talking. Women do most of the listening, even if discussion is tedious. They nod in the right places, and laugh appropriately at jokes, even if they've heard them many times before.

But with a high female literacy rate, educational opportunities and a vibrant feminist discourse, the women of Sri Lanka are well positioned to take a greater role in determining their country's future.

ARTS
Dance

Sri Lanka has a rich dance heritage comprising three main schools: Kandyan dance, masked dance-drama and devil dance.

KANDYAN DANCE

This dance form flourished under the Kandyan kings and became so refined that Buddhist monks admitted it to temple courtyards and it became an integral part of the Kandy Esala Perahera (p167).

Now considered the national dance of Sri Lanka, there are five types of Kandyan dance: *pantheru*, named after a tambourine-like instrument, which was used as an accompaniment to dances after victory in war and is associated with the goddess Pattini; *udekki*, connected to several gods, involves the dancer singing and drumming; *naiyaki*, a graceful dance performed at the lighting of lamps prior to festivals; *ves*, considered the most sacred, is the most frequently seen dance, particularly in the Kandy *perahera* (procession); and *vannamas*, inspired by nature and deities.

The best-known costume of male Kandyan dancers is a wide skirtlike garment. The dancer's bare chest is covered with necklaces of silver and ivory, while the arms and ankles wear bangles of beaten silver. The dances are energetic performances with great leaps and back flips accompanied by the complex rhythms of the *geta bera*, a Kandyan tapering double-ended drum that yields different tones from monkey hide at one end and cow hide at the other.

Deities and Demons by Nandadeva Wijesekera features vivid illustrations of past (sometimes enduring) Sri Lankan customs. For an enjoyable read you'll need to abandon all notions of syntax and feminism.

MASKED DANCE-DRAMA

There are four folk-drama dance forms: *kolam, sokari, nadagam* and *pasu*. The best known of these is the *kolam* (Tamil for costume or guise). *Kolam* has numerous characters (up to 53), which have many grotesque and exaggerated deformities, including bulging eyes and nostrils that issue forth tusks and cobras.

Performances, with a cast of singers and drummers, are traditionally held over several nights at New Year (late April). After songs in praise of Buddha, the master of ceremonies explains the origin of the *kolam* – a pregnant Indian Queen had cravings to see a masked dance-drama.

Of the many *kolam* plays, the two best-known are the *Sandakinduru Katava* and the *Gothayimbala Katava*. In the first, a king who is out hunting kills a man-bird creature who is later restored to life by the Buddha. In the second, a demon who falls in love with a married woman is beheaded by her avenging husband. The demon regenerates itself over and over, until the husband is rescued from the dilemma by a forest deity. You're most likely to see *kolam* and devil dancing at Ambalangoda.

MASKS FOR DANCE & FESTIVALS

There are three basic types of mask: *kolam, sanni* and *raksha*.

The *kolam* mask – a form of disguise – is used in *kolam* masked dance-dramas, in which all the characters wear masks. *Kolam* masks are generally for dance, not for sale to tourists.

The second mask type, *sanni,* is worn by dancers to impersonate and exorcise disease demons that range from rheumatism, boils or blindness to gruesome conditions of bile and phlegm. The whole grotesque ensemble is bordered by two cobras, and other cobras sprout from the demon's head.

Raksha masks are used in processions and festivals. There are about 25 varieties, including the common *naga raksha* (cobra) masks, in which a demonic face, complete with protruding eyeballs, lolling tongue and pointed teeth, is topped with a coiffure of writhing cobras. The *gurulu raksha* mask developed from the legend of the Rakshasas, an ancient Lankan people ruled by Rawana of the Ramayana. The Rakshasas assumed the form of cobras to subjugate their enemies, who pleaded for help from the *gurulu*, a bird that preyed on snakes.

Most masks are made from a light balsa-type wood called *kaduru,* which is smoke-dried before the mask is carved. The mask's base colour is yellow, with other colours added as desired. Finally, it is glazed with a mixture of resin powder and oil.

The best place to watch masks being made is Ambalangoda, which also has some museums that detail the mask-making process (p122).

DEVIL DANCE

Traditionally, devil dancing was performed to free a person from evil spirits or bad luck. There are many types of devil dance: *sanni yakku* exorcises the disease demon, *kohomba kankariya* ensures prosperity, and the *bali* honours heavenly beings.

Three beings must be appeased in these ceremonies: demons, deities and semidemons. Before the dance begins, palm-leaf shrines dedicated to each of the beings are built outside the victim's house. The beings must be tempted out of these and into an arena. The dancers (all men) go through an astounding athletic routine, costumed in red headdresses hung with palm leaves and with white cloths wound tightly round their hips (which stays firm despite their gyrations). All the while, bare-chested drummers beat out a frantic rhythm on the *yak bera* (a double-ended, cylindrical drum). At the climax of their routine the dancers put on masks representing the demons, and the demon considered to be causing the distress is questioned and confronted by the chief exorcist. He exhorts, threatens and sometimes even bribes the demon to force it away.

Theatre

Theatre moved into the cities when a Parsi theatre company from Bombay (Mumbai) introduced *nurti* (new theatre) to Colombo audiences in the 19th century. *Nurti* was a blend of European and Indian theatrical conventions: stage scenery, painted backdrops and wings, an enclosed theatre, costumes, and music and song. It was to spawn a new profession – play writing – with writers drawing inspiration from Sanskrit drama and other sources, including Shakespeare.

The arrival of cinema almost killed off theatre. However, a breakthrough came in 1956 with *Maname* (King's Name), a play written by university professor Ediriweera Sarachchandra. It was staged in *nadagam*, a form of Sinhalese drama that developed from Catholic pageants. In *nadagam* the absence of masks and the inclusion of different musical forms enabled a greater audience connection with the plays. This combination of familiar folk tale and accessible staging made the play an instant hit and marked the beginning of a new era of experimentation and creativity. Sarachchandra is recognised as the father of modern Sri Lankan theatre.

Today, Sri Lankan theatre is undertaking many innovative ventures on contemporary issues, particularly on the healing of trauma in the aftermath of conflict. Such projects are sponsored by the Alliance Française, the British Council and the Goethe Institute. It's worthwhile checking out what's on when you arrive in Colombo; see p81 for details.

If you're in the Hill Country in May look out for *Kamankoothu*, an ancient folk drama that depicts the story of Kama, the Hindu god of love (akin to Cupid). The performance lasts for several days, with whole villages taking part.

Courageous, poetic and with a strong sense of place, Chandani Lokugé's novels *If the Moon Smiled* and *Turtle Nest* tackle the alarming and the elegant while evoking past and present Sri Lanka.

Literature

Sri Lanka has a rich literary tradition drawn from Sinhalese and Tamil cultures, with colonisation also having a marked influence.

Contemporary writing tends to deal with the trauma of war and with romance – perhaps as a means of escape from war.

SINHALESE LITERATURE

Sri Lankan literature has never shied away from depicting humanity's flaws, as well as its nobility. The first works of Sinhalese literature were composed by monks, since it was they who were educated and literate.

OLA & THE SINHALA SCRIPT

The elegant swirls and flourishes of the 58-letter Sinhala script developed partly due to the nature of the *ola* (the young leaves of the talipot palm), Sri Lanka's first writing material. Tough, with a distinct fibre, the leaves tend to be split by straight lines, but swirls don't cause damage.

Before they are used, the *ola* are boiled, dried, rolled and stretched. A steel-tipped stylus etches the writing, after which the leaf is buffed with a sticky blend of charcoal and *dummala* oil, made from fossilised resin from the paddy fields. Most of the resin is wiped off, emphasising the blackened letters. The resin also preserves the leaves, which can last as long as 500 years. The Sinhalese classics, the Pali canon, the Mahavamsa and numerous Jataka tales were engraved on *ola*.

You can sometimes see *ola* being inscribed by students outside the National Museum in Colombo.

Without computers and electric light they accomplished extraordinary feats in recounting the tales of others. The earliest surviving texts date from the 10th century AD and focus on the study of Pali and Buddhism. In two major works, the Mahavamsa and the Culavamsa (Minor Chronicle), the monks recorded Sinhalese history. Generally regarded as part history, part myth, the chronicles relate the arrival of Vijaya, the lives of the royals and the coming of Buddhism. The monks demonstrated shrewd insight into human nature as they depicted centuries of history – relationships, betrayal, loss, death, patricide, tragedy and drama are all there. The Thupavamsa (Chronicle of the Great Stupa) records the construction of the huge Ruvanvelisaya Dagoba (p250) in Anuradhapura. In the 13th century the works of Gurulugomi (who wrote in almost pure Sinhala) began a transition from Pali to Sinhala in Sri Lankan literature.

Poetry was an early literary form; the graffiti on the Sigiriya mirror wall (p235) attests to that. The Jatakas, tales of the Buddha's past lives, were also recorded in verse. *Samdesha*, a popular genre originating in India, centred on themes of love and travel, describing poems that were transported between lovers on monsoonal winds. Poems also explored the peace of the Buddha and the ravages of war.

From the mid-19th century, literary endeavours went beyond the traditional, mostly religious subjects, and towards the end of the century, printing presses produced the newspapers, periodicals and the first novels. The novel *Meena* appeared in 1905. Written by Aluthgamage Simon De Silva, its theme of young love was popular with some, controversial with others. Years later this work was translated into English and published in the USA by the author's grandson. Works by Buddhist writer and political activist Piyadasa Sirisena, as well as those by Martin Wickramasinghe and WA Silva, were very popular in the early part of the 20th century. Wickramasinghe's *Gamperaliya* (Overturning of the Village), which subsequently developed into a trilogy, received much critical praise for its exploration of Western influence on village life. Many European works were translated into Sinhala, including Leonard Woolf's *A Village in the Jungle*.

Elephant dung is part of a curious concoction that is made into paper for stationery, artwork and books.

TAMIL LITERATURE

Tamil writing emanates from a strong literary tradition dating back over 2000 years. It shares its literary origins with Sanskrit, but while Sanskrit ceased to be a spoken language, Tamil continued and survived – still voiced and written much as it has been for many centuries. The first Tamil writing was poetry, possibly derived from songs. One of the most loved Tamil works, *The Kural*, was written by the poet Tiruvalur. While its writing is dated anywhere from 200 BC to AD 600, its 1330 couplets advocating compassion are as relevant today as when they were written.

The period from the late centuries BC to early centuries AD was a particularly fruitful time for Tamil literature, with the Sangam – the academy of literature in Tamil Nadu (India) – nurturing a rapidly growing literary scene. Many works from this time are included in *Pattuppattu* (Ten Idylls) and *Ettuttohai* (Eight Anthologies). Sri Lankan Tamils date their first poet, Eelattu Poothanthevanar, from the Sangam period, his work being found in the anthologies. Two epics, *Silappadhikaram* and *Manimekhalai*, considered comparable in distinction with the Ramayana and Mahabharata, were produced by Tamil poets of the late Sangam period.

As the Sangam period progressed, all the major styles of literature were in vogue, especially the epic and the poem, which invariably took a highly moral stance. The sciences, including astrology and medicine, was also a favoured topic.

Having drawn upon these rich literary beginnings, Sri Lankan Tamil writing has developed a keen sense of place as well as a strong awareness of the Tamils' social and political context. It has also been a significant influence within the Tamil diaspora. Through the colonial years, particularly the British period, Tamil writing explored and analysed the colonial experience. Tamil newspapers, begun in the 1930s, were well established by the 1940s, enabling greater debate and dissemination of views – important in the preindependence climate.

The two decades post independence saw a lively literary debate that mostly focused on politics. This vibrant literary movement was hit by a massive blow in 1981 when the library in Jaffna was burnt down by a Sinhalese mob. Thousands of works, including ancient *ola* (the young leaves of the talipot palm) manuscripts, were lost. Local and global efforts have re-established the library, which opened in March 2004. However, this attack, combined with the general ethnic violence has led to Resistance Literature – writing that aims to not only protect and promote Tamil language and literature but also to explore it as a means of retaining identity and dignity. It aims further to record violent activity while contesting attempts at suppression.

On declaration of the cease-fire in 2002, Tamils immediately began activities to reinvigorate their literary culture. Just 10 months later the Trincomalee Literary Festival celebrated Tamil language, literature and culture, reinforcing the significance of these to Tamil identity and belonging.

In Pradeep Jeganathan's *At the Water's Edge* you get to feel Sri Lanka's raw edge. The writing in these seven short stories is raw too, but it says much in few words.

CONTEMPORARY LITERATURE

Much of Sri Lanka's more recent literature centres on romance and ethnic conflict. *Born to Labour* by CV Vellupillai describes the lives of tea-estate workers, while, according to some travellers, *Medusa's Hair* by Gannanath Obeyesekere is a must for understanding Kataragama's fire-walking ceremony. In fact, Obeyesekere is a good option at any time; although somewhat verbose, his work provides fascinating insights into the lesser-known aspects of Sri Lankan culture. For an entrée into the Burgher community, look at Carl Muller's *The Jam Fruit Tree,* for which he won the 1993 Gratiaen Prize. Jean Arasanayagam's poetry and short stories provide vivid and intimate accounts into the upheavals in Sri Lanka.

The country's best-known writer is Arthur C Clarke, who made his home here in the 1950s. His *The Foundations of Paradise,* set on an imaginary island, features places remarkably like Adam's Peak and Sigiriya.

Sri Lankan children have been raised on the folk tales of Mahadenamutta, a village know-all who somehow acquired numerous sycophants. Mahadenamutta is the ideal character for satirical pieces about the exploits of current politicians. They're witty articles that are possibly more reliable than the actual news. Look out for the articles in newspaper features.

Many Sri Lankan writers have migrated to other lands and written evocative and courageous works about their native land. *Funny Boy* and *Cinnamon Gardens* by Shyam Selvadurai explore relationships and societal expectations, particularly in regard to gay issues. *Cinnamon Gardens*, at times prescriptive and stereotypical, is a gutsy account of caste life in early-20th-century Sri Lanka. Selvadurai has done his research and packed it in – a little too obviously at times. For one Sri Lankan critic, the 'feminist' character was right on the mark because in spite of her attempts at liberation (bike riding) she still wore pretty saris! His latest novel, *Swimming in the Monsoon Sea*, deals with similar subject matter.

Monkfish Moon, a book of nine short stories by Romesh Gunesekera, provides a diverse glimpse at Sri Lanka's ethnic conflict. Gunesekera was nominated for the Booker Prize for his novel *Reef*, which also examines lives changed irrevocably by war.

See the sidebar reviews and p19 for more titles.

Cinema

The first Sri Lankan–made film, *Kadavunu Poronduwa* (Broken Promise), was shown in Colombo in 1947, allowing audiences to hear Sinhala spoken on screen for the first time. Movies continued to be produced mostly in Indian studios, though, until director Sirisena Wimalaweera opened a studio in Sri Lanka in 1951. Lester James Peries' first feature film, *Rekawa* (Line of Destiny), is considered the first truly Sinhalese film. It attempted to realistically portray Sri Lankan life and used its filming technique to express this – it was the first film in Sri Lanka shot outside a studio.

Contemporary Sri Lankan directors tend to explore themes directly related to war. *Death on a Full Moon Day*, made in 2000 by Prasanna Vithanage, explores the story of a father who refuses to accept the death of his soldier son.

Today, in spite of government support, the local film industry struggles to compete with Indian movies and TV.

Films shot on location in Sri Lanka include *Elephant Walk*, which starred Elizabeth Taylor and Peter Finch, and David Lean's *Bridge on the River Kwai*. More recently Sri Lanka has been used as a setting in *Indiana Jones and the Temple of Doom* and *Mountbatten: The Last Viceroy*.

Music

Sri Lankan music has been influenced by Buddhism and Hinduism, the rhythms of the African slaves, the melodies of Europe and the energy of India.

Initially *baila*s (folk tunes with an African beat) were accompanied by guitar and the beat of drums or handclapping. Now electrified instruments strum the accompaniment. The most popular contemporary *baila* singer is Desmond de Silva. Although currently living in England, he still inspires many Sri Lankan bands, including Shanaka and his Sri Lankan Vibes, who incorporate *baila*, hip-hop, pop and classical Sri Lankan music. You may hear them in Colombo, Kandy or Dambulla.

One of Sri Lanka's best-known composers is Ananda Samarakone (1911–62), who wrote the Sri Lankan national anthem. Samarakone studied in India, where the work of the great poet and composer Tagore, who had transformed Indian writing and musical composition by refusing to work within their traditional forms, had a significant impact on him. Inspired, Samarakone introduced new musical and lyrical forms that

To find out what's happening with Sri Lankan rock, go to www .clublk.us for information, downloads and blogs.

involved great complexity. Today, he is considered to be the inspiration for much of Sri Lanka's current music.

Until the late 1990s Sri Lanka's popular music was mainly film music, Hindi pop and imitations of Western pop. Many locals longed for a more home-grown style. For some, their longings materialised when heavy-metal band Stigmata burst onto the scene. Stigmata's latest work, *Lucid,* while still promoted as heavy metal, is a more placid piece with interesting harmonies. Other popular and influential bands are Bathiya and Santhush, Iraj and Samitha, and Centigradz, whose *Dark Angel* jumped quickly to the top of the charts on release. Most popular music could be described as hip-hop meets Hindi pop meets soft Western pop. Look for the Rock Saturday events held regularly at various venues; you'll see them listed in the newspapers, and on numerous posters on walls and poles.

For more traditional sounds, be at the Kandy temple at dawn, where you'll hear the shrill conch shell as it announces morning *puja.* There, and throughout the island, you'll hear the animated rhythms of the Kandy drums, particularly at wedding celebrations.

For those with a classical bent, the **Sri Lankan Symphony Orchestra** (SOSL; ☎ in Colombo 011-268 2033; solsnet@yahoo.com; 204 De Saram Pl, Col 10) may have little resonance – nevertheless, it's still quite an experience! Sadly, the annual concert for the Pinnawala elephants has ceased. Contact the Orchestra for a concert schedule.

Geoffrey Bawa: The Complete Works, by David Robson, is a comprehensive book with stunning images. Detailing the life and work of the acclaimed architect, Robson cleverly demonstrates how Bawa's early life influenced his later work.

Architecture

Sri Lankan architecture is an expression of ancient and modern, aesthetic and functional. The simplest and most economical structure is the *cadjan* (coconut-frond matting) dwelling, made from timber frames covered with woven coconut fronds. No doubt they're similar to the structures favoured in ancient times by ordinary people. Particularly suited to Sri Lanka's climate, the *cadjan* dwellings' availability and low cost made them especially effective after the 2004 tsunami.

BUDDHIST

One of the most striking features of Sri Lanka's architectural landscape is the dagoba – those smooth, lime-washed bell-shaped structures that protrude above the tree line along the coast and dot the dry zone at Anuradhapura. The dagoba is actually a chamber for holding 'relics', the corporal remains

GEOFFREY BAWA – 'BRINGING POETRY TO PLACE'

The most famous of Sri Lanka's architects, Geoffrey Bawa (1919–2003) fused ancient and modern influences in his work. Architect Ranjith Dayaratne described it as 'bringing poetry to place'.

Using courtyards and pathways, Bawa developed pleasing connections between the interior and exterior of his structures. These connections frequently included contemplative spaces, as well as framed areas that enabled glimpses of spaces yet to be entered.

His designs were based within the environment. And he was not averse to the environment claiming his structures – at times he encouraged jungle growth along walls and roofs.

While Bawa created aesthetic beauty, he was also concerned with the functional aspects of architecture, opening and exposing structures to air and light while ensuring shelter and protection from harsh climatic elements.

His approach was important not only for its originality but also for its influence on architecture in Sri Lanka and abroad.

Bawa's work included the new parliament house in Colombo, the Lighthouse Hotel (p136) in Galle, the Kandalama Hotel (p233) in Dambulla, and Hotel Serendib (p119) in Bentota.

or possessions of the Buddha or enlightened monks, along with other sacred material. In ancient times, the *hataraes kotuwa,* a square structure above the lower bell shape, contained the relics but later they were lodged in a granite piece (known as the mystic stone) just below the spire. You can see these stones at museums in Anuradhapura (p253) and Mihintale (p258).

Rising from the *hataraes kotuwa* is the furled ceremonial parasol called the *chatta.* The dagoba is very often surrounded by a *vahalakada* (platform), used by devotees to make a clockwise circuit; stairways to the *vahalakada* pass through gates situated at the cardinal points.

Dagobas are made of solid brick, which is then plastered and lime-washed. Early dagobas were probably simple structures, but they became increasingly sophisticated. The Ruvanvelisaya and Mirisavatiya Dagobas, built in the 2nd century in Anuradhapura by King Dutugemunu, had their foundations established well below ground (stamped down by elephants, legend has it). The Jetavanarama Dagoba in Anuradhapura, which dates from the 3rd century and is the focus of a gigantic reconstruction project, is nearly as high as Egypt's Great Pyramid of Khufu (Cheops). As it is mainly a repository for relics, the dagoba is not usually entered.

To compare the Sri Lankan stupa with those in other Buddhist countries see www.bud dhamind.info/leftside /arty/build/styles.htm.

A uniquely Sinhalese architectural concept is the *vatadage* (circular relic house). Today you can see *vatadages* in Anuradhapura and Polonnaruwa, but perhaps the finest example is at Medirigiriya. The *vatadage* consists of a small central dagoba flanked by images of the Buddha and encircled by columns. Some people believe that long ago these columns may have supported a wooden roof, but all traces of early wooden architecture have disappeared.

Another peculiarly Sinhalese style is the *gedige,* a hollow temple with thick walls topped by a trussed roof. Often the walls are so thick that stairways can be built into them. There are a number of *gediges* in Anuradhapura and Polonnaruwa, and a restored one at Nalanda (p230).

The Temple of the Sacred Tooth Relic (p166) is a magnificent example of Kandyan architecture. Surrounded by a large moat, long since dried up, from outside its most obvious feature is a *pathiruppuwa,* an octagonal structure from where the king traditionally delivered important public communications. Inside, the lower of the temple's two storeys contains an open pillared area that leads to several smaller shrines. The Audience Hall is a large impressive space with columns, edged with paintings and reliefs.

HINDU

For more-detailed information on Sri Lankan art visit www.artsrilanka.org.

In Sri Lanka, Hindu temples, known as *kovils,* are mostly dedicated to Shiva or Murugan. They consist of a prayer hall and shrine room, and there is a covered space that allows worshippers to take the ritual clockwise walk. The *sikhara,* a central edifice that is usually dome- or pyramid-shaped, towers above the shrine room. Walls and domes may be covered with ornate murals. Some temples also have *gopurams* (gateway towers). The *gopurams* soar towards the heavens in a glitz of sculpted, brightly painted deities and saints.

EUROPEAN

The colonising Europeans all made an impact on Sri Lanka's architecture. The Portuguese influence can be seen in the high-pitched roofs and covered verandas. This style continued well after the Dutch defeated the Portuguese because, barred from administrative duties, they turned to the building trade to earn a living. The Dutch influence, characterised by fort ramparts and the broad sturdy walls of churches and administrative buildings, is, however, far more apparent. These solid features are often softened by ornamental edifices, small arches and, in the case of churches, stained-glass windows. The historic Fort (p133) in Galle has wonderful examples of Dutch style. The Dutch changed the Portuguese forts to suit their own architectural requirements, and the English continued the tradition. The English style is particularly apparent in the buildings in hill stations such as Nuwara Eliya, which positively cry out 'England'.

For stunning images that evoke the splendour of Sri Lanka, its festivals, architecture, landscape and much more, see any of Dominic Sansoni's books.

Painting & Sculpture

Images of the Buddha dominate the work of Sri Lankan sculptors. Limestone, which is plentiful, was used for early works (which means they haven't weathered well), but a variety of other materials has been used over the centuries, including jade, rock crystal, marble, emerald, pink quartz, ivory, coral and sometimes wood or metal. The Buddha is represented in three poses – sitting, standing or lying – with his hands arranged in various *mudras* (positions): *dhyana mudra,* the meditative pose, where hands rest lightly in the lap, with the right hand on the left hand; *abhaya mudra,* with right hand raised, conveying protection; and *vitarka mudra,* where the index finger touches the thumb, symbolising teaching.

The staircases at Sri Lanka's ancient temples and palaces reveal a wealth of finely sculpted detail, with the elaborately carved moonstones a notable feature (see Symbols of Sri Lanka, p46). The bottom of either side of a staircase often has guardstones. A mythical beast, *makara* (a cross between a lion, a pig and an elephant) often stretches its form along the balustrade.

For a fuller listing of Sri Lankan galleries see www.leisuretimes.lk /leisuretimes_files /galleries.jsp.

Other notable examples of sculpture include the four *vahalkadas* (solid panels) at the Kantaka Chetiya (p256) at Mihintale.

Painting, like dance and music, was not encouraged by orthodox Buddhists, yet artists (influenced by Indian conventions) *did* paint; the best-known example appears in the form of the shapely nymphs on the walls of Sigiriya (p235). On the whole, painting centred on sacred themes, with the best examples to be seen at Dambulla and Polonnaruwa, and on the walls and ceilings of many temples. By the 13th century, painting as an art form appears to have declined.

Kolams (also called *rangoli*), the rice-flour designs that adorn thresholds in Tamil areas, are much more than mere decoration. Meaning 'guise' in Tamil, *kolams* are drawn by the women of the household at sunrise. The rice flour may be eaten by small creatures – symbolising a reverence for all life, even the most apparently insignificant. This gesture is doubly blessed, as it is extremely auspicious to give as your first act of the day.

Visit the well-set-up site www.craftrevival.org /SouthAsia/SriLanka /Crafts/Pottery.htm for information on pottery, pictures of pots and places to see them.

Sri Lanka is rapidly developing a vibrant contemporary art scene. Locally woven and dyed fabrics are fashioned into striking garments, while numerous new art galleries, mainly in Colombo, exhibit work that is uniquely Sri Lankan: strong and evocative, and expressing traditional themes in modern styles. The **Sapumal Foundation** (Map pp84-5; 2/34 Barnes Pl, Col 7; ☺ 10am-1pm Thu-Sat) exhibits contemporary Sri Lankan art, while the **Gallery Cafe** (Map pp84-5; ☎ 011-258 2162; 2 Alfred House Rd) has exhibitions of painting and photography. See p90 for more art galleries in Colombo. For a taste of some of Sri Lanka's stunning textiles and design, visit **Barefoot** (Map pp84-5; ☎ 011-258 0114; www.barefootceylon.com/home.htm; 704 Galle Rd, Col 3) and **Yolland Collection** (Map pp84-5; ☎ 011-540300; Crescat Boulevard, 89 Galle Rd, Col 3). See p102 for details of other shops selling Sri Lankan crafts.

Pottery

The art of crafting pots, often made of red terracotta with symbolic designs, encompasses beauty, utility and unique style. The pottery industry has recently received a boost with increased government funding.

RESPONSIBLE TRAVEL

- You may see beggars in Sri Lanka, but not often and not many. You may, however, be approached by people claiming to be collecting money for charity. Children may also ask for sweets, but if you respond you will encourage begging. It's best to donate to a reputable charity.
- On a sad note, thousands of Sri Lankan children are sexually abused by locals as well as foreigners. If you suspect that such crimes are happening follow the reporting procedures at the website for **End Child Prostitution & Trafficking** (ECPAT; www.ecpat.net).
- At temples, always remove shoes (and usually head coverings) and dress respectfully.
- Always use your right hand when giving or receiving.
- Avoid plastic bags. They're everywhere in Sri Lanka and badly damage the environment.
- For information on responsible hiking, diving and snorkelling, see p64.

SPORT

It's a cliché, but true – cricket is another religion in Sri Lanka. Sri Lankans may play volleyball, netball, soccer, tennis and other sports, but cricket outruns them all. Cricketers are current-day deities. Innings, wickets and scores are mantras throughout the nation, and cricket pitches (including on road sides and in forest clearings) are temples. Sri Lanka's 1996 World Cup win boosted its cricket reputation nationally and internationally.

It's easy to see a big match – the main venue is the Premadasa Stadium in Kettarama, Colombo. Other venues include the Sinhalese Sports Club (SSC) in Cinnamon Gardens, Colombo, and ovals at Moratuwa, Borella (Sara Stadium), Kandy, Dambulla and Galle. Check the local newspapers to catch a club match or international game at almost any time of year.

One entirely sedentary sport enjoyed by many Sri Lankans is betting on British horse and dog racing! With racing in Sri Lanka frowned upon by the Buddhist establishment, you'll see people in hole-in-the-wall betting shops avidly studying the day's races in Aintree, Ascot and Hackney. Race commentaries are beamed from Britain starting at about 6pm. This passion is one reason for the mushrooming of satellite dishes, but the betting bug may take a dive as the government imposes new taxes.

The Net teems with cricket sites where player pics vie for space with facts. For tongue-in-cheek but reliable information go to news.bbc.co.uk/sportacademy/bsp/hi/cricket/rules/html/default.stm.

MEDIA

The media in Sri Lanka comes in Sinhala-, Tamil- and English-language forms, and is both state and privately owned. After peace negotiations began in 2002, the government approved a radio license for the formerly clandestine Tamil radio station 'Voice of the Tigers'. See the daily newspapers for radio and TV programmes.

The media is generally seen as open and unafraid to be critical, but there are also claims of bias. State-controlled media is accused of government propaganda, and counteraccusations are levelled at the private media. More serious are journalists' claims that they fear retribution for their reporting. Sadly their fears are well founded, as they have suffered assaults, threats and even death. In 2004, three journalists were killed – two allegedly for articles they had written, and one while on duty.

The journalists' allegations have been investigated by the international organisation Reporters without Borders and by the local Free Media Movement. The results of their investigations have been submitted to the government, requesting that justice be administered.

Freer than print media and public broadcasts is the Internet, where Sri Lankans can read and write whatever they like.

Sri Lankans can choose from eight daily newspapers, nine radio stations and 10 TV channels. For quick links to the media visit www.abyznewslinks.com/srila.htm.

Environment

THE LAND

Shaped like a teardrop falling from the southern end of India, the island country of Sri Lanka stretches 433km from north to south, and measures only 244km at its widest point. At 66,000 sq km it is roughly the same size as Ireland or Tasmania.

The southern centre of the island is dominated by mountains and hills, which taper down to coastal plains. The highest mountain is broadbacked Mt Pidurutalagala (2524m), rising above Sri Lanka's tea-growing capital, Nuwara Eliya. However, the pyramid profile of 2243m-high Adam's Peak (Sri Pada) is better known and far more spectacular.

Hundred of streams and rivers carry rain from the south central mountains down to the rice-growing plains. The Mahaweli Ganga, Sri Lanka's longest river, has its source close to Adam's Peak and runs 860km before emptying into the sea near Trincomalee.

The rolling plains of the north central and northern Sri Lanka extend from the Hill Country all the way to the northern tip of the island. This region is much drier than the rest of the island.

Hundreds of lagoons, marshes and beaches punctuate Sri Lanka's Indian Ocean coastline, with the most picturesque beaches found on the southwest, south and east coasts. A group of low, flat islands lies off Jaffna.

> The Mahaweli Ganga drains 16% of the island's fresh water and is the primary source for all irrigation in the dry zone.

WILDLIFE
Animals

Sri Lanka boasts 92 mammal species, including leopards, monkeys and elephants. Other interesting mammals include sloth bears, loris, porcupines, jackals, dugongs and flying foxes. In addition the country has registered 242 species of butterflies, 435 species of birds, 107 species of fish and 81 species of snakes.

> Although the section on Sri Lanka is rather small, *Field Guide to the Mammals of the Indian Subcontinent*, by KK Gurung and Raj Singh, is one of the few guides that detail Sri Lankan mammals.

PRIMATES

The common langur, also known as the Hanuman or grey langur, is a slender, long-tailed monkey that bounds through the tree tops with remarkable agility. Troops of 15 to 20 forage mostly in the trees but will descend to the ground to collect fallen fruit. The endemic purple-faced langur has a black brown body and limbs. It has been proposed that several species of monkey, including the shaggy bear monkeys of the mountain forests, are subspecies of the langur. Open forest, dense jungle and temples are all prime habitats.

Noisy troops of toque macaques occupy most of the island. The monkeys' heads have a distinctive thatch of hair parted down the middle.

The striking slender loris is a small, slow-moving, brown grey primate. According to superstition, its large, close-set eyes have the power to induce love! It snatches insects, amphibians, reptiles, birds and small mammals with a lightning-quick lunge, and supplements its diet with fruits and leaves. It is usually solitary, but is occasionally found in pairs.

PREDATORY ANIMALS

The sloth bear is typically black with a white v-shaped blaze across the chest; its powerful forearms end in great curved claws, which are used for climbing and ripping apart termite mounds.

The golden jackal is a well-known fringe dweller. Shy and shrewd, it is mostly nocturnal; eerie howling at dusk signals the beginning of the night's activity. Notorious as a scavenger, the jackal is also an opportunistic hunter of small mammals, birds, reptiles and insects. Occasionally a large pack will congregate and run down larger prey, such as deer.

The wide distribution of the leopard attests to the adaptability of this predator. It is an agile climber and will drag its prey high up a tree to avoid scavengers. The leopard's diet can be quite diverse, ranging from insects and amphibians to large deer, although some leopards become partial to certain meats. This solitary creature roams within a defined territory, and most activity, particularly hunting, occurs at dawn or dusk. Sri Lanka has a subspecies endemic to the country, the *Panthera pardus kotika*.

Common palm civets are catlike hunters related to weasels. Long-bodied with short limbs and a very long tail, the palm civet has a speckled grey coat with indistinct longitudinal stripes or spots of a lighter colour. The palm civet is also known as the toddy cat because of its taste for fermenting coconut-palm sap.

Mongooses look like ferrets, and have a speckled grey body colour. They prey on snakes, frogs, birds and small mammals, and also eat fruit and birds' eggs. They hunt during both the day and night, usually alone but sometimes in pairs.

An armour plating of large, overlapping scales distinguishes the Indian pangolin. The grey scales, made from modified hair, cover the top of its head and the top and sides of its body. The shy pangolin ventures out at night to raid termite mounds and ant nests. When threatened, it curls itself into a ball, its tail tightly enveloping its vulnerable belly.

The Department of Forestry & Environmental Science at the University of Sri Jayewardenepura maintains www.environmentlanka.com, a website that displays photos of Sri Lankan wildlife and essays on key environmental issues.

BOAR & DEER

The omnivorous wild boar of Sri Lanka is closely related to the slightly hairier wild boar of Europe. A strip of long black bristles, which rises when the animal is excited, runs down its spine. The elongated tusks of the upper and lower jaw, more pronounced in the male, are formidable weapons. Wild boars are common in open forests and near cultivated land.

The sambar is a big, brown and shaggy-coated deer with a mane. More active by night than day, sambar can be observed at dawn and dusk, usually near water. A matriarch hind will lead a group of 10 to 20 deer. The mature male, or stag, leads a solitary life apart from the rutting season (November to December). Prior to the rut he develops antlers, which are used in ritualistic combat with other males.

Chital deer have reddish brown backs and sides with rows of white spots. They graze in herds of 10 to 30, which may include two or three mature stags. Chital frequent open forest and places where forest meets grassland or cultivated land. Often they can be seen with langurs; the chital feed on fruit dropped by the monkeys, and both gain security from the extra eyes, ears and noses.

OTHER MAMMALS

The five-striped palm squirrel has a grey brown body and a long, bushy grey tail. These squirrels are more commonly seen in gardens and town parks than native forest. They eat fruit, nuts, flowers, shoots, insects and birds' eggs. Their scurrying and bounding is accompanied by shrill, high-pitched chatter, and much flicking of their bushy tails.

The Indian flying fox is a fruit-eating bat with an impressive 1.2m wingspan. Camps (groups of roosting bats), most often found in very large trees, can number up to several hundred bats. They decamp soon after sunset.

THE ROYAL PACHYDERM

Elephants occupy a special place in Sri Lankan culture. In ancient times elephants were Crown property and killing one was a terrible offence. Legend has it that elephants stamped down the foundations of the great dagobas (stupas) at Anuradhapura, and elephant iconography is common in Sri Lankan religious and secular art. Even today elephants are held in great affection and the Maligawa tusker, which carries the sacred tooth relic on the final night of the Kandy Esala Perahera, is perhaps the most venerated of all.

There are some 2500 wild elephants in Sri Lanka (compared with 12,000 in 1900), plus about 300 domesticated elephants (most of which were born in the wild). There are two subspecies of the Asian elephant: *Elephas maximus maximus* (Ceylon elephant) and *Elephas maximus vilaliya* (Ceylon marsh elephant). The Asian elephant is smaller than the African elephant; it also has a rounder back, smaller ears, one 'lip' rather than two on the tip of its trunk and four nails rather than three on its hind feet. In Sri Lanka, most females and many males are tuskless. Asian elephants congregate in family groups of up to 10 led by an adult female. Males, banished from the family group upon maturity, may form bachelor herds.

Farmers in elephant country face an ever present threat from animals that may trample their crops, destroy their buildings and even take their lives. During the cultivation season farmers conduct around-the-clock vigils for up to three months to scare off the unwelcome raiders. For farmers on the breadline, elephants are a luxury they can't afford; one solution to the problem is swift and adequate compensation for elephant-inflicted damage. Arming farmers is occasionally mooted, but this would surely hasten the demise of elephants in Sri Lanka. Creating elephant corridors is another option, as has been done with the creation of Kaudulla National Park. Problem elephants are sometimes relocated, but seem to have a knack for finding their way back.

REPTILES & FISH

Sri Lanka has many species of large reptiles, including 83 species of snakes.

Mugger crocodiles can be seen on the banks of rivers, lakes and marshes. If a pond dries up, muggers will march great distances to reach water. They feed on fish, amphibians, birds, and mammals such as young deer. Muggers are social creatures, especially during mating season.

Seven venomous snakes are found in Sri Lanka: Russell's viper, green pit viper, hump-nosed viper, saw-scaled viper, common krait, Ceylon krait and cobra.

The water monitor is distinguished by its sheer size and colourful markings – black with yellow dappling on its back and a pale yellow belly. This scavenger is an expert swimmer, and is particularly fond of crocodile eggs and bird eggs. It swallows its prey whole, mostly unchewed.

The Indian cobra is the famous hooded snake associated with the subcontinent's snake charmers. This highly venomous snake avoids confrontation and will usually retreat if threatened. Cobras are mostly nocturnal and feed on amphibians, reptiles and mammals, particularly mice and rats.

Some 54 species of fish are found in Sri Lanka's waterways and marshlands, including prized aquarium varieties such as the red scissor-tail barb and the ornate paradise fish. The British introduced several kinds of fish, including trout, which is still common around Horton Plains National Park (p205). There are myriad colourful tropical marine fish.

Divers and snorkellers will find Dr Charles Anderson's well-illustrated *Common Reef Fishes of Sri Lanka* to be of interest.

Sri Lanka has five species of marine turtle, all endangered: the leatherback, the olive ridley, the loggerhead, the hawksbill and the green. Though protected, they face significant threats from poachers, and environmental hazards caused by pollution and coastal development.

BIRDS

A tropical climate, long isolation from the Asian mainland and a diversity of habitats have helped endow Sri Lanka with an astonishing abundance of birdlife. There are more than 400 bird species, 26 of which are unique

---

TIPS FOR BIRD-WATCHERS

Visit a variety of habitats – rainforest, urban parks, and bodies of water in the dry zone – to see the full diversity of birdlife in Sri Lanka.

February to March is the best time for bird-watching – you miss the monsoons and the migrant birds are still visiting. Water birds are active for most of the day. Although morning is always the best time to go bird-watching, you will see noisy flocks of birds preparing to roost in the evening.

A pair of binoculars is an invaluable tool to help with identification. Small models can be bought cheaply duty-free and don't weigh much.

Consider taking a tour with a specialist if you're keen to see the endemic species and achieve a healthy bird-watching tally, particularly if time is short.

---

to Sri Lanka, while others are found only in Sri Lanka and adjacent South India. Of the estimated 198 migrant species, most of which stay here from August to April, the waders (sandpipers, plovers etc) are the long-distance champions, making the journey from their breeding grounds in the Arctic tundra.

Reference books on Sri Lanka's birds include *A Selection of the Birds of Sri Lanka*, by John and Judy Banks, a slim, well-illustrated book that's perfect for amateur bird-watchers. *A Photographic Guide to Birds of Sri Lanka*, by Gehan de Silva Wijeyeratne, Deepal Warakagoda and TSU de Zylva, is a notch above; it's a pocket-sized book jam-packed with colour photos. *A Field Guide to the Birds of Sri Lanka*, by John Harrison, is a hardback with colour illustrations; it's pricey, but is one of the best field guides available.

Cities, Towns & Villages

Food scraps and gardens around dwellings attract insects, which in turn attract many birds. The call of the black house crow *(Corvus splendens)* is one of the first bird sounds you'll hear in Sri Lanka. Like the common myna and house sparrow, this species is ubiquitous around settlements. The common swallow *(Hirundo rustica)* can be seen chasing insects over virtually any open space, while Loten's sunbirds *(Nectarinia lotenia)*, little creatures with iridescent plumage and a sharp down-curved bill, are often seen flitting in flower gardens. The black-headed oriole *(Oriolus xanthornus)* has a bright yellow back and belly, a black head, an orange beak and yellow-and-black wings. It usually hides in the treetops; its frequent singing is a giveaway. Some species, such as house swifts *(Apus affinis)*, are so accustomed to humans that they are only rarely found away from settlements.

You'll see many bird species at Viharamahadevi Park (p90) in central Colombo, and the beautiful Peradeniya Botanic Gardens (p188) near Kandy. Sigiriya village (p233) is also home to dozens of species.

Countryside

A surprising variety of birds can be seen on rice paddies, in open wooded areas and by the roadside. These birds are often lured by the insects that crops and livestock attract. The shiny black drongos *(Dicrurus macrocercus)* have forked tails; noisy and ostentatious, they're often seen swooping after flying insects. Tiny black palm swifts *(Cypsiurus balasiensis)* sweep low over the fields chasing prey, while white cattle egrets *(Bubulcus ibis)*, whose breeding plumage is actually fawn coloured, pluck lice from water buffalo. Egrets also flock around farmers as they plough. Brahminy kites *(Haliastur indus)* may be spotted flying overhead. Adults of this species have a white head and chest and chestnut brown wings and belly. Green

Sri Lanka's first new bird discovery in 132 years occurred in 2001. Many birders are calling the small, orange-feathered owl the Serendib Owl.

bee-eaters *(Merops orientalis)* are often seen in pairs, perched near the ground or flitting around catching insects. You can identify this bird by the black stripe on each side of its head, its aqua-coloured throat and chin, the orange on the back of its head, and its green wings. The Ceylon junglefowl *(Gallus lafayettii)*, an endemic relative of the domestic chicken, is widespread in remote areas but rarely found near settlements.

Most of these species are easily spotted from the comfort of a bus seat.

Sri Lanka has a large proportion of endemic species: 23% of the flowering plants and 16% of the mammals on the island are native to the island.

Wetlands, Waterways & Tanks

In the dry regions, bodies of water and their fringe vegetation provide an important habitat for many birds. You can't miss the clumsy-looking painted stork *(Mycteria leucocephala)*, with its distinctive orange face and pink rump feathers. Great egrets *(Casmerodius albus)*, huge white birds with yellow beaks, pick off fish with deadly precision. Spoonbills *(Platalea leucorodia)* swish their peculiar flattened bills from side to side, snapping up small creatures.

Little cormorants *(Phalacrocorax niger)* are regularly seen in large flocks. The little cormorant is smaller and less heavily built than the Indian cormorant *(Phalacrocorax fuscicollis)*, and has a shorter neck and beak. Both birds are dark brown to black and are often seen with their wings stretched out to dry. Keep an eye out for the Indian darter

---

RESPONSIBLE ACTIVITIES
RESPONSIBLE DIVING & SNORKELLING

Sri Lanka is a wonderful place for diving and snorkelling, but it is important to observe a few simple rules to minimise your impact, and help preserve the ecology and beauty of marine areas:

- Don't use anchors on a reef, and take care not to ground boats on coral. Encourage dive operators and regulatory bodies to establish permanent moorings at popular dive sites.

- Avoid touching living marine organisms with your body or dragging equipment across reefs. Polyps are damaged even by gentle contact. Never stand on corals, even if they look solid and robust. If you must hold onto the reef, only touch exposed rock or dead coral.

- Be conscious of your fins. Even without contact the surge from heavy fin strokes near a reef can damage delicate organisms. When treading water in shallow reef areas, avoid kicking up clouds of sand. Settling sand can easily smother delicate organisms.

- Practise and maintain proper buoyancy control. Major damage can be done by divers descending too fast and colliding with the reef. Make sure you're correctly weighted and that your weight belt is positioned so you stay horizontal in the water. If you have not dived for a while, have a practice dive in a pool before heading out. Be aware that buoyancy can change over the period of an extended trip; initially you may breathe harder and need more weight, but a few days later you may breathe more easily and need less weight.

- Take great care in underwater caves. Spend as little time in them as possible, as your air bubbles may be caught beneath the roof and leave previously submerged organisms high and dry. Take turns to inspect the interior of small caves to lessen the chances of contact.

- Ensure that you take home all your rubbish and any litter you may find. Plastic in particular is a serious menace to marine life – turtles can mistake it for jellyfish and eat it.

- Resist the temptation to feed the fish. You may disturb their normal eating habits or encourage aggressive behaviour.

- Minimise your disturbance of marine animals. In particular, do not ride on the backs of turtles as this causes them great anxiety. Similarly, discourage your boat driver from circling around turtles, which also puts them under stress.

(Anhinga melanogaster), which has a lanky brown neck and spears fish underwater with its daggerlike bill. It is also known as the snake bird because of its peculiar habit of swimming like a snake.

The common kingfisher *(Alcedo atthis)*, with striking blue plumage and a tan belly and flank, is often seen skimming the water or watching for fish.

The dark-brown-and-white pheasant-tailed jacana *(Hydrophasianus chirurgus)* trots across lily pads on incredibly long, slender toes. Its long tail feathers are shed after the breeding season.

The greater flamingo *(Phoenicopterus ruber)* has a short bent beak, spindly legs and white-and-pink plumage. It is mostly found in Bundala National Park (p152).

Virtually any tank (artificial lake) or large body of water is host to a selection of water birds. Try the tanks at Anuradhapura (p247) and Polonnaruwa (p237). Bundala National Park (p152) and Yala National Park (p156) are also particularly good spots.

What Tree Is That?, by Sriyanie Miththapala and PA Miththapala, contains handy sketches of common trees and shrubs in Sri Lanka, and includes English, Sinhala and botanical names.

Rainforests & Jungle
Most of Sri Lanka's endemic birds are found in the rainforests of the hill zone. A walk in the forest can be eerily quiet until you encounter a feeding party, and then all hell breaks loose! Birds of many species travel in flocks, foraging in the forest canopy and among the leaf litter of the forest floor.

RESPONSIBLE HIKING

Sri Lanka offers plenty of scope for great hiking; please consider the following tips to help minimise your impact on the environment.

Rubbish

- Carry out all your rubbish. Don't overlook items such as silver paper, orange peel, cigarette butts and plastic wrappers. Make an effort to carry out rubbish left by others.

- Never bury your rubbish; digging disturbs soil and ground cover, and encourages erosion. Buried rubbish will more than likely be dug up by animals, who may be injured or poisoned by it. It may also take years to decompose.

- Minimise the waste you must carry out by taking minimal packaging and taking no more food than you need. If you can't buy in bulk, unpack small-portion packages and combine their contents in one container before your trip. Take reusable containers or stuff sacks.

- On longer walks, don't rely on plastic water bottles, as their disposal is a major problem. Use iodine drops or purification tablets instead.

Human Waste Disposal

- Contamination of water sources by human faeces can lead to the transmission of hepatitis, typhoid and intestinal parasites such as giardia and roundworms.

- Where there is no toilet, bury your waste. Dig a small hole 15cm (6in) deep and at least 100m (320ft) from any watercourse. Consider carrying a lightweight trowel for this purpose. Cover the waste with soil and a rock, and carry out your toilet paper.

Erosion

- Hillsides and mountain slopes, especially at high altitudes, are prone to erosion. It is important to stick to existing tracks and avoid short cuts that bypass a switchback.

- If a well-used track passes through a mud patch, walk through the mud; walking around the edge will increase the size of the patch.

You'll probably see noisy orange-billed babblers *(Turdoides rufescens),* which have brown plumage and orange beaks (hence their name). Then there's the Ceylon paradise flycatcher *(Terpsiphone paradisi ceylonensis),* which has a distinctive chestnut-coloured back and tail, white chest and black-crested head. The male of this species has a long, showy tail. You may also see the black Ceylon crested drongo *(Dicrurus paradiseus ceylonicus)* with its deeply forked tail and noisy chattering, or if you are lucky, the beautiful blue-and-chestnut Ceylon blue magpie *(Urocissa ornata).* Noisy flocks of blossom-headed parakeets *(Psittacula cyanocephala)* are often seen flying between patches of forest in the lower hills.

Sinharaja Forest Reserve (p221) contains many endemic species, while others are found at Horton Plains National Park (p205). Udawattakelle Sanctuary (p168) in Kandy is also rewarding, and is easy to reach as well.

ENDANGERED SPECIES

Red Databook, produced by the World Conservation Union (formerly the IUCN), lists 43 animal species as threatened in Sri Lanka. They include the two subspecies of Asian elephant, the sloth bear and the leopard. All five of Sri Lanka's turtle species are threatened, as is the estuarine crocodile and the mild-mannered dugong, both of which are killed for their meat. Also under threat are several species of birds, fish and insects.

Plants

The southwestern wet zone is tropical rainforest with dense undergrowth and a tall canopy of hardwood trees, including ebony, teak and silkwood. Here also are some of the most spectacular orchids and many of the plants used in traditional Ayurvedic medicine. The central hill zone has cloud forests and some rare highland areas populated by hardy grasslands and elfin (stunted) forests. The remainder of the island forms the arid dry zone, with a sparser cover of trees and shrubs, and grasslands that may erupt into bloom with the first rains.

The sacred bodhi tree *(Ficus religiosa)* was brought from India when Mahinda introduced the teachings of the Buddha to Sri Lanka. Saplings are planted in most Buddhist temples in Sri Lanka. The shape of a turned-over leaf is said to have inspired the shape of the dagoba (stupa). Also often found around Buddhist temples is the *sal,* also known as the cannonball tree. You'll understand how the tree got its name when you see the huge woody fruits clinging to the trunk. The frangipani is common throughout the island; its sweet-scented white, pink or yellow flowers are used as Buddhist temple offerings. You'll also see plenty of scarlet and magenta bougainvilleas in gardens. In the Hill Country there are many eucalyptus trees, which have often been planted to provide shade at tea estates.

Fruit trees such as mangoes, papayas and bananas grow in many private gardens in Sri Lanka, but the jackfruit and the *del* (breadfruit) will catch your eye in particular. The jackfruit is a tall evergreen with the world's largest fruit; green and knobbly skinned, the fruit weigh up to 30kg and hang close to the trunk. The *del* is the jackfruit's smaller relative.

NATIONAL PARKS & RESERVES

More than 2000 years ago royalty ensured certain areas were protected from any human activity by declaring them sanctuaries. The oldest of these, Mihintale, was created by King Devanampiya Tissa in the 3rd century BC and was the first wildlife sanctuary in the world. Almost every province in the kingdom of Kandy had such *udawattakelle* (sanctuaries). All animals and plants in these sanctuaries were left undisturbed.

Supporting conservation and environmental awareness, the Green Movement of Sri Lanka is a consortium of 147 Sri Lankan groups that are involved in natural resource management; check out its website at www.greensl.net.

MAJOR NATIONAL PARKS & RESERVES

Park	Area	Features	Best Time to Visit
Bundala National Park (p152)	6216 hectares	coastal lagoon, migratory birds, elephants	May-Sep
Gal Oya National Park (p278)	62,936 hectares	grasslands, evergreen forest, deer, Senanayake Samudra (tank), elephants, sloth bears, leopards, water buffaloes	Dec-Sep
Horton Plains National Park (p205)	3160 hectares	mossy forests, marshy grasslands, World's End precipice	Jan-Mar
Kaudulla National Park p245)	6656 hectares	Kaudulla Tank, evergreen forest, scrub jungle, grassy plains, elephants, leopards, sambar deer, fishing cats, rusty spotted cats, sloth bears	Jan-Mar
Minneriya National Park (p245)	8890 hectares	Minneriya Tank, toque macaque, sambar deer, elephant, waterfowl	Jun-Sep
Sinharaja Forest Reserve (p221)	18,899 hectares	Unesco World Heritage Site, sambar, rainforest, leopard, purple-faced langurs, barking deer, 147 recorded bird species	Aug-Sep, Jan-Mar
Uda Walawe National Park (p220)	30,821 hectares	grassland, thorn scrub, elephants, spotted deer, water buffaloes, wild boar	May-Sep
Wilpattu National Park (p109)	131,693 hectares	dense jungle, scrub, saltgrass, elephants, leopards, sloth bears, deer, crocodiles	Jan-Mar
Yala East National Park (p275)	18,149 hectares	grassland, jungle, lagoons, mangrove swamp, waterfowl	Dec-Sep
Yala National Park (p156)	14,101 hectares	tropical thornforest, lagoons, coral reef, elephants, sloth bears, leopards, water buffaloes, crested serpent eagles, lesser flamingos	May-Sep

Today's system of parks and reserves is mostly a synthesis of traditionally protected areas and those established by the British. There are 100 areas protected by the government, covering 8% of the island and divided into three types: national parks, strict nature reserves (where no visitors are allowed) and nature reserves, in which human habitation is permitted. Some parks in the northern and northeastern parts of Sri Lanka are currently unprotected; they have no onsite rangers and are being exploited by armed poachers and loggers. See above for specific details on Sri Lanka's national parks.

ENVIRONMENTAL ISSUES

At the beginning of the 20th century about 70% of the island was covered by natural forest. By 1998 this had shrunk to about 24%. *Chena* (shifting cultivation) is blamed for a good part of this deforestation, but irrigation schemes and clearance for cultivation have also been contributing factors. In recent decades the biggest danger to the island's forests has been illegal logging.

Gem mining, sand mining and the destruction of coral reefs to feed lime kilns have also degraded the environment. On the west coast, prawn farming has done major damage to the coastal ecology between Chilaw and Puttalam.

Eighty-two per cent of the land is controlled by the state in some form or other; the majority of natural forests are under state jurisdiction. There is a raft of legislation to combat destructive activity and to protect sensitive areas. Sri Lanka is a signatory to the Ramsar Convention on Wetlands and Bundala National Park (p152) has been recognised internationally under this convention. Sinharaja Forest Reserve (p221) is a World Heritage Site – saved after being logged during the early 1970s. Sri Lanka has two marine sanctuaries: the Bar Reef (west of Kalpitiya peninsula) and the Hikkaduwa Marine Sanctuary.

Although the 2004 tsunami had catastrophic consequences for human society along Sri Lanka's coasts, its effects on marine life were minimal. Damage to coral reefs, for example, has been estimated at 5% or less. In a few cases the tsunami altered the shapes of lagoons, coves and other coastal features, but most mangroves survived and the flora and fauna habituated to these areas live on relatively unperturbed.

In 1991, Sri Lanka became one of the first countries in the world to impose a total ban on genetically modified foods.

Food & Drink

Sri Lanka boasts a unique and exciting cuisine, shaped by the bounty of the island and the varied tastes introduced by traders and invaders. Yet, in spite of this, Sri Lankan cuisine is little known and often confused with other culinary styles. The distinctiveness of the island's cuisine comes from the freshness of its herbs and spices and the methods used to grind, pound, roast, temper and combine. Roasting the spices a little more, or a little less, delivers a very different outcome. The oil that distributes the flavours throughout the dish may be vegetable, sesame or, for a richer taste, coconut. Varieties of rice offer different textures, fragrances and flavours. Curries may be prepared within delicious sauces, or they may be 'dry'.

Regional differences in cuisine are more about availability of ingredients than ethnicity. In the North, the palmyra tree reigns, and its roots, flowers, fruits and seeds produce dishes ranging from curries to syrups, sweets, cakes and snacks. In the South, rice is considered indispensable; fish and jackfruit are popular too. In the fertile Hill Country there are vegetables and mutton, but fewer fish and fewer spices.

But it's really the personal touch that creates the food's uniqueness. The same ingredients and the same methods produce radically different results as each cook conjures up a cuisine with their own particular magic.

In text and images, Vinodini de Silva's *Cultural Rhapsody, Ceremonial Food and Rituals of Sri Lanka* celebrates the cuisine customs of Sri Lanka across cultures, religions and regions.

STAPLES & SPECIALITIES

Rice is the main staple of Sri Lankan cuisine, and it is served in numerous ways – plain, spiced, in meat juices, with curd (buffalo-milk yoghurt) or tamarind, or with milk. It's usually eaten, in some form or other, at every meal. Rice flour often forms the basis of two popular Sri Lankan dishes: hoppers (also called *ah-ppa* or *appam*), which are bowl-shaped pancakes, and dosas (thosai), the paper-thin pancakes that are often served stuffed with spiced vegetables.

Popular breakfasts include hoppers, bread dipped in curry, and *pittu* (*puttu* in Tamil) – the latter a mixture of rice flour and coconut steamed in a bamboo mould. *Kola kanda* (porridge of rice, coconut, green vegetables and herbs) is nutritious, and although it has fallen from favour it is now regaining popularity.

At lunch or dinner you can try some short eats (p72), eat from a streetside hut, or dine on a banquet of rice and curry.

Rice & Curry

Sri Lankan rice and curry usually includes a variety of small spiced dishes made from vegetables, meat or fish. They're generally served with accompaniments like chutney and *sambol* – a term that describes any condiment made from ingredients pounded with chilli.

Local spices flavour Sri Lankan curry, and most curries include chilli, turmeric, cinnamon, cardamom, coriander, *rampe* (pandanus leaves), curry leaves, mustard, tamarind and coconut milk; dried fish is also frequently used to season dishes.

The many varieties of rice are often cooked with subtle spices.

Sri Lankan food is slow to prepare, hot to consume. Having endured centuries of Western whinging about spicy food, Sri Lankans have tempered it for Western palates, but if you like it hot, they'll oblige. If it's not hot enough just add some *pol sambol*, a condiment of chilli and coconut. If you don't like it hot, you'll still have a range of delicious possibilities – the

The beautifully produced *Sri Lankan Flavours*, by talented chef Channa Dassanayaka, offers recipes and personal stories of Sinhalese people and food.

lighter the colour the lighter the heat. But if your mouth suddenly explodes from chilli fire, just have some rice, yoghurt or cucumber. Alcohol's a good antidote, too, as it dissolves chilli oil – maybe the British lager louts, with their vindaloo and beer extravaganzas, have got it right!

Because Sri Lankan food takes some time to prepare, order early, state exactly what you want and leave the cooks to work their magic.

Sri Lanka exports over 11 million metric tons per year of seafood; almost 400 tons of that is crab and lobster.

Fish & Seafood

After the 2004 tsunami many people naturally avoided seafood, but they're gradually returning to the produce of the sea. Excellent fish and prawns are widespread, and in many coastal towns you'll find crab and lobster. Seer, a tuna-type fish, is always a favourite. A southern speciality is the popular *ambulthiyal* (sour fish curry), made with *goraka,* a sour fruit.

Other Specialities

Sri Lankans love their hoppers. These bowl-shaped pancakes are skilfully fried over a high flame and are sometimes served with an egg or banana in the middle. String hoppers are tangles of steamed noodles, often used instead of rice as a curry dip.

Recipes of the Jaffna Tamils, edited by Nesa Eliezer, is a culinary journey through Tamil Sri Lanka. It is lovingly compiled from recipes and stories of spice-laden dishes contributed by local and expat Tamils.

Chilli lovers will thrive on 'devilled' dishes, where meat is infused with chilli. *Lamprais* is made from rice, meat and vegetables, all slowly baked in a banana leaf; open the leaf to release the aroma and tempt the senses.

Desserts & Sweets

Sri Lankans love to indulge their sweet tooths; sweets were traditionally eaten at the beginning of the meal but this is rare now. *Wattalappam* (*vattalappam* in Tamil), a coconut-milk and egg pudding with jaggery and cardamom, is a favourite dessert, while curd with *kitul* (syrup from the *kitul* palm; also called treacle) is good at any time. You can buy curd in clay pots with a handy carry rope; the pots are so attractive you'll want to keep them. Hardened *kitul* is jaggery, a candy and all-purpose sweetener. See p75 for a list of other desserts and sweets.

Fruit

Sri Lanka has a wide variety of fruit: passion fruit, avocados, mangoes, melons, pineapples and guavas are just a few. Try a sweet red banana or papaya with lime for a delicious start to the day, or check out some of the many products of the ever-versatile coconut (p110).

Sri Lanka produces over 12,000 metric tons per year of cinnamon – two-thirds of the world's supply. It's mostly cultivated on land plots that are smaller than 2 hectares.

The wooden-shelled woodapple is used for refreshing drinks, dessert toppings and jam. The infamous spiky-skinned durian smells – but doesn't taste – like a blocked sewer. Rambutan is so sought after that growers guard their trees to outwit poachers. Mangosteen tastes like strawberries and grapes combined, and Queen Victoria is said to have offered a considerable prize for one. You'll get one (and more) from July to September. The jackfruit, with its orange-yellow segments, is the world's biggest fruit. It tastes good fresh, or in curry.

DRINKS
Nonalcoholic Drinks

In Sri Lanka's heat it's always wise to have water with you, whether boiled or bottled. Guesthouses will usually arrange the boiling for you. Sri Lanka also has a ready supply of bottled water.

Most Sri Lankans drink tea with plenty of sugar. If you don't have a sweet tooth you'll need to be assertive just to lower the dose. When made with fresh tea leaves, it's a wonderfully aromatic drink.

Sri Lankans don't drink coffee, so it may be best if you don't drink it either; unless you're staying in a top-end hotel, Colombo is the only place you'll get a good espresso.

Lime juice is excellent. Have it with soda water (but ask for the salt or sugar to be separate, otherwise you could be in for another major sugar kick). And the local Elephant House ginger beer is not just a thirst quencher – it's marketed as having Ayurvedic qualities (see p320 for more information on Ayurveda). Another favourite drink is *faluda*, a syrup and milk drink that often contains jelly pieces.

A refreshing, natural option is *thambili* (king coconut), for sale at stalls everywhere.

Alcoholic Drinks

Local (Lion Lager, Carlsberg and Three Coins) and imported beers are available; Three Coins is a premium beer, and therefore will cost a little more. The local wines are syrupy sweet.

Other local alcoholic beverages include toddy, a drink made from the sap of palm trees. It has a bitter (or sharp) taste a bit like cider. There are three types of toddy: toddy made from coconut palms, toddy from *kitul* palms, and toddy from palmyras. Toddy dens are on village outskirts, where men can drink without disturbing others.

Fermented and refined toddy becomes arrack. It's produced in a variety of qualities – some are real firewater. Kalutara, 40km south of Colombo, is the toddy and arrack capital. The best mixer for arrack is the local ginger ale.

If you like a drink, remember that alcohol isn't sold on *poya* (full moon) holidays.

CELEBRATIONS

As a symbol of life and fertility, rice is the food for festivities. The Buddha is said to have derived energy from *kiri bath* (coconut-milk rice) and subsequently achieved nirvana. *Kiri bath* is the baby's first solid food; it's also the food the new bride and groom feed each other, and it's the festive food for New Year.

Dumplings are a popular celebration food, but imagine them landing on your head! This is a custom in the north involving *kolukattai* (dumplings with edges pressed to resemble teeth) being dropped gently on a toddler's head while the family make wishes for the infant to develop healthy teeth. Dumplings are also a favourite of Ganesh; sweet dumplings, *mothagam*, are offered to him in prayer.

Hindus celebrate the harvest at Thai Pongal, in January. *Pongal* (milk boiled with rice and jaggery) is offered to the sun god in thanksgiving. Later, the rice is eaten in celebration of the harvest and its life-sustaining qualities.

Ramadan ends with the breaking of the fast and the Eid-ul-Fitr festival. Muslims eat dates in memory of the Prophet Mohammed, and then *congee* (rice cooked with spices, coconut milk and meat). The food itself is not as important as its significance – a reminder to strive for equality for all. On Eid-ul-Fitr, Muslims share food (often the rice dish biryani) with family, friends and neighbours.

Aurudu (Sri Lankan New Year) is another time for celebration. After the sacred activities, feasting begins with *kiri bath* followed by *kaung* (oil cake), a Sri Lankan favourite. Try it, if you enjoy sweet oil coating your palate! Once again it's not the food that's important but its significance – reconciliation and harmony among family, friends and neighbours.

Toddy (prior to fermentation) is an excellent animal food. In recent years, Sri Lankan toddy tappers have shared their expertise with farmers in Vietnam, whose animals can now take advantage of this excellent food source.

Toddy tappers can tap up to 100 trees per day, and each tree may yield from 550L to 800L per year.

Many Sri Lankans value the gotukola plant for its medicinal properties; it has been used to treat AIDS, restore memory loss and promote intelligence.

WHERE TO EAT & DRINK

There's absolutely no doubt that the best place to eat in Sri Lanka is the home. Whether rich or poor, luxurious or simple, home-prepared food has a variety and zing that excites and satisfies. Perhaps this is why Sri Lanka has not traditionally had a restaurant culture. Tourism has changed this, and in the cities you'll find the usual restaurants, cafés and bars. Outside the cities you'll find numerous places, often aesthetically located and constructed, where you'll enjoy a range of local and Western dishes. Family-run guesthouses are the next best thing to home dining. No amount of trouble is spared in satisfying guests, so just explain your likes and dislikes, and enjoy the result. In the larger upmarket hotels, traditional-style banquets are very popular. And in most places you can dine as quickly or as slowly as you like, feeling at ease whether you're alone or with others.

Except in Colombo, most places close early so it's best to check if you're planning to eat late. Most sit-down restaurants add 15% tax to the bill, and many also add a 10% service charge. However, the people waiting on you earn minuscule salaries and tips are usually appreciated.

Interested in the amount of manganese in tea, the annual production of okra, or the major markets for desiccated coconut? Then visit www .srilankabusiness.com. Within this slow and convoluted portal are some statistical gems.

Quick Eats

If you're in a hurry try some short eats. These are a selection of meat-stuffed rolls, meat-and-vegetable patties (called cutlets), pastries and *vadai* (called *vaddai* in Sinhala, these are deep-fried doughnut-shaped snacks made from lentil flour and spices) – they're placed on the table, you eat what you want and the bill is totalled according to what's left.

Streetside huts (called *kadé* or boutiques by the Sinhalese, and *unavakam* by Tamils) sell *kotthu rotti*, a doughy pancake that is chopped and fried with fillings ranging from chilli and onion to bacon and egg. You'll soon become attuned to the evening chop-chop sounds of the *kotthu rotti* maker.

Also available from the *kadé* are lunch packets, a real Sri Lankan favourite. These are food parcels and are sold all over the country between 11am and 2pm. Inside you'll usually find rice, curry (generally chicken, fish or beef, though if you're vegetarian you'll get an egg), curried vegetables and *sambol*.

For heaps of Sri Lankan recipes visit www.info lanka.com/recipes. New recipes are continually coming online, and there are a few other cuisines tossed in as well.

VEGETARIANS & VEGANS

Vegetarian food is widely available, and there are appetising vegetable curries made from banana (ash plantain), banana flower, breadfruit, jackfruit, mangoes, potatoes, beans and pumpkins, to name just a few. An accompaniment of *mallung* (spiced green leaves, lightly stir-fried) is common, as is *parripu* curry (*paruppa kari* in Tamil), a pulse curry. Some dishes have dried Maldive fish in them, so you may wish to check this if fish is not part of your diet.

EATING WITH KIDS

Sri Lankans love children and children are welcome almost anywhere. They may thrive on the local food but if not, Sri Lankan hospitality means that people will go to any length to please them. Most places have Western-style dishes and there are the usual pizza, hamburger and chicken outlets in Colombo.

If you're wanting to introduce your children to Sri Lankan food and you're meeting some resistance, try a breakfast of *pittu*; the coconut-rice combination will be kind to their palates and the round shape may entice them. Also try hoppers (either the pancake or the string variety). Cashew nut curry is another possibility, and curd and treacle make an

---

DOS & DON'TS

- Always use your right hand to give and to receive.
- It's acceptable to use or to ask for cutlery. However, if eating with your hand, always use your right hand.
- It's acceptable to drink holding a glass in your left hand.
- Always wash your hands before you eat, for the sake of courtesy as well as hygiene.
- If you're invited home for a meal, remove your shoes before entering the home (although some people no longer follow this custom).

---

excellent dessert. A *bonda* (deep-fried ball made from lentil flour and spices) makes a good snack.

For more information on travelling with children, see p322.

HABITS & CUSTOMS

Eating Sri Lankan style is one of life's greatest pleasures. It may be a breakfast hopper at the open-air *kadé*, where the hopper maker, squatting beside a fire, gently flips the pancake from the griddle. Do you want banana? If so, a banana will be removed from the hand hanging near your head and carefully placed within the hopper. You can then devour the light, crunchy hopper and the fleshy fruit. Wash it down with hot tea and you have the perfect breakfast in a perfect setting.

The rice and curry meal is a banquet *par excellence*. Social events usually begin with light eats and chatter. The main food comes later (often much later), when rice and myriad small curries are set out before you in an artistic display that is visually and aromatically stunning.

Sri Lankans say that it's only by eating with fingers that you can fully enjoy the texture of the food. If you want to try this, there's a particular etiquette. Once everyone is served you can use the fingertips of your right hand to eat the food on your plate. Separate a little rice and gradually add some curry to form a mouthful-sized wad of food. Lift the wad and place it all in your mouth. Don't let the food pass the middle knuckles on your fingers and try not to drop any on the way to your mouth. This may sound difficult, but you'll soon become adept at it. Don't take a bone to your mouth to remove meat; remove the meat first with your fingers and only take mouthful-sized quantities to your mouth. In the more upmarket places you'll receive a finger bowl, but otherwise just visit the washroom.

In traditional homes men and visitors may eat first, while the women will eat later. It's normal to take a small gift (chocolates, biscuits or arrack) if you're invited home for a meal. Don't be concerned if it's put aside, as gifts are not usually opened in front of the giver. And if you're out to talk business, it's customary to talk first, then eat.

European custom may suggest a slow end to the dining experience. Not so in Sri Lanka, where they up and leave immediately after they've finished eating.

EAT YOUR WORDS

Getting the food you want in Sri Lanka is not so hard, as many people speak English. But if you'd like to try the local lingo, here are a few phrases. For guidance on pronunciation take a look at p351. Just remember that language and culture are of vital importance to many Sri Lankans, so try to speak Sinhala to Sinhalese and Tamil to Tamils.

Sri Lanka is the third-largest producer of tea in the world – 300,000 tons per year. For more interesting facts on Sri Lanka's tea, visit www.pureceylontea.com/srilankatea.htm.

Wanting to know more about curry ingredients? Visit www.asiafood.org for detailed information on spices, staples and specialities.

If you want to try your hand at Sri Lankan cooking you'll find over 200 recipes at www.lankalink.net/cgi-bin/recipes/srilankan/book.cgi?Display.

Useful Phrases

Sinhala phrases are shown first, followed by Tamil phrases.

May we see the menu?
menoo eka balanna puluvandha?   *unavu pattiyalai paarppomaa?*

What's the local speciality?
mehe visheshayen hadhana dhe   *ingu kidaikkak koodiya visheida unavu*
monavaadha?   *enna?*

Could you recommend something?
monavadha hondha kiyala obata kiyanna   *neengal ethaiyum shifaarsu seivingala?*
puluvandha?

What dishes are available today, please?
kahmata monarada thiyennay?   *sappida enna irukkiradu?*

I'd like to order rice and curry, please
bahth denna   *sorum kariyum tharungal*

I'm vegetarian
mama elavalu vitharai kanne   *naan shaiva unavu shaappidupavan*

I don't eat meat
mama mas kanne naha   *naan iraichchi shappiduvathillai*

I don't eat chicken, fish or ham
mama kukul mas, maalu, ho ham kanne naha   *naan koli, meen, pandri iraichchi*
                                                    shaapiduvathillai

I'm allergic to (peanuts)
mata (ratakaju) apathyayi   *(nilak kadalai) enakku alejee*

No ice in my drink, please
karunaakarala maghe beema ekata ais   *enadu paanaththil ais poda vendaam*
dhamanna epaa

That was delicious!
eka harima rasai!   *adhu nalla rushi!*

Please bring a/the ...
... karunaakarala gennah   *... konda varungal*

bill
bila   *bill*

fork
gaarappuvak   *mul karandi*

glass of water
vathura veedhuruvak   *thanni oru glass*

knife
pihiyak   *kaththi*

plate
pingaanak   *oru plate*

Food Glossary

Food items are shown with the Sinhala name first, then the Tamil name, followed by a definition. Some foods only have a Tamil name, while others are the same in both languages.

RICE & BREADS

ah-ppa	*appam*	hopper (bowl-shaped pancake)
doon thel bath	*nei choru*	ghee rice with green peas
kiri bath	*paat choru*	coconut-milk rice
kotthu rotti	*kotthu rotti*	*rotti* chopped and fried with meat and vegetables
maalu paan	*maalu paan*	bread rolls stuffed with fish
masala dosa	*masala dosa*	*dosa* stuffed with spiced vegetables

pittu	*puttu*	rice flour and coconut steamed in a bamboo mould
rotti	*rotti*	doughy pancake
—	*thayir saatham*	curd (buffalo-milk yoghurt) rice
thosai	*dosa*	paper-thin rice- and lentil-flour pancake

VEGETABLE & FRUIT DISHES

ala thel dala	*urulakkilangu poriyal*	fried spicy potatoes
alukehelkan uyala	*vaalaikkal kari*	green banana curry
kangkung	*pashali keerai kari*	spinach with chilli
kiri kos	*palaakkai kari*	young jackfruit curry
—	*marakarl*	mixed vegetables in a mild creamy sauce
murungah curry	*murungakkaai kari*	drumstick (fruit of the *kelor* tree) curry
nelum ala uyala	*thaamarai kilangu kari*	lotus roots in curry
parripu curry	*paruppa kari*	thick curry made from pulses
pathola curry	*pidalanggaai kari*	snake-gourd curry
umbah uyala	*maanggaai kari*	mango curry

MEAT

elu mus curry	*aattiraichi kari*	mutton curry
kukul mas hodhi	*kodzhi kari*	chicken curry
lamprais	*lamprais*	meat and vegetables baked with rice in a banana leaf
ooru mas miris badun	*pandri iraichi kari*	devilled pork

FISH

dhallo uyala	*kanawu meen kari*	cuttlefish black curry
kakuluwo uyala	*nandu kari*	crab curry
dhallo badhun	*kanavaai potiyal*	fried squid
—	*kool*	a dish akin to soup, combining many ingredients
malu hodhi	*meen kari*	fish curry

SIDE DISHES & ACCOMPANIMENTS

—	*kekkairikkal thayir pachadi*	cucumber and yoghurt
lunu miris	*maashi sambol*	onion and fish *sambol*
mallung	*sundal*	spiced green leaves, lightly stir-fried
pol sambol	*thengaapu sambol*	coconut *sambol*
sambol	*sambol*	chilli condiment
seeni sambol	*seeni sambol*	sweet onion *sambol*
—	*semparathappu-thayir pachadi*	hibiscus flower and yoghurt

SWEETS

ali gyata pera	*butter fruit dessert*	avocado dessert
kiri aluwa	*alva*	sweetmeat made from rice flour, treacle and sometimes cashews
kiri dodol	*dhodhal*	coconut-milk, cashew and jaggery sweets
—	*laddu*	balls of flour sweetened with jaggery and deep-fried
—	*payasam*	sago cooked in coconut milk and jaggery (may contain nuts)
—	*rasavalli kilangu pudding*	yam pudding
thala guli	*ellu pahu*	sesame sweet balls
wattalappam	*vattalappam*	coconut milk, egg, cardamom and jaggery pudding

SNACKS

bhoodhi	bonda	deep-fried ball made from lentil flour and spices
godambah	rolles	meat and vegetables wrapped in pastry
mas patis	iraichi patis	deep-fried beef pasties
polos cutlets	pinchu pilaakkai cutlets	jackfruit cutlets
vaddai	vadai	deep-fried doughnut-shaped snack of spiced lentil flour

GENERAL

co-ppuwa	glass	glass
han-duh	karandi	spoon
kiri	paal	milk
koh-pi	kahpee	coffee
lunu	uppu	salt
palathuru	paadham	fruit
seeni	seeree	sugar
thay	te-neer/plan-tea	tea
vathura	than-neer	water
vendhuwa	kooppai	bowl

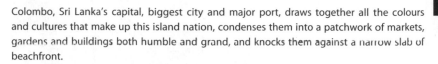

Colombo

Colombo, Sri Lanka's capital, biggest city and major port, draws together all the colours and cultures that make up this island nation, condenses them into a patchwork of markets, gardens and buildings both humble and grand, and knocks them against a narrow slab of beachfront.

Many visitors will appreciate Colombo's colonial heritage, its fine dining and shopping opportunities, and the dash of urban buzz in an overwhelmingly rural country. Others will tire quickly of the diesel fumes and the modern buildings on Galle Rd, the city's main artery. If you're only on a short trip to Sri Lanka, you may wish to pass by Colombo, but if you have the time – say at least two days – there are plenty of cultural and historical attractions in areas such as Fort, Cinnamon Gardens and Pettah.

Colombo is the political, economic and cultural centre of Sri Lanka, so if you need to extend your visa or buy a plane ticket, you'll find yourself here. The city was the scene of quite a few bombings during the war years, but security has been relaxed since a cease-fire was declared and peace talks began.

HIGHLIGHTS

- Chewing, sipping and slurping your way through the huge variety of **food** (p97) on offer
- Elbowing your way through the street-stall 'boutiques' in **Pettah** (p89)
- Relishing peaceful **Viharamahadevi Park** (p90) after navigating the darting three-wheelers and the jungle of streets
- Taking a sunset promenade on **Galle Face Green** (p90)
- Visiting Hindu **kovils** (p91) during the Thai Pongal festival or watching elephants and dancers parade during the Navam Perahera at **Gangaramaya Temple** (p91)

■ TELEPHONE CODE: 011 ■ POPULATION: 2.2 MILLION

COLOMBO

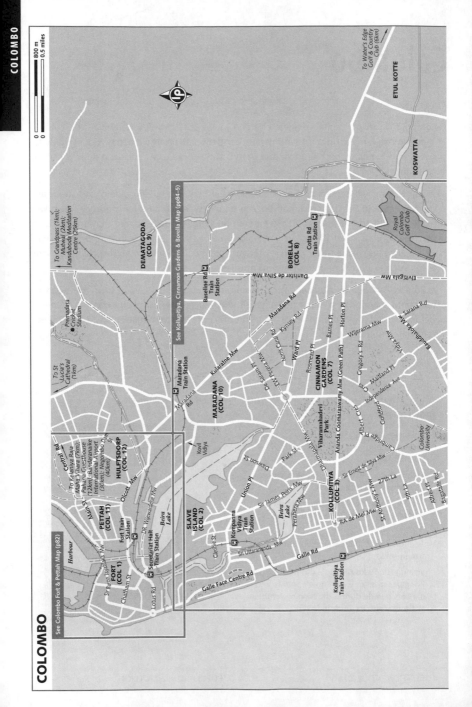

See Colombo Fort & Pettah Map (p82)

See Kollupitiya, Cinnamon Gardens & Borella Map (pp84-5)

0   800 m
0   0.5 miles

To Water's Edge
Golf & Country
Club (6km)

ETUL KOTTE

KOSWATTA

Royal
Colombo
Golf Club

DEMATAGODA
(COL 9)

BORELLA
(COL 8)

Cotta Rd
Train Station

Danister de Silva Mw

Elvitigala Mw

To Grandpass (1km);
Mutuel (2km);
Kanduboda Meditation
Centre (25km)

Premadasa
Cricket
Stadium

Baseline Rd
Train Station

Maradana Rd

Kynsey Rd

Ward Pl

Barnes Pl

Horton Pl

Wijerama Mw

Sarana Rd

Bauddhaloka Mw

Vidya Mw

Kularatne Mw

North Canal Rd

DR Perera Rd

EW Perera Mw

Rosmead Pl

CINNAMON
GARDENS
(COL 7)

Gregory's Rd

Maitland Pl

Independence Ave

Colombo
University

To St
Lucia's
Cathedral
(1km)

Maradana
Train Station

Maradana
Rd

MARADANA
(COL 10)

Kovil
Vidya

Park St

Dawson St

Union Pl

Viharamahadevi
Park

Ananda Coomaraswamy Mw (Green Path)

Albert Cres

Guildford Cres

Cambridge Pl

To Kelaniya Raja
Maha Vihara (7km);
Pettah Bus Stand;
Bandaranaike
International Airport
(30km); Negombo Da
(40km)

Central Rd

Main St

Olcott Mw

HULFTSDORP
(COL 12)

PETTAH
(COL 11)

Fort Train
Station

Beira
Lake

SLAVE
ISLAND
(COL 2)

Kompanna
Vidya
Train
Station

Clarke St

Sri James Peiris Mw

Perahera Mw

Beira
Lake

Dharmapala Mw

RA de Mel Mw

Sir Ernest de Silva Mw

KOLLUPITIYA
(COL 3)

St Anthony's Mw

Alfred Pl

27th La

5th La

Bagatalle Rd

Harbour

Sir Baron Jayatilaka Mw

Chatham St

Secretariat Halt
Train Station

DR Wijewardene Mw

Lotus Rd

FORT
(COL 1)

Galle Face Centre Rd

Sri Uttarananda Mw

Galle Rd

Kollupitiya
Train Station

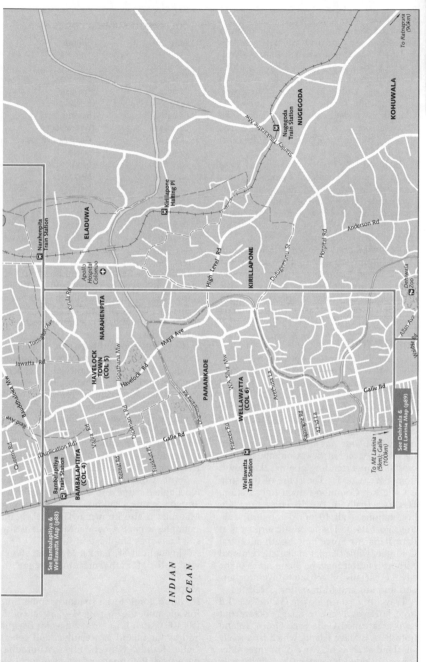

HISTORY

As far back as the 5th century, Colombo served as a sea port for trade between Asia and the West. During the 8th century, Arab traders settled near the port and, in 1505, the Portuguese arrived. By the mid-17th century the Dutch had taken over, growing cinnamon in the area now known as Cinnamon Gardens, but it wasn't until the British arrived that the town became a city. In 1815 Colombo was proclaimed the capital of Ceylon.

During the 1870s the breakwaters were built and Fort was created by flooding surrounding wetlands. Colombo was peacefully handed over when Sri Lanka achieved independence in 1948. A new parliament was built in Sri Jayawardenepura-Kotte, an outer suburb of Colombo, in 1982.

Isolated Liberation Tigers of Tamil Eelam (LTTE) bomb attacks in Fort during the 1990s caused Colombo's major businesses and institutions to disperse across the city. These days Colombo is spreading north and south along the coast as people migrate to the city to work.

ORIENTATION

Colombo is split into 15 postal code areas, which are often used to identify the specific districts. Pettah, for example, is also referred to as Colombo 11 (or just Col 11), Slave Island is referred to as Col 2, and so on. See right for a full listing of codes. Once you've got a few directions down, it is relatively easy to find your way around the city. From the visitor's point of view, Colombo is a long coastal strip extending about 12km south from Fort (Col 1). The spine of this strip is Galle Rd. Colombo's main train station, Fort, is actually in Pettah, as are the main bus stations – all 10 or 15 minutes' walk from Fort itself. The domestic airport is at Ratmalana Air Force Base, south of central Colombo, while Bandaranaike International Airport is at Katunayake, 30km north of the city. For details on getting to/from the airport and bus and train stations, see p104.

Travelling south down Galle Face Rd from Fort you come to a large oceanfront lawn area called Galle Face Green. Inland from here is Slave Island, which isn't really an island at all as only two of its three sides are surrounded by water (though it really was used for keeping slaves in the Dutch

COLOMBO'S SUBURB CODES	
Zone	**Suburb**
Colombo 1	Fort
Colombo 2	Slave Island
Colombo 3	Kollupitiya
Colombo 4	Bambalapitiya
Colombo 5	Havelock Town
Colombo 6	Wellawatta
Colombo 7	Cinnamon Gardens
Colombo 8	Borella
Colombo 9	Dematagoda
Colombo 10	Maradana
Colombo 11	Pettah
Colombo 12	Hulftsdorp
Colombo 13	Kotahena
Colombo 14	Grandpass
Colombo 15	Mutwal

colonial era). South is neighbouring Kollupitiya, followed by Bambalapitiya, Wellawatta, Dehiwala and finally the old beach resort of Mt Lavinia, which isn't officially part of Colombo but is definitely within its urban sprawl.

If you turn inland (east) from Kollupitiya you'll soon find yourself in Cinnamon Gardens, home of the national art gallery, museum, university, Viharamahadevi Park, some of the most exclusive residential quarters and many embassies.

Finding addresses is complicated by the fact that street numbers start again each time you move into a new district. Thus there will be a '100 Galle Rd' in several different neighbourhoods.

Some Colombo streets have both an old English name and a postindependence Sinhala name. Ananda Coomaraswamy Mawatha is also known as Green Path, for example, while RA de Mel Mawatha is also still known as Duplication Rd.

Throughout Sri Lanka, Mw is an abbreviation for Mawatha, meaning 'Avenue'.

Maps

If you're going to be spending some time in Colombo, the 96-page *A–Z Street Guide* (Rs 400) extends as far south as Mt Lavinia and as far inland as Kelaniya, and covers Galle, Kandy, Nuwara Eliya, Anuradhapura and Polonnaruwa. It also includes information on Colombo's suburban and inner-city buses. Its main competitor, *A to Z Colombo* (Rs 170), has only 45 pages and doesn't cover Mt Lavinia, but for central Colombo it is more detailed and more accurate. Both publications are available from bookshops.

INFORMATION
Bookshops

Colombo has some excellent bookshops. Top-end hotels also often have bookshops where you'll find up-to-date foreign magazines and newspapers.

Barefoot (Map pp84-5; ☎ 258 9305; 704 Galle Rd, Col 3) Better known for its textiles, this shop carries a broad range of quality books on local art, culture, travel and literature.

Bibliomania (Map p82; ☎ 243 2881; 32 Hospital St, Col 1) Jam-packed with a random selection of second-hand fiction and a mixed bag of magazines, educational books and more. Most are in English. Prices are often the best in the city.

Bookland (Map pp84-5; ☎ 256 5248; 430-432 Galle Rd, Col 3) Offers the usual range of books about Sri Lanka, plus English titles and magazines.

Buddhist Book Centre (Map pp84-5; ☎ 268 9786; 380 Bauddhaloka Mawatha, Col 7) Filled with books on Buddhism; about a third of the stock is in English.

Lake House Bookshop (Map pp84-5; ☎ 257 4418; Liberty Plaza, RA de Mel Mawatha, Col 3) Colombo's oldest bookshop has an extensive range of books, along with foreign and local magazines and newspapers.

MD Gunasena Bookshop (Map p88; ☎ 255 3379; 27 Galle Rd, Col 4) Gunasena's ambitious-looking outlet is opposite Majestic City; it carries a decent selection of titles.

Vijitha Yapa Bookshop Crescat Boulevard (Map pp84-5; 89 Galle Rd, Col 3); Unity Plaza (Map p88; ☎ 259 6960; Galle Rd, Col 4) Stocks a comprehensive collection of foreign and local novels, magazines and pictorial tomes on Sri Lanka. The branch in Crescat Boulevard shopping centre is smaller.

Cultural Centres

Alliance Française (Map pp84-5; ☎ 269 4162; 11 Barnes Pl, Col 7) Hosts seminars, and shows films at 3pm on Tuesday and 6pm on Wednesday. Has a library.

American Information Resource Center (Map pp84-5; ☎ 233 2725; 44 Galle Rd, Col 3) Periodically hosts films and seminars, and offers a library and Internet access (per day Rs 100).

COLOMBO IN...

One Day

Start off the day while it's still relatively cool with a ramble through the aromatic markets of **Pettah** (p89), testing fruit for ripeness, buying fresh coconut juice and watching the locals haggle. While you're in the neighbourhood, learn about Sri Lanka's colonial history at the **Dutch Period Museum** (p89) and enjoy this restored mansion's garden.

Kill the proverbial two birds with lunch at **Gallery Cafe** (p99) after perusing the arts and crafts at **Paradise Road Cafe** (p100), both housed in the former offices of acclaimed Sri Lankan architect Geoffrey Bawa.

In the afternoon take in the Colombo's most visually impressive Buddhist temple, **Kelaniya Raja Maha Vihara** (p91). Take a stroll along the oceanfront with Sri Lankan families at **Galle Face Green** (p90) as the sun sets, followed by a cold Lion Lager or cocktail at the courtyard bar of **Galle Face Hotel** (p95).

Two Days

Breakfast with Colombo's high society at **Barista** (p98) or grab a *kotthu rotti* (doughy pancakes chopped and fried with a variety of ingredients) on the street before tackling the recently renovated **National Museum** (p90). Clear your head of historical overload with a walk across adjacent **Viharamahadevi Park** (p90).

If you have time for two temples, explore the contrasts between the humble Bawa-designed **Seema Malakaya** (p91) on Beira Lake, and the grand **Gangaramaya Temple** (p91) nearby. Go native for lunch with South Indian *idlis* (spongy fermented rice cakes) and dosas (paper-thin rice and lentil-flour pancakes) at **Amaravathi** (p98) or Sri Lankan hoppers (bowl-shaped pancakes) and *pittu* (rice flour and coconut steamed in a bamboo mould) at **Palmyrah** (p98).

To get an idea of how British Colombo looked at its zenith, take a walk north along York St in **Fort** (p89), past row after row of grand Victorian shop-houses, to the **Grand Oriental Hotel** (p93). Have a drink at the hotel's **Harbour Room** (p97) and check out the namesake views.

COLOMBO

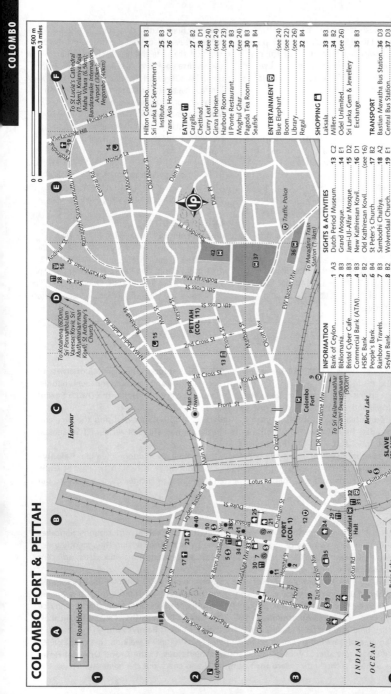

COLOMBO FORT & PETTAH

INFORMATION
Bank of Ceylon...................................1	A3
Bibliomania.......................................2	B3
Bristol Cyber Cafe.............................3	B3
Commercial Bank (ATM)....................4	B3
HSBC Bank..5	B2
People's Bank...................................6	B4
Rainbow Travels...............................7	B3
Seylan Bank......................................8	B2
Standard Chartered Grindlays	
Bank..9	C3
Survey Department Map Sales	
Centre..10	B2
Tourist Police..................................11	B3
Tourist Police..................................12	B3

SIGHTS & ACTIVITIES
Dutch Period Museum......................13	C2
Grand Mosque..................................14	E1
Jami-Ul-Alfaz Mosque......................15	D2
New Kathiresan Kovil.......................16	D1
Old Kathiresan Kovil...............(see 16)	
St Peter's Church.............................17	B2
Sambodhi Chaitya............................18	A2
Wolvendaal Church...........................19	E1

SLEEPING
Ceylon Continental Hotel................20	A3
Colombo YMCA...............................21	B3
Galadari Hotel.................................22	A3
Grand Oriental Hotel.......................23	B2

EATING
Hilton Colombo...............................24	B3
Sri Lanka Ex-Servicemen's	
Institute.......................................25	B3
Trans Asia Hotel.............................26	C4
Cargills..27	B2
Chettinad......................................28	D1
Curry Leaf................................(see 24)	
Ginza Hohsen.........................(see 24)	
Harbour Room........................(see 23)	
Il Ponte Restaurant................(see 24)	
Moghul Ghat....................................29	B3
Pagoda Tea Room............................30	B3
Seafish..31	B4

ENTERTAINMENT
Blue Elephant...........................(see 24)	
Boom......................................(see 22)	
Library....................................(see 26)	
Regal...32	B4

SHOPPING
Laksala..33	B3
Millers..34	B2
Odel Unlimited........................(see 26)	
Sri Lanka Gem & Jewellery	
Exchange.......................................35	B3

TRANSPORT
Bastian Mawatha Bus Station........36	D3
Central Bus Station..........................37	D3
Indian Airlines.................................38	B2
Kuwait Airways...............................39	A3
LTU International.............................40	B2
Malaysia Airlines.............................41	B2
Saunders Pl Bus Station...................42	D2
SriLankan Airlines...................(see 35)	

British Council (Map pp84–5; ☎ 258 1171; 49 Alfred House Gardens, Col 3) Puts on regular free cultural events, including films (usually Friday and Saturday), exhibitions, concerts and lectures. There is a library as well.

Goethe Institut (Map pp84–5; ☎ 269 4562; 39 Gregory's Rd, Col 7) Offers German language courses, screens German films and puts on music concerts, seminars and more.

Russian Centre (Map pp84–5; ☎ 268 5440; 10 Independence Ave, Col 7) Has one of the city's best auditoriums, which is often used by visiting musical performers.

Emergency Services
Accident Service (☎ 269 1111)
Fire & Rescue Service (☎ 242 2222)
Medi-Calls Ambulance (☎ 257 5475)
Police (☎ 243 3333)
Red Cross Ambulance (☎ 269 5434, 269 1095)
Tourist Police (Map p82; ☎ 243 3342; Bank of Ceylon Mawatha, Col 1) Has its main office at the police station in Fort.

Internet Access
Shops offering Internet services are found all over the city. On Galle Rd you're rarely more than walking distance from one, and each shopping centre has at least one. Access is cheap; most places charge around Rs 60 per hour. A few places we've found especially accommodating:

Berty's Cyber Cafe (Map pp84–5; 380 Galle Rd, Col 3)
Bristol Cyber Cafe (Map p82; 8/3/4 Bristol St, Col 1) Opposite the YMCA.
Cafe@Internet (Map pp84–5; 491 Galle Rd, Col 3)
Infotech Internet (Map p88; 46 Galle Rd, Col 6)
Rainbow Travels (Map pp84–5; 113 Chatham St, Col 1)

Colombo has recently begun sprouting public wi-fi spots. Some allow free wi-fi access, while others require the purchase of access codes. So far it's available at Bandaranaike International Airport, Gallery Cafe (p99), Barista (p98), Barefoot Garden Cafe (p99) and Cricket Club Cafe (p99).

Left Luggage
Left luggage services are available at the Fort train station's **cloakroom** (Map p82; per bag per day Rs 20; ⏱ 4.30am-11.30pm). As you approach the station from Olcott Mawatha it's on the extreme left of the building, up a flight of stairs.

Media
LT, distributed free at hotels, shops, bars and restaurants aiming for the expat market, carries listings of bars, clubs, restaurants, galleries and cultural events. *Linc* is a comparatively inferior free magazine with a smattering of information tucked between advertisements and advertorials. *Travel Lanka* has information about concerts, plays, and lectures held by cultural centres.

Hands on Colombo, updated annually by Dinesh Kulatunga and Peter Kamps, and the American Women's Association's *Colombo Handbook*, serve the expat community with listings and reviews of everything from dentists to jewellers.

Medical Services
Avoid government hospitals such as Colombo General, if you can. The following private hospitals have relatively high standards and English-speaking doctors.

Apollo Hospital Colombo (Map pp78–9; ☎ 453 0000; cnr Vijaya Kumaratunga Mawatha & Park Rd, Col 5) Established in 2002, this medical facility contains a bank and food centre as well as the usual.

Asha Central Hospital Colombo (☎ 269 6411; 57 Horton Pl, Col 7)

Nawaloka Hospital (Map pp84–5; ☎ 254 4444; 23 Sri Saugathodaya Mawatha, Col 2)

Osu Sala (Map pp84–5; ☎ 269 4716; 255 Union Pl, Col 2; ⏱ 24hr) This is the only nonhospital pharmacy open round the clock.

Money
There are banks and ATMs all over the city, and several 24-hour bank branches in the arrivals hall at the Bandaranaike International Airport.

There are several moneychangers in Fort; their offices are concentrated in and around Chatham St and Mudalige Mawatha. Their cash-only rates are a little higher than you would get in a bank. You can change cash or travellers cheques at reduced rates in the main hotels.

NationsTrust Bank/American Express (Map pp84–5; ☎ 441 4141; 104 Dharmapala Mawatha, Col 7) sells travellers cheques.

Post
Sri Lanka Post (Map p82; DR Wijewardhana Mawatha, Col 1; ⏱ 7am-6pm, poste restante 7am-9pm, stamps & telephone 24hr) was moved out of its historic premises on Janadhipathi Mawatha for security reasons in 2000 and has changed locations several times since then. The poste restante holds mail for two months – call ☎ 232 6203 to see

COLOMBO

KOLLUPITIYA, CINNAMON GARDENS & BORELLA

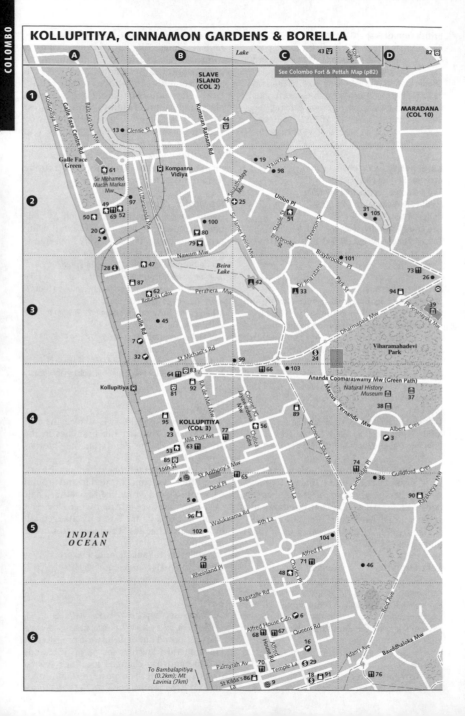

COLOMBO

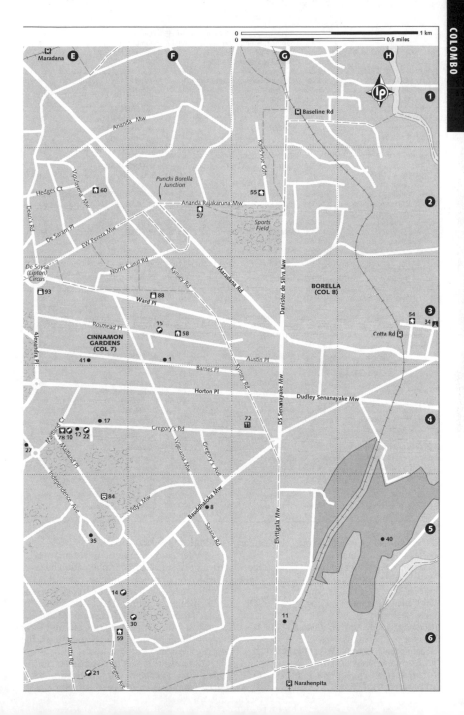

COLOMBO

if there's anything awaiting you. See p330 for postal and parcel rates.

If you are sending home anything of particular value you should consider using a courier service. Reliable couriers:

DHL Worldwide Express (Map pp84–5; ☎ 230 4304; Keells, 130 Glennie St, Col 2)

IML (Map pp84–5; ☎ 233 7733; 140 Vauxhall St, Col 2) UPS agent.

Mountain Hawk Express (Map pp84–5; ☎ 252 2222; 300 Galle Rd, Col 3) FedEx agent.

TNT Express (Ace Cargo; Map pp84–5; ☎ 244 5331; 315 Vauxhall St, Col 2)

Telephone & Fax

For international calls there are many relatively pricey private communication bureaus (which often have fax machines). A cheaper option is using the card-operated international direct dialling (IDD) telephones, of which there are many in Colombo.

Most Internet centres in Colombo offer web-phone services, which cost about the same as regular Internet access.

All five-star hotels have business centres that offer a range of communication services, from email and fax to telephone.

For domestic calls, **Sri Lanka Post** (Map p82; DR Wijewardhana Mawatha, Col 1; 7am-6pm, telephone 24hr) sells Sri Lanka Telecom phonecards; calls from these cardphones (found in post offices only) are slighter cheaper than those from the private cardphones. However, it's probably more convenient to use one of the yellow Lanka Pay or Tritel cardphones.

See p332 for general information on phone services.

Tourist Information
Sri Lanka Tourist Board (SLTB; Map pp84-5; 243 7059; www.srilankatourism.org; 80 Galle Rd, Col 3; 9am-4.45pm Mon-Fri, 9am-12.30pm Sat) The country's national tourism office. The staff can help with hotel bookings, answer questions and hand out leaflets. It also maintains a 24-hour booth at the international airport.

Travel Agencies
Colombo's plethora of travel agencies can help organise car hire, city tours or tours elsewhere in Sri Lanka. Following are some of the biggest operators, plus some recommended niche-market companies.

A Baur & Co Ltd (244 8087; www.baurs.com; Baur's Bldg, 5 Upper Chatham St, Col 1) One of the few companies specialising in bird-watching tours.

Adventure Asia (536 8468; 338 TB Jaya Mawatha, Col 10) A relatively young company specialising in white-water rafting, kayaking and bicycling tours.

Adventure Sports Lanka (279 1584; http://action lanka.com; 366/3 Rendapola Horagahakanda Lane, Talagama, Koswatta) Arranges outdoor activities including white-water rafting, kayaking, diving, mountain biking and walks.

Aitken Spence Travels (230 8021; www.aitken spencetravels.com; Vauxhall Bldg, 305 Vauxhall St, Col 2) One of the biggest tour operators; organises tour packages, hires out cars and drivers, and books hotels.

Jetwing Travels (234 5700; www.jetwing.net; Jetwing House, 46/26 Nawam Mawatha, Col 2) Another big operator; has a large chain of upmarket hotels and organises tours within Sri Lanka and to the Maldives.

JF Tours & Travels (258 7996; www.jftours.com; 189 Bauddhaloka Mawatha, Col 4) Specialises in steam-train tours (groups only), and booking train tickets in general.

Quickshaws Tours (258 3133; www.quickshaws .com; 3 Kalinga Pl, Col 5) Organises standard tours but specialises in personalised tours with a car and driver.

DANGERS & ANNOYANCES
Crime
While violence towards foreigners is uncommon, it helps to tell someone where you are going and when to expect you back.

Women in particular are urged to take care at night. Even couples should be very cautious about walking along lonely beach areas, such as those near Mt Lavinia, after dark.

Solo women should be careful when taking taxis and three-wheelers at night; if, as sometimes happens, your taxi turns up with two men inside, call another. Travellers should also avoid taking three-wheelers between the airport and Colombo at night; robberies are not unknown.

Watch out for pickpockets when on public transport. Never get on a bus or train with your shoulder bag unzipped – in fact, don't even walk down the road with it in that state. If you are carrying valuables such as a passport, travellers cheques or reasonably large amounts of cash, keep them out of sight and out of reach in a money belt or a pouch under your clothes. Bum bags, besides being a fashion error, are far too conspicuous.

See p334 for tips for women travellers riding buses and trains in Colombo and elsewhere in Sri Lanka.

Ethnic Tension
Since the February 2002 cease-fire no civilian areas of Colombo have been hit by (alleged) LTTE bombings. However, in July 2004 a woman detonated a bomb in a Kollupitiya police station, killing herself and four policemen, and critically injuring 11 people. There have been no additional incidents since then, but if hostilities should flare up again, the Fort and Pettah areas are the traditional targets.

Scams
Touts (sometimes disguised as officials) gather inside the second arrivals hall waiting for jet-lagged visitors to emerge. You may be approached with claims that, for some reason or another (eg a bomb's just gone off somewhere), it's dangerous to travel any further unaccompanied. The pitch is that the tourists should, for their own safety, sign up for a tour on the spot. This can end up being a convenient scam if you do want to take a tour, but if you want to travel independently double-check the current security situation with the Sri Lanka Tourist Board's information desk in the first arrivals hall.

COLOMBO

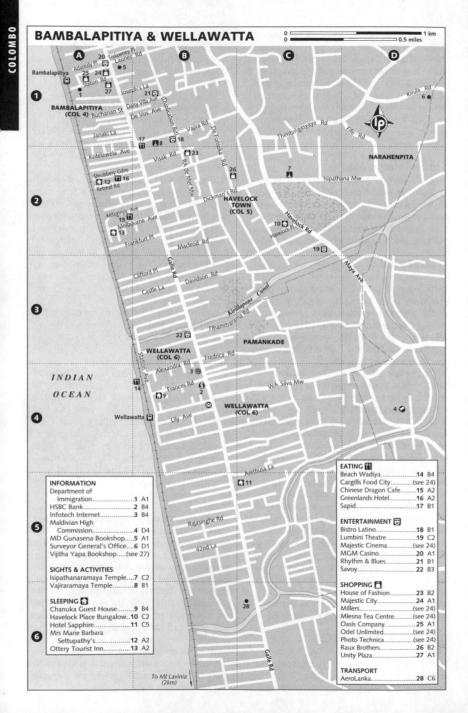

BAMBALAPITIYA & WELLAWATTA

Touts

Colombo has its share of touts and con artists. Fort train station is a favourite hangout and the touts here are particularly skilful and persuasive. Galle Face Green is another favourite hunting ground. You are likely to be approached at some stage by someone who, after striking up a conversation, asks for a donation for a school for the blind or some such cause – these people are invariably con artists.

SIGHTS

Wags may claim there's nothing to see in Colombo but most people will find plenty of diversion. The Fort district is where most of the historical sights are concentrated, Pettah is the place for street markets and bazaars, while almost everything else – including temples and churches – is scattered around the city.

Fort

During the European era Fort (Map p82) was indeed a fort, surrounded by the sea on two sides and a moat on the landward sides. Today it's a curious mix of brash modern structures such as the World Trade Center, venerable red-brick institutions such as Cargills and Millers, and buildings from a variety of other eras. The security presence is heavy here, curtailing vehicle access and some pedestrian access. Fort can be eerily quiet in spots, though vendors still line the Cargills side of York St, selling everything from fluorescent alarm clocks to padded bras. The lack of traffic at least makes it easy to take a walk around.

There's also a harbour (off limits) and the large white dagoba (stupa) of **Sambodhi Chaitiya**, perched about 20m off the ground on stilts – a landmark for sea travellers.

A good landmark in Fort is the clock tower at the junction of Chatham St and Janadhipathi Mawatha (once Queen St), which was originally a lighthouse.

Pettah

Immediately inland from Fort, the bustling bazaar of Pettah (Map p82) is one of the oldest districts in Colombo and one of the most ethnically mixed places in the country. You name it, and a boutique (street stall) will be selling it in Pettah. Each thoroughfare has its own speciality; Gabo's Lane and

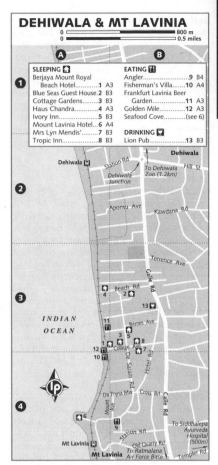

DEHIWALA & MT LAVINIA

0	800 m
0	0.5 miles

SLEEPING 🏠
Berjaya Mount Royal
    Beach Hotel..............**1** A3
Blue Seas Guest House.**2** B3
Cottage Gardens........**3** B3
Haus Chandra............**4** A3
Ivory Inn.....................**5** B3
Mount Lavinia Hotel...**6** A4
Mrs Lyn Mendis'........**7** B3
Tropic Inn..................**8** B3

EATING 🍴
Angler.........................**9** B4
Fisherman's Villa.......**10** A4
Frankfurt Lavinia Beer
    Garden..................**11** A3
Golden Mile..............**12** A3
Seafood Cove...........(see 6)

DRINKING 🍷
Lion Pub....................**13** B3

5th Cross St specialise in Ayurvedic medicines, while jewellery stores line 2nd Cross St. Leading up to major holidays such as Christmas, the Pettah crowds reach Biblical proportions. If crowds leave you cold, *poya* (full moon) days are a good time to have a look around. Pettah also harbours many religious buildings (p91).

The **Dutch Period Museum** (Map p82; ☎ 244 8466; 95 Prince St; adult/child Rs 65/35; 🕙 9am-5pm Sat-Thu) was originally the 17th-century residence of the Dutch governor and has since been used as a Catholic seminary, a military hospital, a police station and a post office. The well-restored mansion contains a lovely garden courtyard. Exhibits include Dutch colonial furniture and other artefacts.

National Museum

Housed in a fine 1877-vintage building in Viharamahadevi Park, the **museum** (Map pp84–5; Albert Cres, Col 7; adult/child Rs 500/250; ⊙ 9am-5pm Sat-Thu) displays a collection of ancient royal regalia, Sinhalese artwork (sculptures, carvings and so on), antique furniture and china, and *ola* (leaves of the talipot palm) manuscripts. There are fascinating 19th-century reproductions of English paintings of Sri Lanka, and an excellent collection of antique demon masks.

Galle Face Green

Immediately south of Fort is Galle Face Green (Map pp84–5), a long stretch of lawn facing the sea. It was originally cleared by the Dutch to give the cannons of Fort a clear line of fire. Today its broad lawns are a popular rendezvous spot; on weekdays it's dotted with joggers, kite flyers and walkers, and on weekends (especially Sunday evenings) food vendors gather to feed the hordes.

The remaining structures of the 19th-century **Colombo Club** face the green from the grounds of Taj Samudra hotel; the club's rooms are still used for functions. At opposite ends of the green are delightful old Galle Face Hotel and monolithic Ceylon Continental Hotel.

Cinnamon Gardens

About 5km south of Fort and 2km inland, Cinnamon Gardens (Map pp84–5) is Colombo's ritziest address. A century ago it was covered in cinnamon plantations. Today it contains elegant tree-lined streets and the posh mansions of the wealthy and powerful, as well as the city's biggest park, several sports grounds and a cluster of museums and galleries.

The centrepiece of Cinnamon Gardens is the 50-acre **University of Colombo** (also called the University of Ceylon) campus, which originally opened as the Ceylon Medical School in 1870.

VIHARAMAHADEVI PARK

This is Colombo's biggest park, originally called Victoria Park but renamed in the 1950s after the mother of King Dutugemunu (see p153). It's notable for its superb flowering trees, which bloom in March, April and early May. The broad Ananda Coomaraswamy Mawatha cuts across the middle of the park, while Colombo's white-domed **Old Town Hall** (also called White House) overlooks the park from the northeast. Working elephants sometimes spend the night in the park, happily chomping on palm branches.

INDEPENDENCE HALL

Critics lambast this modern recreation of a Kandyan audience hall as a concrete non-entity, but it's a rather impressive structure nonetheless, and makes a good photo opportunity. As the name suggests, it was built to commemorate Sri Lanka's independence in 1948. The parkland surrounding it is painstakingly well kept.

Art Galleries

The **National Art Gallery** (Map pp84–5; 106 Ananda Coomaraswamy Mawatha, Col 7; admission free; ⊙ 9am-5pm, closed poya days) is next door to the Natural History Museum in Viharamahadevi Park. The permanent collection mostly consists of portraits, but there are also some temporary exhibitions by Sri Lankan artists.

The stylish **Lionel Wendt Centre** (Map pp84–5; 18 Guildford Cres, Col 7; admission varies; ⊙ 9am-1pm & 2-4pm Mon-Fri) has contemporary art and craft exhibitions. It stages musical performances and has occasional sales of antiques and other items.

The **Sapumal Foundation** (Map pp84–5; 2/34 Barnes Pl, Col 7; admission free; ⊙ 10am-1pm Thu-Sat) is located in what was once the home of artist Harry Pieris. Today this rambling tile-roofed bungalow is packed with some of the best examples of Sri Lankan art from the 1920s onwards.

Art galleries are sometimes attached to upmarket cafés, including **Gallery Cafe** (p99) and **Commons** (p100).

Dehiwala Zoo

By the standards of the developing world, this **zoo** (☎ 271 2751; Dehiwala; adult/child Rs 500/250; ⊙ 8.30am-6pm), 10km south of Fort, treats its animals well enough. Over the last five years the 70-year-old zoo has undergone a much-needed face-lift, developing facilities for smaller animals, including a walk-in aviary and a butterfly park. The major attraction is the elephant show at 5.15pm, when elephants troop on stage in true trunk-to-tail fashion and perform a series of feats of elephantine agility. An aquarium displays over 500 varieties of aquatic life. A new veterinary hospital is due to be completed by the end of 2006.

You can get to the zoo on bus 118 from Dehiwala train station.

Galle Road

Galle Rd – the 'backbone' of Colombo – runs from north to south along practically the entire length of the city. Yes, it can be choked with air pollution (depending on sea breezes), and it is lined with some of the city's worst architecture. But hold your breath and launch in – you'll find some yummy restaurants, shopping centres brimming with goodies and, near the northern end, the Indian and British high commissions, the US embassy and the prime minister's fortified official residence, **Temple Trees** (Map pp84–5).

Places of Worship

BUDDHIST TEMPLES

Most of Colombo's Buddhist temples date from the late 19th-century Buddhist Revival, a period when Sri Lankan Buddhists resisted the flooding of the island by Christian missionaries.

The most important Buddhist centre is the **Kelaniya Raja Maha Vihara**, 7km northeast of Fort, just off the Kandy road. Even if the thought of seeing yet another temple sends you reaching for the arrack, this one is worth the effort. The original temple was destroyed by Indian invaders, restored, destroyed again by the Portuguese, and restored again in the 18th and 19th centuries. It's mostly known for its very fine reclining Buddha. The dagoba, which (unusually) is hollow, is the focus of the Duruthu Perahera (Duruthu Procession) in January each year. To reach the temple take bus 235 from in front of the traffic-police station, which is just northeast of the Bastian Mawatha bus station.

Another important Buddhist centre is the sprawling **Gangaramaya Temple** (Map pp84–5; ☎ 243 9505; Sri Jinaratana Rd, Col 2), near Beira Lake. Run by one of Sri Lanka's more politically adept monks, the ever expanding temple complex has a library, a **museum** (donation Rs 100) and an extraordinarily eclectic array of bejewelled and gilded gifts presented by devotees and well-wishers over the years. Most of the Buddha images on display in the temple were donated by Buddhists from Thailand, Myanmar and Japan. Gangaramaya is the

focus of the Navam Perahera (p93) on the February *poya* day each year.

The small but captivating **Seema Malakaya** (Map pp84–5) on Beira Lake comprises two island pavilions, designed by Geoffrey Bawa in 1985 and run by Gangaramaya Temple. The pavilions – one filled with Thai bronze Buddhas, the other centred on a bodhi tree and four Brahmanist images – are especially striking when illuminated at night.

The **Vajiraramaya Temple** (Map p88; Vajira Rd, Col 4) has been a centre of Buddhist learning since 1901. From here Sri Lankan monks have taken the Buddha's message to Western countries, and on Sundays the complex is thronged with thousands of children taking Buddhism school.

The modern **Gotami Vihara** (Map pp84–5), 6km southeast of Fort near Cotta Rd train station in Borella, has some outstanding Jataka (Buddha life stories) murals by modern artist George Keyt. The **Isipathanaramaya Temple** (Map p88; Isipathana Mawatha, Col 5) has particularly beautiful frescoes.

HINDU TEMPLES

Known as *kovil*, Hindu temples are numerous in Colombo. On Sea St, the goldsmiths' street in Pettah, **New Kathiresan Kovil** (Map p82) and **Old Kathiresan Kovil**, both dedicated to the war god Murugan (Skanda), are the starting point for the annual Hindu Vel festival held in July/August, when the huge *vel* (trident) chariot is dragged to various *kovils* on Galle Rd in Bambalapitiya.

In Kotahena, northeast of Fort, you'll find the **Sri Ponnambalam Vanesar Kovil**, which is built of South Indian granite, and the **Sri Muthumariamman Kovil** (Kotahena St, Col 13). The **Sri Kailawasanathar Swami Devasthanam** (Map pp84–5), apparently the oldest Hindu temple in Colombo, has shrines to Shiva and Ganesh; it's at Captain's Gardens, 600m west of Maradana station off DR Wijewardena Mawatha. There is also the huge **Sri Shiva Subramaniam Swami Kovil** (Map pp84–5; Kew Rd, Col 2).

During the harvest festival of Thai Pongal (held in January) devotees flock to these temples, which become even more colourful and lively.

MOSQUES

The **Grand Mosque** (Map p82; New Moor St, Col 11) is the most important of Colombo's many mosques. In Pettah you'll also find the

COLOMBO

decorative 1909 **Jami-Ul-Alfar Mosque** (Map p82; cnr 2nd Cross & Bankshall Sts, Col 11), which has candy-striped red-and-white brickwork. There are many mosques in Slave Island, dating from the British days, when a Malay army regiment was stationed here.

CHURCHES

The 1749 **Wolvendaal Church** (Map p82; Wolvendaal Lane, Col 11) is the most important Dutch building in Sri Lanka. When the church was built, this now-crowded inner-city district was a wilderness beyond the city walls. The Europeans mistook the packs of roaming jackals for wolves, and the area became known as Wolf's Dale, or Wolvendaal in Dutch. The church is in the form of a Greek cross, with walls 1.5m thick, but the real treasure is its Dutch furniture. The Dutch governors had a special pew made with elegant carved ebony chairs, and the workmanship in the wooden pulpit, baptismal font and lectern is just as beautiful. The stone floor includes the elaborate tombstones of five Dutch governors, moved here from an older Dutch church in Fort in 1813. The congregation dwindled as the Burghers emigrated, but it still holds services – in Sinhala, English and Tamil – on Sunday mornings.

St Peter's Church (Map p82), near the Grand Oriental Hotel in Fort, was converted from the Dutch governor's banquet hall and was first used as a church in 1804.

The enormous **St Lucia's Cathedral** (St Lucia's St, Kotahena) lies in the Catholic heart of the Kotahena district. The biggest church in Sri Lanka, it can hold up to 5000 worshippers. The interior is plain but the immense domed mass of the church is impressive.

One of the city's most interesting shrines is **St Anthony's Church** (St Anthony's Mawatha, Kotahena). Outside it looks like a typical Portuguese Catholic church, but inside the atmosphere is distinctly subcontinental. There are queues of devotees offering *puja* (prayers or offerings) to a dozen ornate statues behind glass cases; a statue of St Anthony endowed with miraculous qualities is the centre of devotions. Mothers often bring pubescent daughters here to pray for protection from evil spirits that might take advantage of the girl's nascent sexuality. The church seems to be as popular with Hindu and Buddhist mothers as it is with Catholics. Photography is frowned upon.

ACTIVITIES
Swimming

The only Colombo beach where you'd consider swimming is in Mt Lavinia, a somewhat faded resort area 11km south of Fort – and even that's borderline, with a severe undertow at times and some foul waterways issuing into the ocean just to the north.

Visitors can use the pools at several top-end Colombo hotels for a fee. One of the nicest spots is the outdoor saltwater pool right by the seafront at **Galle Face Hotel** (Map pp84-5; 2 Kollupitiya Rd); it costs nonguests Rs 250. A dip in the magnificently positioned pool at **Mount Lavinia Hotel** (Map p89; 100 Hotel Rd) will cost Rs 500 and includes access to the hotel's private stretch of beach. Or head to **Berjaya Mount Royal Beach Hotel** (☎ 273 9610; 36 College Ave), which charges nonguests Rs 350.

The large pool at **Water's Edge Golf & Country Club** (☎ 440 2302; 316 Etul Kotte Rd, Battaramulla; nonmember club admission per day adult/child US$10/8) is also open to the public.

Meditation

Kanduboda Meditation Centre (☎ 244 5518, 2570 306; kandubod@sltnet.lk), 25km outside Colombo in Delgoda, is a major centre for meditation instruction in the style of the late Mahasi Sayadaw. Accommodation and meals are offered free of charge, though donations are expected. Most meditators stay for an initial three-week training period, after which they can meditate on their own for as long as they like. White clothing (available on loan at no charge) must be worn. The Pugoda bus 224 passes the centre.

Golf

Royal Colombo Golf Club (Map pp84-5; ☎ 269 5431; Borella; greens fee weekday/weekend & holiday Rs 2500/3500, club hire Rs 600-1000, caddy Rs 350) has an 18-hole golf course at the Ridgeway Golf Links dating from 1879 – it was the third club in the British Empire to earn the 'royal' appellation. It's quite an institution, with 300-odd staff. The links are in good condition. Visitors are welcome, but ring in advance to let the club know that you're coming. Caddies are compulsory. Men must wear collars, decent shorts or trousers with zippers, while for women there's a one-word dress code: decency. The elegant clubhouse has a bar, a restaurant and a broad veranda.

Water's Edge Golf & Country Club (☎ 440 2302; 316 Etul Kotte Rd, Battaramulla; greens fee US$14), in Kotte on the eastern edge of Colombo, has a modern 18-hole golf course.

Ayurveda & Spas

Siddhalepa Ayurveda Hospital (☎ 273 8622; Templers Rd) in Mount Lavinia is a full-service Ayurvedic health centre.

The relatively new 450-sq-m **Aryana Spa** (☎ 440 2302; 316 Etul Kotte Rd, Battaramulla), at Water's Edge Golf & Country Club, offers a menu of Sri Lankan, Thai and Balinese treatments at very reasonable rates. **Taj Airport Garden Hotel** (☎ 225 2950; www.tajairportgardensrilanka.com), out near Bandaranaike International Airport, houses another Aryana Spa.

FESTIVALS & EVENTS

The **Duruthu Perahera** is held at the Kelaniya Raja Maha Vihara (p91) on the January *poya*. The **Navam Perahera**, on the February *poya*, is led by 50 elephants; it starts from the Gangaramaya Temple (p91) and is held around Viharamahadevi Park and Beira Lake. During the **Vel**, the gilded chariot of Murugan (Skanda), the Hindu war god, is ceremonially hauled from the Kathiresan *kovil* in Sea St, Pettah, to a *kovil* at Bambalapitiya.

See p326 for more information on festivals in Colombo.

SLEEPING

Colombo has a range of accommodation options: there are cheapies (some of which are forlorn and overpriced), a small but growing collection of midrange places, and so many top-end options you won't know where to start. Rates for top-end hotels in the city fluctuate widely depending on time of year, whether there are any conventions in town and how far in advance you book. Budget and midrange places tend to have more-stable room pricing.

If you head to Fort you'll find the big hotels and their fancy restaurants and nightclubs, plus some spartan budget digs. Slave Island has hectic streets, a heavy police presence and small dwellings jammed in between office blocks.

Kollupitiya covers Galle Face Green, the ritziest stretch of Galle Rd with the highest security. The other chunk of Kollupitiya follows noisy Galle Rd south, and is lined with larger shops, restaurants and businesses; inland, expensive dwellings mix with commercial buildings.

Moving into Bambalapitiya, Galle Rd starts losing some of its gloss: the buildings are smaller, footpaths are busier, and shops abound. By Wellawatta, Galle Rd has lost all pretentiousness. Here, small shops and elbowing shoppers vie for space, and even the odd cow wends its way through the busy traffic. It's one of the most colourful parts of Colombo.

Within leafy Cinnamon Gardens you'll find stately public buildings, posh houses and embassies.

Borella and Maradana are a bit out of the way but give an idea of what life is like in middle-class Colombo.

Mt Lavinia is an ageing beach resort with a beachfront lined with restaurants. This is a decent spot to avoid busy Colombo and, with Fort's skyline visible from the end of the beach, you'll feel like you're close to the action.

Fort & Slave Island
BUDGET
Colombo YMCA (Map p82; ☎ 232 5252; fax 243 6263; 39 Bristol St, Col 1; dm/s Rs 200/250, s/d with fan Rs 400/500, r with fan & bathroom Rs 800) This is a basic institutional place with cramped 16-bed male-only dorms, and a few single and double rooms that are open to both men and women. There are no lockers, so you'll have to chain up your gear it or risk it. There's a Rs 10 daily membership charge as well as a Rs 100 key deposit. Billiard tables, a gym and other facilities are available (for a fee), and there's an inexpensive cafeteria that serves Sri Lankan and Western food (meals Rs 100 to 150); it's open for lunch.

Sri Lanka Ex-Servicemen's Institute (Map p82; ☎ 242 2650; Bristol St, Col 1; dm/s/d Rs 200/400/850) Virtually next door to the YMCA, this is an option for male travellers if the YMCA is full. It has rickety bunks in a basic 10-bed dorm and coffinlike double rooms. The bar sells the cheapest beer in the Fort.

MIDRANGE & TOP END
Grand Oriental Hotel (Map p82; ☎ 232 0391/2; goh@sltnet.lk; 2 York St, Col 1; s/d/ste US$60/70/110) Opposite the harbour, this was Colombo's finest hotel 100 years ago when Bella Sidney Woolf wrote 'if you waited long enough in the hall…you would meet everyone worth

COLOMBO

knowing.' Most rooms have been stripped of original features and renovated like a Spanish motel; the suites are pleasant but the standard rooms are boxy. There are superb views from the 4th-floor restaurant, Harbour Room (p97).

Hilton Colombo Residence (Map pp84-5; ☎ 230 0613; colomboresidence@hilton.com; 200 Union Pl, Col 2; 2-/3-bedroom apt per month from US$2520/2990; ✂ 🖳 🐕) The city's most luxurious full-service apartment complex, the Hilton offers 175 fully furnished apartments in a 34-storey tower. Amenities include parking for guests, a tennis court, pool, squash court, gym and private restaurant and bar. There is a shopping arcade on the ground floor.

Galadari Hotel (Map p82; ☎ 254 4544; www.galadarihotel.lk; 64 Lotus Rd, Col 1; s US$80-100, d US$90-120, ste US$140-160; ✂ 🖳 🐕) This hotel is very popular with travellers from India, Malaysia and the Middle East. Although the décor is a bit tacky, the 446 rooms are comfortable and offer good city views. Restaurants include the Sheherezade Arabic Restaurant, and the Crab Claw (Chinese cuisine). The lobby-level nightclub, Boom, is one of the city's busiest.

Ceylon Continental Hotel (Map p82; ☎ 242 1221; www.colombocontinental.com; 48 Janadhipathi Mawatha; s/d/ste US$85/90/140; 🖳 🐕) Beautifully located, the 250-room Continental faces the sea on one side and the north end of Galle Face Green on another. The rooms are very comfortable but a tad on the small side.

Hilton Colombo (Map p82; ☎ 249 2492; www.hilton.com; 2 Sir Chittampalam A Gardiner Mawatha, Col 2; s/d standard US$180/200, executive US$215/225; 🐕) Among business travellers this place is known as the city's most efficient and most comfortable business hotel. With six restaurants (one of which is open round the clock), a karaoke bar, a disco, a pub, a 24-hour business centre, a fully equipped sports-and-fitness club and even a masseur at hand, you needn't even leave the hotel.

Trans Asia Hotel (Map p82; ☎ 249 1000; www.transasiahotel.com; 115 Sir Chittampalam A Gardiner Mawatha, Col 2; r US$150-180, ste US$240-260; ✂ 🖳 🐕) This modern, function-oriented hotel is a favoured location for conventions. The lobby is particularly grandiose, and the swimming pool is huge. The hotel's Library nightclub and Royal Thai restaurant are popular with moneyed locals. Lower rates may be available if you book through the hotel's website.

Kollupitiya

BUDGET

YWCA National Headquarters (Map pp84-5; ☎ 232 3498; fax 243 4575; natywca@sltnet.lk; 7 Rotunda Gardens; s/d incl breakfast women only Rs 400/800, mixed Rs 1000/1700) This place has eight tidy, basic rooms that surround a leafy courtyard. It's a secure, homely refuge for female travellers; men can stay if they're with a female companion. There are women-only rooms with shared bathroom, while mixed rooms have private bathrooms. There's a cheap cafeteria (meals Rs 100 to 150), open from Monday to Saturday for breakfast, lunch and dinner.

MIDRANGE

Colombo House (Map pp84-5; ☎ 257 4900; colombohse@eureka.lk; 26 Charles Pl; s/d/tr Rs 1500/1900/2000, with air-con Rs 2000/2400/2500; ✂) Lying on a quiet leafy street not far from the University of Colombo, this ageing but attractive mansion has four large rooms.

Mrs Padmini Nanayakkara's (Map pp84-5; ☎ 071 278758; 20 Chelsea Gardens; s/d incl breakfast Rs 1500/2250) This place offers three cute rooms in one of Colombo's classier neighbourhoods. The house has some elegant furniture and a pretty little garden. Mrs Nanayakkara speaks fluent French.

Hotel Renuka & Renuka City Hotel (Map pp84-5; ☎ 257 3598; www.renukahotel.com; 328 Galle Rd; s/d US$55/75; ✂ 🐕) Possibly the best-value midrange hotel in Colombo, the Renuka is split into the older Hotel Renuka and the newer Renuka City Hotel. Although the 80 spotless rooms a little dated, they are in good condition. Added to this are two excellent, reasonably priced restaurants: Palmyrah (p98), serving Sri Lankan cuisine, and Namaste (p98), serving North Indian food. The swimming pool is around 50m from the hotel towards the sea.

Galle Face Court Suites (Map pp84-5; ☎ 239 6666; miguel@srilankainstyle.com; 23 Galle Face Crt II; r US$60) Centrally located off Galle Rd, almost opposite the High Commission of India, Galle Face Court Suites has two comfortably decorated rooms with a good-sized living-and-entertaining area. This would be a good choice for someone needing a very private serviced apartment.

TOP END

Holiday Inn (Map pp84-5; ☎ 242 2001-10; holiday@sri.lanka.net; 30 Sir Mohamed Macan Markar Mawatha; s/d

---

THE AUTHOR'S CHOICE

Galle Face Hotel & Galle Face Regency
(Map pp84-5; ☎ 254 1010-6; www.gallefacehotel
.com; 2 Kollupitiya Rd; hotel r US$94-120, regency
ste US$263-1260; ⬛ 🖳) The hotel that epito-
mises Colombo is this 142-year-old *grande
dame*, facing Galle Face Green to the north
and the sea to the west. The sweeping stairways, high ceilings and grass courtyard buf-
feted by sea breezes look much the same as
they did nearly 100 years ago. Just about
everyone who visits Colombo shows up for
a drink at the Veranda bar at some point,
whether or not they stay at the hotel. While
the northern wing still maintains an atmosphere of faded decadence, the southern
wing has recently undergone a total renovation and now caters to discerning tastes
with a wine lounge, a state-of-the-art spa,
and a fusion restaurant, 1864 (p98).

US$94/114; ⬛ 🖳) A step down from most
other top-end hotels, this hotel has all the
mod cons but is smaller and less grandiose.
It has 94 rooms. Discounts are fairly easy to
come by if you book in advance, lowering
the cost of doubles to around US$80.

Taj Samudra (Map pp84-5; ☎ 244 6622; www.taj
hotels.com; 25 Galle Face Centre Rd; s/d with pool views
US$90/98, with sea views US$120/140; ⬛ 🖳) This
is a vast edifice with elegant public areas and
a well-tended 12-acre garden. The remaining
buildings of the colonial-era Colombo Club
still stand near the entrance. The hotel has
a 24-hour coffee shop, a restaurant serving
North Indian cuisine, another with Canton-
ese and Sichuan dishes, and a steak house.

Cinnamon Grand Hotel (Map pp84-5; ☎ 243 7437;
www.cinnamonhotels.com; 77 Galle Rd; s/d US$116/132;
⬛ 🖳) Formerly the Colombo Plaza
Hotel and, before that, the Lanka Oberoi,
this five-star hotel occupies 10 acres and was
completely refurbished in 2005. It's a short
distance from Galle Face Green.

Bambalapitiya, Havelock Town & Wellawatta

Mrs Marie Barbara Settupathy's (Map p88; ☎ 258
7964; jbs@slt.lk; 23/2 Shrubbery Gardens, Col 4; s/d incl
breakfast Rs 850/1000) The Settupathys offer five
clean and tidy rooms. There's a sitting area
with a TV and a minuscule pebble courtyard. To find the Settupathys' house, look

for the church on the left as you come down
Shrubbery Gardens. The guesthouse is at
the end of the alley next to the church.

Chanuka Guest House (Map p88; ☎ 258 5883;
29 Frances Rd, Col 6; s/d Rs 550/660, r with hot water Rs
800) Though the five rooms are bland they're
very clean and the owners are friendly.

Ottery Tourist Inn (Map p88; ☎ 258 3727; 29 Melbourne Ave, Col 4; s/d Rs 350/700) This 1920s-era
lodging house is a short walk from the
coast. It's run-down and the staff is dif-
fident at best, but the eight rooms are spacious, and it's doubtful you'll find closer to
the sea for this price.

Havelock Place Bungalow (Map p88; ☎ 258 5191;
www.bungalow.lk; 6-8 Havelock Pl, Col 5; r/ste US$100/140;
⬛ 🖳) This handsome boutique hotel
has six rooms, refined décor, comfy lounge
areas and a garden. The outdoor café here
is also well worth a visit.

Hotel Sapphire (Map p88; ☎ 238 3306; sapphire@
slt.lk; 371 Galle Rd, Col 6; s/d/tr incl breakfast US$68/81/96;
⬛ 🖳) The 40 rooms here have fridge
and satellite TV as well as an overwhelm-
ing 1970s feel.

Cinnamon Gardens

Parisare (Map pp84-5; ☎ 269 4749; sunsep@visualnet
.lk; 97/1 Rosmead Pl; s/d Rs 750/1500, deluxe Rs 1000/2000)
This modern home houses two upstairs
rooms and a deluxe downstairs room with
a private garden. All rooms have hot water.
Parisare is very popular – book ahead.

Ranjit Samarasinghe's (Map pp84-5; ☎ 250 2403,
071 234 7400; ranjitksam@hotmail.com; 53/19 Torrington Ave;
s/d Rs 1600/2000, with air-con Rs 2200/2500; ⬛) This
guesthouse is modern and airy with a small
leafy courtyard and a wealth of books on
Buddhism. There are three homely rooms,
two with attached bathrooms. All rooms
have air-con, though you have to pay extra
to use it. Finding the house is a bit tricky.
Coming down Torrington Ave from Bauddhaloka Mawatha, look for the mosque on
the right, then take the first left at a small
playground, and then the first right. It's the
second house on the left.

Borella & Maradana

Mrs A Jayawardhana's (Map pp84-5; ☎ 269 3820;
samera@sri.lanka.net; 42 Kuruppu Rd, Col 8; r Rs 850-1000)
This is an unpretentious family home with
three tidy rooms, a large garden, an excellent library of books on Buddhism and good
Sinhalese food. Two rooms share a bathroom

while the other room has a private bathroom. The guesthouse is a bit out of the way: you can get here by train to Cotta Rd train station, or catch a bus from Fort (bus 168, 174 or 177). A three-wheeler from Fort will cost about Rs 350; ask the driver to head to the Cotta Rd train station. If you ring, the family may be able to arrange to pick you up from the Pettah bus stations or Fort train station.

Mrs Swarna Jayaratne's (Map pp84-5; ☎ 269 5665; indcom@sltnet.lk; 70 Ananda Rajakaruna Mawatha, Col 8; s/d Rs 1050/1350, with air-con 1550/1850; ✂) Mrs Jayaratne's guesthouse features two clean rooms with a shared bathroom. There's an attached guest sitting area with satellite TV, a balcony and a small patch of lawn. To get here catch bus 103 or 171 (Rs 6 from Fort train station) and get off at Punchi Borella Junction.

Rendlesham Tourist Accommodation (Map pp84-5; ☎ 268 4985; 165 Vipulasena Mawatha, Col 10; s/d incl breakfast Rs 1800/2400; ✂) This is a fine old villa packed with antiques. The handsome guest rooms have air-con, and the garden is crammed with parrots and pot plants. The glamorous owner, Mrs Suriya de Livera, is a fashion designer. Rendlesham is situated on a little alley that runs off Vipulasena Mawatha, close to the corner of Hedges Ct.

Mrs Chitrangi de Fonseka's (Map pp84-5; ☎ /fax 269 7919; 7 Karlshrue Gardens, Col 10; r US$40-65; ✂) This is a modern home bubbling with eccentricity, including chintzy décor, lots of porcelain and an indoor fountain. The three spacious rooms have TV, air-con, and laptop and phone connections, and there's a fully equipped guest kitchen. Bus 103 or 171 from Fort will take you nearby; get off at Punchi Borella Junction.

Mt Lavinia
BUDGET
Blue Seas Guest House (Map p89; ☎ 271 6298; 6/9 De Saram Rd; s/d/tr incl breakfast Rs 1035/1380/1725) This large house down a quiet lane has 12 clean, simple and spacious rooms, some with balconies. There's a large sitting room decked out with colonial furniture, and a garden. Guests praise the staff members for their helpful attitude.

MIDRANGE
Haus Chandra (Map p89; ☎ 273 2755; hauschandra@wow.lk; 37 Beach Rd; s/d/ste/villas US$33/46/65/125, all incl breakfast; ✂ 🖳 🖥) This place has a mix-

ture of suites, a colonial villa and standard hotel rooms with air-con, TV, telephone and fridge; some rooms can be cramped so check them out before you book in. The two-person suites have antique furnishings, carpets and a fully equipped kitchen. The charming villa – an older Colombo-style house – sleeps six and comes with a kitchen.

Mrs Lyn Mendis' (Map p89; ☎ 273 2446; ranmal@bigfoot.com; 11 College Ave; s/d incl breakfast Rs 1750/2000; ✂) Opposite Tropic Inn, Mrs Mendis' is a clean, peaceful and friendly guesthouse. There's a light-filled guest sitting area and a kitchen complete with stove and fridge.

Tropic Inn (Map p89; ☎ 273 8653; www.tropicinn .com; 30 College Ave; s/d incl breakfast US$23/25; ✂ 🖳) This multistorey hotel features 20 clean rooms in a simple, stylish building. There's an internal courtyard and many of the rooms have a balcony; all rooms have cable TV.

Cottage Gardens (Map p89; ☎ 273 2478; aquila@eureka.lk; 42-48 College Ave; bungalows US$21) This place offers five charming self-contained bungalows – each equipped with cooking facilities and a fridge – set in a small garden.

Ivory Inn (Map p89; ☎ 271 5006; 21 Barnes Ave; s/d Rs 1500/2500, with air-con Rs 1650/2750, all incl breakfast; ✂) This a motel-like place that has 16 basic rooms with balconies; some have a view to the sea. There's a small garden but, overall, this place lacks character.

TOP END
Mount Lavinia Hotel (Map p89; ☎ 271 5221-7; www .mountlaviniahotel.com; 100 Hotel Rd; governor's wing s US$100-120, d US$120-140, s/d sea & garden wing US$130/150, bay wing US$160/180; ✂ 🖳) Built in 1836 as the residence of the British governor, this magnificently marbled hotel overlooks the sea. About a third of the hotel – the part referred to as the 'governor's wing' – has colonial architecture; the remainder is modern. There's a private sandy beach and a beautifully positioned pool and terrace. Many of the staff members are students at the hotel school on the premises. Locals still refer to this hotel as 'Galkissa', the district name before Mt Lavinia was established.

Berjaya Mount Royal Beach Hotel (Map p89; ☎ 273 9610-5; www.berjayaresorts.com; 36 College Ave; s/d US$75/80; ✂ 🖳) This is a fading 1970s resort hotel where the rooms are dated but comfortable. In a nutshell, you're paying for its prime beach position.

Airport

Hotel Goodwood Plaza (☎ 225 2561; Canada Friendship Rd, Katunayake; s/d incl breakfast Rs 2000/2200) The basic motel-like rooms here are decent value, given the proximity to the airport. The hotel offers a shuttle (Rs 200) to and from the airport.

Taj Airport Garden (☎ 225 2950; www.tajairport gardensrilanka.com; s/d US$105/110; 🕃 🖳 🖳) The 120-room Taj is 10 minutes' drive from the airport in the free hotel shuttle. The hotel has a 24-hour coffee shop, a Chinese restaurant and a pub. Lower rates are available through the hotel's website.

EATING

Colombo unsurprisingly boasts the best selection of restaurants in Sri Lanka. In addition to good Sri Lankan food, you'll find North and South Indian, German, Swiss, French, Italian, Malaysian, Japanese, Chinese and Korean cuisines. Some of the best restaurants are in the five-star hotels, but the real innovation is coming from the independent cafés and restaurants that are bringing a mix of cuisines to Colombo's wealthier classes.

For cheap, tasty food it's hard to beat a lunch packet. Sold between about 11am and 2pm on street corners and footpaths all over the city, the lunch packet contains rice and curry, usually made from vegetables, with fish or chicken as optional extras. It generally costs between Rs 75 and Rs 100. Restaurants will also prepare your meal for you to take away; ask for a parcel.

Fort, Pettah & Slave Island

BUDGET

Colombo YMCA (Map p82; 39 Bristol St, Col 1; meals Rs 100-150; 🕒 lunch) The cheap cafeteria at this hostel (p93) serves tasty Sri Lankan and Western dishes.

Pagoda Tea Room (Map p82; ☎ 232 5252; 105 Chatham St, Col 1; dishes Rs 75-150) Hungry like the wolf? Duran Duran filmed its classic 1980s video for that very song in this venerable establishment. It's one of the oldest eating establishments in Fort and the service is graciously old-fashioned. Although there's a variety of Sri Lankan, Malaysian, Chinese and Western dishes, the main focus on its inexpensive pastries. This is a sister establishment to Green Cabin (p98), where most of the food is prepared.

Chettinad (Map p82; 293 Sea St, Col 11; rice & curry Rs 60-70; 🕃) Enjoy cheap South Indian and Sri Lankan food at this place in the heart of Pettah. The downstairs dining room is open to the street, and the menu is veg only. Upstairs is air-con and offers both veg and nonveg meals; prices are about Rs 10 more than those downstairs. Bombay sweets are sold from a glass case in the lobby.

Cargills (Map p82; York St, Col 1) The original store of this countrywide chain has a food court offering Sri Lankan, Indian, Thai, Malay and Chinese cuisines, all scooped from steam trays.

MIDRANGE

Harbour Room (Map p82; ☎ 232 0391/2; 2 York St, Col 1; dishes Rs 350-600, buffets Rs 800) Overlooking the city harbour from the 4th floor of Grand Oriental Hotel, this blandly decorated hotel dining room is worth visiting for its superb views. The menu covers all the usual Sri Lankan, Chinese and Western bases. Inexpensive lunch buffets are served on weekdays; there are dinner buffets daily.

Seafish (Map p82; ☎ 232 6915; 15 Sir Chittampalam A Gardiner Mawatha, Col 1; mains Rs 700-1400) At the end of an alley on the southern edge of Fort, the venerable Seafish serves honest seafood in a faded colonial-club setting.

Lotus Leaf (Map pp84-5; ☎ 479 3100; 466 Union Pl, Col 2; dishes Rs 75-150; 🕃) This brasserie-style eatery, popular with students, serves fresh, reasonably priced Sri Lankan cuisine. The upstairs dining room has air-con.

Il Ponte (Map p82; ☎ 249 2492; 2 Sir Chittampalam A Gardiner Mawatha, Col 1; mains Rs 600-800) This light, airy restaurant in Hilton Colombo has a range of Italian and continental dishes, imported wines and beers, and a good salad bar.

TOP END

Hilton Colombo has possibly the best array of upscale international restaurants in the city. **Curry Leaf** (Map p82; ☎ 249 2492; 2 Sir Chittampalam A Gardiner Mawatha, Col 1; buffet Rs 950; 🕒 dinner only), tucked away in a lovely garden that recreates the atmosphere of a traditional village, serves excellent Sri Lankan food. It also has an arrack bar. **Moghul Ghar** (mains Rs 600-1000) specialises in Pakistani halal cuisine, and **Ginza Hohsen** (dishes Rs 1000-1600) serves sushi and other Japanese fare (made with all-imported ingredients).

COLOMBO

Kollupitiya

BUDGET

YWCA National Headquarters (Map pp84-5; ☎ 232 3498; 7 Rotunda Gardens; dishes Rs 100-150) The busy cafeteria at this hostel (p94) offers a wide variety of dirt-cheap eats.

Amaravathi (Map pp84-5; ☎ 257 7418; 2 Mile Post Ave; meals from Rs 125; ✂) This place offers attentive service and arguably the best South Indian cuisine in the capital for very reasonable prices. The menu includes three different vegetarian thalis ('all-you-can-eat' plates of rice, curries and accompaniments), plus a varied selection of veg and nonveg Madras- and Andhra-style dishes.

Crescat Boulevard (Map pp84-5; 89 Galle Rd; dishes Rs 135-250; ✂) A couple of minutes from Cinnamon Grand Hotel, this shopping centre has a good food hall downstairs. You have a choice of Sri Lankan, Chinese, Malaysian or Indian cuisine – or burgers. Service is efficient, the surroundings are clean (with clean toilets nearby), and the prices are moderate.

Fab (Map pp84-5; ☎ 257 3348; 474 Galle Rd; pastries Rs 25-45, dishes Rs 65-150) Upper-middle-class Colombo residents fill the Fab in the afternoon for tea, pastries, cakes and Western and Eastern snacks, all of which are cut above the similar fare at Green Cabin and Pagoda Tea Room. There are four other branches around the city, but this is the original and the most popular.

Green Cabin (Map pp84-5; ☎ 258 8811; 453 Galle Rd; dishes Rs 75-300) This place is a bit of an institution in the local restaurant trade. It's well known for both its baked goods and its inexpensive Sri Lankan, Indian and Chinese dishes; the lunchtime buffet is excellent value – the mango curry, if it's on, is very good. For a snack try the vegetable pastries or the bacon-and-egg pies.

Self-caterers can head to **Beema** (Map pp84-5; RA de Mel Mawatha) on the 2nd floor of the big market building near Liberty Plaza. It's an indoor place with fruit, vegetables and a good range of imported foods at very competitive prices. **Keells** (Map pp84-5; Crescat Boulevard 89 Galle Rd; Liberty Plaza RA de Mel Mawatha) is a supermarket popular with expats.

MIDRANGE

Palmyrah (Map pp84-5; 328 Galle Rd; dishes Rs 200-500; ✂) In a nondescript kitchen in the basement of Hotel Renuka a chef is whipping up some of the finest Sri Lankan curries in Colombo, along with a selection of South Indian specialities. Don't miss the stellar *wattalappam* (coconut milk, egg, cardamom and jaggery pudding).

Namaste (Map pp84-5; 328 Galle Rd; dishes Rs 300-600) This recent addition to Hotel Renuka does for North Indian cuisine what the Palmyrah does for Sri Lankan and South Indian food – it provides the highest standards at affordable prices.

Siam House (Map pp84-5; ☎ 257 6993; 55 Abdul Gaffoor Mawatha; dishes Rs 250-500) The décor at this great place is simple but the Thai food is excellent and the service is good. It's located in a villa on a side street off RA de Mel Mawatha.

Chesa Swiss (Map pp84-5; ☎ 257 3877; 3 Deal Pl; mains from Rs 400; ✆ 7-11pm Tue-Sun) This place attracts regulars with sturdy Swiss fare (such as sliced venison in Cognac-pepper sauce), efficient service and its cosy, clean atmosphere. A good selection of imported wines and beers is available.

Sakura (Map pp84-5; ☎ 257 3877; 15 Rheinland Pl; dishes Rs 250-350) The food at Sakura, Colombo's oldest Japanese restaurant, is simply prepared yet very tasty. If you sit at the bar you can switch between watching the sushi chef and the delightfully weird Japanese game shows on the TV. Occasionally there are karaoke videos. There is also a private dining room with tatami mats.

German Restaurant (Map pp84-5; ☎ 242 1577; 11 Sir Mohamed Macan Markar Mawatha; dishes Rs 400-600; ✆ 6pm-midnight) Opposite Galle Face Hotel, this simply named eatery does all things German. You may wish to visit during the happy hour (7pm to 8pm) to sample the draught German beer and wines.

Kafé Kent (Kent Cafe; Map pp84-5; ☎ 255 2837; 35 Bagatalle Rd; dishes Rs 200-500) This cosy restaurant includes several areas for a drink, and multiple dining rooms for a quiet dinner. It's a good spot for women travellers.

TOP END

1864 (Map pp84-5; ☎ 254 1010; 2 Kollupitiya Rd, Col 3; mains around Rs 1500) One of the most talked-about restaurant debuts in Colombo, this place in Galle Face Regency wows its customers with a fusion of Indian, Italian and Japanese cuisines.

Barista (Map pp84-5; ☎ 535 8849; The Piazza, 2 Kollupitiya Rd, Col 3; coffees Rs 45-75, sandwiches Rs 375; 💻)

Sip perfect cappuccinos alongside the city's young, beautiful and wealthy in this large espresso bar and deli that's attached to the new shopping wing of Galle Face Regency.

Gallery Cafe (Map p84-5; ☎ 258 2162; 2 Alfred House Rd; mains Rs 420-1100; 🖳) The historic building that houses Gallery Cafe used to be an office for Sri Lanka's most famous architect, Geoffrey Bawa. Entry is through a series of colonnaded courtyards featuring ornamental pools; from the outer latticed gate you can gaze right through to the inner courtyard. There are exhibitions of paintings and photography in the courtyards, as well as in the building. The open-air café area looks over a pebbled courtyard, while the lounge-bar is where Bawa's old office used to be – in fact, his desk is still there. It's definitely one of the places to be seen in Colombo, but more importantly it's a stunning spot and a terrific retreat from the bustle of Colombo. On a par with the décor, the Sri Lankan–inspired dishes focus on fresh ingredients and bold, clean flavours. As a cheaper option, come for an afternoon coffee.

Cricket Club Cafe (Map pp84-5; ☎ 250 1384; 34 Queens Rd; meals Rs 600-900; ⏰ 11.30am-2am; 🖳) This older-style bungalow with a garden and veranda is one of Colombo's most popular places to meet, drink and eat. It is packed with cricket memorabilia, needless to say. Options range from pasta to seafood to burgers with salad and chips. There's a good bar and an excellent selection of beers and wines.

Sea Spray (Map pp84-5; ☎ 254 1010; 2 Kollupitiya Rd; buffet lunch/dinner Rs 600/900) This quaint oceanside restaurant in Galle Face Hotel specialises in barbecued seafood. The outside tables are close enough to the sea to hear the surf.

Barefoot Garden Cafe (Map pp84-5; ☎ 258 9305; 704 Galle Rd; sandwiches Rs 300-500, meals Rs 600-800; 🖳) Located in the courtyard of the well-known Barefoot gallery (p102), this café serves sandwiches, snacks such as falafel in pita bread, and daily specials that usually include one Sri Lankan, one Thai, one Malay-Indonesian and several Western dishes. There's also a wine list.

Bambalapitiya, Havelock Town & Wellawatta

Greenlands Hotel (Map p88; ☎ 258 1986; 3A Shrubbery Gardens, Col 4; meals from Rs 120; 🍴) Despite its hospital-ward-like interior, Greenlands whips up very good, fresh South Indian

---

THE AUTHOR'S CHOICE

Beach Wadiya (Map p88; ☎ 258 8568; 2 Station Ave, Col 6; mains from Rs 400) Maybe it's the way the staff greets every arriving diner as if they were family. Or it might be because you feel equally welcome whether you're wearing a T-shirt or a tux. Whatever the appeal, come early to pick a table inside the weather-beaten beach shack or outside in the sand, order a chilled Three Coins beer while a waiter fills you in on the day's catch, and receive your specially customised grilled or fried seafood platter.

---

food. Divided in to a busy semi-open-air canteen area and a separate air-con dining room, this place is popular with locals. The prices are so low you won't mind that you may have to beg to be served.

Shanti Vihar (Map pp84-5; ☎ 258 02243; Havelock Rd, Col 5; meals Rs 90-145; 🍴) This place's deliciously spicy vegetarian food and very reasonable prices make it popular with locals and foreigners alike. It's a basic, well-worn eatery, though there is a fancier air-con section. The menu's South Indian offerings are especially good: masala dosa (curried vegetables inside a paper-thin lentil-flour pancake) for Rs 60, curd *vadai* (a deep-fried lentil-flour patty with yoghurt) for Rs 25 and Madras thalis for Rs 90. Shanti Vihar also has a home-delivery service.

Sapid (Map p88; 145 Galle Rd, Col 4; dishes Rs 100-300; 🍴) From the outside, Sapid's glassed-in dining rooms gives the place the look of a New York deli, but inside it's tasty and fast Sri Lankan food.

Chinese Dragon Cafe (Map p88; ☎ 250 3637; 11 Milagiriya Ave, Col 4; dishes Rs 200-400) Colombo probably has more Chinese restaurants than Sri Lankan ones, and this spot, housed in an old mansion, is one of the more popular because of its inexpensive rice and noodle dishes.

Majestic City (Map p88; Galle Rd, Col 4; 🍴) A good spot for a cheap but reasonable quality lunch in the food hall in the basement of this shopping centre, where you can choose from Malaysian, Chinese, Sri Lankan, Western fast food and Indian. There's a play area for children next to the eating area, and the complex also has a good Cargills Food City on the ground floor.

COLOMBO

Cinnamon Gardens

MIDRANGE

Paradise Road Cafe (Map pp84-5; ☎ 268 6043; 213 Dharmapala Mawatha; light meals Rs 250-450) Part of the shop of the same name (p103), this café serves great coffee, milk shakes, cakes and light meals (such as quiche and spaghetti) in an airy veranda-style atmosphere upstairs. It's just southwest of De Soysa (Lipton) Circus.

Delifrance (Map pp84-5; coffee & lunch Rs 500; Crescat Boulevard 89 Galle Rd, Col 3; Odel Unlimited 5 Alexandra Pl, Col 7) This busy café, on the ground floor of the very popular Odel Unlimited store, is delighted to siphon off your shopping change. There's also an outlet in Crescat Boulevard.

Mahout Café (Map pp84-5; ☎ 269 1056; 61 Ward Place; light meals Rs 400-500) In the mezzanine of Elephant Walk, this is a pleasantly casual spot for lunch or afternoon tea. The menu emphasises Mediterranean and Sri Lankan cuisines.

Commons (Map pp84-5; ☎ 257 4384; 74A Dharmapala Mawatha; light meals Rs 400-500) Part garden, part gallery and part café (with large, soft sofas), this is a safe retreat for women and for tired visitors generally. It's a perfect spot to take a break or to settle in with a sandwich and coffee while reading the Sunday papers. There's a good selection for the sweet-toothed, including fudge brownies and a delicious brunch that features pancakes, bacon and syrup.

TOP END

Number 18 (Map pp84-5; ☎ 269 4000; 18 Cambridge Pl; dishes Rs 500-1500) Local designer and hotelier Taru Fanseca has transformed this '60s-vintage bank governor's residence into a chic eatery with minimalist décor. Australian Russell Gronow is the man behind the menu, which blends Pacific Rim and Mediterranean influences. Also available is a variety of wines and exotic cocktails, including the Turkish delight martini.

Le Palace (Map pp84-5; ☎ 269 5920; 79 Gregory's Rd; dishes Rs 600-900) In a beautiful old mansion in one of Colombo's most exclusive streets, this place specialises in first-class pastries and baked goods, and has 15 international set menus ranging from Mexican to Malaysian. If you are coming here by taxi or three-wheeler, ask the driver to take you via the Kynsey Rd entrance; much of the street is closed to traffic.

Mt Lavinia

The beachfront here is lined with restaurants focusing on what most Mt Lavinia visitors expect: fresh seafood. Note that some restaurants have limited menus on weekdays because most local tourists come on the weekend.

Angler (Map p89; 71 Hotel Rd; dishes Rs 350-1000) Casual and friendly, this is a good choice for reliable and reasonably priced seafood, and a range of Sri Lankan and Western dishes.

Frankfurt Lavinia Beer Garden (Map p89; ☎ 271 6034; 34/8A De Saram Rd; mains Rs 400-1000) As the name suggests, German food – including delicious home-made sausages – is the speciality here. It's on the same lane as Blue Seas Guest House.

Fisherman's Villa (Map p89; ☎ 074 202821; 43/19 College Ave, Mt Lavinia; mains Rs 500-1500) Set in a wooden pavilion, this beachfront restaurant offers well-prepared seafood dishes cooked in Western, Sri Lankan and Thai styles.

Golden Mile (Map p89; ☎ 273 3997; 43/14 College Rd; mains Rs 600-1700) In a timber-framed, partially open-air building right on the beach, Golden Mile has become the most popular evening hang-out in Mt Lavinia for well-funded Sri Lankan weekenders. While the seafood and modern Sri Lankan menu (including a few vegetarian items) isn't stellar, the snappy service keeps them coming back.

Seafood Cove (Map p89; ☎ 271 5221-7; 100 Hotel Rd; mains Rs 800-2100) Enjoy Mt Lavinia's prettiest ocean view at Mt Lavinia Hotel's elegant beachfront restaurant.

DRINKING

Galle Face Hotel (Map pp84-5; 2 Kollupitiya Rd, Col 3; ☾ 11am-midnight) Favourite gathering spots for a drink at this venerable institution (p95) include Veranda, a no-nonsense bar on the inside veranda, and the Checkerboard, a cluster of tables on the courtyard lawn facing the sea. Or go the whole hog and quaff imported wine while smoking Cuban cigars and nibbling French cheeses in the hotel's new wine lounge.

Clancy's Irish Pub (Map pp84-5; ☎ 268 2945; 29 Maitland Cres, Col 7; ☾ 11am-3.30am) Colombo's stab at Irishness offers pub grub and a variety of beers and ales, including Guinness. It's a popular spot, with regular quiz nights, live music on weekends and a few couches to sink into. Upstairs, Shooters Sports &

Music Lounge has several billiards tables, a bar and a 150-inch TV screen for sport fans. All drinks are discounted 50% during the daily 6pm to 8pm happy hour.

Molly's Irish Pub & Restaurant (Map pp84-5; ☎ 254 3966; 46/38 Nawam Mawatha, Col 2; ✆ 10.30am-3.30am) Like Clancy's, this pub (tucked away in a small office area) has regular quiz nights, live music, pub meals, happy hours and retro dance nights.

White Horse (Map pp84-5; ☎ 230 4922; 2 Nawam Mawatha, Col 2; ✆ 10am-2pm) Close enough to Molly's that you could lead a conga line between them, White Horse is a sparse, modern space with stainless–steel décor, and low couches and tables. On Friday nights the mixed crowd of locals and expats often spills out onto the street.

Bistro Latino (Map p88; ☎ 258 0063; 21 RA de Mel Mawatha, Col 4; ✆ 6.30pm-2am) This wine bar serves tapas (Rs 300 to 800) and plays recorded Latin jazz and salsa. The staff offers free salsa-dancing lessons.

Cricket Club Cafe (Map pp84-5; 34 Queens Rd, Col 3; ✆ 11.30am-2am) This café (p99) has yet another bar in which you can drink to colonial nostalgia, in this case while surrounded by cricket memorabilia.

Sri Lanka Ex-Servicemen's Institute (Map p82; 29 Bristol St, Col 1; ✆ 11am-11pm) The plain bar at the back of this hostel's (p93) lobby serves Lion Lager at about the lowest prices you'll find outside a grocery store, but you're not paying for atmosphere. Solo women travellers are advised against drinking here.

Lion Pub (Map p89; Galle Rd, Mt Lavinia; ✆ 11am-2am) Locals and tourists alike neck Lion Lager at this casual little bar that's not far from the beach.

ENTERTAINMENT

Although the long years of war put a dampener on Colombo's nightlife, since the 2002 cease-fire a small but vigorous group of clubs has loosened up the city's young and wealthy. A big night out might start at a restaurant or pub, segue into revelry at a nightclub, and finally collapse in a heap at a casino.

Casinos

Gaming is legal in Colombo, but only for foreign passport–holders. All five of the city's casinos are found in Bambalapitiya and Kollupitiya. Incentives to lure punters include free meals and drinks, plus free transport to and from the casino; bets at most tables start at Rs 500. Most casinos are open 24 hours. Despite bearing identical names, those listed alphabetically below have no relationship with the casinos in Las Vegas.

Bally's Casino (Map pp84-5; ☎ 257 3497; 14 Dharmapala Mawatha, Col 3) Near Liberty Plaza.

Bellagio Casino (☎ 257 5271; 430 RA de Mel Mawatha, Col 3)

MGM Casino (Map p88; ☎ 259 1319; 772 Galle Rd, Col 4) Near Majestic City.

Ritz Club (☎ 234 1496; 5 Galle Face Terrace, Col 3)

Star Dust (Map pp84-5; ☎ 257 3493; 15th Lane, Galle Rd, Col 3)

Cinemas

TV and video have largely killed off the cinema scene – many old movie houses are hanging on by catering to the raincoat brigade with lurid skin flicks such as *Craving Desire* and *House of Pleasure*; if the title doesn't tip you off, a notice on the marquee reading 'Strictly for Adults' will. Most of these films are either Hollywood backlot or B-grade Indian (both Hindi and Tamil) productions, often featuring the story of a busty victim seeking vengeance with heavy weaponry. Expensive scenes (explosions etc) are spliced in from other films. Sinhalese films are also popular, but production values are similarly low.

There are four nonsleazy cinemas that show Hollywood blockbusters, although often quite a while after they've been released elsewhere in the world. The air-con systems and volume tend to be turned up high. **Majestic Cinema** (Map p88; ☎ 258 1759; 4th fl, Majestic City, Galle Rd, Col 4) is the most modern and has the best screens. **Liberty Cinema** (Map pp84-5; ☎ 232 5264; Dharmapala Mawatha, Col 3), **Savoy** (Map p88; ☎ 258 9621; Galle Rd, Col 6) and **Regal** (Map p82; ☎ 243 2936; 8 Sir Chittampalam A Gardiner Mawatha, Col 2), opposite the original Lake House Bookshop, are also safe bets. Shows run in the morning and evening (usually starting at 6.30pm or 7pm). Tickets cost Rs 150 for adults and Rs 100 for children under 12.

The foreign cultural centres show arthouse films; see *LT, Travel Lanka* and the *Linc* for what's on. Regal, which is opposite colonial-era Lake House, is a common screening location for local film festivals.

Nightclubs

Most of Colombo's dance-oriented nightlife centres on the top hotels. All clubs have a cover charge of about Rs 500 to 600 (which usually includes one drink). The dress code is fashion-conscious but casual; entry is usually restricted to mixed couples and single women. Things get going at about 11pm and continue through to 6am.

Blue Elephant (Map p82; Hilton Colombo, 2 Sir Chittampalam A Gardiner Mawatha, Col 1)

Boom (Map p82; Galadari Hotel, 64 Lotus Rd, Col 1)

Cascades (Map pp84–5; Cinnamon Grand Hotel, 77 Galle Rd, Col 3)

Library (Map p82; Trans Asia Hotel, Sir Chittampalam A Gardiner Mawatha, Col 2)

My Kind of Place (Map pp84–5; Taj Samudra, 25 Galle Face Centre Rd, Col 3)

Live music

Both Molly's Irish Pub & Restaurant (p101) and Clancy's Irish Pub (p100) host live local bands most nights, while Rhythm & Blues (Map p88; 19/1 Daisy Villa Ave, Col 4; weekend cover charge Rs 500) has live rock, R&B and blues nightly. Despite the Daisy Villa Ave address, Rhythm & Blues is on Duplication Rd.

Sport

Sri Lanka Cricket (☎ 472 2235; sl.cricinfo.com; 35 Maitland Pl, Col 7) The top sport in Sri Lanka is, without a doubt, cricket. You can buy tickets for major games from Sri Lanka Cricket, either online or at the office next to Sinhalese Sports Club.

Theatre

Foreign cultural centres such as the British Council occasionally host live theatre performances. These are advertised in newspapers and magazines such as *LT*, as well as at cafés and hotels frequented by expats. The following places, listed alphabetically, are some other notable theatres in Colombo.

Elphinstone Theatre (Map pp84–5; ☎ 243 3635; Maradana Rd, Col 7) This finely restored 80-year-old theatre maintains a busy programme that includes music, theatre and films.

Lionel Wendt Centre (Map pp84–5; ☎ 269 5794; 18 Guilford Cres, Col 10) Among other events, this gallery (p90) occasionally hosts live theatre.

Lumbini Theatre (Map p88; Havelock Rd, Col 5) This is the city's oldest theatre and one of the only places where you'll find modern Sinhala performances.

SHOPPING
Handicrafts

If you missed out on buying Sri Lanka's plentiful handicrafts while travelling, don't worry – just about everything is available in Colombo. The better shops can easily arrange shipping.

Laksala (Map p82; ☎ 232 9247; 60 York St, Col 1) Run by the Sri Lankan Handicraft Board (a government institute promoting traditional craft skills), Laksala has two floors showcasing all manner of traditional Sri Lankan crafts, including leather goods, silverwork, furniture, brass, batik and woodcarvings. The prices are decent and clearly marked, so there's no need to bargain.

Lanka Hands (Map pp84–5; ☎ 451 2311; 135 Bauddhaloka Mawatha, Col 4) Here you'll find a good variety of local crafts including jewellery, Sinhalese masks, brightly painted wooden toys and puzzles, cane furniture and basketry, drums and more. The prices are reasonable.

Lakpahana (Map pp84–5; ☎ 269 8211; 21 Rajakeeya Mawatha, Col 7) As with Laksala and Lanka Hands, this Cinnamon Gardens showroom carries traditionally crafted items, including lacework, jewellery, batik and masks, as well as tea.

Fabrics & Clothing

Sri Lanka has a thriving weaving industry that produces both hand- and machine-woven fabrics, and is a major garment manufacturer. All manner of clothing, ranging from beach wear to padded jackets, is sold in Colombo. Many of the items are Western-style clothes – you'd be able to find them in department stores all over the world – while others you'll only find here.

Barefoot (Map pp84–5; ☎ 258 0114; www.barefoot ceylon.com/home.htm; 704 Galle Rd, Col 3) Designer Barbara Sansoni's beautifully laid-out shop, located in an old villa, is justly popular for its bright hand-loomed textiles, which are fashioned into bedspreads, cushions, serviettes and other household items (or sold by the metre). You'll also find textile-covered notebooks, lamp shades and albums, and a large selection of stylish, simple clothing.

Oasis Company (Map p88; ☎ 269 7097; 18 Station Rd, Col 4) You'll find goods similar those of Barefoot here, but some of the textiles are block-printed; there are carpets, too.

Odel Unlimited (Cinnamon Gardens Map pp84–5; 5 Alexandra Pl, Col 7; Majestic City Map p88; Galle Rd, Col 4;

Trans Asia Hotel Map p82; 115 Sir Chittampalam Gardiner A Mawatha, Col 2) Head here to shop with the glamorous. You'll find everything from homewares, designer-label clothing and sportswear to banana soap.

House of Fashion (Map p88; ☎ 250 4639; cnr RA de Mel Mawatha & Visak Rd, Col 4) This three-storey surplus outlet for the nation's garment industry is the place to go for serious clothes shopping. Many items are hugely discounted.

Collectables

Paradise Road (Map pp84-5; ☎ 268 6043; 213 Dharmapala Mawatha, Col 7) In addition to a variety of colonial and Sri Lankan antiques you'll find a good selection of original houseware here. Paradise Road's Gallery Cafe (p99) carries a similar array of collectables. Both are excellent places to look for small gifts to take home.

Elephant Walk (Map pp84-5; ☎ 269 1056; 61 Ward Pl, Col 7) Similar in scope to Paradise Road, this well-decorated shop housed in a Bawa-designed bungalow carries hand-crafted houseware, furniture, lamps and stationery, and gourmet food items.

Raux Brothers (Map p88; ☎ 533 9016; 7 De Fonseka Rd, Col 5) This 45-year-old antiques showroom, located in a large, beautiful colonial house, stocks an impressive range of furniture, and artworks crafted from wood. There are genuine antiques and handcrafted new pieces. This is the best antique house in the city, if you can afford it.

Kandyan Antiques (Map pp84-5; ☎ 451 0981; 36 Sir Ernest de Silva Mawatha, Col 7) Some of the antiques here are genuine, while others are skilful copies; the staff can tell you which is which if the price tags don't make it obvious. There's also a good selection of Buddhist and Hindu religious art.

Gems & Jewellery

There are many gem dealers and jewellers along Galle Rd and RA de Mel Mawatha, and on Sea St, Pettah, where the shops can be on a tiny scale. The biggest outlets employ the most silver-tongued salespeople in the business.

Sri Lanka Gem & Jewellery Exchange (Map p82; ☎ 239 1132; www.slgemexchange.com; 4th & 5th fl, East Low Block, World Trade Center, Bank of Ceylon Mw, Col 1) This is your safest bet for price and authenticity. It contains 41 government-approved shops plus a gem-testing laboratory.

Tea

Ceylon tea is sold in just about every place that sells foodstuffs, from minimarts to supermarkets. For the best quality and selection head to a **Mlesna Tea Centre** (Crescat Boulevard Map pp84-5; 89 Galle Rd, Col 3; Liberty Plaza Map pp84-5; RA de Mel Mawatha, Col 3; Majestic City Map p88; Galle Rd, Col 4) or a Dilmah Tea Shop, located inside **Odel Unlimited** (Cinnamon Gardens Map pp84-5; 5 Alexandra Pl, Col 7; Majestic City Map p88; Galle Rd, Col 4; Trans Asia Hotel Map p82; 115 Sir Chittampalam Gardiner A Mawatha, Col 2). In these outlets you'll find a variety of teas packed in airtight canisters, ceramic containers and wooden or cardboard boxes, along with strainers, china and other tea-making paraphernalia.

Photographic Supplies & Repairs

The following places, listed in alphabetical order, sell photographic supplies such as film and memory cards; also try stores in luxury hotels.

Crescat Boulevard (Map pp84-5; 89 Galle Rd, Col 3)
Liberty Plaza (Map pp84-5; RA de Mel Mawatha, Col 3)
Majestic City (Map p88; Galle Rd, Col 4)
Millers (Fort Map p82; ☎ 232 9151; York St; Majestic City Map p88; Galle Rd, Col 4) For print and slide film.

The following stores have been recommended for camera repairs.

Photoflex (Map pp84-5; ☎ 258 7824; 1st fl, 451/2, Galle Rd, Col 3)
Photo Technica (Kollupitiya Map pp84-5; ☎ 257 6271; 288 Galle Rd, Col 3; Liberty Plaza Map pp84-5; RA de Mel Mawatha, Col 3; Majestic City Map p88; Galle Rd, Col 4)

GETTING THERE & AWAY

Colombo is the international gateway to Sri Lanka, and it is also the centre of the island's bus and rail networks. You may find leaving Colombo by train is easier than by bus, though trains are usually less frequent and a little more expensive than buses. There's more order at the train stations than at the bus stations, and there's often less overcrowding once on board.

Air

Colombo's domestic airport is at Ratmalana Air Force Base, south of Mt Lavinia. There is no public transport to or from this airport, but AeroLanka runs its own shuttle bus. Because of the air force presence security is heavy and you need to check in two hours before takeoff.

COLOMBO

Expo Aviation (Map pp84–5; ☎ 257 6941; info@ expoavi.com; 464 Galle Rd, Col 3) and **AeroLanka** (☎ 250 5632; www.aerolanka.com; 500 Galle Rd, Col 6) operate flights between Colombo and Jaffna (one way Rs 6900), while AeroLanka also flies to Trincomalee (one way Rs 4890). At the time of writing, however, AeroLanka had temporarily suspended flights to Trinco.

Bandaranaike International Airport is at Katunayake, 30km north of the city and about 2km east of the Colombo–Negombo road. For information on international flights see p336.

Bus

Colombo has three main bus terminals, all just east of Fort train station on the south edge of Pettah (Map p82). Long-distance buses leave from chaotic Bastian Mawatha

---

SELECTED BUS DESTINATIONS FROM COLOMBO

From Bastian Mawatha

Ambalangoda Rs 36, two hours.
Galle Regular/air-con Rs 63/130, three hours.
Hikkaduwa Regular/air-con Rs 54/110, two to three hours.
Kandy Regular Rs 70 to 120, air-con Rs 140, 2½ to 3½ hours.
Kataragama Regular/air-con Rs 146/280, 10 hours.
Matara Regular/air-con Rs 84/170, four to five hours.
Nuwara Eliya Rs 220, six hours.
Tangalla Regular/air-con Rs 104/210, six hours.
Trincomalee Regular/air-con Rs 200/240, six to seven hours.

From Saunders Pl

Anuradhapura CTB/intercity bus Rs 107/210, five hours.
Badulla Rs 22, seven hours.
Haputale Rs 265, six hours.
Kurunegala Regular/intercity Rs 45/84, four to five hours.
Negombo Regular/air-con Rs 28/42, one to two hours.
Ratnapura CTB/intercity bus Rs 46/100, three hours.
Polonnaruwa Regular/air-con Rs 170/230, six hours.

---

station and Saunders Pl station; Central Bus Station on Olcott Mawatha is where many suburban buses start and stop. See left for details of selected services.

Train

The main train station, Colombo Fort, is within walking distance of the city centre. Trains in transit often stop only for two or three minutes. See opposite for details of services.

There's an **information office** (☎ 244 0048; ⏱ 9am-5pm Mon-Fri, 9am-1pm Sat), in fact a branch office of JF Tours, at the front of Fort station. The helpful staff know everything about transport in and out of Colombo. Or you could try the information desk in the station. There is left-luggage storage at the station's **cloakroom** (per bag per day Rs 20; ⏱ 4.30am-11.30pm). Fort station is crawling with touts waiting to hook you up with their 'uncle's' hotel in Kandy or down the coast.

GETTING AROUND
To/From the Airport

To get to the domestic airport at Ratmalana Air Force Base AeroLanka offers free shuttle service if you hold its tickets; otherwise you'll have to take a taxi.

Taxis and buses are the most convenient forms of transport to and from Bandaranaike International Airport. If you're arriving in the dead of the night it's best to book a room and let the hotel or guesthouse know what time you'll be arriving. Staff *should* be able to organise a driver to pick you up from the airport, though it's easy enough to jump in a taxi. Bus 187 to the airport departs the Bastian Mawatha station from 6am until 9pm (Rs 25). The buses are easy to find, as there are men screaming out 'Airport! Airport!' whenever one is filling up. From the airport they leave every 30 minutes between 4.30am and 11pm. Taxi drivers will tell you there is no public transport.

There is no bus directly to Negombo from the airport but you can catch an air-con bus to Katunayake junction (Rs 8), from where you can catch a bus to Negombo (intercity express Rs 15). Buses from Negombo head to the airport every 15 to 20 minutes from about 5am to 9pm – again, change buses at the junction. The trip takes about 45 minutes.

MAIN TRAINS FROM FORT

Destination	Departure time	Fare (Rs) 3rd class	2nd class	1st class	Duration (hr)
Anuradhapura	5.45am, 2pm	120	215	420	5
Anuradhapura (Intercity Express)	3.55pm	160	290	520	4
Anuradhapura (Night Mail)	9.30pm	175	309	520	5
Batticaloa (Intercity Express)	7.30pm	218	393	697	9 10
Badulla via Kandy (Podi Menike)	5.55am	190	343	580	9
Badulla via Peradeniya Junction (Udarata Menike)	9.45am	190	343	580	9
Badulla (Night Mail)	7.40pm, 10pm	190	343	580	9
Kandy via Peradeniya Junction	7am, 3.25pm	80	125	250	2½
Kandy via Rambukkana	5.55am, 10.30am, 12.40pm, 4.55pm, 5.50pm, 7.40pm	61	150	—	3
Matara via Bentota, Hikkaduwa & Galle	7.10am, 9am, 4pm, 10.30am, 2.05pm, 5pm, 5.52pm	72	180	—	4
Negombo	4.30am, 5.20am, 6am, 8.40am, 9.25am, 1pm, 1.45pm, 2.50pm, 4.55pm, 5.20pm, 5.35pm, 5.40pm, 6.20pm, 6.55pm, 8.20pm	21	—	—	2
Polonnaruwa	6.15am, 10.30pm	54	147	331	6-9
Trincomalee	6.15am, 10.30pm	194	347	587	8
Vavuniya via Anuradhapura	5.45am, 2pm	120	218	420	6
Vavuniya (Intercity Express)	3.55pm	160	290	560	4

It's possible, although not particularly convenient, to catch a commuter train to Colombo. The station is near the turn-off from the main road, about 500m from the terminal.

If you want a taxi, head to the Ceylon Tourist Board's **information desk** (24hr), in the first arrivals hall after you exit through customs, and find out the latest fixed rates. At the time of writing a one-way fare was Rs 1010 to Colombo (40 minutes to 1½ hours); Rs 600 to Negombo (20 minutes); and Rs 3300 to Kandy (two to three hours). After you've exited the second arrivals hall that's full of hotel and hire-car agencies, you'll be pounced on by an army of taxi drivers – take your pick, as you'll know what to pay. Taxis to the airport cost more –

around Rs 1500 from Colombo (Rs 1800 from Mt Lavinia), Rs 800 from Negombo and Rs 3500 from Kandy.

Avoid taking a three-wheeler between the airport and Colombo; it's a long, miserable journey and you'll be sucking in exhaust fumes all the way. Three-wheeler fares between the airport and Negombo should be around Rs 400 (30 minutes). Three-wheelers may not pick up passengers from the terminal but you can catch one on the road outside the airport.

Public Transport
BUS
The *A–Z Street Guide* contains a detailed table and a map showing bus routes in Colombo. The Central Transport Board (CTB)

and private bus companies operate parallel services. A timetable is not necessary – the buses can hardly be described as running to one. Buses going down Galle Rd from Fort or Pettah include 100, 101, 102 and 400, and can be picked up at the Central Bus Station. Fares vary from Rs 4 to 25, depending on distance.

Private semiluxury and luxury buses are a recent addition to the Galle Rd service, although they are far fewer in number than the regular buses. Sometimes they have a destination sign in English in the front window. Generally they have curtains and soft seats. The fare is about twice that for ordinary buses, but still a bargain.

TRAIN

You can use the train to get to the suburbs dotted along Galle Rd – Kollupitiya, Bambalapitiya, Wellawatta, Dehiwala and Mt Lavinia – and to avoid the smog, noise and hassle of bus travel. The Kelani Valley line could be used to get to outlying suburbs such as Narahenpita (via Cotta Rd station) from Fort. Timetables are clearly marked at the stations, though if you just turn up you shouldn't have to wait long. If you board the train at Fort train station, double-check that it stops at all stations or you may end up speeding to Galle. Train fares are fixed and are usually marginally lower than bus fares. A taxi from Fort train station to Galle Face Hotel (a little over 2km) should cost about Rs 150 (less if a meter is used).

Taxi

Some taxis are metered, but often the driver won't use the meter – agree on the fare before setting off. Getting to Mt Lavinia, for example, should cost around Rs 650.

A less fraught alternative is using one of Colombo's radio cab companies; they take anywhere from five to 20 minutes to arrive. All have air-con cars with meters and average Rs 40 to 44 per kilometre. Reliable companies include **Ace Cabs** (☎ 281 8818), **GNTC** (☎ 268 8688) and **Cool Kangaroo** (☎ 258 8588).

Three-Wheeler

Everywhere you look you'll see a three-wheeler, often referred to as Bajaj after one of the Indian manufacturers. Darting through traffic in one of these might be called exhilarating by some and downright reckless by others.

As a rule of thumb you should pay no more than Rs 40 per kilometre, but agree on a fare before getting in. At times three-wheeler drivers will try their luck by asking for a ridiculous initial fare in the hope that you haven't got a clue. Try rolling your eyes and heading for another three-wheeler. From Fort, expect to pay Rs 150 to 200 to get to Cinnamon Gardens, Rs 300 to Bambalapitiya and Rs 500 to 550 to Mt Lavinia.

You'll generally get a better price hailing a three-wheeler on the street than using one that's waiting outside a hotel or sitting at a three-wheeler stand.

Keep in mind that it's often cheaper and less frustrating to take a metered taxi.

West Coast

Sri Lanka's west coast has two personalities, split figuratively and literally by the behemoth that is Colombo. In the north, the old beach town of Negombo still welcomes travellers looking for a sandy respite near the airport. Head further north, however, and you enter a sparsely populated land of coconut plantations and fishing villages. Past the old market town of Puttalam is Wilpattu National Park, a remarkable place of elephants and leopards that is re-emerging as an important destination after years of war.

Going south from Colombo, the capital seems to drag on forever. But after about 40km the traffic thins enough to create a sense of open road, and you begin to see stretches of the beautiful coast, lined with rocks, sand or both. Simple guesthouses intermingle with resorts. Some visitors cleanse their bodies at Ayurvedic spas, while others use their beachside idyll to cleanse their soul.

The tsunami hit hard here, especially in the low-lying areas beyond Ambalangoda, but the region is working hard on its long-term recovery and travellers are welcomed. Hikkaduwa was the country's original laid-back backpacker town, and it continues to exude a mellow vibe. Its long beaches inspire relaxation, while those looking for more activity can enjoy snorkelling and diving amid coral – or try riding some of the often-excellent waves.

Whether it's exploring the outer regions to the north or joining the sun seekers in the south, the west coast has much to offer travellers. If you're pushing on to the South, you may find your plans delayed by your discoveries here.

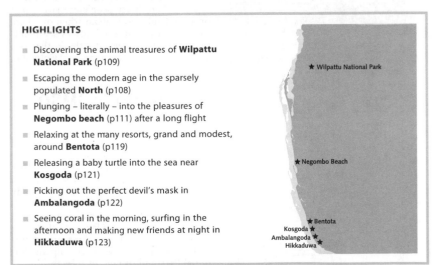

HIGHLIGHTS

- Discovering the animal treasures of **Wilpattu National Park** (p109)
- Escaping the modern age in the sparsely populated **North** (p108)
- Plunging – literally – into the pleasures of **Negombo beach** (p111) after a long flight
- Relaxing at the many resorts, grand and modest, around **Bentota** (p119)
- Releasing a baby turtle into the sea near **Kosgoda** (p121)
- Picking out the perfect devil's mask in **Ambalangoda** (p122)
- Seeing coral in the morning, surfing in the afternoon and making new friends at night in **Hikkaduwa** (p123)

★ Wilpattu National Park
★ Negombo Beach
★ Bentota
Kosgoda ★
Ambalangoda ★
Hikkaduwa ★

WEST COAST

THE 2004 TSUNAMI – AFTERMATH IN THE WEST

The tsunami caused significant damage at many places along the coast south of Colombo. However, the waters were fickle, and some beachside places were untouched while others were completely wiped out. Damage can be found around Beruwela, Bentota, Kosgoda and Ambalangoda. Between Ambalangoda and Hikkaduwa is where some of the most significant loss of life occurred. It was here that a train was trapped and thousands of people lost their lives. The land will look scoured and scarred for a long time to come, and it will also take years for many people to live in proper homes once again.

Expect more hotels and guesthouses to open each year as damaged places begin to rebuild. Initial efforts to enforce a buffer zone between the sea and developed areas have mostly been abandoned, though many beaches now sport highly unattractive protective berms.

Dangers & Annoyances

All along the west coast you have to watch out for dangerous currents, undertows and rip tides, particularly with the bigger seas during the wet season, which runs from April or May to October or November. Watch where other people are swimming or ask reliable locals about when or where to go for a dip. In some places sea pollution is another deterrent – the further you are from town centres, especially Colombo, the better.

NORTH OF COLOMBO

The A3 heads north out of Colombo, skirting old Dutch canals, sandy beaches and wildlife refuges. Close to the Bandaranaike International Airport, on the outskirts of Colombo, the pleasant beach town of Negombo makes a good first stop for many visitors to the country, while further north the west coast is rural and green – just watch out for coconuts falling in the many palm plantations. In the far north of this region the chief attraction is Wilpattu National Park and its myriad animals.

WILPATTU NATIONAL PARK

Covered in dense pockets of jungle scrub interspersed with small clearings, and tanks that shrink in the dry season and swell in the monsoon, **Wilpattu National Park** (admission per person Rs 600, plus per vehicle Rs 120, plus per group service charge Rs 600, plus 15% tax; ☼ 6am-6pm) is home to up to 50 elephants and 50 or more leopards, as well as spotted deer, sloth bears, wild pigs, crocodiles and more. At 1085 sq km, it is Sri Lanka's largest national park.

Like much of the country, recent history has not been kind to the park. At one time it was the most visited in the country, but it was closed due to ethnic violence in 1985. In the following years it was a base for rebels and poaching was rife. However, the park reopened with a new visitors centre and an enthusiastic staff in 2003.

Research on the park's animals is only just starting again, so animal counts are more speculative than factual. But visitors usually have a good chance of seeing some wildlife, especially from January to May. In fact, on the drive to the park from Puttalam, you'll see fences designed to keep marauding elephants out of farmland (you'll also see lots of abandoned homes). Peacocks and mongooses are everywhere.

This national park is definitely worth a visit if you enjoy animal spotting, albeit in primitive conditions. It still remains very uncrowded.

Information

The **park office** (☎ 025-225 7893; ☼ 6am-4.30pm) has helpful staff, a few displays and a snack stand. Elephants often visit the nearby tank at dusk. Be sure to pick up a copy of the excellent colour map.

Guides are essential. Fees for a guide and a 4WD vehicle (which seats up to four) are negotiable but should run to roughly Rs 2000 for a half-day and Rs 4000 for a full day. You can arrange them through your accommodation in Puttalam or Anuradhapura, or you will find some waiting at the turn-off from the Puttalam–Anuradhapura Rd.

Sights & Activities

There are 100km of very rugged roads inside the park, and another 200km of trails. In the park's centre there is a grouping of tanks and lakes that is the focus for most visitors, as it has the greatest concentration of wildlife. A visit to this area can be accomplished in half a day. In a full day's journey you can cover a good portion of the park, including a visit to the remote beach at **Kudiramale Point**.

Throughout the park expect to see *villus*, depressions in the ground that fill with water in the rainy season and then contract or disappear during the dry season (May to September). These are magnets for animals and numerous bird species. There's some good tropical forest near the entrance.

Sleeping

Many visitors base themselves in either Puttalam or Anuradhapura, where hotels can easily arrange guides and visits. Alternatively, groups of up to 10 can camp inside the park at one of five primitive sites for Rs 690 per night. Book at the park office. You'll need to bring your own gear.

Like Yala National Park, Wilpattu has some rather expensive bungalows. These are scattered around the park, but tend to be about 15km from the park office, and situated near water. Costs (after park admission) are US$24 per person per night, plus US$2 per person for linens and US$30 per group for 'service'. These basic huts come with drinking water and don't have electricity. Reservations are made through the **Department of Wildlife Conservation** (Map pp84-5; ☎ 011-269 4241; www.dwlc.lk; 18 Gregory's Rd, Col 7).

At the park's turn-off on the Puttalam–Anuradhapura Rd, **Preshamel Safari Hotel** (☎ in Anuradhapura 025-225 7699, in Colombo 011-252 1866; preshmel@sltnet.lk; r per person incl breakfast Rs 1500) has five rooms that define 'basic'. There's food available at night. Management will organise all-inclusive two-day camping safaris into the park for Rs 10,000 per two people.

Getting There & Away

The turn-off to the park on the rough but paved Puttalam–Anuradhapura Rd (A12) is 26km northeast of Puttalam and 20km southwest of Anuradhapura. A further 8km of rough road leads to the park entrance and office at the barely discernable village of Hunuwilagama.

Buses on the main road between Puttalam and Anuradhapura stop at the junction (Rs 25, one hour), which is approximately halfway between the two towns. One of the waiting guides will be more than happy to take you into the park for a negotiable fee.

PUTTALAM & AROUND

☎ 032 / pop 42,000

The old trading, pearling and fishing town of Puttalam is a scruffy, neglected market town in its modern incarnation. You can use it as a base for trips into Wilpattu National Park, but you will probably prefer Anuradhapura.

A Portuguese regiment of soldiers from Mozambique originally settled the village of **Sellankandal**, about 10km inland from Puttalam. As late as the 1930s, Sellankandal villagers still spoke a version of Portuguese and sang Afro-Portuguese *bailas* (folk songs). You might see some people of mixed-African descent in Puttlam; there is also a large Muslim population.

The turn-off to the peninsula towns of Kalpitiya and Talawila is south of Puttalam, and leads past saltpans and a salt factory. The somewhat preserved Dutch fort on the peninsula road dates from 1670 and is still manned by the Sri Lankan army. To the north of Kalpitiya a string of islands guards Dutch Bay and Portugal Bay. The saltpans and thin coconut plantations on the peninsula are home to a herd of wild donkeys.

At **Talawila** there's a Catholic shrine to St Anne. The church features satinwood pillars and is pleasantly situated on the seafront. Thousands of pilgrims come here in March and July, when major festivals honouring St Anne are held. The festivals include huge processions, healing services and a fair.

Accommodation in Puttalam is basic.

Senatilake Guest Inn (☎ 226 5403; 81A Kurunegala Rd; r Rs 800-1800; ⌘) has 10 rooms, some of which are fan-only; the restaurant is good and the bus station is some 300m away.

It feels like the country at the 14-room **Dammika Holiday Resort** (☎ 226 5192; 51 Good Shed Rd; r with/without air-con Rs 1650/1000; ⌘), 1km south of the town centre off the Colombo road and 100m from the train station. Meals in the pleasant dining rooms cost about Rs 300.

---

101 USES FOR A COCONUT

Sri Lankan cuisine wouldn't be the same without the rich, white flesh of the coconut kernel. Grated coconut is made into *pol sambol* (*pol* means coconut in Sinhala), a fiery condiment laced with chilli. But minus the chilli it can be sprinkled over a curry to reduce it to something less explosive. Dried, the scrapings are known as *copra*, which is exported and used to make confectionery. Coconut oil is extracted from *copra*, and *poonac* (the desiccated residue) is used as fodder for animals.

The flesh of a newly opened coconut can be squeezed to produce a creamy white milk that adds a silky richness to curries; *pol hodda*, for example, is a spicy gravy made from coconut milk. Delicious *kiri bath* (rice cooked in coconut milk) is traditionally the first solid food fed to a baby and is essential at weddings and other celebrations.

The bud on top of the coconut's stem, called the *bada*, can be pickled and eaten.

Piles of *thambili* (king coconuts) are a familiar sight along roadsides. The liquid they contain is sweet and refreshing, and cheaper than a soft drink. *Kurumba* (young green coconuts) are slightly less sweet.

To make the drink known as toddy, agile toddy tappers move from coconut palm to coconut palm like tightrope artists, extracting the trees' sap. Toddy trees are not permitted to bear fruit; the opened flowers are bound and bent over, and their sap is drawn off after about three weeks. Every morning and evening the toddy tappers go from flower to flower, changing the pots. One palm yields an average of 270L of toddy annually, and a good tapper can get about a month's sap from one flower. Fermented and distilled, toddy becomes arrack, a popular honey-coloured alcoholic drink that causes many a curse the morning after.

In rural areas you can still see *cadjan* (coconut-frond matting) roofing, fencing made from dried coconut palm branches, and roof supports made from coconut wood. The coconut's fibrous husk yields fibres that can be woven into rope, matting and upholstery, while *ekel* brooms are made from the tough mid-rib of the coconut frond.

The shells are sculpted into tacky souvenirs such as monkeys and elephants, and bowls made from polished coconut shells are widely available. The versatile shells also fulfil a spiritual role – they're often smashed at temples to bring good fortune.

You can sit on the shady verandas of the **Rest House** (☎ /fax 226 5299; Beach Rd; r with/without air-con Rs 1500/1000; 🔀) and watch cows graze on the grounds. The eight large rooms in this old place are gloomy but clean. The bar-restaurant is popular; the bus station is 500m away.

There are frequent buses to Colombo (regular/air-con Rs 71/140, three hours). For Anuradhapura (Rs 45, two hours) you may have to change at Kala Oya, on the boundary between Western Province and North-Central Province.

There's infrequent train service to and from Colombo (2nd/3rd class Rs 127/68, 3½ hours). The station is 1km south of town.

PUTTALAM TO NEGOMBO

Although the A3 stays close to the coast, there are few ocean views from the road. Rather, when heading south to Negombo you pass through an endless series of co-conut plantations, which have their own rhythmic beauty. Look for the coconut harvesters using knives mounted on sticks as tall as the trees. Other sights include numerous large rivers and lots of green countryside. The road itself, which lacks the killer traffic found between Negombo and Colombo, is in excellent condition.

Udappuwa, south of Puttalam, has an important temple and also features a complex of three shrines. A colourful festival is held here in August, when devotees test their strength by walking on red-hot coals.

Twelve kilometres to the south of Udappuwa, **Chilaw** has a strong Roman Catholic flavour, and has elaborate statues to religious figures and local cardinals in the centre.

Munneswaram, 5km to the east of Chilaw, has a rather interesting Hindu temple that is an important centre of pilgrimage. There are three shrines at this complex; the central one is dedicated to Shiva. A major festival, also featuring fire walking, occurs here in August.

Thirty kilometres north from Negombo is **Mahawewa**, a village renowned for its batiks while, further south, the towns of **Waikkal** and **Marawila** have a few package-tour beach hotels. Just north of Negombo, **Kochchikade** is home to numerous large roof-tile factories, whose smoky furnaces are fuelled by a dwindling supply of firewood.

Buses are frequent all along the A3.

NEGOMBO

☎ 031 / pop 125,000

Negombo is a modest beach town located close to Bandaranaike International Airport. In many ways it is a more salubrious introduction to the country than Colombo, and it's a pleasant alternative to the monster traffic into and through the capital. In fact, some budget-conscious sun seekers just stay here, although doing this means missing the much nicer beaches to the south.

Bustling Negombo town is a historically interesting place, strongly influenced by the Catholic Church. The narrow strip of land to the south of the lagoon and the many canals make for good exploring.

The Dutch captured the town from the Portuguese in 1640, lost it, then captured it again in 1644. The British then took it from them in 1796 without a struggle. Negombo was one of the most important sources of cinnamon during the Dutch era, and there are still reminders of the European days.

Orientation

The busy centre of Negombo town lies to the west of the bus and train stations. Most places to stay, however, line the main road that heads north from the town centre, running almost parallel to the beach. Closer to town, the road is called Lewis Pl; going 1km north of the centre, it becomes Porutota Rd. Called Ethukala, this neighbourhood has cafés, restaurants and tourist shops. As you go north the hotels become generally pricier and nicer. Along most of road are footpaths that are good for relaxed strolling.

A breakwater divides the beach; to the north, hotels regularly clean the sand and it's all very neat. To the south, the beach is a bit more natural; it's not as clean and is often covered with various weeds.

Information

In the centre of town you'll find the post office (Map p112), a **Bank of Ceylon** (Map p112; Broadway) and a **Vijitha Yapa Bookshop** (Map p112; 135 Broadway), which has English-language novels, magazines, guidebooks and maps. There are numerous Internet and telephone offices scattered along Lewis Pl and Porutota Rd, as well as near the bus and train stations. If this is your first stop in Sri Lanka, hotels can fix you up with guides and drivers for trips elsewhere in the country.

WEST COAST

WEST COAST

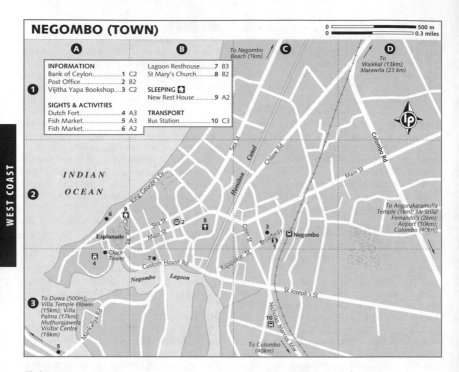

Sights

Close to the seafront near the lagoon are the ruins of the old **Dutch fort** (Map p112), which has a fine gateway inscribed with the date 1678. Also here is a green, called Esplanade, where cricket matches are a big attraction.

Several old Dutch buildings are still in use, including the **Lagoon Resthouse** (Map p112; Custom House Rd).

Each day, fishermen take their *oruvas* (outrigger canoes) and go out in search of the fish for which Negombo is well known. They're a fine sight as they sweep home into the lagoon after a fishing trip. Fish auctions on the beach and sales at the **fish market** (Map p112) near the fort are common – the shark catch is brought in to the beach in the early afternoon. The catch is not all from the open sea: Negombo is at the northern end of a lagoon that is renowned for its lobsters, crabs and prawns. Across the lagoon bridge there's a second **fish market** (Map p112). If you can stagger out of bed at 6am it's a good place to watch the fishing boats return with their catches. If you're hanging

around the markets you won't have to wait long before you're invited to go out on an *oruva* or another kind of vessel; expect to pay around Rs 700 per boat per hour. A **Fishers' Festival** is held here in late July.

Negombo is dotted with churches – so successfully were the locals converted to Catholicism that the town is often known as 'Little Rome' (and another reason for the moniker is that many of the residents receive money from relatives working in Italy). **St Mary's Church** (Map p112), in the town centre, has very good ceiling paintings by a local artist. East of town the **Angurukaramulla Temple**, with its 6m-long reclining Buddha, is also worth seeing. A three-wheeler from Lewis Pl should cost Rs 400 return. The island of **Duwa**, joined to Negombo by the lagoon bridge, is famed for its Easter passion play.

The Dutch showed their love of **canals** here as nowhere else in Sri Lanka. Canals extend from Negombo all the way south to Colombo and north to Puttalam, a total distance of over 120km. You can hire a bicycle in Negombo from various hotels and ride the canal-side paths for some distance, enjoying the views and small villages. The road over the lagoon bridge continues as a small coastal road between lagoon and ocean almost all the way to Colombo.

Sleeping

There are plenty of places along the beach in the budget and midrange categories. You can also find a couple of higher-priced places here and in Waikkal. Generally the closer the accommodation is to town, the rougher it is around the edges. Beware of a couple of places with hourly rates.

BUDGET

Ocean View (Map p112; ☎ 223 8689; oceanview@wow .lk; 104 Lewis Pl; r Rs 700-2200; 🔀) This place has 13 neat and clean rooms. The more expensive ones, all with balconies, are in a newer wing; some have air-con. There are views from the rooftop, and the family that runs the place is charming and helpful.

Jeero's Guest House (Map p113; ☎ 223 4210; 239 Lewis Pl; r Rs 800-900) The four clean and cheery rooms at this family-run place are enlivened by wooden ceilings. The cheaper rooms face away from the sea. Potted plants abound.

Hotel Silver Sands (Map p113; ☎ 222 2880; silver sands@dialogsl.net; 229 Lewis Pl; r Rs 750-1200, with air-con Rs 1700; 🔀) This hotel has a Moorish touch with its arched walkways and central courtyard garden. The 15 rooms have their own balcony or patio. There's a nice area by the beach for a beer.

Beach Villa Guest House (Map p113; ☎ 222 2833; www.beachvillasrilanka.com; 3/2 Senavirathna Mawatha; r Rs 500-1700; 🔀) On the beach near a spot popular with cricket-playing local kids, this place has cheerfully gaudy décor, and a bar and restaurant downstairs. The 16 rooms are clean, if chaotic. Cheaper rooms are fan only.

Dephani Guest House (Map p113; ☎ 223 4359; deph anie@slt.lk; 189/15 Lewis Pl; r Rs 880-1200) This spot has 12 clean rooms, some with colonial-style furnishings. Upstairs rooms have a balcony and more light. There's a garden opening onto the beach, and a restaurant.

Star Beach (Map p113; ☎ 222 2606; 83/3 Lewis Pl; r Rs 700-1200) A decent, if dated, guesthouse on the beach. The 14 rooms are clean and three of these face the sea; some have hot water.

New Rest House (Map p112; ☎ 222 2299; 14 Circular Rd; s/d with fan Rs 900/1500, with air-con Rs 1000/1600; 🔀) In the old part of town, this atmospheric

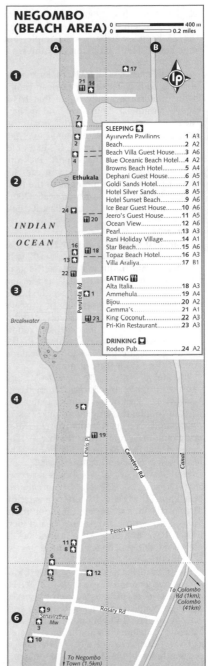

NEGOMBO (BEACH AREA)

SLEEPING 🛏		
Ayurveda Pavilions	1	A3
Beach	2	A2
Beach Villa Guest House	3	A6
Blue Oceanic Beach Hotel	4	A2
Browns Beach Hotel	5	A4
Dephani Guest House	6	A5
Goldi Sands Hotel	7	A1
Hotel Silver Sands	8	A5
Hotel Sunset Beach	9	A6
Ice Bear Guest House	10	A6
Jeero's Guest House	11	A5
Ocean View	12	A6
Pearl	13	A3
Rani Holiday Village	14	A1
Star Beach	15	A6
Topaz Beach Hotel	16	A3
Villa Araliya	17	B1

EATING 🍴		
Alta Italia	18	A3
Ammehula	19	A4
Bijou	20	A2
Gemma's	21	A1
King Coconut	22	A3
Pri-Kin Restaurant	23	A3

DRINKING 🍷		
Rodeo Pub	24	A2

INDIAN OCEAN

Ethukala

Broadwater

Perutota Rd

Lewis Pl

Cemetery Rd

Canal

Perera Pl

Rosary Rd

Senavirathna Mw

To Colombo Rd (1km); Colombo (41km)

To Negombo Town (1.5km)

WEST COAST

relic has lots of history and colonial charm (Queen Elizabeth II stayed in no 7 in 1958). The 25 rooms are bare and simple, but some have balconies looking over the sea – and the fish market.

Mr Srilal Fernando's (☎ 222 2481; 67 Parakrama Rd, Kurana; d Rs 750-1250) There are six clean rooms in this handsome family home that has a vaguely Pompeian courtyard and garden. The genial owner does a good Truman Capote impression, while the name may put the ABBA tune in your mind. It's in a quiet neighbourhood near the airport. Pick-ups from the airport cost Rs 550; you can also take a Colombo–Negombo bus to the RAC Motors Kurana bus stop and walk 700m east. Dinner costs Rs 450, breakfast Rs 250.

MIDRANGE

Ice Bear Guest House (Map p113; ☎ 223 3862; www .icebearhotel.com; 103/2 Lewis Pl; r incl breakfast US$14-35; ✂) A gorgeous traditional villa with lots of colour and flair (or 'Swissness', as the sign says). The beautiful gardens face the beach and there are regular tastings of produce from the coconut tree. The décor is delightfully funky, and the more expensive rooms have fridges and air-con. Muesli in the morning is home-made; elaborate seafood dinners (Rs 545) feature at night.

Villa Araliya (Map p113; ☎ 227 7650; villa.aralia@ wow.lk; 154/1 Porutota Rd; r Rs 2200-5000, apt Rs 8000-11,000; ✂ ✈) Run by a charming Dutch–Sri Lankan couple, this tidy guesthouse has 12 rooms and five apartments in two-storey brick buildings away from the beach. The smart décor includes nice tile floors. The restaurant is good and features pasta.

Pearl (Map p113; ☎ 487 2824; www.pearl-negombo .com; 13 Porutota Rd; s/d US$36/50; ✂) A great little beach hotel that belies its concrete exterior. The six spacious rooms are excellent; room 6 has a tub with a spectacular beach view (others have showers). All come with a CD player and fridge. The restaurant serves excellent seafood.

Browns Beach Hotel (Map p113; ☎ 222 2031; www .aitkenspencehotels.com; 175 Lewis Pl; s/d US$70-80; ✂ ✈) This 1970s place is so well-preserved that in a couple more years it will be stylishly retro. The 140 rooms all have views, balconies, satellite TVs and fridges. There's a private beach area with a bar on the sand, a popular lunch buffet (Rs 750) and, on many nights, live music and DJs.

Goldi Sands Hotel (Map p113; ☎ 227 9021; www .goldisands.com; Porutota Rd; s/d US$50/55; ✂ ✈) A remodelled lobby complete with jellyfish mural fronts 70 standard rooms. All have a fridge, a satellite TV and a balcony with garden or beach views. The swimming pool boasts an all-too-rare water slide. Breakfast is US$5.

Topaz Beach Hotel (Map p113; ☎ 227 9265; topaz@ sltnet.lk; 21 Porutota Rd; r US$25-60; ✂ ✈) The plain exterior of this four-storey L-shaped block hints at the 30 clean but bland rooms inside. Some have air-con; all feature balconies, views and an earnest staff.

Hotel Sunset Beach (Map p113; ☎ 222 2350; www .hotelsunsetbeach.com; 5 Senavirathna Mawatha; r US$40-48; ✂ ✈) The rooms in these three-storey blocks enjoy a beachfront pool (though avoid the rooms hidden by the pool structure). Most rooms have balconies and terraces with sea views. It's a sparkling white, busy place, but it lacks character.

Rani Holiday Village (Map p113; ☎ 074 870718; ranihv@slt.net.lk; 154/9 Porutota Rd; r Rs 3500-5000; ✂ ✈) Off the beach, this place has modern studio apartments set around a small pool. The double-room villas have hot water and kitchens with a fridge; the 33 units each have satellite TV, hot water and a fridge.

TOP END

Ayurveda Pavilions (Map p113; ☎ 487 0764; www .ayurvedapavilions.com; Porutota Rd; villas from US$250; ✂ ✈) There are 12 villas in this walled compound that's across from the beach. The units are large, with minimalist yet luxurious furnishings and huge bathrooms. Rates include various treatments and spa sessions, yoga and cooking classes.

Beach (Map p113; ☎ 227 3500; www.jetwinghotels .com; Porutota Rd; r US$90-200; ✂ ▯ ✈) The décor here is as minimalist as the name. The priciest place in Negombo may be a bit too pricey unless you get a deal. Still, the 73 rooms at this massively rebuilt older hotel are attractive, with beige and natural wood décor. Luxuries include DVD players, a library, high-speed Internet and balconies with views. There's also a good spa.

Blue Oceanic Beach Hotel (Map p113; ☎ 227 9000; www.jetwinghotels.com; Porutota Rd; r US$85-180; ✂ ✈) This standard resort hotel of early-'80s vintage has 108 rooms with balconies or terraces in three-storey blocks. The décor is an attractive mix of gold and blue. The grounds are shady.

Eating & Drinking

There are lots of restaurants and cafés of varying quality along Porutota Rd and Lewis Pl. Some are rather good.

Alta Italia (Map p113; ☎ 227 9206; 36 Porutota Rd; meals Rs 300-1000; ☺ lunch & dinner) The best restaurant in town, this Italian-run place is a tropical trattoria complete with lovely rattan chairs and a long menu that includes fresh pasta, seafood grills and pizza. Try the authentic risotto and finish with a *limoncello* or grappa. Or sample from the espresso machine, steaming behind the counter.

Bijou (Map p113; ☎ 531 9577; Porutota Rd; mains Rs 300-1000) You'll know this place is Swiss-owned when you see fondue on the menu. But the real star is the massive lobster platter (Rs 850). There's a long list of Western and German specialities.

Pri-Kin Restaurant (Map p113; ☎ 227 8646; 10 Porutota Rd; mains Rs 250-450) Chinese cuisine is the real focus of this open-air place, although you can also get Western and local meals. For dessert, don't pass up the fried bananas and ice cream.

Ammehula (Map p113; ☎ 487 3065; 286 Lewis Pl; meals Rs 200-400) The young owners of this café create a delightful and playful vibe. They claim the name means 'Go Away!' and the menu features a cartoon turtle cussing about how all the good fish come here. Besides seafood dishes there are sandwiches and a long breakfast menu that includes Dutch pancakes. The bar stays open as late 2am some nights.

Gemma's (Map p113; ☎ 077 627 7852; 154 Porutota Rd; dishes Rs 150-400; ☺ 10am-6pm) A bright and airy coffee-and-tea shop with home-made cakes and sandwiches.

Rodeo Pub (Map p113; ☎ 077 774 6474; 35 Porutota Rd; dishes Rs 300-700) Blathering expats quaffing cheap brews are the highlight of this cheery open-air dive. 'Riders on the Storm' seems to be on continuous loop, and the small menu includes steaks and breakfasts. Go for one of the pavement tables near the cactus out the front. Depending on the condition of the patrons, this place can stay open past 1am.

King Coconut (Map p113; ☎ 227 8043; 11 Porutota Rd; mains Rs 300-1000) This is a lively, popular spot beside the beach. There's a menu of curries and seafood, but this place is probably best just for enjoying a drink and the view.

The larger hotels have standard resort fare. For excellent food try the restaurants at the smaller **Ice Bear Guest House** (Map p113; ☎ 223 3862; www.icebearhotel.com; 103/2 Lewis Pl; mains Rs 300-1000), **Villa Araliya** (Map p113; ☎ 227 7650; villa.aralia@wow.lk; 154/10 Porutota Rd; mains Rs 300-1000) and **Pearl** (Map p113; ☎ 487 2824; www.pearl-negombo.com; 13 Porutota Rd; mains Rs 300-1000).

Getting There & Away

Central Transport Board (CTB), private and intercity express buses run between Negombo and Saunders Pl, Colombo (regular/air-con Rs 28/42, one to two hours, every 20 minutes). Long queues form at the bus station on weekend evenings, when day-trippers return to the capital. There are also trains to Colombo (Rs 21, 1½ hours), but they're slower and rarer than the buses. You can get a taxi between Negombo and Colombo for about Rs 2500. Any hotel, guesthouse or travel agent will arrange a taxi for you.

For Kandy take a bus to Veyangoda (Rs 20, two hours) and change to a Kandy train.

Getting Around

Bus 270, for the Bandaranaike International Airport (Rs 11, 45 minutes), leaves every 15 minutes from about 5am to 9pm. A taxi costs about Rs 700; the journey takes about 20 minutes.

To get from the bus station to Lewis Pl or Porutota Rd, you can catch a Kochchikade-bound bus.

A three-wheeler costs about Rs 150 to the middle of Lewis Pl from either the bus or train stations.

AROUND NEGOMBO
Waikkal & Marawila
☎ 031

The towns of Waikkal and Marawila lie about 3km inland of the coast on the A3. There are several mostly upmarket waterside hotels, which are self-contained and walled off from the local communities. It's a very different scene from the bars and tourist shops at Negombo. On the plus side, the nearby beaches are long and golden, and the terrain flat and palm covered.

On the coast near Waikkal, **Ranweli Holiday Village** (☎ 222 2136; http://ecoclub.com/ranweli/; r US$90-120) is a spacious beach resort with an ecological bent; it boasts of its recycling and other ecofriendly practices. Reached by a short ferry punt across the old Dutch canal, the hotel arranges canoeing, bird-watching tours, nature walks and other environmental activities. Most of the rooms are in separate bungalows with a small lounge, balcony, and lagoon or sea views.

Club Hotel Dolphin (☎ 227 8565; www.serendibleisure.com; r from US$80; ☒ ☒) is a vast beachfront resort near Waikkal, with 76 rooms and 50 cottages on spacious grounds. There's a gigantic pool and a palm-studded lawn. Activities include resort standards like karaoke, and there are buffet meals.

Heading north towards Marawila, **Sanmeli Beach Hotel** (☎ 225 4766; fax 225 4768; r from US$30; ☒ ☒) is an older 20-room place on a remote stretch of coast. It's a good place to come if you're on the lam or get a very good deal. Rooms are a bit tatty.

The hotel furthest north is massive, all-inclusive **Club Palm Bay** (☎ 225 4956; palm bay@lankacom.net; Talwilawella; r from US$120; ☒ ☒), about 3.5km off the main road (from Talwilawella junction). The resort's 104 rooms are on huge grounds flanked by beaches and lagoons. Many of the clientele seem to pass the day in the enormous swimming pool (in between bouts at the buffet).

Most people reach Waikkal and Marawila by taxi or car and driver.

South of Negombo

The narrow belt of land between the gulf and lagoon south of Negombo is sometimes called **Pamunugama**, after its biggest settlement. It's a lovely strip of coconut palms, old Portuguese-style churches, cross-dotted cemeteries on dunes, and pockets of tidy houses. There are some small hotels along here. The beach is steep, and swimming could be perilous – consult the locals before wading in.

This is also home to one of the best stretches of the old and straight-as-an-arrow **Dutch Canal** that runs along this entire length of coast. It's lined with small factories, fishing villages, mansions, nature areas and more. Hiring a bike in Negombo is an ideal way to tour this area.

Muthurajawela Marsh (which evocatively translates as 'Supreme Field of Pearls') is a little-known gem of a wetland at the southern end of Negombo's lagoon. The area had been a rich rice-growing basin before the Portuguese constructed a canal that ruined the fields with sea water. Over the centuries, Mother Nature turned Muthurajawela into Sri Lanka's biggest saline wetland, home to

purple herons, cormorants and kingfishers. However, the marsh is under pressure from encroaching industrial development. The **Muthurajawela Visitor Centre** (☎ in Colombo 011-483 0150; Indigaslanda, Bopitiya, Pamunugama; ☒ 7am-6pm) is at the southern end of the road along Pamunugama, next to the Hamilton Canal. It has displays and a 25-minute video show on the wetland's fauna; it also runs boat trips. A two-hour guided boat ride (Rs 650 per person) through the wetland is highly recommended. You can expect to see over 75 bird species, monkeys, crocs and more.

On the ocean side of the road, 15km south of Negombo, **Villa Temple Flower** (☎ in Colombo 011-223 6755; Pamunugama; r Rs 1600-2000; ☒) has lush gardens, a swimming pool and an ebullient owner. The eight simple and comfy rooms each have a small veranda; two have air-con.

Eighteen kilometres south from Negombo, **Villa Palma** (☎ in Colombo 011-223 6619; www .villa-palma.de; Beach Rd, Pamunugama; r from Rs 3000; ☒ ☒) is located right next to the sea. The 18 rooms are simple, although lurid statuary provides spice. There's a secluded area around the swimming pool that is popular with guests inspired by the statues.

A modern hotel close to the airport, **Taj Airport Garden** (☎ in Colombo 011-225 2950; www .tajairportgardensrilanka.com; 234-238 Colombo-Negombo Rd; r US$60-100; ☒ ☒ ☒) provides a good service for business travellers who don't want to make the journey into the heart of Colombo. It's nothing special, but it is good if you have a late or early departure or arrival. The hotel provides free transfers for the five-minute ride to or from the airport. Arrange in advance.

SOUTH OF COLOMBO

Driving south on Galle Rd (A2), you'll think that Colombo will never end. But about 30km from Colombo's Fort you'll feel you've escaped the capital and its hubbub. Beginning with Wadduwa, there are beach towns big and small along the coast. Most travellers focus on Hikkaduwa, but at some point along the coast you should find a cove, bay or stretch of sand to suit you. Accommodation comes in all shapes, sizes and styles, and Ayurvedic health centres are common. The Galle Rd is generally in good shape, but roads leading off it are often in miserable condition. Look carefully for signs marking tracks leading to hotels. Note that this entire stretch of coast was heavily affected by the tsunami (p108).

KALUTARA & WADDUWA

☎ 034

The town of Kalutara was an important spice-trading centre controlled at various times by the Portuguese, Dutch and British. Today it has a reputation for fine basketware and for the best mangosteens on the island. The fine beaches along here boast some good hotels.

Immediately south of the Kalu Ganga bridge on the main road is the impressive **Gangatilaka Vihara**, which has a hollow dagoba (stupa) with an interesting painted interior. By the road there's a small shrine and bodhi tree where drivers often stop to make offerings to ensure a safe journey.

Kalutara and Wadduwa, located 8km to the north of Kalutara, have a number of resorts, but there's little to halt travellers who are en route to more laid-back beach spots further south. All the places below are well off Galle Rd, and are on the beach.

The slick **Siddhalepa Ayurveda Health Resort** (☎ 229 6967; www.ayurvedaresort.com; Samanthara Rd, Wadduwa; 1-week packages from US$1200; ☒ ☒) is run by Siddhalepa, the respected Ayurvedic hospital in Mt Lavinia. It offers everything from stress relief to detoxification, and sets the mood with piped sitar music. Prices include all meals, treatments and accommodation in plush rooms with satellite TV etc.

The following four hotels are near the 38km marker.

Tangerine Beach Hotel (☎ 222 2982; www.tangerinehotels.com; De Abrew Rd, Waskaduwa, Kalutara North; r incl half-board from Rs 3500; ☒ ☒) is a busy, friendly place with 172 comfy modern rooms set around a large pool. The hotel's entrance is beautified by lotus flowers blooming in small ponds.

Run by the same company as the Tangerine Beach Hotel, **Royal Palms Hotel** (☎ 222 8113; www.tangerinehotels.com; De Abrew Rd, Kalutara North; s/d US$100/103; ☒ ☒ ☒) has 123 immaculate rooms. It has lavish gardens and feels a bit formal with its air-con lobby.

The great value **Hibiscus Beach Hotel** (☎ 558 2271; www.hibiscusbeachhotel.com; De Abrew Rd, Kalutara North; r US$35-75; ☒ ☒ ☒) has 56 smallish rooms with satellite TVs and fridges. The hotel is 500m north of the Royal Palms.

Blue Water (☎ 038-223 5067; www.bluewatersrilanka .com; Thalpitiya, Wadduwa; r US$110-200; ☒ ☒ ☒) Following the current fad for Asian minimalism, the Blue Water is serene and elegant. The 100 rooms are spare in décor and feature slick tile floors, although note that some face away from the beach. The pool is enormous, and facilities include squash, tennis and a health club. There's wi-fi.

There are frequent buses to Kalutara and Wadduwa along the main coastal road.

BERUWELA & MORAGALLE

☎ 034

Beruwela and Bentota have been developed into Sri Lanka's chief package-tour-resort zone. There's little to attract independent travellers here. Moragalle is technically slightly north of Beruwela, but the towns have practically merged. Throughout this area there is a lot of tsunami damage; many hotels are closed for good. Large fishing boats washed far inland are destined to become part of the landscape.

The first recorded Muslim settlement on the island took place at Beruwela in 1024. The **Kechimalai Mosque**, on a headland north of the hotel strip, is said to be built on the site of the landing and is the focus for a major **Eid-ul-Fitr** festival at the end of Ramadan. It's part of a fascinating collection of mosques, churches and temples out by the fishing port and beach.

Sleeping

The tourist hotels are all very much aimed at the package groups that come to Sri Lanka to escape the European winter. The hotels have various facilities including tennis and water sports.

Ypsylon Guest House (☎ 227 6132; www.ypsylon-sri lanka.de; Beruwela; s/d €24/42; ☒) On a rocky patch of the shore, the two-storey buildings here house 25 clean rooms, all with sea views. The restaurant is good and many people come for the dive shop. It charges €25 per dive.

Hotel Sumadai (☎ 227 6404; info@sumadai.com; 61 Maradana Rd, Beruwela; s/d incl half-board €27/39; ☒) Split in two buildings – one facing the ocean and the other a large lagoon – the 20 rooms here are spotless and basic. Four with air-con cost an extra Rs 500. Some have balconies with views.

Barberyn Beach Ayurveda Resort (☎ 227 6036; www.barberyn.com; Moragalle) This beachside Ayurvedic resort has bags of character. Mid-range in price, it was heavily damaged by the tsunami but should reopen during 2006.

Tropical Villas Hotel (☎ 227 6780; www.jetwing.net; Galle Rd, Moragalle; r US$85-110; ✷ 🖳 🖳) This place does not have direct access to the beach, but it has a good pool. The 52 rooms are stylish; set around a quiet, leafy garden, each has a separate lounge with satellite TV.

Getting There & Away
Aluthgama is the main transport hub serving Beruwela and Moragalle. See p121 for details. Local buses link all the towns along Galle Rd.

ALUTHGAMA, BENTOTA & INDURUWA
☎ 034
Bentota's beach is one of the best on the west coast, protected from Galle Rd by the broad sweep of the Bentota Ganga. While it is dominated by big package hotels, it also has a number of smaller places catering to independent travellers. There are more such places in Aluthgama, a small town on the main road between Beruwela and Bentota.

Aluthgama has a raucous fish market, local shops and the main train station in the area. Induruwa doesn't really have a centre – it's spread out along the coast.

Orientation
Just south of the town centre of Aluthgama, the main road crosses the Bentota Ganga into Bentota, where there's the Bentota resort centre on the seaward side, with tourist facilities, shops and a few restaurants. From the bridge, the river turns north to flow parallel to the coast for a few hundred metres, divided from the sea only by a narrow spit of land that is home to some resorts (they're reachable by boat across the river). Induruwa is 5km south of Bentota.

Information
There are Internet facilities in the big hotels, and others are sprinkled throughout the towns. A good one is the eponymous **Internet Cafe** (☎ 227 5003; 201 Galle Rd; per min Rs 4) in Aluthgama. Just north of the river, the **Commercial Bank** (339 Galle Rd) has an international ATM. At the Bentota resort centre there's a post office. The **Cargills Food City**

(☎ 227 1921; 331 Galle Rd, Aluthgama) sells a wide range of goods and has a pharmacy.

Sights
In addition to **beaches** that are as fine as those at Beruwela, Bentota and Aluthgama enjoy the calm waters of the **Bentota Ganga**, which are good for water sports.

Aluthgama has a bustling **market** every Monday, located across the train line, towards Dharga Town. A few kilometres inland on the south bank of the river is the **Galapota Temple**, said to date from the 12th century. To reach it, cross the bridge and take the side road to your left after 500m. The temple is signposted.

Fine beaches continue several kilometres south from Bentota. Induruwa has a small cluster of places to stay on a lovely, quiet length of beach, at the north end of which is the **Turtle Research Project**, one of the turtle hatcheries in the area (p121).

Ten kilometres inland from Bentota is the pretty **Brief Garden** (☎ 227 0462; admission Rs 125; ⏱ 8am-5pm). It used to be the home of Bevis Bawa, brother of renowned architect Geoffrey Bawa. Bawa's house is the highlight, and it has an eclectic range of artwork on display – from homoerotic sculpture to a wonderful mural of Sri Lankan life in the style of Marc Chagall. The mural was created by Australian artist Donald Friend, who originally came for six days but stayed six years. Other, more short-term, guests included Vivien Leigh and Laurence Olivier, who stayed here during the filming of *Elephant Walk* in 1953. The beautiful garden covers 2 hectares. To get here follow the road south from Aluthgama to Matagama Rd and turn inland to the Muslim village of Dharga Town. From here you will periodically see yellow signs saying 'Brief', but as everyone knows this place, it's easy enough to ask directions. You do need your own transport, though – a three-wheeler from Aluthgama should cost about Rs 500 return and a taxi about Rs 700 return.

Activities
The vast lagoon and river mouth make this an excellent area for water sports. Windsurfing, water-skiing, jet-skiing, deep-sea fishing and everything else watery are offered by local operators. **Sunshine Water Sports Center** (☎ 428 9379; River Ave, Aluthgama) is an independ-

ent shop right on the water near the Hotel Sunil Lanka. Besides renting out a wide range of equipment, the shop runs courses include windsurfing (Rs 8500, six hours). There are also snorkelling tours.

All the large resorts have their own water-sports operators. **Club Inter Sport** (☎ 227 5176), in the Bentota Beach Hotel, is open to non-guests and offers everything from squash and archery to banana-boat rides (Rs 2000 per ride) and surfing lessons.

Boat journeys along the Bentota Ganga are quite popular. Tours travel through the intricate coves and islands on the lower stretches of the river, which is home to more than 100 bird species plus a wide variety of amphibian and reptile species. Most trips go for three hours and charge Rs 500 to 700 per person, with a minimum of five people per boat. There are also five-hour dinner cruises for around US$20 per person. All hotels can point you to operators.

One attraction of this part of the coast is the huge variety of fish (including large specimens such as barracuda), which seem unperturbed by the presence of divers. Major hotels in the area can provide details of local diving outfits.

Sleeping

Accommodation is scattered all along the coast from Aluthgama to Induruwa. Budget places to sleep are not plentiful, but there are plenty of choices further south in Hikkaduwa.

ALUTHGAMA

Hotel Sunil Lanka (☎ 558 2535; http://www.boutique srilanka.com/hotel-overview.php?HotelId=545; River Ave; r Rs 2300-2500; 🕮) This river-side hotel has six sparkling-white rooms, four with air-con. One room has a waterbed, so you can feel the motion of the ocean. There's a nice grassy common area.

Terrena Lodge (☎ 428 9015; terrenalodge@sltnet.lk; River Ave; s/d Rs 1900/2000) Handsomely furnished, this place has five colourful, clean rooms. There is a pretty garden leading down to a river-side dining area, and the Austrian owners have installed a tiny but properly woodsy Austrian bar.

Hotel Hemadan (☎ 227 5320; www.hemadan.dk; 25 River Ave; r Rs 1400-2100; 🕮) This nice, Danish-owned property has 10 large, clean rooms in an ageing building. There's a leafy court-

yard and prime river-viewing opportunities. Better rooms have balconies and/or air-con. There are free boat shuttles across the river to the ocean-side beach.

Hotel Ceysands (☎ 227 5073; ceysandsgm@sltnet .lk; r from US$75; 🕮 🕮) This large resort hotel has a prime position on the spit of land between the ocean and the river. It's popular with tour groups, who seem to never leave the sand. You arrive and leave via a five-minute boat ride.

BENTOTA
Midrange

Hotel Susantha (☎ 227 5324; www.hotelsusanthas.com; Holiday Resort Rd; r US$24-40; 🕮 🕮) This place has 18 clean, moderately sized rooms (some of which are bungalows) in a leafy garden setting. More-expensive rooms include air-con and fridge; older rooms have comfy rattan loungers. It's only a short walk over the train tracks to the beach. The restaurant is justifiably popular for its Western and local food.

Southern Palm Villa (☎ 227 0752; www.spvhotel .com; r Rs 1700-3500; 🕮) Behind Taj Exotica (and across the train tracks), this simple place has 15 clean rooms (with linens for the 'Eden Hotel'), some with air-con. It's not the newest building around, but it's kept tidy and the grounds are spacious. Some rooms have balconies from which you can hear – but not see – the surf. It's a short walk to the beach.

Ayubowan (☎ 227 5913; www.ayubowan.ch; 171 Galle Rd, Bentota South; r €20-35; 🕮 🕮 🕮) This place isn't right beside the beach but the four large, spotless bungalows are set in a pretty garden that has a large pool and views across rice fields. It's a good place for dinner, and has an interesting Swiss-Italian-Asian menu. There's a resident masseur, as well. One room has air-con, and all have fridge.

Lihiniya Surf Hotel (☎ 227 5126; www.thesurfhotel .com; r incl half-board US$50-80; 🕮 🕮 🕮) This is a middle-of-the-range package-tour resort, and the 86 rooms are clean but bland.

Top End

Hotel Serendib (☎ 227 5248; www.serendibleisure .com; r US$55-90; 🕮 🕮 🕮) Designed by noted Sri Lankan architect Geoffrey Bawa (p56), this hotel has 90 distinctive rooms. Some have vast terraces with trees bisecting the roof, while others have balconies. All have beach views and fridge, but none have TV – which is part of the charm. There's dramatic sculpture around a pond off the entrance. All in all a good value package-oriented hotel.

Bentota Beach Hotel (☎ 227 5176; www.johnkeells hotels.com; r from US$150; ⚡ ⌨ ⚑ ✆) This is another Bawa-designed hotel. The 133 rooms are large and of top-end standard, and all have beach views from a balcony or terrace. The lobby has a dramatic entrance and colourful batik lining the ceiling. Nonguests can use the swimming pool here for Rs 275.

Taj Exotica (☎ 227 5650; www.tajhotels.com; r US$140-250; ⚡ ⌨ ✆) Although it lacks the architectural panache of Hotel Serendib or Bentota Beach Hotel, this 162-room hotel is plenty luxurious. There's lots of marble, fountains, and rooms with satellite TV, fridge etc. Brass and rattan abounds.

Club Villa (☎ 227 5312; www.club-villa.com; 138/15 Galle Rd; r incl half-board US$65-150; ⚡ ⌨ ✆) This is a spacious, elegant, 19th-century Dutch-style villa with a big coconut-grove garden, gentle fountains and a swimming pool. The 15 rooms are luxurious yet restrained; the best ones have balconies and air-con. It's located near the 63km marker of Galle Rd; the beach is a two-minute walk away.

Villa Mohotti Walauwa (☎ 428 7008; www.villa mohotti.com; 138/18 Galle Rd; r from US$195; ⚡ ⌨ ✆) Next door to Club Villa, this is a stunning 19th-century villa done up in traditional style with discreet modern details. The 10 rooms are large, elegantly furnished and attentively cared for. This was the beach home of Geoffrey Bawa for a while, so his touches are everywhere. The swimming pool is tiny; the beach a short walk away.

Taruvillas Taprobana (☎ 0777 748 064; www .taruvillas.com; 146/4 Galle Rd; r from US$120; ⚡ ⌨ ✆) One of the best boutique hotels in Sri Lanka, this place has the *Hip Hotel* shtick down. There are nine designer rooms with classic black-and-white photographs hung on whitewashed walls. It's like staying at your publisher's tasteful beachside retreat.

Ayurveda Walauwa (☎ 227 5372; www.sribudhasa .com; 1-week packages from US$1300; ⚡ ⌨ ✆) Just south of Club Villa, this walled resort is on the land side of Galle Rd – but the lack of a beach may help you concentrate on your Ayurvedic cure. The 20 rooms are basic, with tile floors and a good sitting area. Bathrooms have numerous rolls of toilet paper. This health centre tempers its regimen with extras like a large pool.

INDURUWA

Niroga Herbal Resort (☎ 227 0312; 14-day packages from €1000) As unadorned as your colon after a good enema, Niroga is easily the most intense and authentic Ayurvedic centre on the coast. The eight rooms are fan-only because air-con conflicts with the treatments. The staff are genial and caring, and you can take internally and externally cleansed body down to the beach out the front.

Long Beach Cottage (☎ 227 5773; hanjayas@yahoo .de; 550 Galle Rd; r Rs 800) About 200m north of Induruwa train station, this has five slightly faded rooms (three upstairs with shared balcony, and two downstairs) with four-poster beds. There's a pretty, albeit chaotic, garden fronting the beach. The lovely hosts will arrange pick-ups in Aluthgama.

Induruwa Beach Resort (☎ 227 5445; www.villa oceanhotels.com; Kaikawala; s/d US$45/48; ⚡ ⌨ ✆) Revel in this oxymoronic 'modern' hotel that's become old-fashioned. The 90 large rooms are comfortable.

Saman Villas (☎ 227 5435; www.samanvilla.com; Aturuwella; units from US$180; ⚡ ⌨ ✆) There are 27 luxury suites at this superb little boutique hotel, which has a Japanese-style garden with cascading ponds, great views and a superbly sited pool. The plush chalets have a private garden, open-air bathroom, CD player and satellite TV.

Eating

Hotel Susantha (☎ 227 5324; Holiday Resort Rd; mains Rs 200-1000) The restaurant at this hotel (p119) serves excellent Eastern and Western food. You can enjoy seafood specialities under the stars. This is one hotel restaurant that draws large crowds of nonguests.

Golden Grill (☎ 227 5455; Bentota; meals Rs 250-750) This traditional-style Chinese seafood place has a pleasant spot beside the river, near the resorts. Waiters in bow ties lend an elegant air. The best tables overlook the water.

Many places offer only half- and full-board packages, discouraging customers from seeking food outside their friendly confines. However, many of the hotels, especially the top-end ones, have great restaurants that feature evening buffets. **Hotel Serendib** (☎ 227 5248; www.serendiblei sure.com), for instance, has a fine Italian buffet many nights. Among the more sedate places, **Ayubowan** (☎ 227 5913; www.ayubowan.ch; 171 Galle Rd, Bentota South) has a good restaurant.

WEST COAST

Getting There & Around

Beruwela and Bentota are both on the main Colombo–Matara railway line, but Aluthgama, the town sandwiched between them, is the station to go to as many trains do not make stops at these smaller stations. Aluthgama has five or six express trains daily to Colombo (2nd/3rd class Rs 64/32, 1½ to two hours), and a similar number to Hikkaduwa (2nd/3rd class Rs 35/23, one hour), Galle (2nd/3rd class Rs 64/32, 1½ hours) and Matara. There is also service to Kandy (2nd/3rd class Rs 90/170, 1½ to two hours). Avoid the other, slower trains.

When you get off the train at the unusual middle platform station you'll hear the usual boring tales from the touts and fixers that the hotel of your choice is 'closed', 'washed away' and/or 'putrid'. Just ignore them.

Aluthgama is also the best place to pick up a bus, although there is no trouble getting *off* any bus anywhere along the Galle Rd. There is frequent service to both Colombo (regular/air-con Rs 32/60, one to 1½ hours) and Galle (regular/air-con Rs 40/70, 1½ hours).

Three-wheelers are available from Aluthgama; fees range from Rs 50 for a local trip to Rs 300 for the jaunt to Induruwa.

KOSGODA

The tsunami was hard on the coast around Kosgoda, which is about 5km south of Induruwa. Villages suffered but the impact on tourism was limited as this attractive stretch of beach and coast had seen little development. The exception to this was the grave damage suffered by the local turtle hatcheries, the area's one big tourism draw.

HATCHING TURTLES

Five species of sea turtles lay eggs along the coasts of Sri Lanka. The green turtle is the most common, followed by the olive ridley and the hawksbill. The leatherback and loggerhead are both huge, reaching 2m and more in length. During what should be long lives (if they don't end up in a net, soup pot etc), turtles make numerous visits to the beaches of the south coast to lay eggs in the sand. A few weeks later, hundreds of baby turtles make, as the many lurid nature specials will tell you, what is a perilous journey back to the water.

Most of the tiny turtles are quickly gobbled up by birds, fish, people and other critters with gullets. And many never hatch at all, since human egg poachers work overtime to satisfy the demand for turtle omelettes. The turtle hatcheries on the coast aim to increase the odds for the turtles by paying locals for the eggs at a rate slightly above what they fetch in the market (roughly Rs 5 to 10). The eggs are then incubated by the hatchery until they hatch. After a short stay in a tank (supposedly for protection against parasites), the babies are released under the cover of darkness to foil at least some of the birds.

The Kosgoda turtle hatcheries were all wiped out by the tsunami. But each is rebuilding with the help of volunteers. While some naysayers in the scientific community question the benefits of the hatcheries, there's no denying that turtles of any age are awfully cute and make for an entertaining visit. Three of the following hatcheries are in and around Kosgoda; the fourth is north of Kosgoda, near Induwara. They're sufficiently different from each other, so you could easily take in all four. Visits rarely last more than about 20 minutes. Expect to see babies, as well as veterans who have been injured by nets and other calamities.

Kosgoda Turtle Centre (☎ 077 683 5427; admission Rs 100; ☼ 8am-6pm) Located behind a group of new homes built by a German woman for tsunami victims, this very basic place is hands-on and has some charming staff. There's an old albino turtle that has survived both man (nets) and nature (tsunami). Look for a sign on the west side of the Galle Rd, 500m south of the 73km marker.

Kosgoda Turtle Conservation Project (☎ 226 4567; admission Rs 200; ☼ 8am-6pm) On the beach side of Galle Rd, just north of Kosgoda, this volunteer-run operation has been here for 18 years. It's a very simple affair.

Kosgoda Turtle Hatchery (☎ 225 8667; admission Rs 200; ☼ 7am-7pm) Turn down a small track at the 73km marker to find this operation, located in a quiet spot right on the beach. Arrive at 6.30pm and you can help release the day's hatchlings into the ocean.

Turtle Research Project (☎ 227 1062; Induwara; admission Rs 200; ☼ 6am-6.30pm) Undamaged by the tsunami, this facility feels more commercial and established than the Kosgoda operations.

WEST COAST

AMBALANGODA & AROUND
☎ 091

Ambalangoda is a fair-sized town, but its touristy near-neighbour, Hikkaduwa, over-shadows it as a destination. It does, however, have a beautiful sweep of sandy beach to its north, some famous mask carvers, local cultural centres and a bustling fish market. Crafts include hand-woven cotton and finely carved wooden doors, screens and lintels. If you want to see a traditional dance per-formance (p50), Ambalangoda is the place to go. Genuine devil dances – which drive out spirits causing illness – still occur ir-regularly in the hinterland villages. Visitors are welcome, though you do have to expect more curiosity and less English from the vil-lagers. The real catch is finding one of these dances, but ask around and count on good luck from the gods.

This coast was hit hard by the tsunami. The proximity of the Galle Rd, with its vil-lages and the railway along the coast, meant that the waves caused enormous damage and loss of life. Evidence of the tragedy is continu-ous from the 88km to 94km markers.

The barren land between the 94km and 96km markers was once densely populated and covered with thick foliage. One of the starkest reminders of the disaster is near the 95km marker: three cars from a train that was inundated by the waters, killing up to 1500 passengers. The area is now a staging zone for long-term relief efforts, and there are many refugee camps here. The battered red train cars are both a popular tourist at-traction and a shrine. Desperate locals post signs, which include phrases like 'Need help rebuilding' and 'Entire family lost'. No-one questions their validity.

Information
In Ambalangoda town, the **Commercial Bank** (Galle Rd) has an international ATM.

Sights & Activities
Ambalangoda is the centre of much of Sri Lanka's traditional culture. There are two mask shops (with free museums) on either side of the intersection of Galle Rd and Main St, 800m north of the train and bus stations. Each is owned by a son of the fa-mous mask-carver Ariyapala. The **Ariyapala Mask Museum** (☎ Galle Rd & Main St; ☒ 8.30am-⁀eum, with dioramas

and explanations in English. It also sells the booklet *The Ambalangoda Mask Museum*, if you want to delve into the mysterious world of dance, legend and exorcism, and the psychology behind the masks. **Ariyapala Traditional Masks** (432 Galle Rd; ☒ 9am-5pm) is the other shop. The pieces on sale at both are rather expensive.

MH Mettananda (☎ 225 8810; Galle Rd; ☒ 9am-5pm), who has a shop about 500m north of the stations, is one of the good mask carvers in Ambalangoda.

Dudley Silva (☎ 225 9411; 53 Elpitiya Rd; ☒ 9am-5.30pm) is a good place for batik – and the 140-year-old house is an attraction in itself. There's a signpost a little past MH Metta-nanda's shop as you head south towards the centre of town.

School of Dance (☎ 225 8948; bandu@sri.lanka.net; cnr Galle Rd & Main St) teaches the southern forms of dance such as *kolam* (masked dance-drama) as well as South Indian dance trad-itions. It's located across the intersection from the Ariyapala Mask Museum, with which it's affiliated. The school is run by Bandu Wijesuriya, a descendant of a long line of famous mask carvers. Anyone can join the classes; there's a fee of Rs 500 per hour for foreigners. Wijesuriya also teaches mask carving and painting, as well as trad-itional drumming and singing. Students can stay in hostel-style rooms for Rs 750 per night.

Sailatalarama Vihara lies 7km inland from Ambalangoda. This temple sits on a domed hill with broad views over plantations and lakes towards the ranges of the Province of Sabaragamuwa. The temple has a 35m-long sleeping Buddha statue, built by donations. Pilgrims approach the dagobas and *devales* (shrines) via 208 steps, but there's also a road to the top. The statue is new and not the most outstanding example of its type, but it's worth coming here for the rural scenery and the views. A taxi from Ambalangoda should cost about Rs 700 return, plus extra for waiting time of an hour or so.

Sleeping & Eating
Most places are north of the centre – note that Main St is one block west of Galle Rd, but the streets also intersect at the very north end of Main St, where Galle Rd veers west.

Sumudu Tourist Guest House (☎ 225 8832; 418 Main St, Patabendimulla; r with fan/air-con Rs 850/1200;

⊗) Near the intersection with Galle Rd, this large, cool, old-style house is run by a friendly family. There are six pleasant, clean rooms, one of which has hot water. Meals are available. It's a 10-minute walk to the beach; a three-wheeler to or from the bus station should cost Rs 70.

Piya Nivasa (☎ 225 8146; Galle Rd; s/d Rs 500/750) About halfway between Ambalangoda and Hikkaduwa, this 19th-century colonial mansion was one of the few structures in the area to survive the tsunami. It's opposite the beach. The six clean rooms are great value, and you can eat your meals in the family's sitting room. From the Ambalangoda bus or train station a three-wheeler should cost around Rs 100. Otherwise you can catch a Hikkaduwa-bound bus and ask the driver to let you off at the doorstep (the house is easily spotted).

Shangrela (☎ 225 8342; 38 Sea Beach Rd; r Rs 750-1500) A modern, spotless place in an area of many refugee encampments. It has 25 rooms and sweeping views of the beach across the dirt road. Meals are available, and the manager can arrange boat trips and tours to waterfalls.

Dream Beach Resort (☎ 225 8873; dbra@sltnet.lk; 509 Galle Rd; s/d Rs 2200/2900; 🖳) Close to a photogenic stretch of beach, this hotel has some truly strange mushroom-shaped lamps in the lobby. It also has a wide garden and a pool under coconut palms. The 25 rooms, situated in a multistorey building, are plain and spacious with balconies.

Getting There & Away

Ambalangoda is on the main transport route between Colombo and Hikkaduwa, Galle and the South. Buses to and from Colombo (Rs 36, two hours) are common. Trains to Colombo (2nd/3rd class Rs 66/34, two hours) stop here less often. There are frequent buses to and from Hikkaduwa (Rs 12, 15 minutes) and beyond.

HIKKADUWA & AROUND

☎ 091

Hikkaduwa has long been among the most popular of Sri Lanka's beach spots. Its proximity to the capital (98km from the Fort) helps – many people come here direct from the airport to start their classic Asian beach holiday. And it's got a definite fun vibe, especially at its southern end, where there are dozens of affordable guesthouses built along a beautiful stretch of wide beach. At night, backpackers wander the sand from one café to the next, enjoying the sunset and the pleasures beyond.

This popularity has caused Hikkaduwa to swallow the villages south of it for a distance of more than 4km. The downside of this is that busy Galle Rd ploughs right through the middle of everything, which makes strolling amid the shops and restaurants along the road unpleasant.

People in search of watery fun will find many choices. There's a variety of beaches, sea-coral for snorkellers, and good waves for board- and body-surfers. During the May to October monsoon season many places close and the water can get quite rough.

Although Hikkaduwa was damaged by the tsunami – especially the commercial parts at the north end – it escaped the devastation of places further north.

Orientation

Services such as the train and bus stations, banks, the post office and non-tourist-oriented shops congregate in the northern end of Hikkaduwa proper, which was the original settlement. Further south is where the first tourist hotels, guesthouses and restaurants opened up, but this area now seems overdeveloped and unappealing compared with Wewala and Narigama (around 2km south of the stations), where most independent travellers stay. These areas are more relaxed and spread out, and have better beaches than Hikkaduwa proper. South of Narigama the waters tend to be rougher and less safe for bathing – but there are even more guesthouses scattered along the beach and on the road as far as Dodanduwa, only 14km from Galle.

Information

Fittingly located in the commercial district, **Commercial Bank** (Galle Rd) has an international ATM, and you can change money or travellers cheques at the nearby **Bank of Ceylon** (Galle Rd). There are various moneychangers along Galle Rd that are open daily, but it may pay to check the exchange rate in a newspaper beforehand, and to count your money.

The main **post office** (Baddegama Rd) is a five-minute walk inland from the bus station.

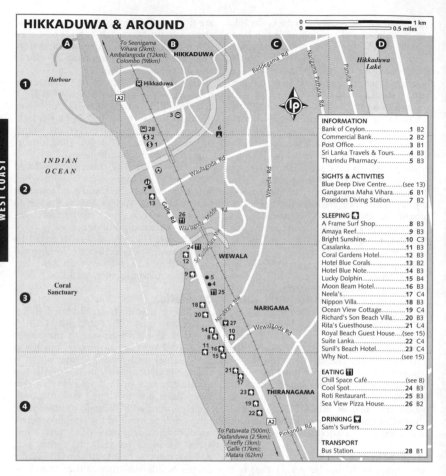

HIKKADUWA & AROUND

INFORMATION	
Bank of Ceylon..................1	B2
Commercial Bank..................2	B2
Post Office..................3	B1
Sri Lanka Travels & Tours........4	B3
Tharindu Pharmacy..............5	B3

SIGHTS & ACTIVITIES	
Blue Deep Dive Centre........(see 13)	
Gangarama Maha Vihara.........6	B1
Poseidon Diving Station.........7	B2

SLEEPING	
A Frame Surf Shop.................8	B3
Amaya Reef.........................9	B3
Bright Sunshine...................10	C3
Casalanka..........................11	B3
Coral Gardens Hotel............12	B3
Hotel Blue Corals................13	B2
Hotel Blue Note..................14	B3
Lucky Dolphin.....................15	B4
Moon Beam Hotel................16	B3
Neela's..............................17	C4
Nippon Villa.......................18	B3
Ocean View Cottage............19	C4
Richard's Son Beach Villa.....20	B3
Rita's Guesthouse.................21	C4
Royal Beach Guest House....(see 15)	
Suite Lanka.........................22	C4
Sunil's Beach Hotel..............23	C4
Why Not...........................(see 15)	

EATING	
Chill Space Café.................(see 8)	
Cool Spot..........................24	B3
Roti Restaurant...................25	B3
Sea View Pizza House..........26	B2

DRINKING	
Sam's Surfers.....................27	C3

TRANSPORT	
Bus Station........................28	B1

There are numerous IDD telephone bureaus on Hikkaduwa's main street, many of them with Internet facilities. **Sri Lanka Travels & Tours** (☎ 227 7354; 371 Galle Rd) offers Internet (Rs 2 per minute) and, like many other places in town, organises tours of the island.

Tharindu Pharmacy (☎ 545 1426; 238 Galle Rd) has a basic selection of medicines.

From tourist libraries along Galle Rd you can borrow books written in numerous European languages. There's usually a small fee (Rs 100) per read, plus a deposit (say Rs 300), which is refunded on the safe return of the book. Shops selling all manner of souvenirs and cheap cotton clothes can be found along Galle Rd.

Sights & Activities

For many people a visit to Hikkaduwa begins and ends on the beach – especially if they've just arrived from somewhere cold. The widest bit of sand extends north and south from Narigama. Here you'll find a few simple lounge chairs that you can rent – or even use for free if they're part of a café. But don't expect a chaotic scene – there are a few vendors but it's pretty relaxed.

The sands at Wewala are narrower and steeper, but this is where you'll see surfers in action.

CORAL SANCTUARY

Hikkaduwa's over-exploited 'coral sanctuary' stretches out from the string of 'Coral' hotels at the north end of the strip to a group of rocks a couple of hundred metres offshore. You can swim out to the rocks from the Coral Gardens Hotel, where the reef runs straight out from the shore. The water over the reef is never more than 3m or 4m deep. Many visitors have been disappointed with the coral and the lack of fish; in many places the coral has died due to being disturbed or broken. Bleaching caused by oceanic and atmospheric conditions struck the reef in 1998, affecting about half the coral, but it is now recovering. The tsunami caused some further damage, but the real problem was the enormous amount of debris that ended up in the coral when the waters receded. Fortunately the local diving community spent months cleaning things up.

It's easy to see the coral. Dive shops and many hotels and guesthouses rent out snorkelling gear for around Rs 200 a day, or less. Stay alert in the water so you don't, say, get run over by a glass-bottomed boat (not a recommended vehicle for viewing the reef anyway, given the boats' running-into-coral proclivities).

SCUBA DIVING

The diving season runs from November to April. Both the companies listed here offer Professional Association of Diving Instructors (PADI) courses for similar prices (open water for US$320, advanced for US$220), plus a selection of dives such as wreck dives, night dives and trips for those who just want to try out diving. The tsunami and the ensuing drop in business took a toll on operators, but as business returns there should be many more places than those listed here.

Because many people use Hikkaduwa as a base for exploring the country, dive shops also offer tours to other parts of Sri Lanka.
Blue Deep Dive Centre (☎ 074 383190; bluedeepdive@yahoo.co.uk; 332 Galle Rd) This centre, at Hotel Blue Corals, runs PADI courses and two-day discovery courses (US$70, equipment included).
Poseiden Diving Station (☎ 227 7294; www.divingsrilanka.com; Galle Rd) This large school and dive shop has its own guesthouse and offers a full range of PADI courses. Single dives are US$25.

WATER SPORTS

Wewala, south of the coral sanctuary, has good surfing from November to April. The action draws surfers – serious and beginner –

from around the globe. This, combined with the nice beaches and casually energetic nightlife, makes Hikkaduwa Sri Lanka's most popular surf spot. One note: be sure to find out where the coral lies before you head out – it's just centimetres below the surface.

A Frame Surf Shop (☎ 545 8131; www.mambo.nu; 434 Galle Rd), located in A Frame Surf Shop guesthouse (p126), repairs boards and has a large selection of surfing gear. It rents out a variety of boards in good shape from Rs 600 per day. It also offers surfing tours throughout the island under the moniker 'Mambo Surf Tours'. The staff here is quite friendly and in addition to the large shop, there's a cool café. Surfers: if you're heading anywhere in the south, this is the last place where you can get gear or essentials like wax.

Many places to stay, such as **Why Not** (☎ 438 3325; Galle Rd; r Rs 1000-1500), also rent out boards.

Body-surfing is popular through much of the year and you can pretty much seek out the waves of your choice all along the beach.

Kitesurfing is growing in popularity, especially in the months when the waves are mild. **Lucky Dolphin** (☎ 227 5272; info@kiten.nl; 533 Galle Rd), a guesthouse in Narigama (p126), rents out kitesurfing gear and offers lessons (four hours for US$50).

INLAND ATTRACTIONS

To take a break from the beach scene just walk or cycle along any of the minor roads heading inland. They lead to a calmer, completely different, rural world. Just off Baddegama Rd is **Gangarama Maha Vihara**. This is an interesting Buddhist temple that has lots of popular educational paintings that are the work of one man over nearly a decade. The monks are happy to show you around. A further 2km along Baddegama Rd you come to **Hikkaduwa Lake**, home to monitor lizards and a lot of birdlife. Boat tours can sometimes be organised on the lake; ask around.

About 2km north of Hikkaduwa is **Seenigama Vihara**, perched on its own island. It's one of only two temples in the country where victims of theft can seek retribution. People who have been robbed visit the temple and buy a specially prepared oil made with chilli and pepper. With the oil they light a lamp in their homes and recite a mantra. Sooner or later, maybe within weeks, the thief will be identified when they're struck down with misfortune, such as having a bicycle accident or being hit on the head by a falling coconut.

Sleeping

Virtually all of Hikkaduwa's places to stay are strung out along Galle Rd. The best way to find something to suit is simply to wander down the road (or beach) and look at a variety of rooms. All budget accommodation prices can be bargained over. Those given here are what you'd expect to pay in the high season; out of season the same room may go for half the quoted price. Prices also vary according to which stretch of the strip you're on – down the Narigama end, where the sands are wider, room rates tend to be higher. In the high season the best-value, smaller places fill up quickly; you may need to make a booking a few days ahead.

Most plots of land along the strip are quite narrow, which means that guesthouses will only have a few pricey rooms with views of the water. In contrast, rooms closest to the road get a lot of noise, so be sure to get a room well away from the traffic. Many places are jammed right up against each other.

Finally, Hikkaduwa is not a place for those looking for a top-end resort. There's a collection of ageing resort-style hotels at the north end of the strip (all of which have 'Coral' in the name), but you'll have a more enjoyable experience at the guesthouses to the south.

BUDGET

Unless otherwise noted, expect fans, mosquito nets, cold water and private bathrooms at these places.

Richard's Son Beach Villa (☎ 227 7184; Galle Rd; r Rs 600-800) Unlike most places locally, this small one-storey guesthouse has a huge garden planted with coconut palms and other trees. There are hammocks hanging about, and an overall mellow vibe. The eight rooms are small but clean. There's no food.

Lucky Dolphin (☎ 227 5272; info@kiten.nl; 533 Galle Rd; r Rs 800-1500, apt Rs 1500-2500) You may well feel like a propitious porpoise at this good value place. The standard rooms are in bungalows and are large and have hot water. The apartment, however, is the real steal: it's huge, sleeps numerous folks (bring on the keg!) and has a full kitchen, plus good views.

Poseiden Diving Station (☎ 227 7294; www.diving srilanka.com; Galle Rd; r US$12-21) This popular dive school (p125) has 12 basic rooms. Those upstairs have views and nicely tiled bathrooms.

Bright Sunshine (☎ 077 902 1921; 501 Galle Rd; s/d Rs 800/1200) This place has six very clean and airy rooms. Although there's no garden and it's across the road from the beach, the owners are delightful and very keen to please.

Why Not (☎ 438 3325; Galle Rd; r Rs 1000-1500) Well, why not? This place is very good value. The five rooms are large and set in a mellow one-storey compound. There are whimsical touches about, like the elephant doorstops. Surfboards are available for rent from the surfer owners.

Neela's (☎ 227 7496; ritas@sltnet.lk; 634 Galle Rd; r Rs 1000-2000) The six rooms here are basic but comfortable and clean. The real draw, however, is the location in the heart of the Narigama beach scene. The café is popular.

MIDRANGE

Many places in the midrange category are not far removed from their budget guesthouse roots. Room quality can vary wildly as a result of years of piecemeal additions. Unless otherwise noted, expect hot water in rooms.

Moon Beam Hotel (☎ 545 0657; hotelmoonbeam@ hotmail.com; 548/1 Galle Rd; r Rs 2500-4000; ⚡) A friendly, professional operation. There are 20 rooms on the narrow site, with three having great beach views. More-expensive rooms have air-con, but ask to see a few. There's a big tree out the front, which provides some cover from Galle Rd. The restaurant is highly recommended.

A Frame Surf Shop (☎ 545 8131; www.mambo.nu; 434 Galle Rd; r 2000-4800; ⚡) A growing empire of 15 rooms, this is also home to the popular surf shop and the even more popular Chill Space Café. The great variety of rooms are large and clean; more money buys you air-con and better views. Ask to see several rooms. There are cheap long-term rates available for surfers.

Ocean View Cottage (☎ 227 7237; www.oceanview cottage.net; Galle Rd; r Rs 1500-4000; ⚡) The large grassy expanse leading down to the beach is the real attraction here. There are 12 rooms in this three-storey, family-run block; six have air-con and all have fridge. Everything is spotless.

Suite Lanka (☎ 227 7136; suitelanka@hotmail.com; Galle Rd; r €50-70; 🛏 🛁) This is a small, friendly hotel with seven very good rooms. The small pool is set in a shaded garden next to the beachfront. Rooms have colonial touches; those upstairs are brighter.

Royal Beach Guest House (☎ 545 8485; Galle Rd; r Rs 1500-2500; 🛏) This low-key place has 12 rooms (six with air-con) in one-storey blocks set around an open yard. Although the place itself is quiet, you couldn't get more in the middle of the Narigama action if you tried.

Hotel Blue Note (☎ 227 7016; bluenote@eureka.lk; 424 Galle Rd; r Rs 1500-2000) Not as claustrophobic as the rooms in some other places, those here are in bungalows set around a sandy garden. Everything is clean, though nothing special, and rooms only have cold water and fans. The roadside café is popular.

Amaya Reef (☎ 438 3244; www.amayaresorts.com; 400 Galle Rd; r US$75; 🛏 🛁) The closest thing Hikkaduwa has to a top-end resort, the Amaya is an older hotel that was rebuilt and reopened in 2005. It features the currently *de rigueur* Asian minimalist style throughout. Rooms are good value and have flat-screen TVs, fridges, desks and stylish bathrooms. Fans of the original Star Trek series will note the pool's resemblance to the Starfleet insignia.

Rita's Guesthouse (☎ 227 7496; Galle Rd; r Rs 1800-3000) There are 28 rooms in two- and three-storey blocks on this rather tight site. Better rooms have little sitting areas outside. Budget rooms are not such good value, as they lack hot water.

Sunil's Beach Hotel (☎ 227 7186; www.sunilbeach .com; Galle Rd; r €18-25; 🛏 🛁) This is a standard-issue package-tour complex with a fenced garden surrounding an L-shaped pool. The 62 rooms are large and have a balcony (air-con adds €8 to room rates). There is less character here than at the better family-run places.

Nippon Villa (☎ 227 7103; 412 Galle Rd; r Rs 2000-5000; 🛏) This place has a small courtyard in a colourful, quite handsome building. The 23 rooms are airy and clean but slightly overpriced – especially the six with air-con.

Hotel Blue Corals (☎ 227 7679; bluecorals@itmin .com; 332 Galle Rd; s/d US$40/50; 🛏 🛁) A busy, older resort-style hotel with a pool and 42 rooms. The rooms with balconies are good value; the ones without aren't. This end of town is away from the groovy beach scene.

Coral Gardens Hotel (☎ 227 7023; www.johnkeells hotels.com; s/d from US$64/78; 🛏 🛁) The rapidly ageing '80s décor goes with the package-tour vibe at this five-storey resort-style hotel. The only elevators in town serve 154 large rooms with views but, sadly, no balconies.

Eating & Drinking

Most of Hikkaduwa's best places to eat are connected to hotels and guesthouses. Down on the sandy shores of Narigama you can table-hop from one spot to the next through the night. Many places are good just for a drink and a few stay open past 11pm – but don't expect any raves here.

Moon Beam Restaurant (☎ 545 0657; 548/1 Galle Rd; mains Rs 300-500) This hotel (opposite) has the most attractive restaurant on the beach. It has a salty, open-air nautical décor, and tables where you can curl your toes in the sand. The seafood is excellent. It's also a good place for a sunset drink.

Hotel Blue Note (☎ 227 7016; 424 Galle Rd; mains Rs 300-800) The NASA-sized satellite dish on the roof tells you that this roadside café, located at the hotel of the same name (left), is a couch potato's dream. Enjoy over 500 channels of TV joy while you sample local and Western foods. As a bonus, there's draught beer on tap. Now you just need to get control of the remote.

Cool Spot (327 Galle Rd; mains Rs 200-800) This family-run place has been serving up fresh seafood from a vintage roadside house at the north end of the strip since 1972. There's a cool porch where you can peruse the blackboard menu and delight to specialities like garlic prawns and the bulging seafood platter.

Chill Space Café (☎ 545 8131; 434 Galle Rd; meals Rs 100-1000) This popular beachside café in the A Frame Surf Shop (opposite) features shakes, snacks, seafood and more. There are free beach chairs and showers for swimmers, while under the roof there's a pool table and a skateboard ramp. It's a fun, popular spot; some nights there's music.

Firefly (☎ 077 302 7559; 364 Galle Rd; meals Rs 300-1300) Set in an old Dutch colonial building, Firefly hopes to be Hikkaduwa's hippest joint. Of course, first you have to find it (between the 104km and 105km markers in Dodanduwa). Following the trend in distinctly trendier locales, Firefly is a place where you can get a meal, chill on sofas or have a drink at the bar. Lunch sees paninis; dinner, a complex Asian-fusion menu.

Neela's (☎ 227 5312; 634 Galle Rd; mains Rs 150-400) The café here is as simple as the adjoining guesthouse (p126), but that doesn't mean it skimps on quality. Seafood treats like calamari are delicious. Many people laze away the hours here over snacks and beers.

Sea View Pizza House (☎ 227 7014; 297 Galle Rd; mains around Rs 200) This welcoming spot has a short list of pizzas, plus decent pastas and seafood. It's a real find at the north end of town.

Roti Restaurant (☎ 491 1540; 373 Galle Rd; meals Rs 70) A hole in the wall right on the road, it sells 59 kinds of *rottis* (doughy pancakes), ranging from garlic chicken to banana. There are also fresh, good shakes and lassis.

Sam's Surfers (Roger's Garage; 403 Galle Rd) A laid-back bar that shows recent movies every night at 7.30pm. At other times, conspiracy fans rejoice as Fox News is shown via satellite dish. There's a pool table, and cheap beer and snacks.

Getting There & Away
BUS
There are frequent buses from Colombo (regular/air-con Rs 54/110, two to three hours). Buses also operate frequently to Ambalangoda (Rs 13, 15 minutes) and Galle (Rs 13, 30 minutes). Buses to Galle or beyond will drop you south of the bus station along the guesthouse strip. When leaving Hikkaduwa you stand more chance of a seat if you start at the bus station.

MOTORCYCLE
Motorcycles are readily available for rent in Hikkaduwa. Depending on the size of the machine and your negotiating skills expect to pay roughly Rs 600 to 1500 per day; ask at your hotel or guesthouse.

TAXI
Most of the taxis in Hikkaduwa are minibuses able to hold about eight passengers, so they can be quite cheap if there's a group of you. Most gather in front of the top-end hotels. Some sample fares are Galle Rs 1000, Unawatuna Rs 1200, Tangalla Rs 2000 to 2400, Colombo Rs 2000 to 2400, and Bandaranaike International Airport Rs 2800.

TRAIN
The trains can get very crowded; avoid the really slow ones that stop everywhere. Check at the station for express departure times. Service on the coast line is fairly frequent; some destinations include Colombo (2nd/3rd class Rs 91/43, two to three hours), Galle (2nd/3rd class Rs 19/10, 30 minutes) and beyond to Matara.

There's one direct express to Kandy each day (2nd/3rd class Rs 200/107, six hours).

Getting Around
A three-wheeler from the train or bus stations to Wewala or Narigama costs about Rs 100. Once you're settled in, a bicycle is a nice way to get around; it's easy to hire a bike for Rs 100 to 150 a day.

The South

The South needs to figure prominently in any traveller's visit to Sri Lanka. The Unesco-listed old port town of Galle is fast gaining international fame as one of the best-preserved examples of colonial life in Asia. The streets of the 17th-century Fort are lined with old, unrestored buildings that vividly show the influences of the Dutch, Portuguese, British, Muslims and the many other peoples and cultures that have passed through. As upmarket hotels open, Galle is on the cusp of becoming something much bigger.

Just around a rocky headland from Galle, Unawatuna has shaken off the devastation of the tsunami (even if the memories linger) and continues to be the idyllic beach town of many a traveller's dreams. The perfect crescent of sand inspires a languor that can last for days, if not weeks. Just east, luxurious, picture-perfect villas welcome the well-heeled.

Among the smattering of villages and coastal towns between Unawatuna and Tangalla there are bare-bones guesthouses fronting the amazing surfing breaks at Midigama, and character-filled family-run resorts on their own little coves. The popular beach town of Tangalla, with its long stretches of white sands, will be reborn as the tsunami devastation recedes over time. At the far corner of the island, Yala National Park is the place to see leopards, elephants, monkeys and much more amid its remote savanna plains.

As you head east along the south coast the road becomes less and less crowded, and it becomes easier and easier to feel part of local life. Stretches of dramatic coast alternate with the lush green interior, and there are many important places of local culture, like the temples at Kataragama.

THE SOUTH

HIGHLIGHTS

- Wandering the atmospheric streets of **Galle** (p130)
- Living the colonial life in a restored Galle mansion such as **Galle Fort Hotel** (p135)
- Lounging away the days on the white sand of **Unawatuna** (p138)
- Finding your own perfect hidden resort along the coast west of **Tangalla** (p147)
- Surfing the breaks at **Midigama** (p142)
- Taking a yoghurt break on the **road to Tissamaharama** (p152)
- Spotting big game in **Yala National Park** (p156)
- Making your penance at the **Kataragama festival** (p159)

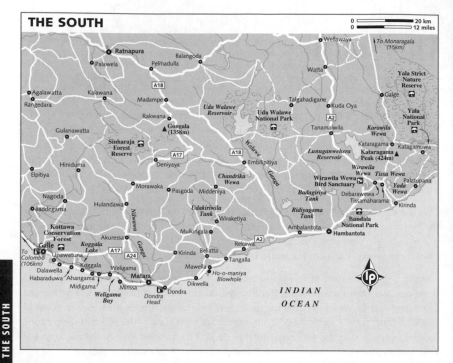

THE SOUTH

GALLE

☎ 091 / pop 91,000

Galle (pronounced gawl in English, and gaar-le in Sinhala) is a living time capsule. It has a vibrant commercial district that's also shambolic and often charmless, but pass through one of the Fort gates and you are transported back to the Dutch colonial era.

Built by the Dutch beginning in 1663, the 36-hectare Fort occupies most of the promontory that forms the older part of Galle. Described by the notoriously hard-to-please Paul Theroux as being 'garlanded with red hibiscus and smelling of the palm-scented ocean,' the Fort is an amazing collection of structures and culture dating back through the centuries. Just wandering the streets at random yields one architectural surprise after another. And be sure to take in the dramatic views of town and ocean from the encircling walls. Unesco has recognised Fort as a World Heritage Site.

A key part of the Fort's allure, however, is that it isn't just a pretty place. Rather, it remains a working community: there are administrative offices, courts, export com-

panies and lots of regular folks populating the streets. There's a definite energy in the air, and tourism takes a back seat. However, this may not be the case for long. Some excellent boutique hotels have opened and locals are busily selling their often amazing unrestored vintage buildings to foreigners and speculators. The Fort is definitely one of those places that in a few years will have people saying: 'Oh you should have seen it before.' So hurry up and visit before 'before' is past.

Galle is easily reached as a day trip from Hikkaduwa and Unawatuna. But an increasing number of travellers are staying within the atmospheric walls of the Fort, instead choosing to make day trips to the beach towns.

History

Although Anuradhapura and Polonnaruwa are much older than Galle, they are effectively abandoned cities – the modern towns are divorced from the ancient ruins. In contrast, both old and new Galle have remained vibrant.

THE 2004 TSUNAMI – AFTERMATH IN THE SOUTH

The south coast was heavily affected by the tsunami. You won't go far without seeing the effects, whether they are the 'temporary' encampments of people who lost their homes, boats washed far ashore or open land where there were once villages. Much of Galle was damaged, although the walls of the Fort lived up to their name and protected the historic old town. The popular beach resort of Unawatuna was virtually wiped out, but was rebuilt quickly thanks to foreign generosity. Further east, Tangalla suffered heavily and many once-popular beach guesthouses have vanished. In the sparsely populated areas past hard-hit Hambantota the waters changed the shape of the coast, although areas such as Yala National Park proved resilient to nature's forces.

Wherever you go, every person has a harrowing story of survival and loss. Although you'll see large signs along the main road proclaiming the involvement of various international programs, their efforts are often harder to discern. And talk of a buffer zone between the surf and beachside buildings proved to be just that – talk.

Historians believe Galle may have been the city of Tarshish – where King Solomon obtained gems and spices – but it became prominent only with the arrival of the Europeans. In 1505 a Portuguese fleet bound for the Maldives was blown off course and took shelter in the harbour. Apparently, on hearing a cock (*galo* in Portuguese) crowing, they gave the town its name. Another slightly less dubious story is that the name is derived from the Sinhala word *gala* (rock).

In 1589, during one of their periodic squabbles with the kingdom of Kandy, the Portuguese built a small fort, which they named Santa Cruz. Later they extended it with a series of bastions and walls, but the Dutch, who took Galle in 1640, destroyed most traces of the Portuguese presence.

After the construction of the Fort in the 17th century Galle was the main port for Sri Lanka for more than 200 years, and was an important stop for boats and ships travelling between Europe and Asia. However, by the time Galle passed into British hands in 1796, commercial interest was turning to Colombo. The construction of breakwaters in Colombo's harbour in the late 19th century sealed Galle's status as a secondary harbour, though it still handles some shipping and yachts.

For an interesting take on local history, buy a copy of *Galle: As Quiet As Asleep* by Norah Roberts, Galle's long-time librarian.

Orientation

Sri Lanka's fourth-biggest town, Galle is 116km south of Colombo. The old town, or Fort, occupies most of the south-pointing promontory. Where the promontory meets the 'mainland' is the centre of the new town, with the bus and train stations, shops and banks. The two areas are divided by the grassy expanse of Galle International Cricket Stadium. Galle has a busy market area in the new town, on Main St.

The Fort's walls did a fine job of protecting the old town from the tsunami, while the newer commercial district was battered but rapidly recovered. However, residential areas near the water suffered heavily, scores of people died and 'temporary' housing looks to become a permanent part of the future.

Information

Galle is a good source of supplies and other essentials for those heading east along the coast.

Places offering IDD services are common, and many phone places also offer Internet access. There is no shortage of banks with international ATMs, both in the Fort and the new town.

Cargills Food City (☎ 223 3212; 3rd fl, 26 P&J City, Gamini Mawatha) This supermarket also has a pharmacy.

Commercial Bank (Church St) Has an international ATM.

Galle Library (Church St) Seems almost as old as the Fort. Has a small collection and students eager to try out their English.

Hatton National Bank (Wackwella St) Has an international ATM.

Lexcom (☎ 438 5521; 4th fl, 26 P&J City, Gamini Mawatha; per min Rs 4) An Internet café in the same building as Cargills Food City, with good connections.

Main post office (Main St; per min Rs 4) Has a poste restante counter and an air-con Internet centre. It's near the market.

Post Office (Church St) A small branch office.

Sampath Bank (Wackwella St) Has an international ATM.

GALLE

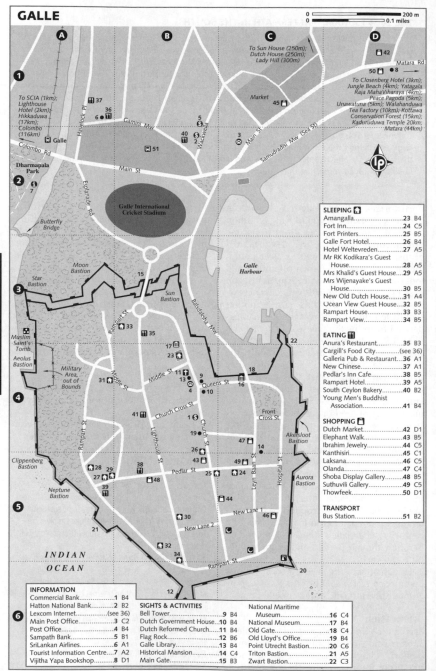

0 _____ 200 m
0 _____ 0.1 miles

SLEEPING 🏠
Amangalla..........................23 B4
Fort Inn.............................24 C5
Fort Printers......................25 B5
Galle Fort Hotel..................26 B4
Hotel Weltevreden..............27 A5
Mr RK Kodikara's Guest
    House............................28 A5
Mrs Khalid's Guest House....29 A5
Mrs Wijenayake's Guest
    House............................30 B5
New Old Dutch House.........31 A4
Ocean View Guest House....32 B5
Rampart House...................33 B3
Rampart View....................34 B5

EATING 🍴
Anura's Restaurant.............35 B3
Cargill's Food City.........(see 36)
Galleria Pub & Restaurant...36 A1
New Chinese......................37 A1
Pedlar's Inn Cafe...............38 B5
Rampart Hotel....................39 A5
South Ceylon Bakery..........40 B2
Young Men's Buddhist
    Association....................41 B4

SHOPPING 🛍
Dutch Market.....................42 D1
Elephant Walk...................43 B5
Ibrahim Jewelry.................44 C5
Kanthisiri..........................45 C1
Laksana............................46 C5
Olanda.............................47 C4
Shoba Display Gallery.........48 B5
Suthuvili Gallery................49 C5
Thowfeek..........................50 D1

TRANSPORT
Bus Station.......................51 B2

INFORMATION
Commercial Bank...................1 B4
Hatton National Bank............2 B2
Lexcom Internet...............(see 36)
Main Post Office...................3 C2
Post Office...........................4 B4
Sampath Bank......................5 B1
SriLankan Airlines................6 A1
Tourist Information Centre.....7 A2
Vijitha Yapa Bookshop..........8 D1

SIGHTS & ACTIVITIES
Bell Tower...........................9 B4
Dutch Government House....10 B4
Dutch Reformed Church......11 B4
Flag Rock...........................12 B6
Galle Library......................13 B4
Historical Mansion.............14 C4
Main Gate..........................15 B3

National Maritime
    Museum........................16 C4
National Museum...............17 B4
Old Gate............................18 C4
Old Lloyd's Office...............19 B4
Point Utrecht Bastion..........20 C6
Triton Bastion....................21 A5
Zwart Bastion....................22 C3

SriLankan Airlines (☎ 224 6942; 3rd fl, 16 Gamini Mawatha) You can book flights here; it also offers a full range of travel services.

Vijitha Yapa Bookshop (☎ 238 1181; 170 Main St) Small shop with novels, magazines, maps and guidebooks.

Dangers & Annoyances

Galle has legions of bamboozlers, fixers, flimflammers and other characters looking to pull a scam. Be prepared to fend off all sorts of fabricated stories, such as the Fort is closed, or there are no buses to Unawatuna, or predictably, tsunami tragedies. The usual aim is to set you up for the centuries-old gem scam, where you pay absurdly high prices for gemstones, or buy a fake, or are asked to buy gems and resell them for a profit in other countries.

Numerous touts hang around the train and bus stations. But you'll also find them in the Fort and along the walls. A firm 'I have no interest in anything you have to offer,' should do the trick – at least by the fourth repetition.

Sights

The Fort area is home to about 400 houses, churches, mosques, temples and many old commercial and government buildings. To really experience it, wander the walls and streets, making your own discoveries as you go. And don't neglect the new town: there are all manner of interesting shops and markets along Main St and Matara Rd.

THE FORT WALLS

One of the most pleasant strolls you can take in town is the circuit of the Fort walls at dusk. As the daytime heat fades away, you can walk almost the complete circuit of the Fort along the top of the wall in an easy hour or two. You'll be in the company of a few other travellers, lots of locals, shyly courting couples and plenty of kids diving into the protected waters. The views are great.

The **Main Gate** in the northern stretch of the wall is a comparatively recent addition – it was built by the British in 1873 to handle the heavier flow of traffic into the old town. This part of the wall, the most heavily fortified because it faced the land, was originally built with a moat by the Portuguese, and was then substantially enlarged by the Dutch, who in 1667 split the wall into separate Star, Moon and Sun Bastions.

Following the Fort wall clockwise you soon come to the **Old Gate**. The British coat of arms tops the entrance on the outer side. Inside, the letters VOC, standing for Verenigde Oostindische Compagnie (Dutch East India Company), are inscribed in the stone with the date 1669, flanked by two lions and topped by a cock. Just beyond the gate is the **Zwart Bastion** (Black Bastion), thought to be Portuguese-built and the oldest of the Fort bastions.

The eastern section of the wall ends at the **Point Utrecht Bastion**, close to the powder magazine. The bastion is topped by an 18m-high lighthouse, which was built in 1938.

Flag Rock, at the end of the next stretch of wall, was once a Portuguese bastion. During the Dutch period approaching ships were signalled from the bastion, warning them of dangerous rocks – hence its name. Musket shots were fired from Pigeon Island, close to the rock, to further alert ships to the danger. On the **Triton Bastion** there used to be a windmill that drew up sea water, which was sprayed from carts to keep the dust down on the city streets. This part of the wall is a great place to be at sunset. There's a series of other bastions, as well as the tomb of a Muslim saint outside the wall, before you arrive back at your starting point.

INSIDE THE FORT

Most of the older buildings within the Fort date from the Dutch era. Many of the streets still bear their Dutch names, or are direct translations. The Dutch also built an intricate sewer system that was flushed out daily by the tide. With true colonial efficiency, they then bred musk rats in the sewers, which were exported for their musk oil. There's a large Muslim community living and working inside the Fort, particularly at the southern end of the walled town. Many shops close for a couple of hours around noon on Friday for prayer time.

The **Dutch Reformed Church** (Groote Kerk, Great Church; cnr Church & Middle Sts; ☯ 9am-5pm), near New Oriental Hotel, was originally built in 1640, but the present building dates from 1752 to 1755. Its floor is paved with gravestones from the old Dutch cemetery (the oldest dates from 1662); the friendly caretaker will tell you where remains are held in the walls and under the floor. The organ from 1760 still sits in the building and the impressive pulpit, made from calamander wood from Malaysia, is an interesting piece. Services are held each Sunday. The Dutch government has helped restore many parts, including the brilliant azure ceiling, to their original lustre.

The ultraposh hotel **Amangalla** (opposite) was built in 1684 to house the Dutch governor and officers. As **New Oriental Hotel** it was the lodging of choice for first-class P&O passengers travelling to and from Europe in the 19th century.

Near the Dutch Reformed Church are a **bell tower** (built in 1901) and the old **Dutch Government House**, now awaiting refurbishment. A slab over the doorway bears the date 1683 and Galle's ubiquitous cock symbol. Look for the **Old Lloyd's Office**, with its preserved ship arrival board, in the 19th-century commercial building just north of Galle Fort Hotel.

Entered via the Old Gate, the **National Maritime Museum** (admission Rs 65; ☺ 9am-5pm Sat-Wed) is inside the thick, solid walls of former storehouses. The dusty exhibits are poorly displayed, but have a certain kitsch appeal: fibreglass whales, pickled sea creatures, models of catamarans. There's an exhibit on the pilgrimages that fishermen from this area once made to Kataragama in the hope that they could increase their catches.

The **National Museum** (Church St; admission Rs 45; ☺ 9am-5pm Wed-Sun) is housed in an old Dutch building near the Main Gate. It has sad displays of traditional masks, information on the lace-making process, a few examples of the luxury items that once passed through the port, and religious items, including a relic casket.

The **Historical Mansion** (31-39 Leyn Baan St; ☺ 9am-5.30pm Mon-Thu, Sat & Sun, 10am-noon & 2.30-5.30pm Fri), in a well-restored Dutch house, is not really a museum, as many of the exhibits have price tags. It's a junkyard of colonial artefacts, including collections of antique typewriters, VOC china, spectacles and jewellery. There's also a gem shop.

Tours

Somebody's going to start offering walking tours of Galle and make a killing. Until then you can explore on your own.

Across from the train station you'll see a small building bearing the sign 'Tourist Information Centre'. It's official status

has been in doubt since the tsunami, but inside you'll find guides ready to offer their services and arrange tours of the region (for a price).

Sleeping

As testament to Galle's fast-rising star, there are several new boutique hotels inside the Fort. The Fort is also a bastion of character-filled guesthouses, where the real characters are often the owners. There are some nice upmarket places in the hills above town and along the coast in both directions.

FORT
Budget

Mrs Wijenayake's Guest House (Beach Haven; ☎ 223 4663; thalith@sri.lanka.net; 65 Lighthouse St; r Rs 600-3000; 🖭) This is a modern home with 10 tidy rooms and a rooftop deck. The cheaper rooms are in the family home, and the larger, more expensive ones are upstairs at the back, with sitting areas on the balcony. The family is welcoming and still remembers the extended stay by Lonely Planet cofounder Tony Wheeler in 1977.

Hotel Weltevreden (☎ 222 2650; piyasen2@sltnet.lk; 104 Pedlar St; s/d Rs 600/750) A heritage-listed Dutch building, Hotel Weltevreden has characterful rooms surrounding a leafy central courtyard, and a pretty garden. The welcoming hosts are happy to make your meals.

Mr RK Kodikara's Guest House (☎ 222 2351; kodi.galle@penpal.lk; 29 Rampart St; r Rs 600-1100) This is a charming ramshackle mansion overlooking the ramparts. There are four clean, simple rooms downstairs, a suite upstairs, and two value-for-money rooms with views over the ramparts. If you're tall, Mr Kodikara (a real charmer) has made 2m-long beds with timber from the old roof.

Rampart House (☎ 223 4448; 3 Rampart St; r from Rs 500) This is a large 1970s home with a variety of rooms; the triples have a view of the ramparts. One room has a small study, another has a small balcony, bathtub and hot water, and there's a single downstairs. There isn't a sign outside; look for the street number on the fence post.

Rampart View (☎ 438 0566; rampartview@hotmail.com; 37 Rampart St; r Rs 1300-2000; 🖭) This place, in a prime corner location, has some of Galle's best views of the ramparts. The five rooms are basic, although the pricier ones have air-con.

Midrange

Fort Inn (☎ 224 8094, 0777 394820; rasikafortinn@yahoo .com; 31 Pedlar St; r Rs 1500) The three rooms are smallish at this simple, family-run place. But the welcome is warm and you can observe the lively Pedlar St action from the large balcony out the front.

New Old Dutch House (☎ 438 5032; www.newold dutchhouse.lk; 21 Middle St; r US$25-45; ✷) An old new place close to the sea where you can enjoy breakfast under papaw trees and listen to the ocean's waves break on the rocks below the ramparts. The eight suite rooms are modern, all-white and come with satellite TV and fridge. Cheaper rooms share bathrooms and are fan only.

Mrs Khalid's Guest House (Huize Bruisen de Zee; ☎ 223 4907; sabrik@sltnet.lk; 102 Pedlar St; r Rs 1500-2500) This tastefully restored Dutch house has a stylish sitting area. There are four hot-water rooms, two of which have balconies and sea views. The guesthouse is popular with nongovernmental organisation (NGO) workers, and Mrs Khalid's meals get good reviews.

Ocean View Guest House (☎ 224 2717; 80 Lighthouse St; r from Rs 2800; ✷) Two of the six comfortable and modern rooms here have views over the ramparts. The cheapest are fan only. There's a fine patio for relaxing. The guesthouse is entered from Rampart St.

THE AUTHOR'S CHOICE

Galle Fort Hotel (☎ 223 2870; www.gallefort hotel.com; 28 Church St; r US$150-250; ✷ ▢ ▨) Christopher Ong and Karl Steinberg have transformed a derelict 17th-century Dutch merchant's house into one of the finest boutique hotels in Sri Lanka. The 14 rooms are all different, with each room's design reflecting the part of the vast L-shaped structure it occupies. Some have two levels, others stretch across entire floors, and all are very comfortable. Linens are exquisite and there are antiques everywhere. What you won't find are distractions like TVs – rather, you can enjoy the large courtyard pool and the hospitality of the accommodating owners and smooth-as-silk staff. The restaurant serves excellent food and the bar is a stylish meeting place. The hotel also rents out several luxurious villas and has its own spa.

Top End

The Fort is regaining some of the upmarket cachet it enjoyed during the colonial era.

Fort Printers (☎ 224 7977; www.thefortprinters .com; 39 Pedlar St; ste US$200-250; ✷ ▢ ▨) This 18th-century mansion was once used by printers, and you can still see the enormous wooden beams used to support the presses. There are five large suites here, each with an enormous tub and open bathroom. Luxuries include satellite TV, and vast and stylish public spaces.

Amangalla (☎ 223 3388; www.amanresorts.com; cnr Middle & Church Sts; r US$450-650; ✷ ▢ ▨) There's nary a backpacker here now, although they once roamed the halls of the grand old New Oriental Hotel. The Amanresorts group has massively restored and rebuilt the property, paying homage to its 19th-century status as one of the most luxurious hotels in Asia. Several old rooms have been combined into each of the 27 large suites, which have traditional décor accented by period fittings. New areas past the gardens hold a huge pool and spa. Service is top end as well and, even if the hotel is not in your budget, you may at least want to hang out in the lobby for a drink.

OUT OF TOWN
Midrange

Lady Hill (☎ 224 4322; www.ladyhillsl.com; 29 Upper Dickson Rd; r from US$60; ✷ ▨) This excellent-value hotel combines a 19th-century vicarage with good rooms and a modern wing of 12 spotless rooms with balconies and sweeping views of Galle. Situated in the quiet hills above the new town, five minutes away by three-wheeler, it's a cool, shaded and airy place. There's also a rooftop bar-restaurant, and all rooms include satellite TV and fridge.

Closenberg Hotel (☎ 222 4313; www.closenburg hotel.com; 11 Closenberg Rd; r incl breakfast US$50-125; ✷) Built as a 19th-century P&O captain's residence in the heyday of British mercantile supremacy, this lovely bougainvillea-bedecked hotel, east of the centre, sits out on a promontory with views over Galle beach and the Fort. Four rooms in the original building are filled with antiques and are a real step back in time, while the 16 rooms in a modern wing have balconies overlooking the beach. Breakfast is served on the wide, shady veranda.

Top End

Sun House (☎ 222 2624; www.thesunhouse.com; 18 Upper Dickson Rd; r from US$150; ✿ 🖳) This gracious old villa, built in the 1860s by a Scottish spice merchant, has been renovated with superb taste and attention to detail. Located on the shady hill above the new town, the hotel has wonderful views towards the Fort on one side and the port on the other. There's a large, well-kept garden that's popular with hummingbirds. The food is excellent, and so is the hospitality.

Dutch House (Doornberg; ☎ 438 0275; www.thesunhouse.com/doornberg.html; 23 Upper Dickson Rd; ste US$350; ✿ 🖳) A former residence of a Dutch admiral, this place was built in 1712 and has been beautifully restored with colonial furniture. The four suites each have a private garden, Fort views, a bathtub and a romantic net-covered four-poster bed. There's a pool, a croquet green, garden dining and more. Owned by the same people as Sun House (who also manage lovely Taprobane Island – see p144), Dutch House sits on the same shady hill as its sibling property.

Lighthouse Hotel (☎ 222 3744; www.jetwinghotels.com; Galle Rd; r US$230-350; ✿ 🖳) Designed by Geoffrey Bawa, this 63-room resort has a prime position on the seafront, 2km from town on the Colombo side. It beautifully blends Dutch colonial style with modern design. Check out the vast staircase sculpture *The Portuguese Arriving in Ceylon under a Cloud*, which features a Nero-like king at the top. The bar is very attractive, and the restaurant has great views.

Eating & Drinking

Many of the places to stay in Galle have good places to eat. As the scene heats up in the Fort, expect the options there to multiply. Nightlife remains very subdued.

FORT

Galle Fort Hotel (☎ 223 2870; 28 Church St; meals from US$10) The restaurant at this hotel (p135) serves superb Asian fusion cuisine at tables set along the deep inner veranda. The dinner menu changes nightly. At other times there are baked goods, classic breakfast dishes, salads and sandwiches. The bar, overlooking Church St, feels like a colonial retreat. It's popular with the expat community.

Pedlar's Inn Cafe (☎ 077 314 1477; 92 Pedlar St; meals Rs 120-220) A groovy little place in an old colonial house. Shakes, coffees and sandwiches can be enjoyed at long tables that are good for lounging.

Anura's Restaurant (☎ 222 4354; 9 Lighthouse St; mains Rs 220-300) This friendly, family-run hang-out serves local food and pizza from a tiny kitchen sheltered by beads.

Young Men's Buddhist Association (YMBA; Lighthouse St; meals Rs 50-100; ✆ lunch) Housed in another mouldering colonial gem of a building, the YMBA is a local social club that has a wonderful café hidden away on the main floor. The superb curries are served at communal tables.

Mrs Khalid's Guest House (Huize Bruisen de Zee; ☎ 223 4907; 102 Pedlar St; meals from Rs 300; ✆ dinner) Mrs Khalid's meals get the thumbs up from travellers; she'll cook Persian and Moroccan food as well as rice, curry and other local treats. Located at the guesthouse (p135), this restaurant does not permit alcohol. You must book in advance.

Rampart Hotel (☎ 074 380103; 31 Rampart St; mains from Rs 300) This ancient place has an ornately carved wooden staircase that would make redevelopers drool. But you won't drool over the long menu of dull Chinese, local and Western fare served in the cavernous dining room on the 2nd floor. Rather, come here for a drink and the amazing sunset views.

NEW TOWN

Galleria Pub & Restaurant (☎ 438 5555; 26 P&J City, Gamini Mawatha; meals Rs 200-400) Locals and travellers are attracted to this top-floor restaurant overlooking the cricket stadium and Fort. Pizza, pasta and sandwiches are the main items on the menu. You can enjoy your drinks under the air-con breeze inside or under the stars outside. On weekends there's music.

South Ceylon Bakery (☎ 223 4500; 6 Gamini Mawatha; mains Rs 50-200) Opposite the bus station, this open-air place serves casual fare in a tidy setting. The chicken soup is balm for the soul and there are many other fresh items on display.

New Chinese (☎ 222 3091; 14 Havelock Pl; mains Rs 120-250) A budget stand-by by the train tracks, this has very reasonable and filling Western, Chinese and Sri Lankan food.

Cargills Food City (☎ 223 3212; 3rd fl, 26 P&J City, Gamini Mawatha) This is a good spot to stock up on supplies for your journey through the South.

OUT OF TOWN

Lady Hill (☎ 224 4322; 29 Upper Dickson Rd; meals from Rs 600; ⏱ lunch & dinner) This charming hotel (p135) serves meals in the old vicarage, or up on the roof with its panoramic views. The food's also worth a second look.

Lighthouse Hotel (☎ 222 3744; Galle Rd; mains from US$8) The Cinnamon Room restaurant at this resort (opposite) smells just like its namesake spice. It serves elaborate versions of local specialities in a stunning room with views of the surf crashing on the rocks. Book ahead.

Shopping

Galle's history makes it a natural spot for antique shopping, and you'll find several places inside the Fort. Besides the requisite gem shops, there's a growing number of boutique shops and galleries.

Olanda (☎ 223 4398; 30 Leyn Baan St) Dutch-period furniture and reproductions, including carved window and door lintels, are among the treasures you'll find here. Brass door hinges, Buddhist and Hindu statues, and ceramic door knobs (from Rs 150) will be easier to take home.

Laksana (30 Hospital St) Another place with a good selection of antiques and art works.

Elephant Walk (30 Church St) Fragrant spices and potions, fine paper goods and high-end collectable art works make this gem of a shop a browser's treat.

Shoba Display Gallery (☎ 222 4351; 67 Pedlar St) Handcrafted art works and other fine items – 80% made right in the shop – are the specialities here. It's a serene and beautiful place.

Suthuvili Gallery (Pedlar St) This small shop has simple displays of elaborate and beautiful polychromatic masks.

Ibrahim Jewelry (☎ 223 4253; Church St) A recommended jeweller that is several cuts above (ahem) the omnipresent gemstone vendors.

Kanthisiri (☎ 223 4361; 19-23 Main St) This is a huge and bustling fabric vendor. The cottons are top quality and come in a dizzying array of patterns. Six metres of fine silk is a mere Rs 3500 and, best of all, prices are fixed.

Thowfeek (☎ 238 4002; 108-110 Main St) Exceptionally cheap prices on name-brand clothes. The store is above a vendor selling cheap kitchenware.

South Ceylon Industrial Agency & Handicraft Factories (SCIA; ☎ 223 4304; 73A Kandewatta Rd) This place employs traditional craftspeople from villages that specialise in the various handicrafts. You can watch jewellery, leatherwork, batik, lace and machine embroidery being created. And yes, gemstones are polished. Prices are negotiable. A three-wheeler from the station costs about Rs 100.

Look for the **Dutch Market** (Main St), which sells Galle's freshest fruits and vegetables under a 300-year-old columned roof. There are other fresh food markets along Main St, as well as a busy row of shops, many selling excellent merchandise at dirt-cheap prices. The entire area is worth a wander and a browse.

Getting There & Around

There are plenty of buses linking the towns along the coastal road. They leave from the bus station in the centre of Galle, opposite the cricket stadium. Major destinations include Colombo (regular/air-con Rs 63/130, three hours), Hikkaduwa (Rs 17, 30 minutes), Unawatuna (Rs 10, 10 minutes) and Matara (Rs 26, one hour).

There are express passenger trains to Colombo's Maradana station (2nd/3rd class Rs 108/58, three hours) from the town's vaguely art deco train station. Local trains serve Hikkaduwa (2nd/3rd class Rs 19/10, 30 minutes) and Matara (2nd/3rd class Rs 42/23, one to 1½ hours). There's a daily express to Kandy (2nd/3rd class Rs 217/115, 6½ hours).

A three-wheeler between Galle and anywhere in Unawatuna costs about Rs 200 to 250.

Although you won't need one for the Fort, a three-wheeler eases covering distances in the heat of the day, and makes it simple to navigate the town and nearby sights. At your accommodation arrange for one with an English-speaking driver or find your own (well, they'll find you). Expect to pay Rs 350 to 400 per hour – negotiable, of course.

AROUND GALLE

Huge and glistening, the **Peace Pagoda** was the gift of a Japanese Buddhist monk in 2005. It can be seen on a precipice at the east end of the bay. Take the first turn after the water ends as you drive east and follow a tree-lined track for about 1km. Along the way, you can visit isolated **Jungle Beach**, which can be reached down a steep path that begins by a huge tree (see Map p139).

The road heading north passes the **Kottawa Conservation Forest**, a 14-hectare wet evergreen forest about 15km northeast of Galle. There are walking tracks in the forest, but first get permission from the forest department office near the gate. Wear good walking shoes and trousers: the leeches are ferocious. Trees are identified with their botanical names, making this a good opportunity to get to know your Sri Lankan flora. In the small-sized park is a swimming spot fed by a waterfall.

On the way to the forest you can stop at **Walahanduwa Tea Factory** (☎ 438 1856; admission Rs 200; ☺ 7am-5pm Mon-Sat), a huge government-run complex that reeks of its produce. Closer to the park you'll find yet more tea factories tucked away in the hills. Some offer tastings.

About 10km east of Kottawa the 10m-high seated Buddha at **Kaduruduwa Temple** (donation Rs 100) rises above the surrounding paddy fields.

Just 4km inland from Unawatuna the **Yatagala Raja Maha Viharaya** (donation Rs 100) is a quiet rock temple with a 9m reclining Buddha. The mural-covered walls are painted in the typical style of the Kandyan period. The site is reached by almost 100 steps; monks have been living here for at least 1500 years.

UNAWATUNA
☎ 091
Lying behind a crescent of beach lapped by turquoise waters, Unawatuna's setting is so perfect it could be a cliché. Easily the most popular beach town in the South, Unawatuna doesn't offer the same opportunities for surfing or diving as other parts of the coast but the waves are good for swimming and the sands are clean and white.

Unawatuna has a classic mellow traveller vibe and pretty much every bit of development is aimed at the mostly young visitors who flock here. With the coast road a kilometre away, Unawatuna isn't plagued by the same kinds of traffic irritations found at many other beach towns. It's quiet, which only adds to the allure. At night people wander the beach, sipping cold beers at the many simple beachside cafés.

In late 2004, however, this idyllic scene turned horrible. The tsunami caused major damage, washing away many of the guesthouses and killing hundreds. Thanks to generous donations from foreigners who had vacationed here, as well as the efforts of teams of foreign volunteers, who were drawn by Unawatuna's natural allures, reconstruction happened faster here than any other place in Sri Lanka.

Unfortunately, the calamity was not turned into an opportunity to right some of the previous excesses of development. Business owners ignored plans for a setback from the water and rebuilt their places right on the sand. Some guesthouses sit on the high-tide mark. This, coupled with an unsightly pile of rocks dumped in the middle of the beach, detracts from the area's natural beauty.

Orientation & Information
Unawatuna is mostly strung along small Wella Dewala Rd and its tributaries, which lead off the main Galle–Matara coast road. Formal names for these little tracks are not commonly used.

For most goods and services you'll have to make the short trip to Galle, as there are only a couple of rudimentary huts selling bottled water and crisps. Many places offer Internet access; **Full Moon Resort** (☎ 223 3091; ☺ 9am-midnight) has the fastest connections in town (Rs 4 per minute).

Sights & Activities
Most people spend a lot of their time lying around the beach or slouching in cafés. To actually see something requires activity.

WATER SPORTS
Unawatuna has active surf much of the year, making body-surfing a popular – and cheap – activity. All the regular cautions about rip tides and suchlike apply.

You can hire snorkelling equipment from some of the beachfront places (or borrow it from guesthouses) to explore a small reef that's a short distance from the west end of the beach.

There are several interesting wreck dives around Unawatuna, as well as reef and cave diving. The wreck dives include the *Lord Nelson*, a cargo ship wrecked about 10 years ago, which has a 15m-long cabin to explore. The 33m-long *Rangoon* is one hour south of Unawatuna. The following places run diving courses and trips.

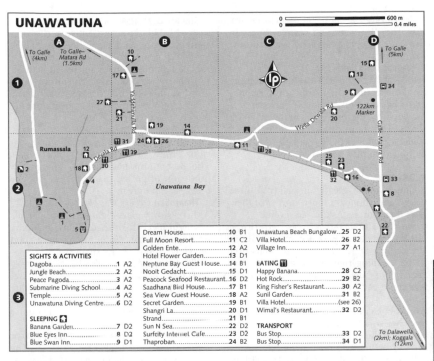

UNAWATUNA

SIGHTS & ACTIVITIES
Dagoba.................................1 A2
Jungle Beach.......................2 A2
Peace Pagoda......................3 A2
Submarine Diving School.....4 A2
Temple................................5 A2
Unawatuna Diving Centre....6 D2

SLEEPING
Banana Garden....................7 D2
Blue Eyes Inn.......................8 D2
Blue Swan Inn......................9 D1

Dream House........................10 B1
Full Moon Resort..................11 C2
Golden Ente.........................12 A2
Hotel Flower Garden.............13 D1
Neptune Bay Guest House....14 B1
Nooit Gedacht.....................15 D1
Peacock Seafood Restaurant..16 D2
Saadhana Bird House...........17 B1
Sea View Guest House..........18 A2
Secret Garden......................19 B1
Shangri La............................20 D1
Strand..................................21 B1
Sun N Sea............................22 D2
Surfcity Internet Cafe...........23 D2
Thaproban............................24 B2

Unawatuna Beach Bungalow...25 D2
Villa Hotel.............................26 B2
Village Inn.............................27 A1

EATING
Happy Banana.......................28 C2
Hot Rock...............................29 B2
King Fisher's Restaurant.........30 A2
Sunil Garden.........................31 B2
Villa Hotel.......................(see 26)
Wimal's Restaurant...............32 D2

TRANSPORT
Bus Stop...............................33 D2
Bus Stop...............................34 D1

Submarine Diving School (☎ 0777 196753) Rents out snorkelling gear for Rs 150 per hour or Rs 700 per day, and offers tours from Rs 2000. A Professional Association of Diving Instructors' (PADI) Open Water course costs US$300, while one dive costs US$30. A picture on the wall shows the many family members lost to the tsunami.

Unawatuna Diving Centre (☎ 0777 903430; www .unawatunadiving.com) Runs PADI courses from €300. Also rents out equipment and offers single dives. It has a good café on the water.

WALKING

You can take some interesting walks over the rocks rising from the west end of the beach or up the hill behind Yaddehimulla Rd to catch views to the other side of the promontory. The rocky outcrop on the west end of the beach, **Rumassala**, is known for its protected medicinal herbs – legend has it that Hanuman dropped herbs carried from the Himalaya here. The temple right on the promontory is fenced off, but you can wander up to the **dagoba** (stupa) on top of the hill and on to the huge **Peace Pagoda** and isolated **Jungle Beach**; see p137 for more details.

Sleeping

Unawatuna is packed with budget places to stay. Modest midrange places are becoming more common; for top-end places and villas continue a bit east along the coast towards Koggala.

BUDGET

Stay a few metres away from the beach for big savings. Unless noted all the places below are cold-water only.

Peacock Seafood Restaurant (☎ 075 384998; r Rs 1000-1200) Right on the beach, this place has stunning views, making the six otherwise plain rooms good value.

Surfcity Internet Cafe (☎ 224 6305/6; www.surf city1.net; r Rs 1200-1800) There are nine rooms above the namesake café. Three have hot water and all have places to sit outside and relax, although views are limited.

Village Inn (☎ /fax 222 5375; r Rs 500-1000) This inn has an assortment of 13 rooms spread over three buildings. The picks of the bunch are the rooms with balconies or verandas. The owners have some harrowing tsunami stories and welcome guests gratefully.

THE SOUTH

Golden Ente (☎ 074 381228; Devala Rd; r Rs 700-1000) The nine neat and simple rooms in this three-storey block each have their own balcony or veranda. It's good value.

Saadhana Bird House (☎ 222 4953; birdhouse_una watuna@hotmail.com; r Rs 1000-1500) Located away from the beach, this family-run place has pretty basic rooms, although personality is provided by the bug-eyed Bratz character sheets. The room on the top floor, with a rooftop lawn and peekaboo bathroom, can be your own bird house.

MIDRANGE
Rooms can vary greatly in quality at these places, and some are more worthy of their rates than others. Ask to see several.

Sun N Sea (☎ 228 3200; muharam@sltnet.lk; r US$25-100; ✷) The most stylish accommodation in Unawatuna, Sun N Sea has 10 rooms in a simple building right above the water. The views across the bay are superb. Furnishings are in easy-on-the-eye beiges, while the furniture is easy-on-the-backside rattan. A remnant of a door is displayed in the lobby – the charismatic owner Muharam Perera clung to it during the tsunami. There's also a decent restaurant.

Nooit Gedacht (☎ 222 3449; nooitged@sltnet.lk; Galle-Matara Rd; r Rs 2000-3000; ✷ ▯ ▨) Set back from Galle–Matara Rd, this 1735 Dutch colonial mansion has lovely gardens and a small pool, as well as lots of antique furniture, heavy timber panelling and loads of character. A four-bed family apartment, costing Rs 6000, is large and airy. The hotel is affiliated with a Dutch archaeology organisation doing work in Galle harbour.

Full Moon Resort (☎ 223 3091; r Rs 1200-2400; ✷ ▯) Built so close to the beach that some rooms have water at the door, the Full Moon has a range of 19 rooms, including some with air-con. The manager, Andrea Quintarelli, became a celebrity in Italy after his story of surviving the tsunami became a media sensation. The resort has a good restaurant.

Shangri La (☎ 438 4252; www.shangrila.lk; r from Rs 1500; ▯) A large compound set among coconut palms, the ever-growing Shangri La has four rooms and four cabanas. The personable owners have created a delightful atmosphere that's popular with NGO workers and long-term visitors. There's a spa with flotation tanks, a good bar with a pool table, and a sun deck.

Strand (☎ 222 4358; www.lanka.net/strand; r Rs 1000-5000; ✷) This is an attractive early-20th-century house set in large gardens. There are five charming rooms, and an apartment, ideal for families, that's furnished with atmospheric colonial-style furniture. One unit has air-con; the 'Nest' (Rs 3000) has a wrap-around veranda and is the pick of the bunch. The owner is a hoot.

Blue Swan Inn (☎ /fax 222 4691; Wella Dewala Rd; r Rs 1500-2000; ✷) A large, modern and spacious family home with four nice rooms. The best room has air-con, though the profusion of potted plants means that the breezes aren't great.

Thaproban (☎ 438 1722; r Rs 2800-4500; ✷ ▯) A three-storey place right on the beach, this has eight nicely furnished rooms, including four with air-con. Some rooms have good sea views and there's a small spa.

Villa Hotel (☎ 224 7253; thevilla@slt.lk; r incl breakfast Rs 6300; ✷ ▯) A three-storey hotel, set almost in the surf. All rooms have satellite TV, large fridge, attractive wooden floors and comfy loungers. There's also a popular beachside restaurant.

Neptune Bay Guest House (☎ 223 4014; www.neptunebayhotel.com; r Rs 1500-4000; ✷ ▯ ▨) The most ambitious hotel in the heart of Unawatuna, this imposing three-storey block has 24 large rooms with balconies and an elevated pool with views of the surf. More-expensive rooms have satellite TV and air-con.

Hotel Flower Garden (☎ 222 5286; www.hotelflowergarden.com; Wella Dewala Rd; r Rs 1500-3000; ✷ ▨) There are lots of flowers growing in the gardens of this popular place, located 300m from the beach. It has 25 rooms spread among several cabanas; more money buys you more room. The pool is quite large.

Banana Garden (☎ 438 1089; www.banana-garden.com; r Rs 1800-5000; ✷) The 10 rooms here vary greatly in quality. The cheaper ones only have cold water, but some of these have truly stunning views across the bay. More-expensive rooms come with hot water and air-con.

Sea View Guest House (☎ 222 4376; www.seaview.slt.lk; r Rs 2000-5000; ✷) One of Unawatuna's longest-running guesthouses, this has 16 comfortable rooms spread over one- and two-storey buildings. The grounds are spacious and rooms have balconies or patios; some rooms have air-con. During the high season, rates include half-board.

Unawatuna Beach Bungalow (☎ 222 4327; una watunabeachbungalow@yahoo.com; r Rs 1100-3000; ⌘) This place has a garden and eight well-kept rooms with beach-facing balconies. The singles are good value, and the doubles come with air-con.

Secret Garden (☎ 472 1007; www.secretgardenvil la.lk; r US$36-84) Past a prominent sign, this pleasant, old-style place is really only semi-secret, although the garden is nice. It has four big bedrooms and two cute bungalows, and there's a domed meditation pagoda.

Dream House (☎ 438 1541; dreamhouse@libero.it; r incl breakfast US$50) A delightful Italian-run guesthouse that has four spacious rooms with colonial ambience, four-poster beds, private balconies and a profusion of pillows in a panoply of colours. It's well back from the beach and very private.

Blue Eyes Inn (☎ 438 0445; Galle-Matara Rd; r Rs 1500-2500) At the east end of the beach, Blue Eyes is very well run. It has six large rooms, and the apartment is good for families. The food is recommended.

Eating & Drinking

Almost all places to stay provide meals or have restaurants. The best way to choose from the many places on the beach may be to simply stroll around and see what looks good. Most places are good for a drink – see which ones are in favour when you're there. Just don't expect much past midnight.

Sun N Sea (☎ 228 3200; meals from Rs 500) The dining area at this hotel (opposite) looks across the bay. Meals are a few cuts above the norm and focus on salads and seafood. The bar is a good place for a G&T.

Happy Banana (☎ 223 2776; meals Rs 300-1000) A fairly elaborate beachfront restaurant with plenty of appeal. The menu consist of a long list of seafood treats, and meals are well prepared. Ready to move beyond Lion Lager? Champagne is Rs 3000.

Full Moon Resort (☎ 223 3091; meals Rs 250-800) Thanks to the Italian owners, the standard of pasta is high at this café, located on the sand in front of the resort (opposite). It's a good place to take a new friend for dinner.

Sunil Garden (☎ 0777 472441; meals Rs 200-500) Set back from the beach, the Garden is busily re-growing after the tsunami. Sunil is a delight and he sets a festive mood while cooking up seafood, pasta and more. On many nights he leads live music. This is *the* place for a beer.

King Fisher's Restaurant (meals Rs 250-1000) It doesn't get much more simple than this thatched-roof place, right on the sand. The seafood, however, is more complex, including some excellent lobster dishes.

Wimal's Restaurant (☎ 077 301 6655; mains Rs 200-400) A simple seafood and sandwich place with great banana smoothies. It has a great location right above the surf and sand.

Hot Rock (☎ 224 2685; meals Rs 250-350) A classic bare-bones beachside seafood restaurant with delightful owners.

Villa Hotel (☎ 224 7253; mains Rs 200-1000) The food at this hotel (opposite) is good, and there's plenty to choose from as the menu is long even by the we'll-cook-anything-you'll-pay-for standard. The only downside to the prime beachfront location is the unsightly fence. Perhaps suggest the hotel removes it.

Getting There & Away

Coming by bus from Galle (Rs 10, 10 minutes) you can get off at the small road that leads into town, or get off at the next stop, where the ocean meets the main road, and walk in along the beach. A three-wheeler to or from Galle costs Rs 200 to 250. A taxi from Unawatuna to Bandaranaike International Airport costs from Rs 3500 and can take up to five hours, depending on traffic through Colombo.

UNAWATUNA TO KOGGALA
☎ 091

Beyond Unawatuna the road runs close to the coast through Dalawella, Koggala and on to Ahangama and beyond. There are numerous beautiful stretches of beach and picturesque coves in this area, as well as a number of attractive, secluded places to stay (including many renowned villas).

Along this part of the coast you will see stilt fishermen if the tides are running right (often around 6am to 8.30am, and 4pm to 6pm). Each fisherman has a pole firmly embedded in the sea bottom, close to the shore. When the sea and fish are flowing in the right direction the fishermen perch on their poles and cast their lines. Stilt positions are passed down from father to son and are highly coveted. The fishermen expect payment if you photograph them.

THE SOUTH

Sights & Activities

Just before Koggala there's a **WWII airstrip**. Beside the airstrip a small road turns inland, past a **Free Trade Zone**. The large **Koggala Lake**, next to the road, is alive with birdlife and dotted with islands, one of which features a Buddhist temple that attracts many visitors on *poya* (full moon) days. You can take a catamaran ride on the lake for Rs 400 per person per hour.

A visit to the lake's **Ananda spice garden** (☎ 228 3805; 🕑 7am-7pm) will provide you with the chance to buy all manner of home remedies and to see how cinnamon is grown. The catamaran and spice garden are managed by the same people. The return trip (including waiting time) by three-wheeler from Unawatuna to the spice garden should cost Rs 500.

Near the beachside behemoth called Hotel Horizon and the 113km marker, west of Koggala, is the **Martin Wickramasinghe Folk Art Museum** (admission Rs 50; 🕑 9am-5pm), set back from the road. It includes the house where this respected Sinhalese author was born. The exhibits are interesting and well displayed, with information in English and Sinhala. Among them is a good section on dance (including costumes and instruments), puppets, *kolam* (masked dance-drama) masks, kitchen utensils and carriages (including one to be pulled by an elephant). The bookshop sells the author's works, many of which deal with local culture.

Just east of Koggala the **Kataluwa Purwarama temple** feels like the temple time forgot. Dating from the 13th century, it has some recently restored murals. A friendly monk will open the building and explain the murals, if you ask. Some of the Jataka tales (episodes from the Buddha's lives) painted here are said to be 200 years old. The turn-off to the temple is in Kataluwa – you'll see the signs on the inland side of the road. Continue a couple of kilometres inland and ask for directions.

Sleeping & Eating

Sri Gemunu Guest House (☎ 228 3202; www.sri-gemunu.com; r incl half-board Rs 3200-4400; 🍴) This slightly stylish place has 21 rooms in new and old two- and three-storey blocks. There's a pleasant garden and a small beach. Cheaper rooms are fan only, while more expensive ones have satellite TV and air-con.

Wijaya Beach Cottage (☎ 228 3610; lizinsrilanka@yahoo.co.uk; r incl breakfast Rs 1800-2200) A few hundred metres on from the Sri Gemunu, this place has 18 pleasant rooms and cabanas. Enjoy the sandy, palm tree–shaded garden, swim at the small beach or chill on the terrace with the friendly owners.

Apa Villa (☎ 438 1411; www.villa-srilanka.com; ste US$195-660; 🌀 🖥 🐾) This glamorous compound has seven luxurious suites in a spacious and relaxed complex of villas right on the beach. The design is minimalist yet also posh. The pool runs right out to the private beach, and the library is well-stocked with guidebooks, due to the owner's association with a Singapore publisher.

Some of the walled beachside compounds on the road east of Unawatuna are rental villas where you and your best friends can enjoy a luxurious holiday in chic surroundings with your own staff to serve you. Some are so large that you'll need a lot of best friends. **Villa-srilanka.com** (☎ 228 2372; www.villa-srilanka.com) is a Galle-based management company that represents many of the villas. Although not cheap, many can become reasonable deals with several couples.

Frequent buses stop along the main road.

AHANGAMA & MIDIGAMA

☎ 091

This is Sri Lanka's surfers' paradise, known for its powerful left break. For the best surfing in Ahangama, head straight out from Kabalana Beach Hotel; in Midigama, look for the breaks near the 139km marker. The whole area is popular with surfers as it's cheap to stay here and the breaks are never crowded. But apart from surfing, the area doesn't have wide appeal; the beaches can be pretty thin and there's no real concentration of places that appeal to travellers.

Note that the water covers lots of rocks, coral and other hazards. Also, besides a few guesthouses offering battered boards for rent (Rs 450 to 600 per day), there are no places selling surf gear or offering repairs – you'll have to go to Hikkaduwa.

One worthwhile stop on this stretch of coast is the **Sea Turtle Farm & Hatchery** (☎ 0777 836115; admission Rs 150; 🕑 7am-7pm), midway between the 128km and 129km posts, where you can see baby turtles that are ready for release into the ocean here. For a description of turtle hatcheries, see p121.

Sleeping & Eating

AHANGAMA

Many surfers stay in Ahangama and ride the waves in Midigama.

Ahangama Easy Beach (☎ 228 2028; easyb@sltnet .lk; r Rs 2100-3800; ✷) A Norwegian-run place close to a couple of surfing points, this has views of the beach, eight bright and beachy rooms, Italian coffee and a good restaurant. The best rooms are in cabanas with air-con. Snorkelling gear, boogie boards and surfboards may be rented.

Kabalana Beach Hotel (☎ 223 6365; www.kabal anahotel.com; s/d US$40/45; ✷ ✷) One of the best surf breaks is right in front of this attractive 23-room hotel. Antiques mix with amenities such as satellite TVs in the hotel's large rooms; ask for one with a view. There's not much beach but that makes it all the more easy to start paddling out on one of the rental boards.

Villa Gaetano (☎ 228 3968; vgaetano@sltnet.lk; r US$8-19; ✷ ✷) Just after the 137km post, this place is right on the beach. The rooms are large and the four rooms upstairs at the front have balconies and great views. Some rooms have air-con and hot water. Surfboards are available.

Surfers Dream (☎ 0777 551614; r Rs 1200) If a surfer dreams of a cheap, clean bed then this place, run by the owners of Villa Gaetano, is a dream come true. The house, set back from the road, has four basic rooms featuring surfing décor.

Hotel Club Lanka (☎ 228 3296; fax 228 3361; r US$35-45; ✷ ✷) On the beach, this no-frills resort has 32 simple but stylish rooms; eight have air-con, and most have ocean views. There's a large pool and grassy gardens, a nice beach and stilt fishermen out the front.

MIDIGAMA

There are a couple of cheap guesthouses at the prime surfing break at the 139km marker, but not much else. The tsunami washed much away.

Jayaniki Surf Dreams (☎ 0777 239955; r Rs 530) Seven rooms share bathrooms at this family-run joint right on the water. It is as basic as you can get. Rental surfboards are available.

Hot Tuna (☎ 228 3411; r with/without bathroom Rs 500/400) This is a friendly family home with slightly dark but reasonable rooms.

Villa Samsara (☎ 225 1144; members.aon.at/sam sara; r per person incl full board €77) At the 140km

marker, this is a walled country house. Austrian-owned, it has four spotless rooms furnished in colonial style. There's a large tranquil sitting area, and a palm-studded lawn that fronts the beach. Ring in advance as it's not set up for drop-ins.

Getting There & Away

There are frequent buses along the southern coastal road connecting Ahangama and Midigama with other towns between Galle and Matara, and points beyond. The bus from Galle costs Rs 15 to Midigama. Many Colombo–Matara trains stop at Ahangama. Only a few local trains stop at Midigama.

WELIGAMA
☎ 041

About 30km east of Galle, the town of Weligama (which means 'Sandy Village') has a fine sandy sweep of bay – just as its name suggests. It's a busy fishing town, and you could easily spend a day wandering around, getting a feel for local life. The commercial area is small but vibrant; the fish stalls are both smelly and interesting.

Close to the shore – so close you can walk out to it at low tide – is a tiny island known as Taprobane. It looks like an ideal artist's or writer's retreat, which indeed it once was: novelist Paul Bowles wrote *The Spider's House* here in the 1950s. Even better, the island was once owned by the French Count de Maunay-Talvande. You can stay here (p144).

The road divides to go through Weligama, with one branch running along the coast, and the other running parallel through the town centre, a short distance inland. To reach the centre from the coast road, turn inland 500m east of Taprobane. The bus and train stations are in the middle of town.

Sights & Activities

Scenic though the bay is, Weligama beach is a bit shabby and not geared for sunbathers. It's primarily a fishing village, with **catamarans** lining the western end of the bay. You can organise an hour-long ride in one – expect to pay Rs 2000 per catamaran – by approaching a fisherman along the beach. Fishermen will also take you out in motorboats to see sharks and dolphins. This four-hour trip costs about Rs 5000 per person, but that's highly negotiable.

Snorkelling at Weligama is good, or you can scuba dive. **Bavarian Divers** (☎ 225 2708; www.cbg.de/bavariandivers), in Bay Beach Hotel, runs PADI courses (US$350) as well as excursions such as wreck dives. These can include the sunken yacht that belonged to the shop's amiable owner.

Turning inland west of the centre takes you to **Kustaraja**, a large rock-carved figure in a peaceful small park. The statue, said to date from the 8th century, may represent a king who was mysteriously cured of leprosy, or it may represent Avalokitesvara, the most beloved of the Bodhisattvas (the divine beings who seek to help others reach enlightenment).

Weligama is known for its **lacework**, and stalls are located on the main road along the coast. You can spend anything from Rs 100 for a small lace doily to Rs 5000 for a large, finely worked tablecloth.

Sleeping & Eating

Taprobane Island (☎ in Galle 091-222 2624; www .taprobaneisland.com; island US$1000; 🖭) Your own island, and this one comes with a staff of six and an infinity swimming pool! There are five large bedrooms here, so five couples could bring the rate closer to earth (and that's before you bargain). Run by the same people who manage the posh Sun House in Galle, this is a fantasy property with stunning views, balconies and verandas galore, antiques and more. You shuttle to shore via boat, but most guests never leave (until check-out time that is).

Bay Beach Hotel (☎ 225 0201; www.baybeachhotel .com; r Rs 3800; 🖭 🖭) On the Galle end of the bay, this has an attractive swimming pool and extensive gardens. The 40 standard rooms are plain but have good views of the fishing boats out the front.

Weligama Bay Inn (☎ 225 0299; 247 New Matara Rd; r incl breakfast US$26-36; 🖭) This is a simple and modern place near Taprobane Island. It has a wide veranda and pleasant green gardens; some rooms have air-con and views across the busy road to the sea.

Samaru Beach House (☎ 225 1417; 544 New Matara Rd; r Rs 800-1200) Located at about the middle of the bay, this eight-room place is close to the beach. The better rooms have a veranda. Bikes and surfboards may be rented; the latter can be used right out the front.

Neptune Guest House (☎ 225 0803; r Rs 1500-4500; 🖭) There's a range of units at this attractive place right on the beach. Older units are fan only while newer rooms are in two-storey units with views. The bar-restaurant is a cut above average and has an elaborate nautical theme, complete with lots of brass and polished wood. Have a few cold ones and make believe you're a salty pirate.

Crystal Villa (☎ 225 0635; www.holidays-srilanka .com; Matara Rd; r US$50-60, bungalows US$60-70, all incl half-board; 🖭 🖭) This is a modern place facing the sea. Set on spacious grounds with a huge pool, it has four rooms and two bungalows with fairly basic furnishings.

Getting There & Away

There are frequent buses to Galle (Rs 15, one hour) and Matara (Rs 19, 30 minutes). Weligama is on the Colombo–Matara train line; destinations include Colombo (2nd/ 3rd class Rs 136/73, four hours), Galle (2nd/3rd class Rs 29/16, one hour) and Matara (2nd/3rd class Rs 40/18, 30 minutes).

MIRISSA
☎ 041

Sleepy Mirissa, 4km southeast of Weligama on the Matara road, has a headland dividing its small fishing harbour from a beautiful curve of sandy beach with calm, clear waters. It's a low-key, peaceful spot that was once the preserve of backpackers but is now becoming more popular as travellers seek out quieter alternatives to Unawatuna and Hikkaduwa. The tsunami caused much damage along the coast here.

Most of the places to stay are on the beach. You'll need to go to Matara for most services, although there are Internet and phone places, and small markets near the 149km marker.

Sights & Activities

The water at Mirissa is clear and excellent for snorkelling. The best stretch is at the west end of the bay, along the jagged coastline, where there are many fish. The south side of the bay yields flat-bottom coral and, sometimes, sea turtles. Surfing is also good at the west end of the bay. Ask your guesthouse or hotel if it has gear that you can rent.

The rocky outcrop to the east of the bay, Parrot Rock, is the perfect place to watch the sunset, and it's also a popular fishing spot.

There are pleasant walks around Mirissa. One heads up a steep series of steps from the main road to the small **Kandavahari temple**, while the headland is a good spot to view Weligama Bay. About 6km inland there's a **snake farm** with an Ayurvedic practitioner. Ask your guesthouse how to get there.

Some guesthouses organise boat trips on a lake that's about 2km inland.

Sleeping & Eating

Meals are available at all of these places. Unless noted, rooms only have cold water. Look for signs along the main road.

Villa Sea View (☎ 077 604 6653; r Rs 1000-1500) The seven rooms at this hillside place are pretty simple, but what separates them are the views. The Rs 1500 rooms have idyllic views over palm trees to the bay below (though note that some of these rooms bake in the morning sun). There's a veranda and a nice garden swing.

Calm Rest (☎ /fax 225 2546; Suranda Rd; r/cabanas incl breakfast Rs 1500/2500) The place is exactly as it's named. Four good-quality cabanas and seven rooms are set in a peaceful and immaculate garden about 300m from the beach. Fans are available on request.

Ocean Moon (☎ 225 2328; r/cabanas Rs 550/1100) A very simple place that has nine cabanas with verandas set on a lawn leading to the beach. The three rooms are inside the family home.

Mirissa Beach Inn (☎ 225 0410; beachinn@sltnet .lk; r Rs 900-1400) This inn has bungalows close to the beach, as well as rooms in a three-storey building – you can just about pick the coconuts from the balcony. The newer upstairs rooms are best.

Amarasinghe's (☎ 225 1204; chana7@sltnet.lk; r Rs 300-1500) This pleasant, lush spot is away from the guesthouse hub on the beach. There are 10 rooms; the cheapest share bathrooms. Three bungalows are spacious and comfortable and have fridges. Herbs are labelled in the garden and the meals are superb. It's signposted from the main road; a three-wheeler from the turn-off costs Rs 40.

Mount Garden (☎ 225 1079; r Rs 500-1400; ⚟ ▢) This superfriendly family home, set back from the beach, has 10 rooms; the better

ones have air-con and hot water. It's signposted on an inland road near the eastern end of Mirissa.

Giragala Village (☎ 225 0496; nissanka.g@lycosmail .com; r €17-20) Almost opposite the road heading to Mount Garden, this simple place has a stunning setting that fronts Parrot Rock. The 17 rooms (only some have hot water) look onto the large, palm tree–shaded grounds. Grab a hammock and enjoy the view.

Getting There & Away

The bus fare from Weligama is Rs 10; a three-wheeler costs Rs 200. From Matara the bus far is Rs 12; a three-wheeler costs Rs 300. If you're heading to Colombo it's better to catch a bus to Matara and change, as many buses will be full by the time they pass through Mirissa.

MATARA

☎ 041 / pop 44,000

Matara, 160km from Colombo, is a busy, sprawling commercial town. The main attractions are its ramparts and well-preserved Dutch fort. Beaches in Matara proper are nothing special, but the one in Polhena, 3km towards Colombo, is clean, white and inviting. Polhena has a good coral reef that you can snorkel to, and there's a surfing point. Swimming in the Nilwala Ganga (Nilwala River) is not recommended; crocodiles are active and hungry.

The tsunami caused much damage locally; Polhena was hit hard, as was the old town inside the ramparts.

Orientation & Information

Matara is bisected by the Nilwala Ganga. Shops are located along Anagarika Dharmapala Mawatha, and Old Tangalla and New Tangalla Rds.

Cargills Food City (☎ 222 9815) Near Bandaranayaka Mawatha, this place has traveller supplies and a pharmacy.
Commercial Bank (Station Rd) Has an international ATM.
Mighty Vision Computer Systems (☎ 222 0330; 171 Anagarika Dharmapala Mawatha; per hour Rs 180) Offers Internet facilities.
Post office (New Tangalla Rd) Near the bus station.
Sampath Bank (Anagarika Dharmapala Mawatha) Has an international ATM.
Vijitha Yapa Bookshop (25A 1/1 Anagarika Dharmapala Mawatha) Good selection of novels, magazines, maps and guidebooks.

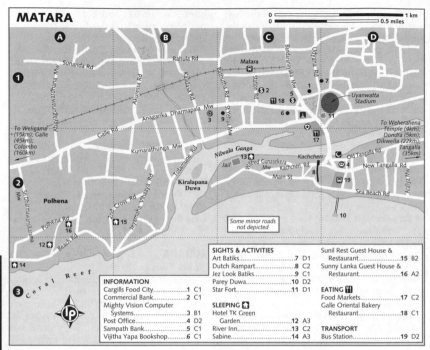

MATARA

Sights

Seeing all Matara has to offer shouldn't take more than an hour or two. A pedestrian bridge near the bus station leads to a small island, **Parey Dewa** (Rock in Water), which is home to a tiny Buddhist temple. Four monks live out here and you can stop by and say hello.

The smallish **Dutch rampart** occupies the promontory separating the Nilwala Ganga from the sea. Built in the 18th century to protect the VOC's *kachcheri* (administrative office), its structure is a little peculiar – it was originally meant to be a fort, but cost-cutting dictated otherwise. Inside the rampart are quiet vestiges of old Matara. Wander the few streets and you'll see the odd colonial gem – though its real charm is that it is quieter than modern Matara.

The **Star Fort** (🕙 10am-5pm), about 350m from the main rampart gate, was built by the Dutch to compensate for deficiencies in the rampart. However, it's so small it could only have protected a handful of bureaucrats. The date of construction (1765) is embossed over the main gate, along with the VOC company insignia and the coat of arms of the governor of the day. Look for the two carved lions that guard the entrance gates. You can also spot the slots that once secured the drawbridge beams.

The fort, built for 12 large cannons, is surrounded by a stagnant moat. Inside there's a dusty model replica of the site, a well, and the remains of the original quarters. There are also two eerie prisoners' quarters. For a tip, a guide will show you around the fort (this takes five minutes). The Star Fort was used as an administrative building and was never attacked. It was the last major defensive construction by the VOC in Sri Lanka.

Sleeping
MATARA

Matara has several places to stay, but most are not very nice.

River Inn (☎ 222 2215; 96/1 Wilfred Gunasekera Mawatha; s/d from Rs 440/660) There are eight tidy cold-water rooms in this three-storey building in the old town. Rooms upstairs have river views. It's peaceful and shady, and you'd never know you were next to the city jail.

POLHENA

Many travellers stay in Polhena, about 3km southwest of the centre. Most places serve meals and have cold water and fans. Note that the area is a warren of small tracks, so you may need to ask for directions. A three-wheeler from Matara costs Rs 200.

Sabine (☎ 222 7951; Beach Rd; r Rs 500) In a prime spot right at the surf, this small place has three rooms in bungalows, as well as hammocks and cheap eats. The charmer of an owner organises snorkelling tours and other trips.

Hotel TK Green Garden (☎ 222 2603; 116/1 Beach Rd; s/d from Rs 660/990) This hotel has 11 neat and tidy rooms and a large grassy garden. Rooms in the two-storey block have balconies or patios.

Sunny Lanka Guest House & Restaurant (☎ 222 3504; 93 Polhena Rd; s/d Rs 400/440) This is a friendly, relaxed place set in small compound. The six rooms are basic and clean. You can rent scuba-diving and snorkelling gear, as well as bicycles.

Sunil Rest Guest House & Restaurant (☎ 222 1983; 16/3A Second Cross Rd; r Rs 400-1000) The delightful family running this place has extended its empire over several buildings. Cheaper rooms are in the buildings (one quite tall!) set back from the beach down a track. Two other buildings are right at the surf. You can organise diving trips and gear rental here.

Eating

Just north of the bridge on the main road you'll see food markets and several fruit vendors with gorgeous displays of produce. Otherwise, dining choices are limited to some simple joints along the main road.

Galle Oriental Bakery Restaurant (41 Anagarika Dharmapala Mawatha; mains from Rs 50) The best option in the centre is a classic old place with a carved wooden interior and display cases bulging with baked and savoury treats. The soups and curries are good.

Shopping

Matara has two places that are a dream come true for anyone interested in batik. **Jez Look Batiks** (☎ 222 2142; 12 St Yehiya Mawatha) has large displays and offers lessons. **Art Batiks** (☎ 222 4488; 58/6 Udyana Rd) is run by an older couple who have dedicated a good part of their house to batik displays. Both places sell fabric at good prices.

Getting There & Away

BUS

The Matara bus station is a vast multilevel place. Look for tiny destination signs over the various queuing pens. As Matara is a regional transport hub, service is frequent in all directions. The following are some of the major destinations.

Amapara Rs 168, eight hours.
Badulla Rs 135, 5½ hours.
Colombo Regular/air-con Rs 84/170, four to five hours.
Galle Rs 26, two hours.
Ratnapura Rs 105, 4½ hours.
Tangalla Rs 23, 1½ to two hours.

TRAIN

Matara's **train station** (☎ 222 2271) is the end of the coastal railway line. Destinations include Galle (2nd/3rd class Rs 42/23, one to 1½ hours) and Colombo (1st/2nd/3rd class Rs 270/148/79, four hours), as well as Vavuniya (for Anuradhapura; 2nd/3rd class Rs 372/194, 10 hours) and Kandy (2nd/3rd class Rs 255/135, seven hours).

MATARA TO TANGALLA

There are several other places of interest just off the 35km of road from Matara to Tangalla, including two superb examples of what one visitor labelled 'neo-Buddhist kitsch'. Another impressive sight is the Ruhuna University campus at Meddawatte, on the main road a few kilometres east of Matara.

Overall, this stretch of road is in good shape, and verdant inland views alternate with stretches of coast. Dikwella is a small market town midway along the route.

Sights & Activities

WEHERAHENA TEMPLE

Just as you leave the outskirts of Matara, a turn inland will take you to this gaudy **temple** (admission by donation), where an artificial cave is decorated with about 200 comic-book-like scenes from the Buddha's life. There's also a huge Buddha statue.

At the time of the late November or early December *poya*, a *perahera* (procession) of dancers and elephants is held at the temple to celebrate the anniversary of its founding. Foreigners should pay Rs 1000 to 1500 for tickets.

You can get here from Matara on bus 349; a three-wheeler will charge Rs 300 from Matara's bus station.

THE SOUTH

DONDRA

About 5km southeast of Matara you come to the town of Dondra. Travel south from the main road for 1.2km and you'll reach the lighthouse at the southernmost point of Sri Lanka. There are good views from here, and a humdrum café nearby.

Buses from Matara will drop you in the centre of Dondra. From here you can three-wheel it or walk to the lighthouse.

WEWURUKANNALA VIHARA

If the Weherahena Temple is 'Marvel Comics meets Lord Buddha', then here it's Walt Disney who runs into him. At the town of Dikwella, 22km from Matara, a road turns inland towards Beliatta. About 1.5km along you come to a 50m-high seated Buddha figure – the largest in Sri Lanka.

The **temple** (admission Rs 50) has three parts. The oldest is about 250 years old but is of no particular interest. The next part, a real hall of horrors, has life-sized models of demons and sinners shown in gory detail. Punishments include being dunked in boiling cauldrons, sawn in half, disembowelled and so on. Finally there's the gigantic seated figure, which was constructed in the 1960s. As if to prove that it really is as high as an eight-storey building, what should be right behind it but an eight-storey building? You can climb up inside and peer right into the Buddha's head. The walls of the backing building have been painted with hundreds of scenes of events in the Buddha's lives. There's also an interesting clock in the adjoining building, made by a prisoner over 70 years ago.

Puja (offerings or prayers) is held every morning and evening. There's usually a resident monk here to show you around. Tips are appreciated.

You can reach the temple on any Matara–Tangalla bus that goes via Beliatta. The fare from either town is Rs 15.

HO-O-MANIYA BLOWHOLE

About 6km northeast of Dikwella, near the 186km post, a road heads off for 1km to the (sometimes) spectacular Ho-o-maniya blowhole. During the southwest monsoon (June is the best time) high seas can force water 23m up through a natural chimney in the rocks, then up to 18m in the air. At other times the blowhole is disappointing.

Sleeping & Eating

There are places to stay in all categories scattered along this stretch of coast. Some are quite nice, and are isolated from the main road. Look for signs and watch the kilometre markers as you go; the following places are listed in the order you will reach them when travelling to Tangalla.

Dickwella Village Resort (☎ 041-225 5271; www.dickwellavillage.net; r incl half-board US$70-120; ✕ 🖳 ⚑) A spectacularly sited resort on a headland on the Matara side of Dikwella. The 67 comfortably stylish rooms have been entirely rebuilt since the tsunami and feature terraces and stunning sea views. This place has buckets more personality than many large resorts – there's even a candle-lit guitar pavilion and lots of spa and healing services. It's near the 178km marker.

Claughton (☎ 041-225 5087; www.srilankayellowpages.com/claughton; r incl half-board US$90-120; ✕ 🖳 ⚑) This beautiful villa sits on a knoll and has a distinctly Mediterranean flavour. The garden runs down to a secluded beach and there's a fine swimming pool with sweeping views. The décor combines black and white, which contrasts nicely with the lush foliage and azure waters beyond. One of the three rooms has air-con, and the bathrooms are large with great tubs. You can rent out the entire property. The turn-off is 500m east of the 184km marker.

Nugaya Restaurant (☎ 041-225 5087; meals Rs 150-500) Down the hill a little from the Claughton and owned by the same people, this restaurant has good views and serves well-prepared seafood dishes.

Kadolana Beach Resort (☎ 041-2256140; r Rs 2000-3300; ✕) The eight large rooms at this mellow place are right on the beach. Views from the two-storey block are great, with the Ho-o-maniya blowhole in the distance. There's a small café. The turn-off is the same as for Claughton.

Manahara Beach Cottage & Cabanas (☎/fax 047-224 0585; r incl half-board US$35-45; ✕ ⚑) Just west of the 189km post and about 6km west of Tangalla, this has 10 spacious cabanas and rooms. There's also a large leafy garden, a big pool and beach frontage. It's a quiet spot and makes a good getaway.

Surya Garden (☎ 0777 147818; srilankas@tiscalinet .it; r €30-35) Sri Lankan charm meats Italian flair at this personable little place, set 100m back from the beach. The three cabanas have large, open bathrooms with plants, hot water and large sinks. Not surprisingly, the menu features a lot of very tasty pastas. The turn-off is at the 189km marker.

Eva Lanka (☎ 047-224 0940; www.eva.lk; s/d chalets incl half-board US$120/132; ✷ 🖭 🕿) This Italian-owned hotel has 29 stylish rooms and chalets in a beautiful setting on the beach. There are three swimming pools throughout the lush multilevel garden, a water slide, sports, games and a restaurant, which includes a pizzeria. There are elaborate shell mosaics made by the owner's mother throughout the property, and the hotel is wheelchair-friendly. The turn-off to the steep entrance is at the 191km marker.

Amanwella (☎ 047-224 1333; www.amanresorts .com; ste from US$550; ✷ 🖭 🕿) Easily the most luxurious resort in Sri Lanka, the Amanwella opened in 2005. Each of the 30 suites has its own private pool and is comfortable to such an extent that you may need to be prised out on check-out day. The design is dramatic; the open-air bathrooms are all natural stone. All of the units have ocean views, and some are right on the beach. Service is superb, and the food and beverages are as you'd expect. The resort entrance is near the 193km marker.

TANGALLA
☎ 047
Situated 195km from Colombo, Tangalla (also spelt Tangalle, but usually pronounced *ten*-gol) is one of the nicest spots along the coast, particularly if you just want somewhere to relax and soak up the sun. The town itself is an easy-going place with some reminders of Dutch days.

From Tangalla the white sands of Medaketiya Beach stretch for more than 3km northeast. Heading southwest there is a whole series of smaller bays and beaches. From a distance it looks idyllic, but up close it is another story. Tangalla suffered grievously from the tsunami. Thousands died in the area and hundreds of homes were destroyed, especially going northeast from the Kirama Oya. Scores of oceanfront guesthouses (with owners, guests and staff) were washed away along Medaketiya Beach. Rebuilding has been very slow, although at some point more places to stay should reappear along this gorgeous beach. In the meantime, everybody has their own tale of loss.

Information
Shopping is fairly limited. The main post office is west of the Rest House and there is an agency post office opposite the main bus station. **Hatton National Bank** (Main Rd) has an international ATM. There are Internet and phone places on Main Rd near the bus station.

Sights & Activities
There are some reminders of the colonial era on the knoll just south of the centre. The shady **Rest House** was once home for the Dutch administrators. It's one of the oldest resthouses in the country, originally built (as a plate on the front steps indicates) in 1774. As you round the head, note the many large boats now permanently stranded high above the surf – this will give an idea of how far inland the tsunami came here.

Out by Matara Rd, a **pond** covered with lotus flowers offers a serene respite from development.

The bay just on the town side of Tangalla Bay Hotel is probably the most sheltered beach, although right beside the Rest House there is a tiny bay with a swimming area that is shallow and generally calm. There are some basic changing rooms on the grass, and it's popular with snorkellers. There is a picturesque and fairly secluded bay by Palm Paradise Cabanas, near the village of Goyambokka. Medaketiya Beach is beautiful but it drops off sharply and can have dangerous currents.

Sleeping
Most of the places to stay on the Matara side of Tangalla survived the 2004 tsunami, helped by their locations on hills and on protected bays. It will take several years for a new group of guesthouses to emerge along Medaketiya Beach, although a few places rebuilt fairly quickly.

MEDAKETIYA BEACH
Lagoon Paradise Beach Resort (☎ 224 2509; fax 224 2286; r Rs 1500-2500) Near the lagoon at the far end of the beach, 3km from town, this rebuilt place has 10 rooms and two cabanas done up in cheery shades of orange. Rooms have cold-water bathrooms. The friendly staff serves good food in the café. A three-wheeler from town costs Rs 100.

King Fisher (☎ 224 2472; r Rs 500-650) This is a colourful German-run place close to the

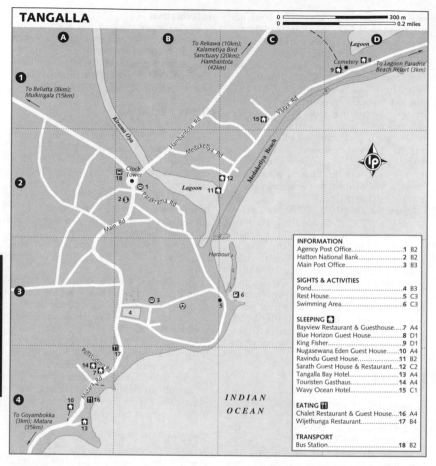

TANGALLA

To Rekawa (10km);
Kalametiya Bird
Sanctuary (20km);
Hambantota
(42km)

To Beliatta (8km);
Mulkirigala (15km)

To Lagoon Paradise
Beach Resort (3km)

To Goyambokka
(3km); Matara
(35km)

Harbour

INDIAN
OCEAN

INFORMATION
Agency Post Office..............................1 B2
Hatton National Bank.........................2 B2
Main Post Office...................................3 B3

SIGHTS & ACTIVITIES
Pond..4 B3
Rest House..5 C3
Swimming Area......................................6 C3

SLEEPING
Bayview Restaurant & Guesthouse.....7 A4
Blue Horizon Guest House..................8 D1
King Fisher..9 D1
Nugasewana Eden Guest House.......10 A4
Ravindu Guest House..........................11 B2
Sarath Guest House & Restaurant....12 C2
Tangalla Bay Hotel..............................13 A4
Touristen Gasthaus.............................14 A4
Wavy Ocean Hotel...............................15 C1

EATING
Chalet Restaurant & Guest House....16 A4
Wijethunga Restaurant......................17 B4

TRANSPORT
Bus Station...18 B2

beach. Its rooms are neat and the indoor-outdoor dining room has lovely views. Better rooms have their own cold-water bathrooms.

Wavy Ocean Hotel (☎ 224 2680; r Rs 700-1100) This hotel has a range of very simple rooms with their own bathrooms. The beach – and a permanently beached trawler – is right outside the door. The guys running the place have energy to spare.

Blue Horizon Guest House (☎ 224 0721; r Rs 1000-1500) The six cold-water rooms here are in a multilevel building across from the beach. There are elevated open-air common areas where you can have a snack or just hang.

Ravindu Guest House (☎ 567 0560; r Rs 500) There are five very simple rooms here. A

shrine to the owner's family – lost to the tsunami – is at the front.

Sarath Guest House & Restaurant (☎ 224 2630; r Rs 800) This is a lively family home with six clean, neat rooms and shared bathrooms.

TANGALLA

The following options are above the beach, just south of the centre.

Bayview Restaurant & Guesthouse (☎ 224 2431; 230 Matara Rd; r Rs 650-1200) With excellent views over the bay, this place has two rooms and a cabana. The young owner, Ruwan, runs a hopping café.

Nugasewana Eden Guest House (☎ 224 0389; www.nugasewana.com; Matara Rd; r from Rs 440, s/d with air-con Rs 1430/1650;) The former Tourist

Guest House is opposite the big Tangalla Bay Hotel. It has eight stylish rooms with hot water, including some with sea-facing balconies and air-con.

Touristen Gasthaus (☎ 224 0370; wkapila@sltnet .lk; 19 Pallikkudawa Rd; r Rs 1100-2500; ✕) This guesthouse has a leafy garden and six spotless rooms, including three with balconies facing the sea. One of the rooms has a kitchen; another has air-con.

Chalet Restaurant & Guest House (☎ 224 0452; Matara Rd; r Rs 800-1200) There are three simple rooms at this restaurant (right), each with a cold-water bathroom and postcard-ready views of the bay.

Tangalla Bay Hotel (☎ 224 0683; accountstbh@ sltnet.lk; r US$23-32; ✕ ☎) A 1970s monstrosity built to look like a boat (you can get lost for hours looking for the poop deck), it's kitsch and dated in an endearing kind of way. It certainly has a great location right on a promontory, and the service is good and the pool has a view. The 28 rooms vary in quality (all have hot water, some have air-con); ask to see several.

GOYAMBOKKA
About 3km towards Matara on the main road you'll come to a signposted turn-off at Goyambokka, and a road lined with several guesthouses. This is a quiet leafy area with a beach that feels private. You can ask any Matara-bound bus to drop you at the turn-off. A three-wheeler from Tangalla bus station costs Rs 150.

Rocky Point Beach Bungalows (☎ 224 0834; rockypointbeach@yahoo.com; r incl breakfast US$25-30) At the end of the road, this popular, relaxed spot has great views overlooking a small beach. The five rooms and three bungalows are in a large garden. There's a restaurant (with board games), and you can rent boogie boards.

Palm Paradise Cabanas (☎ 224 0338; www.palm paradisecabanas.net; s/d incl half-board €30/40; ☐) There are 22 lovely cabanas here, scattered around a secluded beachside palm grove. All have their own sitting area, breezy veranda and hot water. There's an open-air bar and a good restaurant. Bicycles can be rented here for Rs 200 per day.

Goyambokka Guest House (☎/fax 224 0838; r incl breakfast Rs 1000-1600) Further on from Palm Paradise Cabanas, this place has four small, spotless rooms with screens on the

windows. It's away from the beach, but there's a pretty garden and a small shared veranda.

Calm Garden Cabanas (☎ 224 0523; r incl breakfast Rs 1000-1600) This is a family-run affair, back from the beach. The three cabanas are pretty simple, and there's a large garden. It's about 200m up the track from the turn-off.

Eating
Just about all guesthouses serve food. The following places are central.

Bayview Guesthouse & Restaurant (☎ 224 2431; 230 Matara Rd; r Rs 650-1200) The energetic vibe at this guesthouse-café keeps the place packed out with travellers, NGO workers and others. It's the place in town for a beer.

Wijethunga Restaurant (Matara Rd; meals Rs 50-150) This is a local place with good rice and curry. It's just near the popular lookout spot on the Matara road.

Chalet Restaurant & Guest House (☎ 224 0452; Matara Rd; mains Rs 175-320) A popular lunch stop with an extensive seafood menu and great views across the bay (ignore Tangalla Bay Hotel). Omelettes, sandwiches and other casual fare are also available.

Further afield, try **Lagoon Paradise Beach Resort** (☎ 224 2509; fax 224 2286; mains Rs 200-800) and **Palm Paradise Cabanas** (☎ 224 0338; www .palmparadisecabanas.net; mains Rs 200-800).

Getting There & Away
Tangalla is serviced by bus; the following are some of the major destinations.
Colombo Regular/air-con Rs 104/210, six hours.
Galle Regular/air-con Rs 48/100, two hours.
Hambantota Rs 24, one hour.
Matara Rs 23, 1½ to two hours.
Tissamaharama Rs 54, three hours.

MULKIRIGALA
The rock temple at **Mulkirigala** (admission Rs 100; �)6am-6pm), about 16km northwest of Tangalla, has a little of Dambulla and Sigiriya about it. Steps lead up to a series of cleftlike caves in the huge rock. As with Dambulla, the caves shelter large reclining Buddhas, together with other, smaller, sitting and standing figures, and wall paintings. You can then continue on your barefoot way to a dagoba perched on top of the rock, where there are fine views over the surrounding country. There is a Buddhist school for young monks nearby.

THE SOUTH

Pali manuscripts found in the monastic library by a British official in 1826 were used for the first translation of the Mahavamsa (Great Chronicle), which unlocked Sri Lanka's early history for Europeans.

Mulkirigala can be reached by bus from Tangalla via either Beliatta or Wiraketiya (depending on the departures, it might be quicker to go via Wiraketiya than to wait for the Beliatta bus). A three-wheeler from Tangalla costs about Rs 600 for a return trip.

HAMBANTOTA
☎ 047 / pop 11,200
Travelling between Tangalla and Hambantota you move from a wet zone into a dry zone, which continues right across Yala National Park. Hambantota is a commercial town with little going for it, although there are some magnificent sweeps of beach both east and west of the town's small promontory. A large collection of outrigger fishing boats is often beached on the sands. The fish market near the bus station is interesting.

Hambantota's main claim to fame is that it was home to Leonard Woolf, the husband of Virginia Woolf, when he served as government agent from 1908 to 1911. He documented some of his experiences in *A Village in the Jungle*.

Hambantota has a large number of Malay Muslims, many of whom speak Malay as well as Tamil and Sinhala. A major industry is the production of salt by evaporating sea water from shallow saltpans. You will see these pans alongside the road on the east side of Hambantota as you turn inland from the coast.

The tsunami was hard on locals. Much of the area north of the centre was wiped clean, along with the area's minimal tourist infrastructure.

The **Hatton National Bank** (47 Wilmot St), about 200m up from the clock tower, has an international ATM. **Cargills Food City** (☎ 222 2267; Main Rd) has the usual travellers' supplies and a pharmacy.

Hambantota has a few touts angling to take travellers to Bundala or Yala National Parks. Ignore them as this is best arranged with your guesthouse in Tissamaharama.

Hambantota Rest House (☎ /fax 222 0299; r US$24-36; 🍽) is nicely situated on the promontory overlooking the town and beach, about 300m south of the bus station. The

rooms in the historic wing are slightly palatial, definitely musty and are certainly the pick of the bunch. The restaurant is the best eating choice locally. A three-wheeler from the centre costs Rs 30.

Oasis Hotel (☎ 222 0650; www.oasis-ayurveda.de; Sisilasagama; s/d US$60/70; 🍽 🌊) is a modern, well-run resort with 52 rooms. There's a large swimming pool and sloping gardens sheltered from the beach by dunes. Various meal plans are available and there's an on-site spa. It's about 7km along the main road before you reach Hambantota from Tangalla.

The bus station is by the fish market in the town centre. Destinations include Tangalla (Rs 24, one hour) and Tissamaharama (Rs 21, one hour).

BUNDALA NATIONAL PARK
Bundala is an important wetland **sanctuary** (adult/child US$8.40/4.20, plus per vehicle Rs 72, plus per group Rs 144) that has been recognised under the Ramsar Convention on Wetlands, but it has always been less visited than Yala. It shelters some 150 species of bird within its 62-sq-km area, with many birds journeying from Siberia and the Rann of Kutch in India to winter here, arriving between August and April. It's also a winter home to the greater flamingo, and up to 2000 have been recorded here at one time. At most times you can see wild peacocks crossing the road.

As well as sheltering a small population of elephants (between 25 and 60 depending on the season), Bundala provides sanctuary to civets, giant squirrels and crocodiles. Between October and January four of Sri Lanka's five species of marine turtle (olive ridley, green, leatherback and loggerhead) lay their eggs on the coast.

Bundala's lagoons, beaches, sand dunes and scrubby jungle stretch nearly 20km along a coastal strip, starting just east of Hambantota. The main road east of Hambantota passes along Bundala's northern boundary, but it was severely damaged by the tsunami, and access is difficult. On the road to Tissamaharama look for the parking area near the signposted entrance to the park. You will usually see some guides and drivers here; a four-hour, five-person 4WD trip costs a negotiable Rs 2500, plus the entry fees.

Between Hambantota and Tissa are a number of roadside stalls selling delicious curd (buffalo-milk yoghurt) and treacle.

TISSAMAHARAMA

☎ 047

Usually called Tissa, the busy town of Tissamaharama is surrounded by rice paddies that are dotted with ancient temples. Yala National Park is the main reason most visitors come to Tissa, so there are plenty of 'safari' touts lurking at guesthouses and bus stops, and everybody else trying to get their cut of the safari business.

Orientation

If you're coming via Hambantota or Wellawaya you'll pass the village of Deberawewa (look for the clock tower) about 2km before Tissa. Ignore the 'Tissamaharama' signs here and the accommodation touts who board buses and advise travellers to get off because 'this is Tissa'. Most places to stay are closer to the real Tissa, so go there.

Information

Nearly all the facilities are on Main Rd, where you'll find an agency post office. There's not much in the way of shopping but there are some useful services. **Hatton**

National Bank (Main Rd) and **Peoples Bank** (Main Rd) have international ATMs. Internet connections are slow but **Dhammika Communication** (☎ 223 9185; Main Rd; per min Rs 5) and **Sakura Communication** (☎ 223 7915; Main Rd; per min Rs 5) are friendly places for surfing and phone calls.

Sights

The **Tissa Wewa** (Tissa Tank), about 1.5km from the town centre, is thought to date from the 3rd century BC.

The large white restored **dagoba** between Tissa town centre and the *wewa* is believed to have been built by Kavantissa, a king of the kingdom of Ruhunu, which centred on Tissamaharama. The dagoba has a circumference of 165m and stands 55.8m high. It is thought to have held a sacred tooth relic and forehead bone relic. A small bookshop sells books on Buddhism.

Next to the dagoba is a **statue** of Queen Viharamahadevi. According to legend, Viharamahadevi was sent to sea by her father, King Devanampiya Tissa, as penance after he killed a monk. Unharmed, the daughter landed at Kirinda, about 10km south of

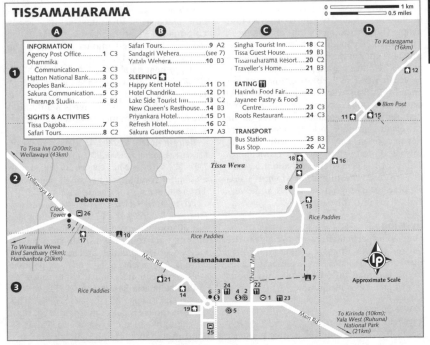

TISSAMAHARAMA

INFORMATION	
Agency Post Office...........1 C3	
Dhammika	
Communication..........2 C3	
Hatton National Bank....3 C3	
Peoples Bank.................4 C3	
Sakura Communication....5 C3	
Tharanga Studio.............6 B3	
SIGHTS & ACTIVITIES	
Tissa Dagoba.................7 C3	
Safari Tours...................8 C2	

Safari Tours.......................9 A2
Sandagiri Wehera.............(see 7)
Yatala Wehera.................10 D3

SLEEPING
Happy Kent Hotel..............11 D1
Hotel Chandrika................12 D1
Lake Side Tourist Inn.........13 C2
New Queen's Resthouse.....14 B3
Priyankara Hotel...............15 D1
Refresh Hotel...................16 D2
Sakura Guesthouse...........17 A3

Singha Tourist Inn............18 C2
Tissa Guest House............19 B3
Tissamaharama Resort......20 C2
Traveller's Home...............21 B3

EATING
Hasindu Food Fair............22 C3
Jayanee Pastry & Food
Centre.........................23 C3
Roots Restaurant..............24 C3

TRANSPORT
Bus Station......................25 B3
Bus Stop.........................26 A2

0 ————— 1 km
0 ————— 0.5 miles

To Kataragama (16km)

To Tissa Inn (200m); Wellawaya (43km)

Tissa Wewa

Deberawewa

Clock Tower

To Wirawila Wewa Bird Sanctuary (5km); Hambantota (20km)

Rice Paddies

Tissamaharama

Rice Paddies

Approximate Scale

To Kirinda (10km); Yala West (Ruhuna) National Park (21km)

8km Post

Rice Paddies

Vihara Mw

Main Rd

Wellawaya Rd

Tissa, and subsequently married Kavantissa. Their son, Dutugemunu, was the Sinhalese hero who liberated Anuradhapura from Indian invaders in the 2nd century BC.

The **Sandagiri Wehera**, an unrestored dagoba set behind the Tissa dagoba, is also credited to Kavantissa. A walk around the dagoba will give you insight into the construction of the great dagobas.

Next to the Tissa–Deberawewa road is **Yatala Wehera**, built 2300 years ago by King Yatala Tissa, who fled Anuradhapura after a palace plot and founded the Ruhunu kingdom. There's a small **museum** (admission free) next to the dagoba; its hours vary.

Tours

Tours of Yala National Park are easily arranged in Tissa. Perhaps too easily. Touts push safaris from the moment you arrive in Tissa. The easiest thing to do is to arrange a safari through your accommodation, as this gives you a bit more certainty that the guide will do a good job. Alternatively, you can go to one of the gatherings of safari touts at Tissa Wewa and at the clock tower, but this can be a bit of a carnival-like experience.

Generally expect to pay about Rs 2500 to 3000 for a half-day safari for up to four people (not including the raft of park fees). This will get you the services of a guide, who should also double as a driver. There's no need to hire both a guide and a driver, as you'll need to hire an animal tracker once in Yala anyway. Check out the 4WD before you book a safari; obviously avoid rust buckets, but also look for some of the newer and grander models, which feature elevated, open seats that help with spotting animals. Good drivers provide binoculars.

Expect to leave your hotel about 5.30am so as to catch the animals at dawn. It's also possible to arrange dusk safaris and overnight trips into the park.

Sleeping

There's no particular reason to be near the centre, so you might consider the pretty area around Tissa Wewa – the best places are on the road to Kataragama. Just about every place has a restaurant.

TOWN CENTRE

Traveller's Home (☎ 223 7958; supuncj@sltnet.lk; r Rs 350-1800; ✷) Surrounded by rice paddies,

this is just off Main Rd, about halfway between Tissa and Deberawewa. It's friendly, neat and basic. The seven varying rooms have features ranging from shared bath to posh air-con. There are free bicycles for guests, and a safari display.

New Queen's Resthouse (☎ 223 7264; s/d Rs 550/ 650, with air-con Rs 1000/1100; ✷) Off Main Rd, this is an eclectic building with a nice terrace and seven basic rooms, although the bidets lend continental flair. It's an easy walk from the bus station.

Tissa Guest House (☎ 223 7057; Molawatte Rd; r Rs 850) Found near the bus station, this is a pleasant family home, with four clean guest rooms and a colourful garden. Check in at the owner's photography shop, Tharanga Studio, on Main Rd near the bus station.

TISSA WEWA

Most of Tissa's accommodation is near the Tissa Wewa, about 1.5km from the centre of Tissa. It's easy enough to get into town by bus (Rs 10) or by three-wheeler (Rs 70) from this area.

Hotel Chandrika (☎ 223 7143; www.chandrikaho tels.com; Kataragama Rd; s/d Rs 1700/2100, with air-con Rs 2200/2600; ✷) This is a quiet and comfortable place with 20 rooms facing a lovely colonnaded veranda and a courtyard-style garden. There are rumours of a pool. The restaurant is a tad formal but good.

Happy Kent Hotel (☎ 223 7085; r Rs 1700-2700; ✷ ⌷) This growing place has 14 decent rooms (some with air-con) in cottages and a main building. The owner is helpful and the raised pool is a nice reward after a day's safari.

Refresh Hotel (☎ 223 7357; refresh@sri.lanka.net; Kataragama Rd; s/d Rs 1800/2200, with air-con Rs 2400/ 2800; ✷) The spot has five colourful, stylish and quiet rooms facing a small courtyard. The restaurant's food is delicious.

Priyankara Hotel (☎ 223 7206; priyankarahotel.com; Kataragama Rd; r US$29-40; ✷) This modern place has 30 rooms served by a copious number of staff. Each room has a small balcony with views over rice paddies, and some have satellite TV and fridge. The restaurant has a Western menu; it's popular with groups.

Tissamaharama Resort (☎ 223 7299; www.cey lonhotels.lk; Kataragama Rd; r US$44-64; ✷ ⌷) This old guesthouse is delightfully situated, right on the banks of the Tissa Wewa. It has 57 comfortable rooms (some with air-con) in a three-storey block, a pool (Rs 200 for non-guests) and a pleasant open-air restaurant and bar. This place is the number one choice for groups, so it pays to book ahead.

Singha Tourist Inn (☎ 223 7090; s/d Rs 500/850, with air-con Rs 1150/1550; ☒) A no-frills place with a palm-studded lawn reaching down to the tank's edge. It has 11 basic rooms (some are a bit dark).

Lake Side Tourist Inn (☎ 223 7216; s/d Rs 900/1200, with air-con Rs 1250/1650; ☒) This spot has views to the tank from some of its 24 rooms. The rooms have simple furniture but vary in quality, so check out a few. This place is quite popular with groups.

DEBERAWEWA

It's fairly relaxed at the west end of Tissa.

Tissa Inn (☎ 223 7233; tissainn@sltnet.lk; Wellawaya Rd; s/d Rs 850/950; ☒ ▢) Fifteen hundred metres from the Deberawewa clock tower, this has a touch of class for a very reasonable price. The newer rooms have French windows and a balcony, while the older rooms have a veranda. There are tables under the trees, and the guesthouse is popular with wedding parties.

Sakura Guesthouse (☎ 223 7198; s/d from Rs 400/600, cottages Rs 750) Near a creek, this spot is a friendly, traditional family home set in spacious, quiet grounds. There are three cold-water rooms plus two 'cottages' that sleep three. The family will pick you up (for free) from the bus station in Tissa or Debera-wewa. A three-wheeler from the Tissa bus station will cost Rs 100.

Eating

Refresh Hotel (☎ 223 7357; Kataragama Rd; mains Rs 200-450) The menu is down-to-earth but the preparation is stellar at this hotel's (opposite) restaurant. Curries, omelettes and sandwiches are presented with colour and flair. It does big business with nonguests and is a good place for a Lion Lager.

Jayanee Pastry & Food Centre (Main St; mains Rs 60-120) Run by a friendly young family, this small, simple place has a Rs 75 lunch buffet and very good rice and curry for dinner, as well as fresh juices.

Hasindu Food Fair (12 Vihara Mawatha; mains Rs 50-100) A dark and cool lunch spot in the centre of town, with tasty rice and curry.

Roots Restaurant (☎ 437 8755; mains Rs 60-250) Set a few metres off Main Rd, this very re-laxed open-air place serves rice and curry. It's a good spot to have a chat and down a Lion Lager.

Getting There & Away

The road from Hambantota is sealed but pretty rough. Few buses go directly to the Hill Country, and if you can't get one you'll need to change at Wirawila junction (Rs 11, 30 minutes) and/or at Wellawaya (Rs 44). There are no buses to Yala National Park. Other major bus destinations from Tissa include Colombo (regular/air-con Rs 138/210, nine hours), Hambantota (Rs 21, one hour) and Kataragama (Rs 18, one hour).

AROUND TISSAMAHARAMA
Wirawila Wewa Bird Sanctuary

Between the northern and southern turn-offs to Tissa, the Hambantota–Wellawaya road runs on a causeway across the large Wirawila Wewa. This extensive sheet of water forms the Wirawila Wewa Bird Sanctuary. The best time for bird-watching is early morning. See p62 for information on the bird species found in the area.

From Hambantota or Tissa you can get a bus to Wirawila junction on the south side of the tank and walk north; from Tissa you can also go to Pandegamu on the north side and walk south.

Kirinda

About 10km south of Tissa, Kirinda has a fine beach and a Buddhist shrine on the huge round rocks. Kirinda was used as a land base by Arthur Clarke's party when diving for the *Great Basses* wreck (see Clarke's *The Treasure of the Reef*). It can make an interesting pause on the way to or from Yala. The road here passes through savanna; it's flat and feels remote. A few cattle graze and dunes shimmer in the distance.

Suduweli (☎ 072-263 1059; r Rs 400, with bathroom from Rs 700, bungalows Rs 1000-1500) is on a peaceful farm with a shady garden. The bungalows' verandas look towards the paddy and lake. The friendly Sri Lankan–German couple and their dogs will share their home and local expertise (the dogs got bushes down!). There's a motorcycle and a bicycle available, and a 4WD for safaris into Yala.

There is a bus from Tissa to Kirinda every half-hour or so (Rs 10). A three-wheeler from Tissa costs about Rs 500.

YALA NATIONAL PARK

It's not Kenya, but Yala National Park (also known as Ruhunu) is a major draw in Sri Lanka for its opportunity to see herds of elephants, leopards and an array of other animals, including reptiles and birds. For many people, a safari here is an essential part of their visit to the island.

Information

The entrance fees for **Yala National Park** (adult/child US$14/7, plus per vehicle tracker fee Rs 120, service charge US$6, plus overall tax 15%; ⏱ 6am-6.30pm 16 Oct-31 Aug) are payable at the main office, which is near the entrance, some 21km from Tissa. There are a few displays here of the pickled and stuffed variety. The road from Tissa

is rough but passable, although a 4WD is necessary once in the park. Realistically the only way to visit the park is as part of a safari (see p154). Part of the entrance fee includes the services of an animal tracker; their quality varies. Tips are both expected and usually earned; Rs 100 to 200 each for the tracker and driver is average.

Sights

Yala combines a strict nature reserve with a national park, bringing the total protected area to 126,786 hectares of scrub, plains, brackish lagoons and rocky outcrops. It is divided into five blocks, with the most visited being Block I (14,101 hectares). Also known as Yala West, this block was origin-

YALA NATIONAL PARK

0 —————— 2 km
0 —————— 1 mile

ally a reserve for hunters, and was given over to conservation in 1938.

With over 35 leopards, Yala West has one of the world's densest leopard populations. *Panthera pardus kotiya*, the subspecies you may well see, is unique to Sri Lanka. The best time to spot leopards is February to June or July, when the water levels in the park are low. Elephants are also well-known inhabitants (the best time to spot them is also between February and July), and you'll probably see sloth bears, sambars, spotted deer, boars, crocodiles, buffaloes, mongooses, jackals and monkeys.

Around 150 species of birds have been recorded at Yala, many of which are visitors escaping the northern winter. These birds include white-winged black terns, curlews and pintails. Locals include jungle fowl, hornbills and orioles.

If you visit between October and December you're guaranteed to see a lot of birdlife, deer and crocodiles – anything else will be a bonus. Whatever the season, dawn and dusk are the best times of day to view animals.

Yala contains the remains of a once thriving human community. A monastic settlement, **Situlpahuwa**, appears to have housed 12,000 inhabitants. Now restored, it's an important pilgrimage site. A 1st-century BC *vihara* (Buddhist complex) – **Magul Maha Vihara** – and a 2nd-century BC *chetiya* (Buddhist shrine) – **Akasa Chetiya** – point to a well-established community, believed to have been part of the ancient Ruhunu kingdom.

Sleeping

Although most of the park was untouched by the tsunami, two resorts near the shore were demolished.

There are six appallingly expensive bungalows scattered about inside the park. Costs (after park admission) are US$24 per person per night plus US$2 per person for linens and US$30 per group for 'service'. The basic huts come with drinking water and don't have electricity. You can make reservations through the **Department of Wildlife Conservation** (☎ 011-269 4241; www.dwlc.lk; 18 Gregory's Rd, Col 7).

Alternatively, groups up to 10 people can camp inside the park at one of two primitive sites for Rs 690 per night. Book at the park office. You'll need to bring your own supplies and gear.

Just outside of the entrance, **Yala Village Hotel** (☎ 047-223 9450; www.johnkeellshotels.com; s/d US$90/95, full board per person US$30; ⌨ ⌘) offers posh accommodation amid the sand dunes near the rugged coast. Rooms are in individual bungalows, which come with satellite TV and fridge. A blackboard near the entrance lists the day's animal sightings, and there's a cool rooftop bar that has views in all directions. There's little else out here.

KATARAGAMA

☎ 047

Fifteen kilometres northeast of Tissa (past lots of woodcarving stands) is Kataragama. Along with Adam's Peak (Sri Pada), this is the most important religious pilgrimage site in Sri Lanka. It is a holy place for Buddhists, Muslims and Hindus, and the sprawling religious complex across the Menik Ganga contains buildings of all three religions. It is difficult to sort fact from legend at Kataragama. Many believe that King Dutugemunu built a shrine to the Kataragama Deviyo (the resident god) here in the 2nd century BC, and the Buddhist Kirivehera dagoba dates back to the 1st century BC, but the site has been significant for longer.

In July and August, the predominantly Hindu **Kataragama festival** draws thousands of devotees, who make the pilgrimage over a two-week period (see The Long Walk to Kataragama, p159).

Apart from festival time, the town is busiest at weekends and on *poya* days. At these times it may be difficult to find accommodation, and the place will be buzzing. At other times it can feel like a ghost town. If you're staying in Tissamaharama you may just want to visit on a day trip.

Information

There's a **Bank of Ceylon** (Tissa Rd), which has an international ATM, and a **post office** (Tissa Rd). Don't expect much help from the information office in the religious complex.

Sights

The most important shrine is the **Maha Devale**, which supposedly contains the lance of the six-faced, 12-armed Hindu war god, Murugan (Skanda), who is seen as identical

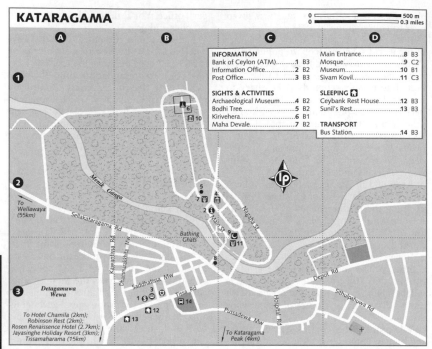

KATARAGAMA

0   500 m
0   0.3 miles

INFORMATION
Bank of Ceylon (ATM)..........1 B3
Information Office................2 B2
Post Office.........................3 B3

SIGHTS & ACTIVITIES
Archaeological Museum........4 B2
Bodhi Tree..........................5 B2
Kirivehara...........................6 B1
Maha Devale.......................7 B2

Main Entrance......................8 B3
Mosque..............................9 C2
Museum.............................10 B1
Sivam Kovil.........................11 C3

SLEEPING
Ceybank Rest House............12 B3
Sunil's Rest.........................13 B3

TRANSPORT
Bus Station.........................14 B3

to the Kataragama Deviyo. Followers make offerings at daily *pujas* at 4.30am, 10.30am and 6.30pm (no 4.30am offering on Saturday). The **Kirivehara** and **Sivam Kovil** shrines are dedicated to the Buddha and Ganesh (the remover of obstacles and champion of intellectual pursuits) respectively; there is also a bodhi tree.

The Muslim area, close to the entrance, features a beautiful small **mosque** with coloured tilework and wooden lintels, and tombs of two holy men.

Apart from the shrines, there are some other points of interest inside the temple complex. An **archaeological museum** (admission by donation; ⏰ 10.30am-12.30pm & 6.30-9pm) has a collection of Hindu and Buddhist religious items, as well as huge fibreglass models of statues from around Sri Lanka. A small **museum** has a display of Buddhist statues.

Sleeping & Eating
The first two places are in town, while the rest are on Tissa Rd.

Ceybank Rest House (☎ 223 5229, reservations 011-254 4315; Tissa Rd; s/d Rs 1250/1500) An airy, well-run

place with 22 simple, clean rooms. Some rooms have views across to Kataragama mountain and others overlook the town. You're supposed to reserve your room from Colombo but there are often on-the-spot vacancies. You'll need to book in for the vegetarian food (no alcohol, meat, fish or eggs allowed). It's close to the temples.

Sunil's Rest (☎ 223 5300; 61 Tissa Rd; r with/without air-con Rs 1800/900; ✷) This clean, family-run place has three rooms, a pleasant garden and an elaborate waterfall feature.

Rosen Renaissance Hotel (☎ 223 6030-3; www.rosenhotelsrilanka.com; Tissa Rd; s/d US$40/50; ✷ ✷) This posh two-storey hotel attracts a lot of tour groups. The 52 rooms have satellite TV and fridge. There's a swimming pool with an underwater music system – requests taken. Pool use for nonguests is Rs 300.

Hotel Chamila (☎ 223 5217; r with/without air-con Rs 1600/1100; ✷) Two- and three-storey blocks hold 40 modern rooms at this kid-friendly (there's a playground!) hotel. The grounds are pretty and the rooms clean and functional. Boozers, note that there's no drinking in the TV lounge, only in the bar.

THE LONG WALK TO KATARAGAMA

Forty-five days before the annual Kataragama festival starts on the Esala *poya* (full moon), a group of Kataragama devotees start walking the length of Sri Lanka for the Pada Yatra pilgrimage. Seeking spiritual development, the pilgrims believe they are walking in the steps of the god Kataragama (also known as Murugan), and the Veddahs, who made the first group pilgrimage on this route.

The route follows the east coast from the Jaffna peninsula, via Trincomalee and Batticaloa to Okanda, then through Yala National Park to Kataragama. It's an arduous trip, and the pilgrims rely on the hospitality of the communities and temples they pass for their food and lodging. During the war, the risks to them were great and the walk was not completed between 1983 and 2002.

Pilgrims arrive in time for the festival's feverish activity. Elephants parade, drummers drum. Vows are made and favours sought by devotees, who demonstrate their sincerity by performing extraordinary acts of penance and self-mortification on one particular night: some swing from hooks that pierce their skin; others roll half-naked over the hot sands near the temple. A few perform the act of walking on beds of red-hot cinders – treading the flowers, as it's called. The fire walkers fast, meditate and pray, bathe in the Menik Ganga (Menik River) and then worship at the Maha Devale before facing their ordeal. Then, fortified by their faith, they step out onto the glowing path while the audience cries out encouragement. The festival officially ends with a water-cutting ceremony (said to bring rain for the harvest) in the Menik Ganga.

Robinson Rest (☎ 223 5175; anjulaj@sltnet.lk; Tissa Rd; r with/without air-con Rs 1300/900; 🔀) Situated about 2km south of Kataragama on the road to Tissa, this place has 20 basic rooms with balconies and verandas. There's also a bar and restaurant.

Jayasinghe Holiday Resort (☎ 223 5146; www .jayasinghehotels.com; Tissa Rd; r with/without air-con US$31/26; 🔀 🖳) This place, 3km from town, has a swimming pool (which can be used by nonguests for Rs 100) and 25 clean, basic rooms. It's well back from the road.

Getting There & Away

To reach Pottuvil (for Arugam Bay), change at Monaragala (Rs 55, two hours). the following are some other major bus destinations from Kataragama.

Colombo Regular/air-con Rs 146/280, 10 hours.
Ella Rs 116, three hours.
Kandy Rs 172, eight hours.
Matara Rs 71, 3½ hours.
Nuwara Eliya Rs 116, five hours.
Tissamaharama Rs 18, one hour.
Wellawaya Rs 49, two hours.

THE SOUTH

The Hill Country

The Hill Country lives in a cool, perpetual spring, away from the often enervating heat and heavy air of the coastal regions or the hot dry air of the central and northern plains. Everything here is green and lush, and much of the region is carpeted with the glowing green of the tea plantations, with montane forest hugging the higher slopes.

Although Sinhalese culture was born in the north of Sri Lanka, following the decline of the Polonnaruwa dynasties in the early 13th century, power shifted southwest to Kotte (near Colombo) and to the Hill Country. The kingdom of Kandy resisted European takeover for more than 300 years after the coastal regions first succumbed to the Portuguese in the 17th century, and the city of Kandy remains the Sinhalese cultural and spiritual centre.

Since the 19th century the region has become home to a large number of Tamils, brought from India by the British to labour on the tea estates. The Tamil culture in the Hill Country is very different from that found in northern Sri Lanka; the Hinduism practiced here is not as strict and there is much less support for the Liberation Tigers of Tamil Eelam (LTTE).

The Hill Country is a relaxed area where it's very easy to find the days just drifting by. Higher up into the hills are many towns that are worth a visit, and an abundance of walks and climbs, refreshing waterfalls and historic sites.

HIGHLIGHTS

- Watching the throbbing throng of elephants, drummers and dancers at the **Kandy Esala Perahera** (p167)
- Meandering around **Kandy Lake** (p165) in the evening
- Slogging up **Adam's Peak** (Sri Pada; p194) to be rewarded by a perfect sunrise
- Rattling through the high tea plantations in a Hill Country train; the trip between **Haputale and Ella** (p216) is particularly lovely
- Hiking through the countryside around **Ella** (p217) while enjoying the views to the plains
- Exploring the pristine **Sinharaja Forest Reserve** (p221) with an expert guide
- Digging up the perfect gem in one of **Ratnapura's gem shops** (p224)
- Rising early to walk through **Horton Plains National Park** (p205) and peer over stunning World's End

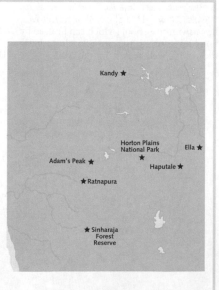

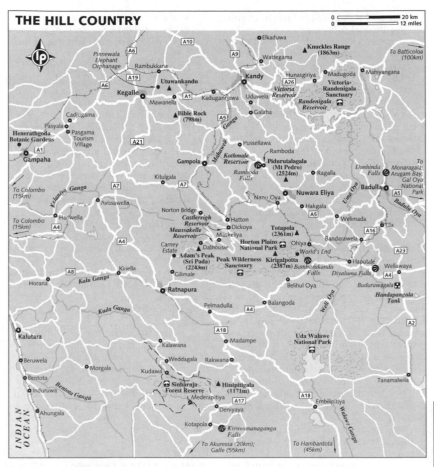

COLOMBO TO KANDY

The **Henerathgoda Botanic Gardens** (☎ 033-222 2316) near Gampaha, off the Colombo–Kandy road about 30km northwest of Colombo, was where the first rubber trees planted in Asia were carefully grown and their potential was proved – some of those original rubber trees are still in the 37-acre gardens today, along with around 400 other plant varieties. It's worth a stop if you have the time and an interest in botany.

Some 47km from Colombo is the village of Pasyala, where there's a turn-off leading to the **Pasgama tourism village** (☎ 033-228 5183; admission US$10), about 1.5km from the main road. This privately owned venture is an attempt to bring to life a pre-1940 settlement showcasing craftspeople, dancers and other features of traditional village life. Some enjoy this place while others see it as corny commercialism – few are delighted by the entry fee. There's a shop selling handicrafts. Hire a three-wheeler from Pasyala to get to the tourism village; it should cost Rs 150 each way.

About 3km further towards Kandy from Pasyala is **Cadjugama**, a village famous for its cashew nuts. Stalls line the road, and brightly clad cashew-nut sellers beckon passing motorists. At the 48km post is **Radawaduwa**, where all sorts of cane items are woven and displayed for sale at roadside stalls.

Kegalle, located 77km from Colombo, is the nearest town to the Pinnewala Elephant

Orphanage (below). A little further on you can see **Utuwankandu**, a prominent rocky hill from which the 19th-century Robin Hood–style highwayman, Saradiel, preyed on travellers until he was caught and executed by the British.

At Kadugannawa, just after the road and railway make their most scenic climbs – with views southwest to the large **Bible Rock** – is a tall pillar erected in memory of Captain Dawson, the English engineer who built the Colombo–Kandy road in 1826.

Pasyala, Cadjugama, Kegalle and Kadugannawa are on the A1 and are all accessible by buses travelling between Colombo and Kandy. The train is useful for getting to the Henerathgoda Botanic Gardens at Gampaha, and Kadugannawa.

Pinnewala Elephant Orphanage

This government-run **orphanage** (adult/child under 12 Rs 500/250, video camera Rs 500; ⊗ 8.30am-5.30pm), near Kegalle, was created to protect abandoned or orphaned elephants. It has now grown into the most popular jumbo attraction in Sri Lanka, and with good reason, for nowhere else except at *peraheras* (processions) are you likely to see so many elephants at close quarters. The elephants are controlled by their *mahouts* (keepers), who ensure they feed at the right times and don't endanger anyone, but otherwise the elephants roam freely around the sanctuary area.

There are usually 60 or so elephants in residence, from babies to young adults. The elephants are led to a nearby river for bathing daily from 10am to noon and from 2pm to 4pm, while meal times are at 9.15am, 1.15pm and 5pm. There's a café and some shops selling snacks, camera film, elephant T-shirts, elephant toys and so on.

A few readers have written to express their distress over the *mahouts'* treatment of the elephants. If you think you might have trouble accepting the *mahouts'* traditional use of the goad – an L-shaped tool with a pointed metal tip – then this is probably not the place for you.

Near the Pinnewala Elephant Orphanage are a couple of **spice gardens**. You can turn up unannounced and a guide will show you around, explaining their uses and growth habits. A tip will be expected and, more often than not, you'll end your tour at the gar-

den's shop for a high-pressure sales pitch. If you're interested in buying Sri Lankan spices you'd be much better off shopping in local markets.

The orphanage is on a good road a few kilometres north of the Colombo–Kandy road. The turn-off is just out of Kegalle on the Kandy side. From Kandy you can take a private bus or Central Transport Board (CTB) bus 662 to Kegalle – get off before Kegalle at Karandupona junction. From the junction catch bus 681 going from Kegalle to Rambukkana and get off at Pinnewala. It's about an hour from Kandy to the junction, and 10 minutes from the junction to Pinnewala. There are also numerous buses between Colombo and Kegalle.

Rambukkana station on the Colombo–Kandy railway is about 3km north of the orphanage. From Rambukkana get a bus going towards Kegalle. Trains leave Kandy at 6.45am (arriving at Rambukkana station at 8.21am), 10.30am (arriving at 12.13pm) and 2.15pm (arriving at 3.43pm). Trains for Kandy leave from Rambukkana at 1.55pm and 2.25pm.

There is also a train from Colombo Fort at 11.30am that terminates in Rambukkana at 1.55pm. If you're heading to Colombo, trains leave Rambukkana at 10am and 11.25am, arriving roughly 2½ hours later.

From Anuradhapura take a bus to Kurunegala, then change to another bus to Rambukkana and travel by three-wheeler the rest of the way.

KANDY
☎ 081 / pop 112,000 / elev 500m
Some say Kandy is the only other real 'city' in Sri Lanka, other than Colombo. The easy-going capital of the Hill Country has a lot to offer – history, culture, forested hills and a touch of urban buzz. Only 115km inland from the capital, climatically it is a world away due to its 500m altitude.

Kandy served as the capital of the last Sinhalese kingdom, which fell to the British in 1815 after defying the Portuguese and Dutch for three centuries. It took the British 11 years to build a road linking Kandy with Colombo, a task they finally completed in 1831.

The town, and the countryside around it, is lush and green and there are many pleasant walks from the town and further afield.

The town centre, close to Kandy's picturesque lake set in a bowl of hills, is a delightful jumble of old shops, antique and gemstone specialists, a bustling market and a very good selection of hotels, guesthouses and restaurants. As night falls the city becomes eerily quiet.

Kandy is particularly well known for the great Kandy Esala Perahera (p167), held over 10 days leading up to the Nikini *poya* (full moon) at the end of the month of Esala (July/August), but has enough attractions to justify a visit at any time of year.

Locally, Kandy is known as either Maha Nuwara (Great City) or just Nuwara (City), which is what some conductors on Kandy-bound buses call out.

Orientation

The focus of Kandy is its lake, with the Temple of the Sacred Tooth Relic (Sri Dalada Maligawa) on its north side. The city centre is immediately north and west of the lake, with the clock tower a handy reference point. The train station, the market and the various bus stations and stops are just a short walk from the lake. The city spreads into the surrounding hills, where many of the places to stay are perched, looking down on the town.

MAPS

The *A–Z Street Guide*, available at bookshops such as Vijitha Yapa (right), contains one of the most detailed maps of Kandy. The tourist office has maps as well but the quality tends to be a bit dodgy. Nelles Verlag produces a reasonable map of Kandy.

Information

BOOKSHOPS

If you're interested in books on Buddhism, visit the friendly people at the Buddhist Publication Society towards the east end of the lake. Local scholars occasionally and monks sometimes give lectures here. It also has a comprehensive library.

Cultural Triangle Office (🕑 9am-12.30pm & 1.30-4pm) Opposite the tourist office, this has a selection of books for sale on the ancient cities. *Kandy*, by Dr Anuradha Seneviratna, is an informative guide to the city's heritage. Also available here is *The Cultural Triangle*, published by Unesco and the Central Cultural Fund, which provides good background information on the ancient sites and monuments.

Mark Bookshop (151/1 Dalada Vidiya) Has a good selection of books about Sri Lanka, as well as fiction and nonfiction. It's poky but the staff are very helpful.
Vijitha Yapa (5 Kotugodelle Vidiya) Good bookshop selling periodicals, newspapers (including foreign papers) and assorted fiction and nonfiction.

CULTURAL CENTRES

Alliance Française (☎ 222 4432; allikandy@sltnet.lk; 642 Peradeniya Rd; 🕑 8.30am-6pm Mon-Sat) To the southwest of town, the Alliance hosts film nights (though in French, the films often have English subtitles), and has books and periodicals. Good coffee is available. Nonmembers are welcome to browse in the library.
British Council (☎ 223 4634; enquiries.kdy@british council.org; 178 DS Senanayake Vidiya; 🕑 9.30am-5pm Tue-Sat) The council has back copies of British newspapers, CDs, videos and DVDs. Although English instruction is the main activity, the council sometimes holds film nights, exhibitions and plays. Nonmembers may read newspapers on presentation of a passport.

INTERNET ACCESS

There are five or six Internet cafés in the town centre; the going rate last we checked was Rs 60 per hour (except at Koffeepot, where the rate was inexplicably triple).
Café@Internet (77 Kotugodelle Vidiya)
Cyber Cottage (1st fl, 154 Kotugodelle Vidiya)
Koffeepot (Ground fl, The Pub, 36 Dalada Vidiya)

MEDICAL SERVICES

Lakeside Adventist Hospital (☎ 224 6295; percydias@yahoo.com; 40 Sangaraja Mawatha) If you need a doctor in Kandy, this hospital offers good, efficient service.

MONEY

Most major Sri Lankan banks have branches in town, and offer ATM service.
Bank of Ceylon (Dalada Vidiya)
Commercial Bank (Kotugodelle Vidiya)
Hatton National Bank (Dalada Vidiya)
HSBC (Kotugodelle Vidiya)

POST

The main post office is over the road from the train station. There are a few smaller, more central post offices, including one at the intersection of Kande Vidiya and DS Senanayake Vidiya. There are numerous private communications bureaus in town.
DHL (☎ 447 9684; 7 Deva Vidiya) offers domestic and international courier services at its office opposite the Cultural Triangle Office.

THE HILL COUNTRY

KANDY

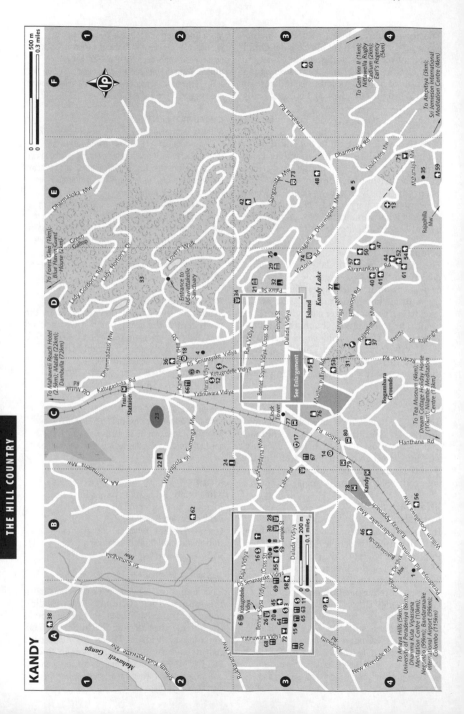

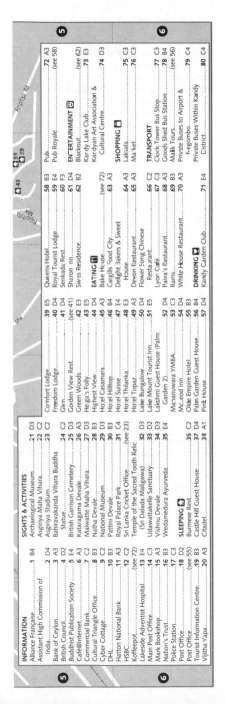

TOURIST INFORMATION

Cultural Triangle Office (9am-12.30pm & 1.30-4pm) Located in an old colonial-era building across the road from the tourist office. Books are available for sale (p163) though not everything displayed is in stock. You can buy Cultural Triangle round-trip tickets that cover many of the sites of the ancient cities here. Within Kandy the round-trip ticket covers the four Hindu *devales* (complexes for worshipping deities; Kataragama, Natha, Pattini and Vishnu), two monasteries (Asgiriya and Malwatte), the National Museum and the Archaeological Museum. It is customary to make a donation (usually Rs 50 and upwards) at the *devales* and monasteries, though you are unlikely to be asked to produce a Cultural Triangle ticket. The National Museum costs Rs 100 to enter without a triangle ticket, while the Archaeological Museum insists on one. See later in this section for more details on these places. For more information on these tickets, see p228.

Tourist Information Centre (222 2661; Palace Sq; 9am-1pm & 1.30-4.15pm Mon Fri) Housed in a rather empty-looking pavilion beside Olde Empire Hotel, this is helpful for information on transport and things to do in the Kandy area, and also has some information on places to stay.

Dangers & Annoyances

The back alleys of the town centre are worth avoiding after dark – they're home to sour bars, gambling dens and the homeless.

Touts are particularly numerous around the train station and the lake. They will generally have a well-rehearsed stock of stories about guesthouses that you shouldn't patronise (presumably because those place won't pay them commission). Another neat trick is the man who says he works at your hotel, who's off shopping for tonight's dinner. Of course he doesn't work at your hotel, and any money you give him for a special meal disappears.

Sights

KANDY LAKE

A lovely centrepiece for the town, Kandy Lake was created in 1807 by Sri Wickrama Rajasinha, the last ruler of the kingdom of Kandy. Several small-scale local chiefs, who protested because their people objected to labouring on the project, were put to death at stakes in the lake bed. The island in the centre was used as Sri Wickrama Rajasinha's personal harem, to which he crossed on a barge. Later the British used it as an ammunition store and added the fortress-style parapet around the perimeter of the lake. On the south shore in front of the Malwatte

THE HILL COUNTRY

Maha Vihara there's a circular enclosure that is the monks' bathhouse.

A cement footpath dotted with benches encircles the lake and is a favourite venue for early-evening strolls.

TEMPLE OF THE SACRED TOOTH RELIC (SRI DALADA MALIGAWA)

Just north of the lake, the **Temple of the Sacred Tooth Relic** (admission Rs 500, still/video camera Rs 150/350; ☾ 6am-5pm, puja 5.30am, 10.15am & 7.15pm) houses Sri Lanka's most important Buddhist relic – a tooth of the Buddha. The temple was damaged when a bomb was detonated – by the Liberation Tigers of Tamil Eelam, according to the government – near the main entrance in early 1998, but the scars have been repaired.

The tooth is said to have been snatched from the flames of the Buddha's funeral pyre in 543 BC, and was smuggled into Sri Lanka during the 4th century AD, hidden in the hair of a princess. At first it was taken to Anuradhapura, but with the ups and downs of Sri Lankan history it moved from place to place before eventually ending up at Kandy. In 1283 it was carried back to India by an invading army but was soon brought back again by King Parakramabahu III.

Gradually, the tooth came to assume more and more importance as a symbol of sovereignty; it was believed that whoever had custody of the tooth relic had the right to rule the island. In the 16th century the Portuguese, in one of their worst spoilsport moods, apparently seized the tooth, took it away and burnt it with Catholic fervour in Goa. 'Not so', say the Sinhalese; the Portuguese had been fobbed off with a replica tooth and the real incisor remained safe. Even today there are rumours that the real tooth is hidden somewhere secure, and that the tooth kept here is a replica.

The Temple of the Sacred Tooth Relic was constructed mainly under Kandyan kings from 1687 to 1707 and from 1747 to 1782, and, in fact, the entire temple complex was part of the Kandyan royal palace. It is an imposing pink structure surrounded by a deep moat. The octagonal tower in the moat was built by Sri Wickrama Rajasinha and used to house an important collection of *ola* (talipot-palm leaf) manuscripts. However, this section of the temple was heavily damaged in the 1998 bomb blast.

The main tooth shrine – a two-storey rectangular building known as the Vaha-hitina Maligawa – occupies the centre of a paved courtyard. The eye-catching gilded roof over the relic chamber was added by President Ranasinghe Premadasa and paid for by Japanese donors. The bomb blast of 1998 has exposed part of the front wall to reveal at least three layers of 18th- to 20th-century paintings depicting the *perahera* and various Jataka (Buddha life stories).

It is impossible to overestimate the importance of this temple to most Sri Lankan Buddhists, who believe they must complete at least one pilgrimage to the temple in their lifetime. Worshipping at the temple is thought to improve one's karmic lot immeasurably.

The tooth shrine itself receives a constant flow of worshippers and flocks of tourists, with fewer tourists in the morning than in the evening. Wear clothes that cover your legs and your shoulders and remove your shoes (which are kept by shoe minders near the entrance).

During *pujas* (offerings or prayers), the heavily guarded room housing the tooth is open to devotees and tourists. However, you don't actually see the tooth. It's kept in a gold casket shaped like a dagoba (stupa), which contains a series of six dagoba caskets of diminishing size and eventually the tooth itself.

Most visitors are only allowed to view the dagboa casket from the doorway, which is around 3m from the actual altar. Guards keep the queue moving so that no-one gets more than 10 or 15 seconds to see the inside of the shrine room. Occasionally you'll see VIPs being invited to enter the inner sanctum for a closer look. Thai and Japanese nationals – because of their country's generous temple donations – may be allowed into the tooth room upon advance request to the temple guardians.

Behind the shrine stands the three-storey **Alut Maligawa**, a newer and larger shrine hall displaying dozens of bronze sitting Buddhas donated by Thai devotees. In fact, the design of this floor is intended to resemble a Thai Buddhist shrine hall as a tribute to the fact that Thai monks re-established Sri Lanka's ordination lineage during the reign of King Kirti Sri Rajasinha. The upper two floors of the Alut Maligawa contain the **Sri**

KANDY ESALA PERAHERA

This *perahera* (procession) is held in Kandy to honour the sacred tooth enshrined in the Temple of the Sacred Tooth Relic. It runs for 10 days in the full-moon month of Esala (July/August), ending on the Nikini *poya* (full moon). The big night of the year in Kandy comes at the culmination of these 10 days of increasingly frenetic activity.

The first six nights are relatively low-key; on the seventh things start to take off as the route lengthens, the procession becomes more and more splendid and accommodation prices go right through the roof.

The procession is actually a combination of five separate *peraheras*. Four of them come from the four Kandy *devales* (complexes for worshipping Hindu or Sri Lankan deities, who are also devotees and servants of the Buddha): Natha, Vishnu, Kataragama and Pattini. The fifth and most splendid *perahera* is that of the Sri Dalada Maligawa itself.

The procession is led by thousands of Kandyan dancers and drummers beating thousands of drums, cracking whips and waving colourful banners. Then come long processions of elephants – 50 or more of them. The brilliantly caparisoned Maligawa tusker is the most splendid of them all – decorated from trunk to toe, he carries a huge canopy that shelters, on the final night, a replica of the sacred relic cask. A carpet-way of white linen is laid in front of the elephant so that he does not step in the dirt.

The Kandy Esala Perahera is the most magnificent annual spectacle in Sri Lanka, and one of the most famous in Asia. It has been an annual event for many centuries and is described by Robert Knox in his 1681 book *An Historical Relation of Ceylon*. There is also a smaller procession on the *poya* day in June, and special *peraheras* may be put on for important occasions. It's essential to book roadside seats for the *perahera* at least a week in advance; prices for such seats range from Rs 3750 to 4750. Once the festival starts, you may be able to get seats about halfway back in the stands quite cheaply.

There's a daylight procession on the first day of the Nikini *poya* month, which marks the end of the Kandy Esala Perahera.

Dalada Museum (admission Rs 100; ⏰ 9am-5pm) with a stunning array of gilded and bejewelled reliquaries and gifts to the temple. There is also a sobering display of photographs of the damage caused by the truck bomb in 1988.

To the north inside the compound, and accessible only via the Temple of the Sacred Tooth Relic, is the 19th-century **Audience Hall**, an open-air pavilion with stone columns carved to look like wooden pillars. Adjacent to this, in the **Rajah Tusker Hall**, you can view the stuffed remains of Rajah, the Maligawa tusker who died in 1988 (see Kandy Esala Perahera, above).

NATIONAL MUSEUM

This **museum** (adult/child under 12 Rs 100/50, camera Rs 150; ⏰ 9am-5pm Sun-Thu) was once the quarters for Kandyan royal concubines and now houses royal regalia and reminders of pre-European Sinhalese life. On display is a copy of the 1815 agreement that handed over the Kandyan provinces to British rule. This document announces a major reason for the event.

...the cruelties and oppressions of the Malabar ruler, in the arbitrary and unjust infliction of bodily tortures and pains of death without trial, and sometimes without accusation or the possibility of a crime, and in the general contempt and contravention of all civil rights, have become flagrant, enormous and intolerable.

Sri Wickrama Rajasinha was therefore declared, 'by the habitual violation of the chief and most sacred duties of a sovereign', to be 'fallen and deposed from office of king' and 'dominion of the Kandyan provinces' was 'vested in...the British Empire'.

The audience hall, notable for the tall pillars supporting its roof, was the site for the convention of Kandyan chiefs that ceded the kingdom to Britain in 1815.

The National Museum, along with the less-interesting Archaeological Museum behind the temple, four *devales* and two monasteries – but not the Temple of the Sacred Tooth Relic itself – together make up

THE HILL COUNTRY

one of Sri Lanka's Cultural Triangle sites. You can buy a Cultural Triangle round-trip ticket at the office across the road from the tourist office (p165).

BRITISH GARRISON CEMETERY

This **cemetery** (donation appreciated; ⏰ 8am-5pm Mon-Sat) is a short walk uphill behind the National Museum. There are 163 graves and probably 500 burials in total here, lovingly cared for by the friends of the cemetery. The amusing and friendly caretaker is more than happy to show people around and provide information about many of the graves. Some of the demises were due to sudden sunstroke, or elephants, or jungle fever. The Cargills of supermarket fame lie here. James McGlashan survived the battle of Waterloo but disregarded instructions given on mosquitoes, which ultimately proved deadlier.

The office, once the chapel of rest, has pamphlets and the old cemetery records.

DEVALES

There are four Kandyan *devales* (complexes for worshipping Hindu or local Sri Lankan deities) to the gods who are followers of Buddha and who protect Sri Lanka. Three of the four *devales* stand close to the Temple of the Sacred Tooth Relic. The 14th-century **Natha Devale** is the oldest. It perches on a stone terrace with a fine *vahalkada* (solid panel of sculpture) gateway. Bodhi trees and dagobas stand in the *devale* grounds, and there's a fine icon in the main shrine. Next to the Natha Devale is the simple **Pattini Devale**, dedicated to the goddess of chastity. The **Vishnu Devale** on the other side of Raja Vidiya is reached by carved steps and features a drumming hall. Vishnu is the guardian of Sri Lanka and an indicator of the intermingling of Hindu and Buddhist beliefs, since he is also one of the three great Hindu gods.

The **Kataragama Devale** is a little way from the others – a brightly painted tower gateway fights for attention with the bustle on Kotugodelle Vidiya. Murugan, the god of war (also called Skanda), appears here with six heads, 12 hands wielding weapons, and riding a peacock.

MONASTERIES

The principal *viharas* (Buddhist complexes) in Kandy have considerable importance – the high priests of the two best known, Malwatte and Asgiriya, are the most important in Sri Lanka. These temples are the headquarters of two of the main Nikayas (orders of monks). The head monks also play an important role in the administration and operation of the Temple of the Sacred Tooth Relic. The **Malwatte Maha Vihara** is directly across the lake from the Temple of the Sacred Tooth Relic, while the **Asgiriya Maha Vihara** is on the hill off Wariyapola Sri Sumanga Mawatha to the northwest of the town centre, and has a large reclining Buddha image.

ELEPHANTS

Elephants can often be seen in and around Kandy. Working elephants might be spotted anywhere, and you may catch the Temple of the Sacred Tooth Relic elephant chained up along the lakeside near the temple. There are elephants in the Riverside Elephant Park (p191) as well.

From Kandy it's a fairly easy trip to the Pinnewala Elephant Orphanage (p162).

UDAWATTAKELLE SANCTUARY

North of the lake is this cool and pleasant **forest** (adult/child under 12 Rs 600/300; ⏰ 7am-5pm). There are lots of huge trees, much bird- and insect life and many monkeys, but visitors are advised to be careful in this woodland if they're alone. Muggers are rare in Sri Lanka but not unknown, and single women especially should take care.

Entry to the sanctuary is seriously overpriced. You enter through the gate, which you reach by turning right after the post office on DS Senanayake Vidiya (there's a sign at the junction). There are clear paths, but it's worth paying attention to the map at the entrance.

TEA MUSEUM

This recently opened **museum** (Map p189; ☎ 070-280 3204; admission Rs 250; ⏰ 8.15am-4.45pm) occupies the 1925-vintage Hanthana Tea Factory, 4km south of Kandy on the Hanthana road. Abandoned for over a decade, it was refurbished as a museum by the Sri Lanka Tea Board and the Planters' Association of Sri Lanka. In addition to a good collection of 19th-century rollers, dryers and other typical tea-factory equipment in their original settings, the museum contains exhibits on the lives and work of tea pioneers James Taylor and Thomas Lipton.

UNIVERSITY OF PERADENIYA
Ten years after the 1842 founding of the University of Ceylon in Colombo, the bulk of the university (Map p189) moved to Peradeniya, 8km south of Kandy. Today around 7800 students are typically enrolled at any given time. The Mahaweli Ganga (Mahaweli River) flows through the leafy green campus.

Activities
AYURVEDA
Wedamedura Ayurveda (☎ 074 479484; www.ayurve dawedamura.com; 7 Mahamaya Mawatha; 1hr massage Rs 800, 2½hr full treatment Rs 4000), southeast of the lake, is a fully licensed Ayurveda treatment facility with both male and female masseurs. Week-long residential packages, including accommodation and food, are also available.

You could also splurge at the Ayurvedic treatment centre at Amaya Hills (Map p189; ☎ 223 3521; amayahills@amayaresorts.com; Heerassagala; facial Rs 1000, oil massage & steam bath Rs 2500). The body oil massage and steam bath takes 1½ hours – the bath is *very* hot. The 40-minute facial treatment includes a massage, sandalwood/turmeric mask and steam. Although Amaya Hills (p193) is a bit far from town you can relax around the pool after the treatment with a drink, and make an afternoon (or morning) of it. A three-wheeler from Kandy should cost Rs 800 return.

GOLF
The Victoria Golf & Country Resort (☎ 237 5570; www.srilankagolf.com; green fees US$35, club hire Rs 1000, caddy per round Rs 350) is 20km east of Kandy. Surrounded on three sides by the Victoria Reservoir and with the Knuckles Range as a backdrop, it's worth coming out here for lunch at the clubhouse just to savour the views. Claimed to be the best golf course in the subcontinent, it's a fairly challenging 18 holes.

MEDITATION
Visitors can learn or practise meditation and study Buddhism at several places in the Kandy area. Ask at the Buddhist Publication Society (☎ 223 7283; www.bps.lk; 54 Sangharaja Mawatha; ⏰ 9am-4.30pm Mon-Fri, 9am-12.30pm Sat), by the lake, for details about courses. Many centres offer free courses but they'd obviously appreciate a donation. Give what you'd normally be paying per day for food and accommodation in Sri Lanka. For details of some of the centres that offer courses, see p192.

SWIMMING
South of Kandy lake, Hotel Suisse (☎ 223 3024; 30 Sangaraja Mawatha; pool fee Rs 150) charges non guests to use the pool (towels included), located in a garden. In the town, Queens Hotel (☎ 223 3290; Dalada Vidiya; pool fee Rs 150) also has an OK pool and a pretty garden. There are some stunningly positioned pools around Kandy, including at: Hotel Thilanka (☎ 223 2429; 3 Sanghamitta Mawatha; pool fee Rs 200) on a terrace looking down on the lake; Hotel Hilltop (☎ 222 4162; 200/21 Bahirawakanda; pool fee Rs 150); Swiss Residence (☎ 447 9054; 23 Bahirawakanda; pool fee Rs 100), the least expensive in town; and Amaya Hills (☎ 223 3521; amayahills@amayaresorts.com; Heerassagala; pool fee Rs 200), southwest of Kandy, from whose terrace you get great views over the countryside.

WALKING
There are many walks around the centre of Kandy, such as up to the Royal Palace Park (admission Rs 50; ⏰ 8.30am-4.30pm), also constructed by Sri Wickrama Rajasinha, overlooking the lake. Further up the hill on Rajapihilla Mawatha there are even better views over the lake, the town and the surrounding hills, which disappear in a series of gentle ranges stretching far into the distance. If you're in the mood for a longer walk there are also a couple of paths, along from Rajapihilla Mawatha, that head up into the hills.

Looming over Kandy, the huge concrete Bahiravokanda Vihara Buddha Statue (admission Rs 150) can be reached by walking 20 minutes uphill from near the police station on Peradeniya Rd. Save your sweat and money – there are no views from the top and the statue is unremarkable.

Sleeping
Kandy has heaps of good guesthouses. In the middle and top brackets there are some lovely, luxurious houses and an increasing number of good hotels. Many places are set on the hills surrounding the town – in some cases 3km or more from the centre – but because of their outstanding locations and views they are worth the effort to get there. See p192 for details.

At the time of the Kandy Esala Perahera, room prices in Kandy can treble or quadruple;

even worse, you may not be able to find a room at all. If you're intent on coming to see the *perahera,* booking far ahead may secure you a more reasonable price.

You'll find the highest concentration of places to stay along or just off Anagarika Dharmapala Mawatha; buses 654, 655 and 698 (or just ask for 'Sanghamitta Mawatha' at the clock tower bus stop) will get you to this area and beyond.

Kandy Hoteliers Association (www.kandyhotels .com) maintains a useful website with details on midrange and top-end accommodation in the city.

BUDGET

Lakshmi Guest House (Palm Garden 2) (☎ 222 2154; www.lakshmipg2.lkguide.com; 57/1/1 Saranankara Rd; r Rs 800-1500) This art deco guesthouse was recently taken over by the friendly owners of Palm Garden and has been completely refurbished. Eleven rooms, ranging in size from relatively small to large, all very clean, are available; six have attached bathrooms. Reasonably priced meals are served on a terrace overlooking the town. Guests have access to Internet. Cars and motorcycles are available for hire.

Pink House (☎ 077 780 9173; 15 Saranankara Rd; r with/without bathroom Rs 700/400) This old stand-by occupies a quaint, one-storey rambling bungalow around a courtyard. The facilities are basic and the rooms well-worn. Choose from seven rooms with shared bathrooms and one with a private bathroom. The owners are very friendly and helpful.

Glen (☎ 223 5342; 58 Saranankara Rd; r with/without bathroom Rs 700/500) This place has clean, homey rooms, two with shared bathroom and one with private bathroom. The couple who own the place are friendly and maintain a pretty garden for use of the guests.

Lake Mount Tourist Inn (☎ 223 3204; hirokow@ sltnet.lk; 195A Rajapihilla Mawatha; r with/without bathroom Rs 1300/1000) Clinical and tidy, and run by a Sri Lankan–Japanese husband and wife, this inn features a variety of rooms and some quiet, tidy lounge areas. Free transport from the bus or train stations is available if you call upon arrival.

Lake Bungalow (☎ 222 2075; shiyan_d@ispkandyan .lk; 22/2B Sangaraja Mawatha; r Rs 550-880, apt Rs 2500) This place offers six clean, cheerful rooms in a multistorey building that looks like a school. In fact, there's a preschool on the

ground floor – here's hoping you like kids. All rooms are decorated with floral prints and have hot water and kitchenettes. You can rent a floor with three bedrooms as an apartment. The rooms look out over the villa of the head abbot of the Malwatte Maha Vihara. It's on a lane off Sangaraja Mawatha, just one street along from Saranankara Rd.

Olde Empire Hotel (☎ 222 4284; fernandovja@ eureka.lk; 21 Temple St; r Rs 400-500) Run by the same family for over a century, this colonial hotel has oodles of faded ambience. Most rooms are very basic and come with shared bathrooms (cold water only); two have attached bathroom. Some of the rooms at the back are a little dingy, but there's a great balcony with old chairs and tables at the front, overlooking the lake. There's a good, dirt-cheap restaurant here. The clientele tends to be Sri Lankan males, and solo female travellers may want to give it a miss unless they're prepared for extra attention.

Mahanuwara YMBA (Young Men's Buddhist Association; ☎ 223 3444; 5 Rajapihilla Mawatha; r with/without bathroom Rs 1150/690) Well located near the lake and town centre, the local YMBA offers 32 basic rooms (only six with attached bathroom) in a three-storey building. There's a small, inexpensive cafeteria on the premises.

McLeod Inn (☎ 222 2832; mcleod@sltnet.lk; 65A Rajapihilla Mawatha; r with/without view Rs 950/1300) Featuring six clean rooms with hot water, some with stunning views, this is a modern place with pleasant lounge areas, good food and a steady following.

Freedom Lodge (☎ 222 3506; freedomamead@yahoo .com; 30 Saranankara Rd; r Rs 1000-1250) Further up on the other side of the road, this place (owned by Tamil Catholics) has three spotless, bright rooms, all with hot water. The double upstairs has a balcony and attracts a higher price. There's a small garden and the hosts are very welcoming.

Green Woods (☎ 223 2970; greenwoodkusum@slt net.lk; 34A Sanghamitta Mawatha; r with/without hot water Rs 1000/800) This quiet house with six guestrooms (only two with hot water) sits on the green verge of Udawattakelle Sanctuary and is popular with birders. The kindly owner keeps a log of birdlife spotted from the balcony and has recently added a rooftop terrace dedicated to bird-watching. The food is excellent, too.

Palm Garden Guest House (☎ 223 3903; www.palm gardenkandy.com; 8 Bogodawatte Rd, Suduhumpola; r

Rs 1000-1500) Owned by a very friendly and industrious Kandy family, this modern and comfortable guesthouse offers 12 spacious rooms, each with its own balcony. The rooms at the back are quieter than those facing the street. The rooftop restaurant-bar is a great spot to relax, and the food – Sri Lankan, Indian and Western – may be the best guesthouse fare in Kandy. The guesthouse also offers reliable car hire (Rs 2750 per day) and personalised tours anywhere in Sri Lanka. It's a Rs 400 three-wheeler ride from the centre of town, on the road to Peradeniya.

Burmese Rest (DS Senanayake Vidiya; s/d Rs 150/300) This former pilgrims' guesthouse, still the cheapest place to stay in Kandy, has six very basic rooms downstairs with shared bathrooms – no showers, just small plastic buckets. Upstairs are four larger rooms with better shared toilet and shower facilities. With advance permission you may use the kitchen to prepare your own food. The monks living here are friendly, and the crumbling courtyard has its charms.

MIDRANGE & TOP END

Sharon Inn (☎ 222 2416; sharon@sltnet.lk; 59 Saranankara Rd; r incl breakfast Rs 2200; 🖳) At the top of Saranankara Rd, this is a particularly well-managed guesthouse. The owners, a Sri Lankan–German couple, keep everything scrupulously clean and are very helpful. The newer rooms upstairs have better views, while the older rooms on the 1st floor are a little more spacious. The guesthouse serves nightly Sri Lankan buffets (Rs 400).

Senkada Rest (☎ 222 9291; www.senkadarest.com; 108 Hewaheta Rd; r Rs1500-1750) A multistorey building tucked into a hillside, Senkada Rest offers a combination of helpful service and well-kept spacious rooms. The owners are happy to arrange free transport to or from your arrival point, with advance notice.

Hotel Casamara (☎ 222 4688; 12 Kotugodelle Vidiya; s/d Rs 2500/3000; 🕳) Conveniently located near the town centre, restaurants and lake, the Casamara features comfortable modern rooms with TV and minibar, plus a rooftop bar with cityscape views.

Golden View Rest (☎ 223 9418; goldenview@sltnet .lk; 46 Saranankara Rd; r with/without view Rs 1000/800, apt with/without air-con Rs 3000/1800) This large family-owned house offers nine very clean, quiet rooms, Chinese food, email access, an Ayurveda treatment room and even a piano. On the top floor the owners have recently added three new air-con rooms with a shared pantry, outdoor dining area and Finnish sauna. The rooms can be rented individually or together as an apartment.

Highest View (☎ /fax 223 3778; 129/3 Saranankara Rd; r Rs 600-1200) This place has clean, plainly decorated rooms with hot water, and a balcony with good views. The rooms without balconies are cheaper; the only complaint is that they're a bit small.

Royal Tourist Lodge (☎ 222 2534; www.royal lodge.srilankaads.com; 201 Rajapihilla Mawatha; r Rs 1250-2000; 🖳) This lodge is a comfortable, modern middle-class home with three guestrooms. The more expensive room has a balcony, and all have hot water. Meals are available if you order in advance.

Comfort Lodge (☎ 074 473707; www.lanka.net /comfort; 197 Rajapihilla Mawatha; s/d Rs 1300/1800) This place has six modern, smallish rooms with all mod cons, including hot water, TV and telephone. There's a large sitting area, a roof garden and cooking facilities.

Castle Hill Guest House (☎ 222 4376; ayoni@sltnet .lk; 22 Rajapihilla Mawatha; r Rs 2750) Overlooking the lake, this is a lovely art deco villa-turned-guesthouse with four rooms, all with

THE AUTHOR'S CHOICE

Queens Hotel (☎ 223 3290; queens@kandy .ccom.lk; Dalada Vidiya; s/d/tr US$30/40/50; 🕳 🖳) If you're assessing comfort-per-rupee, Kandy offers several comfortable yet bland options, but for ambience and location nothing else compares with this 165-year-old Raj relic. Having thus far escaped being taken over and gussied up by an international hotel franchise, the Queens harbours the lost-in-time feel that Yangon's Strand and Bangkok's Oriental long ago relinquished to the accountants. The large rooms have polished floorboards, old-style furniture (bedspreads your grandmother would probably love), telephone, TV and modern bathrooms. This is *the* place to be during the Kandy Esala Perahera (see p167), but any time of year it is a perfect base for exploring Kandy's quaint-cum-seedy town centre, plus it's only a short walk from the Temple of the Sacred Tooth Relic and Royal Palace compound. Kick back with a cold Three Coins at night at the equally antique Pub Royale next door.

THE HILL COUNTRY

bathroom. The rooms are immense, and the lounge room has a piano and French doors to the gardens.

Helga's Folly (☎ 223 4571; www.helgasfolly.com; 32 Frederick E de Silva Mawatha; r US$75-100, ste US$130; 🅧 🅜) Off Rajapihilla Mawatha, this is a deeply eccentric place crammed with palatial furnishings, puffed with comfy cushions and partially lit by wax-dripping candelabras. A long list of celebs stayed here in the post-WWII era; the Stereophonics composed the song 'Madame Helga' after a memorable stay here. It's possibly the only hotel in the world that discourages having too many guests, and package tourists are banned. All rooms have attached bathrooms and private balconies. There's a pool surrounded by fairy statues, and a restaurant where merely curious nonguests can dine.

Hotel Hilltop (☎ 282 2416; hilltop@ispkandyan.lk; 200/21 Bahirawakanda; s/d incl breakfast US$42/54; 🅧 🅜) A five-minute walk off Peradeniya Rd, the Hilltop has 81 colourful rooms, great views over the town and surrounding hills, a peaceful garden with a good-sized, clean swimming pool and a modest Ayurvedic health centre.

Hotel Swiss Residence (☎ 447 9054; jethot@sri .lanka.net; 23 Bahirawakanda; s/d tr incl breakfast US$50/55/60; 🅧 🅜) This multistorey, 40-room hotel sits atop one of the city's highest hills, so virtually every room has a great view. All rooms are equipped with IDD phone, satellite TV and balcony or terrace.

Hotel Suisse (☎ 223 3024; suisse@kandy.ccom.lk; 30 Sangaraja Mawatha; s/d US$55/67; 🅜) South of the lake, this was once a British governor's house before sprouting extra ballrooms and billiards rooms and turning into a rambling hotel. The original wing dates back to the 1840s. The rooms have been updated with satellite TV, minibar and comfy chairs, but six rooms have antique or reproduction furniture for the full colonial attack. Be forewarned that, for such a palatial spot, the beds tend to be rather hard and the pillows rather flat. Although a bit far from the town centre, one can stroll around the lake to the town centre. There are spacious public areas, including a snooker room and a fine garden. On weekends, when Kandyans host wedding parties here, it can be rather busy.

Thilanka (☎ 223 2429; www.hotelthilanka.com; 3 Sanghamitta Mawatha; s/d US$40/45; 🅧 🅜) This rather large but very welcoming hotel overlooks the lake. The older rooms are a bit dark and neglected, while the newer wing offers light, airy rooms and great views. The oldest part of the hotel, including the reception hall, still boasts some of the original features, including elegant tiles and furniture. From the pool area, guests have a good view over the town and lake.

Hotel Topaz (☎ 223 2326; topaz@eureka.lk; Anniewatte; s/d US$58/66; 🅧 🅚 🅜) Way up on top of a hill overlooking the town from the west, about 2km up from Peradeniya Rd, Topaz has 75 rooms (most with air-con). It's rather bland but the superb views and swimming pool help justify the prices.

Citadel (Map pp164-5 ☎ 223 4365/6; htlres@keells .com; 124 Srimath Kuda Ratwatte Mawatha; s/d with air-con US$101/115; 🅧 🅜) A mostly package-tour resort beside the Mahaweli Ganga, 5km west of the town centre, Citadel has 121 rooms with balconies overlooking the river. The swimming pool is worth a visit. A taxi from Kandy costs Rs 400.

Eating

Lyon Café (☎ 222 3073; 27 Peradeniya Rd; dishes Rs 60-120; 🕗 8am-11pm) Among locals this is one of Kandy's most famous restaurants. There are three dining rooms, a fan-cooled room downstairs and two slightly fancier, air-con rooms on two separate floors upstairs. About two-thirds of the menu is Chinese, a third Sri Lankan, but for dinner just about everyone orders the Sino-Sinhalese 'Lyon Special', a huge platter of fried rice, boiled eggs and your choice of devilled meats. One plate will easily feed two or three people (though that doesn't stop most Sri Lankan patrons from downing one platter each).

History Restaurant (☎ 220 2109; 27A Anagarika Dharmapala Mawatha; mains from Rs 300; 🕗 8am-11pm) A high-concept restaurant owned by the same family that owns Bake House and Pub, History is named for the hundreds of black-and-white photos – taken during the 100-year period between 1860 and 1960 – that decorate its walls. The menu offers an eclectic variety of European, Thai, Malay and Italian dishes. The restaurant occupies the 2nd floor of a new building close to the lake. As you climb the stairs, stop off at the 1st floor to see Sri Lanka's first 'show kitchen'.

(Continued on page 185)

ANDERS BLOMQVIST

Pottery shop on the Colombo–Kandy road (p161)

A selection of fabrics, Colombo (p102)

CHRISTINE NIVEN

CHRISTINE NIVEN

Lentils for sale, Galle market (p137)

Fruit stall, Kalutara (p117)

DALLAS STRIBLEY

Stilt fishermen, near Koggala (p141)

Early morning beachside fish
sales, Negombo (p112)

Baby turtle, Kosgoda Turtle Hatchery (p121)

Outrigger fishing boat, Negombo (p111)

MICHAEL AW

Palm trees, Unawatuna (p138)

RICHARD I'ANSON

Fishermen at sunset, Midigama (p142)

MARK DAFFEY

Hanuman langur, Bundala National Park (p152)

Lizards are just some of Sri Lanka's many species of wildlife (p60)

Leopard, Yala National Park (p156)

CHRIS MELLOR

Baby elephant, Pinnewela Elephant Orphanage (p162)

MICHAEL AW

Green bee-eater (p63)

Chital deer, Yala National Park (p156)

JASON EDWARDS

Reclining Buddha statue at Isurumuniya Vihara (p252), Anuradhapura

RICHARD I'ANSON

Fresco (p235), Sigiriya

RICHARD I'ANSON

ERIC L WHEATER

Decorative dagoba, Anuradhapura (p247)

Seated Buddha statue at Gangaramaya Temple (p91), Colombo

RICHARD I'ANSON

One of Sri Lanka's vividly decorated *kovils* (Hindu temples; p57)

GREG ELMS

MARK DAFFEY

Adisham Monastery (p210), Haputale

DALLAS STRIBLEY

Waiter at Galle Face Hotel (p95), Colombo

Opposite: Tea pickers, Nuwara Eliya (p199)

ANDERS BLOMQVIST

Viharamahadevi Park (p90), Colombo

CHRIS MELLOR

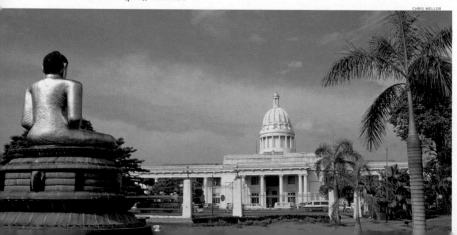

CHRIS MELLOR

Buddhist monks at Malwatte Maha Vihara
(p168), Kandy

Burgher man (p44)

ANTONY GIBLIN

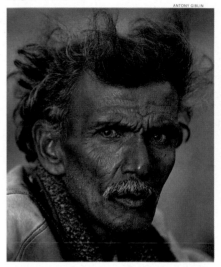

Pilgrims outside Maha Devale (p157), Kataragama

RICHARD I'ANSON

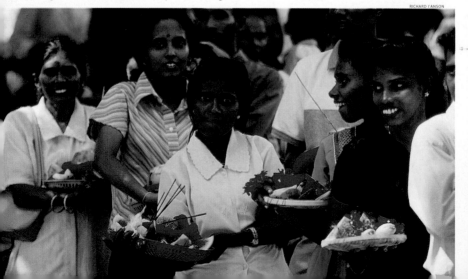

Pilgrims descending Adam's Peak (Sri Pada; p194)

Drummer with *geta bera* (double-ended drum), Kandy (p186)

Worshippers entering a mosque, Galle (p130)

CHRISTINE NIVEN

Spices and vegetables waiting to be cooked

A typical array of meat, vegetables and chillies

RICHARD NEBESKY

RICHARD NEBESKY

Curry served with string hoppers, *rotti*, hoppers and *sambol*

Veddah man with betel nuts, lime and tobacco leaves

DALLAS STRIBL

(Continued from page 172)

Flower Song Chinese Restaurant (☎ 222 3628; 137 Kotugodella Vidiya; dishes Rs 400-700) Another local family favourite, Flower Song does Sri Lankan–style Chinese with old-fashioned service in clean, air-con surroundings.

Olde Empire Hotel (☎ 222 4284; 21 Temple St; dishes Rs 75-150) This hotel's (p170) modest dining hall is full of character and still serves delicious rice and curry, and lunch packets.

Bake House (☎ 223 4868; 36 Dalada Vidiya; dishes Rs 70-150) Downstairs from Pub, and under the same ownership, Bake House is a quick counter-service place with pastries and short eats (plates of pastries and savouries). The bacon-and-egg roll is a good bet any time of day.

Devon Restaurant (Dalada Vidiya; dishes Rs 80-350) Popular with both visitors and locals, the chrome-and-Formica Devon Restaurant offers a wide range of Chinese, Western and Sri Lankan dishes.

White House Restaurant (Dalada Vidiya; mains Rs 100-250) Down the street from Devon, this restaurant is tacky but cheap. It has snacks, drinks and ice cream, or you can fill up on meals such as mixed fried rice, chicken fried noodles and sweet-and-sour chicken.

Paiva's Restaurant (37 Yatinuwara Vidiya; dishes Rs 70-300) Featuring a North Indian menu, Chinese menu and bakery, Paiva's Restaurant offers a seating choice between the airy, busy section downstairs or the office-like surroundings upstairs. There's also an inexpensive lunchtime rice and curry.

Rams (11 DS Senanayake Vidiya; mains Rs 150-250; ☯ 7.30am-10pm) In a new, larger location, Rams continues to serve good South Indian food, including vegetarian thalis ('all-you-can-eat' meals consisting of rice with vegetable curries and pappadams) and a variety of dosas (paper-thin rice- and lentil-flour pancakes) in a wonderfully colourful setting featuring Hindu devotional art.

Delight Bakers & Sweet House (Dalada Vidiya; dishes Rs 60-150) Similar to Bake House, Delight has reasonable bread, pastries, cakes and short eats, and dozens of sweets waiting to march out the door.

Cargills Food City (Dalada Vidiya) Self-caterers can shop for groceries or cheap prepackaged meals here.

Many people eat in their guesthouses, where some of Kandy's tastiest food is to be had. Particular kudos go to the kitchens at **Golden View Rest** (☎ 223 9418; 46 Saranankara Rd), **Sharon Inn** (☎ 222 2416; 59 Saranankara Rd; buffet Rs 400), **Palm Garden Guest House** (☎ 223 3903; 8 Bogodawatte Rd, Suduhumpola) and **Lakshmi Guest House** (☎ 222 2154; 57/1/1 Saranankara Rd). Non-guests are welcome, but should call ahead to make sure there's enough food to go around.

Drinking

In this sacred city the zoning and licensing for pubs, bars and discos is very strict – the typical Kandyan goes to bed early, and looks down on recreational drinking. As well as the places listed below, the top hotels all have bars.

Pub (☎ 232 4868; 36 Dalada Vidiya; ☯ 4pm-midnight) This pub, with a balcony overlooking the street below, is a good place to unwind and meet other travellers over a beer. Stick to beer and cocktails; on our last couple of visits we found the food to be of below-average quality, yet overpriced – and rather slow to arrive.

Pub Royale (Dalada Vidiya; ☯ 5pm midnight) Beside Queens Hotel, this is a large airy bar with old-fashioned flavour. It's a place for a quiet drink, with relatively low prices.

Kandy Garden Club (☎ 222 2675; Sangaraja Mawatha; ☯ 5pm-late) At the far end of the lake, this venerable gentlemen's club is open to visitors, and for a temporary membership fee (Rs 100) you can relax in the bar or on the veranda with a Lion Lager and fried devilled cashews. For a fee, rack up on the old tables in the billiards room, still something of a male bastion.

Entertainment
NIGHTCLUBS

Kandy's two nightclubs are found in hotels. At both, entry for women is free, for mixed couples Rs 400 to 500, and there's usually no entry allowed for men from outside the hotel. Expect dress codes to turn away anyone in shorts, sandals or baseball caps.

Blackout (☎ 447 9054; Swiss Residence, 23 Bahirawakanda) Located in Swiss Residence, this is the only dance club within city limits.

Le Garage (Map p189; ☎ 223 3521-2; Amaya Hills, Heerassagala; ☯ 9pm-2am Fri, to 3am Sat). Twenty minutes' drive southwest of town by three-wheeler (Rs 500), the Amaya Hills disco is open Friday and Saturday nights only.

THE HILL COUNTRY

KANDYAN DANCERS & DRUMMERS

The famed Kandyan dancers are not principally a theatrical performance, but you can see them go through their athletic routines each night at three locales around Kandy.

Kandy Lake Club (admission Rs 300) Located 300m up Sanghamitta Mawatha, this club starts its show at 7pm. It's very popular; the finale is a display of fire-walking. The front seats are usually reserved for groups and if you want to get good seats, turn up at least 20 minutes early. Kandy Lake Club is also a casino.

Kandyan Art Association & Cultural Centre (admission Rs 300) There are shows here at 6pm, which culminate in fire-walking. The auditorium makes it easier to take photographs than at Kandy Lake Club. It's on the northern lake shore.

Mahanuwara YMBA (☎ 223 3444; 5 Rajapihilla Mawatha; admission Rs 300) Southwest of the lake, the YMBA guesthouse (p170) hosts dance shows at 5.45pm.

You can also hear Kandyan drummers every day at the Temple of the Sacred Tooth Relic (p166) and the other temples surrounding it – their drumming signals the start and finish of the daily *puja*.

SPORT

The modest Asgiriya Stadium, north of the town centre, hosts crowds of up to 10,000 cheering fans at international one-day and test matches. Ticket prices depend on the popularity of the two teams. India versus Sri Lanka matches are the most valued; seats in the grandstand can cost up to Rs 2000, while standing room in the public areas will cost Rs 120. Tickets are also sold on the day, or you can book grandstand seats up to a month in advance through the **Sri Lanka Cricket office** (☎ 223 8533; sl.cricinfo.com) at the stadium or online.

If you're a rugby fan and are in Kandy between May and September, you can take in a game or two at the Nittawella rugby grounds. Check with the tourist office for details on who's playing when.

Shopping

The Kandyan Art Association & Cultural Centre (above) has a good selection of local lacquerwork, brassware and other craft items in a colonial-era showroom covered in a patina of age. There are some craftspeople working on the spot.

There's a government-run Laksala arts and crafts shop to the west of the lake that has cheaper prices than those of the Art Association & Cultural Centre, but it has nothing on the big Laksala in Colombo.

Central Kandy has a number of shops selling antique jewellery, silver belts and other items. You can also buy crafts in and around the colourful **main market** (Station Rd). Kandy has a number of batik manufacturers; some of the best and most original are the batik pictures made by **Upali Jayakody** (Peradeniya Rd) and by **Fresco Batiks** (Peradeniya Rd) outside Kandy. You'll find several showrooms purveying antiques and curios in the same general vicinity, including **Dharshana Lanka Arts** (Peradeniya Rd).

Getting There & Away

BUS

Kandy has one main bus station (the manic Goods Shed) and a series of bus stops near the clock tower. It can be hard to work out which one to head to. A rule of thumb worth following is that the Goods Shed has long-distance buses, while local buses, such as to Peradeniya, Ampitiya, Matale and Kegalle, leave from near the clock tower. However, some private intercity express buses (to the airport, Negombo and Colombo, for example) leave from Station Rd between the clock tower and the train station. If you're still confused, ask a passer-by.

Colombo

CTB buses run from the Goods Shed bus station every half-hour till 8.30pm (Rs 70, 3½ hours). There are also ordinary private buses (Rs 80 to 120, three hours), and air-con intercity express buses (Rs 140, 2½ to three hours); both services start at 5.15am and leave when full throughout the day (on average every 45 minutes). The express and ordinary buses leave from stand No 1.

International Airport & Negombo

Private intercity express buses to Bandaranaike International Airport and Negombo leave from the Station Rd bus stop. CTB buses leave from the Goods Shed. The first intercity bus departs at about 6.30am and the last at about 5.30pm. They tend to leave when full, every 20 to 30 minutes. The fare for the three- to 3½-hour journey is Rs 64 for the CTB bus and Rs 140 for the air-con express bus.

Nuwara Eliya & Hatton
Private air-con buses go to Nuwara Eliya, and some go on to Hatton (or you can change in Nuwara Eliya for Hatton). They leave from the Goods Shed bus station every half-hour between 5am and 5pm. The fare is Rs 125.

Haputale & Ella
Change buses at Nuwara Eliya for these destinations.

Ratnapura
Ordinary buses to Ratnapura leave from the Goods Shed every 45 minutes, from 5.30pm to 3.45am; the fare is Rs 67.

Anuradhapura
Buses leave from the Goods Shed bus station. Air-con intercity express buses start running at about 4.30am and depart roughly every half-hour until 6.30pm. The trip takes three hours and costs Rs 150. Ordinary buses take about 30 minutes longer and cost Rs 75. You can also catch an air-con Anuradhapura-bound bus to Dambulla, but you must pay the full amount regardless. The trip to Dambulla on an ordinary private bus costs Rs 40.

Polonnaruwa
Ordinary buses leave the Goods Shed bus station from 4.30am and go roughly every 20 minutes until 6pm. Tickets are Rs 90 and the journey takes three hours, with a change of bus in Dambulla (included in the ticket price). Air-con buses leave three times daily at 9.30am, 11.30am and 1pm and cost Rs 150.

Sigiriya
There's a CTB bus to Sigiriya from the Goods Shed bus station at 10.30am, which returns at 5.30pm (Rs 45). There are a couple of ordinary private buses per day for Rs 52. You can also take one of the more-frequent Polonnaruwa-bound buses, then get off at the Sigiriya junction and take another bus the final 9km to Sigiriya.

TAXI
Many long-distance taxi drivers hang around the Temple of the Sacred Tooth Relic, waiting for work. Your guesthouse or hotel can organise taxi tours but you may be able to get a cheaper deal if you organise it through these chaps. Cars can generally be hired, with a driver and petrol, for approximately

MAIN TRAINS FROM KANDY

Destination	Departure time	3rd-class fares (Rs)	2nd-class fares (Rs)	1st-class fares (Rs)	Duration (hr)
Badulla (Podi Menike)	8.24am, 11.10am	92	171	341	7½
Bandarawela (Podi Menike)	8.24am, 11.10am	76	141	270	6
Colombo (Intercity Express)	6.25am, 3pm	80	125	250	2½
Colombo via Rambukkana	1.40am, 6.40am, 10.30am, 3pm, 4.10pm	61	114	—	3
Ella (Podi Menike)	8.24am, 11.10am	82	152	310	6½
Haputale (Podi Menike)	8.24am, 11.10am	70	121	268	5½
Hatton (Podi Menike)	8.24am, 11.10am	35	64	245	2½
Matale	5.10am, 7.05am, 10.05am, 2.25pm, 5.20pm, 6.55pm	13	—	—	1½
Matara via Bentota & Galle	5.20am	135	225	—	6
Nanu Oya (for Nuwara Eliya) (Podi Menike)	8.24am, 11.10am	51	94	289	4

Rs 2000 to 2500 per day. For a whole van you should expect to pay around Rs 2800 per day.

Some guesthouses advertise day trips to all three Cultural Triangle destinations (Sigiriya, Anuradhapura and Polonnaruwa) but this is an exhausting itinerary for both driver and passengers, and one that encourages manic driving. At least one overnight stay in Anuradhapura, Sigiriya or Polonnaruwa would be a saner – and safer – option.

A taxi to Bandaranaike International Airport costs about Rs 4000 and to Colombo about Rs 3200.

TRAIN
For details of the train services from Kandy see p187. Tickets can be bought and reserved up to 10 days in advance at Kandy's train station from counter 1, which is open from 5.30am to 5.30pm.

Seats are very popular in the 1st-class observation saloon on the Badulla-bound train, which originates in Colombo and after Kandy stops in Hatton (near Adam's Peak), Nanu Oya, Haputale and Ella, yet the official allocation for Kandy boarding is limited to a mere four seats. If you're unable to reserve a seat at the ticket window, it's worth checking with the stationmaster, who has the authority to release further seating for tourists.

Getting Around
BICYCLE
You can hire bicycles from **Malik Tours** (☎ 220 3513; www.palmgardenkandy.com; Palm Garden Guest House, 8 Bogodawatte Rd, Suduhumpola) for Rs 150 per day. Some guesthouses can arrange bicycle hire, as well.

BUS
Buses to outlying parts of Kandy and nearby towns such as Peradeniya, Ampitiya, Matale and Kegalle leave from near the clock tower.

CAR & MOTORCYCLE
You can hire cars and motorcycles for self-drive from **Malik Tours** (☎ 220 3513; www.palm gardenkandy.com; Palm Garden Guest House, 8 Bogoda-watte Rd, Suduhumpola). This well-run company hires out Nissan Charades or Toyota Corollas for Rs 2500 per day with unlimited kilometres. A Honda 250cc motorcycle or similar costs Rs 1250 per day, discounted

to Rs 1000 per day for hires of five days or more. The price includes a helmet and insurance – but double-check with the company. Malik also leads tours around the island and is fluent in French.

TAXI
With metered air-con taxis, **Radio Cabs** (☎ 223 3322) is a comfortable alternative to three-wheelers. However, be aware that you may have to wait some time for your cab, especially if it's raining and demand is heavy. With taxis (vans) that are not metered, settle on a price before you start your journey. On average, taxis cost Rs 40 to 45 per kilometre.

THREE-WHEELER
The standard cost to take a three-wheeler from the train station to places towards the southeast end of the lake is Rs 60 to 100, and as much as Rs 120 to 200 to places a bit further out such as Green Woods. Drivers will ask foreign tourists for much more than this, but if you stick to your guns you'll get the local price.

AROUND KANDY
☎ 081
There are a few things worth seeing around Kandy that can be done in a morning or afternoon trip or – if you're not in a rush – you could take the day.

Sights & Activities
PERADENIYA BOTANIC GARDENS
The **gardens** (adult/student/child under 12 Rs 300/200/ 200; ☺ 7.30am-4.30pm) are 6km from Kandy. Before the British arrived these were royal pleasure gardens; today they're the largest botanic gardens in Sri Lanka, covering 60 hectares and bounded on three sides by a loop of the Mahaweli Ganga. They're beautiful and well worth a visit.

There's a fine collection of orchids and a stately avenue of royal palms that was planted in 1950. A major attraction is the giant Javan fig tree on the great lawn – it covers 1600 sq m. There's an avenue of cannon ball trees and another of cabbage palms. Don't miss the avenue of double coconut palms (coco de mer) – each coconut weighs from 10kg to 20kg. The spice garden, near the entrance, allows you to see nutmeg, cinnamon, cloves and more. The snake creeper close by is also well

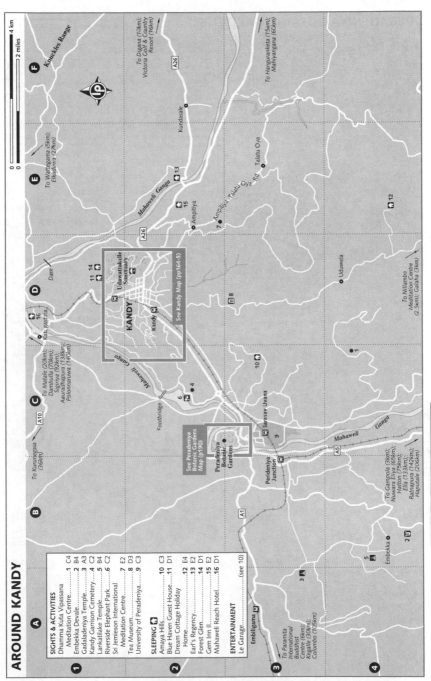

AROUND KANDY

SIGHTS & ACTIVITIES
Dhamma Kuta Vipassana	
Meditation Centre............1	C4
Embekka Devale...............2	B4
Gadaladeniya Temple........3	A3
Kandy Garrison Cemetery...4	C2
Lankatilake Temple...........5	B4
Riverside Elephant Park......6	C2
Sri Jemieson International	
Meditation Centre............7	E2
Tea Museum...................8	D3
University of Peradeniya.....9	C3

SLEEPING
Amaya Hills....................10	C3
Blue Haven Guest House....11	D1
Dream Cottage Holiday	
Home..........................12	E4
Earl's Regency.................13	E2
Forest Glen....................14	D1
Gem Inn II.....................15	E2
Mahaweli Reach Hotel.......16	D1

ENTERTAINMENT
Le Garage..................(see 10)	

THE HILL COUNTRY

PERADENIYA BOTANIC GARDENS

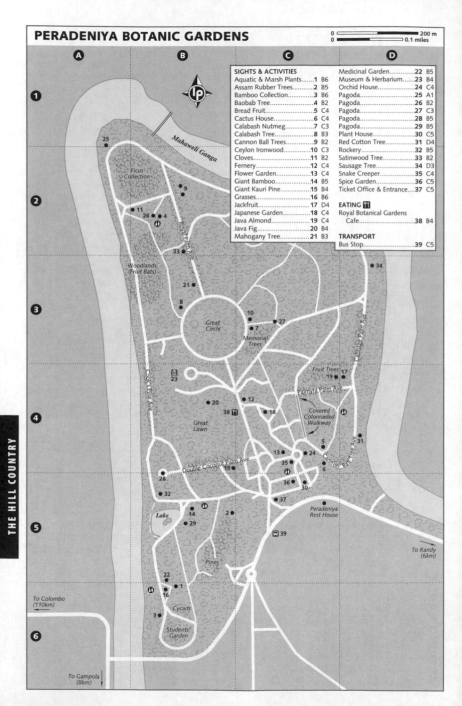

SIGHTS & ACTIVITIES

Aquatic & Marsh Plants......**1**	B6
Assam Rubber Trees...........**2**	B5
Bamboo Collection.............**3**	B6
Baobab Tree......................**4**	B2
Bread Fruit........................**5**	C4
Cactus House....................**6**	C4
Calabash Nutmeg...............**7**	C3
Calabash Tree...................**8**	B3
Cannon Ball Trees..............**9**	B2
Ceylon Ironwood..............**10**	C3
Cloves.............................**11**	B2
Fernery...........................**12**	C4
Flower Garden..................**13**	C4
Giant Bamboo..................**14**	B5
Giant Kauri Pine...............**15**	B4
Grasses...........................**16**	B6
Jackfruit..........................**17**	D4
Japanese Garden..............**18**	C4
Java Almond....................**19**	C4
Java Fig..........................**20**	B4
Mahogany Tree...............**21**	B3

Medicinal Garden.............**22**	B5
Museum & Herbarium......**23**	B4
Orchid House...................**24**	C4
Pagoda...........................**25**	A1
Pagoda...........................**26**	B2
Pagoda...........................**27**	C3
Pagoda...........................**28**	B5
Pagoda...........................**29**	B5
Plant House.....................**30**	C5
Red Cotton Tree..............**31**	D4
Rockery...........................**32**	B5
Satinwood Tree................**33**	B2
Sausage Tree...................**34**	D3
Snake Creeper.................**35**	C4
Spice Garden...................**36**	C5
Ticket Office & Entrance....**37**	C5

EATING 🍴

Royal Botanical Gardens Cafe...............................**38**	B4

TRANSPORT

Bus Stop.........................**39**	C5

PAINTING THE BUDDHA'S EYES

In making a Buddha image, craftsmen leave the *netra pinkama* (eye ritual) until last, and then only paint them in at an auspicious moment, painstakingly charted out by astrologers.

The act of creating the eyes consecrates the Buddha statue. For the *netra pinkama*, the painter, from the Sittaru subcaste of temple craftsmen and artists, is locked into the shrine with an assistant. Rather than looking directly at the face of the image, the painter adds the eyes using a mirror. When the eyes are finished, the painter is blindfolded and led outside to a place where his first gaze can be upon something that can be symbolically destroyed, such as a pool of water, which can be hit with a stick. There is quite a fear of dire consequences if there's a slip-up in the *netra pinkama*. In the 16th century Robert Knox explained the ritual this way: 'Before the eyes are made, it is not accounted a God, but a lump of ordinary metal…the eyes being formed, it is thenceforward a God.'

worth seeing. Then there are the giant bamboo and Assam rubber trees, and who could resist hunting down the sausage tree? You can easily spend a whole day wandering around these gardens.

The Royal Botanical Garden Café (dishes Rs 300 to 600), about 500m north of the entrance, serves good à la carte meals (Western and Sri Lankan) at tables on a roofed veranda. Inside the café is a gift shop with locally made clothes and fabrics.

At the entrance you can buy a copy of the *Illustrated Guide, Royal Botanic Gardens*, which has a map and suggested walks through the gardens. There are other books available too – all decently priced.

Bus 654 from the clock tower bus stop in Kandy will take you to the gardens for Rs 4.50. A three-wheeler from the centre of Kandy to the gardens will set you back about Rs 600 (return trip) and a van will cost Rs 1000.

KANDY GARRISON CEMETERY

This beautifully kept garden **cemetery** (Deveni Rajasinghe; donations accepted; ⏰ 10am-noon, 1-6pm) was founded in 1817 for the interment of British-era colonists and is thus managed by the Commonwealth War Graves Commission. Although there are many 19th-century grave sites, most of the 203 graves date from WWII. The most famous permanent resident of the cemetery is Sir John D'Oyly, a colonial official who planned the bloodless British capture of Kandy in 1815 and then succumbed to cholera in 1824.

This peaceful, rather sad place is close to the River Side Elephant Park, 2km southwest of Kandy.

RIVERSIDE ELEPHANT PARK

Those who don't plan to visit the Pinnewala Elephant Orphanage can engage in close encounters with pachyderms at this **park** (admission Rs 400; ⏰ 7.30am-4.30pm) 4km southwest of Kandy on the Mahaweli Ganga. On our last visit there were six elephants on hand. The admission price includes a short ride, while Rs 1000 buys a longer ride, very popular with Sri Lankan visitors in particular. An 'elephant safari' to Kandy and back costs Rs 2000. The elephants knock off work at around noon and bathe in the river.

A TEMPLE LOOP FROM KANDY

Visiting some of the many temples around Kandy gives you a chance to see a little rural life as well as observe Sri Lankan culture. This particularly pleasant loop will take you to three 14th-century Hindu-Buddhist temples and back, via the botanic gardens. There's quite a bit of walking involved so if you're not in the mood you could narrow down your visit to one or two of the temples listed or take a taxi trip to all three; expect to pay Rs 1500 to 1800 from Kandy.

The first stop is the **Embekka Devale** (admission Rs 100), for which you need to catch bus 643 (to Vatadeniya via Embekka) from near the clock tower in Kandy. The buses run about three times an hour and the village of Embekka is about seven twisting and turning kilometres beyond the botanic gardens, a ride of around an hour from Kandy. From the village you've got a pleasant countryside stroll of about 1km to the temple, built in the 14th century. Its carved wooden pillars, thought to have come from a royal audience hall in the city, are said to be the finest

THE HILL COUNTRY

in the Kandy region. The carvings include swans, eagles, wrestling men and dancing women. A local elephant *perahera* is held here in September.

From here to the **Lankatilake Temple** (admission Rs 100) is a 1.5km stroll along a path through the rice paddies until you see the blue temple loom on the left. From Kandy you can go directly to the Lankatilake Temple on bus 666 or take a Kiribathkumbara or Pilimatalawa bus from the same stop as the Embekka buses. It's a Buddhist and Hindu temple with fine views of the countryside, featuring a Buddha image, Kandy-period paintings, rock-face inscriptions and stone elephant figures. A caretaker will unlock the shrine if it's not already open. A *perahera* is held here in August.

It's a further 3km walk from here to the **Gadaladeniya Temple** (admission Rs 100), or you can catch a bus from Kandy (bus 644, among others, will take you there). Built on a rocky outcrop and covered with small pools, the temple is reached by a series of steps cut into the rock. This Buddhist temple with a Hindu annexe dates from a similar period to that of the Lankatilake Temple and the Embekka Devale. A moonstone (carved stone 'doorstep') marks the entrance. The shrine's murals and some of the statues have been nicely restored. A resident artist will be happy to show you around.

The main Colombo–Kandy road is less than 2km from Gadaladeniya Temple – you reach the road close to the 105km post. It's a pleasant stroll, and from the main road almost any bus will take you to the Peradeniya Botanic Gardens or on to Kandy.

MEDITATION

Nilambe Meditation Centre (☎ 077 775 7216; upul nilambe@yahoo.com), close to Nilambe Bungalow Junction about 13km south of Kandy, can be reached by bus (catch a Delthota bus via Galaha and get off at Office Junction; the trip takes about an hour). It's a pretty spot, with great views. There's a daily schedule of meditation classes, and basic accommodation for about 40 people. You can stay for Rs 400 per day (including food), and although blankets are supplied you may wish to bring a sleeping bag. There's no electricity, so bring a torch. To reach Nilambe from Office Junction you have a steep 3km walk through tea plantations (or a three-wheeler may be at

the junction to take you for Rs 150). A taxi to/from Kandy costs Rs 750. The road up to the centre is a narrow, partially sealed track, so you might want to summon a van rather than a sedan.

Near Ampitiya, 4km southeast of Kandy, the **Sri Jemieson International Meditation Centre** (☎ 222 5057; Ampitiya Samadhi Mawatha) runs free five- and 10-day courses. Phone to find out when the next course starts. There are eight rooms for male students only – this is a monastery and temple. Women must stay off-campus but are welcome to meditate here during the day. To get here catch a Talatu Oya bus from the clock tower bus stop in Kandy. Look for the sign on the right-hand side about 3km along the Ampitiya–Talatu Oya road. There's a 1.2km walk up a winding track to the centre.

Dhamma Kuta Vipassana Meditation Centre (☎ 223 4649; www.beyondthenet.net/dhammakuta; Mowbray, Hindagala) offers free 10-day courses following the SN Goenka system of meditation, but you must book – you can't just turn up. There's dorm accommodation for about 90 students, with separate male and female quarters. Retreat schedules are posted at the Buddhist Publication Society in Kandy. Take a Mahakanda-bound bus from the clock tower bus stop in Kandy and get off at the last stop. There's a small sign at the bottom of the track to the centre. It's a very steep 2km walk, or you can catch a three-wheeler for Rs 150. A taxi from Kandy should cost Rs 400 to 500.

The **Paramita International Buddhist Centre** (☎ 257 0732) at the top of the Bolana Pass, 1km past Kadugannawa on the Colombo road, is another meditation centre. It runs two free fortnight-long meditation programs per month, starting every second Saturday. It has clean accommodation for 15 people (men and women), lush gardens and a library. A typical day kicks off at 4am. Several teachers, including a Dutch monk, lead courses in SN Goenka's Vipassana. A three-wheeler from here to Kadugannawa's train or bus stations will cost Rs 50.

Sleeping

If you want quiet days spent wandering along shaded tracks, with views of rolling hills, then stay just out of Kandy. It's always easy to get into town should you want to – a taxi or three-wheeler is never far away.

BUDGET

Gem Inn II (☎ 222 4239; www.geminn.com; 102/90 Hewaheta Rd, Talwatta; r Rs 600-1400) About 2.5km southeast of Kandy's town centre, this guesthouse is perched on a hillside with wonderful views over the Mahaweli Ganga and the Knuckles Range. There are seven rooms, all looking a bit tired; most have their own balcony. There's a large garden and good food.

Blue Haven Guest House (☎ 223 2453; bluehav travels@sltnet.lk; 30/2 Poorna Lane; s Rs 500-800, d Rs 1000-1200; 🖳) On the north side of the Udawattakelle Sanctuary in Kandy, each of the five rooms has florid décor, hot water and a large airy balcony overlooking the jungle setting. The owner can arrange road trips and walks around Kandy and into the Knuckles Range.

Forest Glen (☎ 222 2239; forestglen@ids.lk; 150/6 Lady Gordon's Dr, Sri Dalada Thapowana Mawatha; r Rs 900-1500; 🔀) Tucked away on a winding road on the edge of Udawattakelle Sanctuary, this is a welcoming guesthouse with good food. The eight rooms feature fans, spotless bathrooms and views over a leafy little valley. Rooms with balconies cost the most.

MIDRANGE & TOP END

Dream Cottage Holiday Home (☎ 071 283626; siribas@ sltnet.lk; Uduwela; s/d Rs 1500/1800) This modern villa is 10km south of Kandy (the road here leads through tea estates), set in the country side at the foot of the Uragala Range. It has intriguing architecture, incorporating two huge boulders, and are three rooms, or you can rent out the whole place for Rs 5000 – it has room for eight. There are frequent minibuses from the clock tower to Uduwela; from there a three-wheeler costs Rs 350. It's on the site of the former Metiyagulla Tea Estate, so ask for that name if no-one in Uduwela seems to have heard of the place.

Mahaweli Reach Hotel (☎ 074 472727; www.mahaweli.com; 35 PBA Weerakoon Mawatha; s/d US$135/150, ste US$250-500; 🔀 🖳) Vying for the honour of being Kandy's best hotel, this palatial white building occupies a beautiful spot on the banks of the Mahaweli Ganga north of town. The 115 spacious rooms have recently been renovated. Facilities include elegant restaurants, tennis and squash courts and a particularly nice swimming pool. International cricket teams stay here, and the hotel sometimes hosts concerts (jazz or classical music, typically).

Amaya Hills (☎ 223 3521; amayahills@amayaresorts .com; Heerassagala; r/ste US$96/184; 🔀 🖳) This imposing, V-shaped hotel sits on a grassy slope high in the hills, 20 minutes' drive southwest of Kandy. The rooms are decorated with Kandyan craftwork, and there's an inviting pool with superb views and a well-equipped Ayurvedic centre, which is also open to nonguests. A disco, Le Garage, is open Saturday nights only.

Earl's Regency (☎ 242 2122; erhotel@sltnet.lk; s/d US$120/140; 🔀 🖳 🖳) Near Kundasale, this is a substantial hotel with all mod cons, great views and immaculate rooms. The rooms have a slick black bathroom and polished floorboards, and most have a balcony. The only drawback is that it's very popular with tour groups, and since there are no restaurants nearby, you may find yourself queuing for buffet meals.

EAST OF KANDY

Most travellers from Kandy go west to Colombo, north to the ancient cities or south to the rest of the Hill Country. It's also possible to go east to Mahiyangana, beyond which you will find Badulla on the edge of the Hill Country and Monaragala on the way to Arugam Bay, Gal Oya National Park and, further north, Batticaloa on the east coast; all are reachable by bus from Kandy.

The Buddha is said to have preached at Mahiyangana and there's a dagoba here to mark the spot. There are two roads to Mahiyangana, on either side of the Mahaweli Ganga and the Victoria and Randenigala Reservoirs. The A26 north road goes past the Victoria Golf Club and the Victoria Reservoir to Madugoda, before twisting through no less than 18 hairpin bends, a dramatic exit from the Hill Country to the Mahaweli lowlands and the dry-zone plains. From the top you have a magnificent view of the Mahaweli Development Project. It makes for one of the country's hairiest bus rides – on the way up you worry about overheating and on the way down you try not to think about the brakes. You usually pass at least one 4WD or truck that didn't make it and that now lies in the jungle beneath.

Drivers prefer the road along the southern shores of the Victoria and Randenigala Reservoirs, which is much faster and in better condition. This road closes at dusk, however, because wild elephants from the nature reserve are attracted to headlights. To travel from Kandy to the hills of Uva Province (including towns such as Ella and Haputale), it's quicker to take this road and then the route south to Badulla than to go via Nuwara Eliya.

Mahiyangana

☎ 055

The town was laid out to serve the new irrigation districts, so it's sprawling and not very densely settled. Besides the **Mahiyangana dagoba** (where, according to legend, the Buddha on his first visit to Lanka preached to the primitive people who then inhabited these parts) there are a couple of passable hotels.

Venjinn Guest House (☎ 225 7151; 42 Rest House Rd; r Rs 500-1200, with air-con Rs 1400-1800; ✱) This place has 10 fairly ordinary rooms, plus an outdoor restaurant and a bar. It's a short three-wheeler ride from the bus station.

Tharuka Inn (☎ 225 7631; 89/1 Padiyathalawa Rd; s/d Rs 1000/1400) About 1km from the bus station on the Ampara road, this is a multistorey building with slow country service. The clean bland rooms (cold water only) will do for a night.

Mahiyangana Rest House (☎ /fax 225 7099; r Rs 1800-2500, with air-con Rs 2500-3000; ✱) On the banks of the Mahaweli Ganga, this is a low-rise building in reasonably clean condition. The rooms with air-con are more spacious than the fan rooms.

Sorabora Village Inn (☎ 225 7149; info@vanity holidays.com; r Rs 500-1700; ✱) This 15-room hotel, restaurant and bar is a popular local option for wedding receptions on weekends, but during the week it's a good, quiet choice.

Mahiyangana is something of a transport hub for the area, and there are regular buses to Badulla (CTB Rs 45), Polonnaruwa (private bus Rs 64), Ampara (CTB and private bus Rs 70), Monaragala (CTB Rs 49) and Kandy (private bus Rs 45, three hours). Travellers from Mahiyangana to Monaragala may need to change buses at Bibile.

Knuckles Range

So named because the range's peaks look like a closed fist, this 1500m-high massif is home to pockets of rare montane forest. The area, which offers some pleasant walks, has been declared a Unesco World Heritage Conservation Area. The Rs 575 entry fee is collected at Hunasgiriya, 27km from Kandy. Hotels and resorts in the Knuckles Range can organise guided hiking trips.

Green View (☎ 077 781 1881; bluehavtravels@slt net.lk; Elkaduwa Rd, Elkaduwa; s Rs 800-1000, d Rs 1000-1200) This seven-room hillside lodge offers spectacular views into a forested mountain valley, with rice fields below. It's a particularly good spot for walks as there is a good network of trails nearby. Nature tours are also available. The Sri Lankan fare here is good, and reasonably priced. By advance arrangement the owners can pick you up at the train or bus stations in Kandy.

Rangala House (☎ 081-240 0294; anewman@sltnet .lk; 92B Bobebila Rd, Makuldeniya, Teldeniya; villa US$340) This former tea planter's bungalow ensconced on a steep forested hillside contains three double rooms, each with attached bath, plus large living and dining room with a fireplace. Guests can prepare their own meals in the large Western-style kitchen or have the resident cook do the work; either way you pay only the actual costs of the raw ingredients purchased. A large swimming pool on the premises is solar-heated.

Hunas Falls Hotel (☎ 081-247 0041, 081-247 6402; www.hunasfallshotel.com; Elkaduwa; r US$120, ste from US$160; ✱ ⚫) A luxury hotel with one of the most spectacular settings in the country, it's 27km out of Kandy, high up in a tea estate at Elkaduwa. It has all the mod cons, including a tennis court, a well-stocked fish pool and plenty of walks in the surrounding hills.

A taxi from Kandy to Elkaduwa should cost Rs 800. Alternatively, take a bus to Wattegama (from near the clock tower in Kandy) and then catch another to Elkaduwa.

ADAM'S PEAK (SRI PADA)

elev 2243m

Located in a beautiful and fascinating area of the southern Hill Country, this lofty peak has sparked the imagination for centuries. It is variously known as Adam's Peak (the place where Adam first set foot on earth after being cast out of heaven), Sri Pada (Sacred Footprint, left by the Buddha as he headed towards paradise) or Samanalakande (Butterfly Mountain, where butterflies go to die). Some believe the huge 'footprint' on the top of the 2243m peak to be that of St Thomas, the early apostle of India, or even of Lord Shiva.

Whichever legend you care to believe, this place has been a pilgrimage centre for over 1000 years. King Parakramabahu and King Nissanka Malla of Polonnaruwa provided *ambalamas* (resting places to shelter weary pilgrims) up the mountain.

These days the pilgrimage season begins on *poya* day in December and runs until **Vesak festival** in May. The busiest period is January and February. At other times the temple on the summit is unused, and between May and October the peak is obscured by clouds for much of the time. During the pilgrimage season a steady stream of pilgrims (and the odd tourist) makes the climb up the countless steps to the top. They leave from the small settlement of Dalhousie (del-*house*), 33km by road southwest of the tea town of Hatton, which is on the Colombo–Kandy–Nuwara Eliya railway and road. The route is illuminated in season by a string of lights, which look very pretty as they snake up the mountainside. Out of season you can still do the walk; you'll just need a torch. Many pilgrims prefer to make the longer, much more tiring – but equally well-marked and lit – seven-hour climb from Ratnapura via the Carney Estate, because of the greater merit thus gained.

It's not only the sacred footprint that pilgrims seek. As the first rays of dawn light up the holy mountain you're treated to an extremely fine view – the Hill Country rises to the east, while to the west the land slopes away to the sea. Colombo, 65km away, is easily visible on a clear day. It's little wonder that English author John Stills, in his book *Jungle Tide*, described the peak as 'one of the vastest and most reverenced cathedrals of the human race'.

Interesting as the ascent is, and beautiful as the dawn is, Adam's Peak saves its *pièce de résistance* for a few minutes after dawn. The sun casts a perfect shadow of the peak onto the misty clouds down towards the coast. As the sun rises higher this eerie triangular shadow races back towards the peak, eventually disappearing into its base.

Activities

You can start the 7km climb from Dalhousie soon after dark – in which case you'll need at least a good sleeping bag to keep you warm overnight at the top – or you can wait till about 2am to start. The climb is up steps most of the way (about 5200 of them), and with plenty of rest stops you'll get to the top in 2½ to four hours. A 2.30am start will easily get you there before dawn, which is around 6.30am. Start on a *poya* day, though, and the throng of pilgrims might add hours to your climb.

From the car park the slope is gradual for the first half-hour or so. You pass under an entrance arch, then by the Japan–Sri Lanka Friendship Dagoba. The pathway then gets steeper and steeper until it becomes a continuous flight of stairs. There are tea houses for rest and refreshments all the way to the top, some of which are open through the night. A handful are open out of season. The authorities have banned litter, alcohol, cigarettes, meat and recorded music so that the atmosphere remains suitably reverent.

Since it can get pretty cold on top, there's little sense in getting to the top too long before the dawn and then having to sit around shivering. Bring warm clothes in any case, including something extra for when you get to the summit, and bring plenty of water with you. Some pilgrims wait for the priests to make a morning offering before they descend, but the sun quickly rises (as does the heat), so it pays not to linger too long.

Many people find the hardest part is coming down again. The endless steps can shake the strongest knees, and if your shoes don't fit well then toe-jam starts to hurt, too. It's a good idea to take a hat – the morning sun gets strong quite fast. Try to remember to stretch your leg muscles, or you'll be limping for the next few days.

Between June and November, when the pathway isn't illuminated and there aren't many people around, travellers are urged to do the hike at least in pairs. Expect to pay around Rs 500 for a guide.

Leeches may be about. A popular method of deterring these unpleasant little beasties is an Ayurvedic balm produced by Siddhalepa Ayurveda Hospital. From the way climbers enthusiastically smear it on, one would think it does for leeches what garlic does for vampires. It costs only a few rupees and is available in Dalhousie and indeed throughout Sri Lanka.

Sleeping & Eating

The area surrounding Adam's Peak has a handful of places to stay. Dalhousie is the best place to start the climb, and it also has the best budget accommodation in the area.

Head to Dikoya (see right) if you're seeking midrange and top-end choices.

Out of pilgrimage season the bus driver may dump you in Dalhousie's bare main square, but during the season the buses stop near the beginning of the walk. In the season there are a few tea shops, some of which stay open all night, where you can get something to eat, buy provisions for the climb, or get a place to sleep (before you start the climb).

About 1.5km before you get to the place where the buses stop, there are a handful of guesthouses (on your left as you approach Adam's Peak). Most are open only during the pilgrimage season.

White House (s/d Rs 400/500) About 100m beyond the River View Wathsala Inn (below), this newer guesthouse has basic but clean rooms. It also has friendly owners who not only lead Adam's Peak climbs but can take visitors trekking down the opposite side of the peak to Ratnapura. Like many guesthouses here it opens only during the main tourist season (December to May). You can swim in the river behind the guesthouse.

Sri Pale (s/d Rs 400/600) The four rooms here are very rustic but have a nice location by a small river. The hosts are a congenial local farming family. It's open only during the pilgrimage season.

Yellow House (☎ /fax 051-222 3958; s/d Rs 400/500) Continuing with the colour/name theme, this place next to Sri Pale offers 12 basic rooms, which are open seasonally.

Punsisi Rest (☎ 070-521101; r Rs 400) Further up the road, closer to the bus stop and above a shop, Punsisi has nine small rooms with hot water. The rooms on the top floor are the best but the stairs are steep and narrow. This one is usually open year-round.

Green House (☎ 051-222 3956; r Rs 400) This is across the bridge at the start of the walking path, and, yes, it's painted green. There are simple clean rooms in a characterful little house. There's also a pretty garden and the host can prepare a herbal bath (Rs 150) for an après-pilgrimage soak. The management offers an 'Adam's Peak full-service package' for Rs 2000 that includes a night's accommodation, meals and guided climb. It's open seasonally.

River View Wathsala Inn (☎ 051-222 5261; www .wathsalainn.net; r Rs 800-2000) This modern, rambling place has 14 large rooms with hot water, and unlike most of the other Dalhousie places it's open year-round. The cheapest rooms have shared bathrooms. The recently expanded restaurant here is popular with tour groups. Rafting and canoeing trips can be arranged.

Getting There & Away

Reaching the base of Adam's Peak is quite simple, and if you're making a night ascent you've got all day to arrive. Buses run to Dalhousie from Kandy (from the Goods Shed bus station), Nuwara Eliya and Colombo in the pilgrimage season. Otherwise, you need first to get to Hatton or to Maskeliya (which is about 20km along the Hatton–Dalhousie road).

Throughout the year there are service to Hatton from Colombo, Kandy (three hours) or Nuwara Eliya. There are also some direct buses from Nuwara Eliya and Colombo to Maskeliya, which enables you to avoid stopping in Hatton, if you wish.

There are buses from Hatton to Dalhousie via Maskeliya every 30 minutes in the pilgrimage season (CTB/private bus Rs 28/40, two hours). Otherwise, you have to take a bus from Hatton to Maskeliya (Rs 12, last departure about 7pm), then another to Dalhousie (Rs 12, last departure about 8.30pm). There are usually hotel touts on, in, above and beside the bus when it terminates at Dalhousie.

The *Podi Menike* and *Udarata Menike* trains from Colombo arrive in Hatton at 11.30am and 2.15pm, respectively. These trains continue to Nanu Oya (for Nuwara Eliya), as do the local trains that leave Hatton at 7.35am and 4.20pm. In the other direction (to Colombo) the *Podi Menike* passes through Haputale and Nanu Oya and reaches Hatton at 2.13pm; the *Udarata Menike* leaves Hatton at 10.55am. Mail train 46 leaves at 10.52pm.

A taxi from Hatton to Dalhousie should cost Rs 600 to 700.

AROUND ADAM'S PEAK

Other than making the pilgrimage up the famous peak, visitors to the area can arrange easier hikes through forests and connecting tea plantations in Dikoya, Hatton and Maskeliya, or do a little boating and fishing on the Castlereagh or Maussakelle Reservoirs. Local tea-estate bungalows can handle the arrangements.

A few tea factories in these districts also offer tours and cuppings (tea tastings). The charming 19th-century Anglican church built on a promontory overlooking the Castlereagh Reservoir is worth a visit for its quaint stone architecture, tiny but atmospheric colonial cemetery and sweeping views of the reservoir and adjoining tea plantations.

Hatton, the main train junction in the area, is a bustling tea-trading town with narrow, crowded streets, a market and a few drinking houses.

Sleeping & Eating

At elevations of around 1200m to 1400m, the area around Dikoya has the Hill Country's best selection of converted tea-estate bungalows. There are a couple of grimy local inns near the train station in Hatton and one or two in Maskeliya, but these are best avoided except as a last resort. If you have your own transport it is possible to do Adam's Peak from Dikoya without needing to stay overnight in Dalhousie.

Upper Glencairn (☎ 051-222 2348; Dikoya; s/d Rs 1250/1500) A grand old place, built in 1906, surrounded by gardens and a working tea estate. The five rooms all have attached hot-water bathrooms. There's a bar and leather couches to sink into in the lounge. Meals are available (breakfast Rs 150, à la carte lunch and dinner around Rs 300 per dish)

Lower Glencairn (☎ 051-222 2342; Dikoya; s/d Rs 1250/1500) Below the main road, this one is rather jaded and shabby compared with its Upper counterpart, but the garden is nice, as are the views. Meals aren't served here but rather at Upper Glencairn, a short walk away.

Castlereagh Family Cottages (☎ 051-222 3607; castle@sltnet.lk; Norton Bridge Rd, Dikoya; cottages Rs 2500-5000) Further along the road to Hatton, look for the sign for this place just after a bridge. The cottages are in a lovely spot under euca-lyptus trees on the edge of the Castlereagh Reservoir. The smaller cottage has a double bed and a room with two bunks. The bigger one has three double rooms, plus a kids' room that could fit six to 10. Both have kitchens and hot water, and are nicely decorated.

Tea Trails (☎ 011-230 3888, 051-492 0401; www.tea trails.com; Dikoya; r US$188-240, ste US$236-405) Partially owned by Dilmah Tea, one of Sri Lanka's largest tea companies, Tea Trails comprises a collection of four colonial-style bungalows built for British tea-estate managers in the late 19th and early 20th centuries. Completely refurbished and opened to visitors in 2005, the bungalows feature four to six large bedrooms each, along with spacious dining and living areas, verandas and gardens with views over Castlereagh Reservoir. Rates include sumptuous Western and Sri Lankan meals prepared by a professional resident chef, along with complimentary wines and single-estate teas. Also on staff are an experienced guide who can lead hikes from bungalow to bungalow (or beyond), and a tea expert who can enlighten guests on the processes involved in growing, picking and curing Ceylon tea.

Getting There & Away

Upper and Lower Glencairn and Castlereagh Family Cottages are along the main road between Hatton and Dikoya and can thus be reached by bus. Tea Trails will arrange pick-up for its guests in Colombo, Kandy or Hatton. A taxi from Hatton to any of these accommodations should cost around Rs 700 to 900.

KITULGALA
☎ 036

Southwest of Kandy and north of Adam's Peak, Kitulgala's main claim to fame is that David Lean filmed his 1957 Oscar-winning epic *Bridge on the River Kwai* here. You can walk down a paved pathway to the site where the filming took place along the banks of the Kelaniya Ganga. The pathway is signposted on the main road, about 1km from Plantation Hotel in the direction of Adam's Peak. It is virtually impossible to head down the path without attracting an entourage of 'guides' who expect a consideration for their troubles. If you know the film you'll recognise some of the places.

Kitulgala's second claim to fame is **whitewater rafting** along the Kelaniya Ganga. The typical trip takes in seven Class 2–3 rapids in 7km for US$30 per person, including transport and lunch. Experienced rafters can opt for more difficult Class 4–5 rapids by special arrangement. You can organise this through Rafter's Retreat (p198) or Plantation Hotel (p198).

The Kelaniya Ganga also has some good **swimming** spots – a popular hole is beside Plantation Hotel.

THE HILL COUNTRY

The area is also famous for birding. According to Rafter's Retreat, 23 of Sri Lanka's 27 endemic bird species inhabit the surrounding forest.

One corner of the dining room at **Kitulgala Rest House** (☎ /fax 228 7528; www.ceylonhotels .lk/kith.html; r with/without air-con US$48/36; ✕) is a veritable shrine to the David Lean epic; black-and-white photos of the stars decorate the walls. Each of the 20 large rooms here has a veranda facing the river. Whitewater rafting and river canoeing can be arranged here.

Further towards Adam's Peak than the Kitulgala Rest House, the eight stylish rooms at **Plantation Hotel** (☎ 228 7575; hauschandra@wow .lk; Kalukohutenna; r with/without air-con US$48/36; ✕) are very comfortable; there's also a restaurant serving 'Western and Eastern' cusine beside the river. Bird-watching and rafting trips can be arranged.

Plantation Hotel also manages **Plantation Resort** (Royal River Resort; ☎ 272 4692; hauschandra@ wow.lk; Eduru Ella; s/d US$48/60; ✕), a collection of open-air dining areas and plush guest rooms built alongside the Ing Oya rapids of the river. All rooms come with fireplaces and river views. The restaurant is popular with day-trippers and tour groups.

Rafter's Retreat (☎ 228 7598; channap@itmin .com; r/cottages incl half-board US$35/54) A beautiful 85-year-old colonial tea-estate bungalow serves as the centre for this guesthouse-cum-rafting outfit. Guests don't stay in the old house but rather in three rooms in an adjacent house, or in 11 rustic wood-plank cottages facing the river. The Rafter's Retreat management can arrange rafting, hiking and birding trips.

It's easy enough to have a quick stop at Kitulgala even if you are travelling by bus. If you're coming from Ratnapura you'll have to change at Avissawella; catch the bus to Hatton and get off at Kitulgala (Rs 32). When you're over Kitulgala, flag a bus to Hatton from the main road (Rs 40).

KANDY TO NUWARA ELIYA

The road from Kandy to Nuwara Eliya climbs nearly 1400m as it winds through jade green tea plantations and past crystalline reservoirs. The 80km of asphalt allows for plenty of stops at waterfalls and tea outlets, not to mention Tamil and Sinhalese villages along the way.

At Pussellawa, 45km from Kandy, the 120-year-old **Pussellawa Rest House** (☎ 031-247 8397; ceylonhotels.lk; r with/without air-con US$35/25; ✕) has four reasonably well-maintained rooms in a colonial-style bungalow with fine views.

Kothmale Reservoir (also known as Puna Oya Reservoir) can be looked down on from a little further up the road. It's a large place created as part of the Mahaweli Development Project, and partly blamed by some locals for unusual climatic conditions in recent years. **Ramboda Falls** (108m), about 1.5km from the road, is a double waterfall created by converging brooks.

Ramboda Falls Hotel (☎ 052-225 9582; r from US$18), about 58km from Kandy, by Ramboda Falls and near the Kothmale Reservoir, is down a very steep driveway to your right as you travel from Kandy. The view you get of the falls from here is quite marvellous and there's a restaurant with a pleasant veranda from which to view them. Tasty and reasonably priced meals are available. If you want to venture further, there's also a narrow path to the falls. Some of the 16 rooms are a bit musty but others are airy and bright with balconies, so do have a look before checking in. Indian movie superstar Amitabh Bachchan once stayed here, and there are photos of him looking inscrutably cool.

On the A5, 5km before Nuwara Eliya, the **Labookellie Tea Factory** (☺ 8am-6.30pm) is a convenient factory to visit as it's right on the roadside and staff will willingly show you around. You can buy boxes of good tea cheaply here and enjoy a free cup of tea with a slice (or two) of their delicious chocolate cake.

Closer to Nuwara Eliya are roadside stalls overflowing with all manner of vegetables, a legacy of Samuel Baker, who first came to the area in 1846 and decided it would make a pleasant summer retreat. He introduced a variety of vegetables here, and they're still grown in abundance today. Also grown in abundance are flowers, which are transported to Colombo and abroad. Along the steep roadside approach to Nuwara Eliya you'll come across children selling flowers. If you don't buy their wares, they hurtle down a path to meet you at each and every hairpin turn until (hopefully) you fork out some cash.

THE TEA HILLS

Tea remains a cornerstone of the Sri Lankan economy and a major export. Tea came to Sri Lanka as an emergency substitute for coffee when the extensive coffee plantations were all but destroyed by a devastating disease in the 19th century. The first Sri Lankan tea was grown in 1867 at the Loolecondera Estate, a little southeast of Kandy, by one James Taylor. Tea needs a warm climate, altitude and sloping terrain – a perfect description of the Hill Country – and today the area is virtually one big tea plantation.

Tea grows on a bush; if it isn't cut it can grow up to 10m high. Tea bushes are pruned back to about 1m in height and squads of Tamil tea pluckers (all women) move through the rows of bushes picking the leaves and buds. These are then 'withered' (demoisturised by blowing air at a fixed temperature through them) either in the old-fashioned multistorey tea factories, where the leaves are spread out on hessian mats, or in modern mechanised troughs. The partly dried leaves are then crushed, which starts a fermentation process. The art in tea production comes in knowing when to stop the fermentation, by 'firing' the tea to produce the final, brown-black leaf. Tours of tea plantations and factories are readily available all over Sri Lanka.

There is a large number of types and varieties of teas, which are graded both by size (from cheap 'dust' through fannings and broken grades to 'leaf' tea) and by quality (with names such as flowery, pekoe or souchong). Tea is further categorised into low-grown, mid-grown or high-grown. The low-grown teas (under 600m) grow strongly and are high in 'body' but low in 'flavour'. The high-grown teas (over 1200m) grow more slowly and are renowned for their subtle flavour. Mid-grown tea is something between the two. Regular commercial teas are usually made by blending various types – a bit of this for flavour, a bit of that for body.

Sri Lanka may grow some very fine tea but most of the best is exported. Only in a small number of hotels, guesthouses and restaurants will you get a quality cup. But you can buy fine teas from plantations or shops to take home with you.

NUWARA ELIYA

☎ 052 / pop 25,966 / elev 1889m

The summer resort of Nuwara Eliya (nu-*rel-iya*, meaning 'City of Light') keeps its colonial hill station atmosphere more completely than any place in the subcontinent. The town centre is a concrete tangle but the outskirts still keep the atmosphere of a misplaced British village, with hedges, rose gardens and red-roofed bungalows sporting twee names. It was a favoured stomping ground for the tea planters – the 'wild men of the hills' as one British governor called them. The old post office, the racecourse, the English country house–styled Hill Club with its hunting pictures, mounted fish and hunting trophies and the 18-hole golf course all somehow seem more British than Britain itself.

Nuwara Eliya has a fair assortment of country-style houses with large gardens – many have been turned over to vegetables, making this one of Sri Lanka's main market-gardening centres.

Come prepared for the evening cool – Nuwara Eliya is much higher than Kandy. In January and February you may find yourself needing to sleep with two blankets and all your clothes on. The town can be grey and grim in a peculiarly Scottish way on rainy days. Nuwara Eliya is the 'in place' for socialites during April, around the Sri Lankan New Year. At that time of year the cost of accommodation – if you can find any at all – goes through the roof. Horse races are held on the picturesque semiderelict racecourse then, too.

The town has an abundance of touts angling to get a commission for a guesthouse or hotel.

History

Originally an uninhabited system of forests and meadows lying in the shadow of Pidurutalagala (aka Mt Pedro, 2524m), Nuwara Eliya became a singularly British creation, having been 'discovered' by colonial officer John Davy in 1819 and chosen as the site for a sanatorium a decade later. The sanatorium's reputation became such that Sir J E Tennent wrote in *Ceylon* in 1859 that 'In the eyes of the European and the invalid, Nuwara Eliya is the Elysium of Ceylon.'

Later the district became known as a spot where 'English' vegetables and fruits such as

NUWARA ELIYA

0   400 m
0   0.2 miles

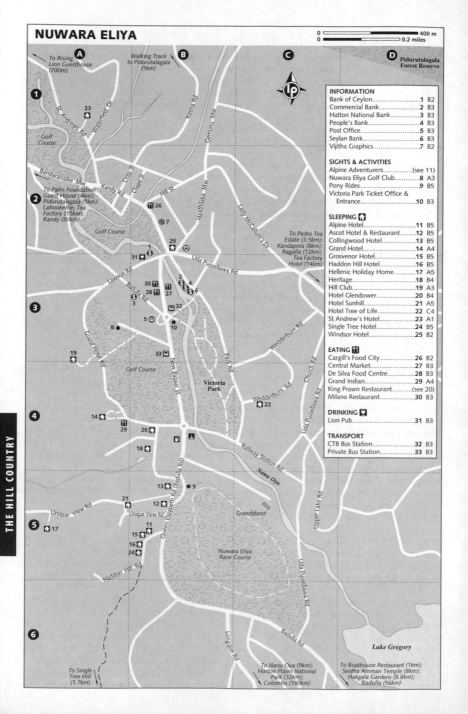

INFORMATION
Bank of Ceylon..............................1 B2
Commercial Bank.......................2 B3
Hatton National Bank................3 B3
People's Bank..............................4 B3
Post Office...................................5 B3
Seylan Bank.................................6 B3
Vijitha Graphics..........................7 B2

SIGHTS & ACTIVITIES
Alpine Adventurers.................(see 11)
Nuwara Eliya Golf Club.............8 A3
Pony Rides...................................9 B5
Victoria Park Ticket Office &
    Entrance................................10 B3

SLEEPING
Alpine Hotel..............................11 B5
Ascot Hotel & Restaurant........12 B5
Collingwood Hotel...................13 B5
Grand Hotel...............................14 A4
Grosvenor Hotel........................15 B5
Haddon Hill Hotel....................16 B5
Hellenic Holiday Home............17 A5
Heritage.....................................18 B4
Hill Club....................................19 A3
Hotel Glendower......................20 B4
Hotel Sunhill.............................21 A5
Hotel Tree of Life.....................22 C4
St Andrew's Hotel....................23 A1
Single Tree Hotel......................24 B5
Windsor Hotel...........................25 B2

EATING
Cargill's Food City....................26 B2
Central Market..........................27 B3
De Silva Food Centre...............28 B3
Grand Indian.............................29 A4
King Prawn Restaurant.........(see 20)
Milano Restaurant....................30 B3

DRINKING
Lion Pub....................................31 B3

TRANSPORT
CTB Bus Station........................32 B3
Private Bus Station...................33 B3

lettuce and strawberries could be successfully grown for consumption by the colonists. Coffee was one of the first crops grown here, but after the island's coffee plantations failed due to disease, the colonists switched to tea. The first tea leaves harvested in Sri Lanka were planted at Loolecondera Estate, in the mountains between Nuwara Eliya and Kandy. As tea experiments proved successful, the town quickly found itself becoming the Hill Country's 'tea capital', a title still proudly borne.

As elsewhere in the Hill Country, most of the labourers on the tea plantations were Tamils, brought from southern India by the British. Although the descendants of these 'plantation Tamils' (as they are sometimes called to distinguish them from Tamils in northern Sri Lanka) have usually stayed out of the ethnic strife endemic to Jaffna and the north, there have been occasional outbreaks of tension between the local Sinhalese and Tamils. The town was partially ransacked during 1983 riots, but the damage has long since been invisible to anyone unaware of what the place looked like previously.

Orientation

CTB buses leave from Railway Station Rd and from the private bus station on New Bazaar St. Over the road is Victoria Park. Further north along New Bazaar St is the central market and a collection of cheap eateries. At the top of the street is the Windsor Hotel and nearby is Bank of Ceylon. If you veer left into Kandy Rd, you will come to Cargills Food City (you can see the golf course on your left). If you head south from the bus station along New Bazaar St, you will enter Queen Elizabeth Rd (also known as Badulla Rd) – many of the cheaper guesthouses are clustered nearby.

Information

The major banks in town can exchange travellers cheques, but only People's Bank has an ATM.

Bank of Ceylon (Lawson Rd)
Commercial Bank (Park Rd)
Hatton National Bank (Badulla Rd)
People's Bank (Park Rd)
Post office (Badulla Rd; 7am-8pm Mon-Sat, closed public holidays) Aside from buying stamps or mailing letters and postcards, you can also conveniently make long-distance phone calls here.

Seylan Bank (Park Rd)
Vijitha Graphics (223 4966; vijithak@sltnet.lk; 28 Daily Fair Trade Complex, Kandy Rd) Internet access.

Sights

The lovely **Victoria Park** (admission Rs 10; dawn-dusk) at the centre of town comes alive with flowers around March to May, and August and September. It's also home to quite a number of Hill Country bird species, including the Kashmir flycatcher, Indian pitta and grey tit.

If you're keen to see where a good, strong cuppa comes from, head to the **Pedro Tea Estate** (admission Rs 50; 8.30am-12.30pm & 2-5pm) about 3.5km east of Nuwara Eliya on the way to Kandapola. Guided tours of the factory, which was originally built in 1885 and still contains much 19th-century engineering to marvel at, run for about a half-hour. Overlooking the plantations there's a pleasant tea house where you can have a tea break. A three-wheeler from Nuwara Eliya should cost Rs 400 to 500 return, including waiting time. Alternatively you could hop on a Ragalla-bound bus (bus 743) from the main bus station in Nuwara Eliya. On the way out you'll pass Hawa Eliya, the site of the Lion brewery (alas, no tours). A side road takes you up to what's locally known as **Lovers Leap** (there are various stories as to who the lovers actually were). From here you get a good view of the countryside.

The **Hakgala Gardens** (adult/student Rs 300/200; 7.30am-5pm), 10km southeast of Nuwara Eliya (and about 200m lower), was originally a plantation of cinchona, the plant from which the antimalarial drug quinine is extracted. Later, the gardens were used for experiments in acclimatising temperate-zone plants to life in the tropics, and were run by the same family for three generations until the 1940s. Today Hakgala is a delightful garden of over 27 hectares, famed for its roses, ferns and medicinal plants.

Legend has it that Hanuman, the monkey god, was sent by Rama to the Himalayas to find a particular medicinal herb. He forgot which herb he was looking for and decided to bring a chunk of the Himalayas back in his jaw, hoping the herb was growing on it. The gardens grow on a rock called Hakgala, which means 'jaw-rock'.

The Hakgala Gardens is a short bus ride from Nuwara Eliya (take a Welimada-bound bus). There are some accommodation options nearby.

On the way out to Hakgala Gardens, near the 83km post, stop off to see the colourful Hindu **Seetha Amman Temple** at Sita Eliya. It's said to mark the spot where Sita was held captive by the demon king Rawana, and where she prayed daily for Rama to come and rescue her. On the rock face across the stream are a number of circular depressions said to be the footprints of Rawana's elephant. Tamil wedding parties make it a point to stop here for *pujas*.

Activities

Grand Hotel, St Andrew's Hotel and Hotel Glendower all have snooker rooms; nonguests can usually play for around Rs 125 to 200 per hour. Holidaying Sri Lankans like to give their children pony rides on the racecourse.

GOLF

Nuwara Eliya Golf Club (☎ 223 4360; fax 222 2835; green fees weekdays till 3pm/weekends & holidays Rs 1900/ 2300, caddie fee per 3hr Rs 700), which spreads north from Grand Hotel Rd, is beautifully kept. It didn't take the tea planters long to lay out land for drives and putts in their holiday town, and the club was founded in 1889. The club has been through tough times but survives to this day. Water – in the form of rivers and streams – comes into play on six holes. You can become a temporary member by paying Rs 100 per day. On weekdays after 3pm green fees drop to less than half for six holes. You can hire golf clubs for Rs 400 per day and golf shoes for Rs 150 per day. The club expects a certain dress code: shirt with collar and slacks or shorts (of a decent length), socks and shoes. Women can wear 'decent' golf attire. The club has a convivial wood-lined bar that almost encourages you to talk in a fake Oxbridge accent. Also on the grounds are a badminton hall and billiard room. Dinner in the dining room includes classic bland English cuisine such as grilled chops with mint for around Rs 300.

CYCLING

Fat-tyre fans will find plenty of steep dirt trails radiating into the hills from the outskirts of town. Most hotels and guesthouses can arrange for **mountain-bike rental** (per day Rs 500).

HORSE RACING

The Sri Lanka Turf Club sponsors horse racing at the 1875-vintage Nuwara Eliya Race Course and during the December–January and April–May high seasons the stands are filled with Sinhalese, Indian and Arab horse-racing fanatics. The most important event every year is the Governor's Cup race, held over the April New Year season. The races usually begin around 10.30am; bets start at Rs 250.

WALKING

Sri Lanka's highest mountain, Pidurutalagala (2524m), rises behind the town. On top stands the island's main TV transmitter, which means the peak is out of bounds to the public. You can walk about 4km up as far as a concrete water tank; beyond here is a high-security zone. Follow the path from Keena Rd, which leads along a little ravine through the exotic eucalyptus forest (which keeps the town supplied with firewood) and into the rare, indigenous cloud-forest. There are a few leopards on the mountain, which sometimes descend to the edges of town and devour some unfortunate pooch.

An alternative walk is to go to **Single Tree Hill** (2100m), which takes about 90 minutes. To get here walk south out of Nuwara Eliya on Queen Elizabeth Rd, go up Haddon Hill Rd as far as the communications tower and then take the left-hand path.

TENNIS

There are tennis courts at the **Hill Club** (☎ 222 2653; hillclub@eureka.lk; per hr Rs 250). The fee includes balls and racquet hire.

Tours

Most hotels and guesthouses in town can arrange day trips by car or 4WD to Horton Plains National Park and World's End. The standard price for up to five passengers is Rs 1700. One of the better 4WD tours is based at **Single Tree Hotel** (☎ 222 3009; 1/8 Haddon Hill Rd). The road is better than it used to be and the trip takes about 1½ hours one way. It costs about the same from Haputale. For more information on this destination, see p205.

Alpine Adventurers (☎ 222 3500; Alpine Hotel, 4 Haddon Hill Rd) specialises in trekking, camping, mountaineering and rafting tours in the area.

Sleeping

Nuwara Eliya is a place where it's worth being a bit choosy about where you lodge, as the budget hotels can be on the dreary side. You'll need blankets to keep warm at night at almost any time of year, owing to the altitude. All places to stay *claim* to have hot water, but in many you have to wait for it to heat up; only a handful have a 24-hour hot-water service. Another way of keeping warm is to get a fire lit in your room, for which you'll be asked to pay Rs 100 or more. Make sure the room has ventilation or an open window, or you may get carbon monoxide poisoning (which can be fatal).

During the 'season', around Sri Lankan New Year in April, rooms are three to five times their normal price. Prices also increase during long-weekend holidays and in August when package tours descend from abroad.

BUDGET

Guesthouses with historic architecture and antique furniture charge higher rates than the more-modern places but aren't necessarily more comfortable.

Single Tree Hotel (☎ 222 3009; 178 Haddon Hill Rd; s/d Rs 1000/1200) The 10 rooms here were recently renovated with lots of wood panelling (upstairs rooms are best), and the helpful owner can arrange all manner of local and regional tours.

Collingwood Hotel (☎ 222 3550; fax 223 4500; 112 Queen Elizabeth Rd; s/d/f Rs 750/1200/3000) The rooms at the front are the best in this colonial-era home that's filled with antique furniture. The family room sleeps six.

Haddon Hill Hotel (☎ 222 3500; 8B Haddon Hill Rd; s/d Rs 900/1200) It won't win prizes for architecture but the rooms are nice and clean and guests can use the kitchen. Some of the rooms have a small balcony.

Ascot Hotel & Restaurant (☎ 222 2708; 120 Queen Elizabeth Rd; r Rs 950) This is one of the least expensive inns in town. Despite an uninviting dirt front yard, it's basically an OK place to stay and all the rooms now have hot water. The owners are very friendly.

MIDRANGE

Hotel Glendower (☎ 222 2501; hotel_glendower@ hotmail.com; 5 Grand Hotel Rd; r/ste Rs 1800/3000; ☐) This rambling colonial house with sizable rooms is a definite cut above its rivals, with

helpful, friendly staff, a pretty garden with a croquet set, a large lounge with soft couches and a fireplace, a cosy English-style bar and a good snooker room upstairs.

Heritage (☎ 222 3053; hritage@slnet.lk; r US$45-55, ste US$70-85) Formerly Ceybank Rest, and once the British governor's mansion, this huge, recently renovated hotel behind Victoria Park and opposite the Nuwara Eliya Race Course offers large airy rooms with colonial-style teak furnishings. A good bar, billiard room and restaurant round out the package. The service seems a bit better and more genuinely friendly than that found at the old posh stand-bys like St Andrew's and Hill Club.

Palm Foundation Guesthouse (☎ 222 4033, 222 2839; www.palmfoundationsrilanka.org; 485/5 Toppass-Kandy Rd; r Rs 1500) This new place outside of town on the road to Kandy offers basic, homey accommodations several kilometres north and several hundred metres above Nuwara Eliya proper. Sunsets and sunrises from the organic garden in the front yard are sublime. Possible adventures include hikes into the surrounding forest and tea gardens. All proceeds go toward the holistic community development activities of Palm Foundation, a local NGO that accepts skilled volunteers with advance notice.

Hotel Sunhill (☎ 222 2878; sunhill@itmin.com; 18 Unique View Rd; r standard/deluxe Rs 1300/2000) This place has boxlike standard rooms but better-value deluxe rooms. The bar has a karaoke machine and can get rather noisy on weekend evenings.

Alpine Hotel (☎ 222 3500; www.alpineecotravels .com; 4 Haddon Hill Rd; s/d/tr Rs 3600/4300/5000; ☐ ☒) The inn has 25 passably decent rooms and a large restaurant. Mountain bikes can be hired for Rs 500 per day. The front desk can arrange hiking, trekking and bird-watching tours for guests.

Grosvenor Hotel (☎ 222 2307; 6 Haddon Hill Rd; s/d incl breakfast Rs 1650/1980) More than 100 years old and once belonging to a colonial governor, the Grosvenor has 10 spacious, simple rooms and a comfortable lounge room.

Hotel Tree of Life (☎ 222 3684; hoteltreeoflife.com; 2 Wedderburn Rd; s/d/tr US$24/32/38; ☒) This 106-year-old colonial-style bungalow features a lovely garden and six well-furnished but faded rooms.

Rising Lion Guesthouse (☎ 222 2083; fax 223 4042; 3 Sri Piyatissapura; r Rs 900-1800) Perched high above town, this place has cheerfully odd taste in furnishings and art. The hosts are very personable and have lots of advice on interesting side trips in the area. The 13 clean, homely rooms all have fireplaces ready, and the more expensive ones have spiffy views. If you ring ahead the staff will pick you up from the bus station for free, or from Nanu Oya for Rs 200.

Hellenic Holiday Home (☎ /fax 223 5872; 49/1 Unique View Rd; s/d Rs 1500/2000) This well-situated place has superb views and 10 modern, carpeted rooms of reasonable quality. A three-wheeler here from the bus station should cost Rs 100.

TOP END

St Andrew's Hotel (☎ 222 2445; www.jetwing.net /andrews; 10 St Andrew's Dr; r US$84-108; ▣) North of town on a beautifully groomed rise overlooking the golf course, this was once a planter's club. There are terraced lawns with white cast-iron furniture, and five-course European dinners are served in the dining room beneath a pressed-copper roof. The rooms are immaculate; during bouts of cold weather the staff offers hot-water bottles for the beds. The difference between the less expensive and more expensive rooms is more substantial than the rates suggest.

Windsor Hotel (☎ 222 2554; fax 222 2889; 2 Kandy Rd; r US$50) One of Nuwara Eliya's landmarks in the middle of town, the Windsor looks a bit jaded from the outside but the interior is more tasteful. The rooms are clean and the staff is friendly.

Hill Club (☎ 222 2653; www.hillclubsrilanka.com; 29 Grand Hotel Rd; r US$40-100, f US$115, ste US$115-140; ▣) A preserve of the British male until 1970, Hill Club now admits Sri Lankans and women but remains very much in the colonial tradition. It's like a living museum of British colonial male privilege – and, in fact, the current members have reciprocal rights with London clubs. Temporary members (Rs 100 per day) are welcome to help keep the tills ringing. Tennis courts are available to guests and nonguests, and the lawns and gardens are immaculate. The suites are very charming but the regular rooms are small and have substandard furnishings given the price. Hence, if you can't afford the suites you'll be better off at Heritage or St Andrew's.

Grand Hotel (☎ 222 2881-7; tangerinetours@eureka .lk; s/d in old wing US$74/92, in new wing US$101/127) Right by the golf course, this is a vast mock-Tudor pile with immaculate lawns, a reading lounge and a wood-panelled billiards room. However, the rooms have lost most of their original features, and the service could still use improvement.

Tea Factory Hotel (☎ 222 3600; ashmres@aitkens pence.lk; Kandapola; s/d US$106/141) This tea factory, 14km east of Nuwara Eliya, has been transformed into a 57-room hotel, leaving bits and pieces of factory machinery as part of the décor. The views from the hotel and the walks around it are very pleasant and from the front desk there's plenty of information available on what to see and do.

Eating & Drinking

Guesthouses and hotels are among the safest bets when it comes to eating and drinking in Nuwara Eliya, as most stand-alone restaurants in the town centre aren't particularly inspiring. Collingwood Hotel, Alpine Hotel and Hotel Sunhill are all good choices in this department.

Grand Indian (Grand Hotel Rd; dishes Rs 150-300) Out the front of Grand Hotel, this modern, glass-walled cafeteria serves excellent and inexpensive Indian food, with northern and southern dishes. Try a cone-shaped *kheema* dosa (dosa with mince) for Rs 215, or a vegetarian thali for Rs 210.

King Prawn Restaurant (Hotel Glendower, 5 Grand Hotel Rd; dishes Rs 250-500) The relaxed dining room of Hotel Glendower serves the best Chinese food in town, perhaps the best outside of Colombo and the beach resorts. All the Chinese standard menu items are available, and the restaurant caters to vegetarians, as well.

De Silva Food Centre (90 New Bazaar St; dishes Rs 120-250) This inexpensive eatery located along a busy main street serves Sri Lankan and Chinese fare.

Milano Restaurant (94 New Bazaar St; dishes Rs 150-350) This is a more middle-class version of De Silva Food Centre, with friendly service and a reliable menu of Sri Lankan, Western and Chinese dishes.

Boathouse Restaurant (Badulla Rd, Lake Gregory; dishes Rs 125-300) Open only during the July–August, December–January and April peak seasons, this is a popular local lakeside bar and restaurant with a nautical theme. There are carrom (a cross between snooker, marbles and air hockey – you flick disks into corner pockets) boards to pass the time.

Hill Club (☎ 222 2653; 29 Grand Hotel Rd; set course dinner US$17, à la carte from US$5) Dinner at Hill Club (opposite) is an event in itself. The five-course set menu focuses on roast beef, rack of lamb and the like, served with all the trimmings promptly at 8pm. You can also order off the à la carte menu for considerably less, but you still have to eat at 8pm. The whole thing is carried off with faded colonial panache: gloved waiters, candles, and linen tablecloths and serviettes. Men must wear a tie and jacket (there are a few on hand, but they sometimes run out) or Sri Lankan national dress. Women must also be suitably attired in a dress or dress slacks; some turn up in evening wear. If you're not staying the night here, you'll have to pay a Rs 100 temporary joining fee. The food doesn't live up to everyone's expectations, especially with such a relatively high price tag, but most people enjoy the experience.

St Andrew's Hotel (☎ 222 2445; 10 St Andrew's Dr; mains Rs 500-1100) Another colonial nostalgia evening-out option is the airy dining room at this hotel (opposite), minus the temporary membership and dress code of Hill Club. As at the latter, the emphasis is on stolid culinary pillars of the British Empire.

Tea Factory Hotel (☎ 222 3600; Kandapola; mains Rs 400-600) Behind the corrugated-iron walls and green doors of the factory-turned-hotel is a cosy bar and restaurant serving quite passable Western and Sri Lankan food. You can work up an appetite by going for a walk in the surrounding tea estate. A taxi here and back costs Rs 700 to 800.

Lion Pub (Lawson St) Almost every town of size in Sri Lanka seems to have a 'Lion Pub', and this version sitting at the edge of the town centre is as good a spot as any for draught lager at local prices.

Self-caterers should head for the central market for fresh produce and to Cargills Food City for canned goods.

Getting There & Away

BUS

The trip from Kandy takes about four hours and costs Rs 125 in a private intercity express bus or van. It's a spectacular climb. Buses leave every 30 minutes to an hour. There are also buses to/from Colombo (intercity express Rs 220, six hours). There are direct CTB buses to Haputale (Rs 50, 2½ hours) a few times daily, or more frequent departures

to Welimada (Rs 23, one hour), where you can change to a Haputale-bound bus (Rs 22). Similarly, for Bandarawela you have a choice of direct CTB bus (Rs 44, three hours) or you can change local buses at Welimada. To get to Matara on the south coast, one intercity express bus (Rs 260, seven to eight hours) leaves each morning around 7.30am.

TRAIN

Nuwara Eliya does not have its own train station, but is served by Nanu Oya, about 9km along the road towards Hatton and Colombo. Buses (Rs 13 to Nuwara Eliya) meet the main trains, so don't get sucked in by touts. You can also always take a taxi (Rs 250 to 300) from the station.

The 8.56am *Podi Menike* from Colombo (via Kandy) reaches Nanu Oya at 1pm. The 9.45am *Udarata Menike* from Colombo (not via Kandy) reaches Nanu Oya at about 3.40pm. Fares onwards to Badulla in 3rd/2nd/1st class cost Rs 30/119/155. Going west, the *Udarata Menike* to Colombo (but not stopping in Kandy) leaves Nanu Oya at 9.35am; the *Podi Menike* leaves at 12.55pm, reaching Kandy at 4.35pm before continuing on to Colombo. Fares to Kandy in 3rd/2nd/1st class cost Rs 51/94/240.

HORTON PLAINS NATIONAL PARK & WORLD'S END

The Horton Plains is a beautiful, silent, strange world with some excellent hikes in the shadows of Sri Lanka's second- and third-highest mountains – Kirigalpotta (2395m) and Totapola (2359m), rearing up from the edges of the plateau. The 'plains' themselves form an undulating plateau over 2000m high, covered by wild grasslands and interspersed with patches of thick forest, rocky outcrops, filigree waterfalls and misty lakes.

The plateau comes to a sudden end at World's End, a stunning escarpment that drops almost straight down for 880m. Unfortunately the view from World's End is often obscured by mist, particularly during the rainy season from April to September. The early morning (between 6am and 10am) is the best time to visit, before the clouds roll in. In the evening and early morning you'll need long trousers and a sweater, but the plains quickly warm up, so take a hat as well. January to March are usually the clearest months, weatherwise.

THE HILL COUNTRY

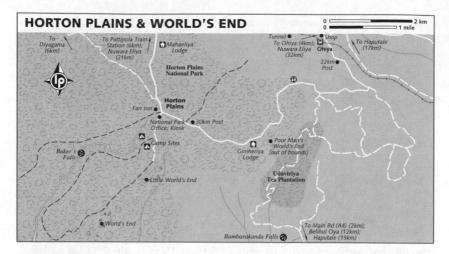

HORTON PLAINS & WORLD'S END

Information

Farr Inn, a local landmark and visitors centre, and the nearby national park office are reachable by road from Ohiya or Nuwara Eliya. Vans and 4WDs can make it up, but smaller cars might not. It's a stiff three-hour walk uphill from Ohiya train station. The **national park office** (☎ 070 522042; adult/child US$12/6; ⏰ 6.30am-6.30pm) is at the start of the track to World's End. Farr Inn itself, which once served as a hunting lodge for high-ranking British colonial officials, is currently being converted into a visitors centre that will contain educational displays.

Sights & Activities

WILDLIFE

As an important watershed and catchment for several year-round rivers and streams, the Horton Plains plays host to a wide range of wildlife. The last few elephants departed the area in the first half of the 20th century, but there are still a few leopards. Sambar deer and wild boar are commonly seen feeding in meadows at dawn and dusk. The shaggy bear-monkey (or purple-faced langur) is sometimes seen in the forest on the Ohiya road, and occasionally in the woods around World's End (its call is a wheezy grunt). You may also come across the endemic toque macaque.

The area is very popular with birdwatchers. Endemic species here include the yellow-eared bulbul, the fantailed warbler, the ashy-headed babbler, the Ceylon hill white-eye, the Ceylon blackbird, the Ceylon white-eyed arrenga, the dusky-blue flycatcher and the Ceylon blue magpie. Birds of prey include the mountain hawk eagle.

A tufty species of grass called *Crosypogon* covers the grasslands, while marshy areas are home to copious bog moss (sphagnum). The umbrella-shaped, white-blossomed keena (*Calophyllum*) stand as the main canopy over montane forest areas. The stunted trees and shrubs are draped in lichen and mosses, giving them a strange, Tolkienesque appearance. Another notable species is *Rhododendron zelanicum*, which has blood-red blossoms. The purple-leafed *Strobilanthes* blossoms once after five years, and then dies.

WORLD'S END

This is the only national park in Sri Lanka where visitors are permitted to walk on their own (on designated trails only). The walk to World's End is about 4km, but the trail loops back to Baker's Falls (2km), from where you can walk to the entrance (another 3.5km); the round trip is 9.5km and usually takes around three hours. Be aware that after about 10am the mist usually comes down – and it's thick. All you can expect to see from World's End after this time is a swirling white wall. Although the ticket gate is open from 6.30am you can actually start walking earlier and pay on the way out. Try to avoid doing this walk on Sunday and public holidays, when it can get crowded. Guides at the national park office expect about Rs 500 to accompany you on the walk – they say there's no fee for the volunteer guides, but expect to donate a similar amount. Some guides are well informed on the area's flora and fauna, and hiring one might be a consideration for solo women travellers.

Wear strong and comfortable walking shoes, a hat and sunglasses. Bring sunscreen (you can get really burnt up here) and lots of water, as well as something to eat. The shop at the park office makes a killing from people who forget to bring supplies. The weather can change very quickly on the plains – one minute it can be sunny and clear, the next chilly and misty. Bring warm clothing just in case. The authorities have cracked down on litter, and it is forbidden to leave the paths. There are no toilets en route to World's End, though there are toilets on the road coming up to Farr Inn from Ohiya train station.

There used to be a free alternative to World's End, dubbed Poor Man's World's End, but it has been fenced off and anyone caught in the area will get a Rs 10,000 fine. Travellers' haunts in Haputale are good sources for innovative ways to see the plains without being slugged with the entry fees, although of course you follow the advice at your own risk.

Tours

Hill Safari Eco-Lodge (right) in Ohiya can arrange guided hikes through the park. Guesthouses in Nuwara Eliya and Haputale also operate trips to Horton's Plains and World's End.

Sleeping & Eating

There are two basic Department of Wildlife Conservation bungalows where you can stay: Giniheriya Lodge, which used to be known as Anderson Lodge, and Mahaeliya Lodge. The bungalows contain 10 beds each, and the charge for foreigners is US$24 per day plus the US$12 park entry, US$2 per group for linen hire and a US$30 per group service charge. You must bring all of your own dry rations and kerosene. The lodges open up only when people are staying, and you must book ahead through the **Department of Wildlife Conservation** (Map pp84-5; ☎ 011-269 4241; www.dwlc.lk; 18 Gregory's Rd, Cinnamon Gardens, Col 7).

There are two camp sites (signposted near the start of the World's End track).

These can also be booked through the Department of Wildlife Conservation. There is water at the sites but nothing else; you must bring everything you need. Because you are inside the World's End park you are obliged to pay the US$12 park entry fee plus the camp-site fee (Rs 600 per day, plus Rs 600 service charge per stay).

A more frugal and possibly more fulfilling alternative would be to stay in nearby Ohiya. **Hill Safari Eco-Lodge** (☎ 071 277 2451; r ind half-board per person Rs 1000), about 1.5km from the Horton Plains junction down a very rough and winding road, has three family rooms with attached bathrooms and hot water. It's a former tea manager's bungalow on the Lower Bray tea estate. Hill Safari offers a seven-day trekking itinerary in the national park.

Opposite the Ohiya train station the first small **shop** (☎ 0777 404658; r Rs 700) you come to has two rooms, if you're desperate. Food is available here at half the price of that at the kiosk near Farr Inn.

Getting There & Away

TAXI

If you don't feel like walking up the road to the park entrance, there is often a taxi waiting at the Ohiya train station. From there, getting to Farr Inn (40 minutes one way) should cost about Rs 1000 return, including waiting time.

It takes about 1½ hours to get from Haputale to Farr Inn by road (Rs 1800 return). From Ohiya the road rises in twists and turns through forest before emerging on the open plains. It's a pleasant journey and on the way through the forest you may catch sight of monkeys.

You can also drive to Farr Inn from Nuwara Eliya, a trip taking about 1½ hours one way (around Rs 1800 by taxi).

There is a 4WD road that goes past the Bambarakanda Falls (the road signposted on the main road between Haputale and Belihul Oya) and emerges near Ohiya train station. It's pretty rough and would probably be impassable in wet weather.

TRAIN & FOOT

Given that the mist comes down at World's End at around 10am, you'll want to get there by at least 9.30am. You can walk to World's End, but it's a 30km round trip from Ohiya with some steep ascents – it's for serious

hikers only. Theoretically it would be possible to catch a night train to Ohiya and start
the walk in the early hours, but as the trains
are often delayed you risk walking 15km
up to World's End only to find the clouds
have rolled in. It would be better to arrive
in Ohiya the day before if you really want to
do the walk. The walk from Ohiya to Farr
Inn is 11.2km, or 2½ to 3½ hours, along
the road – you'll need a torch if you do it
at night. Then you've got another 1½ hours
to World's End. It's a slog but it is doable.
You'll need about two hours for the walk
back down towards Ohiya. You'll sleep well
after you've finished the walk.

You could also catch a taxi from Ohiya
train station to Farr Inn.

The trip up the main road is a pretty walk
with great views and you can be sure you
won't get lost. Near the 27km post you'll
find a toilet block.

Keen walkers can also strike out for Farr
Inn from Pattipola, the next train station
north of Ohiya (a walk of about 10km along
a 4WD track), or from Bambarakanda Falls,
about four hours downhill from the plains
(below). To make this a longer two-day
hike, start from Haputale.

BELIHUL OYA
☎ 045

Belihul Oya is a pretty hillside region worth
passing through on your way to/from the
Hill Country – it's 35km from Haputale
and 57km from Ratnapura. From here you
can walk up to Horton Plains, a seriously
strenuous undertaking.

About 11km towards Haputale, near Kalupahana, are the **Bambarakanda Falls**. (Ask
the bus driver to let you off at Kalupahana.)
At 240m, they're the highest in Sri Lanka.
March and April are the best months for
viewing the falls; at other times the water
may be reduced to a disappointing trickle.
There's a four-hour trail from here to Horton Plains – it's a fair challenge.

Belihul Oya Rest House (☎ 228 7599; Ratnapura-
Haputale Rd; r with/without air-con US$48/30; ☒) has
14 clean but ageing rooms, and is exquisitely
perched beside a stream that rushes down
from Horton Plains. There's a restaurant
here and a lounge packed with comfy chairs
near a natural rock pool – feel like a dip?

River Garden Resort (☎ 228 0222; www.ecoclub
.com/rivergarden/lodge.html; r US$18.50, tent per person

incl half-board US$18.50, lodge US$24.50) has three cottages with spotless rooms set in a shady terraced garden above a stream. The 'ecolodge'
9km up the road sleeps five. A camp site
set in a shady area below the restaurant offers spacious two- to four-person tents with
easy access to swimming in the Belihul Oya.
The camp site also has shared toilets and
showers; some visitors choose to bathe in
the river.

HAPUTALE
☎ 057 / pop 4706 / elev 1580m

Perched at the southern edge of the Hill
Country, the largely Tamil town of Haputale
clings to a long, narrow mountain ridge
with the land falling away steeply on both
sides. The bowl-shaped Uva valley, surrounded by the Idalgashinna and Ohiya
peaks, as well as the Horton Plains plateau,
lies to the north and east of the ridge, while
the foothills of the lower Uva descend from
the other side all the way to the sea. On
a clear day you can see all the way to the
south coast from this ridge, and at night the
Hambantota lighthouse may be visible.

The town centre itself is a squall of traffic and small shops, but a short walk out of
town quickly repays the effort with extraordinary views. The railway hugs one side of
the ridge.

As in many places in the Hill Country, the
legacies of the British planters live on. There
are tea estates on hillsides, and the old plantation bungalows, some of which have lovely
gardens. There's also a pretty little Anglican
church (St Andrew's) on the Bandarawela
road. The headstones in its cemetery make
for interesting reading.

Haputale is a pleasant place with some
good cheap accommodation, and makes a
good base for visiting Horton Plains National Park, exploring other places in the
area, or just taking pleasant walks in cool
mountain air. Guesthouses arrange vans
and 4WDs to Horton Plains for Rs 1700.

Information
The town isn't too small to have a **Bank of
Ceylon** (Station Rd) and a **People's Bank** (Colombo Rd),
where you can change money and travellers
cheques and get cash advances on Visa cards.
The post office is in the centre of town. **Amarasinghe Guest House** (☎ 226 8175; agh777@sltnet
.lk; Thambapillai Ave) has Internet facilities.

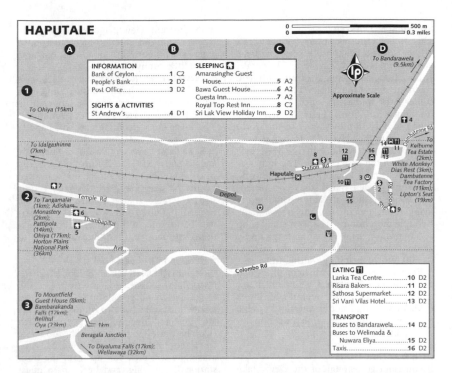

HAPUTALE

0	500 m
0	0.3 miles

INFORMATION
Bank of Ceylon.................1 C2
People's Bank...................2 D2
Post Office.......................3 D2

SIGHTS & ACTIVITIES
St Andrew's.....................4 D1

SLEEPING
Amarasinghe Guest
   House.........................5 A2
Bawa Guest House............6 A2
Cuesta Inn......................7 A2
Royal Top Rest Inn.........8 C2
Sri Lak View Holiday Inn....9 D2

To Bandarawela
(9.5km)

Approximate Scale

To Ohiya (15km)

To Idalgashinna
(7km)

To Kelburne
Tea Estate
(2km);
White Monkey/
Dias Rest (3km);
Dambatenne
Tea Factory
(11km);
Lipton's Seat
(19km)

Haputale

Station Rd

To Tangamalai
(1km); Adisham
Monastery
(2km);
Pattipola
(14km);
Ohiya (17km);
Horton Plains
National Park
(36km)

Temple Rd

Thambapillai

Ave

Depot

Colombo Rd

To Mountfield
Guest House (8km);
Bambarakanda
Falls (12km);
Belihul
Oya (23km)

1km

Beragala Junction

To Diyaluma Falls (17km);
Wellawaya (32km)

EATING
Lanka Tea Centre.............10 D2
Risara Bakers...................11 D2
Sathosa Supermarket........12 D2
Sri Vani Vilas Hotel..........13 D2

TRANSPORT
Buses to Bandarawela........14 D2
Buses to Welimada &
   Nuwara Eliya................15 D2
Taxis...............................16 D2

Sights

DAMBATENNE TEA FACTORY

A few tea factories in this area are happy to have visitors. The most popular, **Dambatenne** (admission Rs 180; closed Sun), was built in 1890 by Sir Thomas Lipton, one of the most famous figures in tea history. A tour through the works educates the visitor on the processes involved in the fermentation, rolling, drying, cutting, sieving and grading of tea. Some of the equipment in use is up to a century old. For further details about tea production, see The Tea Hills, p199.

Although it's 11km from Haputale, the popular factory is easily accessible. A bus (for the estate workers) goes from the bus station for Bandarawela to the factory and back again about every 25 minutes (Rs 10). Alternatively, a taxi there and back costs about Rs 350. If you are fit and energetic this is a great walk, with wonderful views.

DIYALUMA FALLS

Heading towards Wellawaya you'll pass the 171m-high Diyaluma Falls, Sri Lanka's third-highest waterfall, just 5km beyond the town of Koslanda. Cascading down an escarpment of the Koslanda Plateau, the stream is fairly small, though it quickly builds up after a downpour. By bus, take a Wellawaya service from Haputale and get off at Diyaluma (1¼ hours). The falls leap over a cliff face and fall in one clear drop to a pool below – very picturesque and clearly visible from the road.

If you're energetic you can climb up to the beautiful pools and a series of mini falls at the top of the main fall. Walk about 500m down the road from the bottom of the falls and take the estate track that turns sharply back up to the left. From there it's about 20 minutes' walk to a small rubber factory, where you strike off uphill to the left. The track is very indistinct, although there are some white arrows on the rocks – if you're lucky, people in the rubber factory will shout if they see you taking the wrong turn! At the top the path forks: the right branch (more distinct) leads to the pools above the main falls, the left fork to the top of the main falls. The pools above the second set of falls are good for a cool swim.

THE HILL COUNTRY

ADISHAM MONASTERY

This Benedictine **monastery** (admission Rs 60; 🕙 9am-12.30pm & 1.30-4.30pm Sat & Sun, poya days & school holidays) is about 3km west of Haputale. Follow Temple Rd along the ridge until you reach the sign at the Adisham turn-off. The stone-block monastery once belonged to tea planter Sir Thomas Lester Villiers. This is one of only 18 monasteries in the world belonging to the Sylvestrine Congregation, a suborder of the Benedictine fraternity founded in the 13th century. The industrious monks have added lots of stonework, including garden walls, steps and terracing. Inside, visitors are allowed to see the living room and library, and occasionally a couple more rooms. There's a small shop selling produce from the monastery's lovely gardens and orchards. A taxi should cost Rs 300 return, including waiting time.

Before you reach Adisham the road passes through **Tangamalai**, a bird sanctuary and nature reserve. Although it's off limits to visitors, around sunset you'll still be able to see many birds, even sambar deer on occasion, by the roadside.

OTHER ATTRACTIONS

If you can't get enough of the views, take the train to **Idalgashinna** train station, 8km along the railway west of Haputale. You can walk back beside the train tracks enjoying a spectacular view because the land falls away steeply for a great distance on both sides.

Near the Dambatenne tea factory, the **Lipton's Seat** lookout has some claiming that it rivals the views from World's End (and it's free). Take the signed narrow paved road from the tea factory, and climb about 7km through lush tea plantations to the lookout. From the tea factory the ascent should take about 2½ hours.

Some visitors hike along the train lines from Haputale to **Pattipola** (14km, an all-day hike), the highest railway station in Sri Lanka. If you decide to do this, bring along a torch for the long railway tunnels. From Pattipola you can continue via foot or taxi to Ohiya railway station, and from there to the Horton Plains.

Sleeping & Eating

Royal Top Rest Inn (☎ 226 8178; 22 Station Rd; r with/without bathroom Rs 650/550) A short walk from the railway station, this is a friendly place with pleasant views, a cheerfully gaudy living room and simple but clean rooms. There's a restaurant, a small outdoor area and a little sunny shared balcony.

Cuesta Inn (☎ 226 8110; kacp@sltnet.lk; 118 Temple Rd; r Rs 750) This inn has five basic rooms, each with a small balcony, and the large sitting room has superb views over tea plantations. The hosts are welcoming and will happily arrange excursions around the area.

Bawa Guest House (☎ 226 8260; 32 Thambapillai Ave; s Rs 250-350, d Rs 550-600) Run by a friendly Muslim family, this is a basic house nestled on the hillside. There are five cosy rooms with tolerable shared bathrooms in the original building, and two rooms with private bathrooms in the newer building next door. Inexpensive, filling meals (Rs 250 to 400) are available. There's lots of good information in its guest books.

Amarasinghe Guest House (☎ 226 8175; agh777@ sltnet.lk; Thambapillai Ave; r with/without hot water Rs 880/660) This terrific guesthouse, located in a neat white home, has two rooms in a separate block and four modern spotless rooms (with balconies) in the house. The food here (meals Rs 250 to 400) is very good. Mr Amarasinghe will pick you up from the train station if you ring, and he keeps a guest book with some interesting comments and advice.

If you're arriving at the Bawa Guest House or Amarasinghe Guest House by foot, follow Temple Rd until you see a yellow Bawa Guest House sign to the south, just off the side of the road. Go down the first flight of stairs and head along the path (past the mangy truck) for about 250m. You'll come to Bawa first; a further flight of steps will take you in the back way to Amarasinghe Guest House.

Mountfield Guest House (☎ 226 8463; Haldumulla; r Rs 750, whole lodge Rs 2000) Located on the Belihul Oya road, 9km from Haputale, this stone lodge stands close to the road in a little plantation. It has two rooms, both with kitchenettes.

Kelburne Tea Estate (☎ 226 8029; kelburne@eur eka.lk; bungalows Rs 4000-5000) About 2km east of Haputale train station, this is an absolute gem and would be a fine place to unwind for a few days. Three estate bungalows have been made available to visitors, complete with staff (including a cook) and all the trimmings. There's one bungalow with two bedrooms and two bungalows with three bedrooms. Each bungalow comes with huge bathrooms, overstuffed couches and lots of magazines. Meals cost Rs 450 to 600. You must book ahead. A taxi from the train station will cost about Rs 150.

White Monkey/Dias Rest (☎ 071 259 1361; mailva ganamdias@yahoo.co.uk; Thotulagala; s/d incl breakfast Rs 500/700) Three kilometres east of the train station, in Thotulagala, a Tamil family has opened a new guesthouse with one cottage so far. Meals (Rs 200 to 400) are available at reasonable prices. The owner is an experienced guide and has lots of information on local hikes.

Sri Lak View Holiday Inn (☎ 226 8125; Sherwood Rd; r Rs 800-1000) The more expensive rooms at this 11-room lodge have unimpeded views down the back side of the ridge, but general standards seem to drop with every passing year. Only recommended if every other place is full.

You're best off eating in your guesthouse, but there are a number of OK places in town for short eats, dosas, *rottis* (doughy pancakes), and rice and curry, such as the **Lanka Tea Centre** (Temple Rd), opposite the Welimada and Nuwara Eliya bus stand, and the **Sri Vani Vilas Hotel** (Dambatenne Rd), near the Bandarawela bus station. There's also a Sathosa supermarket tucked away on the road to the train station, if you want to buy your own supplies.

Getting There & Away
BUS
There are direct buses to Nuwara Eliya at 7am and 2pm (Rs 50, 3½ hours), but if you miss these buses you'll have to go to Welimada (private bus Rs 30, two hours) and get an onward service. To/from Bandarawela there are frequent buses (Rs 18, one hour) that run into the early evening. There are also express buses to Colombo (Rs 265, six hours).

For the south coast you usually have to change at Wellawaya (Rs 40), 1½ hours down the hill from Haputale. The last bus from Haputale to Wellawaya leaves at about 5pm.

TRAIN
Haputale is on the Colombo–Badulla line, so you can travel directly by train to and from Kandy or Nanu Oya (for Nuwara Eliya). It's 8½ to nine hours to Colombo, 5½ hours to Kandy, 1½ hours to Nanu Oya (3rd/2nd class, Rs 22/40), 40 minutes to Ohiya, 30 minutes to Bandarawela

(3rd/2nd class, Rs 6/11) and two hours to Badulla (3rd/2nd class, Rs 24/44).

The daily train departures in the Badulla direction are at 4.29am, 6.44am, 12.16am, 2.12pm (on *Podi Menike*) and 5.32pm (on *Udarata Menike*). In the Colombo direction the trains depart at 7.56am (*Udarata Menike*), 10.51am (*Podi Menike*), 8.09pm (on the night mail) and 9.30pm. The *Udarata Menike* doesn't go via Kandy.

BANDARAWELA
☎ 057 / pop 7188 / elev 1230m
Bandarawela, 10km north of Haputale but noticeably warmer, is a busy market town that makes a good base for exploring the surrounding area. Due to its agreeable climate, it's a popular area to retire to. Each Sunday morning the town has a lively market.

The focal point of the town is the busy junction just north of the train station. From here Haputale Rd goes southwest; Welimada Rd heads northwest then turns sharply left by a mosque; and Badulla Rd, with the main bus and taxi stops, heads downhill to the east.

Information
The main post office is near the Bandarawela Hotel, and there are plenty of telephone offices on the main streets. Micro Services, located off Welimada Rd, provides Internet access.

Bank of Ceylon (Badulla Rd) Has an ATM.
Commercial Bank (Badulla Rd) Has an ATM.
Hatton National Bank (Badulla Rd) Has an ATM; gives cash advances on MasterCard and Visa.
Woodlands Network (☎ 223 2668; woodlands@sltnet .lk; 38/1C Esplanade Rd) This nonprofit ecotourism centre (p212) has Internet access.

Sights & Activities
DOWA TEMPLE
About 6km east of Bandarawela on the road to Badulla, the charming Dowa Temple is pleasantly situated close to a stream on the right-hand side of the road, with a beautiful 4m-high standing Buddha cut into the rock face below the road. The walls of adjacent cave shrine, cut from solid rock, are covered with excellent Sri Lankan–style Buddhist murals. The temple is easy to miss if you're coming by bus, so ask the bus conductor to tell you when to get off. A three-wheeler or taxi from Bandarawela should cost Rs 400 to 500 return, including waiting time.

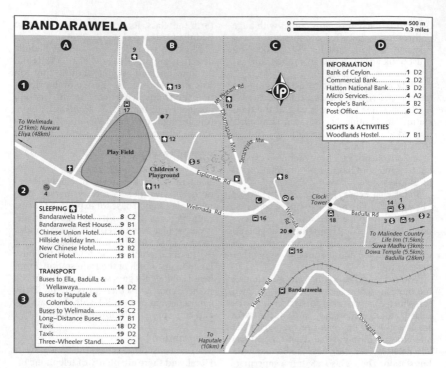

BANDARAWELA

INFORMATION
Bank of Ceylon................1	D2
Commercial Bank................2	D2
Hatton National Bank........3	D2
Micro Services.................4	A2
People's Bank....................5	B2
Post Office.......................6	C2

SIGHTS & ACTIVITIES
Woodlands Hostel..............7	B1

SLEEPING
Bandarawela Hotel..............8	C2
Bandarawela Rest House....9	B1
Chinese Union Hotel.........10	C1
Hillside Holiday Inn...........11	B2
New Chinese Hotel...........12	B2
Orient Hotel....................13	B1

TRANSPORT
Buses to Ella, Badulla & Wellawaya..................14	D2
Buses to Haputale & Colombo.....................15	C3
Buses to Welimada...........16	C2
Long–Distance Buses........17	B1
Taxis...............................18	D2
Taxis...............................19	D2
Three-Wheeler Stand........20	C2

WOODLANDS NETWORK

Founded by the late Dutch priest Harry Haas in 1992, **Woodlands Network** (☎ 223 2668; woodlands@sltnet.lk; 38/1C Esplanade Rd) is one of the most exemplary local-initiative tourism and social action organisations in Sri Lanka. Now headed by Sarojinie Ellawela, the centre offers a wide range of alternative tourism services in the Hill Country. The friendly staff can arrange local and jungle walks, Sri Lankan cooking lessons, meditation classes and visits to temples, forest hermitages, tea plantations, farms and waterfalls. Volunteer work is also available, and the centre sells spices, teas and local handicrafts. It also has a few hostel rooms (right) and can also arrange home stays for groups or individuals.

AYURVEDA

About 3.5km from Bandarawela is an Ayurvedic treatment centre called **Suwa Madhu** (☎ /fax 222 2504; Badulla Rd; head massage Rs 600, full treatment Rs 2600; ⏱ 8am-8pm). It's a large, plush place that caters to tourists. The 1½-hour programme includes a 45-minute oil massage, a steam and a herbal sauna.

Sleeping & Eating
BUDGET

Woodlands Hostel (☎ 223 2668; woodlands@sltnet.lk; 38/1C Esplanade Rd; Rs 500) There are a few simple, clean rooms with shared bathroom in the house that contains this ecotourism centre (left). Guests may use the kitchen; with advance notice meals can also be arranged.

Chinese Union Hotel (☎ 222 2502; 8 Mt Pleasant Rd; r Rs 750, f Rs 1500) Founded by a Chinese immigrant over 60 years ago, this is an old-fashioned place offering five clean rooms in a setting that has changed little over the decades. The restaurant serves good Chinese food ranging from Rs 130 to 260 per dish.

New Chinese Hotel (☎ 223 1767; 32 Esplanade Rd; s/d/tr Rs 850/850/950) This three-storey motel-like structure contains spotless modern rooms that make up in comfort what they lack in character.

Hillside Holiday Inn (☎ 222 2212; 34/10 Welimada Rd; s/d Rs 850/1000) Just off Welimada Rd, this charming old colonial villa has clean, spacious rooms with finely carved wooden doors.

Malindee Country Life Inn (☎ 222 3124; Badulla Rd, Bindunuwela; s/d Rs 900/1200) Rather close to the road, 2km east of town, this is a family-run inn with lots of marble and brass on display. The staff is nice and the foyer–living room is an intriguing place to relax. A three-wheeler from town should cost Rs 75.

MIDRANGE
Orient Hotel (☎ 222 2407; www.orienthotelsl.com; 12 Dharmapala Mawatha; s/d/tr US$27/30/32) The most popular hotel in town with tour groups, the Orient Hotel provides 50 comfortable rooms, along with a billiards hall, karaoke lounge, fitness centre, restaurant and bar.

Bandarawela Rest House (☎ 222 2299; fax 222 2718; s/d/f Rs 1200/1750/2100) This is a quiet spot with nine rooms, a pretty garden and friendly service. The five clean but bland rooms in the newer wing have a shared balcony with a view over the town. There are two decent family rooms in the older wing.

Bandarawela Hotel (☎ 222 2501; bwhotel@sltnet .lk; 14 Welimada Rd; s/d US$47/59) Formerly the tea planters' club, this large chalet-style place opened in 1893 and stopped updating its furnishings around the 1930s. There are vast easy chairs to sink into in the lounge, and bathrooms with lots of hot water in 33 spacious rooms. There is a little courtyard garden with tortoises, as well as a restaurant and bar.

Getting There & Away
BUS
There are infrequent direct buses to Nuwara Eliya (Rs 44) or you can hop on one of the more frequent buses to Welimada (Rs 23) and continue on to Nuwara Eliya (Rs 21) from there. There are also regular buses to Haputale (Rs 18), Ella (Rs 13) and Badulla (Rs 27). Long-distance services include runs to Colombo (Rs 200, six hours), Tissamaharama, Tangalla and Galle. Buses to Tissa, Tangalla and Galle leave from the long-distance station on Esplanade Rd. You can also change at Wellawaya for buses to Tissa or the south coast.

TRAIN
Bandarawela is on the Colombo–Badulla railway line. Trains to Colombo (via Haputale) leave at 7.25am (on *Udarata Menike*), 10.20am (on *Podi Menike,* via Kandy), 2.20pm, 7.33pm and 8.56pm. Trains to Ba-

dulla (via Ella) leave at 5am, 7.15am, 1pm, 2.38pm, 3pm, 5.58pm and 7.15pm.

Destinations include Kandy (3rd/2nd/1st class Rs 31/85/149), Badulla (3rd/2nd/1st class Rs 7.50/19.50/34), Nanu Oya (for Nuwara Eliya; 3rd/2nd class Rs 24/67), Polonnaruwa (3rd/2nd/1st class Rs 76/210/356) and Ella (3rd class only, Rs 7).

ELLA
☎ 057
Sri Lanka is liberally endowed with beautiful views, and Ella has one of the best. The sleepy village is nestled in a valley peering straight through Ella Gap to the plain nearly 1000m below, and across to the coast where, on a clear night, you can see the Great Basses lighthouse. And as if the views weren't enough, Ella is surrounded by hills perfect for walks through tea plantations to temples and waterfalls. Ella only received electricity in 1984.

Information
There's a post office in the centre of the town, but for banking you will need travel to Bandarawela. Rodrigo Communications and RMS Communications on Main St both have Internet and IDD facilities. Rodrigo Communications is also a good source of travel information.

Activities
Ella is a great base for keen walkers who want to explore the surrounding countryside – the views can be spectacular. For more information, see p217.

Sleeping
Touts might approach you on the train with tales that the hotel of your choice is too expensive, closed down, or rat-infested. In fact, every place we visited in Ella was quite acceptable, so don't believe them.

BUDGET
Ella Holiday Inn (☎ 222 8615; tourinfo@sltnet.lk; s/d/tr Rs 800/1000/1500) Recently opened by the same family that runs Rodrigo Communications, this three-storey inn sits in the middle of town and is reached by a footbridge from the main street. Rooms are clean and comfortable, the staff is friendly and the dining room serves good, inexpensive Sri Lankan and Western food.

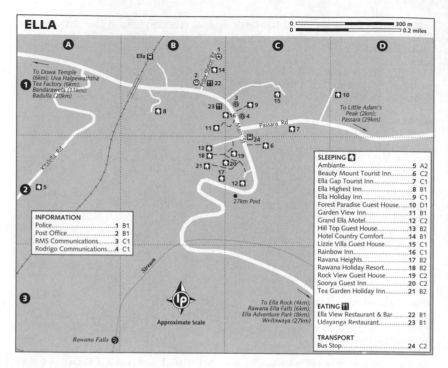

ELLA

INFORMATION
Police	1 B1
Post Office	2 B1
RMS Communications	3 C1
Rodrigo Communications	4 C1

SLEEPING
Ambiante	5 A2
Beauty Mount Tourist Inn	6 C2
Ella Gap Tourist Inn	7 C1
Ella Highest Inn	8 B1
Ella Holiday Inn	9 C1
Forest Paradise Guest House	10 D1
Garden View Inn	11 B1
Grand Ella Motel	12 C2
Hill Top Guest House	13 B2
Hotel Country Comfort	14 B1
Lizzie Villa Guest House	15 C1
Rainbow Inn	16 C1
Ravana Heights	17 B2
Rawana Holiday Resort	18 B2
Rock View Guest House	19 C2
Soorya Guest Inn	20 C2
Tea Garden Holiday Inn	21 B2

EATING
Ella View Restaurant & Bar	22 B1
Udayanga Restaurant	23 B1

TRANSPORT
Bus Stop	24 C2

Lizzie Villa Guest House (☎ 222 8643; s/d/tr Rs 600/1000/1500) Lizzie's is one of the longest-running establishments in Ella. Signposted on the main road, and reached on a 200m dirt track, this place has a hilltop location, a spice garden (the source of much of the home cooking), a shady veranda, and 10 simple, clean rooms with hot water.

Garden View Inn (☎ 222 8792; s/d Rs 500/700) This inn offers three simple rooms with bright, clean bathrooms in a family home. The owner has lots of info on walks in the area. Rice-and-curry meals here are inexpensive, so all in all it's very good value.

Beauty Mount Tourist Inn (☎ 222 8799; r/cottages Rs 500/900) This unpretentious little guesthouse has five rooms, as well as a cute little cottage up the hill, with a kitchen, fridge, one large bedroom and lots of privacy. The owner is a particularly good-natured fellow who likes to serve up home-grown coffee. The rooms are clean enough and the food is cheap.

Rainbow Inn (☎ 222 8788; s/d Rs 500/600, with hot water Rs 550/650) The friendly family here rents out five clean rooms, each painted a different colour (hence the name). The food is tasty and inexpensive.

Ella Highest Inn (☎ 222 8608; s/d Rs 550/750) Set in a tea plantation, this place is a hike up the track from the main road, but it's worth it – you'll get great views of the hilly countryside. The rooms are basic, with small bathrooms.

Soorya Guest Inn (☎ 222 8906; s/d Rs 500/700) This is a clean little place with three rooms, a common balcony and a guest kitchen.

Rock View Guest House (☎ 222 8561; r Rs 600-1000) This is a large old Sri Lankan–style house with four clean but worn rooms set around a large living area. From the terrace there are views to Ella Gap.

Hill Top Guest House (☎ 222 8780; s Rs 600-700, d Rs 800-950) Hill Top has downstairs rooms with verandas surrounded by a garden, as well as upstairs rooms that share a balcony with superb views of Ella Gap. Good Sri Lankan meals are available.

Rawana Holiday Resort (☎ 222 8794; nalan kumara@yahoo.com; r Rs 800-1000) Perched high on a hillside overlooking Ella, this family-run hotel contains six balcony rooms with views, plus four less expensive interior rooms. The

Sri Lankan couple who owns the place is friendly, and the husband cooks very good Sri Lankan cuisine. The house speciality is a delicious garlic-based curry.

Forest Paradise Guest House (☎ 222 8797; forest paradise@123india.com; s/d Rs 800/900) Backed onto a pine forest, this guesthouse has four rooms in a handsome bungalow with clean private bathrooms. The owner arranges trips into the Namunugala Hills, 16km away, for Rs 1000 per person, including a BBQ lunch (minimum three people).

MIDRANGE

Ravana Heights (☎ 222 8888; jith@ravanaheights.com; r US$45) Opposite the 27km post on the Ella–Wellawaya road, this is a terrific little boutique guesthouse with four superclean rooms. It's a stylish, modern home with great service and friendly Sri Lankan–Thai owners. There's a veranda and a pretty garden, and the owners offer various organised excursions. The food is lovely too – if you ring ahead you can have Sri Lankan, Western or Thai dinner here for US$7.50 per person.

Hotel Country Comfort (☎ 222 8500; info@hotel countrycomfort.lk; Police Station Rd; r old Rs 800-100, new Rs 1700-2200) This is an older building with a new annexe. The original building is a beautifully maintained 60-year-old villa, but the rooms here are smaller. The newer wing positively gleams, and the rooms have lots of space, bay windows and modern bathrooms. It's a great choice if you want a little more comfort. It also has a restaurant.

Ambiante (☎ 222 8867; hansasurf.tripod.com/ambi ante/ambiante.htm; Kitalella Rd; r Rs 1200-2000) At the top of a hill, the motel-like row of rooms here all have ample balconies and good views down Ella Gap. It's quite a steep walk from the centre of town; a three-wheeler from the train station should cost Rs 150.

Ella Gap Tourist Inn (☎ 222 8528; Passara Rd; r Rs 1600-2250) This seven-room inn has a very pleasant outdoor restaurant and leafy gardens linking the rooms. The five older rooms are larger and have more charm than the two smaller, newer rooms.

Tea Garden Holiday Inn (☎ 222 8860; s Rs 1000-1500, d Rs 1500-2200) Near Rawana Holiday Resort, this place offers nine clean, spacious rooms. The cheaper rooms are a bit small; the more expensive rooms share a roomy balcony. There are also friendly hosts, excellent food and a leafy communal balcony

with pleasant views to the small Rawana Falls (and decent views through Ella Gap).

Grand Ella Motel (☎ 222 8655; ceylonhotels.lk; s/d/tr old US$51/56/63, new US$72/82/91, all incl breakfast) Formerly Ella Resthouse, Grand Ella Motel has a superb location with great views through Ella Gap from the front lawn. It's run by the government-owned Ceylon Hotels Corporation, and the service tends to be rather uninspired. This place pays hefty commissions so don't be surprised if your driver suggests you stay here. The less expensive rooms are in a rather dark building on the property's lower level.

Ella Adventure Park (☎ 228 7263; wildernesslanka .com; r/treehouses US$55/60) About 9km southeast of Ella on the Wellawaya road, this place is different to the usual cardboard-cut-out hotels. It has log furniture, natural-toned décor, Flintstonesque stone features and a quiet bush setting. The treehouses, though cute, are in need of repair; the cabins are a bit nicer, but the per-day rates are bit over the top. The management organises paragliding, canoeing, rock climbing, abseiling, camping and more. Most guests book in as part of a six-night package (US$1200) that includes all of these activities. A restaurant serves traditional Sri Lankan food.

Eating & Drinking

Ella offers very little in the way of decent restaurants outside of those in the places to stay. All of the guesthouses and hotels serve food, but most ask for at least four hours' advance notice. Our favourites include Ravana Heights, Rawana Holiday Inn, Ambiante and Hotel Country Comfort. The garden dining area at Ella Gap Tourist Inn is especially good for Sri Lankan cuisine, and has perhaps the nicest ambience of any place in town.

Curd (buffalo-milk yoghurt) and treacle (syrup from the *kitul* palm; sometimes misnamed 'honey') is a much advertised local speciality, but, frankly, the shops that serve it here are not very clean and tend to fill up with local drunks.

Udayanga Restaurant (dishes Rs 120-180) This friendly and clean spot has good Sri Lankan and Western food at low prices.

Ella View Restaurant & Bar (dishes Rs 150-300) This dark roadside restaurant is popular with locals and tourists alike, and is one of the only places open past 8pm. Solo female travellers may attract unwanted attention from local men in their cups.

THE HILL COUNTRY

Getting There & Away
BUS & TAXI
The road to Ella leaves the Bandarawela–Badulla road about 9km out of Bandarawela. Buses change schedule fairly often. A couple of old rogues hang around the bus stop asking for foreign coins and occasionally taking money from people to buy bus tickets – don't trust them.

Buses to Bandarawela cost Rs 13 and are fairly frequent. There are infrequent buses to Badulla, although you can always get a bus to Bandarawela and change there for Badulla. It is advisable to catch intercity express buses to Bandarawela, Wellawaya and Badulla. To or from Kandy you must change at Badulla. Alternatively, you could go to Wellawaya, catch the intercity to Nuwara Eliya and then change again for Kandy.

Buses to Matara (CTB/intercity express Rs 80/150) stop at Ella around every hour from about 6.30am until about 2.30pm. The buses are likely to be quite full by the time they reach Ella, though the buses around noon are usually less busy. You can always catch a bus to Wellawaya (Rs 21) and change there for a service to the South or for Monaragala (for Arugam Bay).

It costs Rs 400 to go by taxi from Ella to Bandarawela.

TRAIN
Ella is an hour from Haputale and Badulla on the Colombo–Badulla line. The stretch from Haputale (through Bandarawela) has particularly lovely scenery. Roughly 10km north of Ella, at Demodara, the line performs a complete loop around a hillside and tunnels under itself at a level 30m lower. Ella's train station is quaint, and the fares and timetables well posted.

The main trains to Colombo depart at 6.52am (*Udarata Menike*) and 9.47am (*Podi Menike*). These have a 1st-class observation car; seats inside the car should be booked ahead. Other trains to Colombo depart at 6.50am and 8.23pm (2nd class Rs 230); trains to Kandy (2nd class Rs 152) include departures at 1.07pm and 6.50pm. Destinations on the Kandy line include Bandarawela (Rs 13), Haputale (Rs 23), Nanu Oya (for Nuwara Eliya; Rs 63) and Hatton (Rs 92). Badulla (2nd class Rs 18) departures are at 5.28am, 7.55am, 1.47pm, 3.08pm, 3.28pm (*Podi Menike*) and 6.09pm (*Udarata Menike*).

AROUND ELLA
Some people like to visit the **Dowa Temple** from Ella; for more information, see p211.

Another option is to visit a tea factory; **Uva Halpewaththa Tea Factory** runs tours (Rs 150). To get here catch a bus to Bandarawela, get off at Kumbawela junction and flag a bus going to Badulla. Get off just after the 27km post, near the Halpe temple. From here you've got a 2km walk to the factory. A three-wheeler from Ella will charge Rs 250 return.

The 19m-high **Rawana Ella Falls** are about 6km down Ella Gap towards Wellawaya. During rainy months the water comes leaping down the mountain-side in what is claimed to be the wildest-looking fall in Sri Lanka, but during the dry season it may not flow at all. There are vendors selling food and trinkets, and the invariable array of 'guides' wanting to point out 'the waterfall'. Buses from Ella cost Rs 6 and a three-wheeler will cost Rs 30 return, including waiting time.

Further up the road and to your left as you approach Ella, a side road takes you to a little **temple** and a **cave** that is associated with the Ramayana story. You may visit the temple,

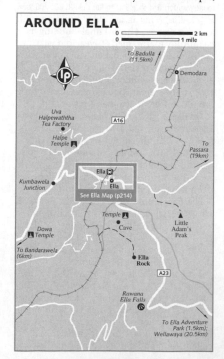

which is part of a monastery, but remember to remove your shoes and hat, and to cover your legs and arms. The cave, located in a cleft in the mountain that rises to Ella Rock, is said to be the very one in which the king of Lanka held Sita captive. Boys often materialise to show you where the track up to the cave starts, but the track is steep, overgrown and slippery. Most people find the cave itself to be a disappointment.

Ella is a great place for walks though it would be inadvisable for women to head off walking alone. A gentle walk will take you to what is locally dubbed **Little Adam's Peak**. Go down the Passara road until you get to the plant shop on your right, just past the 1km post. Follow the track that is on your left as you face the garden shop; Little Adam's Peak is the biggest hill on your right. Take the second path that turns off to your right and follow it to the top of the hill. Part of this path passes through a tea estate. The approximately 4.5km round trip takes about 45 minutes each way.

Walking to **Ella Rock** is rather more demanding. Head along the train tracks (towards Bandarawela) for about 2.5km until you come to the metal bridge where you can see the small **Rawana Falls**. After passing the bridge, turn left towards the falls, cross a log bridge and follow the track up to Ella Rock, where you'll be rewarded with stunning views. The walk (approximately 9km in total) takes about two hours each way.

BADULLA

☎ 055 / pop 42,572 / elev 680m

Badulla marks the southeast extremity of the Hill Country and is a gateway to the east coast. It is one of Sri Lanka's oldest towns, and has a local reputation as a base for black marketeers. The Portuguese occupied it briefly, then torched it upon leaving. For the British it was an important social centre, although the teeming roads have changed the atmosphere quite drastically today. The railway through the Hill Country from Colombo terminates here.

Information

You can change money at **Bank of Ceylon** (Bank Rd), and buy stamps or mail letters at the **post office** (Post Office Rd). Opposite Bank of Ceylon, **Cybrain Computer Systems** (40/1 Bank Rd) offers inexpensive Internet access.

Sights

PLACES OF WORSHIP

Most Sri Lankans visiting Badulla stop at either Muthiyagana Vihara or Kataragama Devale. **Muthiyagana Vihara** is a large Buddhist complex, and includes a whitewashed dagoba that occupies spacious grounds in the southeast quarter of town. During festivals the resident elephant may be paraded around.

At **Kataragama Devale** the main objects of veneration are statues of the gods Kataragama, Saman and Vishnu. Uniquely, the *devale* was constructed in Kandyan style rather than South Indian Tamil style, with a long wooden shrine hall painted with murals depicting a *perahera*.

If you are a history buff, take a look through **St Mark's Church** and peruse the old headstones. Inside the church is a plaque commemorating the elephant hunter Major Rogers, who was killed by lightning.

DUNHINDA FALLS

Five kilometres north of Badulla are the 63m-high **Dunhinda Falls** (admission Rs 25), said to be the most awe-inspiring in the country. The best time to see them is June and July, but they're worth a visit at any time. It's a good spot for a picnic, but watch out for monkeys with lightning reflexes! Buses leave every 30 minutes from Badulla (Rs 16). From the bus stop the falls are about 1km along a clearly defined path. It can be a bit of a scramble, so wear suitable shoes. You can see a lower waterfall on the walk, and there's a good observation spot at the end of the path. There are many snack places on the main road and along the trail. Avoid public holidays and weekends, when the place can get packed. A three-wheeler from town charges Rs 350 for the return trip.

Sleeping & Eating

River Side Holiday Inn (☎ 222 2090; rahinn@sltnet.lk; 27 Lower King St; d/f Rs 990/1650) Badulla's nicest and most efficiently run hotel is a modern affair with a variety of rooms. Some are very good value, others just so-so (although all are clean), so have a look before committing. Also on the premises are a karaoke lounge, a snooker room, plenty of parking and a cheery restaurant serving good Sri Lankan and Chinese cuisine. This is where most tour groups stay.

THE HILL COUNTRY

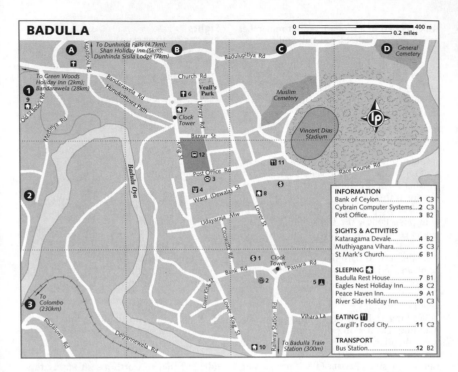

Badulla Rest House (Uda Rest House; ☎ 222 2299; s/d Rs 500/700) Smack in the centre of Badulla, this colonial-era rest house has faded rooms with shared bathrooms (no hot water) set around a grassy courtyard. Inexpensive Sri Lankan meals are available in an adjacent canteen.

Peace Haven Inn (☎ 222 2523; 18 Old St Bedes Rd; s/d Rs 500/700, r with hot water Rs 800) At the western edge of town, this is a modern place with slightly tatty rooms, although it's quieter than Badulla Rest House. A three-wheeler costs about Rs 60 from the bus station, or Rs 100 from the train station. Meals are available.

Eagles Nest Holiday Inn (☎ 222 2841; 159 Lower St; s/d Rs 500/750) This is a no-frills place with quaint rooms set around a courtyard. There's also a bar and liquor outlet, which attracts a clientele that might make a lone woman feel uncomfortable.

Green Woods Holiday Inn (☎ 223 1358; 301 Bandarawela Rd; r with/without air-con Rs 1850/1250; ✷) The third place in Badulla bearing the popular 'Holiday Inn' moniker, this one can be found about 3km from the centre of town

on the road to Bandarawela. The rooms have ceiling-to-floor windows looking out to the countryside, and all have hot water. The rooms by the road are a bit noisy, so try to get a room towards the rear of the hotel. Decent Sri Lankan, Chinese and Western meals are available.

Dunhinda Sisila Lodge (☎ 223 1302; Mahiyangana Rd; s/d Rs 500/900) Close to the falls, this is a curious jumble of buildings by a river – one room has a tree poking through it. There's a natural swimming hole close by. To find it, follow the Dunhinda Falls road past the falls for a further 2.3km. Meals are available.

Shan Holiday Inn (☎ 222 4889; Mahiyangana Rd; r/cottages Rs 2000/2500) Just 300m past the falls entrance, this relatively new establishment has a large open-air restaurant with views of the valley below. Underneath the restaurant are three older cement-walled rooms, while above the restaurant stand three simple cottages with earthen walls.

There are many local nosheries along Lower St, near the intersection with Bazaar St. Self-caterers can buy groceries at **Cargills Food City** (Post Office Rd).

Getting There & Away

BUS

Buses run to Nuwara Eliya (CTB Rs 52) every 40 minutes until 4.30pm, to Bandarawela (private bus Rs 17) every 20 minutes from 6am until 4.50pm, and to Ella (private bus Rs 23) approximately every two hours until 5pm. There are also buses to Colombo (intercity express Rs 22) until 10pm, and to Kandy (CTB/intercity express Rs 100/190) until 2pm. For Monaragala (private bus Rs 64), buses leave every hour until 5.30pm.

TRAIN

The main daily services to Colombo depart Badulla at 5.55am *(Udarata Menike)*, 8.50am *(Podi Menike* via Kandy), 5.50pm (with sleeperettes) and 7.15pm (a slow train). Tickets to Colombo cost Rs 152/268/580 in 3rd/2nd/1st class; tickets to Kandy cost Rs 92/171/380.

WELLAWAYA

☎ 055

By Wellawaya you have left the Hill Country and descended to the dry plains that were once home to the ancient Sinhalese kingdom of Ruhunu. Wellawaya is simply a small crossroads town and, apart from the nearby Buduruwagala carvings, there's not much of interest in the area. Roads run north through the spectacular Ella Gap to the Hill Country; south to Tissamaharama and the coast; east to the coast; and west to Colombo.

Information

There are branches of Hatton National Bank and Bank of Ceylon near the bus station.

Sights

About 5km south of Wellawaya, a side road branches west off the Tissa road to the rock-cut Buddha figures of **Buduruwagala** (admission Rs 100). A small signpost points the way along a 4km road.

The name Buduruwagala is derived from the words for Buddha (Budu), images *(ruva)* and stone *(gala).* The figures are thought to date from around the 10th century, and belong to the Mahayana Buddhist school, which enjoyed a brief heyday in Sri Lanka during this time. The gigantic standing Buddha – at 15m the tallest on the island – in the centre still bears traces of its original

stuccoed robe, and a long streak of orange suggests it was once brightly painted.

The central of the three figures to the Buddha's right is thought to be the Mahayana Buddhist figure Avalokitesvara (the Bodhisattva of compassion). To the left of this white-painted figure is a female figure who is thought to be his consort, Tara. Local legend says the third figure represents Prince Sudhana.

The three figures on the Buddha's left-hand side appear, to an inexpert eye, to be of a rather different style. The crowned figure at the centre of the group is thought to be Maitreya, the future Buddha. To his left stands Vajrapani, who holds a *vajra* (an hourglass-shaped thunderbolt symbol) – an unusual example of the Tantric side of Buddhism in Sri Lanka. The figure to the left may be either Vishnu or Sahampath Brahma. Several of the figures hold up their right hands with two fingers bent down to the palm – a beckoning gesture. You may be joined by a guide, who will expect a tip.

A three-wheeler from Wellawaya costs about Rs 250 return and a taxi Rs 350 to 450 return.

Sleeping & Eating

Little Rose (101 Tissa Rd; r Rs 500-1000) About 1km south of town opposite the road sign announcing Wellawaya, this country home is surrounded by rice paddies and operated by a jolly, welcoming family. Good, inexpensive meals are available. A three-wheeler from the bus station costs about Rs 50.

Wellawaya Rest House (☎ 227 4899; Ella Rd; r with/without air-con Rs 1500/850; 🕃) On the road to Ella, this spot has basic but reasonably clean rooms, and an outdoor café.

Getting There & Away

Wellawaya is a common staging point between the Hill Country and the south and east coasts; you can usually find a connection here until mid-afternoon. Buses to Haputale (Rs 40) start running at around 5am, and the last bus leaves at about 5.30pm. There are regular buses to Monaragala (Rs 28, one hour), with the last bus leaving at about 6.30pm. Buses to Ella (Rs 24) run roughly every 30 minutes until 6pm. If you want to go to Kandy you must catch a bus to Nuwara Eliya and change there. For Tissamaharama you must change at Pannegamanuwa

Junction. There are also buses to Tangalla (Rs 54, three hours) and Colombo (intercity express Rs 225, seven hours).

EMBILIPITIYA

☎ 047

Embilipitiya is a good base for tours to Uda Walawe National Park, as it's only 21km south of the park's ticket office. It's a busy, modern town built to service the surrounding irrigated paddy fields and sugar-cane plantations.

The bus station stands on the main road, in the centre of town. You'll also find branches of Seylan Bank, People's Bank, Commercial Bank and Sampath Bank, all of which have ATMs and can arrange Visa cash advances.

On the main road, about 200m south of the bus station and opposite People's Bank, **Sarathchandra Tourist Guest House** (☎ 223 0044; r with/without air-con Rs 1200/900; 🍴) offers an assortment of clean rooms in the main building as well as in separate cottages. There's also a restaurant and a billiards table. It's a friendly, well-run spot, and offers Uda Walawe tours for Rs 2000 per person (minimum of three people).

Around 1.5km south of the town centre, and 600m south of Sarathchandra Tourist Guest House, **Centauria Tourist Hotel** (☎ 223 0514; centuria@sltnet.lk; s/d/tr Rs 3000/3300/3600; 🍴 🏊) is modern in design yet has an old-fashioned, rambling air. The facilities are excellent – tiled floors, balconies, billiards room and an inviting pool. The restaurant offers buffets when tours stay, otherwise there's à la carte rice and curry, spaghetti bolognaise and more. Uda Walawe 4WD tours cost Rs 2000 per person. A three-wheeler to the hotel from the bus station costs Rs 150.

Buses leave regularly for most destinations from, or near, the bus station. There are CTB buses to Tangalla (Rs 28), Matara (Rs 44) and Ratnapura (Rs 43); the intercity buses cost about twice as much. Colombo intercity buses leave every 30 minutes (Rs 180).

UDA WALAWE NATIONAL PARK

With herds of elephants, wild buffalo, sambar deer and leopards, Uda Walawe is the Sri Lankan national park that best rivals the savanna reserves of Africa. The park's 30,821 hectares centre on the large Uda Walawe Reservoir, fed by the Walawe Ganga.

The entrance to the **park** (per person US$12, plus tracker per vehicle Rs 600; ⏰ 6.30am-6.30pm) is 12km from the Ratnapura–Hambantota road turn-off, and 21km from Embilipitiya. Although most people prefer to take a tour organised by their guesthouse or hotel, if you select a 4WD from one of the many gathered outside the gate, you can expect to pay Rs 1500 for a half-day for up to eight people with driver. Last tickets are usually sold at about 5pm.

Apart from stands of teak near the river, there's little forest in the park. The tall *pohon* grass, which grows in place of the forest, can make wildlife-watching difficult, except during dry months.

This is one of the best places in Sri Lanka to see elephants – there are about 500 in the park in herds of up to 100. There's an elephant-proof fence around the perimeter of the park, preventing elephants from getting out and cattle from getting in. The best time to observe elephant herds is from 6.30am to 10am and again from 4pm to 6.30pm; they're usually near water.

Other creatures that call Uda Walawe home are sambar deer, wild buffaloes (their numbers boosted by domesticated buffaloes), mongooses, bandicoots, foxes, water monitor lizards, crocodiles, sloth bears and the occasional leopard. There are 30 varieties of snake and a wealth of birdlife; northern migrants join the residents between November and April.

A reasonably good little lodge with simple rooms and spacious grounds, **Walawa Park View Hotel** (☎ 047-223 3312; Tanamalwila Rd; r with/without air-con Rs 1400/1000; 🍴) is about 8km from the park on the Embilipitiya road. A 4WD safari costs a reasonable Rs 1500 per half-day.

Walawa Safari Village (☎ 047-223 3201; kinjou@ dialogsl.net; RB Canal Rd; s/d US$15/18, with air-con US$24/28, all incl breakfast; 🍴) is located 3km south of a small junction on the road from Embilipitiya to Uda Walawe – you'll see the sign – and 10km from the park entrance. The clean and basic rooms come in a garden setting. Trips to the park from here also cost Rs 1200 per half-day.

The park has four bungalows and three camp sites along the reservoir and the Walawa Ganga. You must prebook with the **Department of Wildlife Conservation** (Map pp84-5; ☎ 011-269 4241; www.dwlc.lk; 18 Gregory's Rd, Col 7) in Colombo. The bungalows each contain 10 beds; the charge is US$24 per person per day, plus the US$12 park entry, US$2 per group for linen hire and a US$30 per group service charge. You must bring all of your own dry rations and kerosene. Camp sites cost US$6 per site per day, plus a US$6 service charge per trip. Students and children aged between six and 12 years of age pay half-price (kiddies under six are free).

If you're staying at Embilipitiya and wish to organise a tour at the park, catch a bus heading to Tanamalwila (CTB/intercity express Rs 37/80) and ask to be dropped at the gate to the park.

SINHARAJA FOREST RESERVE

The last major undisturbed area of rainforest in Sri Lanka, this forest reserve occupies a broad ridge at the heart of the island's wet zone. On most days the forest conjures copious rain-clouds that replenish its deep soils and balance water resources for much of southwestern Sri Lanka. Recognising its importance to the island's ecosystem, Unesco declared the reserve a World Heritage Site in 1989.

Sinharaja (Lion King) is bordered by rivers: the Koskulana Ganga in the north and the Gin Ganga in the south. An old foot track that goes past the Beverley Estate marks the eastern border, close to the highest peak in the forest, Hinipitigala (1171m). Towards the west the land decreases in elevation.

The reserve comprises 18,899 hectares of natural and modified forest, measuring about 21km east to west and 3.7km north to south. It was once a royal reserve, and some colonial records refer to it as Rajasinghe Forest. It may have been the last redoubt of the Sri Lankan lion.

In 1840 the forest became British crown land and from that time efforts were made to preserve at least some of it. However, in 1971 loggers moved in and began what was called selective logging. The logged native hardwoods were replaced with mahogany (which does not occur naturally here), logging roads and trails snaked into the forest, and a woodchip mill was built. Conservationists lobbied hard for an end to the destruction. In 1977 the government called a halt to all logging; the machinery was dismantled and taken out of the forest, the roads gradually grew over and Sinharaja was saved. Much of the rest

of Sri Lanka's rainforest stands on mountain ridges within a 20km radius of the forest.

There are 22 villages around the forest, and locals are permitted to enter the area to tap palms to make jaggery (a hard brown sweet) and treacle, and to collect dead wood and leaves for fuel and construction. Medicinal plants are collected during specific seasons. Rattan collection is of more concern, as the demand for cane is high. Sinharaja attracts illegal gem miners too, whose abandoned open pits pose a danger to humans and animals and cause erosion. There is also some poaching of wild animals.

Information

Tickets (adult/child Rs 575/290, plus compulsory guide Rs 300) are sold at the main Forest Department office at Kudawa; they're also sold as Deodawa, 5km from Deniyaya on the Matara road. The department offers basic dormlike accommodation.

There are several park access points, but the most relevant to travellers are those via Kudawa in the northwest and via Mederapitiya (reached from Deniyaya) in the southeast.

The drier months (August and September, and January to early April) are the best times to visit the reserve. Hinipitigala stands for most of the year under a constant drizzle, if not an outright downpour, as Sinharaja receives between 3500mm and 5000mm of rain annually, with a minimum of 50mm in even the driest months. There's little seasonal variation in the temperature, which averages about 24°C inside the forest, with humidity at about 87%.

Sights & Activities
WILDLIFE

Sinharaja has a wild profusion of flora, which is still being studied. The canopy trees reach heights of up to 45m, with the next layer down topping 30m. Nearly all the subcanopy trees found here are rare or endangered. More than 65% of the 217 types of trees and woody climbers endemic to Sri Lanka's rainforest are found in Sinharaja.

The largest carnivore here is the leopard. Its presence can usually be gauged only by droppings and tracks, as it is seldom seen. Even rarer are rusty spotted cats and fishing cats. Sambar, barking deer and wild boar can be found on the forest floor. Groups of 10 to 14 purple-faced langurs are fairly common. There are three kinds of squirrel: the flame-striped jungle squirrel, the dusky-striped jungle squirrel and the western giant squirrel. Porcupines and pangolins waddle around the forest floor, mostly unseen. Civets and mongooses are nocturnal, though you may glimpse the occasional mongoose darting through the foliage during the day. Six species of bat have been recorded here.

There are 45 species of reptiles here, 21 of them endemic. Venomous snakes include the green pit viper (which inhabits trees), the hump-nosed viper, and the krait, which lives on the forest floor. One of the most frequently found amphibians is the wrinkled frog, whose croaking is often heard at night.

There is a wealth of birdlife: 147 species have been recorded, with 18 of Sri Lanka's 20 endemic species seen here.

Sinharaja has leeches in abundance. It would be most unusual to walk through the forest and not attract one or more of these unpleasant little critters. In colonial times the British, Dutch and Portuguese armies rated leeches as their worst enemy when they tried to conquer the hinterland (which was then much more forested), and one British writer claimed leeches caused more casualties than all the other animals put together. These days you needn't suffer as much because all guides carry antileech preparations that can be applied to the extremities.

DENIYAYA & AROUND

Kotapola, 6km south of Deniyaya, has a superb early-17th-century **rock temple**. It's well worth the climb. The **Kiruwananaganga Falls**, some of the largest in Sri Lanka (60m high and up to 60m wide), are 5km east of Kotapola on the road towards Urubokka. The **Kolawenigama Temple**, 3km from Pallegama (which is 3km from Deniyaya), is of modest proportions but has a unique structure that resembles Kandy's Temple of the Sacred Tooth Relic. It was built by King Buwanekabahu VII in recognition of the protection given to the tooth relic by the villagers. The shrine has Kandyan-style frescoes.

Sleeping & Eating

It's more convenient to visit the reserve from Deniyaya if you don't have your own wheels, although Kudawa has better accommodation options. **Sena Serasinghe** (☎ 071 200727), a

local guide, is a good source of information on tours of Sinharaja and can help arrange local bed-and-breakfast accommodation.

DENIYAYA

Sinharaja Rest (☎ 041-227 3368; fax 227 3368; Temple Rd; s/d Rs 600/900) Staying here saves a lot of hassle as you can arrange a rainforest walk with Palitha Ratnayaka, a certified guide who is very knowledgeable about the forest. The six rooms at his home are fairly basic, but there's good home cooking and loads of information on Sinharaja. A trip to Sinharaja with Palitha costs Rs 600 per person per day, plus the entry fee and a Rs 800 per person 4WD ride up to Mederapitiya. Nonguests can take his tours, too.

Deniyaya Rest House (☎ 041-227 3600; r Rs 850) Like most rest houses in Deniyaya, this place has a plum position to check out the town's great views; in this case, overlooking the town and the countryside. The large, quaint rooms are in fair condition, if a bit dimly lit, and there's a bar and restaurant on the premises. Staff arrange forest tours through Sinharaja Rest.

Sathmala Ella Rest (☎ 041-227 3481; Pallegama; r Rs 1000-1200) This is a handsome middle-class home in a village about 3.5km from Deniyaya. Run by a friendly family, the guesthouse has 10 modern rooms with private bathrooms; hot water adds Rs 200 to the room price. The staff can arrange tours into the forest for Rs 600 per person, plus entry fees and Rs 800 per group for transport. There's a waterfall about 2km away. A three-wheeler from Deniyaya should cost Rs 150.

KUDAWA

Martin Wijesinghe's (Forest View; r Rs 600) Right on the park's boundary near Kudawa, this is a basic but congenial place. It's about 4km from the ticket office. You can contact Martin by leaving a phone message at the Weddagala post office (☎ 045-222 5528). Martin is an expert on Sinharaja, having worked as a ranger here for years, and is a mine of information. You can get a good rice and curry meal here – vegetarian, as there's no fridge – but if you are coming with your own car it would be a courtesy to bring your own food, which the family will cook for you.

Blue Magpie (☎ 045-250 9391; 115 Pirivena Rd; r Rs 600) This relatively new lodge stands close to the park offices where the road ends.

As at Martin Wijesinghe's, rooms are basic but comfortable. Sri Lankan meals here are excellent.

Singraj Rest (☎ 045-225 5201; Koswatta; r Rs 1500) At Koswatta, 3km from Kalawana, this is a country hotel with seven rooms, a restaurant and a bar – the latter is just about the only entertainment in these parts. The rooms are quite decent, though there's cold water only. Staff can arrange taxis to Sinharaja for Rs 1800 per day. A three-wheeler here from Kalawana costs about Rs 200.

Boulder Garden (☎ 045-225 5812; www.bouldergarden.com; Sinharaja Rd, Koswatta; s/d US$213/252; ☒) This brilliantly designed ecoresort offers 10 rustic suites – two of them in actual caves – built among boulders and streams. The staff run bird-watching tours and hiking trips around 10 hectares of rainforest. Meals are available in a beautiful garden restaurant.

The Forest Department at Kudawa has some bungalows with fairly basic accommodation. Contact the **Forest Department HQ** (☎ 011-286 6633; forest@slt.lk; 82 Rajamalwatte Rd, Battaramulla), in Colombo, for information.

It is far simpler and cheaper to stay with one of the guides based at Kudawa. Sunil Handuwila is one guide who offers accommodation; you can stay at his house (one spare room) for Rs 400 per night.

Getting There & Away
BUS
From Ratnapura to Deniyaya (CTB Rs 80) there are buses roughly every hour from 6.45am until the afternoon. There are also several buses to/from Galle (CTB Rs 80), although you can always catch one of the more frequent buses to Akuressa (Rs 21 from Deniyaya) and change there.

There's an intercity express bus to and from Colombo (Rs 200, 5½ hours); if you want a CTB bus you're better off going to Akuressa or Pelmadulla and changing. For Ella and Nuwara Eliya you must catch a bus to Pelmadulla and change there.

To reach Kalawana you can take a bus from Ratnapura (Rs 60 for an express). For Kudawa you can get a bus all the way from Colombo to Weddagala (4km before Kudawa, Rs 190), and then change in Weddagala to a Kudawa-bound bus.

Wherever you start, try to get moving as early as you can because the roads are often damaged by flooding.

CAR & MOTORCYCLE
If you have a car, the road through Hayes Tea Estate, north of Deniyaya en route to Madampe and Balangoda (for Belihul Oya, Haputale or Ratnapura), is very scenic.

SINHARAJA TO RATNAPURA
The A17 goes north from Deniyaya and passes through **Rakwana**. The view from above the town gives a sweeping panorama across the plains of Uda Walawe National Park, with the escarpment of the Peak Wilderness Sanctuary to the north.

The best place to stay is the **Rakwana Rest House** (☎ 045-224 6299; r Rs 1050), a British-era bungalow with four pleasant rooms, a fine veranda, dining and drinks.

From Rakwana the road reaches a southern spur of the Hill (and tea) Country before hitting the important junction town of Pelmadulla, located between Ratnapura and Haputale.

There are around four buses per day between Rakwana and Ratnapura (Rs 27, two hours), and four between Rakwana and Deniyaya (Rs 48, 3½ hours).

RATNAPURA
☎ 045 / pop 48,230
Sitting near the centre of a number of richly watered valleys between Adam's Peak and Sinharaja Forest Reserve, busy Ratnapura ('City of Gems' in Sanskrit) is famous as a trade hub for the area's ancient wealth of gemstones. The region's wet and humid climate encourages the formation of river beds, which are in turn the perfect environment for gemstones to develop.

The rural scenery surrounding the town is often underappreciated – paddy fields cloak the valley floors, while rubber trees and tea bushes grow on the hills. Many villagers keep old Sinhalese traditions, such as leaving candles outside the front door at dusk to prevent evil spirits from entering.

Ratnapura was the traditional start of the toughest pilgrimages up to Adam's Peak. In clear weather it can be the best place for appreciating the full height of the sacred mountain, since the Hatton side – now the preferred starting point – sits at a higher elevation.

The attractive road route from Ratnapura to Haputale skirts the southern edge of the Hill Country before ascending into the hills.

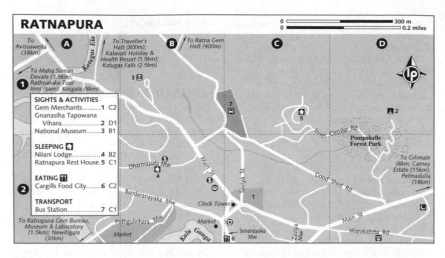

RATNAPURA

SIGHTS & ACTIVITIES
Gem Merchants..........**1** C2
Gnanasiha Tapowana
    Vihara.................**2** D1
National Museum.......**3** B1

SLEEPING 🏠
Nilani Lodge...............**4** B2
Ratnapura Rest House.**5** C1

EATING 🍴
Cargills Food City........**6** C2

TRANSPORT
Bus Station.................**7** C1

Sights

The town's **National Museum** (☎ 222 2451; adult/
child Rs 50/25; 🕑 9am-5pm Sat-Wed) displays the
fossilised remains of various animals (including rhinos and elephants) discovered in
gem pits. There are items of local culture as
well, including gems, fabrics and jewellery.

There are several 'gem museums', which
contain modest displays on gem lore along
with less than modest showrooms where
you're encouraged to purchase 'local' gems
at 'local' prices. One place with relatively
low sales pressure is **Ratnapura Gem Bureau,
Museum & Laboratory** (☎ 222 2469; Pothgulvihara
Mawatha, Getangama; admission free; 🕑 9am-4pm).
There's a good display of local minerals and
gems, as well as information on mining and
polishing. A return three-wheeler trip from
the centre of town should cost about Rs 250
(including waiting time).

The **Maha Saman Devale**, 4km west of the
city, is an architectural treasure well worth
visiting. Perched on a small hill, it boasts a
handsome series of broad courtyards and
multiroofed whitewashed pavilions in the
Kandyan style. Originally built in the 13th
century, the temple was destroyed by the
Portuguese and then rebuilt during Dutch
colonial times. The main sanctuary is dedicated to Saman, while side shrines honour
the Buddha and Pattini. The major festival
is a *perahera* on Esala *poya* (July/August);
it's not as well known as the Kandy Esala
Perahera, with which it coincides. You can
take a three-wheeler from the town centre

for about Rs 80; no need to have the driver
wait as there are usually three-wheelers at
the temple.

The outskirts of town are dotted with
gem mines and, although none cater to tourists per se, your guesthouse should be able
to organise a visit. You can also observe **gem
merchants** selling their wares along Saviya
St northeast of the clock tower. The biggest
local gem market, however, convenes most
mornings (*poya* days being an exception)
in **Newitigala**, a 40-minute drive away (hiring a taxi for half a day should cost around
Rs 1500). Both markets usually run out of
steam by 3pm.

There's a full-sized replica of the **Aukana
Buddha** at the Gnanasiha Tapowana Vihara,
on top of a hill overlooking the town; you
can walk to it through Pompakelle Forest Park. There are some **caves** at Kosgala,
about 8km from town.

You can also use Ratnapura as a base
for a day trip to Sinharaja Forest Reserve.
Expect to pay around Rs 4500 for up to four
people. You'll also be offered day trips to
Uda Walawe National Park but it's really
too long a journey to do in a day.

Activities
GEMOLOGY
Ratna Gem Halt (☎ 222 3745; www.ratnapura-online
.com; 153/5 Outer Circular Rd; courses per day Rs 2000) offers a five-day basic gemology course that
teaches students skills, including how to cut
and polish gemstones.

GEMS

In Ratnapura, gems are still found by ancient methods. Gem miners look for seams of *illama*, a gravel-bearing stratum likely to hold gemstones. It's usually found in the upper reaches of newly buried river beds, as the gems are heavier than gravel so aren't carried to the lower reaches of rivers. On the Colombo–Ratnapura road you'll see countless gem-mining operations in paddy fields beside the road, but there are many more off in the hills and fields around Ratnapura. Different areas have different specialities – villages sometimes have weekly gem markets.

Gem mining is a cooperative effort, requiring men to dig out the *illama*, work the pump and wash the muddy gravel as well as an expert to search through the pebbles. If a stone is found, the profit is divided between all the members of the coop, from the person who supplies the finances to the one up to his neck in mud and water. Children are sometimes sent down the shafts, which can be vertical or horizontal, depending on which way the *illama* runs.

Types of Gems

Every other person you meet in Ratnapura's streets is likely to whisper that they have an unbelievable bargain wrapped up in their pocket. If you're no expert on gemstones the bargain will be on their part, not yours. Synthetic stones are very hard to spot, even for experts.

It's a peculiarity of Sri Lankan gemming that a variety of stones is almost always found in the same pit. A stone's value depends on a number of factors, including rarity, hardness and beauty. Gems are still cut and polished by hand, although modern methods are also coming into use. Some stones are cut and faceted *(en cabochon)*, while others are simply polished. The division between precious and semiprecious stones is purely arbitrary – there is no clear definition of what makes one stone a precious stone and another only semiprecious. Some of the more popular types of stone are listed here.

Corundrums are a group that includes sapphires and rubies, both precious stones and second only to the diamond in hardness. The best and most valuable rubies are red, but these are not found in Sri Lanka in commercial quantities. You will, however, see pink rubies, which are also correctly called pink sapphires. Rubies and sapphires are the same type of stone, with gradations of colour depending on the precise proportions of the chemicals in their make-up. Star rubies and star sapphires are a feature of the Ratnapura gem industry. The stones are comparatively dull, but under light a starburst appears within the gem. Other sapphires can be yellow, orange, white and, most valuably, blue. Sri Lanka has produced three of the world's largest blue sapphires, including the Star of India (displayed at the New York Museum of Natural History). Beware of pink or blue spinels being passed off as sapphires. You can often find corundrums containing 'silk': minute inclusions that give the stone a star effect, particularly with a single light source.

Cat's-eyes and alexandrite are the best-known gems in the **chrysoberyl** group. Cat's-eyes, with their catlike ray known as chatoyancy, vary from green through a honey colour to brown; look for translucence and the clarity and glow of the single ray. Alexandrite is valued for its colour change under natural and artificial light. One rip-off to watch for is tourmalines, which are far less valuable, being sold as cat's-eyes.

The best-known stone in the **beryl** group, the emerald, is not found in Sri Lanka. Aquamarine is found here, and is quite reasonably priced since it is not as hard or lustrous as other stones.

The appearance of a **zircon** can approach that of a diamond, although it is a comparatively soft stone. Zircon comes in a variety of colours, from yellow through orange to brown and green.

Quartz varies from transparent to opaque, and is usually quite well priced. Quartz also varies widely in colour, from purple amethyst to brown smoky quartz, right through to yellow or orange citron.

The moonstone **(feldspar)**, is Sri Lanka's special gem. Usually a smooth, grey colour, it can also be found with a slight shade of blue, although this colouring is rarer.

Among the other precious stones, **spinels** are fairly common but are also quite hard and rather attractive. They come in a variety of colours and can be transparent or opaque. **Garnets** are a sort of poor person's ruby; light-brown garnets are often used in local rings. **Topaz** isn't found in Sri Lanka – if someone offers it to you it'll probably be quartz.

WALKING

One of the oldest routes up Adam's Peak once started at the Maha Saman Devale with the worship of Saman, the patron deity of the trek up the holy mountain. Peak-baggers and pilgrims today pick up the Gilimalai pilgrimage route from the roadhead at Carney Estate, 15km or one hour away from Ratnapura by bus. It takes six to eight hours to reach the top of the peak, and five to seven hours to descend. Leeches are a particular menace on this trail. Before the road was built, the village of **Gilimalai** ('Swallowed Mountain' – there's no view from here) was the first *ambalama* on the journey. The next stop was at **Pallebadole** (elevation 600m), a hill village with a dagoba and pilgrims' lodgings. Further uphill is **Nilihela**, a gorge; pilgrims tell a story of a woman named Nili who tried to save her child from falling over the edge, but fell herself. Pilgrims pause to call out her name, and the eerie echoes send out her answer, ever more faintly. The trail winds up to Diyabetma on the saddle of a ridge, then up the steep final ascent to the footprint on the summit.

Much closer to town there are less arduous walks than to Adam's Peak. Three kilometres north of town are the 6m-high **Katugas Falls**, which are quite pleasant but are crowded on Sundays and public holidays. The lush **Pompakelle Forest Park** lies behind Ratnapura Rest House, and is laced with walking trails through this lush forest.

Sleeping & Eating

Ratnapura Rest House (☎ 222 2299; udarest@stlnet.lk; r incl breakfast Rs 3300) This rest house has the best site in town, right on top of the hill that dominates Ratnapura. The colonial-style rooms are large and bare. Still, the place has heaps of charm with its spacious veranda, bar and grassy garden.

Ratna Gem Halt (☎ 222 3745; www.ratnapura-online.com; 153/5 Outer Circular Rd, r Rs 550-1500) This family-run, seven-room guesthouse north of town wins plaudits for its hospitality, good Sri Lankan food and fine views. The rooms are priced according to which floor they're on – the higher the room the more expensive it is. It's run by a gem dealer, who naturally also has a gem showroom.

Travellers Halt (☎ 222 3092; 30 Outer Circular Rd; r Rs 700-900, with air-con Rs 1200; 🞰) Just over 1km

out of town in the direction of Polhengoda Village, this has nine rooms, two with air-con. The rooms are clean and pleasant and management is keen to arrange tours. A three-wheeler from the bus station should cost Rs 70.

Nilani Lodge (☎ 2222170; hashani@sltnet.lk; 21 Dharmapala Mawatha; s/d Rs 1300/1500, with air-con Rs 1600/1800; 🞰 🖳) This 1970s-era concrete three-storey building has 10 clean, comfy rooms with hot water. The management seems very friendly.

Kalavati Holiday & Health Resort (☎ 222 2465; fax 222 3657; Polhengoda Village; r with/without air-con Rs 2000/1300; 🞰) An Ayurvedic centre 2.5km from the Ratnapura bus station, Kalavati boasts an extensive herb garden and is kitted out with antique furniture. One of the treatments at the Ayurvedic centres is 'gem therapy'. The rooms are basic and could use some treatment themselves, but the gardens help make it a pleasant place to stay. The restaurant has quite an extensive menu, and good food. A three-wheeler from the bus station costs about Rs 100 to 150.

Rathnaloka Tour Inns (☎ 222 2455; ratnaloka@eureka.lk; Kosgala/Kahangama; r standard/deluxe US$32/45; 🞰 🖳) This midrange place 6km from town was built by a gem magnate. Like many of the buildings around town funded by gem wealth, it strives to make a statement, but there's a large garden, an inviting pool, attentive service and a good restaurant. A taxi from Ratnapura should cost Rs 600, a three-wheeler half as much.

There are several eateries around Main St that serve reasonable rice and curry for low prices. There's also a Cargills Food City.

Getting There & Away

Any bus coming from Colombo (CTB/intercity express Rs 46/100, four hours) is likely to be jam-packed. For Hatton or Nuwara Eliya you'll have to catch a bus to Avissawella (Rs 19) and then change there. If you're going to Haputale, Ella and Badulla, you'll probably first have to catch a bus to Balangoda (Rs 28). The CTB bus to Embilipitiya (for Uda Walawe National Park) costs Rs 43. To get to Galle you must change at Matara (Rs 100, 4½ hours). There are also direct buses to and from Kandy (Rs 67, six hours).

The Ancient Cities

North of the Hill Country, in one of the driest parts of the country, lies the original heart of Sri Lankan civilisation. During the golden age of Sinhalese civilisation, it was called Rajarata – the Land of Kings. For 1500 years of dynasties, wars, invasions and religious missions to Asia, increasingly ambitious dams and irrigation systems supported two great cities – Anuradhapura and Polonnaruwa – and many other magnificent examples of the region's Buddhist culture. For almost a thousand years the jungle did its best to reclaim them, but major archaeological excavations over the past century have partially restored their glory. Engineers, too, have patched the irrigation system, marvelling at the skill of the original builders.

A long-running partnership between the Sri Lankan government and Unesco continues to restore the region's ancient sites. The Cultural Triangle project centres on the old capitals of Kandy, Anuradhapura and Polonnaruwa, which are the focus of much local and international tourism.

Kandy is a good starting point for visiting the ancient cities; afterwards you could also continue up the east coast through Ampara, or inland along the fine roads of the Mahaweli irrigation scheme area. You can comfortably explore the area while staying in either Anuradhapura or Polonnaruwa, or you could easily spend a few days in each. Some visitors base themselves Sigiriya or Habarana, which are more or less centrally located for visiting the sites.

HIGHLIGHTS

- Pondering the enigma of **Sigiriya** (p233) while climbing its near-vertical rock face.

- Enjoying the panoramic view of Anuradhapura's great dagoba (stupa) from the top of the sacred hill at **Mihintale** (p255)

- Cycling through the trees and gardens surrounding the 1000-year-old ruins of **Polonnaruwa** (p237) and basking in the serene gaze of the Gal Vihara Buddha

- Admiring the intensely painted murals inside the rock cave temples in **Dambulla** (p231)

- Pausing in the shade of Anuradhapura's **Sri Maha Bodhi** (p250), the sacred bodhi tree and living Buddha relic

Anuradhapura ★ ★Mihintale

Minneriya ★ National Park

Sigiriya ★   ★ Polonnaruwa

Dambulla ★

THE ANCIENT CITIES

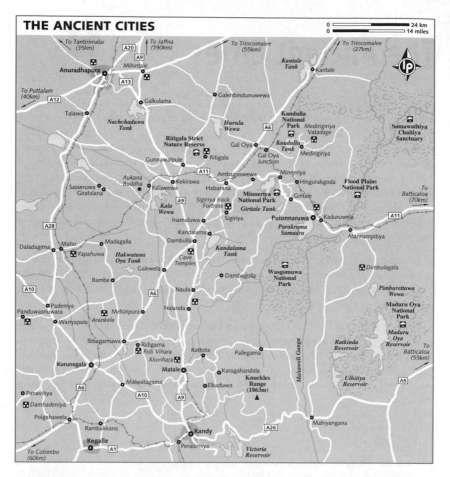

Information

Foreign visitors must purchase tickets to visit the major Cultural Triangle sites as well as a few of the minor ones. You can buy either a 'round ticket' that covers most of the major sites, or individual tickets at the sites themselves. Currently a round ticket costs US$40 (payable either in US dollars or in the rupee equivalent) and covers the following: Anuradhapura, Polonnaruwa, Sigiriya, Ritigala, Medirigiriya and Nalanda, plus a few sites in Kandy (but *not* the Temple of the Sacred Tooth Relic).

The round ticket is valid for 60 days from the date of purchase, and you must finish using your ticket within 14 days of the first time you use it. The ticket entitles you to one day's entry only – if you wish to spend a second day at any site, you pay the full day's fee. If paid for individually, the tickets cost US$20 each for Anuradhapura, Polonnaruwa and Sigiriya; US$10 for Medirigiriya; and US$5 for Ritigala and Nalanda. All foreign nationals and even foreigners with resident visas must pay the full amount. There are no student discounts on the round ticket, though sometimes you can get half-price tickets for individual sites if you sweet-talk the ticket seller. Children under 12 years are charged half price, while those under six get in for free.

Many Buddhist shrines within the Cultural Triangle area, including the Dambulla cave shrines, Sri Maha Bodhi and Mihintale, are run by the Sangha (the community of Buddhist monks) and charge separate entry fees, varying from Rs 100 to 500.

Round tickets can be bought at the Anuradhapura, Polonnaruwa and Nalanda ticket offices. You can also buy them at the **Colombo Cultural Triangle office** (☎ 011-258 7912; 212 Bauddhaloka Mawatha, Col 7) and the Cultural Triangle office in Kandy (p165).

Getting Around

The towns and cities of the Cultural Triangle are well connected by public and private bus, and in some cases by train. Distances are not great and most roads are sealed, so getting around by public transport is relatively comfortable (although buses can be very crowded certain times of day and during holiday periods). Departures between major towns and tourist sites are fairly frequent – you generally won't find yourself waiting hours and hours for a bus or train to depart.

On the other hand, many visitors hire a car and driver to visit the ancient cities. A sedan that can comfortably carry three passengers (four if you don't have much luggage) will cost around Rs 2500 to 2800 per day. For more than four people, a minivan is a better choice; these cost around Rs 3000 to 3500 per day.

MATALE

☎ 066 / pop 37,700

This midsized regional city at the heart of the island lies in a broad, fertile valley at an elevation of 300m. The road to Kandy, 24km south, ascends past paddy fields, areca palm plantations and pepper vines. Other regional specialities include vanilla, rubber, cinchona and cardamom. The area is also famous for *kohila* (a type of watercress) and small, mild chillies. The town's pleasant park includes a monument to the leaders of the 1848 Matale Rebellion – one of the less famous contributions to the Year of Revolutions!

Sights

Not far north of the bus stop for Kandy is an interesting Hindu temple, the **Sri Muthumariamman Thevasthanam** (admission Rs 45). A priest will show you the five enormous, colourful ceremonial chariots pulled along by people during an annual festival.

A drive east through **Knuckles Range**, east of Matale, presents some remarkable mountain views. The B38 heads uphill from the north end of town to a pass near Rattota, while other roads head southwest to the hill villages of Elkaduwa and Karagahandala before winding down to Kandy and the Victoria Reservoir. For more details about Knuckles Range, see p194.

ALUVIHARA

The rock monastery of Aluvihara (also spelt Aluvihare) sits beside the Kandy–Dambulla road, 3km north of Matale. The monastery caves are picturesquely situated among rocks that have fallen from the mountains high above the valley. Legend has it that a giant used three of the rocks as a base for his cooking pot, and the name Aluvihara (Ash Monastery) refers to the ashes from the cooking fire. Ancient drip ledges line the rocks above the frescoed caves, while bats rustle in sheltered corners of the rocks.

The first cave you come to contains a 10m reclining Buddha and impressive lotus-pattern murals on the ceiling. Another is filled with cartoonlike murals of the realms of hell – if you're considering straying from the straight and narrow, you may think twice after seeing the statues of devils meting out an inventive range of punishment to sinners in the afterlife. One scene shows a sexual sinner with his skull cut open and his brains being ladled out by two demons.

Up a flight of rock steps is a cave dedicated to Buddhagosa, the Indian scholar who is supposed to have spent several years here while working on the Tipitaka (Buddhist canon written in Pali, a dialect of Sanskrit). Although histories affirm that Buddhagosa lived in Anuradhapura in the 6th century AD, there's no clear evidence he stayed at Aluvihara. Nonetheless the cave walls are painted with scenes showing Buddhagosa working on *ola* (palm-leaf) manuscripts.

Stairs continue to the summit of the rock bluff, where you'll find a dagoba (stupa) and sweeping views of the surrounding valley.

The Tipitaka was first transcribed from oral and Sinhalese sources into Pali text by a council of monks held at Aluvihara in the 1st century BC. Two thousand years later, in 1848, the monk's library was destroyed by British troops putting down a revolt.

The long process of replacing the *ola* manuscripts still occupies monks, scribes and craftsmen today. You can see their **workshop** (admission Rs 100); the price includes having your name inscribed on a small length of *ola*. See p53 for information about *ola* manuscripts.

A three-wheeler from Matale to Aluvihara will cost about Rs 280 return plus waiting time, and a bus will cost Rs 4.

MATALE HERITAGE CENTRE

About 2km north of Matale, this **heritage centre** (☎ 222 2404; 33 Sir Richard Aluvihara Mawatha) draws on the rich craft traditions of the area, producing quality batik, embroidery, carpentry and brasswork. It occupies a sprawling compound of bungalows, workshops and gardens. The centre's Aluvihare Kitchens does meals for groups of four or more, if you book by phone a day ahead; it costs Rs 550 per person for a banquet with three kinds of rice and up to 25 different curries. A three-wheeler from Matale will cost about Rs 250 return plus waiting time, while a bus will cost Rs 4.

There are many **spice gardens** and several **batik showrooms** along the road between Matale and Aluvihara. The various treats you can expect on a tour of the gardens include milkless cocoa tea sweetened with vanilla and banana, and various creams and potions claimed to make hair shine or cure flatulence. Prices at some spice garden shops are high, so check in a market before you set out so that you can compare prices.

Sleeping & Eating

Rock House Hotel (☎ 222 3239; 17/16A Hulangamuwa Rd; with/without air-con Rs 2000/1200; ✷) Set in a pretty garden, this is a semimodern place just to the south of the Matale Rest House (it is signposted on the main road). There are seven plain rooms sharing a broad balcony, but considering they don't have hot water they're a bit overpriced.

Matale Rest House (☎ 222 2299; thilanka@ids.lk; Park Rd; s/d Rs 1000/1200, r with air-con Rs 1700; ✷) There are 14 clean doubles (with hot water) in this rather institutional building, which lies south of the town centre in the old cantonment (British garrison) area. The resthouse has a broad front lawn and a garden centring on a lovely bodhi tree that predates the hotel. The restaurant's menu includes a lunch buffet if there are enough guests, a mixed grill and a few Chinese dishes; meals cost Rs 300 to 500.

A&C Restaurant (☎ 223 3619; 3/5 Sir Richard Aluvihara Mawatha; meals Rs 250-500; ⏰ lunch) This very special eatery is found on the same turn-off as the Matale Heritage Centre, but you'll need to take a sharp left rather than the road to the centre if you're coming from Matale. With tables on a sheltered veranda, it's an excellent place to stop for lunch if you're travelling by car or van. It's slightly expensive, but the menu is huge and focuses on lots of fresh local produce. Service is excellent.

Getting There & Away

Bus 594 to Matale (private bus/intercity express Rs 33/19) leaves from beside the central clock tower in Kandy. Dambulla or Anuradhapura buses from Kandy or Matale will drop you at Aluvihara or the spice gardens. There are six daily trains on the pretty 28km spur line between Matale and Kandy (Rs 9, 1½ hours).

NALANDA

☎ 066

Nalanda is known for the venerable **Nalanda Gedige** (adult/child US$5/2.50), about 25km north of Matale and 20km before Dambulla. Built in the style of a South Indian Hindu temple, it consists of an entrance hall connected to a taller *shikara* (holy image sanctuary), with a courtyard for circumambulations. There is no sign of Hindu gods, however, and the temple is said to have been used by Buddhists. This is one of the earliest stone buildings constructed in Sri Lanka.

The temple's richly decorated stone-block walls, reassembled from ruins in 1975, are thought to have been fashioned during the 8th to 11th centuries. The plinth bears some of Tantric carvings with sexual poses – the only such sculptures in Sri Lanka – but before you get excited, the carvings are weather beaten and it's difficult to see much. Entry is included in the Cultural Triangle round ticket (see p228).

The site is beside a tank (artificial lake) 1km east of the main road – a sign marks the turn-off near the 49km post. Anuradhapura buses from Kandy or Matale will drop you at the turn-off.

DAMBULLA

☎ 066 / pop 68,200

A service-oriented town at the junction of highways A6 and A9, Dambulla is most well known for the impressive cave temples (officially known as the Royal Rock Temple) atop a massive hill on the edge of town. You can visit it as a day trip on public transport from Kandy, or stop by on your way to or from Sigiriya. If you decide to stay the night, there is decent accommodation for all budgets.

Sights

CAVE TEMPLES

The beautiful **Royal Rock Temple** (adult/child Rs 500/free; ⏰ 7am-7pm) sits 100m to 150m above the road in the southern part of Dambulla. The hike up to the temples begins along a vast, sloping rock face with steps in some places. The ticket office is at the gate near the monstrous Golden Temple, and your receipt is checked at the entrance at the base of the hill; the Cultural Triangle ticket isn't valid here. Photography is allowed inside the caves, but you're not allowed to photograph people. There are superb views over the surrounding countryside from the level of the caves; Sigiriya is clearly visible.

The caves' history as a place of worship is thought to date from around the 1st century BC, when King Valagamba (Vattajamini Ahhaya), driven out of Anuradhapura, took refuge here. When he regained his throne, he had the interior of the caves carved into magnificent rock temples. Further improvements were made by later kings, including King Nissanka Malla, who had the caves' interiors gilded, earning the place the name Ran Giri (Golden Rock).

There are five separate caves containing about 150 Buddha images. Most of the paintings in the temples date from the 19th century.

At the foot of the hill facing the highway stands the modern **Golden Temple**, a very kitschy structure completed in 2000 using Japanese donations. On top of the cube-shaped building sits a 30m-high Buddha image in the *dhammachakka mudra* (dhamma-turning pose). Signs claim it's the largest Buddha in the world, but it's not even the largest in Sri Lanka. A **museum** (adult/child Rs 100/50; ⏰ 7.30am-11.30pm) displays replicas of the cave paintings, imported Buddha images and little else, with only

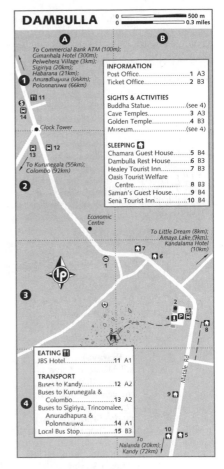

brief labels in Sinhala. Attached is an Internet café and a Buddhist publications bookshop.

Cave I (Devaraja Viharaya)

The first cave, the Temple of the King of the Gods, has a 15m-long reclining Buddha. Ananda, the Buddha's loyal disciple, and other seated Buddhas are depicted nearby. A statue of Vishnu is held in a small shrine within the cave, but it's usually closed.

Cave II (Maharaja Viharaya)

The Temple of the Great King is arguably the most spectacular of the caves. It measures 52m from east to west and 23m from the entrance to the back wall; the highest point

THE ANCIENT CITIES

of the ceiling is 7m. This cave is named after the two statues of kings it contains. There is a painted wooden statue of Valagamba on the left as you enter, and another statue further inside of Nissanka Malla. The cave's main Buddha statue, which appears to have once been covered in gold leaf, is situated under a *makara torana* (archway decorated with dragons), with the right hand raised in *abhaya mudra* (a pose conveying protection). Hindu deities are also represented. The vessel inside the cave collects water that constantly drips from the ceiling of the temple – even during droughts – which is used for sacred rituals. There are brilliantly coloured frescoes of Buddhism's arrival in Sri Lanka, meritorious deeds done by kings and great battles.

Cave III (Maha Alut Viharaya)

This cave, the New Great Temple, was said to have been converted from a storeroom in the 18th century by King Kirti Sri Rajasinghe of Kandy, one of the last of the Kandyan monarchs. This cave, too, is filled with Buddha statues, including a beautiful reclining Buddha, and is separated from Cave II by only a masonry wall.

Cave IV (Pachima Viharaya)

The relatively small Western Cave is not the most westerly cave – that position belongs to Cave V. The central Buddha figure is seated under a *makara torana*, with its hands in *dhyana mudra* (a meditative pose in which the hands are cupped). The small dagoba in the centre was broken into by thieves who believed that it contained jewellery belonging to Queen Somawathie.

Cave V (Devana Alut Viharaya)

This newer cave was once used as a storehouse, but it's now called the Second New Temple. It features a reclining Buddha; Hindu deities including Kataragama (Murugan) and Vishnu are also present.

Sleeping

Because it's an important highway junction as well as a tourist destination, Dambulla boasts a good variety of places to stay.

BUDGET

Healey Tourist Inn (☎ 228 4940; Matale Rd; s/d Rs 400/600) Well located near the post office and within walking distance of the caves and bus station, Healey has good value rooms and friendly management.

Chamara Guest House (☎ 228 4488; Matale Rd; r Rs 900) This is a relaxed place with basic but clean rooms, friendly management and good Sri Lankan food.

Sena Tourist Inn (☎ 228 4421; Matale Rd; s/d Rs 600/800) This inn has six basic rooms in a friendly family house.

Little Dream (☎ 072 618871; s/d Rs 440/660) This is a friendly, laid-back place where you can swim in the nearby Kandalama Tank, bathe in the river or snooze in a hammock. It's about 8km along the road to Amaya Lake (opposite) – a three-wheeler costs Rs 500 from the temple and about Rs 200 from the clock tower, or you can look for the guesthouse's three-wheeler.

Saman's Guest House (☎ 228 4412; Matale Rd; r Rs 700) This little guesthouse has four simple rooms sitting off a central hallway, which is cluttered with antique stuff from the shop at the front.

Oasis Tourist Welfare Centre (☎ 228 4388; r from Rs 400) A cheap place almost directly opposite the entrance to the temple car park, this is dark and rough, but all rooms share a reasonable bathroom. One room with attached bathroom is available.

MIDRANGE

Dambulla Rest House (☎ 222 2299; Matale Rd; d/tr US$25/28, with air-con US$35/38; 🍽) A one-storey affair of semimodern design, this Ceylon Hotels Corporation–operated resthouse offers four large, comfortable rooms, plus a reliable restaurant (meals Rs 500 to 700) and bar. Reader feedback says the food is very good.

Gimanhala Hotel (☎ 228 4864; gimanhala@sltnet.lk; 754 Anuradhapura Rd; r with/without air-con Rs 4300/3400; 🍽 🖳 🌊) About 800m beyond the Colombo junction on the north edge of town, this is a good value midrange hotel. The staff are helpful, the rooms sparkle and there's a swimming pool. The restaurant's daily lunch buffet is popular with tour groups.

Pelwehera Village (☎ 228 4281; r US$20-40; 🍽) Three kilometres north of Dambulla (at Bullagala Junction) and just off the main road, this is a modern place with 10 spotless, bare rooms with hot water. The restaurant serves good food too – it's a nice place to stop for a bite to eat.

TOP END

Amaya Lake (☎ 446 8100; www.amayaresorts.com; villas from US$153; ✷ ✿) Formerly Culture Club, Amaya Lake is a huge, breezy complex comprising 92 stylish villas set in beautiful gardens. Facilities include a pool, tennis and badminton courts, cricket pitch, Ayurvedic spa and bird-watching trails. There are also 11 'ecolodges', which were built with traditional materials and methods, and have solar hot water, adjacent to a traditional village. On the resort premises are two restaurants, one of which serves Ayurvedic cuisine using herbs and vegetables cultivated in the village. The resort can be reached by following the Kandalama road for about 3km from Dambulla and then veering left for another 6km or so.

Kandalama Hotel (☎ 228 4100; www.aitkenspencehotels.com; s/d/tr US$150/175/235; ✷ ✿) If you're interested in modern Sri Lankan architecture, this Geoffrey Bawa–designed place will set your heart racing. It's a huge establishment – 1km from end to end, with 162 rooms and three swimming pools – but the design beautifully complements the landscape. The whole place underwent a major renovation in 2005. The staff offer bird-watching walks and 4WD safaris, and as at Amaya Lake, there's a hotel-supported traditional village, Puranagama.

Eating

JBS Hotel (Anuradhapura Rd; dishes Rs 70-250; ⏱ 24hr) Upstairs in a shop-house next to the Singer store, JBS serves tasty Sri Lankan and Chinese food.

All of the accommodation listed have restaurants. Those with food worth recommending include **Dambulla Rest House** (☎ 222 2299; Matale Rd; meals Rs 500-700), **Chamara Guest House** (☎ 228 4488; Matale Rd), **Pelwehera Village** (☎ 228 4281) and **Gimanhala Hotel** (☎ 228 4864; 754 Anuradhapura Rd).

Getting There & Away

Dambulla is 72km north of Kandy on the road to Anuradhapura. The Colombo to Trincomalee road meets this road 2km north of the cave temple, then splits off from it a couple of kilometres further north, leading to Sigiriya and Polonnaruwa. Because Dambulla is on so many major routes, plenty of buses pass through with varying frequency. However, the nearest

train station is at Habarana, 23km to the north, from where you can catch a Kandy-bound bus to get to Dambulla.

By bus it takes 1½ hours to get to Polonnaruwa (Rs 40, 66km), two hours to Anuradhapura (Rs 40, 68km), and two hours to Kandy (Rs 40). There are buses to Sigiriya (Rs 14, 40 minutes) roughly every 30 minutes. Touts will tell you otherwise to get you into a three-wheeler. The bus takes four hours to get to Colombo (normal/air-con Rs 85/170).

You can flag buses plying this busy route to go between the two parts of Dambulla, or take a three-wheeler for Rs 50.

SIGIRIYA

☎ 066 / pop 1000

Rising 200m straight up over the dusty plains of north central Sri Lanka, the flat-topped rock formation of Sigiriya is not only one of the island's most impressive geological formations but also one of its greatest archaeological legacies. The leafy village that has grown up near its base serves the comings and goings of tourists and pilgrims and is of relatively recent origin.

History

Originally called Sihagiri (Remembrance Rock) and later dubbed Sigiriya (Lion Rock), the rock mass is actually the hardened magma plug of an extinct volcano that long ago eroded away. Pocked with natural cave shelters and rock overhangs – supplemented over the centuries by numerous hand-hewn additions and modifications – the rock may have been inhabited in prehistoric times.

Popular myth says that the formation served royal and military functions during the reign of King Kassapa (AD 477–495), who allegedly built a garden and palace on the summit. According to this theory, King Kassapa sought out an unassailable new residence after overthrowing and murdering his own father, King Dhatusena of Anuradhapura.

A new theory, supported by archaeological, literary, religious and cultural evidence rather than local legend, says that Sigiriya was never a fortress or palace, but rather a long-standing Mahayana and Theravada Buddhist monastery built several centuries before the time of King Kassapa. Monks were using it as a mountain hermitage by the 3rd century BC, and there is abundant evidence to show it had become an important monastery by the 10th century AD. According to *Sigiriya and its Significance: A Mahayana-Theravada Buddhist Monastery,* by Dr Raja De Silva, Sri Lanka's former archaeological commissioner, the ancient site's much treasured frescoes of buxom women were not portraying ladies from Kassapa's court, as was popularly believed. Instead, they were intended to represent Tara Devi, an important Mahayana Buddhist goddess.

After the 14th century, the monastery complex was abandoned. British archaeologist HCP Bell discovered the ruins in 1898, which were further excavated by British explorer John Still in 1907. Whatever exact purposes Sigiriya may have served in the past, the visible ruins today suggest a significant urban site complete with relatively sophisticated architecture, engineering, urban planning, hydraulic technology, gardening and art.

Unesco declared Sigiriya a World Heritage Site in 1982.

Orientation

The village, on the south side of the rock, is just a collection of grocery stores, guesthouses and small restaurants.

Information

The **Centre for Eco-Cultural Studies** (CES; www.ces srilanka.org) and **Sigiriya Ecocultural Tour Guide Association** (Setga; Hotel Rd; ⏰ 8am-6pm) have an information desk with brochures on the region's fauna. These organisations run a range of wildlife and cultural expeditions, including tours of the Sigiriya rock.

Sights

Sigiriya is covered by the Cultural Triangle round ticket (p228); if you don't already have one of these, a single ticket costs US$20 or the rupee equivalent. Both single and round tickets are sold near the site entrance and at Sigiriya Rest House (p236).

Hopeful guides hang around the entrance to the site and will also approach you once you're inside. CES/Setga does a three- to four-hour tour of the royal complex for Rs 350 per person. On a relatively busy day

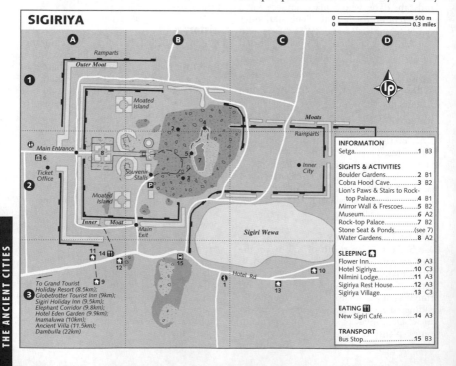

SIGIRIYA

0   500 m
0   0.3 miles

INFORMATION
Setga.....................................**1** B3

SIGHTS & ACTIVITIES
Boulder Gardens..................**2** B1
Cobra Hood Cave.................**3** B2
Lion's Paws & Stairs to Rock-
   top Palace.......................**4** B1
Mirror Wall & Frescoes.......**5** B2
Museum..............................**6** A2
Rock-top Palace..................**7** B2
Stone Seat & Ponds...........(see **7**)
Water Gardens....................**8** A2

SLEEPING 🏠
Flower Inn...........................**9** A3
Hotel Sigiriya......................**10** C3
Nilmini Lodge......................**11** A3
Sigiriya Rest House............**12** A3
Sigiriya Village....................**13** C3

EATING 🍴
New Sigiri Café...................**14** A3

TRANSPORT
Bus Stop..............................**15** B3

you can overhear the commentaries given to tour groups, as long as you can find one in your language.

The site's **archaeological museum** (admission free; 🕑 8am-5pm Wed-Mon), near the entrance, is in poor condition. A small **bookstand** (🕑 8am-4pm) is outside.

An early or late ascent of the rock avoids the main crowds and the fierce heat. Allow at least two hours for the return trip, and more on very busy days. Bring plenty of water and wear a hat, as it's often too windy near the summit to carry an umbrella. The ascent involves a steep climb, so if you're not fit it may be tough. Beware of 'helpers' who latch onto visitors who look as if they may have difficulty. Drinks are available at stalls near the lion's paws for inflated prices.

The verifiable theory that the Sigiriya rock complex was always a Buddhist monastery has not caught on with the locals. Hence the terms traditionally used to describe the various features on the rock city assume it was once a royal palace.

ROYAL GARDENS

The landscaped gardens around Sigiriya consist of water gardens, boulder gardens and terraced gardens.

The usual approach to the rock is through the western (and most elaborate) gate. This takes you through beautiful symmetrical **water gardens**, which extend from the western foot of the rock; bathing pools, little islands with pavilions that were used as dry-season palaces, and trees frame the approach to the rock. The rock rises sheer and mysterious from the jungle. A series of steps leads up through the boulders at its base to the western face, then ascends it steeply.

The **boulder gardens**, closer to the rock, feature rocks that once formed the bases of buildings. The steplike depressions in the sides of boulders were the foundations of brick walls and timber columns. The cistern and audience hall rocks are impressive.

The base of Sigiriya has been landscaped to produce the **terraced gardens**.

COBRA HOOD CAVE

This rocky projection earned its name because the overhang resembles a fully opened cobra's hood. Generally you will pass by this cave after descending the rock on your way to the south gate and the car park. Below the

drip ledge is a 2nd-century-BC inscription that indicates it belonged to Chief Naguli, who would have donated it to a monk. The plastered interior of the cave was once embellished with floral and animal paintings.

FRESCOES

About halfway up the rock there is a modern spiral stairway that leads up from the main route to a long, sheltered gallery in the sheer rock face.

In this niche is a series of paintings of buxom, wasp-waisted women, popularly believed to represent either *apsaras* (celestial nymphs) or King Kassapa's concubines. Modern theory suggests the female forms represent aspects of Tara Devi, the consort of Avalokitesvara – a Bodhisattva (a divine being who chooses to remain on the human plane to help others reach enlightenment) and one of the most important figures in Tantric Buddhism. They are similar in style to the rock paintings at Ajanta in India, but have a specific character in their classical realist style. No one knows the exact dates of the impressive frescoes, though it's unlikely they date as far back as the 5th century (when King Kassapa reigned).

Although there may have been as many as 500 portraits at one time, only 22 remain today – several were badly damaged by a vandal in 1967. Today security is quite tight on the approach to this section of the rock. Protected from the sun in the sheltered gallery, the paintings remain in remarkably good condition, their colours still glowing. They're at their best in the late afternoon light. Flash photography is not allowed.

MIRROR WALL

Beyond the fresco gallery the path clings to the sheer side of the rock and is protected on the outside by a 3m-high wall.

This wall was coated with a smooth glaze upon which visitors of 1000 years ago felt impelled to note their impressions of the women in the gallery above – or so says local legend. The graffiti were inscribed between the 6th and 14th centuries, and 685 of them have been deciphered and published in a two-volume edition, *Sigiri Graffiti,* by Dr S Paranavitana. The graffiti are of great interest to scholars because they show the development of the Sinhala language and script, and because they demonstrate an appreciation of art and beauty. You'll have to look hard beyond the modern mess to see the ancient messages.

One typical graffito reads, 'The ladies who wear golden chains on their breasts beckon me. As I have seen the resplendent ladies, heaven appears to me as not good.' Another, by a female scribbler, reads, 'A deer-eyed young woman of the mountain side arouses anger in my mind. In her hand she had taken a string of pearls and in her looks she has assumed rivalry with us.'

LION'S PAWS
At the northern end of the rock the narrow pathway emerges on to the large platform from which the rock derives its later name – the Lion Rock, Sigiriya. HCP Bell, the British archaeologist responsible for an enormous amount of discovery in Sri Lanka, found the two enormous lion paws when excavating here in 1898. At one time a gigantic brick lion sat at this end of the rock, and the final ascent to the top commenced with a stairway that led between the lion's paws and into its mouth. The lion symbolism serves as a reminder to devotees ascending the rock that Buddha was Sakya-Simha (Lion of the Sakya Clan), and that the truths he spoke of were as powerful as the sound of a lion's roar.

The 5th-century lion has since disappeared, apart from the first steps and the paws. Reaching the top means clambering up across a series of grooves cut into the rock; fortunately there is a handrail.

SUMMIT
The top of the rock covers 1.6 hectares. At one time it was covered with buildings, but only the foundations remain today. The design of this so-called palace, and the magnificent views it commands, suggests that Sigiriya was more a place of residence than a fortress. A 27m-by-21m pond hewn out of the rock looks for all the world like a modern swimming pool, although it may have been used merely for water storage.

De Silva has pointed out that there is no archaeological evidence of a palacelike structure anywhere on the summit. In particular there is a complete absence of stone bases, post holes, visible foundations for cross walls or window sashes, and a lack of lavatory facilities. Instead what you see is an enclosed terrace lying next to the ruins of

a dagoba, suggesting it was a spot reserved for meditation.

A smooth stone slab (the so-called king's throne, possibly another meditation spot) sits 30m away from the ruins of a dagoba. You can sit and gaze across the surrounding jungle as Kassapa – or the Buddhist monks – probably did over 1500 years ago.

Sleeping
BUDGET
Nilmini Lodge (☎ 223 3313; nilmini_lodge@yahoo.com; r with shared/private bathroom Rs 500/800) In the family home here there are six small but comfortable rooms, and a front porch from which you can watch the world go by. The hosts are friendly and the food is good. Guests can use bicycles for free, and the proprietor also offers taxi service in his well-maintained 1957 Morris Minor.

Flower Inn (☎ 078 875 3683; s/d Rs 450/600, r with air-con Rs 1500; ✷) On the same side of the rock as the Sigiriya Rest House and down a path, this six-room lodge is run by a friendly family and has a pretty garden. Living up to its name, the décor is dominated by floral motifs. Good Sri Lankan meals are inexpensive.

Sigiri Holiday Inn (☎ 072 251 5210; sholidayinn@ yahoo.com; Sigiriya Rd; r with/without hot water Rs 1500/ 800) This is a compact and friendly place 500m from the Inamaluwa junction on Sigiriya Rd. With spotless bathrooms and an outdoor restaurant, it's a pleasant spot. Rooms downstairs are smaller and don't have hot water. Keep your windows closed, as monkeys roam the area.

Ancient Villa (☎ 228 5322; ancient@sltnet.lk; r incl breakfast Rs 900-1500) Rustic cabins with antique furniture set the theme here. It's near the 2km post on Sigiriya Rd, about 1.5km from the Inamaluwa junction.

MIDRANGE
Globetrotter Tourist Inn (☎ 078 875 4350; rajaguna8@ sltnet.lk; Sigiriya Rd, Inamaluwa; r with/without air-con Rs 1500/1000; ✷) This relatively new place features friendly father-and-son management and five rooms in separate earthen cottages.

Sigiriya Rest House (☎ 223 1899; ceylonhotels .lk; r with/without air-con US$36/26; ✷) Only about 400m from one side of the rock, this place has a great location. It's one of the Ceylon Hotels Corporation's better-looking resthouses, and the 17 rooms are clean and tastefully decorated in faux colonial.

There's a large, airy restaurant with friendly but slow service. You can buy tickets to the rock here.

Hotel Sigiriya (☎ 228 4811; inquiries@serendible isure.lk; s/d incl breakfast Rs 4600/6300; 🖳) Popular with birders, this 80-room tourist hotel is also a good choice for the splendid views of the rock from the dining room and a large pool (Rs 250 for nonguests), as well as all the usual facilities and comfortable, airy rooms. It's about 1km past the Sigiriya Rest House.

Hotel Eden Garden (☎ /fax 228 4635; eden@digi tech.lk; Sigiriya Rd, Inamaluwa; r Rs 3000, with air-con Rs 3600-4600; 🕃 🖳) Despite the rather ungainly façade, this is a good spot – large, clean rooms, some with balconies, overlook a well-kept garden. There's a pool (Rs 150 for nonguests). Hotel Eden Garden is 100m from the junction, at Inamaluwa.

Grand Tourist Holiday Resort (☎ 567 0136; Sigiriya Rd; r with/without air-con Rs 1500/1000; 🕃) In a peaceful garden setting down a track about 4km from Inamaluwa junction, the resort offers spacious rooms with hot water, and the restaurant, roofed with *cadjan* (coconut-frond matting), serves very good Sri Lankan food.

TOP END

Sigiriya Village (☎ 223 1803; www.sigiriyavillage.lk; r US$152; 🖳) This accommodation has clusters of luxurious rooms in leafy landscaped grounds. The pool (Rs 200 for nonguests) has views of the rock, and an organic garden supplies the hotel's kitchen. It's in the same vicinity as Hotel Sigiriya.

Elephant Corridor (☎ 223 1950; hotel@elephant corridor.com; Kibissa; ste from US$275) It's a cliché to say 'if you have to ask the price, you can't afford it', but truthfully this is one of those occasions. Hidden away on 200 acres of unfenced grasslands wedged between the Kandalama Hills and Pothana Lake, this boutique resort takes its name from the wild elephants that can often be seen wandering through the area. Each of the 21 cavernous, high-ceilinged suites comes equipped with giant-screen TV, a DVD player, binoculars, an artist's easel and pastels, and a private plunge pool. Breakfast/lunch/dinner cost US$8/10/20. Facilities include a spa, a swimming pool, horse riding and a private helipad. The turn-off is 4km from the Inamaluwa junction en route to Sigiriya, down a dirt track and just beyond the Grand Tourist Holiday Resort.

Eating

New Sigiri Café (dishes Rs 125-280) This rustic open-air restaurant caters to tour groups, but the varied menu offering Sri Lankan and Western food is good.

Guesthouses offer meals of home-cooked rice and curry for around Rs 350. **Flower Inn** (☎ 078 875 3683), **Nilmini Lodge** (☎ 223 3313), **Globetrotter Tourist Inn** (☎ 078 875 4350; Sigiriya Rd, Inamaluwa) and **Grand Holiday Tourist Resort** (☎ 56/ 0136; Sigiriya Rd) have especially good food.

Getting There & Away

Sigiriya is about 10km east of the main road between Dambulla and Habarana. The turn-off is at Inamaluwa. In the morning buses run from Dambulla about every 30 minutes from around 7am (Rs 14, 40 minutes), but they are less frequent in the afternoon. The last bus back to Dambulla leaves at around 7pm (but double-check this). A three-wheeler from Dambulla to Sigiriya costs about Rs 400.

POLONNARUWA

☎ 027 / pop 106,000

Once the site of an important royal capital, this town in northeastern central Sri Lanka blossomed into a medium-sized city due to its location along the most important land transport route between Colombo and Batticaloa, and more famously because of its ancient city site, well preserved as a historical park. The fact that it's conveniently close to several national parks also draws a number of visitors.

History

For three centuries Polonnaruwa was a royal capital of both the Chola and Sinhalese kingdoms. Although nearly 1000 years old, it is much younger than Anuradhapura and generally in better repair. The monuments are arranged in a reasonably compact garden setting and their development is easier to follow. All in all, you'll probably find Polonnaruwa the easier of the two ancient capitals to appreciate. It is best to explore by bicycle, which you can rent from several places in town.

The South Indian Chola dynasty made its capital at Polonnaruwa after conquering Anuradhapura in the late 10th century, as Polonnaruwa was a strategically better place to guard against any rebellion from the Ruhunu Sinhalese kingdom in the southeast.

POLONNARUWA

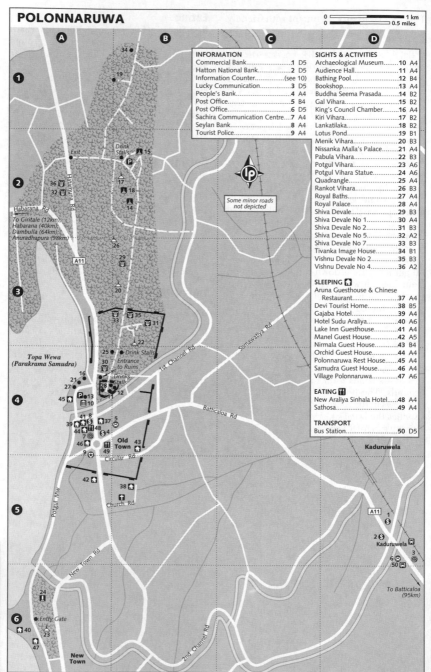

0 — 1 km
0 — 0.5 miles

INFORMATION		
Commercial Bank	1	D5
Hatton National Bank	2	D5
Information Counter	(see 10)	
Lucky Communication	3	D5
People's Bank	4	A4
Post Office	5	B4
Post Office	6	D5
Sachira Communication Centre	7	A4
Seylan Bank	8	A4
Tourist Police	9	A4

SIGHTS & ACTIVITIES		
Archaeological Museum	10	A4
Audience Hall	11	A4
Bathing Pool	12	B4
Bookshop	13	A4
Buddha Seema Prasada	14	B2
Gal Vihara	15	B2
King's Council Chamber	16	A4
Kiri Vihara	17	B2
Lankatilaka	18	B2
Lotus Pond	19	B1
Menik Vihara	20	B3
Nissanka Malla's Palace	21	A4
Pabula Vihara	22	B3
Potgul Vihara	23	A6
Potgul Vihara Statue	24	A6
Quadrangle	25	A4
Rankot Vihara	26	B3
Royal Baths	27	A4
Royal Palace	28	A4
Shiva Devale	29	B3
Shiva Devale No 1	30	A4
Shiva Devale No 2	31	B3
Shiva Devale No 5	32	A2
Shiva Devale No 7	33	B3
Tivanka Image House	34	B1
Vishnu Devale No 2	35	B3
Vishnu Devale No 4	36	A2

SLEEPING		
Aruna Guesthouse & Chinese Restaurant	37	A4
Devi Tourist Home	38	B5
Gajaba Hotel	39	A4
Hotel Sudu Araliya	40	A6
Lake Inn Guesthouse	41	A4
Manel Guest House	42	A5
Nirmala Guest House	43	B4
Orchid Guest House	44	A4
Polonnaruwa Rest House	45	A4
Samudra Guest House	46	A4
Village Polonnaruwa	47	A6

EATING		
New Araliya Sinhala Hotel	48	A4
Sathosa	49	A4

TRANSPORT		
Bus Station	50	D5

Some minor roads
not depicted

It also, apparently, had fewer mosquitoes! When the Sinhalese king Vijayabahu I drove the Cholas off the island in 1070, he kept Polonnaruwa as his capital.

Under King Parakramabahu I (r 1153–86), Polonnaruwa reached its zenith. The king erected huge buildings, planned beautiful parks and, as a crowning achievement, created a 2500-hectare tank, which was so large that it was named the Parakrama Samudra (Sea of Parakrama). The present lake incorporates three older tanks, so it may not be the actual tank he created.

Parakramabahu I was followed by Nissanka Malla (r 1187–96), who virtually bankrupted the kingdom through his attempts to match his predecessors' achievements. By the early 13th century, Polonnaruwa was beginning to prove as susceptible to Indian invasion as Anuradhapura, and eventually it too was abandoned and the centre of Sinhalese power shifted to the western side of the island.

In 1982, Unesco added the ancient city of Polonnaruwa to its World Heritage list.

Orientation

Polonnaruwa has both an old town and, to its south, a sprawling new town. The main areas of ruins start on the northern edge of the old town and spread north. Accommodation is mostly in and around the old town. The main bus and train stations are in Kaduruwela, a few kilometres east of the old town on Batticaloa Rd. However, buses from anywhere except the east go through the old town on their way in, so you can get off there.

The ruins can be conveniently divided into five groups: a small group near the Polonnaruwa Rest House on the banks of the tank; the royal palace group to the east of the Polonnaruwa Rest House; a very compact group a short distance north of the royal palace group, usually known as the quadrangle; a number of structures spread over a wide area further north, known as the northern group; and the small southern group, towards the new town. There are also a few other scattered ruins.

Information

The Cultural Triangle round ticket (p228) is valid for Polonnaruwa. There's an **information counter** (☎ 222 4850; ⏰ 7.30am-6pm) at the museum, near the Polonnaruwa Rest House. You can get maps and brochures and buy tickets to the site; individual entry costs US$20/10 for an adult/child. Near the museum entrance is a well-stocked bookshop. Officially the site closes at 6pm, but in practice you can stay till dark. Tickets are not checked at the Polonnaruwa Rest House group or at the southern group, but the other three groups are within a single big enclosure, which you have to enter from Habarana Rd, just north of the royal palace. Although the ticket technically allows you only one entrance, you can ask a ticket collector to sign and date your ticket so you can enter again. This way you could visit the site in the morning, take a break over midday to avoid the heat, and head back to the site in the late afternoon. Don't believe three-wheeler drivers who say you don't need a ticket if you travel with them.

There's a Seylan Bank near the channel. In Kaduruwela, there are several banks on Batticaloa Rd within 350m of the bus station on the new town side. All banks listed below have ATMs.

Commercial Bank (Batticaloa Rd)
Hatton National Bank (Batticaloa Rd)
Lucky Communication (Kaduruwela) Internet access; opposite the bus station.
People's Bank (Batticaloa Rd)
Post office (Batticaloa Rd) In the centre of the old town.
Sachira Communication Centre (70B Habarana Rd) Internet access.
Seylan Bank (Habarana Rd)

Sights
ARCHAEOLOGICAL MUSEUM

The **Archaeological Museum** (⏰ 9am-6pm), near the Polonnaruwa Rest House, is first class. It's designed so you walk from one end to the other, passing through a series of rooms, each dedicated to a particular theme: the citadel, the outer city, the monastery area and the periphery, and Hindu monuments. The latter room contains a wonderful selection of bronzes. Of particular interest are the scale models of buildings, including the *vatadage* (circular relic house), which show how they might have looked in their heyday – if you follow the theory that they once had wooden roofs. Towards the back of the museum is a small bookshop with a good selection of reading on Sri Lankan archaeology and history, as well as folio-sized books containing temple drawings. To enter, you'll need a current round ticket or a one-day ticket to the site. It's worth visiting before you head out to the site.

ROYAL PALACE GROUP

This group of buildings dates from the reign of Parakramabahu I. Parakramabahu's **Royal Palace** was a magnificent structure measuring 31m by 13m, and is said to have had seven storeys. The 3m-thick walls have holes to receive the floor beams for two higher floors, but if there were another four levels, these must have been made of wood. The roof in this main hall, which had 50 rooms in all, was supported by 30 columns.

Parakramabahu's **Audience Hall** is notable for the frieze of elephants, each of which is in a different position. There are fine lions at the top of the steps.

In the southeast corner of the palace grounds, the **Bathing Pool** (Kumara Pokuna) still has two of its crocodile-mouth spouts remaining.

QUADRANGLE

Only a short stroll north of the royal palace ruins, the area known as the quadrangle is literally that – a compact group of fascinating ruins in a raised-up area bounded by a wall. It's the most concentrated collection of buildings you'll find in the ancient cities. As well as the following ruins, there's a **recumbent image house, chapter house, Bodhisattva shrine** and **bodhi tree shrine**.

In the southeast of the quadrangle, the **vatadage** is typical of its kind. Its outermost terrace is 18m in diameter and the second terrace has four entrances flanked by particularly fine guardstones. The moonstone at the northern entrance is reckoned to be the finest in Polonnaruwa, although not of the same standard as some at Anuradhapura. The four entrances lead to the central dagoba with its four Buddhas. The stone screen is thought to be a later addition, probably by Nissanka Malla.

At the southern end of the quadrangle, the **Thuparama Gedige** is the smallest *gedige* (hollow Buddhist temple with thick walls) in Polonnaruwa, but is also one of the best – and the only one with its roof intact. The building shows a strong Hindu influence and is thought to date from the reign of Parakramabahu I. There are several Buddha images in the inner chamber, but they're barely visible in the late afternoon light.

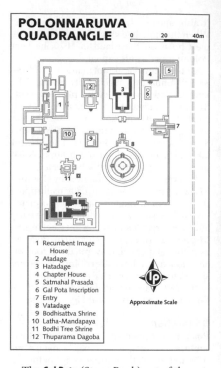

POLONNARUWA QUADRANGLE

0   20   40m

Approximate Scale

1 Recumbent Image House
2 Atadage
3 Hatadage
4 Chapter House
5 Satmahal Prasada
6 Gal Pota Inscription
7 Entry
8 Vatadage
9 Bodhisattva Shrine
10 Latha-Mandapaya
11 Bodhi Tree Shrine
12 Thuparama Dagoba

The **Gal Pota** (Stone Book), ast of the *vatadage*, is a colossal stone representation of an *ola* book. It is nearly 9m long by 1.5m wide, and 40cm to 66cm thick. The inscription on it, the longest such stone inscription in Sri Lanka (and there are many!), indicates that it was a Nissanka Malla publication. Much of it extols his virtues as a king, but it also includes the footnote that the slab, weighing 25 tonnes, was dragged from Mihintale, nearly 100km away!

Also erected by Nissanka Malla, the **Hatadage** is a tooth-relic chamber; it is said to have been built in 60 days.

The busy Nissanka Malla was also responsible for the **Latha-Mandapaya**. This unique structure consists of a latticed stone fence – a curious imitation of a wooden fence with posts and railings – surrounding a very small dagoba. The dagoba is encircled by stone pillars shaped like lotus stalks, topped by unopened buds. It is said that Nissanka Malla sat within this enclosure to listen to chanted Buddhist texts.

Nearly nothing is known about ziggurat-style **Satmahal Prasada**, which may have been influenced by similar Mon-built stupas in Lamphun and Chiang Mai, Thailand. The construction consists of six diminishing storeys (there used to be seven), shaped like a stepped pyramid.

A shrine for the tooth relic, the **Atadage** is the only surviving structure in Polonnaruwa dating from the reign of Vijayabahu I.

CLOSE TO THE QUADRANGLE

Continuing along the road leading north from the quadrangle, a gravel road branches off to the right, just before you reach the city wall. Most of the following structures are on this road, as are many others.

Just south of the quadrangle, the 13th-century Hindu temple **Shiva Devale No 1** displays the Indian influence that returned after Polonnaruwa's Sinhalese florescence. It is notable for the superb quality of its stonework, which fits together with unusual precision. The domed brick roof has collapsed, but when this building was being excavated a number of excellent bronzes, now in the Archaeological Museum (p239), were found.

Similar in style, **Shiva Devale No 2** is the oldest structure in Polonnaruwa and dates from the brief Chola period when the Indian invaders established the city. Unlike so many buildings in the ancient cities, it was built entirely of stone, so the structure today is much as it was when built.

Pabula Vihara, also known as the Parakramabahu Vihara, is a typical dagoba from the period of Parakramabahu I. It is the third-largest dagoba in Polonnaruwa.

NORTHERN GROUP

You will need a bicycle or other transport to comfortably explore these spread-out ruins, all north of the city wall. They include the Gal Vihara, probably the most famous group of Buddha images in Sri Lanka, and the Alahana Pirivena monastic group, which is the subject of a Cultural Triangle restoration project. The Alahana Pirivena group consists of the Rankot Vihara, Lankatilaka, Kiri Vihara, Buddha Seema Prasada and the other structures around them. The name of the group means 'crematory college', since it stood in the royal cremation grounds established by Parakramabahu.

The 54m **Rankot Vihara** dagoba, the largest in Polonnaruwa and the fourth largest on the island, has been ascribed to the reign of King Nissanka Malla. Like the other major dagobas in Anuradhapura and Polonnaruwa, the dome consists of earth fill covered by a brick mantle and plaster. The construction clearly imitates the Anuradhapura style. Surgical instruments found in a nearby ruined 12th-century hospital are said to be similar to those used today.

Buddha Seema Prasada is the highest building in the Alahana Pirivena group, and it was the monastery abbot's convocation hall. This building features a fine *mandapaya* (raised platform with decorative pillars).

Built by Parakramabahu, and later restored by Vijayabahu IV, the huge *gedige* **Lankatilaka** has 17m-high walls, although the roof has collapsed. The cathedral-like aisle leads to a huge standing headless Buddha. The outer walls of the *gedige*, decorated with bas-reliefs, show typical Polonnaruwa structures in their original state.

The building of the dagoba **Kiri Vihara** is credited to Subhadra, King Parakramabahu's queen. Originally known as the Rupavati Chetiya, the present name means 'Milk White' because, when the overgrown jungle was cleared away after 700 years of neglect, the original lime plaster was found to be in perfect condition. It is still the best preserved unrestored dagoba at Polonnaruwa.

Gal Vihara is a group of beautiful Buddha images that probably marks the high point of Sinhalese rock carving. They are part of Parakramabahu's northern monastery. The Gal Vihara consists of four separate images, all cut from one long slab of granite. At one time each was enshrined within a separate enclosure. You can clearly see the sockets cut into the rock behind the standing image, into which wooden beams would have been inserted.

The standing Buddha is 7m tall and is said to be the finest of the series. The unusual position of the arms and sorrowful facial expression led to the theory that it was an image of the Buddha's disciple Ananda, grieving for his master's departure for nirvana, since the reclining image is next to it. The fact that it had its own separate enclosure, and the discovery of other images with the same arm position, has discredited this theory and it is now accepted that all the images are of the Buddha.

The reclining image of the Buddha entering nirvana is 14m long, and the beautiful grain of the stone of the image's face is the most impressive aspect of the Gal Vihara group for many people. Notice the subtle depression in the pillow under the head and the sun-wheel symbol on the pillow end. The other two images are both of the seated Buddha. The one in the small rock cavity is smaller and of inferior quality.

Unfortunately authorities have constructed a very unsightly metal roof structure over the Buddhas at Gal Vihara. This means that some portion of the each statue is always in shade and it's impossible to take a well-exposed photograph.

A track to the left from the northern stretch of road leads to unusual **Lotus Pond**, nearly 8m in diameter, which has five concentric, descending rings of eight petals each. The pool was probably used by monks.

The northern road ends at **Tivanka Image House**. This spectacular image house is, like the Lotus Pond, one of the few surviving structures of the Jetavanarama monastery. Its name means 'thrice bent', and refers to the fact that the Buddha image within is in a three-curve position normally reserved for female statues. The building is notable for the carvings of energetic dwarfs cavorting around the outside, and for the fine frescoes within – the only Polonnaruwa murals to have survived. Some of these date from a later attempt by Parakramabahu III to restore Polonnaruwa, but others are much older.

SOUTHERN GROUP

The small southern group is close to the compound of top-end hotels. By bicycle it's a pleasant ride along the bund of the Topa Wewa (Topa Tank).

Also known as the library dagoba, the **Potgul Vihara** is an unusual structure. A thick-walled, hollow, dagoba-like building, it is thought to have been used to store sacred books. It's effectively a circular *gedige*, and four smaller solid dagobas arranged around this central dome form the popular Sinhalese quincunx arrangement of five objects in the shape of a rectangle – one at each corner and one in the middle.

Another interesting structure in the southern group is the **statue** at the northern end. Standing nearly 4m high, it's an unusually lifelike human representation, in contrast to the normally idealised or stylised Buddha figures. Exactly whom it represents is a subject of some controversy. Some say that the object he is holding is a book and thus the statue is of Agastaya, the Indian religious teacher. The more popular theory is that it is a yoke representing the 'yoke of kingship' and that the bearded, stately figure is Parakramabahu I. The irreverent joke is that the king is really holding a piece of papaya.

REST HOUSE GROUP

A delightful place for a postsightseeing drink is the Polonnaruwa Rest House, situated on a small promontory jutting out into the Topa Wewa. Concentrated a few steps to the north of the Polonnaruwa Rest House are the ruins of the **Nissanka Malla's palace**, which aren't in anywhere near the same state of preservation as the royal palace group.

The **Royal Baths** are the ruins nearest to Polonnaruwa Rest House. Farthest north is the **King's Council Chamber**, where the king's throne, in the shape of a stone lion, once stood. It is now in the Colombo's National Museum (p90). Inscribed into each column in the chamber is the name of the minister whose seat was once beside it. The mound nearby becomes an island when the waters of the tank are high; on it are the ruins of a small summer house used by the king.

Sleeping

BUDGET

Devi Tourist Home (☎ 222 3181; fax 222 3947; Lake View Watte; s/d/tr Rs 550/650/800, r with hot water Rs 1800, with air-con Rs 1900; 🕸) Featuring five spotless rooms around a shady garden, this guesthouse is about 1km south of the old town centre and down Church Rd (there's a sign on the main road). The friendly owner is one of Sri Lanka's small Malay population. Bicycles are available for Rs 175 per day.

Lake Inn Guesthouse (☎ 222 3220; 1 1st Channel Rd; r with/without air-con r Rs 900/1200; 🕸) Just off the main road in the Old Town and next to Seylan Bank, Lake Inn has four dim but passable rooms. Rice and curry meals here cost just Rs 250. The friendly owners hire bicycles for Rs 150 per day.

Samudra Guest House (☎ 222 2817; Habarana Rd; r Rs 500-800) In the old town, this has a range of rooms, including a garden room and cabana at the bottom of the garden. The hosts can organise trips to Minneriya National Park (p245) and Kaudulla National Park (p245). Bicycles can be hired for Rs 150.

Orchid Guest House (☎ 222 5253; 70 Habarana Rd; s/d/f Rs 400/600/750) Near the Samudra, this is not the cleanest option in town, but it's one of the cheapest.

Nirmala Guest House (☎ 222 5163; 65 Circular Rd; s Rs 620, d with/without air-con Rs 1020/740; ✵) This place has clean rooms in both the modern family home and separate buildings.

Aruna Guesthouse & Chinese Restaurant (☎ 222 4661; Habarana Rd; r Rs 600-900) This place has box-like rooms along a long corridor behind a Chinese restaurant. The food is not bad.

Manel Guest House (☎ 222 2481, 077 743 5358; New Town Rd; r Rs 700-900) In a quiet spot just outside the old-town wall, friendly Manel's spacious rooms differ in price according to the bathroom standards. Very good meals are served under the veranda.

MIDRANGE & TOP END

Gajaba Hotel (☎ 222 2394; Kuruppu Gardens, Lake Rd; s/d Rs 875/1250, d/tr with air-con Rs 1500/1875; ✵) In the old town beside the tank, this is a friendly and popular hotel. It has a lovely leafy garden and 23 rooms, of which five come with air-con and two with hot water. Good Sri Lankan food is available. You can hire bicycles for Rs 200 per day.

Polonnaruwa Rest House (☎ 222 2299; http://ceylonhotels.lk; Potgul Mawatha; s/d US$53/58, with view US$71/76, f US$100) On a promontory by the tank and just a short distance from the heart of the ancient city, this resthouse has superb views over the water from the veranda and some of the rooms. There's a fine terrace overlooking the lake where you can sip or sup. The rooms, all with hot water and some with a bathtub, are large and well kept. You may even be able to book the 'Queen's Room', where Queen Elizabeth II kipped in 1954. It has a bar and a restaurant with tasty food and prompt service; breakfast/lunch/dinner costs US$5/7/9.

Village Polonnaruwa (☎ 222 2405; fax 222 5100; Potgul Mawatha; s/d/tr US$95/102/126; ✵ ⛱) On the lakeside just over 2km south of the old town, upmarket Village Polonnaruwa consists of 57 rooms, some of them around a pleasant central courtyard and others in large brick bungalows. Nonguests may use the pool if they purchase a drink or a meal. Also on the premises are a tennis court and a spa.

Hotel Sudu Araliya (☎ 222 4849; www.lanka.net/suduaraliya/; Potgul Mawatha; s/d US$48/60; ✵ ⛭ ⛱) Set by the tank amid lovely landscaped gardens,

this hotel looks good at first pass, but the rooms aren't very well maintained considering the price. It offers an Ayurvedic treatment centre, an overpriced restaurant, bicycle hire and boat trips on the tank.

Eating

New Araliya Sinhala Hotel (Habarana Rd; dishes Rs 50-150) This popular local eatery serves Sri Lankan meals for breakfast, lunch and dinner, including rice and curry, and *kotthu rotti* (doughy pancake chopped and fried with meat and vegetables).

Sathosa (☾ 24hr) This supermarket is opposite the People's Bank.

Guesthouses and hotels are safe bets for good eating in Polonnaruwa, a town not exactly renowned for cuisine. Among the better hotel and guesthouse dining rooms are **Devi Tourist Home** (☎ 222 3181; Lake View Watte), **Gajaba Hotel** (☎ 222 2394; Kuruppu Gardens, Lake Rd), **Polonnaruwa Rest House** (☎ 222 2299; Potgul Mawatha), **Manel Guest House** ((☎ 222 2481, 077 743 5358; New Town Rd) and **Lake Inn Guest House** (☎ 222 3220; 1 1st Channel Rd).

Getting There & Away

BUS

Polonnaruwa's main bus station is actually in Kaduruwela, a few kilometres east of the old town on Batticaloa Rd. Buses to and from the west pass through the old-town centre, but if you're leaving Polonnaruwa and want to make sure of a seat, it's best to start off at Kaduruwela.

Central Transport Board (CTB) buses run regularly to Kandy (Rs 78). Air-con intercity buses to Kandy (Rs 150, four hours) run until 4pm via Dambulla and Habarana. If you want to get to Dambulla, catch this bus.

CTB buses for Anuradhapura (Rs 60, three hours) leave regularly from 5.15am to 4.15pm; there are no air-con buses. Alternatively, you can go to Habarana and pick up another bus there, but a lot of people do this and seats are rare.

There are regular CTB buses to Colombo (Rs 170, six hours) until 7.15pm. The intercity air-con buses (Rs 230) leave every 30 minutes during the day.

TRAIN

Polonnaruwa is on the Colombo–Batticaloa railway line, and is about 30km southeast of Gal Oya, where the line splits from the

Colombo–Trincomalee line. The train station is at Kaduruwela, near the bus station, and in fact the sign over the station entrance reads Kaduruwela Railway Station.

Trains to Colombo (six to seven hours) depart at 8.13am, 8.40pm and 11.27pm. Tickets cost Rs 335 in a 2nd-class sleeper (seat only Rs 285), Rs 560 (seat only Rs 490) in 1st class. For Trincomalee there is a direct train at 3.15pm or you can catch the 8.13am Colombo train and change at Gal Oya for a 12.30pm Trinco-bound train.

Getting Around
There are frequent buses (Rs 8) between the Old Town and Kaduruwela, where the bus and train stations are located. A three-wheeler costs Rs 100.

Bicycles are the ideal transport for getting around Polonnaruwa's monuments, which are surrounded by shady woodland. Bicycles with gears can be hired for about Rs 200 a day from a couple of places in the town's main street. Some guesthouses also hire bicycles (usually gearless) from Rs 150 a day.

For around Rs 500, a car and driver or three-wheeler can be hired for about three hours, which is long enough to have a quick look around the ruins.

AROUND POLONNARUWA
Dimbulagala
Set off the Polonnaruwa–Batticaloa road, about 8km south of Mannampitiya, a rock called **Dimbulagala** or Gunners Quoin stands 545m above the surrounding scrub. There are hundreds of caves cut out of the rock in a Buddhist hermitage that has been occupied almost continuously since the 3rd century BC. The temple at the base of the rock is the first of 15 cave temples that adventurous visitors can explore on their way to the dagoba at the top of the rock.

Giritale
☎ 027 / pop 14,300
Twelve kilometres northwest of Polonnaruwa on the Habarana road, Giritale is a sleepy village alongside the 7th-century Giritale Tank. It's a good base for visiting Polonnaruwa and Minneriya National Park, especially if you have your own transport

A simple place near the tank, **Woodside Tour Inn** (☎ 224 6307; Polonnaruwa Rd; s/d Rs 600/800) has a pretty garden setting and a big mango tree.

The 10 older rooms are bare but fine, and the five new rooms upstairs have balconies from which you can almost smell the mangoes.

Set around a big veranda and a grassed area, **Hotel Hemalee** (☎ 224 6257; Polonnaruwa Rd; s/d Rs 1500/1850; ✷) has 15 rooms, three of which come with air-con. Discounts are available for stays of more than two nights. The restaurant is a bit pricey (rice and curry costs Rs 400) for a hotel in this range.

Giritale Hotel (☎ 224 6311; s/d/tr US$60/71/80, all incl breakfast; ✷) has plain but good value rooms and eight luxury rooms. The restaurant has great views of the Giritale Tank, even if the food is rather mediocre.

The modern **Royal Lotus** (☎ 224 6316; www .lanka.net/jinasena/hotels/royallotus; s/d US$45/52, top fl US$62/69, ste US$67/74; ✷ ⚏) sits high on a hillside, and every room has views of Giritale Tank below. Rooms are large and comfortable, and the public areas are breezy and open, as befits the warm, dry climate.

Several steps up from The Royal Lotus in the posh stake, **Deer Park** (☎ 224 6272; deer park@angsana.com; cottages US$146-228, ste US$702, all incl breakfast; ✷ ⚏) has 77 well-furnished cottages in single units, duplexes and four-unit blocks. All have lovely garden sitting areas, while the most expensive have views of Giritale Tank. The grounds are beautifully maintained. Also on the premises are two restaurants (Sri Lankan and international), a fitness centre, a squash court, a new spa with Ayurvedic, Thai and Balinese treatments, and the Mahout Adventure Club (an ecotourism agency). The resort offers a number of innovative excursions, from a 'champagne and sky' picnic (US$50) to elephant-viewing safaris (US$45) in nearby Minneriya National Park (opposite).

Mandalagiri Vihara
Near Medirigiriya, about 30km north of Polonnaruwa, is the Mandalagiri Vihara, a *vatadage* virtually identical to the one at Polonnaruwa. Whereas the Polonnaruwa *vatadage* is crowded among many other structures, the Mandalagiri Vihara stands alone atop a low hill. Some find it a disappointment, but the site's isolation means that it doesn't attract as many visitors as Polonnaruwa.

An earlier structure may have been built here around the 2nd century, but the one that stands today was constructed in the 7th century by Aggabodhi IV. A granite flight of steps leads up to the *vatadage*, which has concentric circles of 16, 20 and 32 pillars around the dagoba. Four large Buddhas face the four cardinal directions. This *vatadage* is noted for its fine stone screens. There was once a hospital next to the *vatadage* – look for the bath shaped like a coffin.

The site is included in the Cultural Triangle round ticket (p228), or individual tickets cost US$8/4 for an adult/child; it's rare, however, that anyone materialises to check your ticket. Tickets are not sold at the site, so buy one from the museum (p239) in Polonnaruwa before you come.

Mandalagiri Vihara is best visited as a day trip. There are no places to stay or eat, nor are there any worth mentioning in nearby Medirigiriya.

Without your own transport, getting to Medirigiriya is time consuming. It's located about 24km northeast of Minneriya village, which is on the Polonnaruwa–Habarana road. To reach Medirigiriya by bus from Polonnaruwa, Habarana or Dambulla involves at least one change at Giritale, Minneriya or Hingurakgoda, from where you can catch a bus or maybe a three-wheeler. The *vatadage* is 3km from the Medirigiriya bus stop.

NATIONAL PARKS

The national parks situated around Polonnaruwa and Habarana offer excellent access to elephants and other animals without the crowds of Yala National Park. To visit either Minneriya or Kaudulla, you must be accompanied by a licensed guide and you must enter and leave by vehicle. Both parks are well served by tours. Prices range from US$25 to US$35 per person including entry fees and snacks for a four-hour trip from Habarana; more expensive trips usually feature better food and drink or nicer vehicles. From Polonnaruwa, Sigiriya and Giritale, you'll pay about Rs 2000 to Rs 3000 for the 4WD, excluding entry fees. The cost of getting to either park is about the same. However, Habarana is closer to Kaudulla and Polonnaruwa is closer to Minneriya; the less time you spend travelling the longer you have in your chosen park.

Minneriya National Park

Dominated by the ancient Minneriya Tank, this **national park** (adult/child US$12/6, plus service charge US$6, plus per vehicle charge Rs 150) has plenty of scrub and light forest in its 8890 hectares to provide shelter for its toque macaques, sambar deer, leopards and elephants – to name a few. The dry season, from June to September, is the best time to visit. By then, water in the tank has dried up, exposing grasses and shoots to grazing animals; elephants, which number up to 150, come to feed and bathe; and flocks of birds, such as little cormorants and painted storks, fish in the shallow waters.

The park entrance is along the Habarana–Polonnaruwa road. A new visitor centre near the entrance sells tickets and offers a variety of exhibits about the park's natural history.

Kaudulla National Park

This **park** (adult/child US$6/3, plus service charge US$6, plus vehicle charge Rs 150) was opened in 2002 around the ancient Kaudulla Tank. It established a 6656-hectare elephant corridor between Somawathiya Chaitiya National Park and Minneriya National Park. Just 6km off the Habarana–Trincomalee road at Gal Oya junction, it is already a popular safari tour from Polonnaruwa and Habarana because of the good chance of getting up close and personal with elephants. In October there are up to 250 elephants in the park, including herds of juvenile males. There are also leopards, fishing cats, sambar deer, endangered rusty spotted cats and sloth bears.

The best time to visit is from August to December. A catamaran is available for boat rides on the tank.

HABARANA
☎ 066

The highlights of this small village are a small tank and its central location between all the main sites. It is also a good base for visits to the Minneriya and Kaudulla National Parks, and has a midrange to top-end group of hotels principally aimed at package tourists. Habarana has the nearest train station to Dambulla and Sigiriya.

Elephant rides around the tank can be arranged for a pricey US$20 to US$30 per person per hour. If you're spending the night here, the only free entertainment is to wander along the tank bund spotting birds.

One of the more reliable outfitters for an organised national park trip (which is the only way you can visit the park) is **Piya Special Green Track Elephant & Jeep Safari** (☎ 086-227 0225; Dambulla Rd).

Sleeping & Eating

Habarana Inn (☎ 227 0010; Dambulla Rd; d/f Rs 1200/2000) This basic place is the town's cheapest place to sleep. The seven rooms are fine but nothing special. It's just past the Lodge, on the Dambulla road. The restaurant serves Sri Lankan (rice and curry Rs 395), Western and Chinese dishes.

Habarana Rest House (☎ 227 0003; ceylonhotels.lk; r with/without air-con US$35/25; 🍴) This one-storey resthouse, set in a pleasant garden, has four rooms fronted by a long shaded veranda. It's right on the crossroads where the buses congregate. Meals are available (curry and rice Rs 450).

Both of Habarana's neighbouring top-end resort hotels are part of the Keells group and offer similar services and facilities – pools, bird-watching walks, 4WD and elephant safaris, Ayurvedic treatments and views to the tank.

Village (☎ 227 0046; village@keells.com; s/d from US$63/75; 🍴 🐘) This nice place offers spacious terraced rooms with verandas. The restaurant looks over the swimming pool, and there are also badminton and tennis. The lakefront setting makes for easy bird-watching before breakfast.

Lodge (☎ 227 0011; lodge@keells.com; s/d/tr US$76/88/133; 🍴) The 150 spacious rooms come in vaguely Portuguese colonial-style duplexes stacked side by side or in two levels, and set in 11 hectares of lush landscaping. A nature trail leads to a treehouse platform for viewing birds and monkeys.

Getting There & Away

Buses leave from the crossroads outside the Habarana Rest House. A direct inter-city bus from Colombo costs RS 88. From Habarana there are very frequent departures in all directions; for example, you can pick up the air-con Trinco–Colombo bus, or buses travelling between Anuradhapura and Ampara, Batticaloa and Colombo, or Kandy (via Dambulla) and Trincomalee, but you're not guaranteed a seat. If you are embarking on a long-haul trip, it's best to start as early as possible.

The train station is 1km out of town on the Trincomalee road. There are trains leaving for Polonnaruwa (3rd/2nd class Rs 14/35) and Batticaloa (3rd/2nd class Rs 18/65) at 11.34am, and for Colombo at 12.33am (3rd/2nd class Rs 64/150).

RITIGALA

Deep inside the Ritigala Strict Nature Reserve, off the Anuradhapura–Habarana road, are the partially restored ruins of an extensive monastic and cave complex. The ruins lie on a hill, which at 766m isn't exactly high, but is nevertheless a striking feature in the flat, dry landscape surrounding it. The 24-hectare site is isolated and almost deserted. The site is included in the Cultural Triangle round ticket (p228), or individual tickets cost US$8/4 for an adult/child.

The true meaning of the name Ritigala remains unclear – *gala* means rock in Sinhala, but *riti* may come from the Pali *arittha*, meaning 'safety'. Thus Ritigala was probably a place of refuge, including for kings as long ago as the 4th century BC.

Ritigala also has a place in mythology. It's claimed to be the spot from where Hanuman (the monkey king) leapt to India to tell Rama that he had discovered where Sita was being held by the king of Lanka. Mythology also offers an explanation for the abundance of healing herbs and plants found in Ritigala. It's said that Hanuman, on his way back to Lanka with healing Himalayan herbs for Rama's wounded brother, dropped some over Ritigala.

Monks found Ritigala's caves ideal for a ascetic existence, and more than 70 such caves have been discovered. Royals proved generous patrons, especially King Sena I, who in the 9th century made an endowment of a monastery to the *pamsukulika* (rag robes) monks.

Ritigala was abandoned following the Chola invasions in the 10th and 11th centuries, after which it lay deserted and largely forgotten until it was rediscovered by British surveyors in the 19th century. It was explored and mapped by HCP Bell in 1893.

Sights

Ritigala has none of the usual icons: no bodhi tree, no relic house and no Buddha images. The only embellishments are on the urinals at the forest monastery – it's been conjectured that by urinating on the fine stone carving the monks were demonstrating their contempt for worldly things.

Near the Archaeology Department bungalow are the remains of a *banda pokuna* (tank), which apparently fills with water during the rainy season. From here it's a scramble along a forest path via a donations hall to a **ruined palace** and the **monastery hospital**, where you can still see the grinding stones and huge stone baths. A flagstone path leads upwards; a short detour takes you to what is often described as a stone fort – or, more accurately, a lookout.

The next group of ruins of note are the double-platform structures so characteristic of forest monasteries. Here you can see the **urinal stones**, although they almost certainly weren't always in this exact spot. The two raised stone platforms are supported by stone retaining walls. The platform oriented to the east is rectangular, while the western one is smaller and square; unlike its counterpart, it may have had a roof of some sort. Scholars think they were used for meditation, teaching and ceremony. Someone from the Archaeology Department bungalow will accompany you (and will expect a tip, say Rs 300) but may be reluctant to take you beyond this point – although the ruins extend right up to the top – because of wild animals and dense vegetation.

You'll need at least 1½ hours to see the site properly. Staff at the Archaeology Department bungalow sell tickets to the site and staff check all tickets, although there's no-one present after about 4pm.

Getting There & Away

Ritigala is 14km northwest of Habarana and 42km southeast of Anuradhapura. If you're coming from Habarana, the turn-off is near the 14km post. It's a further 9km to get to the Archaeology Department bungalow (which is 2km past the turn-off at the Wildlife Department bungalow). You need your own transport to get here and the road may be impassable in the wet season (October to January). As this is a very isolated area, you are advised to go in a group.

AUKANA

According to legend, the magnificent 12m-high standing **Aukana Buddha** (admission Rs 250) was sculpted during the reign of Dhatusena in the 5th century, though some sources date it to the 12th or 13th century. Kala Wewa, one of the many gigantic tanks he constructed, is only a couple of kilometres from the statue, and the road to Aukana from the Kekirawa runs along the tank bund for several kilometres. Aukana means

'sun-eating', and dawn, when the first rays light up the huge statue's finely carved features, is the best time to see it.

Note that although the statue is still narrowly joined at the back to the rock face it is cut from, the lotus plinth on which it stands is a separate piece. The Buddha's pose, *ashiva mudra*, signifies blessings, while the burst of fire above his head represents the power of total enlightenment. There's a local story that the statue was so finely carved that a drop of water from its nose would fall (without any breeze) directly between Buddha's feet.

The Aukana Buddha is well known and often visited despite its isolation. Fewer people travel on to another image, also 12m high, although incomplete and of inferior craftwork, at **Sasseruwa**, the site of an ancient cave monastery in the jungle. A legend relates that the two Buddhas were carved at the same time in a competition between master and student. The master's more detailed Aukana Buddha was finished first and the Sasseruwa image was abandoned by the conceding student. Buddha's gesture here is *abhaya mudra*, conveying protection. This statue, sometimes called the Resvehera Buddha, stands in a rectangular hollow in the rock. Sasseruwa is 11km west of Aukana, reached by a rough road.

It's easy to catch a bus from Dambulla or Anuradhapura to Kekirawa, and another from there to Aukana. There are five or six buses a day between Kekirawa and Aukana. Aukana is on the railway line from Colombo to Trincomalee and Polonnaruwa, and the station is just a short walk from the statue. Four trains a day (2nd and 3rd class only) stop here. A van from Kekirawa will set you back about Rs 1500 for a Kekirawa–Aukana–Kalawewa (or back to Kekirawa) circuit; a three-wheeler costs about Rs 700. From Habarana, a van to Aukana will cost about Rs 2000 return.

ANURADHAPURA

☎ 025 / pop 56,600

For over 1000 years, Sinhalese kings – and occasional South Indian interlopers – ruled from the palaces of Anuradhapura. It was the most extensive and important of the Sri Lankan royal capitals, but its size and the length of its history, and the length of time since its downfall make it more difficult to comprehend than younger, shorter-lived

Polonnaruwa. Current-day Anuradhapura is a rather pleasant, planned city. Mature trees shade the main guesthouse areas, and the main street is orderly compared to the ugly concrete agglomerations seen in so many other regional centres.

The modern town was developed in the 20th century. In recent years a seamier side of the sacred city has emerged; the large army population (the town was a staging post for the northern battlefields) has brought an influx of prostitutes. The town has a huge number of guesthouses, many of which cater to the rent-by-the-hour market. The ones listed in this book (hopefully) don't attract that sort of business. The town was also a centre for war profiteering: political and business alliances conspired to loot the nearby forests of valuable timber. Some of the timber came from areas controlled by the Liberation Tigers of Tamil Eelam (LTTE) – evidently the Tigers were happy to cooperate in return for a cut.

History

Anuradhapura first became a capital in 380 BC under Pandukabhaya, but it was under Devanampiya Tissa (r 247–207 BC), during whose reign Buddhism reached Sri Lanka, that it first rose to great importance. Soon Anuradhapura became a great and glittering city, only to fall before a South Indian invasion – a fate that was to befall it repeatedly for more than 1000 years. But before long the Sinhalese hero Dutugemunu led an army from a refuge in the far south to recapture Anuradhapura. The 'Dutu' part of his name, incidentally, means 'undutiful', because his father, fearing for his son's safety, forbade him to attempt to recapture Anuradhapura. Dutugemunu disobeyed him, and later sent his father a woman's ornament to indicate what he thought of his courage.

Dutugemunu (r 161–137 BC) set in motion a vast building program that included some of the most impressive monuments in Anuradhapura today. Other important kings who followed him included Valagamba, who lost his throne in another Indian invasion but later regained it, and Mahasena (r AD 276–303), the last 'great' king of Anuradhapura, who was the builder of the colossal Jetavanarama Dagoba. He also held the record for tank construction, building 16 of them in all, plus a major

canal. Anuradhapura was to survive for another 500 years before finally being replaced by Polonnaruwa, but it was harassed by invasions from South India again and again – invasions made easier by the cleared lands and great roads that were a product of Anuradhapura's importance.

Orientation

The ancient city lies to the northwest of the modern town of Anuradhapura. The main road from Kandy, Dambulla and Polonnaruwa enters the town on the northeastern side then travels south to the centre, which is a spread-out affair with two bus stations – the old bus station (intercity express buses leave from near this station) and the new bus station 2km further south. Buses heading for the new bus station usually call at the old one on the way through, and will also let you off anywhere else along their route.

There are also two train stations. If you're just arriving by train, the northern station is the one most convenient for places to stay and the ruins.

The ancient city is rather spread out. There is one important starting point for exploring it, and that is the Sri Maha Bodhi (the sacred bodhi tree) and the cluster of buildings around it. Because of roadblocks around Sri Maha Bodhi, a bicycle is the best way to explore Anuradhapura. However, you can't take a bicycle everywhere; near the bodhi tree shrine you will have to park your bike and walk. There are plenty of cold drink stalls scattered around the site, as well as plenty of people willing to act as a guide. Most guesthouses in town rent bicycles for around Rs 200 per day.

Remember to remove your shoes and hat before approaching a dagoba or the sacred bodhi tree.

Information

A US$20 entry ticket (or a round ticket for the Cultural Triangle – see p228) is required by foreigners visiting the northern areas of the ancient city. Both types of ticket can be bought at two places: the **ticket office** (☾ 7am-7.30pm) near the Archaeological Museum (p253) on the west side of the city, and a **booth** (Trincomalee Rd; ☾ 7am-7.30pm) near Sri Maha Bodhi. Unfortunately your ticket, whether single or round, is valid for one day's visit only. This is a real shame considering the

ANURADHAPURA

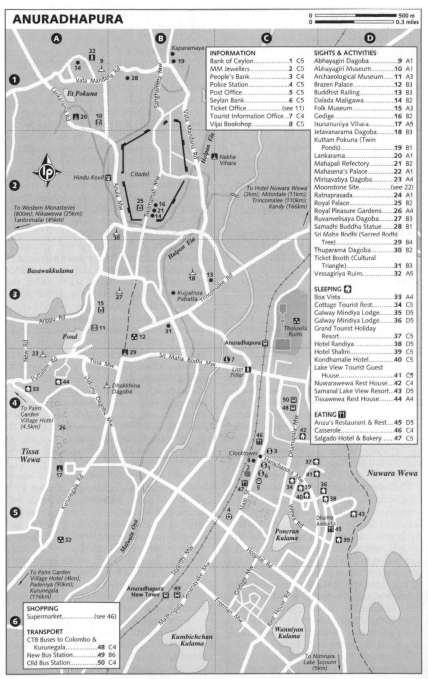

INFORMATION
Bank of Ceylon....................1 C5
MM Jewellers.....................2 C5
People's Bank.....................3 C4
Police Station.....................4 C5
Post Office...........................5 C5
Seylan Bank.......................6 C5
Ticket Office................(see 11)
Tourist Information Office...7 C4
Vijai Bookshop....................0 C5

SIGHTS & ACTIVITIES
Abhayagiri Dagoba..............9 A1
Abhayagiri Museum...........10 A1
Archaeological Museum......11 A3
Brazen Palace.....................12 B3
Buddhist Railing.................13 B3
Dalada Maligawa..............14 B2
Folk Museum......................15 A3
Gedige.................................16 B2
Isurumuniya Vihara...........17 A5
Jetavanarama Dagoba........18 B3
Kuttam Pokuna (Twin
  Ponds).............................19 B1
Lankarama..........................20 A1
Mahapali Refectory............21 B2
Mahasena's Palace.............22 A1
Mirisavatiya Dagoba..........23 A4
Moonstone Site.........(see 22)
Ratnaprasada.....................24 A1
Royal Palace.......................25 B2
Royal Pleasure Gardens......26 A4
Ruvanvelisaya Dagoba.......27 B3
Samadhi Buddha Statue......28 B1
Sri Maha Bodhi (Sacred Bodhi
  Tree)................................29 B4
Thuparama Dagoba............30 B2
Ticket Booth (Cultural
  Triangle).........................31 B3
Vessagiriya Ruins...............32 A5

SLEEPING
Boa Vista............................33 A4
Cottage Tourist Rest...........34 C5
Galway Mindiya Lodge.......35 D5
Galway Miridiya Lodge.......36 D5
Grand Tourist Holiday
  Resort..............................37 C5
Hotel Randiya.....................38 D5
Hotel Shalini.......................39 C5
Kondhamalie Hotel.............40 C5
Lake View Tourist Guest
  House...............................41 C5
Nuwarawewa Rest House....42 C4
Samanal Lake View Resort...43 D5
Tissawewa Rest House........44 A4

EATING
Anzu's Restaurant & Rest....45 D5
Casserole............................46 C4
Salgado Hotel & Bakery......47 C5

SHOPPING
Supermarket.................(see 46)

TRANSPORT
CTB Buses to Colombo &
  Kurunegala.....................48 C4
New Bus Station.................49 B6
Old Bus Station..................50 C4

THE ANCIENT CITIES

ancient city remains are easily worth two or more days of exploration.

You must pay an extra Rs 30 to visit the nearby Folk Museum (p253), and Rs 50 for the Isurumuniya Vihara (p252). Entry to the Sri Maha Bodhi compound area costs Rs 100, but if things aren't busy you may not be approached for the money.

Hotel Shalini (☎ 222 2425; 41/388 Harischandra Mawatha) Has Internet facilities, as do a few other hotels and guesthouses.

People's Bank Changes travellers cheques.

Post Office (Main St)

Seylan Bank (Main St) ATM.

Tourist Information Office (☎ 222 4546; Sri Maha Bodhi Mawatha; ☒ 9am-4.45pm Mon-Fri, 9am-1pm Sat) Offers a rather ordinary map and a couple of brochures, but little else.

Vijai Bookshop (Main St) Has a small but interesting selection of English-language titles in a back room.

Sights

SRI MAHA BODHI

The Sri Maha Bodhi, the sacred bodhi tree, is central to Anuradhapura in both a spiritual and physical sense. The huge tree has grown from a cutting brought from Bodhgaya in India by the Princess Sangamitta, sister of Mahinda (who introduced the Buddha's teachings to Sri Lanka), so it has a connection to the very basis of the Sinhalese religion. This sacred tree serves as a reminder of the force that inspired the creation of all the great buildings at Anuradhapura, and is within walking distance of many of the most interesting monuments. The whole area around the Sri Maha Bodhi, the Brazen Palace and Ruvanvelisaya Dagoba was once probably part of the Maha Vihara (Great Temple).

The sacred bodhi tree is the oldest historically authenticated tree in the world, for it has been tended by an uninterrupted succession of guardians for over 2000 years, even during the periods of Indian occupation. There are not one but many bodhi trees here; the oldest and holiest stands on the top platform. The steps leading up to the tree's platform are very old, but the golden railing around it is quite modern. The railing and other structures around the trees are festooned with prayer flags. Thousands of devotees come to make offerings at weekends and particularly on *poya* (full-moon) days. April is a particularly busy month as pilgrims converge on the site for *snana puja* (offerings or prayers). You

must remove your shoes and your hat before entering this site.

BRAZEN PALACE

So called because it once had a bronze roof, the ruins of the Brazen Palace stand close to the bodhi tree. The remains of 1600 columns are all that is left of this huge palace, said to have had nine storeys and accommodation for 1000 monks and attendants.

It was originally built by Dutugemunu more than 2000 years ago, but through the ages was rebuilt many times, each time a little less grandiosely. The current stand of pillars (now fenced off) is all that remains from the last rebuild – that of Parakramabahu around the 12th century.

RUVANVELISAYA DAGOBA

Behind the Folk Museum, this fine white dagoba is guarded by a wall with a frieze of hundreds of elephants standing shoulder to shoulder. Apart from a few beside the western entrance, most are modern replacements for the originals from 140 BC.

This dagoba is said to be King Dutugemunu's finest construction, but he didn't live to see its completion. However, as he lay on his deathbed, a false bamboo-and-cloth finish to the dagoba was organised by his brother, so that Dutugemunu's final sight could be of his 'completed' masterpiece. Today, after incurring much damage from invading Indian forces, it rises 55m, considerably less than its original height; nor is its form the same as the earlier 'bubble' shape. A limestone statue south of the great dagoba is popularly thought to be of Dutugemunu.

The land around the dagoba is rather like a pleasant green park, dotted with patches of ruins, the remains of ponds and pools, and collections of columns and pillars, all picturesquely leaning in different directions. Slightly southeast of the dagoba, you can see one of Anuradhapura's many monks' refectories. Keeping such a number of monks fed and happy was a full-time job for the lay followers.

THUPARAMA DAGOBA

In a beautiful woodland setting north of the Ruvanvelisaya Dagoba, the Thuparama Dagoba is the oldest dagoba in Sri Lanka – indeed, probably the oldest visible stupa in the world. It was constructed by Devanampiya Tissa in the 3rd century BC and is said to contain the right collarbone of the Buddha. Its 'heap-of-paddy-rice' shape was restored in 1862 in a more conventional bell shape and to a height of 19m.

The surrounding *vatadage*'s slender, capital-topped pillars, perhaps the dagoba's most unique feature, enclose the structure in four concentric circles. Impressions on the dagoba pediments indicate the pillars originally numbered 176, of which 41 still stand. Although some Sri Lankan scholars believe these once supported a conical wooden roof, there is no archaeological evidence for this theory, nor does it follow any known antecedent in south India, whose dagobas were the prototypes for virtually all Sinhalese dagobas.

NORTHERN RUINS

There is quite a long stretch of road, which starts as Anula Mawatha, running north from the Thuparama Dagoba to the next clump of ruins. Coming back you can take an alternative route through the Royal Palace site and then visit the Jetavanarama Dagoba.

Abhayagiri Dagoba

This huge dagoba (confused by some books and maps with the Jetavanarama), created in the 1st or 2nd century BC, was the centrepiece of a monastery of 5000 monks. The name means 'Hill of Protection' or 'Fearless Hill' (though some local guides mistakenly claim 'Giri' was the name of a local Jain monk). The monastery was part of the 'School of the Secret Forest', a heretical sect that studied both Mahayana and Theravada Buddhism. Chinese traveller Faxian (also spelt Fa Hsien) visited in AD 412.

The dagoba was probably rebuilt several times to reach its peak 75m height. It has some interesting bas-reliefs, including one near the western stairway of an elephant pulling up a tree. A large slab with a Buddha footprint can be seen on the northern side of the dagoba, and the eastern and western steps have unusual moonstones made from concentric stone slabs.

Mahasena's Palace

This ruined palace northwest of the Abhayagiri is notable for having the finest carved moonstone in Sri Lanka. Photographers will be disappointed that the railing around it makes it almost impossible to achieve an unshadowed picture. This is a peaceful wooded area full of butterflies, and makes a good place to stop and cool off during a tour of the ruins.

Ratnaprasada

Follow the loop road a little further and you will find the finest guardstones in Anuradhapura. Dating from the 8th century, they depict a cobra king, and demonstrate the final refinement of guardstone design. You can see examples of much earlier guardstone design at the Mirisavatiya Dagoba (p252).

In the 8th century a new order of *tapovana* (ascetic) monks settled in the fringes of the city, among the lowest castes, the rubbish dumps and the burial places. These monasteries were simple but grand structures; ornamentation was saved for toilets, now displayed at the Archaeology Museum (p253). The monks of Ratnaprasada (Gem Palace) monastery gave sanctuary to people in trouble with the authorities, and this led to a major conflict with the king. When court officials at odds with the king took sanctuary in the Ratnaprasada, the king sent his supporters to capture and execute them. The monks, disgusted at this invasion of a sacred place, departed en masse. The general populace, equally disgusted, besieged the Ratnaprasada, captured and executed the king's supporters and forced the king to apologise to the departed monks in order to bring the monks back to the city and restore peace.

To the south of the Ratnaprasada is the Lankarama, a 1st-century-BC *vatadage*.

Samadhi Buddha

After your investigations of guardstones and moonstones, you can continue east from the Abhayagiri to this 4th-century statue, seated in the meditation pose and regarded as one of the finest Buddha statues in Sri Lanka. Pandit Nehru, a prominent leader in India's independence movement, is said to have maintained his composure while imprisoned by the British by regular contemplation of a photo of this statue.

Local authorities recently erected a modern metal roof over the statue, somewhat spoiling the artistic integrity of this masterpiece.

Kuttam Pokuna (Twin Ponds)

The swimming-pool-like Twin Ponds, the finest bathing tanks in Anuradhapura, are east of Sanghamitta Mawatha. They were likely used by monks from the monastery attached to Abhayagiri Dagoba. Although they are referred to as twins, the southern pond, 28m in length, is smaller than the 40m-long northern pond. Water entered the larger pond through the mouth of a *makara* (mythical multispecies beast) and then flowed to the smaller pond through an underground pipe. Note the five-headed cobra figure close to the *makara* and the water-filter system at the northwestern end of the ponds.

Royal Palace

If you return south along Sanghamitta Mawatha, after about 1.5km you'll pass through the Royal Palace site. Built by Vijayabahu I in the 12th century, after Anuradhapura's fall as the Sinhalese capital, the palace is indicative of the attempts made to retain at least a foothold in the old capital.

Close to it are a deep and ancient well and the Mahapali refectory, notable for its immense trough (nearly 3m long and 2m wide) that the lay followers filled with rice for the monks. In the Royal Palace area you can also find the Dalada Maligawa, a tooth-relic temple that may have been the first Temple of the Tooth. The sacred Buddha's tooth originally came to Sri Lanka in AD 313.

JETAVANARAMA DAGOBA

The Jetavanarama Dagoba's massive dome rises from a clearing back towards the Sri Maha Bodhi. Built in the 3rd century by Mahasena, it may have originally stood over 100m high, but today is about 70m, a similar height to the Abhayagiri, with which it is sometimes confused. At the time it was built it was the third-tallest monument in the world, the first two being Egyptian pyramids. An early British guidebook calculated that there were enough bricks in the dagoba's brick core to make a 3m-high wall stretching from London to Edinburgh.

Behind it stand the ruins of a monastery, which housed 3000 monks. One building has door jambs over 8m high still standing, with another 3m underground. At one time, massive doors opened to reveal a large Buddha image.

BUDDHIST RAILING

A little south of the Jetavanarama Dagoba, and on the other side of the road, there is a stone railing built in imitation of a log wall. It encloses a site 42m by 34m, but the building within has long disappeared.

MIRISAVATIYA DAGOBA

Mirisavatiya Dagoba is one of three very interesting sites that can be visited in a stroll or ride along the banks of the Tissa Wewa. This huge dagoba, the first built by Dutugemunu after he captured the city, is across the road from the Tissawewa Rest House. The story goes that Dutugemunu went to bathe in the tank, leaving his ornate sceptre implanted in the bank. When he emerged he found his sceptre, which contained a relic of the Buddha, impossible to pull out. Taking this as an auspicious sign he had the dagoba built. To its northeast was yet another monks' refectory, complete with the usual huge stone troughs into which the faithful poured boiled rice.

ROYAL PLEASURE GARDENS

If you start down the Tissa Wewa bund from the Mirisavatiya, you soon come to the extensive royal pleasure gardens. Known as the Park of the Goldfish, the gardens cover 14 hectares and contain two ponds skilfully designed to fit around the huge boulders in the park. The ponds have fine reliefs of elephants on their sides. It was here that Prince Saliya, the son of Dutugemunu, was said to have met a commoner, Asokamala, whom he married, thereby forsaking his right to the throne.

ISURUMUNIYA VIHARA

This rock temple, dating from the reign of Devanampiya Tissa (r 247–207 BC), has some very fine carvings. One or two of these (including one of elephants playfully splashing water) remain in their original place on the rock face beside a square pool fed from the Tissa Wewa, but most of them have been moved into a small museum within the temple. Best known of the sculptures is the 'lovers', which dates from around the 5th century AD and is built in the artistic style of the Indian Gupta dynasty of the 4th and 5th centuries. It was probably brought here from elsewhere, since it was carved into a separate slab. Popular legend holds that it shows Prince Saliya and Asokamala.

One bas-relief shows a palace scene said to be of Dutugemunu, with Saliya and

Asokamala flanking him, and a third figure, possibly a servant, behind them. There is also a fine sculpture showing a man and the head of a horse. The image house south of the pond has a reclining Buddha cut from the rock. The view over the tank from the top of the temple is superb at sunset. You can't miss the resident colony of bats. You'll be asked for a 'donation' of Rs 50.

South of the Isurumuniya Vihara are extensive remains of the Vessagiriya cave monastery complex, which dates from much the same time.

MUSEUMS
Anuradhapura's **Archaeological Museum** (admission with Cultural Triangle or Anuradhapura ticket free; ⏰ 8am-5pm Wed-Mon, closed public holidays) also houses a ticket office for the ancient city. It's worth visiting for the museum's gorgeous old building, let alone the exhibits inside. It has a restored relic chamber, as found during the excavation of the Kantaka Chetiya Dagoba at nearby Mihintale, and a large-scale model of Thuparama Dagoba's *vataduge* as it might have been if a wooden roof (for which there is no physical or epigraphic evidence) had existed.

In the museum's grounds are the carved squatting plates from Anuradhapura's western monasteries, whose monks had forsaken the luxurious monasteries of their more worldly brothers. To show their contempt for the effete, luxury-loving monks, the monks of the western monasteries carved beautiful stone squat-style toilets, with their brother monks' monasteries represented on the bottom! Their urinals illustrated the god of wealth showering handfuls of coins down the hole.

A short distance north of the Archaeological Museum there's a **Folk Museum** (admission Rs 50; ⏰ 8.30am-5pm Sat-Wed, closed public holidays) with dusty exhibits of country life in Sri Lanka's North Central Province.

The Chinese-funded **Abhayagiri Museum** (admission free; ⏰ 10am-5pm), just to the south of the Abhayagiri Dagoba, commemorates the 5th-century visit of Chinese Buddhist monk Faxian to Anuradhapura. Faxian spent some time living at the Abhayagiri monastery, translating Buddhist texts, which he later brought back to China. The museum, arguably the most interesting in Anuradhapura, contains a collection of squatting plates,

jewellery, pottery and religious sculpture from the site. There is a bookshop selling Cultural Triangle publications.

TANKS
Anuradhapura has three great tanks. **Nuwara Wewa**, on the east side of the city, is the largest, covering about 1200 hectares. It was built around 20 BC and is well away from most of the old city. The 160-hectare **Tissa Wewa** is the southern tank in the old city. The oldest tank, probably dating from around the 4th century BC, is the 120-hectare **Basawakkulama** (the Tamil word for tank is *kulam*) to the north. Off to the northwest of the Basawakkulama are the ruins of the **western monasteries**, where the monks dressed in scraps of clothing taken from corpses and, it's claimed, lived only on rice.

Sleeping
Anuradhapura has a good choice of accommodation, with the greatest concentration of places to stay found off Harischandra Mawatha near the Nuwara Wewa. If you're taking the train to Anuradhapura, be aware that touts begin boarding a few stations before arrival, and will try very hard to steer you away from places not paying them a commission.

BUDGET
Lake View Tourist Guest House (☎ 222 1593; 4C/4 Lake Rd; s/d Rs 700/900, with air-con Rs 1250/1400; 🕮) On a lane off Harischandra Mawatha, almost opposite the Cottage Tourist Rest, this is a friendly place with 10 rooms, some with hot water; the ones in the front of the building looking out towards Mihintale are best. The owners are cheerful, and the Sri Lankan food is good. Bicycle hire is Rs 150 to 200.

Grand Tourist Holiday Resort (☎ 223 5173; granddami@yahoo.com; 4B/2 Lake Rd; r with/without air-con Rs 1500/700; 🕮) Though grandly titled, this is really a large house converted to a tourist bungalow with nine rooms. There's an unobstructed view of Nuwara Wewa from an attractive veranda. Meals are available, and it's a quiet spot.

Samanal Lake View Resort (☎ 222 5092; 388/5 Lake Rd; s/d Rs 900/1100, with air-con Rs 1200/1500; 🕮) Nearby the Grand Tourist Holiday Resort, this friendly three-storey guesthouse offers clean rooms with balconies that have views of the lake, city and temples. It hires out bicycles and offers home-cooked meals as well.

Hotel Shalini (☎ 222 2425; www.hotelshalini.com; 41/388 Harischandra Mawatha; s Rs 559-1305, d Rs 808-1553, r with air-con Rs 1926; ☒ ▣) This place has a cute gingerbread-house-like annexe with a pleasant open-air restaurant, rooftop garden and Internet café. Rooms with hot water are available. You can rent bicycles for Rs 150 a day, or take a tour of Anuradhapura's ancient city for Rs 750 (Rs 1500 for Mihintale and Anuradhapura combined). The friendly owners will pick you up (or drop you off) for free at the bus or train station if you make arrangements in advance.

Milano Tourist Rest (☎ 222 2364; www.milanot rest.com; 596/40 JR Jaya Mawatha; s/d Rs 650/750, r with air-con Rs 1600; ☒) Milano features 12 clean, modern and relatively spacious rooms along with a restaurant serving Sri Lankan, Western and Chinese food. You can hire bicycles for Rs 200 per day.

Cottage Tourist Rest (☎ 223 5363; 38/538 Harischandra Mawatha; s/d/tr Rs 500/750/950) Just past the roundabout, this is a cheap family-run guesthouse with spartan rooms – it might get some street noise.

Kondhamalie Hotel (☎ 222 2029; 42/388 Harischandra Mawatha; r Rs 1250) This hotel has 32 assorted rooms – the rooms in the newer wing are better value than the faded rooms in the older house. Bicycles can be hired, and inexpensive food is available.

Boa Vista (☎ 223 5052; 142 Old Puttalam Rd; s/d/tr Rs 1000/1500/2000, r with air-con Rs 3500; ☒) A sparsely furnished but exceptionally clean hotel run by a Canadian–Sri Lankan couple, who sometimes put people up in their modern flat if there are only a few guests. The location close to the Tissa Wewa and the royal pleasure gardens is a bonus, and the owners offer Sri Lankan and Western meals. Boa Vista doesn't pay touts commissions, so many three-wheeler drivers will tell you the guesthouse is full or closed.

Nimnara Lake Sojourn (☎ /fax 074 580256; www .hotelnimnara.com; 21/146 Wijaya Mawatha, Attikulama; r from Rs 600, with air-con Rs 1500; ☒) On the banks of the Nuwara Wewa 6km south of town, it offers 11 rooms in a new building. The grounds of the guesthouse are rich in birdlife, and there are views across to Mihintale. The owners are helpful and experienced, and the food is noteworthy. There are bicycles for hire. A three-wheeler from town should cost Rs 140, or you can call and the owners will pick you up.

Hotel Nuwara Wewa (☎ 223 5339; s/d Rs 750/1300) With a charming rural location 3km from Anuradhapura (signposted on the left as you head for Mihintale), this three-storey building has nine clean rooms, plus verandas with chairs on each floor overlooking the fields and trees. It is run by an affable family, but not much English is spoken. A three-wheeler from town will cost Rs 100.

MIDRANGE & TOP END

Hotel Randiya (☎ 222 2868; www.hotelrandiya.com; 394/19A Muditha Mawatha; s/d/tr US$17/20/24) A pleasant new addition to the city's lodging choices, the 14-room Hotel Randiya imitates *walawwa* (minor palace) bungalow-style architecture.

Galway Miridiya Lodge (☎ 222 2519; miridiya@slt net.lk; Wasaladantha Mawatha; s/d US$43/46; ☒ ☒) This is a modest two-storey, 39-room modern hotel with a pretty garden running down to the tank. Nonguests may use the pool for Rs 150. This place is popular with groups.

Tissawewa Rest House (☎ 222 2299; hotels@quick shaws.com; d/tr US$35/40, all incl breakfast; ☒) A Raj-era relic with a style all its own, the century-old Tissawewa is authentic right down to the shower railings and claw-foot baths. Besides high-ceilinged lounge areas and verandas, it has 4.4 hectares of gardens with mahogany and teak trees. It also has the advantage of being right in there with the ruins. Since the resthouse stands inside the 'sacred area' alcohol can't be sold, although you can bring your own with you. A big veranda looks out on gardens with lots of monkeys, which have no qualms about stealing your afternoon tea. The 25 quaint rooms are enormous, but try to avoid the annexe, where the shabby rooms are not good value. You can hire bicycles here. As with all resthouses, the set menu is relatively pricey, but the à la carte menu is reasonably priced. Guests can use the swimming pool at the Nuwarawewa Rest House. The hotel is popular with groups, so it would be wise to book ahead.

Nuwarawewa Rest House (☎ 222 3265; hotels@ quickshaws.com; r US$40; ☒ ☒) This place, Anuradhapura's other resthouse, backs on to the Nuwara Wewa. It's pleasant, even though it resembles a 1960s hospital. The 60 rooms cost the same whether or not they face the tank. It has a good, clean pool in the garden – nonguests can swim for Rs 250.

Palm Garden Village Hotel (☎ 222 3961; www.palm gardenvillage.com; Puttalam Rd, Pandulagama; r US$90, villas US$118; ⊠ ⊠) Accommodation at Anuradhapura's top hotel, 6km west of town, is in very spacious rooms in well-designed duplex units or separate villas set in 38 hectares of gardens complete with tennis courts, an Ayurvedic centre, a fitness centre and a Catholic chapel – not to mention resident deer, peacocks and the occasional elephant. The centrepiece is a stunning swimming pool – nonguests who can use it for Rs 250 per day. The suites are almost the same as the standard rooms, except for a bathtub, a TV with local channels and a four-poster bed. A three-wheeler from town costs Rs 350.

Eating
There's little in the way of eating places apart from the guesthouses and hotels.

Anzu's Restaurant (☎ 222 5678; 394/25A Harischandra Mawatha; dishes Rs 175-350) A relaxed house restaurant that's actually down a side street called Dharma Asoka Lane, this place is run by chefs from northern China, which gives it an authenticity that sets it apart from nearly all of the Chinese restaurants out in the provinces.

Salgado Hotel & Bakery (Main St; dishes Rs 35-75) This is an old-fashioned place serving Sri Lankan breakfasts, short eats and biscuits.

Casserole (279 Main St, dishes Rs 70-250; ⊠) A busy, very clean air-con spot serving Sri Lankan, Chinese and Western meals. There's a supermarket downstairs.

Getting There & Away
BUS
Anuradhapura has 'old' and 'new' bus stations – the old bus station is further north, closer to the train station. Private express buses leave from near the old bus station. Buses heading south start at the old bus station and call by the new bus station, while buses heading north to Vavuniya and east to Trincomalee start from the new bus station. It is easier to get a good seat from the starting point. There are departures to Trinco (Rs 47, 3½ hours) from early morning; to Kandy (CTB/intercity bus Rs 75/150, three hours), via Kekirawa and Dambulla, every hour or so until about 5pm; and to Polonnaruwa (Rs 46, three hours) every hour from around 5.30am to 6pm. Buses to Kurunegala (CTB/intercity bus Rs 45/100, two hours) leave every 30

minutes from about 6am; those to Colombo (CTB/intercity bus Rs 107/210, five hours) leave every 30 minutes between 4.30am and 7pm. For Puttalam you may have to catch a bus to Kala Oya (private bus Rs 20), and then another bus on to Puttalam (Rs 27). Buses to Kala Oya go past the road to Wilpattu National Park (get off at Maragahawewa and change for Hunuwilagama).

TRAIN
Anuradhapura has two train stations; the main Anuradhapura station and the smaller Anuradhapura New Town further to the south. Trains to Colombo depart at 7am, 8.40am, 2.30pm and 11.40pm. First-class seats are available on the 7am intercity express and the 2.30pm and 11.40pm trains. It takes four to five hours to reach Colombo, all being well. Prices are Rs 102 for a seat in 3rd class, Rs 191/309 in 2nd class for a seat/ sleeper and Rs 420/520 in 1st class for a seat/ sleeper. For Matara (9½ hours) and Galle (3rd/2nd class Rs 154/291, 8½ hours) catch the *Rajarata Rajini* at 5am. You can also travel between Anuradhapura and Kandy by any train, changing at Polgahawela.

Getting Around
The city is too spread out to investigate on foot. A three-hour taxi trip costs about Rs 900 and a three-wheeler about Rs 650, but a bicycle (Rs 150 to Rs 200 a day) is the nicest and most leisurely way to explore the ruins. There's also a terrific bike track along the bund of Nuwara Wewa. You can hire bicycles at resthouses and several guesthouses.

Numerous buses run between the old and new bus stations, via Main St.

MIHINTALE
☎ 025
Thirteen kilometres east of Anuradhapura on the Trinco road, Mihintale is of enormous significance to the Sinhalese because it is where Buddhism originated in Sri Lanka. In 247 BC, King Devanampiya Tissa of Anuradhapura met Mahinda, son of the great Indian Buddhist emperor Ashoka, while deer hunting around the hill at Mihintale, and was converted to Buddhism.

Exploring Mihintale does involve quite a climb, so you would be wise to visit it early in the morning or late in the afternoon to avoid the midday heat. There are seven authorised guides, who charge around Rs 350 for a ton of information over two hours or so. It pays off if you have a deep interest in Buddhism and the site's history.

Each year a great festival, the **Poson Poya**, is held at Mihintale on the Poson full-moon night (usually in June).

Sights

HOSPITAL

A ruined hospital and the remains of a quincunx of buildings, laid out like the five dots on a dice, flank the roadway before you reach the base of the steps. The hospital consisted of a number of cells. A *bat oruwa* (large stone trough) sits among the ruins. The interior is carved in the shape of a human form, and the patient would climb into this to be immersed in healing oils. There are more examples of these troughs in the museum (p258). Clay urns, used for storing herbs and grinding stones, from the site can be seen in the museum. Inscriptions have revealed that the hospital had its specialists – there is reference to a *mandova*, a bone and muscle specialist, and to a *puhunda vedek*, a leech doctor.

STAIRWAY

In a series of flights, 1840 ancient granite slab steps lead majestically up the hillside. The first flight is the widest and shallowest. Higher up the steps are narrower and steeper. If you have a problem with stairs, Old Rd from the west avoids most of them.

KANTAKA CHETIYA

At the first landing a smaller flight of steps leads to this partly ruined dagoba off to the right. It's 12m high (originally it was higher than 30m) and 130m around at its base. A Brahmi inscription found nearby records donations for the dagoba. While exactly who built it is open to conjecture, Devanampiya Tissa (r 247–207 BC) had 68 cave monasteries built, and the dagoba would have been constructed near these. King Laji Tissa (r 59–50 BC) enlarged it. So the dagoba was built sometime in between, and is certainly one of the oldest at Mihintale. It is noteworthy for its friezes (see opposite). Four stone flower altars stand at each of the cardinal points, and surrounding these are well-preserved sculptures of dwarfs, geese

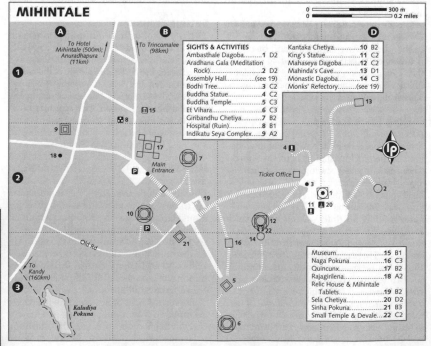

MIHINTALE

0 —— 300 m
0 —— 0.2 miles

SIGHTS & ACTIVITIES
Ambasthale Dagoba	1	D2
Aradhana Gala (Meditation Rock)	2	D2
Assembly Hall	(see 19)	
Bodhi Tree	3	C2
Buddha Statue	4	C2
Buddha Temple	5	C3
Et Vihara	6	C3
Giribandhu Chetiya	7	B2
Hospital (Ruin)	8	B1
Indikatu Seya Complex	9	A2

Kantaka Chetiya	10	B2
King's Statue	11	C2
Mahaseya Dagoba	12	C2
Mahinda's Cave	13	D1
Monastic Dagoba	14	C3
Monks' Refectory	(see 19)	

Museum	15	B1
Naga Pokuna	16	C3
Quincunx	17	B2
Rajagirilena	18	A2
Relic House & Mihintale Tablets	19	B2
Sela Chetiya	20	D2
Sinha Pokuna	21	B3
Small Temple & Devale	22	C2

To Hotel Mihintale (500m); Anuradhapura (11km)

To Trincomalee (98km)

Main Entrance

Ticket Office

Old Rd

To Kandy (160km)

Kaludiya Pokuna

SCULPTURAL SYMBOLISM

The four *vahalkadas* (solid panels of sculpture) at the Kantaka Chetiya are among the oldest and best preserved in the country, and are the only ones to be found at Mihintale.

Vahalkadas face each of the four cardinal directions and comprise a series of bands, each containing some sort of ornamentation. The upper part usually contained niches in which were placed sculptures of divine beings. At either end of each *vahalkada* is a pillar topped with the figure of an animal, such as an elephant or a lion. How or why these sculptural creations came into being is subject to speculation, but one theory is that they evolved from simple flower altars. Others suggest they were an adaptation from Hindu temple design.

The cardinal points in traditional sculptural work are represented by specific animals: an elephant on the east, a horse on the west, a lion on the north, and a bull on the south. In addition to these beasts, sculptures also feature dwarfs (sometimes depicted with animal heads), geese (said to have the power to choose between good and evil), elephants (often shown as though supporting the full weight of the superstructure), and *naga* (serpents, said to possess magical powers). Floral designs, apart from the lotus, are said to be primarily ornamental.

and other figures. Excavation of the dagoba began in 1934, at which time there was virtually no sign of it to the untrained eye. You can see a reconstruction of its interior design in the museum in Anuradhapura.

South of the Kantaka Chetiya, where a big boulder is cleft by a cave, if you look up you'll see what is thought to be the oldest inscription in Sri Lanka, predating Pali. The inscription dedicates the mountain's shelters to meditation, now and for eternity. Through the cave, ledges on the cliff face acted as meditation retreats for the numerous monks once resident here. There are around 70 different sites for contemplation.

RELIC HOUSE & MONKS' REFECTORY
At the top of the next flight of steps, on the second landing, is the monks' refectory with huge stone troughs that the lay followers kept filled with rice for the monks.

Nearby, at a place identified as the monastery's relic house, are two inscribed stone slabs erected during the reign of King Mahinda IV (r 975–91). The inscriptions lay down the rules relating to the relic house and the conduct of those responsible for it. One inscription clearly states that nothing belonging to the relic house shall be lent or sold. Another confirms the amount of land to be given in exchange for a reliable supply of oil and wicks for lamps and flowers for offerings. Also known as the Mihintale tablets, these inscribed stones define the duties of the monastery's many servants: which servants gather firewood and cook, which servants cook but only on firewood

gathered by others, and so on. There are also rules for monks: they should rise at dawn, clean their teeth, put on their robes, meditate and then go to have their breakfast (boiled rice) at the refectory, but only after reciting certain portions of the scriptures. Looking back from the relic house you get an excellent view of Anuradhapura.

ASSEMBLY HALL
On the same level as the relic house, this hall, also known as the convocation hall, is where monks met to discuss matters of common interest. The most senior monk would have presided over the discussions, and the raised dais in the middle of the hall was apparently where this person sat. Sixty-four stone pillars once supported the roof. Conservation of this site began in 1948. The main path to the Ambasthale Dagoba leads from here.

SINHA POKUNA
Just below the monks' refectory on the second landing, and near the entrance if you are coming via the old road, is a small pool surmounted by a 2m-high rampant lion, reckoned to be one of the best pieces of animal carving in the country. Anyone placing one hand on each paw would be right in line for the stream of water from the lion's mouth. There are some fine friezes around this pool.

AMBASTHALE DAGOBA
The final steep stairway, lined with frangipani trees, leads to the place where Mahinda and the king met. The **Ambasthale Dagoba**

MAHINDA'S RIDDLE

Before Mahinda initiated King Devanampiya Tissa into Buddhism, he needed to gauge the king's intelligence. He decided to test the king with a riddle. Pointing to a tree he asked him the name of the tree. 'This tree is called a mango', replied the king. 'Is there yet another mango beside this?' asked Mahinda. 'There are many mango trees', responded the king. 'And are there yet other trees besides this mango and the other mangoes?' asked Mahinda. 'There are many trees, but those are trees which are not mangoes', said the king. 'And are there, besides the other mangoes and those trees which are not mangoes, yet other trees?' asked Mahinda. 'There is this mango tree', said the king, who as a result passed the test.

(admission Rs 250) is built over the spot where Mahinda stood. Nearby stands a statue of the king in the place where he stood. On the opposite side of the dagoba from the statue is a cloister, and behind that a large, white sitting Buddha. Stone pillars surround the dagoba and may once have been used to hold offerings (or if you believe the local theory, to support a wooden roof). You must remove your shoes and hat, and umbrellas aren't allowed. The shoe minders expect a compensation of around Rs 15.

The name Ambasthale means 'Mango Tree' and refers to a riddle that Mahinda used to test the king's intelligence (above).

Nearby is the **Sela Chetiya**, which has a stone rendering of the Buddha's footprint. It's surrounded by a railing festooned with prayer flags left by pilgrims, who have also scattered coins here.

MAHASEYA DAGOBA

A stone pathway to the southwest of the Ambasthale Dagoba leads up to a higher dagoba (arguably the largest at Mihintale), thought to have been built to house relics of Mahinda. The bodhi tree to the left of the base of the steps is said to be one of the oldest surviving ones. From here there is a view over the lakes and trees to Anuradhapura, a horizon studded with the domes and spikes of all the massive dagobas. The sunsets here are something else. A small temple at the foot of the dagoba has a reclining Buddha

and Technicolor modern frescoes – donations are anticipated. A room at the side is a *devale* (Hindu complex) with statues of major gods – Ganesh, Vishnu, Murugan (Skanda) and Saman.

MAHINDA'S CAVE

There is a path leading northeast from the Ambasthale Dagoba down to a cave where there is a large flat stone. This is said to be where Mahinda lived and the stone is claimed to be where he rested. The track to the cave is hard on tender bare feet.

ARADHANA GALA

To the east of the Ambasthale Dagoba is a steep path over sun-heated rock leading up to a point where there are great views. A railing goes up most of the way. Aradhana Gala means 'Meditation Rock'.

NAGA POKUNA

Halfway back down the steep flight of steps from the Ambasthale Dagoba, a path leads to the left, around the side of the hill topped by the Mahaseya Dagoba. Here you'll find the Naga Pokuna (Snake Pool), so called because of a five-headed cobra carved in low relief on the rock face of the pool. Its tail is said to reach down to the bottom of the pool. If you continue on from here you eventually loop back to the second landing.

ET VIHARA

At an even higher elevation (309m) than the Mahaseya Dagoba are the remains of a dagoba called Et Vihara (literally, 'Elephant Temple'). The origin of the name is open to conjecture, but it may have been named after the monastery nearby. The Mihintale tablets mention Et Vihara and its image house. There are good views from here, especially of Kaludiya Pokuna (opposite).

MUSEUM

There is a small **museum** (admission free; ⏰ 9am–5pm Wed-Mon, closed public holidays) on the road leading to the stairs, virtually opposite the ruins of the hospital. There are several rooms, each one dedicated to particular finds, including bronze figurines, fragments of frescoes and remnants of stone tubs from the hospital. The collection includes a replica of the interior of an 8th-century dagoba and a 9th-century gold-plated *ola* manuscript. Pottery fragments from China and Persia are also on display.

INDIKATU SEYA COMPLEX
Back on the road leading to Old Rd, and outside the site proper, are the remains of a monastery enclosed in the ruins of a stone wall. Inside are two dagobas, the larger known as Indikatu Seya (Dagoba of the Needle). Evidence suggests that this monastery was active in fostering Mahayana Buddhism. The main dagoba's structure differs from others in Mihintale; for example, it's built on a square platform.

Nearby is a hill that's been dubbed Rajagirilena (Royal Cave Hill) after the caves found here with Brahmi inscriptions in them. One of the caves bears the name of Devanampiya Tissa. A flight of steps leads up to the caves.

KALUDIYA POKUNA
Further south along the same road is the Kaludiya Pokuna (Dark Water Pool). This artificial pool was carefully constructed to look realistic, and features a rock-carved bathhouse and the ruins of a small monastery. It's a peaceful place.

Sleeping & Eating
Hotel Mihintale (☎ 226 6599; ceylonhotels.lk; r with/without air con US$36/26; ✖) Run by the Ceylon Hotels Corporation, this is on the main road near the turn-off to the site. This is the only hotel in Mihintale. There are 10 mostly large and clean rooms, and the staff are slightly hapless but friendly. The setting is pleasant. Moderately priced meals are available. The pavilion café at the front is a good place to pause for a cool drink and a toilet stop.

Getting There & Away
It's a fairly short bus ride (Rs 10) from Anuradhapura's new bus station to Mihintale. A taxi there and back, with two hours to climb the stairs, costs about Rs 800; a three-wheeler is about Rs 600. It takes less than an hour to cycle here.

YAPAHUWA
Although it's only roughly half the height of Sigiriya and receives far fewer tourists, this **rock fortress** (admission Rs 200) rising 100m from the surrounding plain is quite impressive in its own right. The granite outcropping

of Yapahuwa (pronounced yaa-pow-a), also known as Fire Rock, was used in the early 13th century as a defensible refuge against the invading South Indian armies. Between 1272 and 1284, King Bhuvanekabahu I used the rock as his capital and kept Sri Lanka's sacred Buddha tooth relic here. Indian invaders from the Pandavan dynasty captured Yapahuwa in 2184 and carried the tooth relic to south India, only for it to be recovered in 1288 by King Parakramabahu I.

Yapahuwa's steep ornamental staircase, which led up to the ledge holding the tooth temple, is one of its finest features. One of the lions near the top of the staircase appears on the Rs 10 note. The porches on the stairway had very fine pierced-stone windows, one of which is now in the museum in Colombo; the other is in the museum on site. Reliefs of dancers, musicians and animals are evidence of South Indian influence. The view from the top of the staircase is wonderful. Climbing right up to the top of the rock is not really feasible as it's very overgrown.

There is a **museum** of sorts to the right of the site entrance. On display are stone sculptures of Vishnu and Kali, fragments of pottery and the carved stone screen, but signs are in Sinhala. Behind the museum is something more fascinating – a **cave temple** that contains some 13th-century frescoes. The repetition of images across a geometric grid also appears in Indian Buddhist sites, such as Ajanta (inland from Mumbai) and Alchi (in Ladakh). Also in the temple are wooden Buddha images and an image made of bronze. The temple is usually locked, but a monk will open it for you if you ask, although you are expected to make a donation. Photography is not allowed.

A guide will attach himself to you in anticipation of a tip.

Yapahuwa is 4km from Maho railway junction, where the Trincomalee line splits from the Colombo–Anuradhapura line, and about 5km from the Anuradhapura–Kurunegala road. It's possible to take a three-wheeler from the Anuradhapura–Kurunegala road to the site, although occasional buses do travel to here from Maho. A three-wheeler from Maho costs Rs 200 one way. A three-wheeler from the main road and back would cost about Rs 600 with waiting time. Most trains going to and from Colombo stop at Maho.

PADENIYA

About 85km south of Anuradhapura and 25km northwest of Kurunegala, where the Puttalam and Anuradhapura roads branch off, is the Kandyan-style **Padeniya Raja Mahavihara** (donations appreciated), which is worth popping into if you're passing by. It's a pretty, medieval temple with 28 carved pillars and a stunning elaborate door (said to be the largest in Sri Lanka) to the main shrine. There is also a clay image house and a library, as well as a preaching hall with an unusual carved wooden pulpit.

PANDUWASNUWARA

About 17km southwest of Padeniya, on the road between Wariyapola and Chilaw, are the 12th-century remains of the temporary capital of Parakramabahu I. It's nothing on the scale of Anuradhapura or Polonnaruwa, but it's worth stopping in if you're heading past. The sprawling site, covering some 20 hectares, hasn't been fully excavated. The turn-off to the site is at Panduwasnuwara village, where there is a small **museum** (donation expected). Most of the signs are in Sinhala.

Approaching the site, the first thing you'll see is the moat and the massive citadel wall. After that the road swings to the right and past the remains of the palace, where there are signs in English and Sinhala. Nearby, and indeed throughout the site, are the remains of image houses and dagobas as well as evidence of living quarters for monks. Follow the road past the school and veer left; you will shortly come to a restored tooth temple with a bodhi tree and, beyond that, the remains of a round palace (apparently once multistoreyed) enclosed in a circular moat.

There are many stories about who lived in this palace and why it was built. Legend has it that it kept the king's daughter away from men who would desire her, as it had been prophesised that if she bore a son, he would eventually claim the throne. Another story is that it was built to house the king's wives and, intriguingly, that there was once a secret tunnel that led from the king's palace and under the moat to the queens' palace. However attractive these stories are, they are merely that, and the fact remains that no-one really knows why this place was built.

Buses run between Kurunegala (via Wariyapola) and Chilaw on a regular basis, and it would be possible to be dropped off at Panduwasnuwara village and to walk the remaining 1km. However, it's far more practical to come with your own transport.

RIDIGAMA & RIDI VIHARA

Literally the 'Silver Temple', **Ridi Vihara** (donation Rs 100) is so named because it was here that silver ore was discovered in the 2nd century BC. Although not on the beaten track, it's well worth a visit to see its wonderful frescoes and the unusual Dutch (Delft) tiles in the main cave.

Legend has it that King Dutugemunu, who reigned in the 2nd century BC, lacked the funds to finish an important dagoba in Anuradhapura. The discovery of silver ore at the place now known as Ridigama allowed him to complete the work, and as a token of his gratitude he established a temple in the cave where the ore was discovered, and to put in this cave a gold-plated statue of the Buddha. The golden statue is still in the main cave, called the **Pahala Vihara** (Lower Temple). Also within the Pahala Vihara is a 9m recumbent Buddha that rests on a platform decorated with a series of blue-and-white tiles, which were a gift from the Dutch consul. The tiles depict scenes from the Bible, including Adam and Eve being banished from the Garden of Eden, and the transfiguration of Christ. You can also see what remains of a beautiful piece of ivory carving over the lintel. Unfortunately, this and other pieces of art have been subject to vandalism over the years.

The nearby **Uda Vihara** (Upper Temple) was built by King Kirthi Sri Rajasinghe. The entrance has a Kandyan-period moonstone. It's interesting to try to pick out some of the clever visual tricks used by the fresco artists; in one case, what appears to be an elephant at a distance reveals itself on closer inspection to be a formation of nine maidens. Hindu deities and images of the Buddha are represented in the caves.

The huge boulder that looms over the whole temple complex is attractive to the local wild bee population; you can see their nests bulging below the overhang. It's said that those who enter the temple with impure hearts will get stung, so watch out.

Just beyond the temple courtyard is what used to be a hermit's retreat. It now houses only a small shrine, but there's a skilfully carved pillared porch.

Although there are no signs banning flash photography, you should, of course, refrain from using a flash inside the caves in order to preserve the frescoes. Remember, this is not an entertainment for tourists but a working temple, and you should dress and behave appropriately. Cover your shoulders and legs, remove your shoes and hat and conduct yourself as you would be expected to in a place of worship.

Outside the temple complex you can see an abandoned dagoba at the top of a smooth rocky outcrop. On the way up, to your right, is an ancient inscription in the stone, said to have been etched on King Dutugemunu's behalf. An easy 10-minute walk starts to the right of this abandoned dagoba (as you are walking up to it). Head past a modern pavilion to an abandoned bungalow; nearby, on the top of the cliff, is a slab from which you get the most magnificent views.

Ridi Vihara is east of the Kurunegala–Dambulla road. If you are coming by car from Kurunegala, the turn-off to Ridigama village is on your right just past Ibbagamuwa village. The temple is about 2km from Ridigama via Temple Junction. Buses run between Kurunegala and Ridigama village (Rs 14, approximately every 45 minutes). From the village you can take a three-wheeler to the temple (approximately Rs 400 return, including waiting time).

KURUNEGALA

☎ 037 / pop 29,000

Kurunegala is an important crossroads town on the routes between Colombo and Anuradhapura, and Kandy and Puttalam. The town itself is not particularly interesting, but the region around Kurunegala is rich in archaeological sites and temples.

The large, smooth rocky outcrops that loom over the low-rise buildings are a striking feature of this city. Named for the animals they appear to resemble (Tortoise Rock, Lion Rock etc), the outcrops are, unsurprisingly, endowed with mythological status; it's said that they were formed when animals that were endangering the free supply of water to the town were turned into stone.

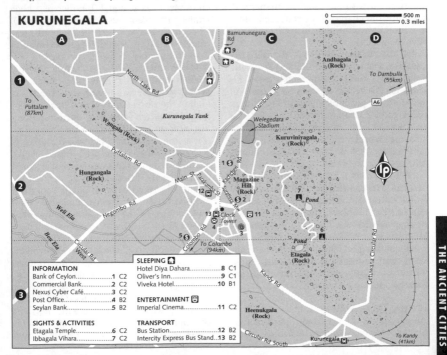

KURUNEGALA

INFORMATION		
Bank of Ceylon	1	C2
Commercial Bank	2	C2
Nexus Cyber Café	3	C2
Post Office	4	B2
Seylan Bank	5	B2

SIGHTS & ACTIVITIES		
Etagala Temple	6	C2
Ibbagala Vihara	7	C2

SLEEPING		
Hotel Diya Dahara	8	C1
Oliver's Inn	9	C1
Viveka Hotel	10	B1

ENTERTAINMENT		
Imperial Cinema	11	C2

TRANSPORT		
Bus Station	12	B2
Intercity Express Bus Stand	13	B2

Information

Bank of Ceylon (Kachcheri Rd) Changes travellers cheques; it's 450m north of the post office.
Commercial Bank (Suratissa Mawatha) ATM.
Nexus Cyber Café (60 Kandy Rd) Internet access.
Post office (Colombo Rd) In town.
Seylan Bank (Colombo Rd) ATM.

Sights

There's a road going up **Etagala**, a large black boulder on the eastern side of the city. The views are extensive from here. On the way up you pass a small shrine, **Ibbagala Vihara**, and at the head of the road there is a **temple** named after the rock itself. The town also boasts the fine old **Imperial Cinema**, which still pulls a crowd to dramas and romance today.

Sleeping & Eating

There are a few hotels around town, but the most pleasant are around the lake. A three-wheeler to these places from town should cost Rs 60 to 100 from the train station.

Oliver's Inn (☎ 222 3452; fax 222 0092; 2 Bamunune-gara Rd; r with/without air-con Rs 1000/550, ✷) This is a 1960s suburban kit home with five rooms, one of them with air-con. The manager is a friendly old chap and the staff are helpful too. It's just around the corner from Hotel Diya Dahara.

Hotel Diya Dahara (☎ 526 6662; diyadahara2004@yahoo.com; 7 North Lake Rd; s/d Rs 1200/1750) Featuring seven rooms with hot water and balcony, it's a little expensive for what you get in terms of the rooms alone, but there's a pretty garden, and a good restaurant beside the lake. The grandiose building across the road is under the same management, and has a honeymoon suite for Rs 3850 and large singles/doubles with air-con for Rs 1650/2200.

Hotel Viveka (☎ 222 2897; www.hotelviveka.com; 64 North Lake Rd; r with/without air-con Rs 2200/1500; ✷) This 150-year-old villa, kept up with lots of spit and polish, boasts an elegant veranda looking over the lake. The six rooms are spartan cubes with new bathrooms. Some interesting framed photographs grace the main room, and the hotel has Kurunegala's most convivial bar and restaurant. Weddings are often held here on weekends.

Getting There & Away

Intercity buses depart from a yard behind the clock tower. You may be dropped here when you arrive. Intercity express buses

heading to Anuradhapura (CTB/express Rs 45/100, two hours) leave every 30 minutes between 6am and 5.30pm. CTB buses for Chilaw (Rs 35, 2½ hours) leave every 30 minutes between 6am and 7pm. There are CTB and express buses to Colombo (express Rs 84, four to five hours) and Kandy (express Rs 64, one hour). Local buses and buses to Negombo (Rs 60, 3½ hours) leave from the nearby bus station on Puttalam Rd.

The train station, 2km from the town centre, sees frequent visits from trains on the Northern Line. There are eight trains between Kurunegala and Colombo daily (2nd/1st class Rs 98/150, two to three hours) and four trains daily to Anuradhapura (2nd/1st class Rs 84/125, three hours).

DAMBADENIYA

For a short time in the mid-13th century this small town was the site of the capital of Parakramabahu II (r 1236–70). Apart from six ponds, there is little to see in terms of palace remains. About 400m east of the centre of town is a **temple** (Vijayasundarama) with wall paintings said to date from when Dambadeniya served as a capital (but there is a huge amount of recent 'restorative' paint work). The temple is also where the tooth relic was exhibited. More archaeological excavation work in this area has been scheduled.

If you have your own transport you may enjoy a detour to a little-visited site called **Panavitiya**, where an *ambalama* (rest hall) was built in the 18th century. The *ambalama* belonged to an era when people travelled long distances on foot. The structure is very simple; a stone platform (4m by 3m) supports a wooden pillar frame, with raised planks running around the sides so people could (and still can) sit facing into the centre.

The 26 carved wooden pillars support a modern tiled roof. The original also had a roof, judging by the tile fragments that were buried in the ground. Unfortunately white ants have invaded some pillars. The carvings depict lotus flowers, wrestlers, women greeting one another, snakes in combat, dancers, men chatting and deer.

To get to Panavitiya, look carefully for the Quinco Highland Sales Outlet sign (there's a white milk bottle with the sign) 4km north of Dambadeniya. The turn-off is opposite this sign. Panavitiya is 3km down this road, near a temple.

The East

Visiting eastern Sri Lanka is travelling as it used to be: tropical lushness, unexplored beaches and scattered jungle ruins that feel way off the beaten track. The main tourist draw is Arugam Bay, a laid-back hang-out that's also Sri Lanka's top surfing spot. The hinterland is full of wildlife, and you're virtually assured of seeing wild elephants at Ampara. Eccentrically craggy forest-scapes tumble into mesmerising vistas of paddy fields as you head north. The coastline leads on to Batticaloa and Trincomalee via chaotic strip villages and beautiful lagoons, uncleared tsunami debris and paradisal beaches. The best-developed beaches are at Uppuveli and Nilaveli, and you can find some real accommodation bargains here in the rainy low season, which runs from October to April. But while swimming is OK in the low season, stick to the dry season (May to September) for surfing or snorkelling.

So few foreign travellers bother to visit the east coast that you're likely to find a very heartfelt welcome and a great generosity of spirit. But you'll need to tread gently. Ethnic conflicts remain unresolved – not just between Sinhalese and Tamils, but also between Tamils and Muslims, and between Tamil factions. For inquisitive travellers, learning about these complex interrelationships is part of the excitement. But sensitivity and tact are crucial.

Meanwhile, some roads remain closed or controlled by the Liberation Tigers of Tamil Eelam (LTTE). Checkpoints are common. At the time of research, soldiers gave us grins and merry waves rather than shakedowns or body searches. But keep an eye on the situation – as the recent violence has shown, renewed civil war is not entirely off the menu.

HIGHLIGHTS

- Chilling out at a beach barbecue after a day's splashing or surfing in **Arugam Bay** (p270)
- Watching the **wild elephants** (p276) arrive at Ampara's Peace Pagoda
- Discovering rarely visited ruins, spotting wildlife and spying birds throughout the region
- Finding a beach of your own north of beguiling **Batticaloa** (p284) or around **Trincomalee** (p290)
- Enjoying the locals' wide-eyed astonishment when they discover you're not a nongovernment organisation (NGO) aid worker
- Climbing **Kudimbigala** (p275) for a Sigiriya-style experience all of your own

Trincomalee ★

★ Batticaloa

Ampara ★

★ Arugam Bay

Kudimbigala ★

THE EAST

BUTTALA

☎ 055

Little more than an overgrown crossroads, Buttala is ideal for viewing the lovely scenery and visiting the uncrowded temples and ruins in the vicinity. Historically this area was part of the ancient Ruhunu kingdom, and is believed to have been an important staging point before King Dutugemunu's much hyped battle with the Tamil king Elara. The name means 'Rice Mound', in reference to the area's agricultural bounty. Today the main industry is sugar cane.

Buttala's attractions lie in the surrounding countryside, but it's worth strolling up picturesque little Temple Rd to visit the idyllically peaceful **Dolapeela Vihara** (a *vihara* is a Buddhist complex), with its small whitewashed dagoba (stupa), 800-year-old bodhi tree and worn old moonstone.

Information

Buttala Pharmacy (Badalkumbura Rd; ☺ 8am-9.30pm) at the central crossroads offers IDD phone calls and one slow Internet computer (Rs 6 per minute).

Sleeping

Lakanji Holiday Inn (☎ 227 3691/2; Temple Rd; d with fan Rs 650-850, with air-con Rs 1450) The four best upper-floor rooms are all newly built with clean, well-tiled floors and a shared balcony looking down on mango and palm trees. It's delightfully quiet, despite being a mere 200m north of the town centre, but the access lane is very dark at night. Cheaper rooms are much more tatty.

Tourist Home (☎ 227 3919; 10/7 Temple Rd; tr Rs 450) Large, good value, if slightly musty, rooms fill a large bungalow in the garden beside the Lakjani. Each has toilet, shower and fan. Darmakirti, the manager, speaks good English and is relatively knowledgeable about the area.

Hansika Guest Inn (☎ 227 3443; Wellawaya Rd; d Rs 650-1000) This recently built low-rise house at the western edge of town has five neat, clean fan-cooled rooms. It's 1km from the crossroads, and 200m west of a checkpoint chicane. Attractively surrounded by paddy fields, it's great for watching the clouds of giant fruit bats at sunset. Room prices vary by size, not quality. Nets are new and effective against predictably prevalent mosquitoes. A reasonable variety of food is served

---

THE 2004 TSUNAMI – AFTERMATH IN THE EAST

The East bore the brunt of the December 2004 tsunami, yet it seems to have received the least help in rebuilding. Certainly, there are still dozens of NGO workers racing about in huge 4WDs, and donations of fishing dinghies have been so overgenerous that some villagers have reportedly gathered a small fleet. However, rehousing has been relatively slow and highly controversial; what use is a home 8km inland to a fisherman who has no transport to reach the sea? Such sites were originally chosen because of a blanket exclusion zone preventing rebuilding within 200m of the sea. However, in the lead up to the November 2005 election the 200m rule was softened or removed altogether in many places. That only added to the nightmare for rebuilding planners, whose carefully surveyed inland resettlement-village sites now seem irrelevant. The complex relationships between Muslim and Tamil villagers has compounded the difficulties of reconstruction. Meanwhile, aid workers preferring to operate from the perceived safety of mostly Sinhalese Ampara are sometimes seen as out of touch with local realities.

For years to come you're likely to see ruined beachside buildings, especially in hard-hit areas like Kalmunai. Much more has been done to rebuild Arugam Bay's sea-facing properties, but considerable destruction remains. Central Batticaloa and Trincomalee both survived fairly intact, but Nilaveli beach has only recently scrabbled back to life and Kalkudah beach remains virtually deserted. Some owners of reconstructed beach hotels keep photos of their tsunami-wrecked buildings, and Hotel Club Oceanic in rebuilt Uppuveli marks the tsunami high-water line on its wall.

---

in the large, if rather characterless, dining room (mains Rs 130 to 300).

Eating

Lanka Chinese (☎ 492 0315; Okampitiya Rd; mains from Rs 140; 🕑 9am-midnight) This restaurant's beautifully inviting porch drips with foliage and naturally artistic contorted branches. Inside, the atmosphere is much less special, with underlit dining booths set behind a central drinking den. Nonetheless the food is tasty and the portions are generous. Beer is available (Rs 100), but it's not cold.

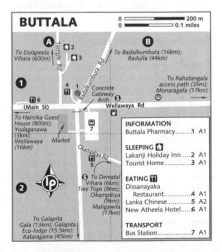

Dissanayaka Restaurant (☎ 227 3876; mains from Rs 120; 🕑 8am-10.30pm) This place has a bland atmosphere but serves great devilled dishes. It's in an alley off the central crossroads.

New Atheela Hotel (Wellawaya Rd; meals from Rs 50; 🕑 6am-10pm) One of several cheap places that serves fresh hoppers (bowl-shaped pancakes) in the evenings.

Getting There & Away

Buttala is the logical junction for transferring between the Hill Country or east coast and Kataragama in the South. Frequent Wellawaya–Monaragala buses intersect here with ten daily Badalkumbura–Kataragama buses. The last buses to Kataragama (Rs 40, 1¼ hours) leave at 4pm and (some days) at 5.30pm.

AROUND BUTTALA
Yudaganawa (Udhagannawa)

One of the biggest yet least known of Sri Lanka's Buddhist dagobas lies quietly hidden in a forest clearing at Yudaganawa, just 3km west of Buttala. Only the bottom third remains, topped with *cadjan* (matting made from coconut fronds), but the setting is charming. It's 1.5km off Wellawaya Rd. Just before reaching the main site you'll pass the moss-encrusted ruins of the much smaller 12th-century Chulangani Vihara, with a pudding-shaped dagoba and fragments of a decapitated 7th-century Buddha.

Maligawila & Dematal Vihara

Two inscrutable **ancient statues** (admission free; ☺ dawn-dusk) stand in an appealingly shady forest glade at Maligawila (mali-*ga*-wila). The site is delightful and the village so diffuse that it's virtually invisible apart from the archaeological site's car park. A path from the back of the car park burrows between stalls selling fruit and offerings, continuing into the partly manicured woodland. Here are the extensive 7th-century remnants of Pathma Vihara. To reach the statues, walk five minutes to a five-way junction, where you meet the degraded asphalt of Siyawasa Mawatha. Turn right up that track to reach the first statue, the 10m-high **Maitreya Bodhisattva** (Avalokitesvara), which stands very impressively atop a great five-storey stone temple tower. It was reconstituted between 1989 and 1991 from over 100 fragments unearthed in the 1950s. Sadly, it's shaded by a banal corrugated canopy.

Walk 10 minutes in the opposite direction to find an 11m-tall **Buddha statue**, considered by some to be the tallest freestanding ancient Buddha in existence. Free of ugly modern covers, he elegantly commands an enclosure containing very aged bricks and a moonstone.

Maligawila is 9km southeast of Okkampitiya, a small village famous for its small-scale gem pits. Direct Maligawila buses run surprisingly frequently from Monaragala (Rs 23, 70 minutes, last bus at 5.30pm), and six times daily from Buttala, which is slightly nearer (last bus at 4.45pm). Of the latter, four go via Kumbukkana, but two use the shorter, narrower and much more scenic road passing delightful **Dematal Vihara**, a gorgeous temple lost in a sea of picturesque rural paddy fields.

Weliara Ridge

The spiky **Weliara Ridge** leading south from near Buttala is dotted with barely visible ruins and many caves. Most were Buddhist retreats in the era of the Ruhunu kingdom, and some are now used again for the same purpose. One of the best known is **Rahatangala**, two hours' hike by an initially well-trodden trail that starts beside a temple 2km east of Buttala on the Monaragala road. Further south, **Arhat Kanda**, the scenic 'Hills of Enlightenment', can be accessed on guided hikes ($14) from Tree Tops (right).

Staying at **Tree Tops** (☎ 077 703 6554; www.tree topsjunglelodge.com; per person all-inclusive US$49), an extraordinarily isolated eco-lodge at base of the Weliara Ridge, 8km from Buttala, is a philosophical statement. This is intensely personal communing with nature: enjoy the starlight, and listen for wild elephants in the ebony trees right behind the sole twin-bed bungalow. That bungalow is simple (no electricity) but comfy, and has hammocks on the terrace. If you're the type who finds it liberating rather than invasive to bathe at a private open-air well with great forest views, Tree Tops is your kind of place. While prices seem high, remember that the whole place is likely to be working just for you. Food (vegetarian, except by special request) and drinks (including an evening cocktail) are included in the price.

At a pinch, two more guests could occupy a tiny, delightfully wobbly tree house if they value views over space and don't suffer from vertigo. But this version of a *chena* perch (used by farmer-guards trying to protect their fields), offers no more than a mattress and mosquito net in a tree.

Dropping in to Tree Tops without reservations is neither wise nor welcomed, as food and staff won't be ready; send an email at least a week in advance. There's no phone signal at Tree Tops, so phoning will only work if the owner happens to go into town.

A three-wheeler to Tree Tops from Buttala costs Rs 350. If the track degrades, as it has in previous years, you might have to walk the last kilometre or two, especially in the rainy season.

Buttala to Kataragama

Roughly following the course of the **Menik Ganga** (River of Gems), this road is especially scenic in its northern section, where it runs parallel to a spiky dragon's-back ridge of forest-topped mini mountains. These reach a curious crescendo at **Galapita Gala** (Rock on a Rock). Here a weird rocky hook, shaped like a giant cashew, is plonked on a bigger outcrop, creating a silhouette that looks something like a huge tortoise's head. As with most such formations, there's a small Buddhist hermit's retreat on top.

A couple of kilometres away, located in splendid, idyllic isolation, is **Galapita Ecolodge** (☎ 077 316 4167; www.galapita.com; full board per person US$70). Although it's actually very simple (there's no electricity), the elegant design gives this place the feeling of a multistar getaway. The adobe-finished rooms and tree houses mostly overlook the lily-pond-flanked river as it cuts into living rock. One of the outdoor showers is fashioned out of hollow tree branches. Although there's little to do here, that's really the point. You can wander the sugar-cane fields or take a guided hike up to Galapita Gala, but just splashing in the river or groping for gemstones is pleasure enough for a day or two. Bookings are made through Colombo's **Paradise Lanka** (Map p88; ☎ 011-250 8755; paradiselanka@sltnet.lk; 62 Havelock Rd, Col 5). Galapita Eco-lodge is 1.5km west of the 31km marker.

Further south the land becomes flat, and all habitation peters out as the road cuts through the scrubby forest of Yala National Park. There's no permit required, assuming you stay on the road, though if you want to enter the park proper from the gate beside the Galge army camp you'll have to pay.

MONARAGALA
☎ 055

Dripping with green foliage, the centre of Monaragala nestles beneath Peacock Rock, a round-topped hunk of forest-covered mountain. The town then straggles 3km west along Wellawaya Rd (A4) to Hulanduwa Junction, where the road meets the A22 to Bibile and Badulla.

Mainly seen as a transit point for reaching Arugam Bay, the town is nonetheless a friendly and attractive place once you get off the busy main road. It's also an alternative place from which to visit the impressive statues and ruins at Maligawila.

Information
Commercial Bank (Bus Station Rd) and several other banks dotted along Wellawaya Rd all have ATMs. In the market area, **Samudura Communications** (☎ 227 6765; per hr Rs 80; ☯ 7.30am-8pm) has the cheapest Internet connection for miles around.

Sights & Activities
An easy but beautiful hike starts near the bus station; walk five minutes past a colourful little Hindu **Ganesh Temple** to the ageing **rubber factory**, then veer left to a charming rock-paved footpath that climbs between attractive boulder fields through Monaragala's famous rubber plantations.

If you're at a loose end, visit **Popunagala Vihara**, located at the 249km post, 1km west of Hulanduwa Junction. Here, on a low rocky outcrop, a blindingly white 14m-tall **Buddha statue** is 'growing' out of a concrete lotus.

Sleeping & Eating
Victory Inn (☎ /fax 227 6100; 65 Wellawaya Rd; s with fan Rs 1210, d with fan/air-con Rs 1420/2970; ☯) Monaragala's main hotel complex offers small but neatly, tiled modern boxlike rooms above a decent restaurant (which serves beer). The takeaway out the front offers pretty much the same food at cheaper prices.

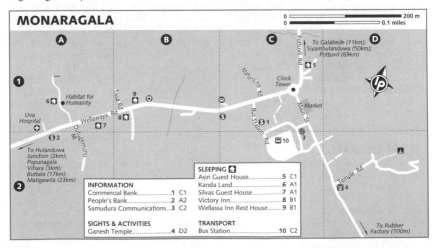

Wellassa Inn Rest House (☎ 227 6815; Wellaway Rd; tw Rs 650) Set behind a lovingly tended garden, this older place has a few functional, slightly worn but sensibly priced rooms. They have little sitting areas out the back but no views. Served around a small ornamental pool, meals are available if you order ahead.

Kanda Land (☎ 227 6925; tw Rs 300) These ultrabasic, ageing rooms have bucket baths in the shared bathrooms, but they are cheap and very clean. The owners speak English, and their son can lead guided walks in the rubber plantations. The unmarked building is opposite Habitat for Humanity in a dead-end lane off Wellawaya Rd.

Silvas Guest House (☎ 227 6296; Wellawaya Rd; tw/tr Rs 500/600) This place has very ordinary rooms with mosquito nets, and bathrooms whose toilets don't always flush too efficiently.

Asiri Guest House (☎ 227 6618; d/tr Rs 500/600) This guesthouse is central yet reasonably quiet, but the toilets and fans are dodgy and the clientele isn't always salubrious. The attached beer garden is relatively pleasant for a sunset drink.

For very cheap meals there are various fly-friendly dives around the bus station area.

Getting There & Away

The most reliable buses to Pottuvil (for Arugam Bay) depart at 8.30am, 11.15am and 12.15pm. Alternatively, take a bus to Siyambulanduwa and change. To Ampara, buses leave roughly twice-hourly until 2.45pm using two possible routes: via Siyambulanduwa (for Arugam Bay) or via Inginyagala (for the Gal Oya National Park). Colombo-bound intercity buses (Rs 220, seven hours) run at roughly 45-minute intervals until late, though there are gaps in the schedule. For the south coast, buses leave roughly hourly to Matara (4½ hours). Services run very frequently to Wellawaya (Rs 40, 50 minutes) for the Hill Country, passing though Buttala; change in Buttala for Kataragama.

EAST OF MONARAGALA

The A4 winds laboriously east around the forested bulk of Peacock Rock, passing endless habitation – although houses are so hidden by trees that you'd hardly notice even a village. At **Galabede** (Galabadda, Bisokotuwa; admission free) there's a gently attractive step well, the remnant of a 12th-century palace complex.

It's 100m south of the road, between the 264km and 265km posts.

Siyambulanduwa

The bus stand of Siyambulanduwa (often abbreviated to Siyambulan – pronounced syam-bulan) is where the A4 and A25 roads meet. There's nothing to see, but coming here improves your options for transport to Pottuvil and Arugam Bay.

If you're stranded overnight, **Nethmini Guest & Rest** (☎ 072 250 7523; Ampara Rd; s Rs 1000, tw Rs 750-1000; 🕮) is very acceptable, guarded by concrete mini-elephants on a manicured, suburban-style lawn. Rooms 3 and 4 are air-conditioned at no extra charge. The Rs 750 rooms share a bathroom. It's on the A25, around 1.5km north of the bus stand.

There's a cheap drink-and-snacks 'hotel' at the bus stand. Just 100m north, thatched **Ilukgedara Restaurant** (Ampara Rd; beers Rs 100; 🕘 8am-10pm) looks misleadingly inviting. In fact, this is primarily an arrack-drinking den, but check out the ageing poster of the Spice Girls, Hindu bindis added to each forehead.

Last buses depart for Ampara at 4pm, for Panama (via Arugam Bay) at 5pm, and for Monaragala at 9.10pm. A three-wheeler to Arugam Bay costs Rs 600, or around Rs 1000 with side trips to the various sites en route.

Siyambulanduwa to Ampara

Forest-smothered rocky outcrops soar above the road for the first 20km of this lushly gorgeous route. This is most dramatic around Nine Mile Junction, where the vast cliff face of **Govindahela** rises above the road to the east. Once a refuge used by the 13th-century king Buvenekabahu, the mountain so impressed colonial Brits that they nicknamed it Westminster Abbey. Another rather grand outcrop occurs at **Wadinagala** (wadi-nag-ala). Just north of the town (at the 27km post), a small but asphalted road short-cuts to Inginyagala. Around 3.5km up that side road, the modest **Panathgoda Rock Temple** offers bucolic views across the paddy fields from its pretty little lily pond. The site is unmarked, 300m west of the road.

At the 36km post on the A25, the photogenic **Ekgal Aru Reservoir** is overlooked by the beautifully situated but spartan and old-fashioned **Ekgaloya Circuit Bungalow** (s/d/tr US$75/100/130). Even if it weren't so overpriced, the fact that you must prepay at the **Department of Wildlife Conservation** (Map pp84-5; ☎ 011-269 4241; www.dwlc.lk; 18 Gregory's Rd, Col 7) is enough to put off most tourists from overnighting here.

Public transport to Ampara veers east at the sugar-processing town of Hingurana rather than following the A25 through Varipattanchenai. So jump off the bus at Hingurana if you want to find a three-wheeler to Deegawapi (p278).

Siyambulanduwa to Pottuvil

Though tourists rarely bother stopping, there are several minor attractions en route to Pottuvil. The **Tharulengala Cave Temple** at Ulannugeh has concrete steps leading up to a very eroded reclining Buddha, fashioned from ancient mud. The site is fairly pretty, though dense foliage limits views of the tank (artificial lake) and the paddy fields below. It's 1.5km north of the A4 at the 299km marker. Further east the road passes through the small **Lahugala National Park**. Although the park itself is not open to tourists, large groups of elephants are often visible across the tank that lies just behind Lahugala hospital (at the 306km post).

About 12km before Pottuvil lies an evocative 'lost-in-the-jungle' ruin called the **Magul Maha Vihara** (donation requested). Built by King Dathusena (473–453 BC), the ruin is often (if mistakenly) described as the wedding site of Queen Viharamahadevi. The ruins feature a *vatadage* (circular relic house) in a cross-shaped raised area at the southwest corner. Large stones at the base are carved as crouched lions. The site is 1km south of the A4 between 308km and 309km posts. To reach the ruins, walk five minutes south from the car park, passing hefty stone slabs that lead down to an ancient tank.

POTTUVIL

☎ 063

Majority-Muslim Pottuvil is the southernmost sizable town on the east coast. For most tourists it's simply the transport hub for reaching Arugam Bay, just 3km further south, where all the accommodation is located. However, Pottuvil does have two banks near the bus stand (no ATMs), and a decent market; its **main post office** (Panama Rd; ⏰ 8am-5pm Mon-Sat) has Internet (Rs 8 per minute).

Hidden away in the backstreets are the ancient ruins of **Mudu Maha Vihara**. This delightful little site, partly submerged in the encroaching sand dunes, features a fine 3m-high standing Buddha statue whose eroded face stares at two smaller, better-conserved Bodhisattva figures. The **beach** just behind is wide, beautiful and undeveloped, though unshaded. Access from the southbound main road towards Arugam Bay is via the second street to the left (east) after the 1km post (signed in bright yellow in local script). Pass a small green mosque, and at the T-junction beyond turn left then immediately right.

A hexagonal **ecology information hut** by the lagoon in Pottuvil's northernmost Kottukal area is the starting point for delightful two-hour **mangrove tours** (www.arugambay.com/pages /eco.html; tours per person Rs 1500). Outrigger canoes take pairs of visitors across the lagoon – a peaceful punt with lovely heron-watching opportunities. You get dropped off at an environmentally important, if dull, mangrove nursery and (much more interestingly) on a deserted sand bar dotted with handsome rocks, located in front of a beautiful curve of beach. This point is also accessible by a sandy road, and the nearby headland is well known to surfers as **Pottuvil Point**. Note that mangrove tours are much easier to arrange from the **Arugam Bay Hillton Guest House** (☎ /fax 224 8189; www.arugambay.lk) – the price includes transfers from there anyway.

Buses depart for Colombo (Rs 320, 10 hours) via Monaragala at 6.45am and

5.30pm. Otherwise take one of several daily departures to Monaragala or Siyambulanduwa (Rs 40, 1½ hours) and change.

To Batticaloa there's a bus at noon, or make short hops via Akkaraipattu (Rs 40, 1½ hours) and Kalmunai.

Buses heading to Panama via Arugam Bay (Rs 20) run when full, but as it's only Rs 100 to Arugam Bay by three-wheeler it's rarely worth the wait. However, if you're arriving on a bus from Siyambulanduwa or Monaragala bound for Panama via Arugam bay, don't believe touts who say the bus will wait an hour in Pottuvil. It usually continues on within 10 minutes.

ARUGAM BAY
☎ 063

Lovely Arugam Bay (aru-*gam*-beh) is the east coast's most traveller-friendly destination. It's basically a single laid-back strip of beach accommodation, following the Panama road and backed by the Muslim village of Sinna Ulla.

From April to October it has the best surfing waves in Sri Lanka, but Arugam Bay is also a great place to unwind, eat seafood and enjoy a mellow party scene. During the low season (November to April) things get very quiet, though NGO types still come for weekend getaways and the sea is better for swimming. At any time of year the surrounding region offers some superb opportunities for viewing birdlife, crocodiles and elephants.

Information
At the time of writing the nearest banks were in Pottuvil, though a Bank of Ceylon was being built into the front of Siam View Beach Hotel beside the beautifully air-conditioned, if fiercely expensive, **Internet Café** (☎ 224 8195; per min Rs 10; ⏰ 9am-1.30pm & 3-9pm; ✷). Surf & Sun's surf shop also plans to provide Internet access. The nearest post office is 500m southwest, between Arugam Bay and Pasarichenai.

Dangers & Annoyances
Single women might receive unwanted attention on the beaches, and there have been some cases of attempted sexual assault in secluded areas, particularly south behind the surf point. Use normal common sense. There is a tourist police post on the beach behind Siam View.

Activities
SURFING
Arugam Bay offers consistent surf from April to September, with some good days until November. The surf does not produce high-performance waves but there are good right-breaking waves of up to 1.6m, and it's a good place to learn to surf. With a water temperature of 24°C to 28°C year-round, you don't need a wet suit. The main promontory on the south curl of Arugam Bay (near Mambo's) is arguably the best surf spot: it's easy to reach and has a long, sectioned wave rolling north. But there are many more breaks of similar quality, including Pottuvil Point, to the north of Arugam Bay (Rs 800 return by three-wheeler); Pasarichenai Beach, near Crocodile Rock (Rs 250, 3km south of Arugam Bay); and various others further south, including Peanut Farm, Panama and Okanda.

From November till early March the waves die off but you might find surf a few days a month off the main beach.

Places that rent out boards:

A-bay Surf Shop (☎ 077 707 0307, 077 958 5008; boogie boards Rs 250-300, surfboards Rs 400-500) Rents out boards, fixes broken fins, and arranges scooter and motorbike hire.

Aloha (boogie boards Rs 450, surfboards Rs 700-1200) This guesthouse (p273) has about the best quality boards available. Johnson, the manager, is a local surf champion.

Surf & Sun (short/long boards per half-day Rs 250/400) The very surf-savvy owners of this guesthouse (p273) organise various surfing excursions, including multiday trips using their own Land Rovers.

Mambos (boogie/surfboards per hr Rs 100/200) The boards at this guesthouse (p272) are expensive, but OK for beginners wanting just a quick splash.

SWIMMING
Seas are OK for swimming during the low season, but ask local advice before plunging in at lesser-known beaches where rips might be strong.

WALKING & CYCLING
It's possible to walk right around the surf point and down the mostly undeveloped Pasarichenai Beach to long, low Crocodile Rock. When water levels are low you can ford the nearby creek and continue to Elephant Rock, which you can climb for beach views and the possibility of spotting elephants, especially at dusk. Further inland, reached by a confusing, twisting track south

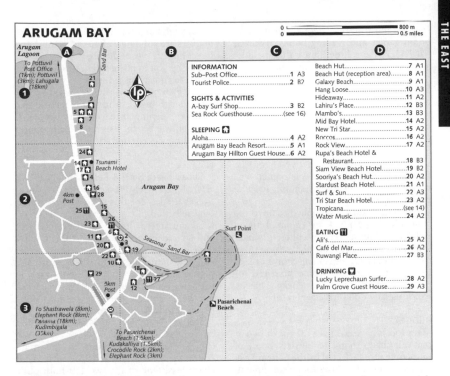

ARUGAM BAY

INFORMATION	
Sub–Post Office	1 A3
Tourist Police	2 B2

SIGHTS & ACTIVITIES	
A-bay Surf Shop	3 B2
Sea Rock Guesthouse	(see 16)

SLEEPING	
Aloha	4 A2
Arugam Bay Beach Resort	5 A1
Arugam Bay Hillton Guest House	6 A2

Beach Hut	7 A1
Beach Hut (reception area)	8 A1
Galaxy Beach	9 A1
Hang Loose	10 A3
Hideaway	11 A2
Lahiru's Place	12 B3
Mambo's	13 B3
Mid Bay Hotel	14 A2
New Tri Star	15 A2
Roccos	16 A2
Rock View	17 A2
Rupa's Beach Hotel & Restaurant	18 B3
Siam View Beach Hotel	19 B2
Sooriya's Beach Hut	20 A2
Stardust Beach Hotel	21 A1
Surf & Sun	22 A3
Tri Star Beach Hotel	23 A2
Tropicana	(see 14)
Water Music	24 A2

EATING	
Ali's	25 A2
Café del Mar	26 A2
Ruwangi Place	27 B3

DRINKING	
Lucky Leprechaun Surfer	28 A2
Palm Grove Guest House	29 A3

of Elephant Rock, is the ancient if somewhat underwhelming cave-temple complex of Shastrawela. Like so many places in the region, this spot is mythically linked with Queen Viharamahadevi. With a bicycle it's accessible from the Panama road, though the last section (behind an army camp) gets rough and steep. The Panama road makes for pleasant, if very hot, cycling.

NATURE-WATCHING

The highly recommended mangrove tours (Rs 1500 including transfers) on Pottuvil Lagoon (p269) are sold from the Arugam Bay Hillton Guest House (p273). This splendid grass-roots initiative supplements the incomes of local fishermen, and a percentage of profits is donated to an important mangrove replanting programme.

The Hillton also plans sea safaris (around Rs 2000) to see whales and dolphins, but you can organise the trip for yourself by calling the **United Deep Sea Fishermen's Co-operative Society** (☎ 0777 845266).

Several guesthouses offer tours to the Yala East National Park, but these get pretty expensive and, unless you have a specialist interest, the excellent wildlife-watching possibilities outside the park will probably satisfy you at a vastly lower cost.

Ask guesthouses about crocodile tours or just head to Panama and take a three-wheeler to Crocodile Lake. Along the way there's a high chance of seeing elephants. There's a good chance of seeing crocodiles and elephants around Crocodile Rock on Pasarichenai Beach, just south of Arugam Bay proper. To see bigger groups of elephants, although at greater distance, head to Lahugala National Park (p269).

For **bird-watching**, the various nearby lagoons are marvellous for waterfowl and waders, while brahminy kites regularly soar above the surf point.

TAMIL LESSONS

Inquire at **Sea Rock Guesthouse** (☎ 224 8341) about Tamil lessons.

GAMES & PASTIMES

Aloha (☎ 224 8379) has table football, **Galaxy Beach** (☎ 224 8415) has a badminton set and several guesthouses keep a selection of board games and reading books. **Hideaway** (☎ 224 8259) has a little library that includes some practical bird-watching guides.

Sleeping

Note that many of the restaurants have rooms, and most of the guesthouses serve meals; the line between the two is blurred. Many other places were under construction or reconstruction at the time of writing, so expect plenty of new alternatives. Spookily, the Tsunami Beach Hotel was named well before the 2004 disaster. It should soon be up and running again soon.

The term 'cabana' is applied to anything from ultrabasic plank or *cadjan* huts to rather luxurious full-facility concrete bungalows. Prices quoted are for high season (May to September). Off-season discounts of 20% to 35% are common. Come prepared for power cuts with a torch for cheaper places, which usually don't have generators.

BUDGET

Many locals have erected a cabana or two or rent out cheap rooms to tourists. Some of the people most affected by the tsunami ask for donations of mattresses or equipment; while perhaps understandable, this makes for an uncomfortable atmosphere and such places have not been reviewed here.

Beach Hut (☎ 224 8202; cabanas Rs 350-800) It's hard to beat this place for atmosphere, budget-level great value, excellent food and thoroughly friendly management. The reception area is slightly set back from the beach with a few rooms, including two two-storey *cadjan* affairs with a bathroom downstairs and an airy bedroom above. The tightly grouped knot of basic shared-facility huts has an even better location – they're right on the beachfront. Remarkably, some of these well-designed high-stilt cabanas survived the tsunami, which washed underneath. Lamps are somewhat understrength. Free bicycle use for guests.

Lahiru's Place (☎ 077 900 5322; d Rs 350-650) Extremely basic, but this place is popular for having the cheapest huts close to the surf point. Many guests rave about the iced coffee and the mashed potatoes.

Mambo's (☎ 077 782 2524; s/d Rs 1000/2000) Uniquely located right next to the main surf point, the four single-bed cabanas here are

ultrarough bare-plank shacks, but the three doubles are solid new affairs with toilet and fan. The café closes during the low season, requiring you to make a dark trek across the beach to find your dinner.

Rock View (☎ 077 642 4616; tw/cabana Rs 700/1500) This guesthouse's sturdy, concrete-floored cabana, sleeping three or four people, is right on the beach. Its private bathroom is appealingly decorated with shell fragments. Cheaper rooms are tucked behind the quiet restaurant.

Rupa's Beach Hotel & Restaurant (☎ 077 666 0934; cabanas Rs 1000-1200, bungalows Rs 2000) Location is the key for this somewhat overhuddled selection of basic cabanas, which have solid concreted floors, small double beds and shared bathrooms. Each cabana has a table on the small porch area. The sturdier concrete bungalows with tiled floors and private facilities are not the best option in the price range. The café has Western food, but the potentially lovely view of the fishing beach is marred by chicken wire.

Sooriya's Beach Hut (☎ 224 8232; s with/without bathroom Rs 600/400, tw with/without bathroom Rs 900/600) The boxy old rooms in the main concrete house are sensibly priced, if charmless. One of the two top-floor basic *cadjan*-walled rooms surveys the town, with glimpses of beach. Ram, the wise and charming owner, is a fascinating character with the looks of a sadhu. The phone line is awaiting reconnection.

Other recommendations:

Hang Loose (☎ 224 8225, 077 606 5097; d with shared toilet Rs 400, d/tr with private toilet Rs 800/900) Bare bulbs, fan and shared showers. There are no mosquito nets. The restaurant closes during Ramadan.

Tropicana (☎ 224 8242; tw Rs 800) Five basic but fresh, brand-new fan-cooled huts with outside WC. Near, but not on the beach.

Mid Bay Hotel (☎ 224 8390; d Rs 1000) Big unadorned fan-cooled rooms with private bathrooms but no mosquito nets. Prices halve during the low season.

Arugam Bay Beach Resort (☎ 224 8405; d Rs 1000-1500) Reasonable, if somewhat roughly finished, concrete cabanas without beach views.

MIDRANGE

Hideaway (☎ 224 8259; tissara@eureka.lk; d/cabanas/bungalows Rs 2200/2500/3000) This recommended NGO favourite has attractive rooms set off lovely wide verandas that drip with bougainvillea. Pleasantly shaped cabanas are bright and have hammocks, while bungalows are more solid and spacious with a chaise longue and a shower that runs off the stonework like a waterfall. It's easy to miss Hideaway because it's hidden at the back of a lush garden.

Surf & Sun (☎ 077 606 5099; www.surfnsunarugam bay.com; cabanas Rs 2500) At night, clever lighting makes this one of the strip's most alluring choices. Comfortable, sturdy double cabanas with tiled floors have that desert island feel, with hammocks on the porch facing the coconut palms. A few cheaper wooden-stilt cabanas are also available. Boss Saman is a delightfully obliging yet laid-back local surfer dude who knows all the breaks on the coast. Internet connection is planned.

Aloha (☎ 224 8379; www.aloha-arugambay.com; cabanas Rs 1500-1800) The characterful cabanas here have straw hats as lamp shades, banana trees growing in some private bath yards, and brilliant upper-storey sitting areas. Lockable chests are ideal for your valuables. There's limited food availability.

Galaxy Beach (☎ 224 8415; d Rs 2500) This nice spot has six very likeable cabanas, as well as some artistry in towel presentation. Each has a lookout-cum-terrace overlooking the beach.

Water Music (☎ 077 905 9064; d with/without bathroom Rs 1600/1200) Two great *cadjan* cabanas with open-air private bathrooms are right on the rock-pocked beach, with wide views round to the distant surf point. Rooms with shared (salty-water) bathrooms are tucked behind the open restaurant area.

Arugam Bay Hillton Guest House (☎ /fax 224 8189; www.arugambay.lk; cabanas Rs 1300, tw Rs 1500-2700, q Rs 3000) Very clean, tiled rooms are somewhat small and dark downstairs, but brighter and with surf-point glimpses upstairs. One cabana is right on the beach, while the other is set back but has a upper-storey view platform. Both are made from *cadjan* but have private bathrooms. The Hillton is a popular meeting place and also offers a range of tours (p271).

Tri Star Beach Hotel (☎ 224 8404; bungalows/tw Rs 2500/4500; 🖳 🖳) Newer rooms are oddly paired in semidetached concrete cottages alongside Arugam Bay's only swimming pool. Each room has hot water, BBC World TV and (somewhat weak) air-con, but light bulbs come bare and some terraces face walls. The drastically overpriced older bungalows are due for replacement.

Siam View Beach Hotel (☎ 224 8195; www.arugam .com; r Rs 2500-4000; 🖳) This place was only partially complete at the time of writing, but the beautifully tiled rooms that were operational were impressive. Rooms have stone-floor bathrooms, while fish tanks built into the hotel's southern wall add character. It is German-owned and the subject of much local gossip and jealousy.

Roccos (☎ 077 664 2991; www.roccoshotel.com; d from Rs 2000) Eye-catching lamps made of recycled bottles draw you in at night, and the rear rooms are spacious and well built. Those further forward are more cramped but have sea-facing terraces.

TOP END

Stardust Beach Hotel (☎ 224 8191; www.arugambay .com; d downstairs/upstairs Rs 5400/6400, cabanas Rs 2400) This sturdily attractive, Danish-owned hotel commands a wide area of beach at the lagoon end of the strip. Upstairs rooms have a fridge and a beach-view balcony, while the *cadjan*-walled cabanas have brick floors, desks and lamp shades. The whole place is quietly stylish – but so it should be at these prices. The food is widely recommended (p274), and the yoga hall is being reconstructed.

Kudakalliya (☎ 224 8636; Pasarichenai Beach) This is a luxurious self-contained holiday home quite separate from the rest of Arugam Bay. Located towards Crocodile Rock, it will sleep up to four couples (when completed). Watch crocodiles in the creek behind the house, or survey the wide undeveloped beach from the water-tower lookout point. Beyond two basic shops catering to resettled tsunami victims, there are no dining facilities anywhere near so the kitchen will be useful.

New Tri Star (☎ 224 8454; fax 224 8011; tw Rs 5500; 🖳) This is a discordantly modern hotel that enforces strict halal, no-alcohol rules for its predominantly Muslim clientele. A foyer with marble tables and a stylish café ends in glass doors to the beach. Painted in startling turquoise, rooms are new and well equipped, if slightly undersized.

Eating

Beach Hut (☎ 077 317 9594; meals Rs 100-150, lobster dinner Rs 600) Order ahead and join the convivial communal meal at this guesthouse (opposite). Food here is delicious and superb value. Ranga's occasional seafood or lobster beach barbecues are legendary.

Ruwangi Place (meals Rs 100; ⏰ from 1pm & 7.30pm) This is a single, simple *cadjan* room offering 'The Best Rice and Curry (I Think)'. We agree. The communal all-you-can-eat set vegetarian meal is cheap yet superb. Local pensioner-singer 'Jimmy' often arrives in an arrack haze to informally serenade diners. 'Thanks for pot smoking' says another sign; it's not a spelling mistake. Booking ahead is wise.

Surf & Sun (☎ 077 606 5099; www.surfnsunarugambay .com; mains Rs 280-450) Feast on superb ginger fish (Rs 320) and OK pizza (Rs 380 to 600) in the comfortable mood-lit, surfer-orientated reggae bar-café at this guesthouse (p273). It's open-sided but there are no sea views.

Stardust Beach Restaurant (☎ 224 8191; mains Rs 700-1050) The restaurant at Stardust Beach (above) has a wide menu of consistently excellent international dishes, ranging from paella (Rs 736) to Danish-style burgers (Rs 862), albeit at almost European prices.

Café del Mar (mains Rs 350-600) This is an open-sided five-table restaurant facing the fishing beach, with hammocks, swing seats and a few chill-out cushions. Follow ginger chicken satay (Rs 350) with a rum-pineapple flambé (Rs 200) and the bay's only Lavazza espresso (Rs 150).

Galaxy Beach (☎ 224 8415; mains Rs 350-400) This likeable hotel (p273) serves a flexible menu of Western-fusion cooking from a superclean modern kitchen. It has the best lime-papaya juice (Rs 90) on the beach.

Siam View Beach Hotel (☎ 224 8195; www.arugam .com; mains Rs 350-600) Pizza and authentic, if not truly memorable, Thai food is served at this atmospheric hotel-restaurant (p273). However, the manager's monkey is annoying.

Ali's (☎ 077 917 3961; meals Rs 45-130; ⏰ 7.30am-10pm, Ramadan dusk-10pm) One of several local eateries dotted along the main road offering great breakfast *rottis* (doughy pancakes) and gut-busting yet complexly tasty chicken *kotthu rottis* (*rottis* chopped and fried with a variety of ingredients). On request, staff can also marinate and cook up fish that you've bought from Pottuvil market.

Drinking & Entertainment

Arugam Bay is small: ask other travellers for the party place of the moment.

Siam View Beach Hotel (☎ 224 8195; beers Rs 150; ⏰ 4pm-late) The café-bar in this hotel (p273) serves great locally brewed draught beers

and has a superb two-storey beach bar; the upper-storey Ladies' Lounge is decked out in cushions and is limited to women or 'loving couples'. The hotel is also a long-standing organiser of Thai-style beach parties.

Lucky Leprechaun Surfer (☎ 077 635 1965; beers R150-200; ⏰ 7.30am-10.30pm) Raised high above the beach with fantastic views, this is a great place to watch the waves while being served by Fasmeen, a remarkable Freddie Mercury lookalike. Hammock in centre, whiffs of weed.

Roccos (☎ 077 664 2991) Located in Roccos hotel (p273), this Brit-managed beachside bar-restaurant has music that swerves somewhat schizophrenically from trance-house to soft jazz.

Palm Grove Guest House (☎ 224 8457; beers Rs 110, arrack shots Rs 55; ⏰ 10am-10pm) This is a surprisingly airy place to get slammed with local boozers.

Mambo's (☎ 077 782 2524; ⏰ May-Sep) In season, this hotel (p272) is *the* place for weekend beach parties.

Getting There & Around

Buses to Colombo and Badulla pick up in Arugam Bay at around 6.30am and 12.30pm respectively. Otherwise take a three-wheeler to Pottuvil (whole vehicle Rs 100, per person shared Rs 20) and continue from there.

It's possible to rent motorcycles from some guesthouses and from **A-bay Surf Shop** (☎ 077 707 0307, 077 958 5008; per hr Rs 350). Prices are somewhat random. Order one day ahead.

SOUTH OF ARUGAM BAY
Arugam Bay to Panama

Kilometres of untouched sandy beaches stretch south of Arugam Bay. The roughly asphalted lane to Panama stays somewhat inland but intersects with lagoons where you can spot waterfowl, wading birds, wallowing water buffalo and even the odd elephant. **Panama** is a sleepy little place with an attractive new white **dagoba** at the entry to the village. Panama's wide but unshaded arc of sandy beach is a kilometre east through town, skirting a lagoon and passing a graveyard. There's a surf break but seas are usually too heavy for safe swimming.

The NGO **Sewalanka** (www.sewalanka.org) is planning home stays, but as yet there's no accommodation.

The road from Arugam Bay to Panama is low in places and may be under water in the wet season (beware of crocodiles). If it's not too bad, you can make the trip in a three-wheeler (one way Rs 400) or wait for rare leaving-when-full buses.

Panama to Okanda

The road to Okanda is not asphalted, but it has been newly regraded. Just south of Panama village it crosses paddy fields and a marshy patch that attracts **crocodiles**. However, to see many more crocs, take the unmarked right fork soon after this marsh (the left fork is signed to Kumana). Continue along the sometimes sandy road for 2.5km to fabled **Crocodile Lake** (Kimbulawala), an attractive ancient tank where dozens of the creatures are menacingly visible at dusk.

Continuing on the Okanda road, around 9km from Panama is a tiny but lovingly tended Ganesh (Pillaiyar) shrine. The rocky outcrop behind the shrine is topped with a new Buddha image called **Sanyasi Mulai** in Tamil or **Veheregama** in Sinhala. Ancient steps in the rock suggest considerable antiquity; scurry up for views of the larger-scale rocks at Kudimbigala.

The superb 4700-hectare site of **Kudimbigala Forest Hermitage** is a marvellous jumble of Sigiriya-style outcrops set in dense jungle. Over 200 shrines and hermits' lodgings are set in caves or sealed rocky overhangs here. While none is individually especially interesting, the dagoba-topped summit of the highest rock offers marvellous panoramas across the eccentric landscape and expansive forest canopy. There are glimpses of lagoon and sand bars towards the shore, and the far southwestern horizon is distantly serrated by the spiky Weliara Ridge.

The Kudimbigala access track leads 2km west of the main Okanda track; although the sign at the junction of the road and the initial path has been ripped down, the turning is obvious enough. At the track's end take the path between the single pilgrims' rest building and the dagoba. The cave lip above the first whitewashed shrine has curious 2000-year-old Brahmi runes inscribed across it. From here bear right to find the steep, grooved steps to the highest summit. A metal guide rope helps, but descending could be dangerous in rain. If you're keen, there is a maze of smaller tracks linking

other caves, rocks, and even a wooden 'gong' fashioned from a hollow tree trunk.

No buses go beyond Panama, but the village has its own three-wheeler stand, 200m east of the Okanda junction; drivers ask around Rs 1500 for a half-day excursion to Okanda.

Okanda

The Arugam–Okanda road ends at the entry gate for Yala East National Park. Immediately east of the gate, Okanda is a seasonal settlement for local fishermen and home to the **Murugan Devale** (a *devale* is a complex designed for worshipping a Hindu or Sri Lankan deity). Though relatively small, the main temple has a very colourful *gopuram* (gateway tower), which survived the 2004 tsunami and is a major point on the Pada Yatra pilgrimage to Kataragama (see boxed text, p159). In trouble-free years, thousands of pilgrims gather here during the two weeks before the July *poya* (full moon) before attempting the last, and most dangerous, five-day leg of the 45-day trek from Jaffna.

The temple is of great spiritual importance as it marks the supposed point at which Murugan (Skanda) and his consort Valli arrived in Sri Lanka on stone boats. On the front frieze of the temple you'll see Murugan riding a peacock, with Valli and Dewani (a second consort of Murugan) at his side. He's watched by his mischievous brother Ganesh. Valli has her own tiny shrine on the **Okanda Malai rocks**, which rise directly above the main temple. Folds in those rocks create over 30 small *teertham* (holy pools), in which Valli is believed to have bathed. Pilgrims do the same, despite the water's rather green and stagnant appearance.

Just five minutes' walk from the temple is a sweeping beige white **surfing beach**. It's bracketed by two rocky promontories that devotees consider to be the remnants of Murugan's and Valli's divine stone boats. Surfers often camp on the dunes.

Yala East National Park & Kumana Reserve

This 18,149-hectare **park** (admission permits around Rs 1600; 5.30am-6pm) is much less frequently visited than its busy neighbour, Yala National Park. For the visitor, the result is a less 'zoolike' experience. However, with less manpower to prevent poaching, the range

WE'RE NOT IN KANSAS ANYMORE

Anyone venturing into this region should not forget that most of the east coast remains a potential conflict zone. At the risk of spelling out the blindingly obvious, don't snap unauthorised photographs of soldiers, checkpoints, military posts or potentially strategic sites like ports and bridges. Be aware that many locals will be too nervous to speak openly in public about politics, especially if that involves implied criticism of the feared LTTE. Patience and understanding pay off.

and density of animals is also less. The best-known feature is the 200-hectare **Kumana bird reserve**, an ornithologically rich mangrove swamp some 22km beyond Okanda. May to June is nesting season. The park also includes ruins, deer, elephants and touted-but-rare leopards. There have been sightings of Sri Lanka's very rare black-necked stork. The most famous resident is Okandaraja, a crossed-tusk elephant.

Nonspecialist visitors may find that the permit-free surrounding area has enough crocodiles, elephants and birdlife to render a trip into the park an unnecessary expense.

The **park information centre** (☎ 063-224 8623) at the Okanda gate has a three-dimensional map and reptile-identification posters, but is not enormously helpful.

Some agencies, including Colombo-based **Eco Team** (☎ in Colombo 011-553 3330; www.srilanka ecotourism.com) and **Arugam Bay Hillton Guest House** (☎ /fax in Arugam Bay 063-224 8189; www.arugambay.lk) can arrange camping within the park, starting from Rs 4000 above basic trip costs.

Visits to Yala East get expensive because you'll need to rent a jeep (typically Rs 8000 per day on top of permit charges). No motorcycles are allowed.

POTTUVIL TO BATTICALOA

You can head north from Pottuvil in relatively easy minibus hops via the predominantly Muslim towns of Akkaraipattu and Kalmunai. Although the route parallels the coast, sea views are minimal, and from Pottuvil to Batticaloa villages have merged to form what is virtually one unattractive strip town. Add the still considerable tsunami damage plus **Akkaraipattu**'s communal ten-

sions (which saw grenade attacks between LTTE forces and Muslims in November 2005) and the area doesn't make for an ideal destination. The longer route via Ampara is more picturesque and has more sights; see p268, p269 and p280 for more details.

AMPARA
☎ 063

This reasonably prosperous district capital, patchily dappled with paddy fields, lakes and palm groves, is a possible base for visits to the Gal Oya National Park and various beautiful lakes and tanks in the surrounding countryside. It's a local transport hub, and is currently the base for many NGO workers, who find the town's workmanlike hospitality, good order and lack of Islamic restrictions much easier than the ravaged coastal towns.

Orientation & Information
Ampara is very spread out. DS Senanayake Rd is the main commercial street.

Chan Computer House (☎ 077 717 3987; 75 DS Senanayake Rd; per min Rs 8; ☺ 9am 6pm) Friendly Internet place. You can prepare your emails for free.

Commercial Bank (DS Senanayake Rd; ☺ 9am-3pm Mon-Fri) Has ATM, and changes money. Several other banks towards the clock tower also have ATMs.

Maura Communications (DS Senanayake Rd; per min Rs 8; ☺ 8am-9pm) Internet place. You can also make telephone calls here.

Sights
West beyond the clock tower and bus station, DS Senanayake Rd leads towards Inginyagala, passing scenic Ampara Tank. After about 2km (just after the 25km marker), a short right turn brings you to the graceful **Japanese Peace Pagoda**. Come here just before dusk for an almost certain chance of seeing **wild elephants**. As though on command, they pass as through a narrow passageway right in front of the pagoda. The point is even marked 'Wild Elephant Crossing'. But this is no circus show. There is a palpable sense of awe among those who come to watch; after all, wild elephants killed five humans around Ampara in 2005 alone.

The central Buddhist **Mandala Mahavihara** (Kachcheri Rd) has a large pagoda. Its interior is somewhat tackily painted with Buddhist scenes and a cloud-dotted 'sky', but it's worth a visit to listen to the eerie echoes. **Sri Manika Pillaiyar** (Inginyagala Rd) gives Ganesh

CENTRAL AMPARA

0   500 m
0   0.3 miles

To Maha
Oya (58km);
Dambana (99km);
Kandy (185km)

To Kachcheri (350km);
Buddhangala Rock
Hermitage (7km)

Kandy Rd

Dutugemunu Rd

7

Kachcheri Rd

Cinema Rd

Ampara
Tank

4

Clock
Tower

10

3

DS Senanayake Rd

2

A31

5

To Manika
Pilliyar (1km);
Japanese Peace
Pagoda (2km);
Kondawatawana (5km);
Polowate (16km);
Inginyagala (18km)

11

6th Ave

5th Ave

4th Ave

3rd Ave

2nd Ave

1st Ave

1

9

To Deegawapi (23km);
Kalmunai (29km);
Akiraipattu (43km);
Siyambulanduwa (56km);
Arugam Bay (90km)

Cabada Rd

1st Ave

8

6

INFORMATION
Chan Computer House.....................1 B2
Commercial Bank 2 B2
Maura Communications...................3 A2

SIGHTS & ACTIVITIES
Mandala Mahavihara........................4 B2

SLEEPING
Ariyasiri Rest................................5 B2
Monty Guest House........................6 B3
Rest House..................................7 A1
SMC Guest House..........................8 B3

EATING
Chinese & Western Food Court.........9 B2
New City Food Cabin.....................10 A2

TRANSPORT
Bus Station.................................11 A2

a lovely view across Ampara Tank; it's at the 24km post.

Although it was once known as Digamadulla, after founding king Digayu, today's Ampara shows few signs of its great antiquity. However, one minor historical curiosity is the **inscription stone** housed in the foyer of the *kachcheri* (administrative office). Found at Kondawatawana 5km to the west, it instructs villagers on how to punish crimes (and ploughing errors!).

Sleeping

Monty Guest House (☎ 222 2169; C32 1st Ave; r Rs 650-4000; ⚡) The top choice has obliging staff and 50 rooms of varying quality. The best are full-facility air-con suites with lovely

sitting areas from where you can gaze out across the paddy fields. These have hot water, coffee-making facilities and mini-bars, and are often booked out by NGO workers. The cheapest rooms are contrastingly basic, with very worn paintwork and dodgy shared showers. Rooms in between include drab air-con twins from Rs 1500. Monty's is hidden away in a peaceful, green residential area that's a 10-minute stroll south of Commercial Bank.

Rest House (☎ 222 3612; Dutugemunu Rd; dm Rs 220-303) The five beds in these dorm-style rooms are charged according to how many people sleep in the room; prices range from Rs 303 for one bed to Rs 1028 for all five. It's clean, if institutional, with recently redecorated bathrooms and a peaceful yet central location. To find it, walk two blocks north up Kandy Rd from the clock tower, then turn right. It has a basic bar and dining room.

Ariyasiri Rest (☎ 222 3282; 3rd Ave; s Rs 400, tw 500-900, tr Rs 850-950) This place is visible from DS Senanayake Rd, but is entered through a squalidly narrow crack in the wall of the side street. The entry is enough to put off all but the hardiest customer. Yet, if you dare to squeeze through the first building of demoralisingly cramped dosshouse rooms, you'll find a surprisingly pleasant second house in the rear garden. Rooms here are neat and clean, set off a communal upstairs dining area. Some share sparklingly clean new bathrooms, others have private facilities but are mustier.

SMC Guest House (☎ 222 3589; 1st Ave; d Rs 500) This small fall-back next door to Monty's tends to attract noisy arrack drinkers and by-the-hour custom.

Eating

Chinese & Western Food Court (☎ 222 2215; Gabada Rd; mains Rs 200-450; ⚡ 11.30am-3pm & 6-10.30pm) Set in a tropical garden, this is far-and-away Ampara's most alluring dining place. The wide range of well-cooked dishes includes good stir-fried cuttlefish and excellent 'crumb chicken' – think Kentucky smeared with crushed garlic.

Monty Guest House (☎ 222 2169; buffet Rs 350; ⚡ 6.30-10pm) The six-dish buffet dinners served around a lily-covered pool and bamboo grove at this guesthouse (left) are great for meeting expat visitors. It's reliably tasty, though there's little variation night after night. Don't confuse it with poky little Monty Restaurant on DS Senanayake Rd.

New City Food Cabin (meals Rs 50-130; ⏰ 7am-9pm) The brightest of several budget eateries around the clock tower, this place rings with the deafening knifework of the *kotthu rotti* maker each evening. It also serves tasty fish rolls (Rs 18) and cutlet balls (Rs 12).

Getting There & Away

AIR
For scenic, weather-dependent hops to Colombo's Bandaranaike International Airport, **Sri Lankan Air Taxi** (☎ 019-733 3355; www.srilankan .aero/airtaxi) flies from a small military airport 5km northwest of Ampara town. Planes leave according to demand, most frequently on Mondays and Fridays. It's US$200 per person (50 minutes), or US$800 for the whole plane.

BUS
The bus station is directly south of the clock tower. For Kandy, intercity buses (Rs 255, 4½ hours) leave every 45 minutes from 5.30am; normal buses (Rs 98, six hours) take longer. Buses to Colombo (Rs 300, 10 hours) leave regularly between 4pm and 8pm, some looping north via Kandy, others passing through Monaragala and Ratnapura. The Colombo buses can be prebooked.

For Arugam Bay you could minibus-hop via Akkaraipattu (Rs 32) and Pottuvil. Or, more attractively, leave before 1.15pm on any southbound bus to Siyambulanduwa and change there. For Batticaloa, minibus-hop via Kalmunai (Rs 30).

For the Hill Country there's a 2.30pm service to Nuwara Eliya (Rs 80, 2½ hours), while 6.10am and 2pm buses to Badulla take a superbly scenic country route via Bibile. There are 10 daily buses to Buttala and Monaragala, several continuing to Matara on the south coast.

AROUND AMPARA

☎ 063

Buddhangala
When approached through the secondary-growth scrub from Ampara or viewed across the paddies from the Ampara–Kalmunai road, **Buddhangala Rock Hermitage** (☎ 222 2030; donation appropriate) looks to be little more than a slight bump on the horizon. Yet at around

150m tall, it's the highest point in the area: from the top there's a wide panorama of surprisingly impressive views. Thanks to a very conscientious monk-guide and a useful explanatory pamphlet in English, the site's special spiritual relevance comes to life. Within an ancient cave overhang there's a small but interesting case of museum-style treasures. Revered Buddha relics are concreted into the sizable whitewashed dagoba. Beside the dagoba a squat and unaesthetic concrete building has an eight-frame 'history' of Buddhism in Sri Lanka painted on the ceiling. Frame six shows Dutugemunu's army heading for battle; armed with picnic skewers, the soldiers look rather fey, but the scene is controversial for it's political (rather than religious) focus. Ignoring all this is a large seated Buddha resembling Boy George, complete with karma chameleon aura.

The hermitage is 7km from Ampara; three-wheelers cost Rs 400 return.

Deegawapi
Deegawapi (Dighavapi Cetiya) is the one place in southeastern Sri Lanka that the Buddha supposedly visited in person – and three times at that – making the place of particular spiritual importance to Buddhists. It was built during the reign of King Saddartissa (137–119 BC) and patched up in the 2nd and 18th centuries AD before becoming lost in the jungle. Rediscovered in 1916, it has for decades been at the centre of disputes with the area's predominantly Muslim population, who fear the site could become a bridgehead for Sinhalese colonisation. Deegawapi's aged chief monk was killed in one such spat in 1952.

For many tourists the site isn't quite interesting enough to warrant the lengthy detour. While the vast central dagoba stub is intriguingly massive, its ancient red bricks lack the appealing forest setting of similar Yudaganawa. Nonetheless there is the compensation of a small **archaeological museum** (admission free; ⏰ 8.30am-3.30pm Wed-Mon), and numerous ancient flower altars and jumbled Buddha and elephant carvings ranged around the dagoba's circumference.

Gal Oya National Park & Inginyagala
Scenic rock-pocked and forested hills create a marvellously impressive horizon behind the waters of **Senanayake Samudra**, Sri Lanka's

biggest reservoir. The easiest way to view the scene is to climb the 40m-high dam, accessed at a small guard post opposite the hydropower station, 1km west of the Inginyagala roundabout (at the 41km post). The 78-sq-km sea, formed by the dam in 1948, is the main feature of the 62,936-hectare **Gal Oya National Park**. It supports a local fishing industry, water birds (notably cormorants) and a wide variety of wildlife, including plenty of elephants, which can be spotted in unusually large groups here.

To enter the park you'll need to arrange things with the **park office** (☎ 224 2002; permits per day US$14; ⏰ 24hr), which is in woodland off the main road between the dam and the roundabout. Minimal English is spoken.

The ideal way to visit the park is by boat; however, the park authorities don't allow tourists to charter fishing boats and the park's own craft is currently out of commission. Eventually you should be able to arrange tours through **Safari Inn** (☎ 224 2147; prem_lake@yahoo.com), which is rebuilding to ambitious standards, a decrepit old hotel 300m south of the Inginyagala roundabout. Some ecotour agents advertise Gal Oya trips (see, for example, www.srilankaecotourism.com/galoya_national_park.htm), but in reality departures are rare.

While in Inginyagala, take a look at the well-signed **Fatima Shrine**, whose naive-style Christian statuary fills an attractive garden. It culminates in a Madonna statue on a tall brick pillar, half lost in the tentacles of a banyan tree.

From Ampara several buses per hour run to Inginyagala (Rs 18, 40 minutes) via Polowate. Six daily buses continue to Wadinagala, including the 6pm to Colombo via Siyambulanduwa and Monaragala.

Inginyagala to Bibile

Just 2km east of Inginyagala on the A31 is **Polowate** village, where the recently excavated **Owagiriya Ruins** are 200m south of the main road. Thought to date from King Saddartissa's reign (2nd century BC), they include a 2m decapitated Buddha torso and several pillar stubs, but there's minimal visual wow factor.

The very peaceful B527 jungle road from Polowate to Bibile is one of the most attractive in the region. Some 8km from Polowate it crosses the bund of the picturesque **Namal**

Oya Tank, which still sprouts the stumps of drowned trees. Beyond, it follows the Gal Oya National Park boundary, and after Mullegama there are wonderfully jumbled rocky outcrops draped in lush forest.

Two daily Ampara–Bibile buses (Rs 80, 2½ hours), eventually bound for Badulla, use this road, departing Ampara at 6.15am and 2pm.

Bibile
☎ 055

Busy little Bibile is a typical junction town, but it has a handful of 'ancient' temples, each around 5km from the town centre. Essentially, the temples are relatively modern rural monasteries around some fairly minimal ruins – their charm lies in their peaceful settings and the local monks' total surprise to see tourists at all. The ruins at **Kotasera** are flanked by two curious lemon-yellow prayer houses that look more like Vietnamese Cao Dai churches, while its 200-year-old **image house**, in front of the main dagoba, has some beast and demon reliefs. The approach road through mossy rubber trees and across mountain-backed rice paddies has a few briefly spectacular sections. En route you can make a rough 1km detour to **Badullagamma Monastery**, which has a degraded 500-year old reclining Buddha torso and some faded murals.

Appealingly situated **Nagala Viharaya** (☎ 226 5603) is also very historic, but it is most interesting for offering **meditation retreats**, due to start in 2006. These will be run in a brand-new prayer hall with six simple guest rooms. Before arriving, arrange details with Reverend Sumonasara, who has a Dalai Lama sense of humour and studied at Catford in London. Nagala's **Cobra Rock**, named for its snakes, not its shape, slopes down to a bucolic tank. It's an idyllic spot to watch ox ploughs working the paddies, with the Hill Country rising up as a wide backdrop.

Of Bibile's three guesthouses, the best is **Sisila Rest Inn** (☎ 226 5691; Pitakumbura Rd; tr Rs 550), about 200m down the B527 towards Ampara. The five rooms have clean bathrooms and food available if you order in advance. No English is spoken.

Mecency Chinese (☎ 226 5279; Badulla Rd; meals Rs 55-150; ⏰ 11.30am-2.30pm & 5-9.30pm), above the Abans Electronics store, is marginally Bibile's best eatery. Décor is limited to two drooping palm fronds, but the egg fried rice (Rs 90) is uncommonly excellent.

With twice-hourly buses to Monaragala (1¼ hours), Badulla (Rs 50, 2½ hours), and Mahiyangana (1¾ hours), Bibile is a handy transport hub. The Badulla run is scenically magnificent. Badulla–Batticaloa buses also pass through. The main bus station is at the town's southern edge, 200m south of the Monaragala junction, but most buses trawl through town to the market before finally departing.

Ampara to Mahiyangana

In contrast to the beautiful southerly roads, this route lacks any real scenic splendour. There is eerily deserted scrubland between Uhana and tiny **Maha Oya**, whose one 'attraction' is **Kunuwaturebubule**, a handful of entirely dull volcanically heated wells 2km north of town. If stranded in Maha Oya, **Wijewickrama Restaurant** (☎ 063-224 4001; Kandy Rd; tw Rs 650) has three rooms, one with a grubby private bathroom and noises in the roof.

Regions flanking the A5 and the A26 beyond are much more heavily populated. The latter skirts the southern edge of the **Maduru Oya National Park**, created to protect the water-catchment area of the big **Mahaweli Dam project**, which irrigates a vast new settlement area and was so significant that it featured on some Rs 2 coins. However, the park's creation mean that the **Veddahs** (p43), Sri Lanka's indigenous peoples, were suddenly branded as poachers for continuing their millennia-old hunter-gatherer lifestyle.

DAMBANA

The easiest way to encounter Veddah people is to visit Dambana, just 5km off the A26. Dambana comprises four subvillages, but you'll inevitably be brought to Kotabakina, where there are 10 traditional-style Veddah homes with thatched roofs and mud floors. On arrival you're likely to encounter a gaggle of long-bearded Veddah men beckoning you in. If the chief, Ururuwarige Wanniya-Laeto, is in residence, you'll first be introduced to him. He sits surrounded by photos of his meetings with minor celebrities and of his revered father (ancestors are gods in Veddah religion). The correct Veddah greeting is to say '*Honda Mai*' while grabbing the other's forearms (proving that you are unarmed!). After this, the men will typi-

cally whisk you off to another house to see **dancing** and **archery** displays, while trying to flog you honey, leopards' teeth and rough-hewn medicine cups. Especially without a translator this can feel uncomfortably voyeuristic, somewhat like hill-tribe tours in Thailand. In a well-intentioned but as yet unproven attempt to improve the present situation, an impressive **Veddah Heritage Centre** (Wariga Rukul Pojja; ☉ 7am-5pm), between Kotabakina and Dambana school, is nearing completion. The site includes an authentically styled Veddah house and tree hut, and plans to highlight the tribe's ecofriendly lifestyle, make comparisons with other aboriginal peoples and even offer tastings of *potu-pojja* (stone-baked *rotti*). The idea is to celebrate and perpetuate Veddah culture, though almost by definition any commercialisation of that culture is liable to have the opposite effect.

Although ethnically Sinhalese, casual guide **GEM Jaisundara** (☎ 077 314 2419) speaks Veddah language and some English, and can take keen visitors to Veddah haunts deep in the jungle.

Ampara–Kandy buses and very slow Maha Oya–Mahiyangana minibuses stop at the 90km marker on the A26. Waiting three-wheelers charge Rs 150 return to Kotabakina. A three-wheeler from Mahiyangana costs Rs 350 return.

Ampara to Batticaloa

KALMUNAI

☎ 067

The only reason most tourists stop in Kalmunai is to change buses on the way between Batticaloa and Ampara or Pottuvil. The town does have a strikingly attractive arc of palm-backed beach. However, the whole foreshore is still littered with tsunami-wrecked building foundations, hardly creating a holiday atmosphere. And strong Islamic mores don't exactly encourage bikinis. The easiest beach access is 1km down Rest House Rd, the first asphalted street to the right if you're walking north from the minibus station – the Central Transport Board (CTB) bus station is just across a Y-junction from that minibus station, facing People's Bank.

New **Superstar Tourist Inn** (☎ 222 9022; 23/1 Yard Rd; d Rs 1500-2000; 🞲), in a houselike building, has fresh, air-conditioned rooms, most with hot water units in spacious private bathrooms. Simpler Rs 1500 rooms share a bathroom. Yard Rd is on the left-hand side of Rest House Rd, halfway to the beach. Wind north for around 700m and you'll find the inn set in an attractive garden to the right.

New London Guest House (☎ 222 4525; 103 Rest House Rd; d with fan/air-con Rs 1500/2500; 🕄) is better known but less appealing than Superstar, with clean rooms ranged around an unexotic eating area that can get noisy. The cheaper fan rooms are pretty small and tend to overheat. All have a small bathroom. The beer garden out the front is popular.

KALMUNAI TO BATTICALOA

Minibuses fill rapidly, but the mere 39km takes around 1½ hours. The journey is tediously slow through almost continuous strip villages; you'll get glimpses of lagoon and beach only when crossing the causeways. Many concrete-box Hindu temples along the way have typically colourful décor, including one with a five-headed giant cobra licking a *lingam* (phallic symbol) at **Koddaikallar**.

BATTICALOA

☎ 065

Batticaloa, Batti for short, has no must-see sights. Nonetheless the relatively compact, steamy centre oozes an intangible charm, magnified by the palm-filtered sunlight glancing off the surrounding lagoons. Around town, the beaches are gorgeous if utterly undeveloped.

Orientation

Central Old Batti is a bridge-linked island sheltered within a complex lagoon system. It's gripped from the north by a double-pronged peninsula; the eastern prong (Koddamunai) shares the commercial centre and hosts the train station. Koddamunai itself is linked by a big bridge to a long, beach-edged southern peninsula (Kallady), down which New Batti extends for some 10km towards Kalmunai.

Information

Bank of Ceylon (Covington Rd; 🕄 9am-3pm Mon-Fri)
Commercial Bank (Bar Rd; 🕄 9am-3pm Mon-Fri) Has an ATM.
Internet Café (22 Lloyds Ave; per hr Rs 50; 🕄 8.30am-8.30pm) The very friendly owner speaks Dutch and English.

People's Bank (Advocate's Rd; 🕄 8.30am-3pm Mon-Fri)
Post office (Post Office Rd) One of the colonial-era post boxes here is over 90 years old.
Wisdom Cafe (☎ 222 2963; 70/1 Bar Rd; per 20 min Rs 20-30; 🕄 7.30am-8.30pm) Internet café.

Sights & Activities

OLD BATTI

Wandering around Old Batti is particularly atmospheric late at night: cicadas scream and water drips, but not a soul stirs on the eerily empty streets. Dim street lamps give lugubrious form to shadows in the various colonial edifices like **St Joseph's Convent** (St Mary's St), **St Michael's College** (Central Rd) or the sturdy 1838 **Methodist Church** (Post Office Rd). Of the dozens of churches, the most eye-catching are the huge, unfinished **Our Lady of Sorrows** (Trinco Rd), the vaguely Mexican, earth-toned **St Anthony's** (St Anthony's St) and the grand, turquoise **St Mary's Cathedral** (St Mary's St). St Mary's was rebuilt in 1994 following its partial destruction during fighting between local Tamils and Muslims. Beside Kallady Bridge is the fairly modern **St Sebastian's Church** (Kalmunai Rd), built in the shape of a whale.

Of the many Hindu temples, **Anipandi Sitivigniswara Alayar** (Hospital Rd) is visually the finest, with a magnificent *gopuram* that's decorated with a riotous festival of intertwined god figures.

The 6m-thick walls of Batti's **Dutch fort** (Bazaar St) surround the rambling *kachcheri*. The walls themselves are not especially beautiful but they do have a 1707 **VOC inscription**, standing for Verenigde Oostindische Compagnie (Dutch East India Company), which you can view while walking along the east-facing battlements. Be sure that you ask permission before approaching the fort and again before climbing the walls as parts remain under military control and the whole zone can sometimes become off limits.

A great place to observe the fort is from across the water, beside the tiny **Auliya Mosque** (Lady Manning Dr), with its curious green minaret.

The **Butterfly Peace Garden** (☎ 222 3492; 1A Jesuit St; admission free; 🕄 9am-6.30pm Mon-Tue, 5.30-6.30pm Wed-Sun) is a peaceful little oasis for children, though it primarily aims to provide play therapy for those affected by war and the tsunami.

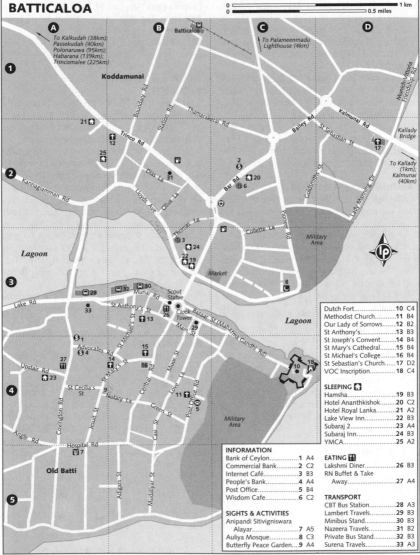

BATTICALOA

INFORMATION
Bank of Ceylon	1	A4
Commercial Bank	2	C2
Internet Café	3	B3
People's Bank	4	A4
Post Office	5	B4
Wisdom Cafe	6	C2

SIGHTS & ACTIVITIES
Anipandi Sitivigniswara Alayar	7	A5
Auliya Mosque	8	C3
Butterfly Peace Garden	9	A4
Dutch Fort	10	C4
Methodist Church	11	B4
Our Lady of Sorrows	12	B2
St Anthony's	13	B3
St Joseph's Convent	14	B4
St Mary's Cathedral	15	B4
St Michael's College	16	B4
St Sebastian's Church	17	D2
VOC Inscription	18	C4

SLEEPING
Hamsha	19	B3
Hotel Ananthkishok	20	C2
Hotel Royal Lanka	21	A2
Lake View Inn	22	B3
Subaraj 2	23	A4
Subaraj Inn	24	B3
YMCA	25	A2

EATING
Lakshmi Diner	26	B3
RN Buffet & Take Away	27	A4

TRANSPORT
CBT Bus Station	28	A3
Lambert Travels	29	B3
Minibus Stand	30	B3
Nazeera Travels	31	B2
Private Bus Stand	32	B3
Surena Travels	33	A3

KALLADY

Kallady has an idyllic strip of beach, but the rubble of tsunami damage remains everywhere. Notice the colourful **Tiruchendur Murugan Alayam temple** (Navalady Rd), which sits near the beach between Third and Fourth Cross Streets. Built in 1984 as a stopping point on the Pada Yatra pilgrimage to Kataragama, its

Murugan image is reputed to have opened its own eyes before the painter could do the job. The structure was slammed by the tsunami, leaving its small *gopuram* leaning at an alarming angle. While visiting the site might seem like car-crash voyeurism, tourists are encouraged – their donations will eventually help to right the tower.

THE LAGOON

Bizarrely, Batti is famous for its **'singing fish'**. Some describe the noise as a dolphin-like clicking and chirruping. Others have likened it to the sound produced by rubbing a moistened finger around the rim of a glass. Whether these were 'sung' by shoals of catfish, clusters of shellfish or various musical crustaceans, nobody's sure. In fact, since the 1960s very few locals have heard the 'singing' at all. Nonetheless the whole comical palaver can be amusing whether or not you actually hear anything; put a nylon string to your ear and dangle the other end in the lagoon water – ideally from a boat.

Some 5km north of central Batti, the 1913 **Palameenmadu lighthouse** was sturdy enough to survive the tsunami. It's not spectacular but its lagoon setting is lovely. To get to the lighthouse, follow Pioneer Rd north then wind along the attractive lagoonside, passing a palm-shaded landing point where outrigger fishermen bring home the catch around noon.

Sleeping

There's nowhere luxurious to stay in Batti. Many options are decidedly poor value by Sri Lankan standards but most are fully booked anyway so reservations are wise.

CENTRAL BATTI

Subaraj Inn (☎ 222 5983; 6/1 Lloyds Ave; s/tw Rs 1230/1980; ✷) In *Only Man Is Vile*, William McGowan gets smuggled into Batti around 1987 to find Subaraj as the only hotel, its outside wall chipped and pocked with bullets fired by the 'peacekeeping' Indian army. These days things are much calmer and the air-conditioned Subaraj is a popular place. The bar and dining area certainly makes it the cosiest central option, but the rooms are damp and often windowless. Beneath new paint the walls have peeling sections. Subaraj 2, the unmarked annex on 1A Upstair Rd, has fresher, more appealing rooms, though they're still somewhat bare and gloomy. Check in at the Subaraj.

Hotel Ananthkishok (☎ 222 7283; top fl, 32 Bar Rd; s Rs 1500; ✷) Because this place is new it's currently in great shape. Unfussy box-like rooms have shiny tiled floors, great air-conditioning and beds just about large enough for a cosy couple. However, many lamp bulbs are already missing, attached

KALLADY

(map) Navalady, 9th Cross St, 8th Cross St Rd, 7th Cross St, 6th Cross St, 5th Cross St, 4th Cross St, 3rd Cross St, 2nd Cross St, New Bar Rd, Lagoon, Bridge View Hotel, To Batticaloa (500m), Riviera Resort, Kallady Bridge, To Kalmunai (39km), INDIAN OCEAN, Beach, Tiruchendur Murugan Alayam Temple

toilets get sprayed by the shower and there's a slight concern with privacy as the flimsy curtains flap open when the fan is running. Management is haphazard.

YMCA (☎ 222 2495; Boundary Rd; tr/5-bed r Rs 900/2000; ✷) The five-bed dormitory-style rooms here have good air-conditioning but are not available on a per-bed basis. The triples are fan-cooled. All have OK private bathrooms, and the position close to the lagoon is attractive, if mosquito prone.

Lake View Inn (☎ 222 2339; 6B Lloyds Ave; tw with/without bathroom Rs 650/550, with bathroom & air-con Rs 1350; ✷) They're hardly appealing but the simplest rooms here are survivable, despite missing window slats – assuming you can persuade the boss to string up a mosquito net. The shared bathrooms aren't jolly. Ground-floor air-con rooms are particularly miserable, dark and musty.

Hamsha (☎ 222 3632; 2 Lloyds Ave; tw Rs 900) There are no nets in these grubby rooms with wet, uncleaned private bathrooms. Entry is via a flimsy metal staircase above a beer shop, and the reception is the 3rd-floor bar. Only the location recommends this place.

Hotel Royal Lanka (☎ 077 326 8279; 155 Trinco Rd; tw from Rs 400) The Rs 600 room with attached bathroom is the least depressing in this drably ordinary local hotel.

KALLADY

Peaceful and walkably close to the beach, these places are a Rs 100 three-wheeler ride from the town centre.

Riviera Resort (☎ 222 2164; New Dutch Bar Rd; s Rs 770, tw Rs 1100-1650) Perched at the water's edge with views of Kallady Bridge and the lagoon, this peaceful spot offers neat and clean, if unsophisticated, double rooms with prices that vary according to lagoon proximity. The Rs 1430 options are possibly the nicest, sharing an old-fashioned dining area, but the Rs 1650 twins each have a little terrace area of their own. Check out the tsunami photo album.

Bridge View Hotel (☎ 222 3723; 63/24 New Dutch Bar Rd; tw with fan/air-con Rs 1000/1800; ⚡) This is good value by Batti standards but less appealing than the Riviera; any bridge views are imagined. The ground-floor rooms beside the restaurant are somewhat nicer than those upstairs.

Eating & Drinking

RN Buffet & Take Away (☎ 222 2684; 42 Covington Rd; lunch buffets Rs 275, mains Rs 110-286; ⏱ 11am-3.30pm & 7-10.30pm; ⚡) This superclean little eatery above a grocery shop offers a six-dish lunch buffet that's not excessively spiced. Dinner is à la carte with devilled dishes, noodles and curries.

Lakshmi Diner (23 Munai Rd; rice & curry Rs 50; ⏱ 5.30am-9pm; ⚡) There's no English sign, but this place, facing a scout statue, is easy to spot. Flies and rubbish-laden floors look off-putting, but the eat-with-your-fingers vegetarian curries are cheap and excellent.

Madras Cafe (Trinco Rd; meals from Rs 60; ⏱ 5.30am-11.30pm; ⚡) Late-night *kotthu rotti*.

The guesthouses **Riviera Resort** (☎ 222 2164; New Dutch Bar Rd; mains Rs 150-350) and **Subaraj Inn** (☎ 222 5983; 6/1 Lloyds Ave; mains Rs 110-400) have recommended places to eat that serve fair local, Chinese and occasional Western options. Both have decent little bars.

Getting There & Away

BUS

CTB buses, private buses and minibuses all have separate but adjacent bus stations on Munai Rd. To prebook Colombo departures (Rs 250, seven hours), use one of several specialist booking offices, including **Lambert Travels** (☎ 222 7204; 60 Bazaar St) and **Surena Travels** (☎ 222 6152; Munai St).

For Polonnaruwa (Rs 50, two hours) there's a noon CTB bus and plenty of private services bound for a variety of eventual destinations. Badulla-bound buses at 6.15am and 11.30am go via Maha Oya. For Arugam Bay or Ampara go in hops via Kalmunai (Rs 30, 1½ hours); there are frequent buses and minibuses. Post buses to Mutur leave at 6.15am and 12.30pm, taking the LTTE-controlled coast road. Trinco buses travel via Habarana; there's a 6am express service (Rs 180, 5½ hours) that departs from outside **Nazeera Travels** (☎ 077 634 0351; 261 Trinco Rd); book your ticket at the agency.

TRAIN

You'll need to book one to 10 days ahead for berths or sleeperettes on the 7.15pm overnight train to Colombo (3rd/2nd/1st class Rs 310/420/700) via Polonnaruwa and Valaichchenai. A day train departs for Colombo at 6.40am.

AROUND BATTICALOA
Kalkudah & Passekudah Beaches
☎ 065

To the north of Batticaloa, two fine curves of swimming beach nuzzle either side of the palm-tipped Kalkudah headland. Long touted as the east coast's touristic crown jewels, they had been recovering from years of civil-war damage when the 2004 tsunami obliterated everything. One day this lovely area is likely to be redeveloped, but for now the few who venture out here have virtually the whole place to themselves.

The smaller, safer, if less majestic, beach is Passekudah, to the north. There's a ghoulish fascination in exploring the concrete skeletons of two former resort hotels that had been sabotaged by the LTTE during the civil war to prevent their use as army strongholds. They're probably free of land mines but it definitely pays to be cautious.

The longer, creamier-coloured **Kalkudah Bay Beach** is one of those paradisal postcard-perfect scenes dotted with occasional fishing boats and backed by palm plantations. The easiest beach approach is now blocked by an army camp at the end of the Valaichchenai–Kalkudah road. To reach the sand, bypass the camp and use the partly rebuilt beach-access lane 800m further southwest.

SLEEPING & EATING

The road southwest from Kalkudah village was once lined with modest hotels. Now only rubble remains amid the palms. The only accommodation now is a pair of basic guesthouses, set back about 2km from the beaches on the Kalkudah–Valaichchenai road. Food is available by advance request.

New Pearl Inn (☎ 225 7987; d/tw Rs 700/700) This place has six unremarkable but acceptable rooms with fan, nets and clean bathrooms, ranged behind a pleasantly airy, if plain, old sitting area.

Simla Inn (☎ 225 7184; r without bathroom Rs 400) Victoria, the owner of Simla Inn, is legendary for her great curries and her incredible perseverance in adversity. Her Simla Inn was the only guesthouse to sit out the raging battles of the 1990s civil war. Then, having finally patched up all the bullet holes, the building got flattened by the 2004 tsunami. Unperturbed, Simla has risen again, 100m west of New Pearl. It's an ultrasimple pair of breeze-block houses without plaster or adornment. Nonetheless the four small rooms are clean and the shared bathrooms functional.

GETTING THERE & AWAY
Three daily buses from Batticaloa (at 8.50am, 11.50am and 3.30pm) run to Kalkudah, passing Simla and New Pearl Inns. The last certain return is 1.30pm, though a 4pm service might run. Slow but much more frequent buses serve Valaichchenai (Rs 28, 1½ hours), which is 5km from the beaches. These get excruciatingly overcrowded between Eravur and Sittandy. Get off in Valaichchenai's market area; although the bus station is 1.5km closer to Kalkudah, finding three-wheelers (Rs 100) is harder there.

Buses on the Colombo–Polonnaruwa–Batti route might drop you off at the Valaichchenai junction on the A15. It's 2km south of Valaichchenai market but just 100m from Valaichchenai train station, where Colombo–Batticaloa trains stop twice daily. Be aware that there is a different train station called Kalkudah: it's tiny and very isolated, 2km southwest of Kalkudah beach on the seldom-used short-cut road from Kumburumoolai. Should you jump off a train here, turn right (north) and walk through the well-marked minefield towards the beach-access road.

Batticaloa to Trincomalee
From Valaichchenai most Trinco-bound traffic cuts inland via Habarana and Kantale, where virtually everyone stops to buy clay pots of locally famous **buffalo curd**. Al-

ternatively, twice-daily post buses take the coast road to Mutur, from where ferries cross Koddiyar Bay to Trinco. The road between Valaichchenai and Mutur has minimal views but does provide the frisson of crossing LTTE territory.

COASTAL ROUTE TO MUTUR
The surprisingly low-key LTTE '**border**' (☯ 6am-7pm) is just north of **Mankerni**, whose unusual modern **church** (Mutur Rd) has a doorway shaped like a silver fish mouth; look east from bus windows. It survived the 2004 tsunami, which hit during the Boxing Day service; virtually the whole village population was safe inside while their houses were washed into oblivion.

At **Panichchankeni** the road crosses a very flimsy causeway – attractive but unreliable in bad weather. The two biggest settlements in the LTTE zone are **Vakerai** (va-*hair*-ra) and **Kathiravely**, both of which have LTTE **martyr memorials**. Severe postwar and post-tsunami poverty means that many people are living in wattle-and-daub or *cadjan* huts. Government control resumes at Mahindapura, where checks can be stringent.

Gently charming features of the trip include the two river-crossings at **Verugal** and **Kiliveddy**, where photogenic little ferries, just big enough for the bus, are pulled across by hand, using metal wires. At Palatoppu, three-wheelers await to whisk pilgrims to **Seruwawila**, where the ancient **dagoba** is believed to contain a fragment of Buddha's

---

ROAD WRECKS
None of Sri Lanka's roads are motorways. But in the east, war and neglect mean some supposed 'highways' are actually potholed wrecks with collapsed bridges that are often bypassed rather than repaired. Post-tsunami donors have been eagerly signing up to rebuild roads across the region (see www.humanitarianinfo.org/sri lanka/docs/Annex-II.pdf), so expect a big improvement by 2008. However, nobody seems keen to rebuild the Mutur–Trinco road – it's now so appalling that buses are routed in a vast loop via Alyuru Junction and Kantale. For tourists, the happy result is an excuse to take the quietly attractive ferry ride across Koddiyar Bay.

forehead. It's briefly, if distantly, visible from the main road.

Beware that there is nowhere to stay between Valaichchenai and Mutur, and there was only very basic local *kadé* (streetside huts) for rather sorry snacks.

MUTUR
☎ 026

The vibrant Muslim village of Mutur (*mood'r*) is not an attraction in itself. However, the Trincomalee boat ride is pleasant, especially in the late afternoon with the low light sparkling off Koddiyar Bay. If stranded in Mutur, the **Jaleel Guesthouse** (☎ 223 8444; Tariq St; tr Rs 600) is survivable, if hardly ideal for single women. It's totally unmarked behind Jaleel Shop on an unpaved street roughly 1km from the port – around halfway to the market where the Batticaloa buses terminate. Ask for directions at the first snack shop to the right on exiting the ferry jetty, or at Jaleel Hotel (a cheap eatery in the market).

Buses to Batticaloa–Mutur (Rs 82, six hours) run twice daily, departing Mutur at 5.30am and 12.45pm, and Batticaloa at 6.15am and 12.30pm. There's a meal stop at Valaichchenai bus station – helpful if you're coming from the Kalkudah beaches.

There's no passable Mutur–Trinco road. Go by boat (Rs 50, one hour); launches currently depart at 7.30am, 11am, 3pm and 4.30pm in both directions, though schedules change fairly regularly. Half an hour before departure, collect a metal tag to guarantee your place in case of overcrowding.

TRINCOMALEE
☎ 026 / pop 57,000

Trincomalee (Trinco) appeals to tourists primarily as the gateway to the fine Uppuveli and Nilaveli beaches. Possibly the site of historic Gokana in the Mahavamsa (Great Chronicle), the town itself is mildly attractive and is situated around several picturesque bays and rocky peninsulas. Its economic trump card is a superb deep-water port, considered to be one of the world's finest. However, this has made it the target for all manner of foreign attacks: the Danish preceded the Portuguese, who desecrated the city's holiest Hindu shrine before losing Trinco to the Dutch. By the British takeover in 1795, the city had changed hands another seven times. It

suffered further attacks in WWII, this time from Japanese bombing raids.

Today the population is a potentially explosive mix of Tamils, Sinhalese and Muslims. Although the city was safe and enjoyably vibrant at the time of research, interethnic tensions erupted again in April 2006, so keep your ear to the ground.

Orientation

Trinco's commercial heart is squeezed into a narrow isthmus that leads south to a large out-of-bounds peninsula occupied by the navy. Historic Trinco is a small thumb of rock jutting northeast, guarded by the remnant walls of Fort Frederick.

Information

Of the several banks along Central Rd, **Commercial Bank** (193 Central Rd) and **Sampath Bank** (262 Central Rd) have the most reliable ATMs. Moneychanger **Thassim Jewellers** (Dockyard Rd; ☯ 9am-7.30pm) opens longer and offers better, commission-free exchange rates than the banks for cash and travellers cheques.

Places offering Internet access:

EdgeNet@Cafe (81A Rajavarothayam St; per hr Rs 50; ☯ 7am-10.30pm)

JSP Internet Cafe (380 Court Rd; per hr Rs 60; ☯ 8am-9pm)

PC Home (358 Court Rd; per hr Rs 60; ☯ 7am-9pm; 🖳) Usually the most reliable option.

Sights & Activities
FORT FREDERICK AREA

Built by the Portuguese, **Fort Frederick** was rebuilt by the Dutch. Today, British insignias crowns the tunnel-like gateway that pierces the fort's massively stout walls. Parts of the fortress are under military jurisdiction, but a stroll up to the big new standing **Buddha statue** at the **Gokana Temple** offers unhampered access to one stretch of the fortifications. Colonial-era buildings within the eastern section now house the *kachcheri*. The road beyond ends at **Swami Rock**, a 130m-high cliff nicknamed Lovers' Leap. On top is revered **Koneswaram Kovil** (☯ lingam viewing 7am-11.30pm & 4-6pm) Although not especially photogenic, it houses the rescued **Swayambhu Lingam** (p288), making it one of Sri Lanka's most spiritually important Hindu sites. The whole area is holy ground so, despite the painful gravel underfoot, you'll need to leave your shoes at the

TRINCOMALEE

INFORMATION
Bank of Ceylon...........**1** C2
Commercial Bank........**2** C2
EdgeNet@Cafe...........**3** C2
JSP Internet Cafe.......(see 4)
PC Home....................**4** C3
Post Office.................**5** C3
Sampath Bank............**6** B2
Thassim Jewellers........**7** C4

SIGHTS & ACTIVITIES
Fort Frederick.................**8** D2
Gokana Temple................**9** D2
Jayasumanarama,,,..........**10** B1
Kali Kovil.......................**11** C2
Kandasamy Kovil............**12** D1
Koneswaram Kovil...........**13** C3
Our Lady of Guadalupe....**14** B1
St Mary's Cathedral.........**15** C3
St Nicholas....................**16** C4
St Stephen's Cemetery.....**17** C3
Seated Buddha Statue......**18** C2

SLEEPING
Chinese Guesthouse.........**19** C3
Dyke Corner Inn..............**20** D3
Harbour View Guest
  House.,,, ...**21** A2
Kumars.........................**22** C3

Medway Hotel................**23** B2
Sunflower.....................**24** C3
Welcombe Hotel............**25** A3

EATING
6 to 9........................(see 4)
Family Needs.................**26** C3
Geeth Me....................**27** C2

TRANSPORT
Bus Station...................**28** C2
Ferry to Mutur...............**29** B3
Sri Lankan Air Taxi Agency....**30** C3

To Colombo (255km)
To Uppuveli (6km);
Nilaveli (15km)
BAY OF BENGAL
Swami Rock
Trincomalee
Station Rd
North Coast Rd
NC Rd (Enampuram Rd)
School La
Central Rd
Main St
Sivapuri Rd
Sivan St
To Airport (China Bay);
Kanniyai Hot Wells (7km);
Velgam Vihara (10km);
Habarana (91km);
Anuradhapura (106km);
Kandy (182km)
Radio Mast
Orr's Hill Lower Rd
4th La
Orr's Hill Central Rd
Konesapuram Rd
Orr's Hill Central
Rd
Orr's Hill Lower Rd
Kachcheri
Back Bay
Clock Tower
Konesar Rd
Gateway
Channel Rd
Mosque Rd
Dockyard Rd
Oval
McHayzer Stadium
Sea View St
Samath St
Sarvamitunar Rd
Huskisson Vidiyalayam
New Moor St
Inner Harbour
Jetty
Wellington Approach
Inner Harbour Rd
Court Rd
Armoury St
College St
Cemetery Rd
Frederick Rd
Dutch Bay
Powder Island
To Mutur
Tidal Causeway
Post Office Rd
Telecom
Aurangzeb St
Lavender St
St Mary's St
Customs Rd
Dyke St
Nevila Rd
Sandy Bay Rd
Dockyard Rd
Manayaweli Cove
Manayaweli Bay
Dhoby Tank
Closed Naval Area

---

car park, located beside a dramatic narrow cleft in the rocks. Geologists can't confirm whether this was created by a divine karate chop from the demon king Rawana.

OTHER RELIGIOUS SIGHTS

Kali Kovil (Dockyard Rd) has the most impressive, eye-catching *gopuram* of Trinco's many Hindu temples. Most others are outwardly rather plain, including the important **Kandasamy Kovil** (Kandasamy Kovil Rd), dedicated to Murugan. However, at sunset *puja* (prayer or offerings) times, chanting and incense billow forth atmospherically from many more.

The biggest Buddhist temple in Trinco, **Jayasumanarama**, is quicker to visit than to

pronounce, but it does have a fine bodhi tree and a pretty whitewashed dagoba. A new **seated Buddha statue** was erected in 2005, right at the busy bus station area. Given finely balanced interethnic relations this was considered a deliberate provocation by local non-Buddhists. Grenades were thrown, tit-for-tat assassinations followed and there were frequent *hartals* (general strikes) for a couple of months. However, the statue remains, wreathed in razor wire and guarded by army gun emplacements. The scene would be make a great photo – however, snapping such a picture would very likely get you interrogated or shot.

Of the churches the 1852 Catholic **St Mary's Cathedral** (St Mary's St) is particularly

RAWANA & THE SWAYAMBHU LINGAM

The radio-mast hill opposite Swami Rock is considered to be the site of the mythical palace of the 10-headed demon king Rawana. He's the Hindu antihero of the Ramayana, infamous for kidnapping Rama's wife Sita. Along with Sita, he supposedly carried to Lanka the Swayambhu Lingam, taken from a Tibetan mountaintop. This *lingam* (phallic symbol) became the object of enormous veneration. However, in 1624, the proselytising Catholic-Portuguese destroyed the surrounding cliff-top temple, tipping the whole structure, *lingam* and all, into the ocean. It was only retrieved in 1962 by a scuba-diving team that included writer Arthur C Clarke. Clarke described the discovery in *The Reefs of Taprobane*. For cameraman Mike Wilson, who first spotted the *lingam*, the experience proved so profound that he renounced his career and family to become Hindu Swami Siva Kalki (see http ://kataragama.org/sivakalki.htm).

attractive, with a sky blue neobaroque frontage and a tiled, towered rear. Anglican church **St Nicholas** (Kandasamy Kovil Rd) is also appealing, while the church **Our Lady of Guadalupe** (NC Rd) rises discordantly from the ruins of its bombed-out former self.

BEACHES & WHALE-WATCHING

Trinco's most famous beaches are at Uppuveli and Nilaveli, but right in the centre, picturesque **Dutch Bay** is also attractive. Swimming is possible despite sometimes-dangerous undertows. However, it's more a place for strolling, and ice-cream sellers cater to the evening *passeggiata*. Don't consider bathing in **Inner Harbour**, where the water is so polluted that at times fish die off en smelly masse. **Manayaweli Cove** is an appealing curl of fishing beach reached by strolling past **Dhoby Tank**, where local washerwomen do their laundry.

You can try organising a whale-watching trip from here, though it's generally easier from Uppuveli, where boatmen are more familiar with tourist interests.

A peculiarity of **Seaview Road** is that if you stand in the middle you can see the sea at either end of the street.

Sleeping

BUDGET

If you just want a bed there are all manner of sordid little dosshouses. These include rooms behind basic restaurants on Central and NC Rds, several places of dubious repute near the bus station and more-attractive places in the back alleys of Green St (though they're ultrabasic and full of transient Indian men). Many Western visitors don't stay in town at all, preferring the accommodation in Uppuveli (p291), just 6km north.

Kumars (☎ 222 7792; 102/2 Post Office Rd; s/d with fan Rs 450/500, tw with air-con Rs 900; ☒) These are neat, good-value rooms located above a prize-winning 'cream-house' café opposite Sihara Cinema.

Sunflower (☎ 222 2963; 154 Post Office Rd; tw with fan/air con Rs 800/1800; ☒) Located above a bakery-café are these rooms, which are pleasant and new, albeit slightly underlit.

Harbour View Guest House (☎ 222 2284; 22 Orr's Hill Lower Rd; tr with fan/air-con Rs 1100/1650; ☒) These rooms are basic but clean with big bathrooms. The best feature is the ramshackle little terrace café area with nice bay views.

Chinese Guesthouse (☎ 222 2455; 312 Dyke Rd; tr Rs 400-500) There are no nets here, and the cheaper downstairs room have a slight 'prison feel' with black-green walls and window bars. However, the upstairs rooms are breezy and newly decorated, and there's a wonderful view of Fort Frederick ramparts from the shared terrace area. Good value.

Dyke Corner Inn (☎ 222 0318; 210/1 Dyke St; s/tw Rs 400/800) This place has small, basic but clean and reasonably bright rooms right on the beach. The bathrooms are shared for now.

MIDRANGE

Welcombe Hotel (☎ 222 3885; welcombe@sltnet.lk; 66 Orr's Hill Lower Rd; s/d/tr US$45/45/60; ☒ ☒ ⓟ) By far the most creative architectural statement in Trinco's hospitality industry, the upmarket Welcombe's semi-Japanese taste for modern angles and lines looks great. However, style doesn't always prove comfortable, as you'll find from your wooden-board armchairs. There's a good restaurant and a wood-panelled pub. The swimming pool could use more-regular cleaning. In a previous incarnation this site was a secretive naval centre rumoured to have harboured a torture chamber.

TRINCO'S CELEBRITY CONNECTIONS

In 1775 young Horatio Nelson, future admiral and column topper, visited Trincomalee (Trinco) and described it as the world's finest port. In 1800 Arthur Wellesley, future Duke of Wellington, arrived in Trinco thinking he was due to lead an attack on the French island of Réunion. Discovering that he was, in fact, to be sent to Egypt, he pre-empted London's command and organised a force to depart for the Middle East from Bombay in advance of orders. However, just before departure he fell ill and didn't join the mission. That proved lucky for him because the *Susannah*, in which he was due to travel, sank without survivors in the Red Sea. Perhaps Napoleon would have won at Waterloo without Wellesley's timely bout of Bombay belly. Locals can't agree where exactly in Trinco Wellesley lodged, but it was probably within Fort Frederick. The Iron Duke is now honoured by a city-centre street named Wellington Approach Rd.

Some minor celebrities are supposedly buried in the rather overgrown **St Stephen's cemetery** (Dockyard Rd). These include author Jane Austen's younger brother (Admiral Sir Charles Austen) and PB Molesworth, a Ceylon railway manager whose amateur astronomy led him to discover Jupiter's Red Spot. If their graves are still there, seeking them out is frustratingly fruitless. The name plates on the headstones have since disappeared, and the Anglican church records that once showed where each grave was have been lost.

Medway Hotel (☎ 222 7655; fax 222 2582; jrstrinc@ slt.lk; 250 Inner Harbour Rd; tw/tr Rs 3025/3575; 🖳 P) The eight sizable rooms here veer towards comfortable with 24-channel TV and (unreliable) hot water. The fragrant frangipani- and hibiscus garden shades you from the views and smells of Inner Harbour bay.

Eating & Drinking

Basic eateries are dotted all over town, especially on NC Rd, Main St and in the busy block of Court St between Customs and Post Office Rds. There are also a couple of comical local party-night restaurants 2km northwest up the road to Anuradhapura, including Hotel Prasand with its zoo of concrete animals. However, few really deserve recommendation. Hotels at nearby Uppuveli (p292) offer a more cosmopolitan alternative.

Welcombe Hotel (☎ 222 3885; welcombe@sltnet.lk; 66 Orr's Hill Lower Rd; mains Rs 500-750) The appealing restaurant at this hotel (opposite) serves some original and mostly successful Western dishes, including lamb chop in wine and rosemary, and jumbo prawns in lemon-garlic butter.

Family Needs (☎ 222 7314; 145A Dockyard Rd; mains Rs 35-200; ⏱ 7-10am, noon-2.30pm & 5-9.30pm) This shack-fronted rice-and-curry place, which you'd never look at twice, actually bakes the east coast's best pizza (Rs 200), with thick, leavened crust and not too much hot pepper. Order well ahead to get it fresh from the oven; availability is irregular.

6 to 9 (360 Court Rd; meals from Rs 60; ⏱ 7am-2pm & 5-9pm) This is a very slight notch above most typical eateries, with a few attempts at décor including dangling plastic chillies and unusual green and-red checkerboard walls. Serves typical noodles, curries and devilled dishes.

Geeth Me (☎ 222 2378; 25 NC Rd; meals Rs 150-600) A rare place offering beer (Rs 100) with meals. Food is fairly standard 'Chinese', but if you dare to wade through the dingy local drinking den at the front there's the underlit luxury of a two-table air-con dining room; it feels like the venue for a late-night poker session in a crime movie.

Getting There & Away
AIR
Scheduled AeroLanka flights to Jaffna and Colombo have been suspended. With a minimum of four passengers, **Sri Lanka Air Taxi** (☎ 019-733 3355; www.srilankan.aero/airtaxi) will fly to Colombo's Bandaranaike International Airport from Trincomalee's China Bay airport (one way US$225). However, customers are relatively rare so you may have to charter the whole plane (one way US$900). You can book tickets in Trinco through the Sri Lanka Air Taxi **agency** (252 Dockyard Rd).

BUS
Private buses to Colombo (Rs 200, seven hours) leave Trinco from 5.30am to 5pm, and from 9pm to midnight. Air-con buses

THE EAST

(Rs 240, six hours) leave approximately every 45 minutes until midnight. You can use these to get anywhere en route, including Habarana, Dambulla or Kurunegala.

For Anuradhapura there are CTB buses at 7am, 9.50am and less reliably at 12.30pm. The last of the eight daily buses to Kandy (six hours) leaves at 2.30pm. Private and CTB buses to Vavuniya (for Jaffna) depart approximately hourly between 5am and 4pm (Rs 80, 4½ hours) using a very rough road. The 1.30pm bus continues to Mannar (Rs 130, seven hours).

Most private buses heading to Batticaloa (5½ hours) leave early in the morning, travelling via Habarana. For the rough coastal route start with the ferry to Mutur (p286).

TRAIN
There are two trains daily between Trinco and Colombo Fort via Habarana. The useful overnight sleeper service leaves Trinco at 8pm (3rd/2nd/1st class Rs 194/347/587, nine hours).

AROUND TRINCOMALEE
☎ 026

Apart from Arugam Bay, the only east coast beaches with any tourist infrastructure are north of Trinco at Nilaveli and Uppuveli. There's much more choice at Uppuveli (6km from Trinco), where you can café-hop along the attractive arc of beach and enjoy horizons that extend south to Swami Rock. Nilaveli is further from Trinco (16km to 18km) and hotels are too spread out to walk easily walk between them all. Nilaveli beach is straighter with a wilder, more deserted feel and is much closer to Pigeon Island, where you can snorkel and dive.

Beaches have golden and grey sands; the 2004 tsunami scoured off the famous powder-white layer that tourist brochures once touted.

From Trinco, or more conveniently from Uppuveli, you can make a mildly interesting excursion to the Velgam Vihara ruins and take a comical splash at the Kanniyai hotel wells.

Uppuveli
Uppuveli is at once a great beach getaway and a sensible, relaxed base for visiting Trinco. Although there are plenty of fairly

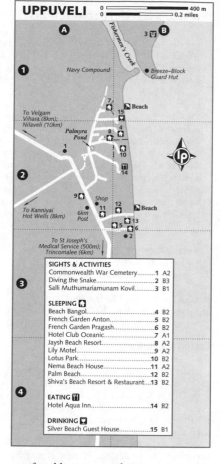

SIGHTS & ACTIVITIES
Commonwealth War Cemetery.........1 A2
Diving the Snake............................2 B3
Salli Muthumariamunam Kovil........3 B1

SLEEPING 🏠
Beach Bangol...............................4 B2
French Garden Anton.....................5 B2
French Garden Pragash...................6 B2
Hotel Club Oceanic.......................7 A1
Jaysh Beach Resort.......................8 A2
Lily Motel...................................9 A2
Lotus Park.................................10 B2
Nema Beach House.......................11 A2
Palm Beach................................12 B2
Shiva's Beach Resort & Restaurant...13 B2

EATING 🍴
Hotel Aqua Inn...........................14 B2

DRINKING 🍸
Silver Beach Guest House..............15 B1

comfortable accommodation options, this remains a village at heart. Ox carts rumble down the rough local tracks between the palm trees, a palmyra production centre has old ladies weaving baskets, and teams of fishermen use the beach for hauling in huge loops of netting.

INFORMATION
There are no banks. As yet the only Internet is a dismally slow, exorbitantly expensive connection at **Hotel Club Oceanic** (per 15 min Rs 150-175).

St Joseph's Medical Service (🕐 24hr) is building an around-the-clock medical centre just south of Uppuveli's hotel area. Payment is mostly donation based.

THE EAST

SIGHTS

If the beach isn't holding your attention you can stroll up to the beautifully kept **Commonwealth War Cemetery** (Nilaveli Rd; donations appreciated; ☺ dawn to dusk). This is the last resting place for over 600 servicemen who died at Trinco during WWII, most of them during a Japanese raid on 9 April 1942 that sank over a dozen vessels. The caretaker likes to show you photographs of a 1995 tree-planting ceremony to mark the replacement of several headstones that were damaged during the 1980s civil war. The hat in the foreground supposedly shades the head of Britain's Princess Anne.

Beachfront **Salli Muthumariamunam Kovil** is 4km by road from Uppuveli but only the shortest hop by boat; it's directly across Fishermen's Creek, masked from view by green-topped rocks. Locals claim that the unexotic breeze-block guard hut on the rocks dates from WWII.

ACTIVITIES

Local boatmen (or hoteliers acting on their behalf) organise whale-and-dolphin-watching trips (Rs 2000) departing at dawn, when sea conditions allow. A popular alternative boat trip takes you out to Pigeon Island (p292) for around Rs 3000, including snorkelling gear. That's not much more than doing the trip via Nilaveli, and it offers the bonus of seeing the whole beach-lined coast en route. Scuba-diving trips also focus on Pigeon Island, but Uppuveli has the coast's two dive shops so it is the place to start. Consistently recommended by readers is **Diving the Snake** (www.divingthesnake .com; ☺ May-Sep), based at the French Garden Pragash guesthouse. Between October to April the seas are rarely suitable for any of the previously mentioned activities.

Swimming is pleasant in the ever-warm seas. When waves are too strong, nonguests can take a dip at the pool of **Hotel Club Oceanic** (☎ 222 2307, 232 0862; Sampaltive Post) for the (relatively hefty) cost of a drink. The Oceanic also has a pool table (Rs 400 per hour), souvenir shop, and an Ayurvedic massage centre.

SLEEPING

Given the heat and humidity here you might find an air-conditioner worth the extra expense.

Budget

Lily Motel (☎ 222 7422; tw Rs 600) This pleasantly airy family house–hotel set in a flower garden has clean, simple rooms with fan and bathroom. Although the house is on the main road, the beach is less than 10 minutes' stroll away.

French Garden Pragash (☎ 222 4546; rajfrench garden@yahoo.com; tw with fan/air-con Rs 1000/1500; 🔀) These unsophisticated but mostly well-kept boxlike rooms have terraces facing directly onto the beach. The east coast's best diving outfit is based here during the high season, Internet is planned for 2006 and there's a little playground for small children.

French Garden Anton (☎ 078 979 1024; d Rs 500) Uppuveli's cheapest offers basic rooms with small bathrooms and narrow queen-sized beds. Some have mosquito nets.

Nema Beach House (☎ 222 7613; Irakkandy Rd; tw from Rs 1000) The darkish rooms here are prone to flooding in the wet season.

Midrange & Top End

Hotel Club Oceanic (☎ 222 2307, 232 0862; www .johnkeellshotels.com; Sampaltive Post; s/d/tr standard US$68/84/99, superior US$76/91/106, chalet US$99/137/175; 🔀 🅿 ☂) Uppuveli's real resort hotel, Club Oceanic commands a fine stretch of curving beach. Located in a two-storey, concrete V-shaped building, the hotel has generally impressive standards of room and service. All rooms have air-con, hot water supplied by new Grohe taps, and closable shower booths (even in the standard rooms). Slight gripes if you're paying full price are the thin walls and lack of in-room safe. However, low-season prices (November to April) as low as US$25 per person are outstanding value, especially for singles.

Lotus Park (☎ 222 5327; www.lotustrinco.com; s/d Rs 3750/4000; 🔀 ☂) Second only to Club Oceanic, this is Uppuveli's top spot for resident foreigners and NGO types. Best are the comfortable bungalows that are splashing distance from the waves; they're the same price as the rooms. All accommodation is air-conditioned and has hot water in the curtainless showers. The irregularly shaped pool is rather too small for serious swimmers.

Palm Beach (☎ 222 1250; tw/tr with fan Rs 1300/ 1500, with air-con 1750/2000, all incl breakfast; 🔀) The attractively tiled, neat new rooms face a garden where squirrels play with lizards on the palm trees. There's an access path to the beach but no direct beach frontage. Food by order.

Shiva's Beach Resort & Restaurant (☎ 078 879 1725; tw with fan Rs 1400, with air-con Rs 1750-2000, all incl breakfast; ✖) These clean, neat, tile-floored rooms here don't have mosquito nets and are rather underlit. An attraction is the simple, thatched beach bar and a hammock amid the coco palms.

Beach Bangol (☎ 222 7599; tw with fan/air-con Rs 1000/2500; ✖) Don't be put off by the battered old building at the approach, as rooms are, in fact, in sturdy new low-rise bungalows. All have sunrise beach views through coconut palms. Air-con rooms have a fridge. The dining room lacks any atmosphere but the food (mains Rs 85 to 200) is decent and the gentlemanly owner is urbane. Foreign students get a 25% discount.

Jaysh Beach Resort (☎ 222 4043; s/tw with fan Rs 2000/3000, with air-con Rs 2500/3500; ✖) This is a new yet somewhat jerry-built place that might be worth considering if you can bargain rates to half-price.

EATING & DRINKING

The only restaurants are in hotels and guesthouses.

Hotel Club Oceanic (☎ 222 2307; www.johnkeells hotels.com; buffet Rs 950) The excellent dinner buffet at this top-end hotel (p291) offers very high standards of Western and local foods, and is a favourite of NGO workers for miles around. Drinks cost (a lot) extra. There's also an à la carte beachfront café.

Lotus Park (☎ 222 5327; www.lotustrinco.com; mains Rs 250-500) Beachfront dining at this hotel (p291) includes some curious, almost-Western dishes like spaghetti with chips. Although our steak was tough as boot leather, other diners reported good experiences.

Hotel Aqua Inn (☎ 222 6302; meals Rs 125-300; ✖ 7.30-10am, 1-2.30pm & 5.30-10.30pm) A pleasant six-table beach café nuzzling against the sand at this otherwise dreary hotel.

Silver Beach Guest House (☎ 222 6305; beers Rs 125) The main attraction of the bare eating area between concrete pillars is that drinks cost less than half the price of those at Club Oceanic next door. Faces the beach.

GETTING THERE & AWAY

Irakkandy-bound minibuses from Trinco's bus terminal run roughly every half-hour, supplemented by occasional small CTB buses. All pass through Uppuveli (Rs 10, 20 minutes) and Nilaveli (Rs 25, 45 minutes). Three-wheelers from Uppuveli cost Rs 150 to Trinco (Rs 200 at night), Rs 250 to Nilaveli, Rs 400 return to Kanniyai hot wells, and around Rs 1000 to loop via Kanniyai to Velgam Vihara and back.

Nilaveli

When Singapore fell to the Japanese during WWII, the British Indian Ocean Fleet retreated to Trincomalee, setting up a massive communications base at Nilaveli. Today there's little left to see, but war hounds can sniff out the stubs of once-huge pylon supports and an engine room (Navy Rd) whose squat, humidity-blackened concrete shell is hidden behind a local house and filled with bats. Fernando at H&U guesthouse (opposite) can show you where it is. Of vastly more interest is the beach, which stretches several kilometres on either side.

SIGHTS & ACTIVITIES
Nilaveli Beach

For years Nilaveli has been considered one of Sri Lanka's most perfect beaches. It certainly has that feeling of paradise-island remoteness, with plenty of bending palms swaying over the golden sand. Post-tsunami, the beach is no longer powdery white and a gully at the back of the beach can form somewhat unsightly pools after rain. Nonetheless the beach remains impressively long and has the off-shore visual focus of Pigeon Island. If you don't need much in the way of entertainment, this could be your kind of getaway.

Pigeon Island

The most common day trip from Nilaveli or Uppuveli is to the dumbbell-shaped **Pigeon Island**, a short boat hop east of Nilaveli Beach Hotel. Here sands remain powdery white, if littered with broken coral fragments. However, it's rather a victim of its own popularity, with graffiti-covered rocks and dozens of picnickers during the high season making this 'desert island' the most crowded place in Nilaveli. Reports are mixed on the quality of Pigeon Island's snorkelling, best from May to September. We saw mostly damaged coral and relatively few fish, but were hampered by rough seas and turbid, low-season waters here and at nearby **Red Rocks** (Coral Island), where

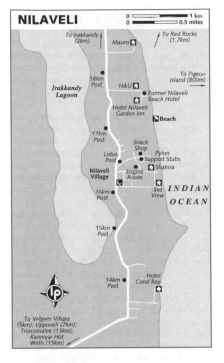

there's only boat-based snorkelling. Regular divers are more enthusiastic.

Boats organised through guesthouses or directly from fishermen typically cost Rs 1500 for a two- to three-hour trip. Add around Rs 200 rental per snorkel or pair of fins. Reportedly there is some appealing scuba diving between May and September off Pigeon Island's coast, with good chances to see manta rays. Currently, the nearest dive operations are based in Uppuveli.

Irakkandy Lagoon

Around 4km north of Nilaveli the main road crosses the mouth of an extensive lagoon system. Views are pleasant from the long narrow bridge (check with the army guard point before walking across). Look to the east for a sand bar and crashing waves, west for mangroves and fishermen in outrigger canoes. Some guesthouses can arrange lagoon boat trips.

SLEEPING & EATING

Note that all Nilaveli accommodation is at least a 400m walk east of the main road, start-ing from the approximate kilometre point noted. At the time of writing, the places reviewed represent all available options. However, more are likely to be (re)developed, including the nearly complete former Nilaveli Beach Hotel. Guesthouses can arrange boat trips and food but there are no alternative dining options.

Mauro (☎ 459 5323, 078 879 1639; s/d/tr/ste Rs 3080/ 3300/3630/4620; 🖭 🖳) This long two-storey building faces a narrow, neatly manicured garden that extends past a very tempting swimming pool to possibly the most attractive stretch of beach, facing Pigeon Island. The comfy new rooms are relatively luxurious, with hot water, stylishly folded towels and stripy bed covers. Save Rs 660 if you don't want air-conditioning, but add Rs 300 per person for breakfast or Rs 700 for half-board. There's a beach-view bar.

Sea View (☎ 492 0016, 071 418 2538) Situated right on the beach, the two-storey Sea View has rooms above an isolated dining-room with luridly blue windows. Views from the rooftop are the best in Nilaveli, though the neat, well-appointed rooms only spy the sea from across access balcony–walkways.

Hotel Nilaveli Garden Inn (☎ /fax 223 2228; www .hotel-garden-inn.de; d with fan/air-con Rs 1870/2970; 🖭) Although set back from the beach about 200m, the Nilaveli Garden offers a touch of style that's lacking in most of the region's hotels. There's lots of airy, open space, the bar-restaurant is decked out with lifebelts, nets and paddles, and the air-con, hot-water rooms are decorated in a tasteful choice of colours and fabrics. The fan rooms are much more ordinary. When the occasional small German tour group visits, an attached Ayurvedic herbal massage centre operates. Ask about scuba-diving trips and all-inclusive packages.

H & U (☎ 222 6254, 0777 54390; www.guesthou se-nilaveli.com; tw Rs 500-900) Just 200m before reaching Nilaveli Beach Hotel, an arch of bougainvillea welcomes you into the tiny H&U, Nilaveli's only backpacker place. Rooms are simple but clean, and have attached bathrooms and mosquito nets. The owner speaks great English and German, and is a knowledgeable local guide.

Hotel Coral Bay (☎ 223 2272; fax 223 2202; d with fan/air-con Rs 2000/2500; 🖭 🖳) This is a beach-facing, low-rise blockhouse where each of the 10 rooms has views towards the ocean and a little sitting area complete with rattan chairs. Rooms are neat but lack mosquito nets. The swimming pool is possibly the best on the east coast, but it lacks any shade or surrounding decoration and the beach is somewhat scraggy. The other slightly off-putting aspect is that without transport you can feel a little stranded here as it's miles from any other guesthouse.

Shahira Hotel (☎ 223 2224, 071 309 0393; tw Rs 1650) Ranged around a garden that's about 150m inland, these 18 simple, clean, if somewhat dark, rooms have veranda sitting areas, fans and towels. The bright dining-room mural survived the tsunami, but the photo album shows how little else did.

GETTING THERE & AWAY
Buses and minbuses to Irakkandy leave Trinco's bus terminal about every half-hour. All pass through Uppuveli (Rs 10) and Nilaveli (Rs 25).

A three-wheeler between Nilaveli and Uppuveli costs Rs 250.

Velgam Vihara
A rough track leads west of the main coast road around halfway between Uppuveli and Nilaveli and bumps a few kilometres through former-war-zone scrub to the pretty Velgam Wewa (Velgam Tank). Just beyond, the isolated Buddhist **Velgam Vihara** (☎ 222 6258; www.geocities.com/welgamweharaya; donation appreciated) dates from around the 2nd century BC, and was embellished in the

10th century AD. There's a moss-crusted, ancient, brick **dagoba** shaped like a pudding dish. But the most striking feature is the human-sized standing **Buddha carving** surveying some valuable inscription stones. A new two-man monastic centre displays gory photos of an attack by the LTTE in 2000.

A 4km-long asphalt access road connects Velgam Vihara to the A12 at the 174km post. This allows you to loop back to Uppuveli or Trinco with a quick side trip to the nearby Kanniyai hot wells and a glimpse of the rocky cockscomb ridge of **Warodiyanagar**, near the 178km post.

Kanniyai Hot Wells
Located some 1.5km southwest of the 176km post on the A12, the **Kanniyai hot wells** (admission Rs 25; ☺ 7.30am-12.30pm & 1.30-6pm) were reputedly created by Vishnu to distract the demon king Rawana during a complex episode of Hindu mythology. You'll need a guide who's a really good storyteller to make this place seem at all interesting. Nonetheless it's mildly amusing to watch horse-playing youths sloshing each other with buckets of the naturally warm water, which rises up into seven totally unaesthetic tiled square pools. There are changing rooms for those who want to join in, and a shedlike 'temple' should the experience move you spiritually. Several war-ruined structures remain brutally bullet pocked. Parking is Rs 10.

Jaffna & the North

Toweringly gaudy Hindu temples, the rapid-fire staccato of spoken Tamil, cupolas heaped on oversized churches, sombrero-sized masala dosas cooking on open-air griddles… Welcome to a different world. The North is a vast cultural contrast to the rest of Sri Lanka. Its flat, low-lying scenery has a sprinkling of minor sights and even a few far-from-home baobab trees, but meeting the industrious, highly educated locals is the most memorable part of a visit. Conversations here fascinatingly underline the gulf of misunderstanding between the Tamil heartland and the Sinhalese South. And seeing battle-scarred Jaffna for yourself vividly brings into relief the reasons for Sri Lanka's intractable conflict.

Tourists are very rare up here. In government-held areas, the myriad checkpoints and army camps can feel intimidating for first-time visitors. But foreigners are rarely stopped. Meanwhile, most of the Vanni region is efficiently run by the Liberation Tigers of Tamil Eelam (LTTE) as virtually a separate country. Crossing this strange statelike entity adds an intriguing frisson to reaching Jaffna. The LTTE's 'terrorist' image needn't scare you off, but sensitivity, tact and open-mindedness are key items for your backpack. So too is a hefty umbrella if you come during the northeastern monsoon (October to January); the rest of the year the region is hot and dry, verging on arid. In sweaty August Jaffna, goes wild during the extraordinary Nallur festival.

At the time of writing there was no sense of danger for travellers in government- or rebel-held zones. However, tensions have since flared again in Sri Lanka, so keep a very careful eye on the news and fast-changing politics of the region.

HIGHLIGHTS

- Pondering the contradictions of **Jaffna** (p304) – its comfortable suburbia, bustling bazaars and war-scarred former centre

- Watching *pujas* (prayers or offerings) or parades at Jaffna's **Nallur Kandaswamy Kovil** (p307), the biggest Hindu temple in Sri Lanka

- Cruising the patchwork of the offshore islands to holy **Nainativu** (p317) or desolate **Delft** (p317)

- Experiencing a country within a country while crossing the former battlefields of **the Vanni** (p297, p303)

- Understanding the roots of Sri Lanka's interminable civil strife by seeing life from the 'other side'

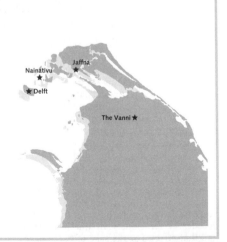

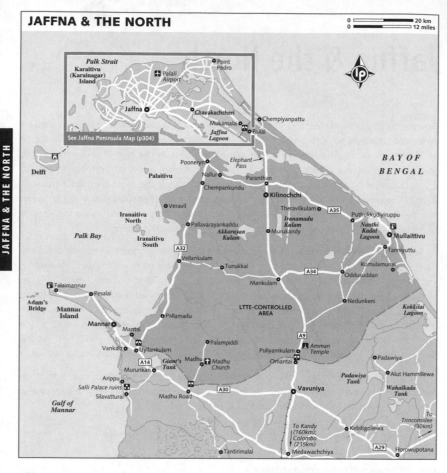

History

When Arab traveller Ibn Batuta visited Ceylon in 1344 he reported that the powerful Hindu-Tamil kingdom of Jaffna extended south as far as Puttalam. Over several centuries territories expanded and retreated, but even under colonial regimes Jaffna, like Kandy, remained highly autonomous. This lasted until the 19th century, when British bureaucrats decided it would be more convenient to administer the whole of Ceylon as a single unit. By independence in 1948 the idea of breaking the island into different states would have seemed preposterous to Sinhalese and Tamil citizens alike. Yet barely 50 years later, insensitive politics and two decades of ferocious civil war has almost had that effect. For the sake of peace nego-

tiations, the LTTE now claims that it will accept autonomy within a federal Sri Lanka rather than outright independence. But the Vanni region it administers (Tamil Eelam)

THE 2004 TSUNAMI – AFTERMATH IN THE NORTH

The 2004 tsunami absolutely devastated the northeastern coast. The LTTE stronghold of Mullaittivu was especially badly ravaged, barely two years after rebuilding itself from the rubble of war. However, as that zone is out of bounds to tourists, the only place you're likely to see tsunami scars in the North is at a few small villages around Manalkadu.

acts almost as a separate nation, leaving the Jaffna peninsula, controlled by the Sri Lanka Army (SLA), physically cut off from the rest of government-held Sri Lanka.

GROWING CONFLICT

As with many world problems, it's easy – if simplistic – to blame the Brits. British managers found Tamils to be agreeably capable at learning English and fulfilling the needs of the colonial administration. This apparent 'favouritism' meant that Tamil candidates were soon overrepresented in universities and public service jobs, creating Sinhalese resentment and contributing to anti-Tamil sentiment in the 1950s. This led eventually to the infamous 1956 'Sinhala only' language policy (p34).

Now it was the Tamils' turn to feel discriminated against. As passions on both sides rose, one of the defining moments came in 1981 when a Sinhalese mob burnt down Jaffna's library, complete with irreplaceable Tamil documents (p309). To the horror of Tamils everywhere this atrocity received minimal public criticism, and thus the seeds were sown for civil war. Small-scale reprisals/terrorism followed. But the world only noticed two years later in 1983, when full-scale anti-Tamil massacres broke out in Colombo.

The horror of this 'Black July' created a groundswell of sympathy for the multiple Tamil resistance groups, and brought notable funding from fellow Tamils in southern India. The LTTE, increasingly the best-organised Tamil resistance group, came to virtually control the North for a while. However, the SLA had pushed it back to Jaffna by 1987, when Sri Lanka welcomed an Indian Peace Keeping Force (IPKF). The welcome didn't last long. The LTTE refused to be disarmed and goaded the Indians into battle, resulting in more ferocious fighting. Human rights nightmares were perpetrated on Tamil civilians by their Indian would-be protectors. Meanwhile, the Sri Lankan government faced vociferous criticism and a Janatha Vimukthi Peramuna (JVP) terrorist backlash for allowing in the Indians at all (p36). In a series of bizarre Machiavellian twists, the Sri Lankan government briefly started supplying arms to the LTTE to get rid of the Indians! The IPKF finally left in 1990. The LTTE, who had hidden

---

BEHIND THE CADJAN CURTAIN

The Soviets had their Iron Curtain. Mao closed a Bamboo one. Now Sri Lanka has the Cadjan Curtain. Behind it lies the LTTE-controlled Vanni region, which they call Tamil Eelam (Tamil Precious Land). There's a Tamil Eelam Bank, an Eelam Law College and a fully developed administration, including customs officers and neatly uniformed police – many of the female agents sport distinctive loops of plaited hair. Until Colombo's recent decision to move the country's clocks back by half an hour, the region even had its own time zone. On the week leading up to Martyr's Day (the 'national' festival on 27 November), red and yellow flags appear everywhere and families flock to LTTE graveyards to honour those who have died in the separatist struggle. Just as the Queen's speech marks a British Christmas, Martyr's Day culminates in Tiger supremo Velupillai Prabhakaran's annual address.

---

out in jungle tunnels based on Vietcong and *Rambo* originals, battled its way back into Jaffna.

Failed attempts at national reconciliation in 1995 resulted in a third phase of war that saw the Tigers once again ejected from Jaffna, where LTTE monuments and graveyards were unceremoniously bulldozed. As ever, the Tigers regrouped in the jungles and mounted renewed terrorist strikes. In 2000, to general astonishment, it launched a full-scale military assault, managing to grab Elephant Pass (the Jaffna peninsula causeway), which it still holds.

APPROXIMATE PEACE

Following a Norwegian-brokered cease-fire of 2002, a certain optimism reigned. Over a quarter of the 800,000 refugees and internally displaced persons who had fled the area since 1983 began to return, bringing an economic boost to devastated Jaffna. Nongovernmental organisations (NGOs) began to deal with an estimated two million land mines.

But large swaths of the Vanni remain too dangerous to farm, and the SLA's nervously tentative hold on the Jaffna peninsula has led to the creation of despised High Security Zones – beaches are no-go areas,

JAFFNA & THE NORTH (side tab)

STAYING SAFE

Isolated killings continue with depressing regularity and the causes of the civil unrest are far from solved. Most of the time all you'll notice is a general sultry calm. But situations could turn dangerous instantly and dramatically. Keep an eye on political developments with www.tamilnet.com.

Many land-mine areas have now been cleared or marked with little red skull-and-crossbones warning signs. But you'd still be extremely unwise to explore any land that's overgrown or fenced off. The same goes for deserted beaches; however, most of the potentially lovely sand on the Jaffna peninsula is off limits anyway to prevent the LTTE from landing weapons.

---

many street-corner homes have been commandeered and whole villages, including port-town Kankesanturai, have been entirely depopulated for military use.

The November 2005 presidential election brought no apparent new hope for lasting peace (see Who Controls Jaffna, p305).

VAVUNIYA

☎ 024

Virtually all transport to and from the north funnels through energetically bustling Vavuniya (*vow*-nya). It makes sense to stay here overnight to get an early start on the cross-Vanni trip to Jaffna. Although there are no real sights, an afternoon here isn't unpleasant and the local people are charmingly hospitable.

Information

Reasonably fast Internet access is available at **SeeNet** (☎ 222 1222; 395/1 Horowapatana Rd; per hr Rs 50; ☑ 7.30am-9pm; ☒) and **Vastec** (☎ 222 2869; 2nd fl, 65 Station Rd; per 15 min/hr Rs 15/40; ☑ 8am-9pm). West of the clock tower, **Sanpath Bank** (Station Rd) and **Commercial Bank** (Station Rd) both have ATMs. For LTTE-permit enquiries, there's a **Tamil Rehabilitation Organisation office** (TRO; ☎ 222 1975; Jaffna Rd).

Sights

The town arcs around a quietly attractive **tank** that is best observed from **Sothida Niliyam Kovil**, a tiled, shedlike Ganesh temple. More photogenic is the **Kandasamy Kovil**

(Kandasamy Kovil Rd), a Murugan (Skanda) temple with a very ornate, if faded, *gopuram* (gateway tower) and a gold-clad image in its sanctum. The **Grand Jummah Mosque** (Horowapatana Rd) might really be pretty grand one day when the building work is finally complete. Also eye-catching is the **Bhagwan Sri Sathya Seva Centre** (www.sathyasai.org), shaded by palms, hibiscus and neem trees in a peaceful side street one block west of the Rest House. It's an ashram of the latter-day Indian guru and Jimi Hendrix–lookalike Sai Baba. On the ashram's colourful lotus balcony stands statues of Buddha, Krishna and a bindhi-browed Jesus. Very multicultural.

Vavuniya's **Archaeological Museum** (☎ 222 4805; 2 Horowapatana Rd; admission free; ☑ 8am-5pm Wed-Mon) is unlikely to impress you if you're arriving from Anuradhapura, but some of the pinched-faced terracotta figures from Kilinochchi (4th to 5th century) are delightfully primitive, while the central hexagonal chamber has some fine 5th-to-8th-century Buddha statues in Mannar limestone.

The quietly charming **Madukanda Vihara** (Horowapatana Rd) is a Rs 100 three-wheeler ride from central Vavuniya, beyond the 3km post on the A29. It was reputedly the fourth resting point in the journey of the sacred Buddha tooth relic from Mullaittivu to Anuradhapura during the 4th-century reign of King Mahsen. Near the white dagoba (stupa) and a 150-year-old bodhi tree, appealing ancient ruins include fine guard stones and lion-and-elephant-decorated banisters. The heavy dressed-stone rectangle that looks like a Palaeolithic swimming pool was probably a *bodhigara* (enclosure for a sacred bodhi tree).

Sleeping

Few Vavuniya hotels have mosquito nets – annoying in the wet season.

BUDGET

Hotel Swarkka (☎ 222 1291; Soosaipillayarkulam Rd; tr with fan/air-con Rs 1000/1500; ☒) The very recent renovations and very good-humoured staff make this the best of many crushingly ordinary box-room guesthouses.

Rest House (☎ 222 2299; Station Rd; s/d Rs 450/500, with air-con Rs 750/800; ☒) This place has plain, decent value rooms with a bar, thick walls behind a beer garden that attracts local ex-office alkies. Not ideal for single women.

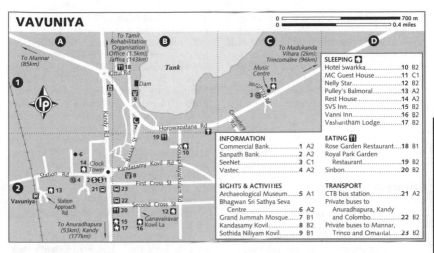

VAVUNIYA

SLEEPING
Hotel Swarkka.................10 B2
MC Guest House..............11 C1
Nelly Star.......................12 B2
Pulley's Balmoral..............13 A2
Rest House.....................15 A2
SVS Inn.........................15 B2
Vanni Inn.......................16 B2
Vashantham Lodge...........17 B2

INFORMATION
Commercial Bank..............1 A2
Sanpath Bank...................2 A2
SeeNet..........................3 C1
Vastec...........................4 A2

SIGHTS & ACTIVITIES
Archaeological Museum......5 A1
Bhagwan Sri Sathya Seva
Centre.........................6 A2
Grand Jummah Mosque......7 B1
Kandasamy Kovil..............8 B2
Sothida Niliyam Kovil..........9 B1

EATING
Rose Garden Restaurant......18 B1
Royal Park Garden
Restaurant....................19 B2
Sinbon.........................20 B2

TRANSPORT
CTB bus station...............21 A2
Private buses to
Anuradhapura, Kandy
and Colombo................22 B2
Private buses to Mannar,
Trinco and Omantai.........23 B2

SVS Inn (☎ 222 2978; Kandy Rd; s/tw with fan from Rs 400/650, tw with air-con Rs 1500; ✷) This inn has cheap, almost clean rooms; those costing over Rs 500 have attached toilet. Air-con twins are small, functional and slightly messy.

Vashantham Lodge (☎ 222 2366; 40 Kandy Rd; r Rs 385-1430; ✷) This concrete purgatory is entered upstairs via a dodgy back passage leading to a cinema. Tatty, if tolerably clean, rooms range from prison-cell singles sharing an outside squat toilet to bearable but entirely unappealing upper rooms with rumbling old air-con.

MIDRANGE

Nelly Star (☎ 222 4477; 84 Second Cross St; r with fan/air-con Rs 1700/2200, VIP Rs 3000; ✷) Striking modernistic architecture with bright orange, custard yellow and royal blue paintwork makes Nelly Star Vavuniya's place of the moment. Standard rooms don't quite live up to expectations but are nonetheless the best in town for now. The VIP rooms are much more spacious and have a minibar, TV and bathtub, plus a little sitting area.

Pulley's Balmoral (☎ 222 2364; Station Approach; s/d with shared bathroom Rs 550/715, tw with private bathroom & fan/air-con Rs 1375/1650; ✷) This old low-rise villa sits in a big palm garden, entered through a snack-stall alley opposite the train station. Air-con rooms are big, well-equipped and freshly decorated, but lack real windows. Food here is good value (meals Rs 50 to 200) and diners may bring their own booze at least until the place gets licensed.

MC Guest House (☎ 222 0445, 077 662 5292; 411 Horowapatana Rd; apt Rs 3300; ✷) Families might consider renting this fairly lovable house with two twin bedrooms (one air-con, both with bathrooms) and basic kitchen. The big, if somewhat sparse, sitting room has flapping plastic floors. Keys are available from the nearby Music Centre, an 85-year-old house.

Vanni Inn (☎ 222 1406; Ganavairavar Kovil Lane; d with fan/air-con Rs 935/1870; ✷) This place has neutral rooms off somewhat depressing corridors; there's good air-con, and it's rarely full.

Eating

Royal Park Garden Restaurant (☎ 222 4026; 200 Horowapatana Rd; meals Rs 125-450; ⌚ 11.30am-10pm) Set behind a brash new wedding palace, the much cosier garden is a great place for dinner when the weather's not unbearably hot. Attractive twinkling lights, outside tables and little pavilions nestle amid ornamental trees, and the Rs 125 mushroom *paneer* masala (mushroom and unfermented cheese curry) is richly delicious. The restaurant has an open-to-view kitchen. No prices on menus.

Rose Garden Restaurant (☎ 222 4473; 8 Kittul Rd; meals Rs 45-300; ⌚ 7.30am-9pm) This is a big, excellent value party-hall restaurant. Food of widely varying styles includes a spicy *tom yam goong* (Thai shrimp soup) that lacks lemon grass but is generously full of shrimps for a mere Rs 80.

Nelly Star (☎ 222 4477; 84 Second Cross St; mains from Rs 150; ✷) The restaurant at this hotel (p299) serves dishes like pizza (Rs 395) and strangely sweet spaghetti (Rs 160). Much better is the eggplant curry (Rs 30), listed as a side dish but a worthy small meal on its own. The dining room doubles as a wedding hall and is often booked for functions.

Sinbon (Kandy Rd; ⏰ 6.30am-8pm; 🔀) This is a modern café ideal for passing the time when you're waiting for a bus. Unusually, local women feel confident enough to come here unchaperoned for coffee (Nescafé Rs 15), cakes or ice-cream sundaes (Rs 50). Next door is an air-conditioned supermarket.

Getting There & Away

BUS

The Central Transport Board (CTB) bus station is close to the clock tower. Private buses to Mannar (Rs 50, 2½ hours), Trinco (Rs 80, four bone-shaking hours) and, on alternate days, Omantai (for Jaffna; see p303 for details) leave from First Cross St, while for Anuradhapura (Rs 34, 1½ hours, at least hourly until 7pm), Kandy (Rs 96 to 106, four hours) and Colombo (bus/air-con minibus Rs 200/250, 5½ hours) they start from Second Cross St. Colombo services run around the clock on the Puttalam route (via Anuradhapura) and until 7pm on the Dambulla route, but some buses will charge full Colombo fares for intermediate drop-offs.

TRAIN

Vavuniya is the northern railhead for the line from Colombo. There are four trains to Colombo daily, plus a 7am Anuradhapura service. Fares to Colombo are Rs 560/290/160 in 1st/2nd/3rd class on the 3.15am slow train, 6.05am express (five hours) and the 1.15pm semiexpress (9½ hours). The convenient overnight sleeper train (seven hours) departs 10pm and costs Rs 520 for a 1st-class berth and Rs 309/175 for a 2nd/3rd class sleeperette. Reserve your tickets at the station between 7am and 10.30am within 10 days of departure.

VAVUNIYA TO MANNAR

Although the army controls the road to Mannar it has little or no presence either side of it. North of the road is effectively a different country, as you'll see if you venture to Madhu Church (opposite). **Murunkan** (at the 60km post) is the only village between Vavuniya and Mannar with shops, a basic guesthouse and three-wheelers for hire.

If you head south from here along the bumpy road to **Arippu** via **Silavatturai** you'll see whole deserted Muslim settlements, left in ruins by LTTE attacks. Off the road lie Mannar's long abandoned oyster-bed **pearl banks**. Unless you're a keen historian, don't let locals persuade you that visiting the **Salli Palace ruins** near Arippu is worth the bone-shattering 40km detour. The remnant brick arches are vaguely picturesque and supposedly 500 years old. However, most of the unkempt structure has already toppled off the sandy cliff onto the long narrow strip of beach below. If you do go, the site is just beyond an unexplained **obelisk** that locals misleadingly call 'the Lighthouse'.

West of Murunkan the main Mannar road follows the edge of the **Giant's Tank**, Sri Lanka's second-largest ancient reservoir. However, you'll need to climb the bank for views across its beautiful bird-attracting waters; it's best to do so beside the small roadside Hindu temple behind which fishermen moor their outrigger canoes in the wet season. Before arranging an informal boat trip double-check with nearby sentry posts that there's no new rule against such ventures.

At Uyilankulam (70km post) there's a **'Crossloading Point'**, where all lorries bound for Tigerland must unload their goods for inspection. The nearby LTTE crossing point is closed to foreign tourists, though ongoing road repairs on the A32 to Pooneryn may eventually change things.

Between the 76km and 77km markers of the Vavuniya–Mannar road is a large military camp and a big, colourful gateway. ID checks are required to pass through the latter on a side road that leads 5km north to **Thirukketeeswaram Kovil**. This is one of Sri Lanka's four most important *kovils* (Hindu temples), supposedly dating from 700 BC. It probably marks the site of ancient Mantota, once one of Lanka's great historic ports, which silted up entirely over the centuries. Today the *kovil* is imposing with a towering, colourful *gopuram* though the present structures look relatively new. It's possible to peep inside during the atmospherically cacophonous *pujas* (prayers or offerings). The *pujas* occur at 5.30am, 8.05am, 12.30pm and 5.30pm, and are busiest on Fridays. Judging from the jigsaw of imported carved stone-work in the yard, a vast new building spree is planned. Ranged around the temple are open-fronted pavilions containing five gigantic floats. These are wheeled out each February for the impressive **Maha Sivarathiri** festival.

Madhu Church

The **Our Lady of Madhu Church** (5.30am-8.30pm) is Sri Lanka's most hallowed Christian shrine. Its revered Madonna-and-child statue was brought here in 1670 by Catholics fleeing from Protestant Dutch persecution in Mannar. The statue rapidly developed a reputation for miracles, notably as a protector against snakebite. Madhu has been a place of pilgrimage ever since. Its 10 annual festivals attract huge crowds of pilgrims, especially around 15 August. Many in the crowds are superstitious non-Christians.

The present church dates from 1872 and has soaring, if unembellished, central columns apparently fashioned from hugely long tree trunks. Outside, its most striking feature is the elongated portico painted cream and duck-egg blue. The church sits in spacious grounds with gnarled old trees. The forest of blue-and-white poles look like snow-drift markers but actually serve to hold lamps and bunting at festival times.

Curiously the all-important Madonna statuette is rather diminutive and Mary's face looks less like a Blessed Virgin than a *Thunderbirds* bad-guy puppet. This doesn't worry worshippers, who mix Christian prayers with *puja*-style veneration. The figure's little metal crown was added in 1924 by a papal legate; the ceremony drew a crowd of 150,000.

Turn at the 47km post, a lonely spot that's nicknamed Madhu road; Madhu itself is 12km north of the Vavuniya–Mannar road. It's within Tamil Eelam, the self-styled (though not officially independent) LTTE-controlled 'country'. If you don't plan to go overland to Jaffna, part of the interest in visiting Madhu is the rigmarole of entering this other world. Start reasonably early in the morning as you are not allowed to stay overnight in Tigerland and frontiers are only open from 7am to 5pm. Border procedures (Rs 2) usually take at least half an hour. By public transport the 10am direct

---

FUN IN TIGERLAND

The members of the LTTE are a clean-living bunch of funsters who don't condone the public consumption of alcohol or tobacco. Other items banned at Madhu, according to signs en route, include sports goods, 'fancy goods', radios, card games, musical instruments and even ice cream.

---

bus from Mannar (Rs 45, two hours) gives you an hour to look around before returning at 1pm. Alternatively you could take a Vavuniya–Mannar bus to Murunkan and then take a three-wheeler (Rs 800 return). Outside festival times there are no three-wheelers reliably stationed at the 47km junction.

MANNAR
☎ 023

The only access to Mannar is by a 3km-long causeway. When the road is low in the water the journey feels like a Biblical miracle. Look left to spy the collapsed rail bridge on the horizon. The LTTE makes periodic attempts to blow up the causeway road bridge too, hoping to isolate Mannar Island – hence all the army checkpoints.

Information

The **Bank of Ceylon** (Palimunai Rd) has no ATM, and that of the **Hatton National Bank** (21 Main St) currently accepts only locally issued cards. The **TRO office** (☎ 223 2186; Main St) occupies a rather bizarrely façaded colonial villa. You could try asking for permits to explore off-limits LTTE areas, but don't get too hopeful.

Sights

The town welcomes you with a glimpse of its Portuguese-Dutch **star fortress** (out of bounds). Mannar's one off-beat attraction is a **baobab tree** (Palimunai Rd), 1.2km northeast of the private bus stand. Quite different from the stout skeletons of typical West African baobabs, this one is shaped like a giant ball with a 19m circumference. It's believed to have been planted in 1477 by Arab traders.

There's not much else for tourists, though **St Sebastian's Church** (Hospital Rd) is rather impressive; if you squint or have been on the

JAFFNA & THE NORTH

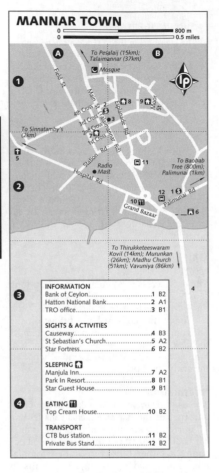

toddy you might think you'd been transported to Florence. Well, almost.

Sleeping & Eating

None of the accommodation options are luxurious, and women travelling alone have reported feeling uncomfortable.

Star Guest House (☎ 223 2177; Moor St; s/tw/tr with fan Rs 350/400/500, tw/tr with air-con Rs 1250/1500; 🞫) The new, clean, if virtually windowless, air-con rooms are the best option available in sweaty Mannar. Some travellers have complained about conditions in the cheaper rooms, which share bathrooms.

Park In Resort (☎ 223 2127; Esplanade Rd; tw/tr with fan Rs 950/800, with air-con Rs 1200/1350; 🞫) This modest but mildly charming colonial-era

house has sloping roofs, a rattan-screened veranda and wooden doors. Except for pre-ordered bread-and-tea breakfasts, no meals are served, despite the sign. Fan triples share bathrooms.

Sinnatamby's (☎ 223 2748; Thavulpadu Rd; tw Rs 500) Some 2km out of the centre via Hospital Rd, the rooms here seem dwarfed by the high roof and lack of intermediate ceiling – walls just end in midair. Though conditions are basic and not ideal for single women, this is the one place that has mosquito nets.

Manjula Inn (☎ 223 2748; 2nd Cross St; r from Rs 500) This place is well located above a small shop in an area popular with NGOs, but the atmosphere is slightly sleazy.

Top Cream House (Grand Bazaar; meals from Rs 50; ⏰ 6am-9pm) Right at the main traffic circle, this ordinary eatery is fly infested but has a relatively extensive and high-quality selection of curries with fresh *rotti* or string hoppers (tangles of steamed noodles). Shrimp curry, shells and all, costs Rs 50.

Getting There & Away

Although death-trap buses head directly to Colombo and there's a daily bus all the way to Trincomalee (Rs 120, 7½ hours), the most convenient access to Mannar is by twice-hourly buses from Vavuniya (Rs 50, 2½ hours). Check both CTB and private bus stands for the next departure.

MANNAR ISLAND

Off Mannar Island's western end, **Adam's Bridge** is a chain of reefs, sandbanks and islets that almost connects Sri Lanka to India. In the Ramayana these were the stepping stones that the monkey king Hanuman used in his bid to rescue Rama's wife Sita. Mannar's proximity to India was once its main tourist draw. Sadly, the Indian ferries that once used a jetty near **Talaimannar** haven't operated since 1984 and are highly unlikely to resume service any time soon.

If you're really seeking sights, try visiting **St Lucia's Church** at Palimunai and **Martyrs' Church** at Pesalai. The latter is named for the unfortunate converts killed when a king of Jaffna caught his son dabbling in St Francis Xavier's Christianity and decided to teach the congregation a bloody lesson. Mannar Island has some **beaches**, but swimming in the sea is locally considered to be a sign of lunacy.

VAVUNIYA TO JAFFNA

For tourists, the A9 is the only permitted land route to cross **Tamil Eelam**, the LTTE-controlled Vanni region (see Behind the Cadjan Curtain, p297). This flat, savanna-like area is today effectively another country, sometimes nicknamed Tigerland. Crossing the area is perfectly feasible and rather intriguing, though you can't explore at liberty without prearranged permission.

The trip is cheapest when made in a series of bus hops. Vavuniya to Jaffna can be done in under six hours if all goes seamlessly (although it's usually easier southbound). Transport connections are best in the mornings, and you'd be wise to start out by around 8am. Once the **frontiers** (7am-5pm) close, those stranded in Tigerland for whatever reason will have to camp down on a concrete floor and wait until the next morning.

The first hop is from Vavuniya to **Omantai** (Rs 25, 25 minutes, twice hourly) on a bus that is run on alternate days by the CTB and private companies. The scenery of overgrown minefields is dotted with army posts and burnt-out buildings but, as fellow passengers are quick to point out, the area was densely populated before the civil war.

At Omantai, women file left, and men right for the **SLA checkpoint**. Beyond you can walk the 700m across no-man's-land or take a Rs 5 shuttle bus to a bus park within Tigerland. Here you jump aboard another bus before dealing with LTTE checks 4km further north at **Puliyankulam** (no stops here southbound). Locals go through counters 10 and 11, but foreigners need to head to counter 2, a special blue hut to the left. Here

you'll apply for what is effectively the Tamil Eelam transit visa. This free transit pass is issued without any awkward questions. However, if you want to stop in Kilinochchi or venture off the A9, you'll need a Rs 1000 passbook, which looks a little like a shortened air ticket. This is usually only issued to those with a specific 'good' reason (tourism isn't sufficient) and you'll generally need to have visited the TRO in Vavuniya beforehand to get back-up documents. (Southbound there's a slightly better chance of getting this pass at Mukamalai but don't hold your breath.)

Armed with your transit pass, proceed through counter 12 for baggage checks, after which you'll receive a chit. Locals have to declare their valuables and pay a series of taxes and duties on all they 'import' to Eelam but foreigners generally get waved through. Return your baggage-checked chit when requested and you are free to board a bus to Mukamalai (Rs 150, 2½ hours). These wait outside and depart when full. Buses are quite frequent in the early morning but much rarer later in the day.

The express bus makes two short temple stops en route. The first is at the **Amman Temple**, where a pot-bellied holy man gets aboard and smears ash blessings on foreheads for a reconstruction-fund donation. On the southern edge of Mankulam, before the Mullaittivu road junction, look left to see the **Captain Pork statue**, honouring an oddly nicknamed suicide bomber. His solo mission destroyed the SLA's Mankulam base in November 1990.

At Murukandy, the very old but particularly tiny **Ankaran Temple** is considered

---

CROSSING TIGERLAND *Mark Elliott*

The LTTE bus décor was as confusingly mixed as my emotions: the Buddha and the Madhu Madonna sat incongruously amid Hindu gods, Chinese Baby posters and a few pictures of LTTE leader Vellupillai Prabhakaran. The distinguished-looking gentleman sitting beside me was obviously a Tiger sympathiser. 'What do you notice?' he asked me, waving generally at the overgrown minefields of Tamil Eelam.

He answered himself. 'No soldiers. No ID checks. We don't want an army to "save" us. Here nobody is harassed. Nobody pushing you around. Here people are free to get on with living.'

When there were ruins he'd bemoan SLA callousness. When there was a paddy field or coconut grove he'd burst with pride that 'the boys' had managed to 'liberate' the land from SLA land mines. At Murukandy, an innocent-looking young man came aboard with twitchy moustache, flip-flops and army-style fatigues. An LTTE 'soldier'. 'You call this a terrorist?' asked my new friend incredulously, yanking playfully on the young man's sleeve. The 'terrorist' simply smiled shyly.

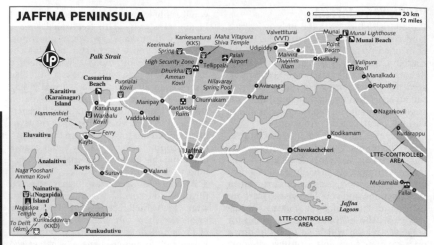

so holy that the road has been diverted to create more room for coconut-cracking pilgrims. Locals consider a prayer here imperative to ensure a safe journey, so virtually all road transport stops, including buses. The atmosphere is lively, with plenty of stalls selling peanuts and dry snacks. Notice truck drivers slapping holy ash on their vehicles as well their brows.

The bus passes without stopping through **Kilinochchi**. It's the only sizable town en route to Jaffna, and is the administrative capital of LTTE-controlled territory. The difficult conditions of life here are most visible at the **Central College** (251km marker), where bombed-out skeletons of the original concrete structures now support thatched roofs so that classes can continue.

North of Kilinochchi, roads branch off to **Mullaittivu**, the LTTE's tsunami-pummelled naval base and former military command centre, and to **Pooneryn**, with its supposedly fine Dutch fortress. The A9 continues north between saltpans and across the **Elephant Pass**, a 1km-long causeway that is the only thing anchoring the Jaffna peninsula to the rest of Sri Lanka. Its capture from the SLA in 2000 was considered the LTTE's most audacious and profound military victory.

The checkpoints for leaving Tigerland are just beyond Pallai in **Mukamalai**. Local bus passengers queue up, but foreigners should nip over to the booth on the left to have their exit pass stamped and collected. Then everyone jumps back on the bus again

for the last 500m across to the **SLA checkpoint**. Men and women queue separately for baggage checks and possibly a little interview. At the end of the checkpoint are buses for Jaffna; there's a choice of frequent minibuses (Rs 40, 55 to 75 minutes) and slower-filling CTB buses (Rs 35, 1½ hours).

JAFFNA
☎ 021 / pop 120,000

Low-rise Jaffna has a compulsively fascinating cityscape. Mostly it's a sprawling patchwork of comfortably middle-class colonial-era suburbs, almost lost in lush foliage and palms. But all this screeches to a halt in the commercial centre, which, in turn, rubs shoulders with the gaping holes and eerie rubble of bombed-out former civic offices. It's an intriguing, friendly and utterly untouristed place that repays gentle exploration. You'll appreciate Jaffna more for its insights into the region's special personality than for any specific sights.

History

For centuries Jaffna (or Yarl) has been Sri Lanka's Hindu-Tamil cultural and religious centre, although the 17th-century Portuguese tried hard to change that. In 1620 they captured Jaffna's King Sangli (whose horseback statue stands on Point Pedro Rd), then set about systematically demolishing the city's fabulous Hindu temples. A substantial wave of mass Christian conversions followed – hence all the beautiful

WHO CONTROLS JAFFNA? *Mark Elliott*

A week before the November 2005 presidential election I interviewed dozens of local Tamils. All told me excitedly that they planned to vote for the opposition 'peace' candidate, Ranil Wickremasinghe. One strong LTTE sympathiser had travelled from Colombo to Jaffna specifically to vote. An almost 100% vote for Wickremasinghe seemed assured among Jaffna district's 400,000-plus electorate.

Then came the bombshell.

The LTTE had originally been noncommittal about the 'irrelevant' election. But a few days before polling day, its line hardened. A boycott was announced. Ominous little fliers announced 'unfortunate repercussions' for Tamils who dared to vote. Suddenly my pro-Wickremasinghe Tamil friends claimed they had 'no interest' in the election!

On polling day an army of international observers sat around to check that voting was free and fair. But there were no voters. Only one vote was cast all day at the station I visited. Jaffna was utterly silent. The only bus that dared to run in contravention of an LTTE travel ban had its windows smashed by 'unknown' youths. Jaffna's turnout was a record-low 0.014%; virtually every Tamil stayed home praying for Wickremasinghe's victory rather than making it happen. He lost by around 180,000 – entirely because of the boycott.

Why would the LTTE want to hand victory to their most vociferous opponent? Many fear it's because the election's victor, Mahinda Rajapakse, is more likely to provide the LTTE with an excuse to restart the war. And few doubt that the LTTE wants to 'liberate' Jaffna. Whatever the reality, the election showed all too graphically just who holds the real power in Jaffna.

churches. Many Hindu temples were not rebuilt until the mid-19th century.

Jaffna surrendered to the Dutch after a bitter three-month siege in 1658. Various Portuguese and Dutch fortifications remain dotted around the peninsula, but most are either ruined or still in military use (and so are inaccessible to tourists).

In 1795 the British took over Jaffna, sowing the seeds of future interethnic unrest by 'favouring' the Jaffna Tamils (p296).

Escalating tensions overwhelmed Jaffna in the early 1980s, and for two decades the city became a no-go war zone. Variously besieged by Tamil guerrillas, SLA troops and the so-called peace-keeping force, the city lost much of its population to emigration. In 1990 the LTTE forced out most Muslims, though around 3000 have now returned.

Somehow Jaffna survived the endless bombings and a crippling blockade (kerosene once retailed here for 20 times the market price). In the sudden peace created by the 2002 accords, Jaffna sprang back to life. Today the town feels 'occupied' but surprisingly calm and relaxed. Although the town has been officially held by the government since 1995, in fact the LTTE wields considerable real power (above). Unlucky Jaffna citizens pay tax twice: both to the government and to the Tigers.

Orientation

Commercial activity is crammed into the bustling, architecturally crapulous 1960s concrete of Hospital, Kasturiya and Kankesanturai (KKS) Rds. Their fascinating ugliness is enhanced by humidity stains and occasional shell holes. Southeast of the fort is an area of Beirut-style shattered buildings that creates a sorrowfully photogenic sense of war horror. Most guesthouses are a world away in the delightfully leafy Nallur and Chundukuli residential areas, notably around Kandy Rd. Jaffna makes for fascinating bicycle rides, but distances are too great and temperatures too sweaty for wandering too far on foot.

Jaffna's addresses have 'old' or 'new' street numbers that can create an apparently nonconsecutive jumble.

Information

INTERNET ACCESS

AeroLanka (6 Modern Market, Hospital Rd; per hr Rs 50; ⌚ 6am-9pm) This airline office (p312) has a reasonably fast connection but few other programs installed on the computers.

Express Net Cafe (328 Stanley Rd; per hr Rs 40; ⌚ 9am-9pm) Neither express nor a café.

Jaffna Public Library (☎ 222 7835; 259 KKS Rd; per hr Rs 30; ⌚ 9am-7pm) Head up the library's (p309) stairs, then right to the back beyond the reference and self-study sections.

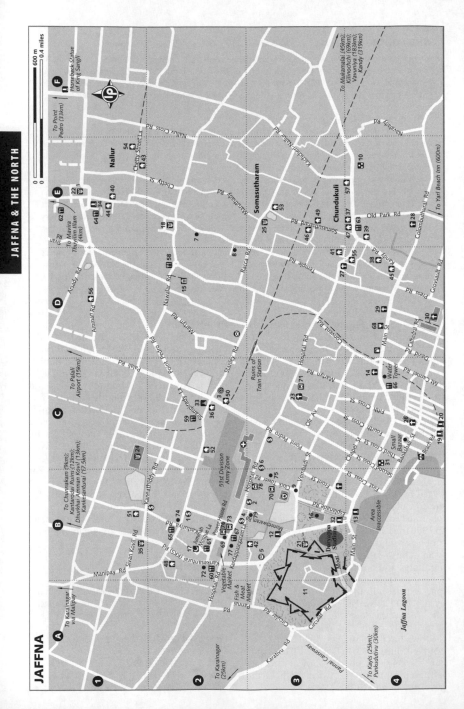

JAFFNA

Theresa Communications (☎ 222 2597; 72A Racca Rd; per min Rs 8; ☺ 8am-7pm or on request)
Universal Link (☎ 222 7286; 127/1 Temple Rd; per hr Rs 30; ☺ variable)

LTTE INFORMATION
TRO office (☎ 222 5125; 141 Temple Rd; ☺ 9am-5pm) Friendly, but not keen on giving LTTE-area permits to tourists.

MONEY
Bank of Ceylon (52 Stanley Rd), **Commercial Bank** (Hospital Rd), **HNB** (Hospital Rd) and **Seylan Bank** (Hospital Rd) all have ATMs.

POST
Post office (Postal Complex, KKS Rd; ☺ 7am-6pm Mon-Fri, 7am-1pm Sat)

Sights
NALLUR KANDASWAMY KOVIL
Much the most impressive religious building in Jaffna, the **Nallur Kandaswamy Kovil** (Temple Rd; donation appropriate; ☺ 4.30am-6pm) is one of Sri Lanka's most significant Hindu temple complexes. The original 15th-century temple was destroyed by the Portuguese, and the current structure dates from 1734.

Get your first view from the east, where the unusual golden-ochre god-encrusted *gopuram* is the focus of Point Pedro Rd. Within, your eye is drawn to the central brassed-framed Murugan image. To the left a succession of tigeresque beams leads towards a colonnaded, stepped holy pool. Other subshrines and murals are somewhat gaudy and naive, but the curious ticking clock on the PA system adds a Hitchcock-style sense of mystery. It's most interesting at **puja** (☺ 5am, 10am, noon, 4pm and 5pm). Men must remove shirts as well as shoes.

The temple is the focus of the country's wildest Hindu festival (25 days in July/August), when pilgrims descend from all across the region. This reaches a climax on day 24, with spectacular parades of juggernaut floats and gruesome self-mutilation by entranced devotees.

Recover from a hard afternoon's prayer at a trio of refreshing ice-cream parlours around the corner.

OTHER HINDU TEMPLES
Jaffna's countless Hindu temples range from tiny shrines to sprawling complexes featuring *mandapaya* (platforms with decorated

pillars) and towering *gopuram*. Those devoted to elephant-headed Ganesh (Pillaiyar) often incorporate attractive ponds. Many more primarily honour Ganesh's brother Murugan. Most temples are easily spotted by vertical red-and-white stripes on the external walls. **Perumal Kovil** (Clock Tower Rd) has the most spectacularly colourful *gopuram* in Jaffna, while that of **Vaitheeswara Kovil** (KKS Rd) is contrastingly sparse, its unusual blue-grey mass standing sentinel at the end of Kannathiddy Rd.

The grey columns of the **Kanabady Kovil** (Nawalar Rd) look dull by day but are appealingly mysterious when half-lit at night. The modest Somasutharam **Pillaiyar Kovil** (Racca Rd) looks picturesque when viewed across its lily pond. The small **Muniyabarar Kovil** (KKS Rd) is nestled above a curve of fortress moat and has an access tunnel into one of the remnant triangles of the outer defence wall (now used as a makeshift toilet).

CHURCHES
Pottering between the many fine churches is a great way to get a sense of Jaffna's charmingly lush back streets and quietly comfortable colonial-era homes.

The grandest church is **St James'** (Main St), a classical Italianate edifice with a silvered central cupola and twin bell towers dripping fish statues.

From Hospital Rd, **Our Lady of Refuge Church** (generally shortened to OLR and pronounced oh-wel-ah) looks like a whitewashed version of a Gloucestershire village church. Its south-facing entrance looks more French. One way or another it maintains a thoroughly European character, right down to the pointed canopy on the wooden pulpit.

St Mary's Cathedral (Cathedral Rd) is astonishingly large. It's built along classical lines, but uses modern materials that don't create any particular grace. It's curious to see banal corrugated-iron roofing held up by such a masterpiece of wooden vaulting.

St John the Baptist's (Hospital Rd) is a fine, column-sided Catholic church. The much smaller Anglican church of **St John's** (Main St) looks like a Sussex chapel, but with the napped flints replaced by cut sandstone chunks in the walls. Appropriately enough there's a cricket pitch ranged behind.

Colonnades and topiary make the **Holy Family Convent** (285 Main St) a beautiful, peaceful

oasis. Founded in 1850 and rebuilt in 1887 by French benefactors, the nearby **St Martin's Seminary** (Main St) looks like a Cambridge college transplanted into a tropical garden.

OTHER PLACES OF WORSHIP
The **Sri Nagavihara International Buddhist Centre** (Stanley Rd) was quickly rebuilt after government forces retook Jaffna from the LTTE in 1995, and it's virtually the only Buddhist structure in Jaffna. Its whitewashed dagoba contains a relic from Kataragama, which was placed inside in 2002. The **Jummah Mosque** (Jummah Mosque Lane) is quirkily colourful.

JAFFNA FORT
On a map, the city's obvious focus is the powerful pentagonal Dutch fort. Nonetheless, from the nearby city centre the fort's ultrasturdy walls are virtually invisible, hidden by wildly overgrown minefields. For much better views look from the Pannai Causeway, or stand on the little bridge on southern Circular Rd where the fortress' eastern moat flows out into the lagoon.

The fort was built in 1680 over an earlier Portuguese original. Defensive triangles added in 1792 produced the classic Vaubanesque star form.

The fort saw much fighting during the recent unrest. In 1990 the LTTE – who then controlled the rest of Jaffna – finally forced out government forces after a grisly 107-day siege. Repeated bombing means that precious little remains of the Dutch church that once stood within, and entry is not permitted anyway. Reaching the inner moat bridge is sometimes possible.

WAR RUINS
East of the fort lies the heartbreaking ruins of what was once central Jaffna's government district. They include several **headless statues** and a **shattered church** (Main St). It seems morbidly appropriate that the main business on battered western Main St is funeral direction. Parallel Bankshall Rd is particularly moving. Perhaps the most photogenic ruin is the **former kachcheri** (administrative office), a romantically gothic collection of old pillars and moss-crusted arches.

Some of Jaffna's best hotels were once along the lagoon, but these are bombed out, occupied by the military or both. The owner of the **Yarl Beach Inn** (p310) has a photo album and plenty of stories to tell. The lagoon is out of bounds, with street access boarded up even in the curious grid of narrow alleys in the fishermen's district. To reach their boats fishermen have to use a single security-checked access point on Beach Rd, west of Third Cross St.

JAFFNA ARCHAEOLOGICAL MUSEUM
This unkempt but interesting **museum** (Nawalar Rd; admission by donation; ⏰ 8.30am-5pm Wed-Mon) is hidden away at the end of a messy garden behind a cubic concrete library building that looks rather like a masonic lodge. At the museum's door are a very rusty pair of Dutch canons from the fort and a set of whale bones. Inside, the most interesting items are 11th-century Buddha torsos found at Kantarodai (p314), a poorly conserved life-sized portrait of Queen Victoria, and the 1845 palanquin of Point Pedro's *mudiyalar* (district governor). He must have been very small.

LTTE SITES
The LTTE built plenty of memorials for its many martyrs. Most memorials were damaged, desecrated or destroyed in 1995 when Jaffna was retaken by the SLA, but since 2002 some have been patched up or rebuilt. A helmet on an upturned gun is a common motif at such places. Perhaps the most sobering is the **Mavira Thuyilim Illam** (Martyrs' Sleeping House) at Kopay, just beyond the city's northeastern limits. Around 2000 grave markers in neat rows commemorate Tiger cadres killed in action; the majority (the smaller memorials) are for Tigers whose bodies have not been retrieved. Eerily there are around 200 headstones as yet unclaimed, suggesting that nobody thinks the war is over yet. The movingly understated box of older tombstone shards commemorates the 1995 SLA bulldozing of the original graveyard.

The monolithic **Thileepan Memorial** celebrates the LTTE's former political officer, Rasaiah Parthipan Thileepan. Seeking concessions from the IPKF in 1987, Thileepan went on a very public hunger strike and died on a plinth right in front of the Nallur Kandaswamy Kovil. The memorial's design (hands with broken chains grasping a flame) is repeated in other parts of town, including the **Martyr's Monolith** (Beach Rd), which commemorates 31 locals killed by the military

in 1986. The nearby statue of a grinning Ray Charles lookalike actually represents **MGR** (MG Ramachandran), a famous Indian-Tamil actor-turned-politician who became an important backer of Tamil rebels between 1983 and 1987. His two-finger V sign represents his offer of two *crore* (200,000,000) Indian rupees (around US$4,000,000) to the LTTE. At the time, the Tiger leaders thought he'd meant two *lakh* (US$40,000), and got a career-changing happy surprise when the funds arrived.

JAFFNA PUBLIC LIBRARY, SJV SELVANAYAKUM MONUMENT & CLOCK TOWER
Symbolically, one of the first major public buildings to be rebuilt once the civil war died down was the **Jaffna Public Library** (Esplanade Rd; ⏰ 9am-7pm). It retains the original neo-Mughal design and is reminiscent of the fine public buildings in New Delhi. The earlier library (inaugurated 1841) had been burnt by progovernment mobs after the violent Jaffna District Council elections of July 1981. Few acts were more significant in the build-up to full-scale civil war, and it has been described as a kind of cultural genocide. The library had contained more than 90,000 volumes,

including irreplaceable Tamil documents such as the one surviving copy of *Yalpanam Vaipavama,* a history of Jaffna.

The strange, top-heavy concrete pillar sitting almost beside the library is the **SJV Selvanayakum Monument** (KKS Rd), celebrating the founder of the Tamil Federal Party. His somewhat Gandhiesque statue stands beside the monument.

Another nearby architectural curiosity is the spindly **clock tower** (Vembadi St), whose Moorish domed top makes it look like it belongs somewhere in North Africa.

Sleeping

There are dozens of guesthouses dotted all over town, though the greatest concentrations are in the leafy Chundukuli and Nallur districts. A map is crucial for finding those in the back lanes. Most guesthouses are adapted from local homes rather than being purpose-built buildings. Jaffna's savvy hoteliers are swift to adjust prices according to demand, so expect considerable fluctuations.

BUDGET

New Rest House (☎ 222 7839; 19 Somasutharam Rd; tw/tr Rs 1000/1000) This place has clean, good value rooms with slightly tatty attached bathrooms in a house-restaurant with great food (breakfast Rs 150, meals Rs 200 to 300).

Theresa Inn (Do Drop Inn; ☎ 222 2597; Theresa-inn@sltnet.lk; 72A Racca Rd; s/tr incl breakfast Rs 750/1250; 🖳 🌣) If you want a home-stay experience, Teresa Inn's three rooms offer a great opportunity to lodge with a local family. The two singles share a bathroom. All have optional air-con, which costs Rs 500 extra if you use it. Joseph speaks English, two free bicycles are available for guests and the communications hut out the front means you can get Internet access on the spot for Rs 8 per minute.

Palan's Lodge (☎ /fax 222 3248; 71 Kandy Rd; tw/q Rs 800/1200; 🌣) The three fan rooms with simple clean bathrooms in a pleasantly homely atmosphere are good value. However, the Rs 1200 supplement for optional air-con seems excessive. No mosquito nets.

Yarl Beach Inn (☎ 222 5490; 8 Old Park Rd; s/tw/tr with fan Rs 500/900/1200, with air-con Rs 1250/2000/3000; 🌣) The poor old Yarl bravely struggles on, despite losing its key assets – the nearby beach (under military occupation) and a former Dutch-era mansion (to 1990 bomb-

ings). Rooms have attached bathrooms and are clean, if ageing. Great seafood dinners are available on advance order. Fan rooms are great value for single travellers and the owner can spin many a heart-rending yarn.

Holiday Resort (☎ 222 5643; St John's Lane; tw with fan/air-con Rs 500/1750; 🌣) This is a four-room getaway in a quiet garden of chirruping caged birds. The rooms share bathrooms and are basic but cheap and clean. The two air-con rooms have such high ceilings that the expense seems wasted. Food is available by advance order.

Green Inn (☎ 222 3898; fax 222 2298; 60 Kandy Rd; tw/q Rs 1250/2000; 🌣) Shelving and rounded mirror units add a tiny bit of character to dowdy rooms, set off the dining room of a dowdy house-restaurant. Optional air-con costs Rs 500 extra. Most rooms have attached bathrooms, though some are tiny cubicles.

APAT Guesthouse (☎ 077 773 8221; 75 Kandy Rd; s/tw/d/tr Rs 385/825/880/990) The rooms here are acceptable at the front but get increasingly dingy further back. Cheaper options share an off-puttingly grimy bathroom. There's a big communal dining table, but no food is available; as a notice reminds guests, 'Why worry?'

Bastian Hotel (☎ /fax 222 2605; 37 Kandy Rd; d/q Rs 825/1650) The basic, presentably clean fan rooms share slightly grubby bathrooms. There are no nets. Much better rooms are available in the associated New Bastian Hotel (opposite).

YMCA (☎ 222 2499; 109 Kandy Rd; s/tw Rs 250/400) The rooms here share unexciting but indoor and frequently-mopped toilets and showers. Some rooms have private toilet for Rs 100 extra. Often full.

If saving money is your only concern, there are several cheap but seriously basic options. Lone women beware.

Anisham Lodge (280 Stanley Rd; s/tr Rs 300/600) Ultrabasic beds in a rather dusty, if characterful and fairly central, older house. Some fans work. Shared toilets and wash booths in the yard behind.

Stanley Lodge (☎ 222 8092; 218 Stanley Rd; r Rs 500) Clean but very basic boxlike rooms with outdoor shared loo.

Sri Balaje Inn (☎ 222 2341; 293 Kasturiya Rd; s Rs 250) Bring your own sheets and bug protection.

MIDRANGE

Sarras Guest House (☎ 222 3627, 077 717 2039; 20 Somasutharam Rd; s Rs 1250-1750, tw/tr Rs 2000/2500; 🌣) This wonderful thick-walled old colonial mansion has been tastefully developed as a comfortable but sensibly priced guesthouse. Each of the four rooms is unique. The top-floor suite is fabulous, while the upstairs single has three sides of windows, polished old floorboards and art deco furniture. Its private bathroom is a short walk along the wraparound balcony. The other rooms have attached bathrooms. All have hot water and towels are provided. Booking ahead is advised, either directly or through Theresa Inn (opposite).

Morgan's Guest House (Maria's, UN Guesthouse; ☎ 222 3666; Temple Rd; tw Rs 3000; 🕃) Art, chests, stylish mirrors and real lamp shades give this four-room place far more character than any standard guesthouse. The best room has hot water and a lovely mosquito-shaded sitting area/veranda. The building is totally unmarked except for '103' (old number) on the red postbox.

GTZ Guesthouse (☎ 222 2203; 238 Temple Rd; tw Rs 2000; 🕃) The neat twin rooms here share big, bright bathrooms, set between pairs of rooms. There's a pleasant lounge, a library of books in German and an eye-opening map of Jaffna district's many minefields.

Jaffna City Hotel (☎ 222 5969; 70 KKS Rd; s/tw Rs 1925/2200; 🕃) The city centre's nicest option is set in a beautiful large garden, complete with silly dolphin fountain. The eight rooms are appealingly smart, except for the discordantly tatty desks. All have hot water. A big 26-room new block is being built behind.

Lux Etoiles (☎ 222 3966; 34 Chetty Street Lane; r Rs 3190-3685) The French-speaking owner has used lots of sash curtains and inexpensive reproduction art to create what he immodestly claims is 'Jaffna's best inn'. The claim might be true but perhaps not enough so to justify the relatively high prices charged. There's hot water, fridge and BBC World TV.

Yarl Paady Residency (☎ 222 6868; 51C Amman Rd; s/tw/tr Rs 1650/1815/2090; 🕃) This is a pleasantly spacious new place with tiled-floor rooms and hot water. Good value. There are free rooms for drivers.

Pillaiyar Inn (☎ /fax 222 2829; 31 Manipay Rd; s/d/ste from Rs 1700/2500/5000; 🕃) With a little better maintenance this breezy three-storey place could be a top choice, but missing door knobs, underlength power cords and crusty carpets that never seem to get vacuumed detract from the generally favourable impression. Some slightly older rooms in the annex are rather less inviting. The location within a central yet quiet garden is great. Food is excellent if you live long enough to await its arrival.

Thinakkural Rest (☎ 222 6476; 45 Chetty Street Lane; tw with fan/air-con Rs 1100/2200; 🕃) The big, clean rooms here have OK private bathrooms; a desk and wardrobe are the only adornments. The fan rooms are a little musty but clean and decent value. The attached bar is unappealing unless you retreat to the hotel's pleasant upstairs terrace.

New Bastian Hotel (☎ 222 7374; 11 Kandy Rd; s Rs 2200, d Rs 2750-3300, tr 3850; 🕃) Entered from beneath a vine trellis, this fairly smart pad has leather sofas in the communal sitting room, and manages to squeeze in a 20-seat conference table upstairs. Rooms are outwardly modern with TV, though not all of the bathrooms have hot water and some walls show signs of premature ageing.

US Guest House (☎ 222 7029; 874 Hospital Rd; d Rs 1500-2500; 🕃) Located in a new shop-house building bristling with antennae, the rooms are clean, green and reasonably well built. However, the garishly clashing colours of settees, bed linen and floor tiles might leave your senses jangling. The rooms have fridge, hot water and Rs 500 optional air-con.

Serendib Inn (☎ 222 6242, 222 3984; 86/1 Point Pedro Rd; s Rs 1100, d Rs 1650-3300; 🕃) The cheaper rooms here are neat but windowless. Somewhat nicer but still underlit doubles are ranged off a pleasant dining area. All rooms have fridge, hot water and optional air-con (Rs 500 extra). No mosquito nets. Car hire is available from Rs 3000 per day.

Eating

Jaffna is a good place to try South Indian–style cuisine. Dosas (paper-thin rice- and lentil-flour pancakes) and red-hued *pittu* (a mixture of rice flour and coconut, steamed in bamboo moulds) are local favourites. Many guesthouses will provide food if you ask in advance. The Pillaiyar Inn (left) and New Rest House (opposite) are particularly good, and keep some food in stock.

Cosy Restaurant (☎ 222 5899; Cosy Hotel, 15 Sirampiradi Lane; mains Rs 90-600; 🕃) Along with its attractively lantern-lit dining terrace, sheltered by *cadjan* (coconut-frond matting), the great attraction here is the tandoori oven. This allows the chef to produce excellent fresh naan (flat breads), as well as succulent chicken tikka (chicken marinated in spices and dry roasted), which is Rs 220 for six chunks; arrive early, as supplies are limited. There's a long menu of alternatives, including somewhat bland kormas and curious 'Swiss' lamb. The attached hotel has functional, slightly musty rooms for Rs 1000/1500 with fan/air-con.

Old Park Restaurant (☎ 222 3790; 40 Kandy Rd; meals Rs 160-600) Although it's a bit like eating in someone's front room, the Old Park offers some of Jaffna's tastiest cuisine and is paradise for garlic lovers. Its small garden is pleasant for a cold beer (Rs 200). It has comfortable air-con guest rooms (twin Rs 2500) if you're too drunk to get home.

Mangos (☎ 222 8294; 359/3 Temple Rd, Nallur; short eats from Rs 15, meals from Rs 60; ⏰ 7am-10pm) Behind a new café that looks somewhat half-finished is a solidly built timber-roofed dining pavilion with open sides. Here you can get good rice-and-curry lunches and traditional South Indian specialities for dinner, including excellent Rs 60 masala dosas (dosas stuffed with spiced vegetables) cooked to order.

Café Yours & TCT Supermarket (☎ 077 922 2829; 527 Nawalar Rd; snacks from Rs 20; ⏰ 7am-10pm) The tiny modern café attached to this Danish-owned supermarket serves reasonable instant coffee (Rs 10) and makes mini pizzas (Rs 50) to order.

Malayan Café (36-38 Grand Bazaar; meals from Rs 50; ⏰ 7am-9pm) This downmarket but wonderfully olde worlde eatery has marble-topped tables, long glass-and-wood cabinets and occasional blasts of incense to bless the in-house shrine. The cheap vegetarian fare is served on banana leaves rather than plates and is eaten by hand. When you're finished, fold up the leaf and post it through the letterbox-shaped waste chute in the hand-washing area.

Sri Palm Beach (☎ 222 6634; 205 Kasturiya Rd; mains Rs 180-350; ⏰ 11.30am-10pm; ✷) This is a comfortably air-conditioned upstairs place with wide, reliable menu. It serves pleasant, if not outstanding, fried chicken '65', as well as masala dosas after 6.30pm.

Thanj Hotel (Main St; snacks from Rs 20; ⏰ 5am-9.30pm) Basic, friendly place for fresh hoppers (bowl-shaped pancakes) in the evening.

Rio Ice Cream (448A Point Pedro Rd; sundaes Rs 40; ⏰ 9am-10pm) This is the biggest and brightest of three popular ice-cream parlours around the Nallur Kandaswamy Kovil.

Three Star Hotel (☎ 222 7125; 162 Hospital Rd; meals from Rs 55; ⏰ 7am-10pm) This typically fly-infested servery has particularly delicious rice-and-curry meals. The vegetable curry is mild, the saffron rice is laced with raisins and for Rs 70 you can add a chunk of prefried chicken.

Food City (175 KKS Rd; ⏰ 8.30am-8.30pm) Central Jaffna's most Western-style supermarket.

Drinking

The unchallenged meeting place for NGO types is the cosy garden bar of **Morgan's Guest House** (Temple Rd; most drinks R200; ⏰ 6-11pm), the unsigned but characterful guesthouse (p311). Pleasant alternatives for a beer include Old Park Restaurant (left) or the garden of the Jaffna City Hotel (p311). The **Rosarian Convent** (☎ 222 3388; 333 Main St; ⏰ 8am-1pm & 2-5.30pm), formerly at 123 Main St, makes Rosario 'wine' (Rs 175 per bottle, takeaway only). Sweet and laced with cinnamon and cloves, it tastes rather like German gluhwein. It also makes startlingly coloured grape 'juice' (Rs 150) and 'nelli crush' (Rs 125), both nonalcoholic fruit cordials with pleasant, if slightly bubble-gum-style, flavours and laxative properties. Add water.

Getting There & Away

AIR

Both **Expo Aviation** (☎ /fax 222 3891; www.expoavi .com; 1E Stanley Rd; ⏰ 8.30am-6.30pm Mon-Sat, 9.30am-5pm Sun) and **AeroLanka** (Hospital Rd ☎ 222 3916; 13 Hospital Rd; Serendib Inn ☎ 222 3984; 86/1 Point Pedro Rd) fly to Colombo's Ratmalana Air Force Base (one way/return Rs 6700/12,000, 75 minutes). Both currently depart daily around 9am, though schedules change frequently. Palali airport is 17km north of Jaffna, but don't try to go to there independently; it's a military installation in an otherwise closed high-security zone. Airfares include a bus shuttle. This departs from an unlikely-looking tin-roofed **shelter** (Hospital Rd) at the Sinhala Maha Vidyalaya. Arrive there three hours before flight departure time for security checks. Bring your own refreshments. Coming *from* Palali, the shuttle drops arriving passengers on Clock Tower Rd.

Several agencies sell air tickets. Try **Manoj Express** (☎ 222 3916, 077 780 1038; 32 Clock Tower Rd; ⏰ 8am-6.30pm) and, for AeroLanka only, **Thampi Travels** (☎ 222 2040; Kandappasegaram Lane; ⏰ 8.30am-6pm) or Serendib Inn (p311).

Jaffna to Trincomalee flights have been suspended.

Ceylinco Travels & Tours (☎ 222 5063; www.ceylinco.lk/travels; 1 Stanley Rd; ☺ 8.30am-5.30pm Mon-Fri, 8.30am-1pm Sat) are agents for SriLankan Airlines. It has proposed a new **SriLankan Air Taxi** (☎ 019-733 3355; www.srilankan.aero/airtaxi) shuttle to Colombo's Bandaranaike International Airport (US$250).

BUS
An extensive CTB network covers the Jaffna peninsula, and routes are duplicated by helpfully numbered private minibuses that leave from a stand behind the bus station. Useful, frequent services include bus 750 to Point Pedro via Nelliady, bus 751 to Point Pedro via Valvettiturai (VVT) and the northbound bus 769 to Dhurkhai Amman Kovil via Chunnakam (for the Kantarodai Ruins). Confusingly, an altogether different bus 769 runs eastwards to Mukamalai (LTTE checkpoint) via Kandy Rd. Take this bus to go anywhere in Sri Lanka beyond the Jaffna peninsula; after crossing the LTTE-controlled Vanni region you'll emerge eventually at Vavuniya in around 5½ to seven hours, depending on waiting times. While this is not too difficult (see p303), those who don't want to make three changes of bus can buy tickets to Colombo (Rs 1100 to 1200, roughly 12 hours) on direct air-con buses or vans. All direct bus services leave Jaffna between 7am and 8am; the return service leaves from Colombo at around 10pm. Agencies that sell Colombo tickets:

Atlas (☎ 222 5464; 77 KKS Rd; ☺ 6.30am-9pm)
Sethu Travels (☎ 222 2822; Three Star Hotel, 162 Main St; ☺ 7am-10pm)
SNJ Travels (☎ 222 2837; Hotel Rolex, Main St)

In Colombo, many agencies on Galle Rd in Wellawatta, including **Sadu Communications** (☎ 077 325 3017), sell these bus tickets. Or contact **SNJ** (☎ 232 1449; 160 Wolvendaal St, Col 13).

Note that when done in hops, the Jaffna–Colombo trip costs under Rs 500. That's less than half the price of a direct bus, and southbound it can even prove quicker!

TAXI
A convenient and relatively good value way to visit Jaffna's hinterland is to rent a van or taxi. If you do this through a guesthouse or travel agent you'll rarely pay more than

CLASSIC CARS

Havana has its classic American cars, maintained in the face of economic boycott. Years of war and isolation means that Jaffna has its less glamorous equivalent – a small fleet of 1960s Austin Cambridge and Morris Minor taxis. Though many are rather run-down, riding in one of these bangers adds a touch of photogenic fun to your trip. But don't expect lower rates; the old cars tend to be fuel inefficient so new air-con vans can actually be cheaper.

if you hire one off the street, and you might also get a driver who speaks a modicum of English. Costs range between Rs 2750 and 4000 per day for up to 100km. Add Rs 25 to 35 per kilometre for extra mileage. Around 130km covers virtually every 'sight' on the peninsula except the offshore islands.

Getting Around
From Kandy Rd, any westbound bus (Rs 4) or minibus (Rs 5) heads to the bus station. Coming back, take the frequent eastbound bus 769 for Chundukuli or bus 750 for Nallur via Point Pedro Rd. Three-wheelers and wonderfully antiquated taxis wait in the centre of Hospital Rd. Three-wheelers cost Rs 50 for short trips, Rs 100 to Nallur or Rs 300 per hour to potter round town. A bicycle is more pleasant for exploring, and several guesthouses will lend or help you find one.

JAFFNA PENINSULA
Bananas, palmyra palms, cassava plantations and even little plots of grapevines characterise the intensively cultivated Jaffna peninsula (Map p304). It's heavily indented with lagoons and wetlands, and dotted with Hindu holy spots, sacred wells and a number of LTTE memorials. Added up this can provide a mildly interesting day trip or two, especially if you rent a van to zip along the confusing web of narrow lanes. However, individually none of the sights are especially memorable and almost all decent beaches are in closed High Security Zones.

Towards Kankesanturai (KKS)
The port of KKS and its once famous Palm Beach are totally out of bounds to tourists, but there are a few places to see en route.

ACRONYM LAND

Tamil names can be quite a mouthful. Handily, the peninsula's longer town names are often abbreviated. Common examples include KKS (Kankesanturai), VVT (Valvettiturai) and KKD (Kurikadduwan). The acronyms don't stop there. Northeast Sri Lanka is often nicknamed NGO land, such is the plethora of nongovernmental organisations trying to help out, post-tsunami. Then there are the myriad players in the ever-shifting fields of politics and Eelam separatism. Official documents can choke on their own acronyms. An example...

'The GOSL and LTTE created the SLMM through signing the CFA on Feb 22nd 2002. Based on the CFA, the NRG and GOSL concluded a SOMA where status, privileges and immunities of SLMM are defined.'

No wonder the public is confused!

Some useful translations:

CFA – Cease-Fire Agreement
EPDP – Eelam People's Democratic Party (www.epdpnews.com); Marxist-leaning Tamil party working with the government
GOSL – Government of Sri Lanka
LTTE – Liberation Tigers of Tamil Eelam; the Tamil Tigers
NRG – Royal Norwegian Government
P-TOMs – Post-Tsunami Operational Management Structures; also known as the Joint Mechanism, this is the means by which aid was at long last be delivered to the desperate coastal communities of LTTE-administered areas.
SLA – Sri Lanka Army
SLMM – Sri Lanka Monitoring Mission; provided by Norway, Sweden, Finland, Denmark and Iceland to oversee the 2002 CFA
SOMA – Status of Mission Agreement
RRR – Relief, Rehabilitation and Reconciliation (www.mrrr.lk)
TRO – Tamils Rehabilitation Organisation (www.troonline.org); the LTTE's self-help humanitarian aid NGO

At Chunnakam bus stand you can pick up a three-wheeler to travel the confusing squiggle of lanes that lead 3km west to the puzzling **Kantarodai Ruins** (Purana Rajamaha Vihara). Here, some two dozen pudding-shaped little dagobas, 1m to 2m in height, grow like mushrooms in a palmyra patch the size of a modest garden. Discovered in 1916, the ruined foundations of many more dagobas are easy to make out. OK, so it's hardly a mind-blowing vista and the dagobas are somewhat crudely patched up but they're probably 2000 years old. Nobody really knows what they were built for. Returning towards Chunnakam, the modest **Kantarodai Pillaiyar Kovil** is attractively located, with its festival chariot parked outside facing the palm-flanked tank.

Beside the KKS road at the 13km marker, the big **Dhurkhai Amman Kovil** is set behind a fairly deep, stepped pool. The temple celebrates the goddess Durga and draws relatively large crowds on Tuesdays. *Puja* is occurs at 7am, 11am, 4pm and 6pm, although in the past they were exactly half an hour late, as the temple worked on LTTE 'Eelam time', which was half an hour behind Sri Lankan time.

The temple is as far as you can go by public transport (northbound bus 769, Rs 18 from Jaffna). A kilometre further north is the start of one of the controversial High Security Zones from which the whole civilian population has been evicted. If you have a car or van, the one way to get a view inside is to request permission to visit the sacred **Keerimalai spring**. This 'miraculous' spring is said to have cured a horse-faced princess of her equine features. Despite waves crashing melodramatically on razor wire behind, the site is about as photogenic as an uncared-for swimming pool. Nonetheless, the trip to get here is one of Sri Lanka's most surreal experiences. It starts with SLA security checks: hand in your phones, cameras and (nerve-rackingly) passport to the duty officer, who places them in an unlocked cubbyhole. You get a worn old pass in return. An assigned soldier-minder then hops aboard your vehicle to stop you straying or exploring the fascinating wreckage en route. Still, you get a good view of abandoned **Tellippalai** just by driving through. Here, bored soldiers shuffle about the otherwise deserted streets, creating an extraordinary war-movie atmosphere that feels like a very real war-movie set. Turn off the KKS road next to the greying *gopuram* of the **Maha Vitapura Shiva Temple**. Just before arriving at Keerimalai spring there's a quick glimpse of **Naguleswaram Kovil**. This spiritually significant temple was bombed by the army in 1990. Some parts have reportedly been repaired, but the visible sections resemble classic Angkor Wat ruins as the jungle creeps into the cracks.

Towards Point Pedro

Travelling by private vehicle you could start out via the Kopay **Maiviri Thuyilim Illam** (p309), and join the Chunnakam–Point Pedro road beside the historic but extremely lacklustre **Nilavaray spring pool**, some 7.5km further north. The water here is supposedly fresh for the first 15m or so, becoming increasingly salty beneath; it's barely worth stopping to look.

In front of Nelliady School is the **gilded statue of 'Captain Miller'** (MMV Rd, Nelliady), nom de guerre of the first Black Tiger (LTTE suicide bomber). On 5 July 1987 he drove an explosives-laden truck into the school, which was then being used as an army camp. Hero or villain, he died taking at least 200 SLA soldiers with him. The statue and some overgrown shattered ruins are 450m north of the Point Pedro road junction, where bus 750 stops.

Ramshackle **Point Pedro** is the Jaffna peninsula's second town, and has a few very faint hints of colonial style. The harbour, located within a military zone, is off limits. However, a kilometre east, more attractive **Munai** remains accessible. From Point Pedro bus station walk 100m south then east, crossing through a curious stone **toll gate** that locals claim dates from the Dutch era. Some 250m beyond, turn left towards the sea up St Anthony's Lane to see the town's two finest **churches**. The coast road continues a kilometre east to **Munai Lighthouse** (no photos), beyond which the fishermen's beach becomes wider and sandier. The nicest area of sand bar is nearly 2km further on, dotted with some curious four-plank lashed fishing rafts. There are also some attractive views towards a lagoon area to the southeast. That's lovely if you don't

look behind you – with tsunami damage, refugee housing and army dugouts in most other directions this is hardly a relaxing place to unroll your bathing towel.

If you have private transport, consider continuing to the much revered **Valipura Kovil**, around 5km southeast of central Point Pedro. It celebrates a surprise visit Vishnu made here in the guise of a fish. The entrance portal is painted in restrained olive and brown tones. Its famous water-cutting festival (a boisterous ceremony where devotees are sprayed in holy water) was revived in October 2004, attracting around 75,000 pilgrims.

Another 6km southeast of the temple is an area of sand dunes that some observers have very exaggeratedly dubbed **Manalkadu Desert**. One mildly interesting sight here is the way one of the dunes has half-submerged the roofless century-old ruins of **St Anthony's Church** in Manalkadu village, 3.5km off the main road. A wonderfully gaudy **new St Anthony's church** in central Manalkadu, 400m beyond, includes a portrait of the Virgin Mary looking rather like a Walt Disney Snow White. However, the formerly picturesque surrounding village is a tragic scene of tsunami devastation, while the lovely beach is currently patrolled by the army.

Valvettiturai (VVT)

On the peninsula's north coast, VVT is an easy stopping point between Jaffna and Point Pedro. This once rich smuggling town is now most famous as the birthplace of the LTTE supreme leader Vellupillai Prabhakaran. The green-walled **Prabhakaran family house** (Vampady Lane) was damaged by security forces in 1985, an attack that also killed 70 VVT citizens and reportedly spurred the LTTE to perform the infamous Anuradhapura killings as reprisal. The house has long since been abandoned and Prabhakaran's parents have fled to India. Nonetheless, somewhat in the style of Jim Morrison's grave, the ruins continue to attract a trickle of tourists and well-wishers from around the world. There's graffiti in Tamil, Sinhalese and English and a painted sign on the gatepost out the front describes Prabhakaran as the 'President of Tamil Eelam'.

To find the house from the bus stop in central VVT, walk west for about 400m, passing the sizable **Amman Kovil** with its fine *gopuram*. Continue 200m to the first asphalted lane on the left. There's a seat around a tree in the middle. Prabhakaran's house is the first on the left up this lane.

Around 8km southeast of VVT, halfway to Nelliady by a circuitous back lane, is the Samurabahe **Mavira Thuyilim Illam**. It's another graveyard for LTTE cadres and is fundamentally similar to the more accessible version at Kopay (p309), but it feels somewhat less stark given the attractive backing of palmyra palms and manicured gardens.

JAFFNA'S OFFSHORE ISLANDS

Jaffna peninsula (Map p304) is surrounded by a series of low-lying islands, many attached to the mainland by a web of causeways. The main pleasure in exploring here is not any specific sight, but the hypnotic quality of the waterscapes and the escapist feeling of a boat ride between them. Long strips of coastal wetland or lagoon are backed by palmyra palms, and the shallow seas are embroidered with fish traps; watch fishermen wading chest-deep to maintain them. Realistically there are two day-trip possibilities. One is to loop around through Karaitivu (Karainagar), ferry-hop to Kayts and return via the causeway. The second and generally more agreeable option is to cross the causeways to Kurikadduwan (KKD), a virtually uninhabited islet off Punkudutivu. From here you can take a ferry to windswept Delft or sacred Nainativu.

Karaitivu (Karainagar) & Kayts

The main attraction of visiting Karaitivu (Karainagar) is the approach across the very low-lying **causeway**, with its views of the fascinating maze of fish traps. Look right at the start of the causeway to spy the towering *gopuram* of **Punnalai Kovil** through the palmyra palms. This Vishnu temple was supposedly founded at the site where a magic turtle mysteriously transformed itself into the radiant rock that remains the temple's central treasure.

Don't let Karaitivu locals persuade you that litter-strewn Casuarina Beach is worth the 3km diversion.

Roughly three buses per hour (bus 782 and bus 785) from Jaffna to **Karainagar town** (Rs 25, one hour) take the western road across Karaitivu, terminating at the colourful **Waribalabu Kovil**. However, for the

ferry to Kayts you'll need the east-coast road. As all the villages on that route have been bombed to bits, buses don't operate. So hop off the Jaffna–Karainagar bus as soon as you see a three-wheeler and charter it for the 6km ride to the tiny jetty. That's within a small naval zone: there's a security check and one traveller reported being turned back, but we experienced no problems here. The wire-pulled ferry contraption runs eight times daily (Rs 5, seven minutes) but be aware that you'll need to wade through knee-deep water on sharp stones, so waterproof sandals would be useful. Ferry access is not currently feasible for cars but bicycles are carried.

From the crossing you get a rather distant view of **Hammenhiel Fort**. Built by the Dutch on its own islet, it looks a little like Alcatraz. The name means 'Heel of the Ham', so-called because the Dutch saw Sri Lanka as shaped like a leg of gammon. It's used by the military so can't be visited.

The ferry arrives at eerie semideserted **Kayts town** between a dozen scuttled fishing boats. The two somewhat noteworthy churches are both visible by walking straight up Sunuvil Rd from the jetty. The first, 300m to the right of the main bus stop, is **St James'**. Over the entrance the sword-brandishing saint is shown riding an oddly smiling horse, while the faintly demonic silver statues of sour-faced angels and apostles above spookily recall a scene from *The Omen*. Some 400m up Sunuvil Rd from the jetty is the grand if dour neobaroque church of **St Mary's** (1895). A little beyond St Mary's the first asphalt lane to the right leads 600m to a waterfront cemetery with better, if still distant, views of Hammenhiel Fort.

Circuitous minibus 780 (Rs 32, 1½ hours) and slightly faster minibus 777 leave for Jaffna roughly every 40 minutes; last services depart 4.20pm, 5.30pm and (theoretically) 6.30pm.

Nainativu & Delft

A long **causeway** links Kayts to the island of Punkudutivu and the drive is delightful. Observe the lagoon fishermen who use wade-out traps and sail little archaic wind-powered canoes that look like miniature Nile feluccas. **Punkudutivu village**, the scene of minor riots in December 2005, has one of Jaffna's most screechingly colourful Hindu temples. Just before the Church of South India a house has its porch supported by two curiously elongated elephant figures. Many other older houses lie in various stages of decay. Smaller causeways link the island to the curiously isolated little ferry dock at **Kurikadduwan (KKD)**, where there are a pair of desultory drink stands but no village. From here there is a choice of destinations. Boats to Delft leave at 10am, returning at 3pm (Rs 50, one hour) but are prone to cancellations. Boats to Nainativu (Rs 15, 17 minutes) are vastly more frequent with sailings every half-hour from 8am to noon, and hourly from 12.30pm to 5.30pm. Often unmarked, Jaffna–KKD minibuses (Rs 35, 1½ hours) depart approximately hourly; the last return is around 5pm.

NAINATIVU (NAGAPIDA)

Known as Nainativu in Tamil and Nagadipa in Sinhalese, this 6km-long lozenge of palmyra groves is holy for both Buddhist and Hindu pilgrims. The term *naga* refers variously to serpent deity figures and to the ancient peoples who once inhabited the island.

Right in front of you as you step off the jetty is the **Naga Pooshani Amman Kovil** complex. While it's not Sri Lanka's most beautiful Hindu temple, its setting amid mature neem trees is very attractive especially viewed from the water, framed by colourful fishing boats. The interior is brought alive by the relief metalwork framing the main image houses and there's an inscription stone explaining the ancient Tamil kings' rules about how to deal with shipwrecked foreigners. The main temple deity is the *naga* goddess Meenakshi, a consort of Shiva. Women hoping to conceive a child come here to seek blessings. This can make

for a fascinating midday *puja*: cacophonous bells, drumming, oboes and conch horns create a trancelike atmosphere. The young women, accompanied by their mothers, are handed chalices full of flower petals, then proceed to the Ganesh subshrine for further prayers before returning to smash coconuts in the culmination of the fertility rite.

Male devotees must remove shirts as well as shoes before entering. An impressive 18-day festival is usually held in early June.

Walk 10 minutes south along the coast road (ID check en route) to find the **Nagadipa temple**, North Sri Lanka's most revered Buddhist pilgrimage site. It is said that the Buddha came here in person to prevent war breaking out between a *naga* king and his nephew over the ownership of a gem-studded throne. The wise Buddha's suggestion of giving the throne to the temple averted a war and created a great centre of pilgrimage. The throne and original temple disappeared long ago but today there is an attractive silver-painted dagoba, set amid waving palms. Just behind, three happy-looking Buddhas sit in a domed temple that looks more like a chapel.

DELFT (NADANTIVU)

The intriguing, windswept island of Delft (Nadantivu) is a 10km ferry ride southwest of KKD. A small, very ruined **Dutch fort** is a short walk from the ferry dock. Behind it is a beach with many exquisite shells. Like Mannar, Delft has a rare, ancient **baobab tree**; it's shaped like an immensely overgrown bamboo shoot.

The hundreds of field-dividing walls are hewn from chunks of brain and fan corals, and local Delft ponies descended from Dutch mounts roam the island.

Directory

CONTENTS

ACCOMMODATION

Sri Lanka has a good range of accommodation options, from rooms in a family home to five-star resorts.

Unlike neighbouring India, only a handful of places in Sri Lanka have dormitory-style rooms. The main accommodation option for solo travellers is single rooms, and they're often doll-sized boxes or cost the same amount as double rooms. On the other hand, most places bigger than a small guesthouse will have a 'family' room with three or four beds for 20% to 50% more than a double.

Prices are very seasonal, particularly in beach resorts. The prices quoted in this guide are high-season rates, and you can often find spectacular bargains in the low season. The 'season', and its prices, has a more or less official starting date – 15 December on the west and south coasts, 1 April on the east coast. The monsoon may have ended well before the season starts. High season ends around March in the South and West, and around September on the east coast. Of course, you can often bargain prices down at any time of the year.

Guesthouses and hotels are in demand during April in Nuwara Eliya, and in Kandy during the Kandy Esala Perahera (July/August). It would certainly pay to book well ahead if you plan to be in these places at these times.

Many places have a variety of rooms at different prices, and it's often worth asking if there are any cheaper rooms available once the staff have shown you their first room or quoted you their first price.

Most guesthouses and hotels can arrange transport or car hire for wherever you want to go, or can tailor a tour for you.

In this guide we place doubles (or equivalent) costing less than Rs 1500 (US$15) a night in the budget category, Rs 1500 to 8000 (US$15 to US$78) in the midrange category and over Rs 8000 in top end. Many midrange and top-end hotels quote room prices in dollars, but will accept the rupee equivalent. Unless stated otherwise, all rooms have a bathroom, fan, and mosquito net or electric 'mat'. Few budget places, except in the Hill Country, have hot water; if budget accommodation does have hot water, it will be mentioned in the review. Midrange places

---

BOOK ACCOMMODATION ONLINE

For more accommodation reviews and recommendations by Lonely Planet authors, check out the online booking service at www.lonelyplanet.com. You'll find the true, insider lowdown on the best places to stay. Reviews are thorough and independent. Best of all, you can book online.

PRACTICALITIES

- **Daily News** (www.dailynews.lk), **Daily Mirror** (www.dailymirror.lk) and the **Island** (www.island.lk) publish national and international news in English daily, while the **Sunday Times** (www .sundaytimes.lk) and **Sunday Observer** (www.sundayobserver.lk) come out weekends.

- Sri Lanka Broadcasting dominates the national AM/FM radio networks with a mix of English-, Sinhala- and Tamil-language programming; Colombo has a few private FM stations that broadcast a variety of music, news and talk. Short-wave radios can pick up the BBC.

- There are seven TV channels, including the state-run SLRC (Sri Lanka Rupavahini Corporation), ITN (Independent Television Network) and privately owned ETV-1, ETV-2, MTV, Swarnawahini and TNL. BBC World Service can be picked up on ETV-1 and StarPlus on ETV-2.

- The electric current is 230V, 50 cycles. Plugs comes two varieties (three round pins, or one flat pin and two round), so carrying an adaptor is necessary even for electrical gear purchased in Sri Lanka. Adaptors are readily available at electrical stores for about Rs 70.

- Sri Lanka uses the international metric system, though some Sri Lankans still express distance in yard and miles. The term *lakh* is often used in place of '100,000'.

---

have hot water; most have air-con too. Many places either have their own restaurant or will provide meals on request.

Guesthouses

You'll find some very inexpensive guesthouses, plus a few in the midrange bracket and even the occasional top-end place. Some guesthouses will rent just a couple of rooms, like the English B&B establishments, while other guesthouses are like small hotels. It's a good idea to pin down exactly what you're getting for your money, or you might be surprised with a bill for every cup of tea.

Apart from the low cost, the 'meeting people' aspect is the big plus of guesthouse accommodation. If you're after privacy, stick to the guesthouses with a separate guest annexe; some guesthouses have separate entrances for guests, while others require you to tiptoe through the lounge after a night on the town.

As many guesthouses are very small, its better to telephone first to see if a room is available rather than simply turning up. If you arrive in a town late at night without booked accommodation, consider a hotel room instead – most guesthouse owners are helpful, but they don't appreciate being woken up by unannounced arrivals.

Hotels

The line between lower-priced hotels and upper-range guesthouses is a blurred one, and not least in name since places that call themselves 'hotels' are really guesthouses, while other small hotels are called inns, lodges, villas and so on. You'll rarely find a double in a hotel for less than Rs 1000 (US$10), and there are places going all the way up the price scale.

The larger hotels are of two basic types: modern resort hotels and older colonial-style places. The latter type definitely has the edge when it comes to atmosphere, and the facilities are often just as good. The newer places pride themselves on luxury facilities such as tennis courts, windsurfing instruction, nightclubs, and prime beach, riverside or hill-top locations, and are mostly geared to package tourists. Resort doubles on the west coast cost from around US$35 up to US$100 plus. People with residency visas get discounts as high as 70% on the FIT (foreign individual tourist) rates at resort hotels, though the saving is more commonly around 30%.

The Ceylon Hotels Corporation operates a number of hotels and resorts around the country, as well as numerous resthouses. Some are well run and good value, while others are marginal and overpriced.

National Parks

The **Department of Wildlife Conservation** (Map pp84-5; ☎ 011-269 4241; www.dwlc.lk; 18 Gregory's Rd, Col 7) has bungalows, each accommodating up to 10 adults and two children, in some national parks, including Yala, Uda Walawe, Wasgomuwa, Wilpattu, Gal Oya and Horton Plains. It costs US$24 per person per

DIRECTORY

night in a bungalow, plus a linen charge of Rs 100 per person per day and a US$30 service charge per group per stay. Students and children six to 12 years of age pay half price (kiddies under six stay for free). You must bring your own dry rations and kerosene. Camp sites cost US$6 per site per day, plus Rs 200 service charge per trip. On top of these costs, there is a park entry fee of US$12 for the most popular parks. You can book up to a month in advance.

The **Wildlife Trust** (Map pp84-5; ☎/fax 011-250 2271; 18 Gregory's Rd, Col 7) maintains bungalows in national parks, and offers some 'nature' tours; see the small shop at the Department of Wildlife Conservation for information. Companies such as **Adventure Sports Lanka** (☎ 279 1584; actionlanka.com; 366/3 Rendapola Horagahakanda Lane, Talagama, Koswatta) also arrange trips to parks.

Resthouses

Originally created for travelling government officials by the Dutch, then developed into a network of wayside inns by the British, resthouses now mostly function as small midrange hotels. They're found all over the country, including in little out-of-the-way towns (where they may be the only accommodation). Although they vary widely in standards and prices (those run by the Ceylon Hotels Corporation are usually well maintained), the best resthouses are old-fashioned, have big rooms, and are usually situated to enjoy the view from the highest hill or across the best stretch of beach. A double costs anywhere from US$10 (Rs 1000) up to US$50 (Rs 5100).

Tea-Estate Bungalows

In the tea-growing areas of the Hill Country, a number of bungalows that were once the homes of British tea-estate managers have been converted into guesthouses or hotels. Despite the 'bungalow' appellation, they're often rambling villas with beautiful gardens and sitting rooms stuffed with antique furniture dating to when Sri Lanka was part of the Raj.

Price-wise the converted tea estate bungalows tend to fall into the midrange category, although a few are very much luxury properties. Tea Trails (p197) organises accommodation at for four magnificently renovated bungalows in the Dikoya area.

ACTIVITIES

Sri Lanka offers a range of activities for those who want to do more than simply sightsee.

Ayurveda

Ayurveda (eye-your-veda) is an ancient system of medicine that uses herbs, oils, metals and animal products to heal and rejuvenate. Heavily influenced by the system of the same name in India, Ayurveda is widely used in Sri Lanka for a range of ailments. Essentially, Ayurveda postulates that the five elements (earth, air, ether, water and light) are linked to the five senses and these in turn shape the nature of an individual's constitution – their *dosha* (life force). Disease and illness occurs when *doshas* are out of balance. The purpose of Ayurvedic treatment is to restore the balance and thus good health.

Traditional Ayurveda clinics patronised by Sri Lankans are very inexpensive, while those facilities orientated towards tourists charge many times more.

Therapeutic treatments often take some time; the patient must be prepared to make a commitment of weeks or months. More commonly, tourists avail themselves of one of the Ayurvedic massage centres attached to major hotels. The full massage treatment involves a head massage with oil, an oil body massage and a steam bath followed by a herbal bath. But this sort of regimen is really only for relaxation.

The standards at some Ayurvedic centres are low; the massage oils may be simple coconut oil and the practitioners may be unqualified, except in some cases as sex workers. As several poisoning cases have resulted from herbal treatments being misadministered, it pays to enquire precisely what the medicine contains and then consult with a conventional physician.

For massage, it may be useful to enquire whether there are both male and female therapists available, as we've received complaints from female readers about sexual advances from male Ayurvedic practitioners. In general it's not an acceptable Ayurvedic practice for males to massage females and vice versa.

Both the University of Colombo and the University of Gampaha offer degrees in Ayurvedic medicine. In this book we've included only clinics where the staff are qualified with degrees.

Cycling

Cycling is a great way to get around in Sri Lanka and mountain biking is also catching on. See p339 for more information.

Diving & Snorkelling

Coral and interesting shipwrecks can be seen at several spots along the west coast, including Hikkaduwa and Tangalla. The reef at Kirinda is said to be in fine shape, but rough seas make it inaccessible for all but a couple of weeks in April and May. There are also reefs at the Basses in the southeast and along the east coast. Pigeon Island off Nilaveli is a fine place to go snorkelling. You can also snorkel at Hikkaduwa, Unawatuna, Mirissa and at Polhena, near Matara.

Diving shops can be found in Colombo and in the major west coast resorts. They hire and sell gear, including snorkelling equipment. PADI courses are also available.

Along the west coast, the best time to dive and snorkel is generally from November to April. On the east coast, the seas are calmest from April to September.

Coral bleaching (where coral loses its algae due to higher-than-average ocean temperatures and regional influences) in 1998 struck about half of the island's reefs. The affected reefs were recovering when the 2004 tsunami struck. However, it is estimated that not more than 5% of the reef systems were affected by the tsunami, and some divers reported that visibility actually improved. See p64 for tips on responsible diving and snorkelling.

Golf

There are three excellent golf courses in Sri Lanka. Green fees and other expenses including club hire comes to about US$40 a day. The most scenic is definitely the Victoria Golf & Country Resort (p169) near Kandy, overlooking the Victoria Reservoir. There is also the historic Nuwara Eliya Golf Club (p202) and the Royal Colombo Golf Club (p92), which has a decent course.

Meditation

Many visitors to Sri Lanka participate in Buddhist meditation retreats. Although you'll find monasteries all over the island where meditation is practiced, the Kandy area is the main centre for such pursuits; see p192 for a list of retreats near Kandy.

There are also listings of places to practice intensive meditation in Sri Lanka at www .vipassana.com/resources/meditation_in _sri_lanka.php and www.mctta.lk/temples /meditation-centers.html.

Surfing

The best surf beach in Sri Lanka is at Arugam Bay on the east coast – surf's up from April to September. Guesthouses and surf shops here can give advice on other surf breaks along this coast. Kirinda, near Tissamaharama is another option.

On the west and south coasts, the best time to surf is from November to April. Hikkaduwa is a long-time favourite for international surfers, and offers gentle breaks for novices. Mirissa is becoming popular too. The point at Midigama is another good, if more isolated, spot.

You can hire surfboards, body boards, wetsuits and anything else you'll need from shops beside the beaches. You can also buy second-hand gear.

Walking

Walking and hiking continue to slowly gain popularity in Sri Lanka. There isn't as much of an organised hiking industry as there is in India, and it's usually a matter of striking out on your own. A few guesthouses in the Hill Country, such as White Monkey/Dias Rest (p211) in Haputale, can arrange guided hikes. Adam's Peak (Sri Pada), Sri Lanka's most sacred mountain, is a good, stiff hike with stunning views as a reward.

White-Water Rafting, Canoeing & Boating

White-water rafting can be done at a few places, notably on the river near Kitulgala in the Hill Country (where *Bridge on the River Kwai* was filmed). **Adventure Sports Lanka** (☎ 011-279 1584; actionlanka.com; 366/3 Rendapola Horagahakanda Lane, Talagama, Koswatta, Colombo) arranges trips. Canoeing trips can also be arranged through this company.

Boat or catamaran trips for sightseeing, bird-watching or fishing are becoming very popular. You can organise excursions in Negombo, Bentota and Weligama.

Windsurfing

Top-end hotels on the west coast are the only places that rent sailboards. Bentota is the best spot to windsurf, and several out-fits there hire out equipment and provide lessons.

BUSINESS HOURS

The working week in offices, including post offices, is usually from 8.30am to 4.30pm Monday to Friday. Some businesses also open until about 1pm on Saturday. Shops normally open from 10am to about 7pm weekdays, and until 3pm on Saturday. Businesses run by Muslims may take an extended lunch break on Friday so staff can attend Friday prayers. Banks are generally open from 9am to 3pm on weekdays, although some banks are open on Saturday. Tourist restaurants are generally open between 8am and 11pm. All exceptions to these opening hours are noted in the reviews.

CHILDREN

Sri Lankans adore children, and hotels and restaurants will happily cater for them. Lonely Planet's *Travel with Children* has lots of road-tested advice for trips with kids.

Practicalities

Sri Lankan hotels and guesthouses invariably have triple rooms, and extra beds are routinely supplied on demand.

If you have a very young child, one dilemma is whether to bring a backpack carrier or a pram. Opinion seems to be divided on this – if you can, bring both. One reader opted for a pram because a backpack would have been too sweaty in the tropical heat; however, prams have to contend with uneven or nonexistent footpaths.

Pharmaceutical supplies, as well as imported baby food and disposable nappies are available at Keells and Cargills Food City supermarkets; however, they can be relatively expensive. Cloth nappies are easier to manage, and hotel staff will get them washed as a matter of course.

Car-rental companies usually have child car seats.

Sights & Activities

There aren't a great many attractions dedicated solely to children. One favourite for kids is the Pinnewala Elephant Orphanage, while the turtle hatcheries on the west coast are also popular. A safari in one of the national parks might also appeal. All top-end hotels have swimming pools and, of course, Sri Lanka is famous for its beaches.

CLIMATE CHARTS

Sri Lanka is tropical, with distinct dry and wet seasons. The seasons are slightly complicated by having two monsoons. From May to August the Yala monsoon brings rain to the island's southwestern half, while the dry season here lasts from December to March. The southwest has the highest

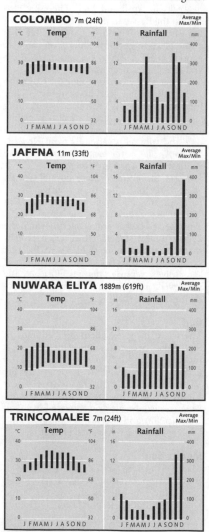

rainfall – up to 4000mm a year. The Maha monsoon blows from October to January, bringing rain to the North and East, while the dry season is from May to September. The North and East are comparatively dry, with around 1000mm of rain annually. There is also an inter-monsoonal period in October and November when rain can occur in many parts of the island.

Colombo and the low-lying coastal regions have an average temperature of 27°C. At Kandy (altitude 500m), the average temperature is 20°C, while Nuwara Eliya (at 1889m) has a temperate 16°C average. The sea stays at around 27°C all year.

COURSES

Woodlands Network (☎ 223 2668; woodlands@sltnet .lk; 38/1C Esplanade Rd) in Bandarawela (p212) is a nonprofit, grass-roots organisation that offers cooking and meditation courses, and volunteer opportunities. See p321 for more on meditation in Sri Lanka.

The **University of Peradeniya** (☎ 081-238 8301; www.pdn.ac.lk) in Kandy has a comprehensive program of Pali and Buddhist studies.

At Sri Lanka's beach resorts, numerous outfits run PADI scuba diving courses. See p321 for Sri Lanka's diving spots.

CUSTOMS

You may bring 2.5L of spirits, 2L of wine, 200 cigarettes or 200g of tobacco, 250mL of perfume, and travel souvenirs (not exceeding US$125 in value for stays of less than 90 days, or up to US$500 for stays between 90 days and a year) into the country. You may take out of the country anything you declared upon entering. Up to 3kg of tea may be exported duty free. For more details, check the customs department website at www.customs.gov.lk.

To export an antique (any article older than 50 years) you need an exemption permit from the Commissioner of Archaeology. We've been told that huge amounts of red tape make it difficult to get the permit; when expats pack up to leave, they've had trouble even for items they brought into Sri Lanka but didn't keep the receipts for. Short-term visitors need to go to the **Department of Archaeology** (Map pp84-5; ☎ 011-266 7155; www.archaeology.gov.lk; National Museum, Albert Cres, Col 7). Inspections and permit issuing are done on Wednesdays only.

DANGERS & ANNOYANCES
Ethnic Tension

The country's ethnic conflict has been widely reported, and many potential visitors have been scared away by the war in the North and East. At the time of research, the situation on the ground was far more relaxed than the old headlines would suggest, and many of the disputed areas had become accessible. You could travel by road, but there were some very specific safety issues in this region – minefields and unexploded ordnance being the most dangerous. Army camps in the North and East were heavily fortified (several old Dutch and Portuguese forts have been garrisoned by the army), and high-security zones such as air bases were completely off limits – definitely not the places to wave around a camera. See the relevant chapters for more information.

All reports were that in the North and East the army and the Liberation Tigers of Tamil Eelam (LTTE) cadres were treating foreigners with respect. Ethnic Sinhalese tourists were almost universally welcomed on visits to Jaffna and other Tamil areas.

However, in April 2006 violence broke out again in the northeast, putting the peace negotiations in jeopardy. The situation is likely to be changing quickly though, so you should check the latest situation with your embassy before you leave.

The war has spawned other risks as well. Thousands of soldiers deserted during the long years of war, and some turned to armed banditry to survive. There have been some isolated but vicious attacks on foreigners by ex-soldiers. Illegal loggers have been stripping forests on the fringes of the conflict zone, and some national parks are

---

GOVERNMENT TRAVEL ADVICE

The following government websites offer travel advisories and information on current hot spots.

Australian Department of Foreign Affairs (☎ 06-6261 3305; www.smartraveller.gov.au)

British Foreign Office (☎ 0845-850 2829; www.fco.gov.uk/travel)

Canadian Department of Foreign Affairs (☎ 800-267 8376; www.dfait-maeci.gc.ca)

US State Department (☎ 888-407 4747, 202-501 4444; http://travel.state.gov)

potentially dangerous, should you stumble across an armed loggers' camp. Before venturing into these areas, go armed with local knowledge and preferably with a local guide.

The government had tried to protect senior politicians from assassination by recruiting dozens of private bodyguards. These armed henchmen soon became political tools, used to intimidate rivals. You're unlikely to meet them, but they're a scary bunch who consider themselves above the law. These goons, and the sons of politicians they're meant to protect, have been accused of several well-publicised bashings in posh Colombo nightclubs.

Theft

With the usual precautions, most people's visit to Sri Lanka is trouble free. However, pickpockets can be active on crowded city buses, notably in Colombo along Galle Rd. They often work together – one to jostle you and the other to pick your pocket or slit your bag, often as you board a bus. All you can do is try to keep a little space around you and hold tight to what you're carrying.

It's often unwise to sleep with your windows open – particularly if you're on the ground floor. Thieves sometimes use long poles with hooks to snaffle items of value. Monkeys are genetically gifted pilferers, and can slip through small gaps and steal food from your room.

One thieves' trick reported by a number of travellers is to take the bottom one or two of a block of travellers cheques, so that you don't notice anything missing until later.

If you do get robbed, go to the police – you won't get your money back but passports and tickets are often jettisoned later. One Australian got her passport back after the pickpockets dropped it in a mailbox!

Touts

Sri Lanka's tourism industry provides an income to many, from the owner of a fancy hotel to the driver of a three-wheeler who drops you at the door. For those at the top of the financial pyramid, the money pours in; for the folks down the bottom, commissions are the name of the game. Touts or, as they like to call themselves, 'friends' or 'guides' lurk around bus and

---

SAFE SWIMMING

Every year drownings occur off Sri Lanka's beaches. If you aren't an experienced swimmer or surfer it's easy to underestimate the dangers – or even to be totally unaware of them. There are few full-time lifesaving patrols, so there's usually no-one to jump in and rescue you. A few common-sense rules should be observed:

- Don't swim out of your depth. If you are a poor swimmer, always stay in the shallows.
- Don't stay in the water when you feel tired.
- Never go swimming under the influence of alcohol or drugs.
- Supervise children at *all* times.
- Watch out for rips. Water brought onto the beach by waves is sucked back to sea and this current can be strong enough to drag you out with it; the bigger the surf, the stronger the rip. Rips in rough surf can sometimes be seen as calm patches in the disturbed water. It's best to check with someone reliable before venturing into the water. If you do get caught in a rip, swim *across* the current if you can – not *against* it. If it's too strong for you to do this, keep afloat and raise a hand so someone on shore can see that you are in distress. A rip eventually weakens; the important thing is not to panic.
- Exercise caution when there is surf.
- Beware of coral; coming into contact with coral can be painful for the swimmer, and fatal for the coral. Always check with someone reliable if you suspect the area you're about to swim in may have coral.
- Never dive into the water. Hazards may be lurking under the surface or the water may not be as deep as it looks. It pays to be cautious.

train stations, waiting to persuade you to go to a hotel or guesthouse of their choice. (The place you want to stay in, you see, is closed, full of giant bugs, overpriced etc.) If you stay at their suggested hotel, the tout will gain a commission, sometimes up to 30% of your bill. This is sometimes subsidised by extra charges to you, but often the hotelier makes do with less money. Saying you have a reservation, whether true or not, is a good ploy to fend off touts. However, many travellers like going with a tout, as often you get a better deal and you don't have the headache of tramping the streets.

The airport is a prime breeding ground for touts (and scams). You may be approached with stories designed to make you sign up for a tour on the spot.

Restaurants also play the commission game: your guide gets a kickback for the lunch you ate. Most gem shops, handicraft stalls and spice gardens, basically any business connected to the tourist industry, also have some kind of commission system set up. Just remember: this is how many make a living – you can help out, or you can spend your money elsewhere. Either way, don't get hung up on beating the commission racket.

Traffic

Sri Lankan drivers – private-bus drivers in particular – can be a real danger. It seems to be acceptable for a bus, car or truck to overtake in the face of oncoming smaller road users – who sometimes simply have to get off the road or risk getting hit. To announce that they are overtaking, or want to overtake, drivers use a series of blasts on loud, shrill horns. If you're walking or cycling along any kind of main road make sure you keep all your senses on alert.

DISABLED TRAVELLERS

Though Sri Lanka is a challenge for disabled travellers, the ever obliging Sri Lankans are always ready to assist. If you have restricted mobility you may find it difficult, if not impossible, to get around on public transport; for example, buses and trains don't have facilities for wheelchairs. Moving around towns and cities can also be difficult for those in a wheelchair or the visually impaired because of the continual

roadworks and very ordinary roads (don't expect many footpaths). A car and driver is the best transport option; if possible, travel with a strong, able-bodied person.

Apart from top-end places, accommodation is generally not geared for wheelchairs. However, many places would be able to provide disabled travellers with rooms and bathrooms that are accessible without stairs. It might take a bit of time to find places with the right facilities, but it is possible. Medical facilities outside Colombo are limited.

Disabled travellers can get in touch with their national support organisation for more information. In the UK, contact **Radar** (☎ 020-7250 3222; 250 City Rd, London EC1V 8AS) or the **Holiday Care Service** (☎ 01293-774 535).

DISCOUNT CARDS

Bad news folks: an International Student ID Card won't get you much. You can't get a discount on the pricey Cultural Triangle round ticket, but you can sometimes get half-price individual site tickets if you sweet-talk the ticket seller. It's the same sad story for seniors, too.

EMBASSIES & CONSULATES
Sri Lankan Embassies & Consulates

There is a full list of Sri Lankan embassies and consulates at the website of the **Ministry of Foreign Affairs** (www.slmfa.gov.lk).

Australia (☎ 02-6239 7041; http://slhcaust.org; 35 Empire Circuit, Forrest, Canberra, ACT 2603)

Belgium (☎ 02-344 5394; sri.lanka@skynet.be; Rue Jules Lejeune 27, 1050 Brussels)

Canada (☎ 613-233 8449; http://srilankahcottawa.org; Ste 1204, 333 Laurier Ave West, Ottawa, Ontario KIP 1C1)

France (☎ 01 55 73 31 13; sl.france@wanadoo.fr; 16 Rue Spontine, 75016 Paris)

Germany (☎ 030-80 90 97 49; www.srilanka-botschaft .de; Niklasstrasse 19, 14163 Berlin)

Italy (☎ 06-855 4560; slembassy@tiscali.it; Via Adige 2, 00198 Rome)

Japan (☎ 03-3440 6911; http://lankaembassy.jp; 2-1-54 Takanawa, Minato-ku, Tokyo 108 0074)

Netherlands (☎ 070-365 5910; mission@infolanka.nl; Jacob de Graefflaan 2, 2517 JM The Hague)

South Africa (☎ 012-460 7702; www.srilanka.co.za; 410 Alexander St, Brooklyn, Pretoria 0181)

UK (☎ 020-7262 1841; www.slhclondon.org; 13 Hyde Park Gardens, London W2 2LU)

USA (☎ 202-483 4026; www.slembassyusa.org; 2148 Wyoming Ave NW, Washington DC 20008)

Embassies & Consulates in Sri Lanka

It's important to realise the limits to what your embassy can do if you're in trouble. Generally speaking, their hands are tied if you've broken Sri Lankan law. In real emergencies you might get some assistance, but only if all other channels have been exhausted. Embassies can recommend hospitals and dentists in a crisis, but they expect you to have insurance to pay for it all.

The following embassies are all in Colombo; if calling from outside the capital, you will need to add the area code 011 to the telephone numbers.

Australia (Map pp84–5; ☎ 269 8767; ahc@sri.lanka .net; 3 Cambridge Pl, Col 7)

Canada (Map pp84–5; ☎ 522 6296; clmbo@international.gc.ca; 6 Gregory's Rd, Col 7)

France (Map pp84–5; ☎ 269 8815; ambfrclb@dree .org; 89 Rosmead Pl, Col 7)

Germany (Map pp84–5; ☎ 258 0431; www.colombo .diplo.de; 40 Alfred House Ave, Col 3)

India (Map pp84–5; ☎ 242 1605; info.colombo@mea .gov.in; 36-38 Galle Rd, Col 3)

Italy (Map pp84–5; ☎ 258 8388; http://sedi.esteri .it/colombo; 55 Jawatta Rd, Col 5)

Japan (Map pp84–5; ☎ 269 3831; www.lk.emb-japan .go.jp; 20 Gregory's Rd, Col 7)

Maldives (Map p88; ☎ 551 6302; www.maldiveshigh com.lk; 23 Kaviratne Pl, Col 8)

Netherlands (Map pp84–5; ☎ 259 6914; nethemb@sri .lanka.net; 25 Torrington Ave, Col 7) Despite the address, the Dutch Embassy is located on the street next to Torrington Ave.

Sweden (Map pp84–5; ☎ 479 5400; ambassaden .colombo@sida.se; 49 Bullers Lane, Col 7)

UK (Map pp84–5; ☎ 243 7336; www.britishhighcom mission.gov.uk/srilanka; 190 Galle Rd, Col 3)

USA (Map pp84–5; ☎ 244 8007; http://colombo .usembassy.gov; 210 Galle Rd, Col 3)

FESTIVALS & EVENTS

Sri Lanka has many Buddhist, Hindu, Christian and Muslim festivals. A full working week is a rarity! Many of the festivals, particularly those on the *poya* (full moon) days, are based on the lunar calendar so the dates vary from year to year according to the Gregorian calendar; see p328 for upcoming *poya* dates.

The dates of Hindu festivals often depend on fiendishly complicated astrological calculations, and the exact dates might not be known until a month or so in advance.

Muslim festivals are timed according to local sightings of various phases of the moon and vary from year to year. During the lunar month of Ramadan that precedes Eid-ul-Fitr, Muslims fast during the day and feast at night, and normal business patterns may be interrupted.

The tourist board publishes information on festivals and events on its website at www.srilankatourism.org. The following are some of the major festivals in Sri Lanka.

JANUARY

Duruthu Perahera Held on the *poya* day in January at the Kelaniya Raja Maha Vihara in Colombo and second in importance only to the huge Kandy *perahera* (procession), this festival celebrates a visit by the Buddha to Sri Lanka.

Thai Pongal Held in mid-January, this Hindu harvest festival honours the Sun God.

FEBRUARY

Navam Perahera First celebrated in 1979, Navam Perahera is one of Sri Lanka's biggest *perahera*s. Held on the February *poya*, it starts from the Gangaramaya Temple and travels around Viharamahadevi Park and Beira Lake in Colombo.

FEBRUARY/MARCH

Maha Sivarathri In late February or early March the Hindu festival of Maha Sivarathri commemorates the marriage of Shiva to Parvati.

MARCH/APRIL

Easter The Christian Good Friday holiday usually falls in April, but can fall in late March. An Easter passion play is performed on the island of Duwa, off Negombo.

Aurudu (New Year) Both New Year's Eve on 13 April and New Year's Day on 14 April are holidays. This occasion for hospitality coincides with the end of the harvest season and the start of the southwest monsoon. See opposite for more details.

MAY

Vesak Poya This two-day holiday – *poya* day and the day after – commemorates the birth, enlightenment and death of Buddha. Puppet shows and open-air theatre performances take place, and the temples are crowded with devotees bringing flowers and offerings. The high point is the lighting of countless paper lanterns and oil lamps. The Adam's Peak pilgrimage season ends at Vesak.

National Heroes' Day Although not a public holiday, 22 May is a day honouring soldiers who have died in the ethnic conflict.

JUNE

Poson Poya The Poson *poya* day celebrates the bringing of Buddhism to Sri Lanka by Mahinda. Anuradhapura

CELEBRATING THE NEW YEAR SRI LANKAN STYLE

On 14 April, when the sun leaves Pisces, the last zodiac sign in its cycle, Buddhist and Hindu Sri Lankans celebrate their new year – Aurudu. Significant tasks, including the lighting of the hearth to cook *kiri bath* (coconut-milk rice), bathing, the first business transaction and the first meal of the new year, are performed at astrologically determined auspicious moments. There are also auspicious colours to be worn and directions to face, all to ensure good fortune for the year ahead.

Aurudu falls at the time when the harvest ends and the fruit trees produce bounteous crops. The festival brings the country to a standstill for almost a week. Public transport is packed on the eve of new year as everyone returns to their parental homes for the celebration. Bread supplies are scarce for a week – bakeries and businesses close down to allow staff to travel home for a few days.

The rituals begin with cleaning the house and lighting the oil lamp. The pounding of the *raban*, a large drum played by several women, sounds the dawning of the new year. The lighting of the hearth is the first ceremonial act for the new year, and even women who are not especially devoted to astrology ensure they light the fire to heat the new pot filled with milk. Families constantly watch the clock, assisted by countdowns on state TV, until it is time to take the first meal for the new year. And just in case you missed it, a shrill chorus of firecrackers reminds everyone that the moment has arrived.

After the other rituals are performed, the family visits friends or joins the games being played in the village, and children ride high on swings hanging from nearby mango or jackfruit trees.

Special Aurudu food is enjoyed during the following days. The ubiquitous plantains (bananas) are a staple, and special additions are *kaung* (oil cake) and *kokis* (a light, crisp sweetmeat of Dutch origin).

Family members exchange gifts after eating, usually clothes (a sari for mother, a shirt or sarong for father and clothing 'kits' for the children), and give sweetmeats or fruit to neighbours. Aurudu sales and markets give Sri Lankans the opportunity to shop for bargains of all sorts.

Aurudu has become deeply embedded in the culture of Sinhalese Buddhist and Tamil Hindu Sri Lankans. It is not celebrated by Buddhists or Hindus anywhere else in the world, and many expat Sri Lankans return to their homeland at this time of year to share the new year and holiday season with their family and friends. The wealthier expats often avoid the heat and humidity by escaping to the cooler hills around Nuwara Eliya, spending the days playing golf and tennis, horse riding or motor racing in the annual hill climb, and partying at night. Accommodation prices here soar at this time of year – if you can find a room at all.

and Mihintale, where Mahinda met and converted the Sinhalese king, are the main sites for this celebration; thousands of white-clad pilgrims climb the stairs to the summit of Mihintale.

JULY/AUGUST

Kandy Esala Perahera The Kandy Esala Perahera, the most important and spectacular festival in Sri Lanka, is the climax of 10 days and nights of celebrations during the month of Esala, ending on the Nikini full moon. This great procession honours the sacred tooth relic of Kandy; see p167 for more details. Smaller *peraheras* are held at other locations around the island.

Vel This festival is held in Colombo and Jaffna. In Colombo, the gilded chariot of Murugan (Skanda), the god of war, complete with his *vel* (trident), is ceremonially hauled from a temple in Sea St, Pettah, to another at Bambalapitiya. In Jaffna the Nallur Kandaswamy Kovil has a 25-day festival in honour of Murugan.

Kataragama Another important Hindu festival is held at Kataragama, where devotees put themselves through the whole gamut of ritual masochism. Many of the devotees have already made the pilgrimage from Jaffna, which reaches Kataragama in time for the festival; see p159 for details.

OCTOBER/NOVEMBER

Deepavali The Hindu festival of lights takes place in late October or early November. Thousands of flickering oil lamps celebrate the triumph of good over evil and the return of Rama after his period of exile.

DECEMBER

Adam's Peak The pilgrimage season, when pilgrims (and the odd tourist) climb Adam's Peak, starts in December.

Unduvap Poya This full-moon day commemorates Sangamitta, who accompanied her brother Mahinda to Sri Lanka and brought a cutting from the sacred Bodhi Tree, which still stands in Anuradhapura today.

DIRECTORY

FOOD

Sri Lankan cuisine has clear links with Indian food, yet it also has many of its own traditions. The staple meal is rice and curry, which comes in all sorts of variations. In Colombo you have a wide array of cuisines from which to choose, while tourist centres such as Hikkaduwa you can get all the usual traveller stand-bys (pizza, french fries and so on). In many other places you'll find a curious kind of fusion cuisine – Sri Lankan meets whatever Western cuisine you dare to choose. Don't be surprised if pasta comes with curry leaves! Sri Lanka rivals any country when it comes to tropical fruits.

Food preparation takes a long time in Sri Lanka; rice and curry can take up to 1½ hours to prepare. Get into the habit of pre-ordering your meal: peruse the menu during the day, order, turn up at the allocated time, and everyone should be happy.

For further information on Sri Lankan cuisine, see p69.

GAY & LESBIAN TRAVELLERS

Male homosexual activity is illegal in Sri Lanka (there is no law against female homosexuality) and the subject is not openly discussed. There have been some convictions in recent years so it would be prudent not to flaunt your sexuality.

According to a gay expat working in Colombo, Sri Lanka is particularly dull when it comes to a gay lifestyle. There are no clubs or pubs where expat or local gays congregate and, besides the 'beach boy' prostitution racket, local gay life is secretive to say the least. Probably the best way to tap into the local gay scene is via the Internet. Check out **Sri Lankan Gay Friends** (www.geocities.com/srilankangay). It provides information on gay and lesbian life in Sri Lanka, as well as a schedule of gay and lesbian events.

Companions on a Journey (coj@sri.lanka.net; PO Box 48, Wattala) is a support organisation for the Sri Lankan gay and lesbian community, based in Colombo. It provides a drop-in centre, a library, film screenings, health-related advice and more. It also lobbies for legislative changes.

Friendship Sri Lanka (c/o Shan Gunawadane, 1049 Pannipitiya Rd, Battaramulla) is orientated towards lesbians and bisexual women.

POYA

Every *poya* or full-moon day is a holiday. *Poya* causes buses, trains and accommodation to fill up, especially if it falls on a Friday or Monday. No alcohol is supposed to be sold on *poya* days, and some establishments close. If you're likely to be thirsty, stock up in advance! Some hotels and guesthouses discreetly provide their needy guests with a bottle of beer 'under the table'.

The *poya* days in the second half of 2006 are 9 August, 7 September, 7 October, 6 November and 6 December. In 2007, *poya* days fall on 3 January, 3 February, 2 April, 2 May, 31 May, 29 June, 31 July, 28 August, 26 September, 26 October, 24 November and 24 December; in the first half of 2008, the dates are 22 January, 21 February, 21 March, 20 April, 20 May, 18 June, 18 July and 16 August.

HOLIDAYS

Independence Day 3 February
Labour Day 1 May
Black Tiger Day 5 July; commemorates the first suicide bombing attack by the Liberation Tigers of Tamil Eelam (LTTE) in 1987 (LTTE areas only)
Heroes Day 27 November; commemorates the death of the first LTTE cadre at Velvettiturai in 1982 (LTTE areas only)
Christmas Day 25 December

INSURANCE

A travel insurance policy to cover theft, loss and medical problems is a good idea. There is a wide variety of policies available, so check the small print. The policies with higher medical expense options are chiefly for countries such as the USA which have extremely high medical costs.

Some policies specifically exclude 'dangerous activities', which can include scuba diving, motorcycling and even trekking. A locally acquired motorcycle licence is not valid under some policies, so again check the fine print carefully.

You may prefer a policy that pays doctors or hospitals directly, rather than you having to pay on the spot and claim later. Check that the policy covers ambulances and an emergency flight home.

Worldwide cover to travellers from over 44 countries is available online at www.lonelyplanet.com/travel_services.

INTERNET ACCESS

You shouldn't have trouble finding Internet facilities in the major tourist towns – even most towns that are off the beaten track have access. Internet access in Colombo is cheap (Rs 60 per hour); elsewhere you'll find places that charge Rs 4 to 10 per minute, occasionally less.

Some larger hotels offer Internet access in the rooms – for a charge (usually much higher than an Internet centre). If you're travelling with a portable computer you can usually plug in at an Internet centre for the same rate as using one of the common terminals. See p19 for a list of websites with good information on Sri Lanka.

LEGAL MATTERS

Sri Lanka's legal system is a complex, almost arcane mix of British, Roman-Dutch and national law. The legal system tends to move fairly slowly, and even a visit to a police station to report a small theft can involve lots of time-consuming form-filling. The tourist police in major towns and tourist spots should be your first point of contact for minor matters such as theft.

Drug use, mainly marijuana but also heroin, is common in tourist centres such as Hikkaduwa, Negombo and Unawatuna. Dabbling is perilous; you can expect to end up in jail if you are caught using anything illegal. Besides the risks, one group of Aussie surfers asked us to warn visitors that 'the dope they sell here is shithouse, mate'.

MAPS

One of the best foreign-produced maps is the Nelles Verlag 1:450,000 (1cm = 4.5km) *Sri Lanka*, which also has maps of Colombo, Anuradhapura, Kandy and Galle. Berndston & Berndston's *Sri Lanka Road Map* is excellent for extra detail on routes and sites. Globetrotter's 1:600,000 (1cm = 6km) *Sri Lanka* has a decent colour country map and a handful of simplified town maps.

The Sri Lankan Survey Department's *Road Map of Sri Lanka* is 1:500,000 (1cm = 5km); it is an excellent overall map and is clear to read. The department also produces a *Road Atlas of Sri Lanka* at the same scale but with 17 town maps at the back. The Survey Department has 82 sheets at 1:50,000 (1cm = 500m) covering the island in British-ordnance-survey style.

In Colombo, the **Survey Department Map Sales Centre** (Map p82; ☎ 011-243 5328; 62 Chatham St, Col 1; ⏱ 9am-4pm Mon-Fri) has a useful selection, including the best Colombo street atlas and the *A to Z Colombo* (Rs 170), which is also available at major bookstores. For the full collection take your passport to the map sales office at the **Surveyor General's Office** (Map p88; ☎ 011-258 5111; Kirula Rd, Narahenpita; ⏱ 9am-4pm Mon-Fri). Both places are closed on government holidays.

MONEY

The Sri Lankan currency is the rupee (Rs), divided into 100 cents. Coins come in denominations of five, 10, 25 and 50 cents and one, two, five and 10 rupees. Notes come in denominations of 10, 20, 50, 100, 200, 500 and 1000 rupees. Break down larger notes (Rs 500) when you change money as most vendors never seem to have change. Dirty or torn notes might not be accepted, except at a bank. See the inside front cover for exchange rates and p18 for typical costs.

ATMs

Commercial Bank has a wide network of ATMs accepting international Visa, Master-Card and Cirrus/Maestro cards. Other options include Bank of Ceylon, NationsTrust Bank, People's Bank, Hatton National Bank, Seylan Bank, Sampath Bank and HSBC. ATMs have spread to all of the cities and major regional centres, though you can't rely on the network paying up every single time.

Black Market

Although a small number of unlicensed moneychangers trade currency at slightly better rates than officially licensed moneychangers, they work mostly with Indians and Sri Lankans doing black-market import-export.

Cash

Any bank or exchange bureau will change major currencies in cash, including US dollars, euros and pounds sterling. Change rupees back into hard currency before you leave the country for the best rates.

Credit Cards

MasterCard and Visa are the most commonly accepted cards. Other major cards such as Amex and Diners Club are also accepted.

DIRECTORY

Moneychangers

Moneychangers can be found in Colombo and the major cities, as well as in tourist centres such as Hikkaduwa. They generally don't charge commission and their rates are usually competitive.

Tipping

Although a 10% service charge is added to food and accommodation bills, this usually goes straight to the owner rather than the worker. So tipping is a customary way of showing your appreciation for services rendered. Drivers expect a tip, as do people who 'guide' you through a site. A rule of thumb is to tip 10% of the total amount due. If there's no money involved use your other thumb for this rule: Rs 10 for the person who minds your shoes at temples, and Rs 20 for a hotel porter.

Travellers Cheques

Fewer people use travellers cheques these days, but major banks still change them – Thomas Cook, Visa and Amex are the most widely accepted. Expect a smallish transaction fee of around Rs 150. Banks in major cities and tourist areas sometimes have special counters for foreign exchange.

PHOTOGRAPHY & VIDEO
Airport Security

Airport X-ray machines won't damage film carried in hand luggage; however, if you want to be on the safe side, put it in a lead-lined bag. Serious photographers won't put their film through any X-ray machine, preferring to put it in clear plastic containers and carry it through by hand. If you do this, be prepared to have each and every canister inspected. Don't leave film in baggage that will go into aircraft holds, as it may be exposed to large doses of X-rays that can damage it.

Film & Equipment

You can buy transparency and print film in Sri Lanka; Cargills Food City (located in large towns) generally has a good supply of both. It pays to check the use-by date before you buy, and to ask for film that's been kept in a fridge. Memory cards are widely available at photo and computer shops in Colombo; see p103 for some recommended places. **Millers** Fort (Map p82;

☎ 232 9151, York St, Col 1); Majestic City (Map p88; Galle Rd, Col 4) in Colombo is a reliable place to have your film developed.

Bring any equipment you'll need. There are a few camera sales places in Colombo, but they may not have what you want. For camera repairs, **Photoflex** (☎ 258 7824; 1st fl, 451/2 Galle Rd, Col 3, Colombo) has been recommended, although many cameras are too advanced these days to be repaired there. The heat and humidity can gum up delicate machinery, so try to keep your camera or video in its case along with moisture-absorbing silica gel crystals when you're not shooting. Taking pictures of wildlife in national parks is usually done in a 4WD, so high-speed film is an advantage.

For useful photography tips see Lonely Planet's *Travel Photography: A Guide to Taking Better Pictures*, by renowned photographer Richard I'Anson, as well as the rest of the *Guide to Taking Better Photos* series, which includes titles such as *Wildlife Photography* and *Urban Photography*.

Restrictions

You aren't allowed to film or photograph dams, airports, road blocks or indeed anything associated with the military. In Colombo, the port and the Fort district are especially sensitive. Take particular care in the North and East, where there are many High Security Zones.

POST

Airmail letters weighing less than 10g sent to the UK, continental Europe or Australia cost Rs 30. The fee rises by Rs 12 for every additional 10g. Airmail letters to North America weighing up to 10g cost Rs 33, plus Rs 17 for every additional 10g. Postcards to these destinations cost Rs 17. Parcels cost Rs 90 and Rs 110 respectively up to 1kg, or a maximum of Rs 475 and Rs 725 for 5kg to 10kg.

It costs Rs 5 to send a letter locally, while local parcels are charged a fixed fee of Rs 10 plus Rs 5 for every 250g or portion thereof.

Private agencies as well as post offices sell stamps. To get up-to-date information on postal rates check out www.slpost.lk.

Ordinary airmail parcels sent from Sri Lanka can take longer than expected – a parcel to Australia can take up to three weeks. If you have something valuable to send home, it may be wiser to use a courier service (for reliable couriers, see p83).

Post offices in larger centres have poste restante, and will generally keep your mail for two months. Amex also has a mail holding service for its clients.

SHOPPING

Sri Lanka has a wide variety of attractive handicrafts on sale. Laksala, a government-run store, is found in most cities and tourist towns. Each store has a good collection of items from all over the country and its stock is generally of reasonable quality, moderately priced and has fixed price tags. There are other handicraft outlets in Colombo; see p102 for details. Street stalls can be found in touristy areas, but you'll need to bargain.

Bargaining

Unless you are shopping at a fixed-price store, you should bargain. Before you hit the open markets, peruse the prices in a fixed-price store for an idea of what to pay. Generally, if someone quotes you a price, halve it. The seller will come down about halfway to your price, and the last price will be a little higher than half the original price.

Batik

The Indonesian art of batik is relatively new in Sri Lanka, but it has been taken to with alacrity. You'll see a wide variety of batiks made and sold around the island. Some of the best and most original are made in the west coast towns of Marawila, Mahawewa and Ambalangoda. Batik pictures start from about Rs 200, and go up to well over Rs 1000. Batik is also used for a variety of clothing items.

Gems

There are countless gem showrooms and private dealers all over the country. In Ratnapura, the centre of the gem trade, everybody and their brother is a part-time gem dealer! It pays to be cautious about authenticity and price; at the government-run gem-testing laboratory in the **Sri Lanka Gem & Jewellery Exchange** (Map p82; ☎ 239 1132; www .slgemexchange.com; 4th & 5th fl, East Low Block, World Trade Center, Col 1), tourists can get any stone tested for free. The only snag with the testing service is that it's not always easy, or practical, to 'borrow' a stone to take it in

for testing before you buy it. However, one reader wrote that a reputable dealer, at least in Colombo, would accompany you to the gem-testing Laboratory for a testing.

There have been letters from readers who have had Sri Lankans try to sell them large amounts of gems with the promise that they can be resold for a big profit in other countries. It's a scam, and unless you happen to be a world-class gem expert you're sure to lose money. Guidebooks from 100 years ago make exactly the same warning.

For more information on the gems found in Sri Lanka, see p225.

Leather

You can find some cheap, good quality leatherwork here – particularly bags and cases. In Colombo, look in the leatherwork and shoe shops around Fort. The bazaar on Olcott Mawatha, beside Fort Station, is cheaper than Laksala for similar-quality goods. Hikkaduwa is also a good place for leather bags.

Masks

Sri Lankan masks are a popular collector's item. They're carved at a number of places, principally along the southwest coast, and are sold all over the island. Ambalangoda is Sri Lanka's mask-carving centre, and you can visit several showroom-workshops there.

Touristy or not, the masks are remarkably well made, good value and look very nice on the wall back home. They're available from key-ring size for a few rupees up to high-quality masks for over Rs 2000. See p51 for more information about Sri Lanka's masks.

Other Souvenirs

If you like to spend, there are countless other purchases waiting to tempt your rupees out of your money belt. The ubiquitous coconut shell is carved into all manner of souvenirs and useful items. Coir (rope fibre from coconut husks) is made into baskets, bags, mats and other items.

Like the Thais and Burmese, Sri Lankans also make lacquerware items such as bowls and ashtrays – layers of lacquer are built up on a light framework, usually of bamboo strips. Kandy is a centre for jewellery and brassware, both antique and modern.

There are some nice chunky silver bracelets, as well as some attractive brass suns and moons – or you could check out a hefty brass elephant-head door knocker. Weligama on the south coast turns out some attractive lacework.

Spices are integral to Sri Lanka's cuisine and Ayurvedic traditions. A visit to a spice garden is an excellent way to discover the alternative uses of familiar spices. You'll see cinnamon, cloves, nutmeg, vanilla beans, cardamom and black pepper, to name just a few. You can buy the pure products, oils or Ayurvedic potions, although the prices are often extortionate; check in local markets beforehand to get an idea of costs.

SOLO TRAVELLERS

Travelling alone isn't a major issue in Sri Lanka, although women should take extra care (see p334 for more information). It's not wise to hike alone in the Hill Country or to walk alone on deserted beaches late at night, as such situations are prime targets for potential thieves.

TELEPHONE

Local calls are timed, and cost about Rs 30 for two minutes, depending on the distance. To call Sri Lanka from abroad, dial your international access code, the country code (☎ 94), the area code (minus '0', which is used when dialling domestically) and the number.

There are no national emergency phone numbers.

International calls can be made from thousands of communications bureaus and booths; many offices also have faxes and Internet access. The cheapest option is a card-operated International Direct Dialling (IDD) telephone, of which there are many in Colombo.

Many villages use what's called a wireless local loop network. This involves having a radio transmitter connected to a land line, allowing a number of subscribers on a 'loop' to use telephones.

Sri Lanka also has a decreasing number of private pay phone operators (right).

Mobile Phones

There are four main network operators. Mobile phones are multiplying like a virus, and coverage is extending beyond the major cities and road corridors into regional areas. GSM phones from Europe, the Middle East and Australasia can be used in Sri Lanka. You can buy a local SIM card for about Rs 2500; local calls on a Sri Lankan SIM card cost about Rs 5 to Rs 7 per minute. Phone rental costs around Rs 3000 per week, cheaper by the month.

Sri Lanka's main mobile-phone companies, roughly in order of size, are **Mobitel** (www.mobitellanka.com), **Dialog GSM** (www.dialog.lk), **Celltel** (www.celltelnet.lk) and **Hutchison Telecom** (www.hutchison.lk).

Phone Codes

All regions have a three-digit area code. In addition, companies operating wireless loop systems also have three- or four-digit prefixes. Calls to these phones cost about the same as to a standard telephone. Mobile phone companies also have separate prefix codes.

Company	Access code
Celltel	☎ 072
Dialog GSM	☎ 0777
Hutchison	☎ 078
Lanka Bell	☎ 075
Mobitel	☎ 071
SLT (WLL)	☎ 070
Suntel	☎ 074

Phonecards

Sri Lanka Telecom sells phonecards, but they can only be used with the card phones found in post offices. There are also phone cards for use in booths operated by Lanka Pay or Tritel, but these booths are relatively rare outside Colombo, since most Sri Lankans either make calls from small privately operated telephone offices or use mobile phones. It's a lot less hassle simply to stop off at a private telephone office and make local calls, even if it costs a hair more.

TIME

Sri Lanka recently changed its time zone; it's now 5½ hours ahead of GMT (the same as India), four hours behind Australian EST and 11 hours ahead of American EST.

TOILETS

All top-end and midrange places to stay have sit-down flush toilets, but if you're staying in budget accommodation you will sometimes find squat toilets, though often there's a choice of commode. In budget digs you might not find toilet paper; it's sold in general stores. Public toilets are scarce, so you'll have to duck into restaurants and hotels.

TOURIST INFORMATION

The Colombo main office of the **Sri Lanka Tourist Board** (SLTB; Map pp84-5; ☎ 011-243 7059; www.srillankatourism.org; 80 Galle Rd, Col 3; ☉ 9am-4.45pm Mon-Fri, 9am-12.30pm Sat) is near the Taj Samudra. The board also runs a **tourist information centre** (☎ 081-222 2661; Palace Sq; ☉ 9am-1pm & 1.30-4.45pm Mon-Fri) in Kandy, as well as a 24-hour **information office** (☎ 011-225 2411) at Bandaranaike International Airport. Staff can help with hotel bookings as well as answer queries and hand out booklets and leaflets. In Colombo the JF Tours office at Fort train station is very helpful.

Among publications provided by SLTB offices inside and outside Sri Lanka is an *Accommodation Guide,* updated every six months, with fairly thorough listings. *Explore Sri Lanka* has feature articles, and information on things to see and places to stay, shop and eat.

Sri Lanka Tourist Board has offices in the following countries:

Australia (☎ 02-6230 6002; fax 6230 6066; 29 Lonsdale St, Braddon, Canberra, ACT 2612)
France (☎ 01 42 60 49 99; ctbparis@compuserve.com; 19 Rue du Quatre Septembre, 75002 Paris)
Germany (☎ 069-28 77 34; ctbfra@t-online.de; Aller-heiligentor 2-4, D-60311 Frankfurt am Main)
Japan (☎ 03-3289 0771; ctb-toky@zaf.att.ne.jp; Dowa Bldg, 7-2-22 Ginza, Chuo-ku, Tokyo)
UK (☎ 020-7930 2627; srilankatourism@aol.com; 26-27 Clareville House, Oxendon St, London SW1Y 4EL)
USA (☎ 732-516 9800; ctbusa@anlusa.com; 111 Wood Ave South, Iselin, New Jersey 08830)

VISAS

Dozens of nationalities, including Australians, New Zealanders, North Americans and virtually all Europeans, receive a tourist visa upon entry, valid for 30 days. It is sometimes possible to obtain a visa for longer than 30 days in your home country; this is more often the case at Sri Lanka's bigger overseas missions, in London and Washington for example. The latest regulations are given at www.immigration.gov.lk.

Extensions can be made at the **Department of Immigration** (Map p88; ☎ 011-250 3629;

VISA EXTENSION FEES	
Country of origin	Cost US$
Australia	27
Canada	50
France	26
Germany	26.80
Italy	35
Netherlands	49
New Zealand	34.50
Switzerland	27.20
UK	54
USA	100

www.immigration.gov.lk; 23 Station Rd, Col 4; ☉ 9am-4.30pm Mon-Fri), near Majestic City shopping centre in Bambalapitiya, Colombo. The last payments are received at 3.30pm. The department sets the cost in US dollars, but you pay in rupees. A visa extension gives you a full three months in the country and you can apply for your extension almost as soon as you arrive (the 30-day visa given upon entry is included in the three months). A further three-month extension is possible, but you must again pay the extension fee plus another Rs 10,000. Extensions beyond this are at the discretion of the department, and incur a Rs 15,000 fee plus the extension fee.

See above for fees for the first 90-day extension.

The whole process takes about an hour. First, go to the 1st-floor office and pick up a visa-extension application form from the person closest to the door. You then work your way along the counter, through six or seven stages of stamps and receipts. Then you wait 30 minutes or so while your passport works its way back down the counter and is returned to you.

You will need your passport, an onward ticket and either a credit card or foreign exchange receipts.

Tourist visas for India can be obtained at the **High Commission of India** (Map pp84-5; ☎ 242 1605; info.colombo@mea.gov.in; 36-38 Galle Rd, Col 3). The cost of a six-month visa depends on your nationality, and you'll need to supply two photos. It takes at least five days to process a tourist visa, but only one day if you are a foreign resident in Sri Lanka. Lines tend to be very long. You can also

---

VOLUNTEER LIFE BEATS TRAVELLING *Brigitte Ellemor*

There was no-one to meet me after midnight at the airport arrivals area – a bus stop was as close as nonauthorised visitors could get to the terminal. The next night, power workers started a four-day strike, leaving homes without fans and water (if they had electric water pumps). Soon after, the government imposed power cuts of up to eight hours a day. Welcome to Sri Lanka!

During later months, a couple of bombs blasted Colombo targets killing dozens of people, a national parliamentarian was assassinated and a curfew was imposed to limit violence during local government elections. Tropical paradise? I think not.

At home in my bedsit flat, I hand-washed clothes on the floor of the shower for 18 months. Outside, I travelled in crazily driven buses crammed full like sardine cans. But for every negative or confusing experience, there was an equally delightful interaction. The family at the general store who understood my charadelike request for candles during the power strike became the people whom I visited if I needed cheering up. My landlady-neighbour delivered the auspicious dish *kiri bath* (coconut-milk rice) on the first day of each month. I enjoyed bathing at private wells in friends' gardens, and the excitement of the national cricket team winning an international tournament was never far away. Most touching were the invitations to witness the cycle of life events and the rituals attached to birth, adolescent rites of passage, marriage and death.

Working as a volunteer in another country is one of the best ways to experience life as it really is for citizens of the country. The opportunity provides unique challenges and rewards, and allows you to move beyond the sometimes superficial encounters and observations of a traveller. If visiting a place renders it part of your consciousness forever, then living in a country for a year or more means it is indelibly marked on your mind and heart. However, the longer-term experience often raises as many questions as it answers, and I doubt I will ever understand Sri Lanka's politics or the long and bloody ethnic conflict.

Living in the 'Third World' brings the inescapable realisation that although life is a struggle for most of the world's people, they generally meet the difficulties with resourcefulness. Like me, Sri Lankans also endure verbal and sometimes physical harassment, the frustration of working in a public sector bureaucracy, and the physical limitations and emotional trauma of living in a country at war with itself, but they generally don't have the opportunity to leave.

---

obtain an Indian visa in Kandy at the **Assistant High Commission of India** (☎ 081-222 4563; ahciknd@mailandnews.com; Box 47, 31 Rajapihilla Mawatha). Kandy makes a good alternative to Colombo because it's not as busy.

VOLUNTEERING

Sri Lanka is a base for many NGOs, and there are about half a dozen major volunteer agencies that operate in Sri Lanka. The best place to start searching for placements is the Web. Check out www.workingabroad.com and www.vso.org.uk.

Woodlands Network (☎ 223 2668; woodlands@sltnet.lk) in Bandarawela (p212) can help arrange volunteer opportunities in the Hill Country.

WOMEN TRAVELLERS

Few Sri Lankan women travel unchaperoned, so lone female travellers may occasionally experience uncomfortable levels of male attention. Covering your legs and shoulders helps you blend in more effectively, though you'll be stared at no matter what you wear. In Colombo you can relax the dress code a little and get away with wearing sleeveless shirts. Lone women travellers may be hassled walking around at night, or while exploring isolated places. Stray hands on crowded buses are something else to watch out for.

However, don't imagine travelling in Sri Lanka is one long hassle. Such unpleasant incidents are the exception, not the rule. Women travellers have the opportunity to enter the society of Sri Lankan women, something that is largely out-of-bounds for male travellers. On the other hand, there are many social environments that are almost exclusively male in character – local bars, for example. If you feel uncomfortable in local eateries or hotels, try to find one where women are working or staying.

Stock up on tampons, as they can be hard to find outside Colombo.

For further comments, see opposite.

WOMEN TRAVELLING IN SRI LANKA   *Jessa Boanas-Dewes*

Before a recent trip to Sri Lanka I was told the country was 'really chilled – way more relaxed than India'. From what I could gather, dressing demurely was a good idea but not essential.

I'd tried to pack long skirts and shirts but decided to get more clothes when I arrived. Unfortunately, finding nonsynthetic clothing that fitted me (or that I vaguely liked!) proved difficult. When I was able to find some clothes, I found that dressing conservatively really made a positive impact on the way I was treated. Sarongs were particularly helpful for creating a baggy layer over a singlet or shirt.

Unabashed staring from men made me feel very uncomfortable and I got the distinct impression that foreign women are regarded as more sexually 'available' than local women, who are carefully chaperoned. It's worth keeping in mind that you'll mostly talk to men, who are the drivers, waiters and hotel owners. Sri Lankan women I encountered were friendly but shy, and they are often starkly absent from the public sphere, so you can't rely on being able to seek shelter in their company. I was glad I'd made the effort to learn some words in Sinhalese – it helped break the ice.

One of the greatest challenges for me was that although so many people were friendly and helpful, some ostensibly 'friendly' conversations veered towards another goal, such as asking for money. 'Are you married, Madam?' was a common question and I found it easier to say 'yes'. Bringing a fake wedding ring and maybe even a photo would have helped; I wasn't asked about my availability while travelling with two male friends.

A female travelling companion didn't get groped (as I did) but found that sometimes men got too close (such as in crowded temples). Her solution was to put her hands on her hips and use her elbows to create more personal space. Unlike other countries in South Asia, trying to publicly shame an offender had no effect. At first, I was under the impression that only foreign women are the subject of sexual harassment. However, I've since learned that unaccompanied Sri Lankan women also have to put up with it, and often carry a spare sari pin to 'accidentally' prick would-be gropers or frottage-artists.

But, overall, these issues were only hiccups in what was otherwise an extremely friendly and chivalrous cultural experience.

Bus & Train Travel

Women travelling solo may find riding the buses and trains extremely trying at times. In Colombo, for example, ordinary buses are so packed that sometimes it's impossible to avoid bodily contact with other passengers. If a sleazebag is making a concerted effort to invade your space, such as it is, you have a few options: put your bag up as a shield; move to another part of the bus if you can; or get off and catch another bus. In Colombo buses are so frequent that you generally don't have to wait long for one that's less crowded. The most important thing in such a situation is to trust your gut instinct; if you feel the need to get off a bus, get off.

Unlike many other Asian countries, shaming the perpertrator seems to have little effect; local women often arm themselves with sari pins to 'accidentally' jab men who attempt to rub lewdly against them. We would strongly suggest that you do not travel on trains alone, as we have received warnings from women who have been sexually assaulted on such trips. Seriously think about finding a travelling companion instead.

Transport

CONTENTS

THINGS CHANGE...

The information in this chapter is particularly vulnerable to change. Check directly with the airline or a travel agent to make sure you understand how a fare (and ticket you may buy) works, and be aware of the security requirements for international travel. Shop carefully. The details given in this chapter should be regarded as pointers and are not a substitute for your own careful, up-to-date research.

GETTING THERE & AWAY

Flights, tours and rail tickets can be booked online through Lonely Planet; see www.lonelyplanet.com/travel_services.

ENTERING THE COUNTRY

Immigration at Bandaranaike International Airport is a straightforward matter of handing your passport over to officials, who will check your visa and stamp your passport with an exit date.

Passport

You must have your passport with you all the time in Sri Lanka; it is the most basic travel document. Before leaving home, check that it will be valid for the entire period you intend to remain overseas. See p333 for information on visas.

AIR
Airports & Airlines

The only international airport in Sri Lanka is **Bandaranaike International Airport** (airport code CMB; ☎ 011-225 2861) at Katunayake, 30km north of Colombo. There are 24-hour money-changing facilities in the arrivals and departures halls. The travel desks in the arrivals hall often have discounts for mid-range and top-end hotels in Negombo and Colombo; you may well be offered a 10- or 20-day package with hotel, van and driver on the spot. There are also bank counters, a few duty-free shops and a cafeteria in the departures lounge, but prices are high.

Sri Lanka isn't quite on the A list for major airlines. Of the bigger European carriers, only Lufthansa flies there. Most of the airlines flying between Europe and Sri Lanka are from the Middle East. A better range of airlines flies between Sri Lanka and Asia (with connections elsewhere).

It's worth reconfirming flights 72 hours in advance in Sri Lanka, as the country is a turning point for flights. Sometimes if a 200-seat plane is scheduled to fly to Sri Lanka but only 80 seats are full, an airline will send a 120-seat plane instead. If there are 200 or so passengers waiting to leave Sri Lanka on that plane, difficulties arise. The passengers who have reconfirmed stand a better chance of leaving Sri Lanka as planned. Absolutely, definitely reconfirm if you're flying with national carrier SriLankan Airlines, as they're notorious for bumping passengers who fail to do so. You'll need the flight number plus a contact address.

AIRLINES FLYING TO & FROM SRI LANKA

All the phone numbers listed below are for the airlines' Colombo offices; add ☎ 011 if calling from elsewhere.

Austrian Airlines (code OS; ☎ 272 5555; www.aua.com; hub Vienna)

Cathay Pacific (code CK; Map pp84-5; ☎ 233 4145; www.cathaypacific.com; hub Hong Kong)

AVOIDING COLOMBO

Although we think Colombo has its good points, some travellers opt to bypass it altogether and take a taxi straight from the airport to Negombo (Rs 600) or to Kandy (Rs 3300).

Condor Airlines (code DE; Map pp84–5; ☎ 232 9804; www.condor.com; hub Frankfurt)

Czech Airlines (code OK; Map pp84–5; ☎ 234 2941; www.csa.cz/en; hub Prague)

Emirates (code EK; Map pp84–5; ☎ 230 0200; www.emirates.com; hub Dubai)

Etihad Airways (code EY; ☎ 476 6500; www.etihadairways.com; hub Abu Dhabi)

Indian Airlines (code IC; Map p82; ☎ 232 6844; www.indian-airlines.nic; hub New Delhi)

Kuwait Airways (code KU; Map p82; ☎ 244 5531; www.kuwait-airways.com; hub Kuwait City)

LTU International Airways (code LT; Map p82; ☎ 473 1366; www.ltu.com; hub Düsseldorf)

Malaysia Airlines (code MH; Map p82; ☎ 234 2291; www.malaysia-airlines.com; hub Subang Jaya)

Qatar Airlines (code QR; Map p82; ☎ 452 5726; www.qatarairways.com; hub Doha)

Royal Jordanian (code RJ; Map pp84–5; ☎ 230 1626; www.rja.com.jo; hub Amman)

SIngapore Airlines (code SQ; Map pp84–5; ☎ 230 0750; www.singaporeair.com; hub Singapore)

SriLankan Airlines (code UL; Map p82; ☎ 242 1161; www.srilankan.lk; hub Colombo)

Thai Airways (code TG; Map pp84–5; ☎ 244 7332; www.thaiair.com; hub Bangkok)

Tickets

The plane ticket will probably be the most expensive item in your trip budget. Some of the cheapest tickets have to be bought months in advance and popular flights sell out quickly.

Colombo is not as good as some other Asian centres for cheap flights, and you may be better off booking your onward tickets before you leave home. For details of travel agencies in Colombo, see p87.

The airport no longer charges a separate departure tax.

Asia
INDIA

SriLankan Airlines flies twice daily between Thiruvananthapuram (Trivandrum) in Kerala and Colombo. One-way/return

fares start at US$119/238. Travelling to Tiruchirappalli (Trichy) in Tamil Nadu costs only slightly more, and there are three weekly flights. Other destinations include Bodhgaya in the northern state of Bihar, and Bangalore in Karnataka. Indian Airlines and SriLankan Airlines have flights between Colombo and Chennai (Madras) for US$155/293 one way/return.

If you're looking for a travel agent in India, **STIC Travels** (www.stictravel.com; Chennai ☎ 044-2433 0211; Delhi ☎ 011-2332 0239; Mumbai ☎ 022-2218 1431) is recommended.

MALDIVES

Many visitors combine a visit to Sri Lanka with a trip to the Maldives. One-way/return fares on SriLankan Airlines flights between Colombo and Male cost US$143/269.

SINGAPORE

The best airfares from Singapore to Colombo are usually with Emirates, at around US$254. SriLankan Airlines, Singapore Airlines, Malaysia Airlines and Thai Airways also fly from Singapore to Colombo (either nonstop or with a stop in Kuala Lumpur) for somewhat higher fares.

THAILAND

A Bangkok–Colombo return flight costs US$511 on Thai Airways, SriLankan Airlines, Cathay Pacific or Malaysia Airlines. One-way flights are not much cheaper.

Australia

SriLankan Airlines' return fares from Sydney are around A$1690, while other airlines cost a bit more. Return fares from Perth cost at least 25% more; Emirates and SriLankan Airlines typically have the best prices.

Flight Centre (☎ 133 133; www.flightcentre.com.au) and **STA Travel** (☎ 1300 733 035; www.statravel.com.au) have offices throughout Australia. Check the *Yellow Pages* and major newspapers for other travel agencies.

Canada

The *Globe & Mail, Toronto Star, Montreal Gazette* and *Vancouver Sun* carry travel agency ads and are good places to look for cheap fares. **Travel CUTS** (☎ 866-246 9762; www.travelcuts.com) is Canada's national student travel agency. For online bookings try www.expedia.ca and www.travelocity.ca.

TRANSPORT

The cheapest return fares for nonstop flights between Vancouver and Colombo start at C$2824 with Cathay Pacific and Sri-Lankan Airlines. Eastern Canada is about as far you can get from Sri Lanka; Cathay Pacific has fares starting from C$3438, with a stop in Hong Kong.

Continental Europe

SriLankan Airlines flies from London to Colombo daily. The main European carriers with flights to Sri Lanka are Czech Airlines (twice weekly from Prague via Dubai) and Austrian Airlines (a seasonal schedule from Vienna, peaking with two or three flights a week around New Year).

FRANCE

SriLankan Airlines has two flights a week between Paris and Colombo. Return flights range in price from €800 to €850.

France has a network of travel agencies that can supply discount tickets to travellers of all ages. Recommended agencies include the following:

Anyway (☎ 08 92 30 23 01; www.anyway.fr in French)
Lastminute (☎ 08 99 78 50 00; www.lastminute.fr in French)
Nouvelles Frontières (☎ 08 25 00 07 47; www.nouvelles-frontieres.fr in French)
OTU Voyages (☎ 01 55 82 32 32; www.otu.fr in French) Agency specialising in students and young people.
Voyageurs du Monde (☎ 08 92 68 83 63; www.vdm.com)

GERMANY

SriLankan Airlines has two weekly flights between Frankfurt and Colombo. Return flights start at €1365. German charter companies with seasonal flights include Condor Airlines (from Frankfurt) and LTU International Airways (from Munich and Frankfurt).

The following travel agencies have been recommended:

Expedia (☎ 01805 007 143; www.expedia.de in German)
Just Travel (☎ 089-747 3330; www.justtravel.de)
Lastminute (☎ 01805 284 366; www.lastminute.de in German)
STA Travel (☎ 06974-303 292; www.statravel.de in German)

New Zealand

Both **Flight Centre** (☎ 0800 243 544; www.flightcentre.co.nz) and **STA Travel** (☎ 0508 782 782; www.statravel.co.nz) have branches throughout the country. A website recommended for online bookings is www.travel.co.nz.

An Auckland–Colombo return flight with Emirates Airlines or SriLankan Airlines should cost around NZ$1700.

UK & Ireland

Discount air travel is big business in London. Advertisements for many agencies appear in the travel pages of the weekend broadsheet newspapers, in *Time Out* and the *Evening Standard*, and in the free magazine *TNT*.

Fares from London to Colombo start at UK£613 return. Emirates, Czech Airlines and Royal Jordanian all have consistently cheap fares. In addition, SriLankan Airlines flies from London to Colombo daily.

Major travel agencies in the UK include the following:

Flight Centre (☎ 0870 499 0040; www.flightcentre.co.uk)
Flightbookers (☎ 0800 082 3000; www.ebookers.com)
North-South Travel (☎ 01245-608 291; www.northsouthtravel.co.uk)
Quest Travel (☎ 0870 442 3542; www.questtravel.com)
STA Travel (☎ 0870 630 026; www.statravel.co.uk)
Trailfinders (☎ 0845 058 5858; www.trailfinders.co.uk)
Travel Bag (☎ 0800 082 5000; www.travelbag.co.uk)

USA

The *New York Times, LA Times, Chicago Tribune* and *San Francisco Chronicle* all have weekly travel sections where you'll find any number of travel agency ads. San Francisco is the discount-ticket capital of America, although some good deals can be found in Los Angeles, New York and other big cities.

A return New York–Colombo flight with SriLankan Airlines or Cathay Pacific costs around US$1650; on Emirates, fares can be as low as US$1390. From Los Angeles, you'll pay US$1370 for a flight with Cathay Pacific (via Hong Kong) or SriLankan Airlines (via Bangkok).

The following sites are recommended for online bookings:

Avia Travel (☎ 800 950 2842; www.aviatravel.com)
Cheap Tickets (☎ 312-260 8100; www.cheaptickets.com)
Expedia (www.expedia.com)
Lowestfare.com (www.lowestfare.com)

SEA

Plans to resume ferry services between Mannar and India come and go with the tide. Any schemes to relaunch the route must wait until the ports are repaired, however, so check with the **Sri Lanka Ports Authority** (www.slpa.lk) for the latest information.

A passenger-ferry service between Tuticorin (Tamil Nadu) and Colombo has also been on the drawing board for some years, but has still not materialised. There has also been talk of ferry services between Chennai and Colombo, and Kochi and Colombo, but no plans have yet come to fruition.

GETTING AROUND

The only regular domestic flights are the flights between Jaffna and Colombo. Flights to Trincomalee were added following the cease-fire a few years ago but were suspended again following the drop in tourism after the 2004 tsunami. The flights are likely to start again if tourism picks up.

Travelling on public transport is therefore mostly a choice between buses and trains. Both are cheap. Trains can be crowded, but it's nothing compared with the seemingly endless numbers of passengers that squash into ordinary buses. Trains are a bit slower than buses, but a seat on a train is preferable to standing on a bus. Even standing on a train is better than standing on a bus.

On the main roads from Colombo to Kandy, Negombo and Galle, buses cover around 40km to 50km per hour. On highways across the plains, it can be 60km or 70km an hour. In the Hill Country, it can slow to just 20km an hour.

All public transport gets particularly crowded around *poya* (full moon) holidays and their nearest weekends, so try to avoid travelling then if you can.

AIR

Sri Lanka has two domestic airlines on the Colombo–Jaffna route: **AeroLanka** (Map p88; ☎ in Colombo 011-250 5632; www.aerolanka.com) and **Expo Aviation** (Map pp84-5; ☎ in Colombo 011-257 6941; info@expoavi.com).

For addresses of airline offices in Colombo and Jaffna, as well as schedules and fares, see p103 and p312. Checking in takes at least 2½ hours due to security measures.

Air taxis are another way of travelling internally. **Sri Lankan Air Taxi** (☎ 019-733 3355; www.srilankan.aero/airtaxi) offers charter services anywhere in the country, including a fairly regular flight to Ampara for US$200.

BICYCLE

Keen cyclists will probably find Sri Lanka a joy, apart from the uphill sections of the Hill Country and the major arteries out of Colombo. When heading out of Colombo in any direction, take a train out beyond the urban corridors before you start cycling.

It's a good idea to start early in the day to avoid the heat, and to take lots of water and sun block. The distances you cover will be limited by the state of the roads – be prepared for a large amount of 'eyes down' cycling.

If you decide to bring your own bicycle, be sure to also bring a supply of spare tyres and tubes as these can suffer from the poor road surfaces. The normal bicycle tyre size in Sri Lanka is 28in by 1.5in. Some imported 27in tyres for 10-speed bikes are available but only in a few shops in Colombo and at high prices. Keep an eye on your bicycle at all times and use a good lock.

When taking a bicycle on a train, every part has to be described on the travel documents, so you should deliver the bicycle at least half an hour before departure. At Colombo's Fort station you may want to allow even more time (up to two hours). It costs about twice the 2nd-class fare to take a bicycle on a train.

Hire

In terms of hired bicycles, those with gears are the exception rather than the rule. You'll find that most range from merely adequate to desperately uncomfortable with dodgy brakes. Bikes imported from China and India are the norm. You should seriously consider bringing your own gear.

The **National Mountain Biking Association** (☎ 011-269 1505) in Colombo acts as a clearing house for information on mountain biking in Sri Lanka, and also arranges guides for individual or custom tours.

Adventure Asia (☎ 536 8468; 338 TB Jaya Mawatha, Col 10) and **Adventure Sports Lanka** (☎ 279 1584; actionlanka.com; 366/3 Rendapola Horagahakanda Lane, Talagama, Koswatta), both based in Colombo, arrange mountain-biking excursions in the Hill Country.

TRANSPORT

Purchase

You can buy mountain bikes at the following bike shops in Colombo. Expect to pay US$100 to US$450 for a new bike, depending on the quality. Most are made in India or China; the Chinese bikes are said to be sturdier and more reliable than the Indian bikes.

City Cycle Stores (☎ 011-250 4632; alamul@slt.lk; 117-119 Dam Str, Col 12)

Cycle Bazaar (☎ 011-268 6255; 82 Danister De Silva Mawatha, Col 8)

Suriyage (☎ 011-269 1505; suri@isplanka.lk; 524 Rider Tower, Maradana Rd, Col 10) Also repairs bikes and occasionally has used mountain bikes for sale for about half the cost of a new bike.

BUS

Bus routes cover about 80% of the nation's 90,000km of roads. There are two kinds of bus in Sri Lanka – Central Transport Board (CTB) buses and private buses. CTB buses are usually painted yellow and ply most long-distance and local routes. Private bus companies have vehicles ranging from late-model Japanese coaches used on intercity-express runs to decrepit old minibuses that sputter and limp along city streets or short runs between towns and villages. Private air-con intercity buses cover all the major routes; for long-distance travel they are by far the most comfortable option.

Bus travel in Sri Lanka can be interesting. Vendors board to sell all sorts of snacks and even books on long-distance routes. Blind singers sometimes get on and work their way down the aisle, warbling away and collecting coins. Beggars may approach passengers with a litany of misfortunes – which they may also sing. Buses sometimes stop at temples so the driver and passengers can donate a few coins.

The first two seats on CTB buses are reserved for 'clergy' (Buddhist monks) and this is never ignored. If you want to guarantee a seat, you'll need to board the bus at the beginning of its journey; Sri Lankans seem to know when to sprint after the right bus as it pulls in, and throw a bag or a handkerchief through the window to reserve a seat.

Finding the right bus at the chaotic bus stations in Colombo and Kandy can be very challenging. Virtually all of the destination signs hung over the bus parking areas are in Sinhala script only, and since there is

no central ticket office, you must locate the right parking area and buy your bus ticket either from a small booth or on board the bus. Probably the best strategy is simply to walk through the station saying the name of your destination until someone leads you to the right bus.

In smaller towns it's much easier, as there are usually separate bus stops for each destination or direction, and your hotel or guesthouse can tell you where these stops are.

Costs

In most cases, private bus companies run services parallel to CTB services. Intercity expresses charge about twice as much as CTB buses, but are more than twice as comfortable, and usually faster. Fares for CTB buses and ordinary private buses are very cheap. The journey between Kandy and Colombo costs Rs 70 on a CTB bus, Rs 80 to 120 on ordinary private buses and Rs 140 on an air-con intercity express. A bus trip from Colombo to Kataragama costs Rs 146 on an ordinary private bus and Rs 280 by intercity express.

Most buses have unbelievably small luggage compartments and they rarely have storage on the roof. For your own sake, travel light. If you have a large pack, you can buy an extra ticket for your bag.

Reservations

Private buses cannot be booked before the day of travel; to book CTB buses you can call ☎ 011-258 1120.

CAR & MOTORCYCLE

Self-drive car hire is possible in Sri Lanka, though it is far more common to hire a car and driver for a day or more. If you're on a relatively short visit to Sri Lanka on a midrange budget, the costs of hiring a car and driver can be quite reasonable.

When planning your itinerary, you can count on covering about 35km per hour in the Hill Country and 55km per hour in most of the rest of the country.

Motorcycling is an alternative for intrepid travellers. Distances are relatively short and some of the roads are a motorcyclist's delight; the trick is to stay off the main highways. The quieter Hill Country roads offer some glorious views, and secondary roads along the coast and the plains are reasonably quick. There are motorcycle-hire agencies

ROAD DISTANCES (KM)

	Anuradhapura	Colombo	Galle	Jaffna	Kandy	Nuwara Eliya	Polonnaruwa	Trincomalee
Anuradhapura	---							
Colombo	206	---						
Galle	322	116	---					
Jaffna	195	396	512	---				
Kandy	138	116	232	320	---			
Nuwara Eliya	216	180	290	398	77	---		
Polonnaruwa	101	216	332	283	140	217	---	
Trincomalee	106	257	373	238	182	259	129	---

in Hikkaduwa and Kandy. In addition to a cash deposit you must provide your passport number and leave your airline ticket as security. The official size limit on imported motorbikes is 350cc.

Driving Licence

An International Driving Permit can be used to roam Sri Lanka's roads, but it's valid for only three months. To extend the permit, turn up at the **Department of Motor Traffic** (Map pp84–5; ☎ 011-269 4331; Elvitigala Mawatha, Narahenpita) in Colombo. You'll need to bring your driving licence and two photos.

Hire

HIRING A CAR & DRIVER

You can find taxi drivers who will happily become your chauffeur for a day or more in all the main tourist centres. Guesthouse owners will probably be able to put you in touch with a driver, or you can ask at travel agencies or big hotels.

Various formulas exist for setting costs, such as rates per kilometre plus a lunch and dinner allowance. The simplest way is to agree on a flat fee with no extras. Expect to pay Rs 2500 to 2800 per day, not including fuel, or more for a newer, air-con vehicle.

At the time of writing, petrol cost Rs 85 per litre, and diesel Rs 46. Rates that include fuel can be arranged from around Rs 3000 per day. Most drivers will expect a tip of about 10%, but of course it's up to you. It pays to meet the driver before you set off, as there

may be a difference between who the travel agent has led you to expect and who turns up. Some travellers find themselves being almost bullied by their driver: the driver chooses where they go, where they stay and what time they leave. Hiring a driver for only two or three days at first can avoid these problems. Drivers seem to prefer spending only three or four days away from home as well.

Some travel agencies may suggest you take a guide along as well. Unless you speak absolutely no English or Sinhala, this is unnecessary.

Be aware that drivers make a fair part of their income from commissions. Most hotels and many guesthouses pay drivers a flat fee or a percentage, although others refuse to. This can lead to disputes between you and the driver over where you're staying the night – they'd prefer to go where the money is. Some hotels have appalling accommodation for drivers – sometimes just a dirty mattress under the stairs. Some of the worst conditions are in the big hotels; drivers share a dormitory and prison-style meals, people come and go all night, and no-one gets a good night's rest. The smarter hotels and guesthouses know that keeping drivers happy is good for their business, and provide decent food and lodgings.

SELF-DRIVE HIRE

Quickshaws Tours (☎ 258 3133; www.quickshaws.com; 3 Kalinga Pl, Col 5) and **Ameri Rent-A-Car** (☎ 258 1594; 30A Temple Lane, Col 3) are two Colombo-based

TRANSPORT

companies offering self-drive car hire. Both have air-con Toyota Corollas from Rs 2400 per day, including insurance, tax and the first 100km; there is a Rs 18 charge for each kilometre in excess of 100km. Discounted weekly rates are also available. Generally you're not allowed to take the car into national parks, wildlife sanctuaries or jungle, or along unsealed roads.

Road Conditions
Although you may see a number of accidents during your time on the road, driving seems fairly safe provided you take care and watch out for other road users. Country roads are often narrow and potholed, with constant pedestrian, bicycle and animal traffic to navigate.

Punctures are a part of life here, so every little village seems to have a repair expert doing an excellent, although rather time-consuming, job.

Road Rules
The speed limit for vehicles is 56km/h in built-up areas and 72km/h in rural areas. Driving is on the left-hand side of the road, as in the UK and Australia. The **Automobile Association of Ceylon** (Map pp84-5; ☎ 011-242 1528; 40 Sir Mohamed Macan Markar Mawatha, Col 3; ⏰ 9.30am-4.30pm Mon-Fri) sells a booklet called *The Highway Code*.

HITCHING
Hitching is never entirely safe in any country in the world, and we don't recommend it. In any case, Sri Lanka's cheap fares make it an unnecessary option. Travellers who do decide to hitch should understand that they are taking a small but potentially serious risk; they can attempt to minimise this risk by travelling in pairs and letting someone know where they are planning to go.

LOCAL TRANSPORT
Many Sri Lankan towns are small enough to walk around. In larger towns, you can get around by bus, taxi or three-wheeler.

Bus
Local buses go to most places, including villages outside main towns, for fares ranging from Rs 4 to 25. Their signboards are usually in Sinhala or Tamil, so you'll have to ask which is the right bus.

Taxi
Sri Lankan taxis are often reconditioned Japanese vans. They're common in all sizable towns and even some villages will be able to dig up a taxi. Only a few are metered, but over longer distances their prices are comparable to those of three-wheelers, and they provide more comfort and security. Radio cabs are available in Kandy and Colombo. You can count on most taxi rides costing around Rs 40 to 50 per kilometre.

Three-Wheeler
These vehicles, known in other parts of Asia as *túk-túks, bajajs* or autorickshaws, are everywhere: turn a corner and you'll find one. Agree (or haggle your heart out) on the fare before you get in. Some keen drivers will offer to take you to the moon, but it's no fun being in a three-wheeler for more an hour; believe us, this comes from hard experience. You may think that the driver is not obeying any road rules; you are probably right.

As a rule of thumb, a three-wheeler should cost no more than Rs 40 per kilometre. Three-wheelers and taxis waiting outside tourist hotels and similar places expect higher than usual fares.

TRAIN
Sri Lanka's rickety railways are a great way to cross the country. Although they are slow, trains travel short distances so there are few overnight or all-day ordeals to contend with. A train ride is almost always more relaxed than a bus ride.

There are three main lines. The coast line runs south from Colombo, past Aluthgama and Hikkaduwa to Galle and Matara. The main line pushes east from Colombo into the Hill Country, through Kandy, Nanu Oya (for Nuwara Eliya) and Ella to Badulla. The northern line launches from Colombo through Anuradhapura to Vavuniya (it once ran beyond Jaffna to the northern tip of Sri Lanka). One branch of the northern line reaches Trincomalee on the east coast, while another branch heads south to Polonnaruwa and Batticaloa.

The Puttalam line runs along the coast north from Colombo, although rail buses run between Chilaw and Puttalam. The Kelani Valley line winds 60km from Colombo to Avissawella.

Trains are often late. For long-distance trains, Sri Lankans sometimes measure the lateness in periods of the day: quarter of a day late, half a day late and so on.

There's a helpful information desk (No 10) at Fort station in Colombo, and also an **information office** (☎ 244 0048; ⏱ 9am-5pm Mon-Fri, 9am-1pm Sat), to the right of the main entrance, run by JF Tours. The staff can provide information on timetables and routes. For details of the main trains leaving Colombo and Kandy, see p105 and p187 respectively. Abbreviated timetables for fast trains can also be found at www.science land.lk/railway/timetb.htm.

Classes

There are three classes on Sri Lankan trains. Third class is dirt cheap and invariably crowded, but with a little luck you'll get a seat on a bench. Second class has padded seats and fans that sometimes work, and it's generally less crowded. There are no 2nd-class sleeping berths, only 'sleeperettes' (fold-down beds in a shared compartment). First class comes in three varieties, all with air-con – coaches, sleeping berths and observation saloons (with large windows) – but is available on relatively few lines.

Costs

As a sample, the intercity express from Kandy to Colombo costs Rs 250 in 1st class or Rs 125 in 2nd class. From Colombo to Anuradhapura, the intercity express costs Rs 520 in 1st class or Rs 290 in 2nd class.

Reservations

You can reserve places in 1st class and on intercity expresses. On four of the daily intercity services between Colombo and Kandy you can also book on 2nd-class sleeperettes.

On weekends and public holidays, it pays to make a booking for 24-seat observation saloons, which only run on the main line, as these carriages often fill up; the booking fee is Rs 50. The best seats to book are Nos 11, 12, 23 and 24, which have full window views. The observation saloon is at the end of the train and jolts around quite a lot.

Reservations can be made at stations up to 10 days before departure. You can book a return ticket up to 14 days before departure.

If travelling more than 80km, you can break your journey at any intermediate station for 24 hours without penalty. However, you must make fresh reservations for seats on the next leg.

TRANSPORT

Health

CONTENTS

While the potential dangers of travelling in Sri Lanka may seem quite ominous, in reality few travellers experience anything more than an upset stomach. Hygiene is generally poor throughout the country, so food- and water-borne illnesses are common. Travellers tend to worry about contracting infectious diseases, but infections rarely cause *serious* illness or death in travellers. Pre-existing medical conditions, such as heart disease, and accidental injury (especially traffic accidents) account for most life-threatening problems.

Fortunately most travellers' illnesses can either be prevented with some common-sense behaviour or be treated easily with a well-stocked traveller's medical kit. The following advice is a general guide only and does not replace the advice of a doctor trained in travel medicine.

BEFORE YOU GO

Pack medications in their original, clearly labelled containers. A signed and dated letter from your physician describing your medical conditions and medications, including generic names, is very useful. If carrying syringes or needles be sure to have a physician's letter documenting their medical necessity. If you have a heart condition bring a copy of your ECG taken just before travelling.

If you take any regular medication bring double your needs in case of loss or theft. You'll be able to buy many medications over the counter in Sri Lanka without a doctor's prescription, but it can be difficult to find some of the newer drugs, particularly the latest antidepressant drugs, blood pressure medications and contraceptive pills.

INSURANCE

Even if you're fit and healthy don't travel without health insurance, as accidents do happen. Declare any existing medical conditions; the insurance company will check if your problem is pre-existing and will not cover you if it is undeclared. You may require extra cover for adventure activities such as rock climbing and scuba diving. If your health insurance doesn't cover you for medical expenses abroad, consider getting extra insurance. If you're uninsured remember that emergency evacuation is expensive; bills of more than US$100,000 are not uncommon.

Find out in advance if your insurance company will make payments directly to providers or reimburse you later for overseas expenditures. (In many countries, doctors expect payment in cash.) Some policies offer a range of medical-expense options; the higher ones are chiefly for countries that have extremely high medical costs, such as the USA. You may prefer a policy that pays doctors or hospitals directly rather than you having to pay on the spot and claim later. If you have to claim later, make sure you keep all documentation. Some policies ask you to call back (reverse charges) to a centre in your home country where an immediate assessment of your problem is made.

VACCINATIONS

Specialised travel-medicine clinics are your best source of information; they stock all available vaccines and will be able to give specific recommendations for you and your trip. The doctors will take into account factors such as past vaccination history, the length of your trip, activities you may be undertaking and underlying medical conditions, such as pregnancy.

Most vaccines don't give immunity until at least two weeks after they're given, so visit a doctor four to eight weeks before departure. Ask your doctor for an International Certificate of Vaccination (aka the 'yellow booklet'), which will list all the vaccinations you've received.

Recommended Vaccinations

The World Health Organization (WHO) recommends the following vaccinations for travellers to Sri Lanka (as well as being up to date with measles, mumps and rubella vaccinations).

Adult diphtheria & tetanus Single booster recommended if none in the previous 10 years. Side effects include sore arm and fever.

Hepatitis A Provides almost 100% protection for up to a year; a booster after 12 months provides at least another 20 years' protection. Mild side effects, such as headache and sore arm, occur in 5% to 10% of people.

Hepatitis B Now considered routine for most travellers. Given as three shots over six months. A rapid schedule is also available, as is a combined vaccination with Hepatitis A. Side effects are mild and uncommon, usually headache and sore arm. In 95% of people lifetime protection results.

Polio In 2004 polio was still present in Sri Lanka. Only one booster is required as an adult for lifetime protection. Inactivated polio vaccine is safe during pregnancy.

Rabies Three injections in all. A booster after one year will then provide 10 years' protection. Side effects are rare – occasionally headache and sore arm.

Typhoid Recommended for all travellers to Sri Lanka, even if you only visit urban areas. The vaccine offers around 70% protection, lasts for two to three years and comes as a single shot. Tablets are also available; however, the injection is usually recommended as it has fewer side effects. Sore arm and fever may occur.

Varicella If you haven't had chickenpox, discuss this vaccination with your doctor.

Immunisations recommended for long-term travellers (more than one month) or those at special risk:

Japanese B Encephalitis Three injections in all. Booster recommended after two years. Sore arm and headache are the most common side effects. Rarely, an allergic reaction of hives and swelling can occur up to 10 days after any of the three doses.

Meningitis Single injection. There are two types of vaccination: the quadravalent vaccine gives two to three years' protection; meningitis group C vaccine gives around 10 years'

protection. Recommended for long-term backpackers aged under 25.

Tuberculosis (TB) A complex issue. Adult long-term travellers are usually recommended to have a TB skin test before and after travel, rather than vaccination. Only one vaccine is given in a lifetime.

Required Vaccinations

The only vaccine required by international regulations is yellow fever. Proof of vaccination will only be required if you have visited a country in the yellow-fever zone within the six days before entering Sri Lanka.

MEDICAL CHECKLIST

Recommended items for a personal medical kit:

- antibacterial cream, eg Muciprocin
- antibiotic for skin infections, eg Amoxicillin/Clavulanate or Cephalexin
- antifungal cream, eg Clotrimazole
- antihistamine: there are many options, eg Cetrizine for day and promethazine for night
- anti-inflammatory, eg ibuprofen
- antiseptic, eg Betadine
- antispasmodic for stomach cramps, eg Buscopan
- contraceptive
- decongestant, eg pseudoephedrine
- DEET-based insect repellent
- diarrhoea medication: consider an oral rehydration solution (eg Gastrolyte), diarrhoea 'stopper' (eg Loperamide) and antinausea medication (eg Prochlorperazine); antibiotics for diarrhoea include Norfloxacin or ciprofloxacin, for bacterial diarrhoea Azithromycin, for giardia or amoebic dysentery Tinidazole
- first-aid items, eg scissors, sticking plasters, bandages, gauze, thermometer (but not mercury), sterile needles and syringes, safety pins and tweezers
- indigestion tablets or liquid, eg Quick Eze or Mylanta
- insect repellent to impregnate clothing and mosquito nets, eg permethrin
- iodine tablets (unless you're pregnant or have a thyroid problem) to purify water
- laxative, eg Coloxyl
- migraine medication if you are a sufferer
- painkiller tablets, eg paracetamol
- steroid cream for allergic or itchy rashes, eg 1% to 2% hydrocortisone
- sunscreen and hat

HEALTH

- throat lozenges
- thrush (vaginal yeast infection) treatment, eg Clotrimazole pessaries or Diflucan tablet
- urinary tract infection treatment such as Ural or equivalent, if you're prone to urinary infections

INTERNET RESOURCES

There is a wealth of travel health advice on the Internet. **Lonely Planet** (www.lonelyplanet.com) is a good place to start. Other suggestions: **Centers for Disease Control & Prevention** (CDC; www.cdc.gov) Good general information.
MD Travel Health (www.mdtravelhealth.com) Provides complete travel health recommendations for every country, updated daily.
World Health Organization (WHO; www.who.int/ith/) Its superb book *International Travel & Health* is revised annually and available online.

FURTHER READING

Lonely Planet's handy pocket-sized *Healthy Travel: Asia & India* is packed with useful information. Other recommended references include *Traveller's Health* by Dr Richard Dawood and *Travelling Well* by Dr Deborah Mills – check out the website of **Travelling Well** (www.travellingwell.com.au).

IN TRANSIT

DEEP VEIN THROMBOSIS (DVT)

DVT occurs when blood clots form in the legs during plane flights, chiefly due to prolonged immobility. The longer the flight the greater the risk. Although most blood clots are reabsorbed uneventfully, some may break off and travel through the blood vessels to the lungs where they could cause life-threatening complications.

The chief symptom of DVT is swelling or pain in the foot, ankle, or calf, usually but not always on just one side. When a blood clot travels to the lungs it may cause chest pain and difficulty in breathing. Travellers with any of these symptoms should seek medical attention immediately.

To prevent the development of DVT on long flights you should walk about the cabin, perform isometric compressions of the leg muscles (ie contract the leg muscles while sitting), drink plenty of fluids and avoid alcohol and tobacco.

JET LAG & MOTION SICKNESS

Jet lag is common when crossing more than five time zones; it results in insomnia, fatigue, malaise or nausea. To avoid jet lag drink plenty of (nonalcoholic) fluids and eat light meals. On arrival, seek exposure to natural sunlight and readjust your schedule (for meals, sleep etc) as soon as possible.

Antihistamines, such as dimenhydrinate (Dramamine), promethazine (Phenergan) and meclizine (Antivert, Bonine), are usually the first choice for treating motion sickness. Their main side effect is drowsiness. A herbal alternative is ginger, which works like a charm for some people.

IN SRI LANKA

AVAILABILITY OF HEALTH CARE

Medical care is hugely variable in Sri Lanka. Colombo has some good clinics; they may be more expensive than local medical facilities but they're worth using because a superior standard of care is offered.

Self-treatment may be appropriate if your problem is minor (eg traveller's diarrhoea), if you are carrying the relevant medication and if you cannot attend a recommended clinic. If you think you may have a serious disease, especially malaria, do not waste time; travel to the nearest quality facility to receive attention. It is always better to be assessed by a doctor than to rely on self-treatment.

Before buying medication over the counter always check the use-by date and ensure the packet is sealed. Don't accept items that have been poorly stored (eg lying in a glass cabinet exposed to the sun).

INFECTIOUS DISEASES

Dengue

This mosquito-borne disease is becomingly increasingly problematic in the tropical world, especially in the cities. As there is no vaccine it can only be prevented by avoiding mosquito bites. The dengue-carrying mosquito bites both day and night so use insect avoidance measures at all times. Symptoms include high fever, severe headache and body ache (dengue was previously known as 'breakbone fever'). Some people develop a rash and experience diarrhoea. There is no specific treatment – just rest and paracetamol; do not take aspirin because it increases the likelihood of haemorrhaging. See a doctor for diagnosis and monitoring.

Hepatitis A

This food- and water-borne virus infects the liver, causing jaundice (yellow skin and eyes), nausea and lethargy. There is no specific treatment for hepatitis A, as you just need to allow time for the liver to heal. All travellers to Sri Lanka should be vaccinated against hepatitis A.

Hepatitis B

The only sexually transmitted disease that can be prevented by vaccination, hepatitis B is spread by body fluids. The long-term consequences can include liver cancer and cirrhosis.

Hepatitis E

Hepatitis E is transmitted through contaminated food and water. It has similar symptoms to hepatitis A but is far less common. It's a severe problem in pregnant women, and can result in the death of both mother and baby. There is currently no vaccine, and prevention is by following safe eating and drinking guidelines.

HIV

HIV is spread via contaminated body fluids. Avoid unsafe sex, unsterile needles (including in medical facilities), and procedures such as tattooing.

Japanese B Encephalitis

This viral disease is transmitted by mosquitoes and is rare in travellers. Like most mosquito-borne diseases, it is becoming a more common problem in many countries affected by mosquitoes. Most cases occur in rural areas, and vaccination is recommended for travellers spending more than one month outside of cities. There is no treatment, and a third of infected people will die, while another third will suffer permanent brain damage.

Malaria

Malaria is caused by a parasite transmitted by the bite of an infected mosquito. The most important symptom of malaria is fever, but general symptoms such as headache, diarrhoea, cough or chills may also occur. Diagnosis can only be made by taking a blood sample.

Two strategies should be combined to prevent malaria – mosquito avoidance and antimalarial medications. Most people who catch malaria are taking inadequate or no antimalarial medication.

Travellers are advised to prevent mosquito bites by taking these steps:

- using a DEET-containing insect repellent on exposed skin – wash this off at night, as long as you are sleeping under a mosquito net; natural repellents such as citronella can be effective but must be applied more frequently than products containing DEET;
- sleeping under a mosquito net impregnated with permethrin;
- choosing accommodation with screens and fans (if not air-conditioned);
- impregnating clothing with permethrin in high-risk areas;
- wearing long sleeves and trousers in light colours;
- using mosquito coils;
- spraying your room with insect repellent before going out for your evening meal.

There are a variety of medications available. The effectiveness of the **chloroquine & Paludrine** combination is limited in many parts of South Asia. Common side effects include nausea (40% of people) and mouth ulcers.

The daily tablet **doxycycline** is a broad-spectrum antibiotic that has the added benefit of helping to prevent a variety of diseases including leptospirosis, tick-borne disease and typhus. Potential side effects include photosensitivity (a tendency to

HEALTH

sunburn), thrush (in women), indigestion, heartburn, nausea and interference with the contraceptive pill. More-serious side effects include ulceration of the oesophagus; you can help prevent this by taking your tablet with a meal and a large glass of water, and never lying down within half an hour of taking it. It must be taken for four weeks after leaving the risk area.

Lariam (Mefloquine) has received much bad press, some of it justified, some not. This weekly tablet suits many people. Serious side effects are rare but include depression, anxiety, psychosis and fits. Anyone with a history of depression, anxiety, other psychological disorders or epilepsy should not take Lariam. If you are pregnant you should consult your doctor before taking Lariam. Tablets must be taken for four weeks after leaving the risk area.

The new drug **Malarone** is a combination of Atovaquone and Proguanil. Side effects are uncommon and mild, most commonly nausea and headache. It is the best tablet for scuba divers and for those on short trips to high-risk areas. It must be taken for one week after leaving the risk area.

Rabies

This uniformly fatal disease is spread by the bite or lick of an infected animal, most commonly a dog or monkey. You should seek medical advice immediately after any animal bite, and begin postexposure treatment. Having a pretravel vaccination means that the postbite treatment is very much simplified. If an animal bites you, gently wash the wound with soap and water and apply iodine-based antiseptic. If you are not prevaccinated you will need to receive rabies immunoglobulin as soon as possible, and this is almost impossible to obtain in much of Sri Lanka.

Tuberculosis

While TB is rare in travellers, those who have significant contact with the local population (such as medical and aid workers and long-term travellers) should take precautions. Vaccination is usually only given to children under the age of five, but adults at risk are recommended to have pre- and post-travel TB testing. The main symptoms are fever, a cough, weight loss, night sweats and tiredness.

Typhoid

This serious bacterial infection is spread via food and water. It gives a high and slowly progressive fever, and a headache, and it may be accompanied by a dry cough and stomach pain. It is diagnosed by blood tests and treated with antibiotics. Vaccination is recommended for all travellers spending more than a week in Sri Lanka. Be aware that vaccination is not 100% effective, so you must still be careful with what you eat and drink.

TRAVELLER'S DIARRHOEA

Traveller's diarrhoea is usually caused by a bacteria (there are numerous potential culprits), and therefore responds promptly to antibiotic treatment. Treatment with antibiotics will depend on your situation – how sick you are, how quickly you need to get better, where you are etc.

Traveller's diarrhoea is defined as the passage of more than three watery bowel actions within 24 hours, plus at least one other symptom, such as fever, cramps, nausea, vomiting or feeling generally unwell.

Treatment consists of staying well hydrated; rehydration solutions like Gastrolyte are the best for this. Antibiotics, such as Norfloxacin, Ciprofloxacin or Azithromycin, will kill the bacteria quickly.

Loperamide is just a 'stopper' and doesn't get to the cause of the problem, though it can be helpful (eg if you have to go on a long bus ride). Don't take Loperamide if you have a fever, or blood in your stools. Seek medical attention quickly if you do not respond to an appropriate antibiotic.

ENVIRONMENTAL HAZARDS
Diving & Surfing

Divers and surfers should seek specialised advice before travelling to ensure their medical kit contains treatment for coral cuts and tropical ear infections, as well as the standard problems. Divers should make sure their insurance covers decompression illness; consider getting specialised dive insurance through an organisation such as **Divers Alert Network** (DAN; www.danseap.org).

Food

Eating in restaurants is the biggest risk for contracting traveller's diarrhoea. Ways to avoid it include eating only freshly cooked

DRINKING WATER

- Never drink tap water.
- Bottled water is generally safe – check the seal is intact at purchase.
- Avoid ice.
- Avoid fresh juices – they may have been watered down.
- Boiling water is the most efficient method of purifying it.
- The best chemical purifier is iodine – it should not be used by pregnant women or those with thyroid problems.
- Water filters should also filter out viruses – ensure your filter has a chemical barrier, such as iodine, and a small pore size, eg less than four microns.

food, and avoiding shellfish and food that has been sitting in buffets. Peel all fruit, cook vegetables, and soak salads in iodine water for at least 20 minutes. Eat in busy restaurants that have a high turnover of customers.

Heat

Much of Sri Lanka is hot year-round. Avoid dehydration and excessive activity in the heat. Take it easy when you first arrive. Don't eat salt tablets (they aggravate the gut); drinking rehydration solution or eating salty food helps.

Dehydration is the main contributor to heat exhaustion. Symptoms include weakness, headache, irritability, nausea, sweaty skin, a fast, weak pulse, and a normal or slightly elevated body temperature. Treatment involves getting out of the heat and sun, fanning the sufferer and applying cool wet cloths to the skin, laying the sufferer flat with their legs raised and rehydrating with water containing a ¼-teaspoon of salt per litre. Recovery is usually rapid but it is common to feel weak for some days afterwards.

Heatstroke is a serious medical emergency. Symptoms come on suddenly and include weakness, nausea, a hot dry body with a body temperature of over 41°C, dizziness, confusion, loss of coordination, fits and eventually collapse and loss of consciousness. Seek medical help and start

cooling by getting the person out of the heat, removing their clothes, fanning them, and applying cool wet cloths or ice to their body, especially to the groin and armpits.

Prickly heat is a common skin rash in the tropics, caused by sweat being trapped under the skin. The result is an itchy rash of tiny lumps. Treat it by moving out of the heat and into an air-conditioned area for a few hours and by having cool showers. Creams and ointments clog the skin so they should be avoided. Locally bought prickly heat powder can be helpful.

Insect Bites & Stings

Bedbugs don't carry disease but their bites are very itchy. They live in the cracks of furniture and walls, and then migrate to the bed at night to feed on you. You can treat the itch with an antihistamine.

Lice inhabit various parts of your body but most commonly your head and pubic area.

Ticks are contracted after walking in rural areas and are commonly found behind the ears, on the belly and in armpits. If you have had a tick bite and experience symptoms, such as a rash at the site of the bite or elsewhere, fever or muscle aches, you should see a doctor. The antimalarial drug doxycycline prevents tick-borne diseases.

Leeches are found in humid rainforest areas. They do not transmit any disease but their bites are often intensely itchy for weeks afterwards and can easily become infected. Apply an iodine-based antiseptic to any leech bite to help prevent infection.

Bee and wasp stings mainly cause problems for people who are allergic to them. Anyone with a serious bee or wasp allergy should carry an adrenaline injection (eg an Epipen) for emergency treatment.

Skin Problems

Fungal rashes are common in humid climates. There are two fungal rashes that affect travellers. The first occurs in moist areas of the body that get less air, such as the groin, armpits and between the toes. It starts as a red patch that slowly spreads and is usually itchy. Treatment involves keeping the skin dry, avoiding chafing and using an antifungal cream, such as Clotrimazole or Lamisil.

Cuts and scratches become easily infected in humid climates. Take meticulous care of

HEALTH

any cuts and scratches to prevent complications such as abscesses. Immediately wash all wounds in clean water and apply antiseptic.

Snakes

There are five species of venomous snakes in Sri Lanka, and it is relatively common to spot them, especially in the dry zone area around Anuradhapura and Polonnaruwa. Be careful when wandering around the ancient ruins. Snake bites do not cause instantaneous death, and antivenins are usually available. Wrap the bitten limb tightly, as you would for a sprained ankle, and then attach a splint to immobilise it. Keep the victim still and seek medical help, if possible with the dead snake for identification.

Sunburn

Even on a cloudy day sunburn can occur rapidly. Always use a strong sunscreen (at least factor 30), making sure to reapply after a swim, and always wear a wide-brimmed hat and sunglasses outdoors. Avoid lying in the sun during the hottest part of the day (10am to 2pm).

WOMEN'S HEALTH

Pregnant women should receive specialised advice before travelling. The ideal time to travel is in the second trimester (between 16 and 28 weeks), when the risk of pregnancy-related problems is at its lowest. Always carry a list of quality medical facilities available at your destination and ensure you continue your standard antenatal care at these facilities. Avoid rural travel in areas with poor transportation and medical facilities. Most of all, ensure travel insurance covers all pregnancy-related issues, including premature labour.

Malaria is a high-risk disease during pregnancy. WHO recommends that pregnant women do *not* travel to areas with malaria that is chloroquine resistant. None of the more effective antimalarial drugs are completely safe in pregnancy.

Traveller's diarrhoea can quickly lead to dehydration and result in inadequate blood flow to the placenta. Many of the drugs used to treat various diarrhoea bugs are not recommended in pregnancy. Azithromycin is considered safe.

Language

CONTENTS

Sinhala and Tamil are both national languages, with English commonly described as a linking language. It's easy to get by in Sri Lanka with English, and the Sri Lankan variety has its own unique characteristics – 'You are having a problem, isn't it, no?' While English may be widely spoken in the main centres, off the beaten track its spread thins. In any case, even a few words of Sinhala or Tamil will win you smiles. People really appreciate the effort when they meet foreigners willing to greet them in their own language.

SRI LANKAN ENGLISH

Like every other country where English is spoken, Sri Lanka has its own peculiar versions of some words and phrases. Life can be a bit confusing if you don't have a grasp of some of the essentials of Sri Lankan English, so we've included a few examples here.

Greetings & Questions
Go and come – farewell greeting, similar to 'see you later'; not taken literally

How? – How are you?
Nothing to do – Can't do anything
What to do? – What can be done about it?; more of a rhetorical question
What country? – Where are you from?

People
batchmate – university classmate
baby/bubba – term used for any child up to about adolescence
to gift – to give a gift
paining – hurting
peon – office helper
uncle/auntie – term of respect for elder

Getting Around
backside – part of the building away from the street
bajaj – three-wheeler
bus halt – bus stop
coloured lights – traffic lights
down south – the areas south of Colombo, especially coastal areas
dropping – being dropped off at a place by a car
get down (from bus/train/three-wheeler) – to alight
hotel – a small, cheap restaurant that doesn't offer accommodation
normal bus – not a private bus
outstation – place beyond a person's home area
petrol shed – petrol/gas station
pick-up (noun) – 4WD utility vehicle
seaside/landside – indicates locations, usually in relation to Galle Rd
two-wheeler – motorcycle
up and down – return trip
up country/Hill Country – Kandy and beyond, tea plantation areas
vehicle – car

Food
bite – snack usually eaten with alcoholic drinks
boutique – a small, hole-in-the-wall shop, usually selling small, inexpensive items
cool spot – traditional, small shop that sells cool drinks and snacks
lunch packet/rice packet – portion of rice and curry wrapped in plastic and newspaper and taken to office or school for lunch
short eats – snack food

Money
buck – rupee
purse – wallet
last price – final price when bargaining

SINHALA

Sinhala is somewhat simplified by the use of many *eka* words. Eka is used more or less similarly to the English definite article 'the' and *ekak* is used like 'a' or 'any'. English words for which there is no Sinhala equivalent have often been incorporated into Sinhala with the simple addition of *eka* or *ekak*. So, if you're in search of a telephone it's simply *telifon ekak* but if it is a specific telephone then you should say *telifon eka*. Similarly, English definitions of people have been included in Sinhala simply by adding *kenek* – if you hire a car the driver is the *draiwar kenek*.

Two useful little Sinhala words are *da* and *ge*. *Da* turns a statement into a question – thus if *nohna* means a lady then *nohna-da* means 'This lady?' or 'Is this the lady?' The suffix *ge* is the Sinhala equivalent of an apostrophe indicating possession; thus 'Tony's book' in Sinhala is *Tony-ge potha*. *Ta* is like the English preposition 'to' – if you want to go 'to the beach' it's *valla-ta*.

As in many other Asian countries, Sri Lankans do not use the multitude of greetings that you find in English ('Hello', 'Good morning', 'How are you?', 'Goodbye'). Saying *aayu-bowan* more or less covers them all. Similarly, there isn't really a Sinhala word for 'Thank you'. You could try *istuh-tee* but it's a bit stiff and formal – a simple smile will often suffice. Appreciation of a meal can be expressed by *bohoma rahay*, which is both a compliment and an expression of appreciation. *Hari sho-ke* translates as 'wonderful', 'terrific' or even 'fine'. A side-to-side wiggle of the head often means 'yes' or 'OK'.

For a more comprehensive guide to the language, pick up a copy of Lonely Planet's *Sinhala Phrasebook*.

FORMS OF ADDRESS

In Sinhala there are more than 20 ways to say 'you' depending on the person's age, social status, sex, position and even how well you know them. The best solution is to simply avoid saying 'you'. The word for Mr is *mahaththeya* – 'Mr Jayewardene' is *Jaye-wardene mahaththeya*. The word for 'Mrs' is *nohna* and it also comes after the person's name. Any non-Eastern foreigner is defined

as white *(sudha)*, so a male foreigner is a *sudha mahaththeya*.

Sinhala is officially written using a cursive script and there are about 50 letters in the alphabet.

PRONUNCIATION

The transliteration system used in this guide to represent the sounds of Sinhala uses the closest English equivalents – they are approximations only. Listening to Sri Lankans is the best way to learn Sinhala pronunciation.

When consonants are doubled they should be pronounced very distinctly, almost as two separate sounds belonging to two separate words. The letters **t** and **d** are pronounced less forcefully than in English, and **g** is pronounced as in 'go', not as in 'rage'. The letter **r** is more like a flap of the tongue against the roof of the mouth – it's not pronounced as an American 'r'.

Vowels

a	as the 'u' in 'cup'; aa is pronounced more like the 'a' in 'father'
e	as in 'met'
i	as in 'bit'
o	as in 'hot'
u	as in 'put', not as in 'hut'

Vowel Combinations

ai	as the word 'eye'
au	as the 'ow' in 'how'

Consonants

dh	one sound, as the 'th' in 'then' (not as in 'thin')
g	as in 'go'
r	a flap of the tongue against the roof of the mouth – not pronounced as an American 'r'
th	one sound, as in 'thin'

ACCOMMODATION

Do you have any rooms available?	*kaamara thiyanawada?*
for one person	*ek-kenek pamanai*
for two people	*den-nek pamanai*
for one night	*ek rayak pamanai*
for two nights	*raya dekak pamanai*
How much is it per night?	*ek ra-yakata kiyada*
How much is it per person?	*ek kenek-kuta kiyada*

Is breakfast included?	udeh keh-emath ekkada?
hotel	hotel eka
guesthouse	gesthaus eka
youth hostel	yut-hostel eka
camping ground	kamping ground eka

CONVERSATION & ESSENTIALS

Hello.	aayu-bowan/hello
Goodbye.	aayu-bowan
Yes.	owu
No.	naha
Please.	karuna kara
Thank you.	istuh-tee
Excuse me.	samah venna
Sorry/Pardon.	kana gaatui
Do you speak English?	oyaa in-ghirisih kata karenawa da?
How much is it?	ehekka keeyada?
What's your name?	oyaaghe nama mokka'da?
My name is ...	maaghe nama ...

EMERGENCIES – SINHALA

Help!	aaney!/aaeeyoh!/ammoh!
Call a doctor!	dostara gen-nanna!
Call the police!	polisiyata kiyanna!
Leave me alone!	mata maghe paduweh inna arinna!
Go away!	methanin yanna!
I'm lost.	maa-meh nativelaa

NUMBERS

0	binduwa
1	eka
2	deka
3	thuna
4	hathara
5	paha
6	haya
7	hatha
8	atta
9	navaya
10	dahaya
100	seeya
200	deh seeya
1000	daaha
2000	deh daaha
100,000	lakshaya
1,000,000	daseh lakshaya
10,000,000	kotiya

SHOPPING & SERVICES

bank	bankuwa
chemist/pharmacy	faahmisiya

SIGNS – SINHALA

Entrance		
etul veema	ඇතුල්වීම
Exit		
pita veema	පිටවීම
Information		
toraturu	තොරතුරු දැන්වුම
Open		
virutai etta	විවෘතව ඇත.
Closed		
vasaa etta	වසා ඇත.
Prohibited		
tahanam	තහනම් වේ.
Police Station		
polis staaneya	පොලිස් ස්ථානය
Rooms Available		
kamara etta	කාමර ඇත.
No Vacancies		
ida netu	කාමර නැත.
Toilets		
vasikili	වැසිකිළ
Men		
purusha	පුරුෂ
Women		
isthree	ස්ත්‍රී

... embassy	... embasiya
my hotel	mang inna hotalaya
market	maakat eka
newsagency	pattara ejensiya
post office	tepul kantohruwa
public telephone	podu dura katanayak
stationers	lipi dravya velendoh
tourist office	sanchaaraka toraturu karyaalayak
big	loku
small	podi, punchi
medicine	behe-yat

What time does it open/close?
ehika kiyatada arinneh/vahanneh?

TIME & DAYS

What time is it?	velaave keeyada?
day	davasa
night	raah
week	sumaanayak
month	maasayak
year	avuurudeh
today	ada (uther)
tomorrow	heta
yesterday	ee-yeh
morning	udai
afternoon	havasa

Monday	sandu-da
Tuesday	angaharuwaa-da
Wednesday	badaa-da
Thursday	braha-spetin-da
Friday	sikuraa-da
Saturday	senasuraa-da
Sunday	iri-da

TRANSPORT
When does does the next ... leave/arrive?
meelanga ... pitaht venne/paminenne?

boat	bohtuwa
bus (city)	bus eka
bus (intercity)	bus eka (nagaraantara)
train	koh-chiya
plane	plane eka

I want to get off.
mama methana bahinawa
I'd like a one-way ticket.
mata tani gaman tikat ekak ganna ohna
I'd like a return ticket.
mata yaam-eem tikat ekak ganna ohna

1st class	palamu veni paantiya
2nd class	deveni paantiya
3rd class	tunveni paantiya
timetable	kaala satahana
bus stop	bus nevathuma/bus hohlt eka
train station	dumriya pala
ferry terminal	totu pala

I'd like to hire ...
mata ... ekak bad-dhata ganna ohna

| a car | kar (eka) |
| a bicycle | baisikeleya |

Directions

Where is (a/the) ...?	... koheda?
Go straight ahead.	kelinma issarahata yaanna
Turn left.	wamata harenna
Turn right.	dakunata harenna
near	lan-ghai
far	durai

TAMIL

The vocabulary of Sri Lankan Tamil is much the same as that of South India – the written form is identical, using the traditional cursive script – but there are marked differences in pronunciation between speakers from the two regions. The transliteration system used in this guide is intended to represent the sounds of Sri Lankan Tamil using the Roman alphabet – as with all such systems it is an approximate guide only. The best way to improve your pronunciation is to listen to the way Sri Lankans themselves speak the language.

PRONUNCIATION
Vowels

a	as the 'u' in 'cup'; aa is pronounced as the 'a' in 'father'
e	as in 'met'
i	as in 'bit'
o	as in 'hot'
u	as in 'put'

Vowel Combinations

| ai | as in 'eye' |
| au | as in 'how' |

Consonants
Most consonants are fairly similar to their English counterparts. The following are a few that may cause confusion:

dh	one sound, as the 'th' in 'then' (not as in 'thin')
g	as in 'go'
r	a flap of the tongue against the roof of the mouth – not pronounced as an American 'r'
s	as in 'sit'
th	one sound, as in 'thin'

ACCOMMODATION
Do you have any rooms available?
ingu room kideikkumaa?
for one/two people
oruvarukku/iruvarukku
for one/two nights
oru/irandu iravukku
How much is it per night/per person?
oru iravukku/oru aalukku evvalavur?
Is breakfast included?
kaalei unavum sehrtha?

hotel	hotehl
guesthouse	virun-dhinar vidhudheh
youth hostel	ilainar vidhudheh
camping ground	mukhaamidum idahm

CONVERSATION & ESSENTIALS

| Hello. | vanakkam |
| Goodbye. | poytu varukirehn |

Yes.	aam
No.	il-lay
Please.	tayavu saydhu
Thank you.	nandri
That's fine, you're welcome.	nalladu varukha
Excuse me.	mannikavum
Sorry/Pardon.	mannikavum
Do you speak English?	nin-gal aangilam paysu-virhalaa?
How much is it?	adhu evvalavu?
What's your name?	ungal peyr en-na?
My name is ...	en peyr ...

EMERGENCIES – TAMIL

Help!	udavi!
Call a doctor!	daktarai kuppidunga!
Call the police!	polisai kuppidunga!
Leave me alone!	enna taniyaahu irukkavidunga!
Go away!	pohn-goh!/poi-vidu!
I'm lost.	naan vali tavari-vittehn

NUMBERS

0	saifer
1	ondru
2	iranduh
3	muundruh
4	naan-guh
5	ainduh
6	aaruh
7	ealluh
8	ettu
9	onbaduh
10	pat-tuh
100	nooruh
1000	aayirem
2000	irandaayirem
100,000	oru latcham
1,000,000	pattuh lat-chem
10,000,000	kohdee

SHOPPING & SERVICES

bank	vanghee
chemist/pharmacy	marunduh kadhai/pharmacy
... embassy	... tudharalayem
my hotel	enadu hotehl
market	maarket
newsagency	niyuz paper vitku-midam
post office	tafaal nilayem
public telephone	podhu tolai-pessee
stationers	eludhuporul vitku-midam
tourist office	toorist nilayem

SIGNS – TAMIL

Entrance	
vahli ullay	வழி உள்ளே
Exit	
vahli veliyeh	வழி வெளியே
Information	
tahavwel	தகவல்
Open	
thirandul-ladhu	திறந்துள்ளது
Closed	
adek-kappattulladhu	அடைக்கப்பட்டுள்ளது
Prohibited	
anumadee-illay	அனுமதி இல்லை
Police Station	
kaav'l nilayem	காவல் நிலையம்
Rooms Available	
arekahl undu	அறைகள் உண்டு
Full, No Vacancies	
illay, kaali illay	நிரம்பியுள்ளது, காலி இல்லை
Toilets	
kahlippadem	மலசலகூடம்
Men	
aan	ஆண்
Women	
pen	பெண்

big	periyeh
small	siriyeh
medicine	marunduh

What time does it open/close?
et-thana manikka tirakhum/mudhum?

TIME & DAYS

What time is it?	mani eth-tanai?
day	pahel
night	iravu
week	vaarem
month	maadhem
year	varudem
today	indru
tomorrow	naalay
yesterday	neh-truh
morning	kaalai
afternoon	pit-pahel
Monday	tin-gal
Tuesday	sevvaay

Wednesday	budahn	1st class	mudalahaam vahuppu
Thursday	viyaalin	2nd class	irandaam vahuppu
Friday	vellee	luggage lockers	porul vaikku-midam
Saturday	san-nee	timetable	haala attavanay
Sunday	naayiru	bus/trolley stop	baas nilayem
		train station	rayill nilayem

TRANSPORT

What time does the next ... leave/arrive?
eththanai manikku aduththa ... sellum/varum?

boat	padakhu/boat
bus (city)	baas (naharam/ul-loor)
bus (intercity)	baas (veliyoor)
train	rayill

I want to get off.
naan iranga vendum
I'd like a one-way ticket.
enakku oru vahly tikket veynum
I'd like a return ticket.
enakku iru vahlay tikket veynum

I'd like to hire ...
enakku ... vaadakhaikku vaynum

a car	car
a bicycle	sai-kul

Directions

Where is it?	adhu en-ghe irukkaradhu?
Where is a/the ...?	... en-ghe?
Go straight ahead.	neraha sellavum
Turn left.	valadhur pakkam tirumbavum
Turn right.	itadhu pakkam thirumbavum
near	aruhil
far	tu-rahm

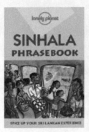

Also available from Lonely Planet:
Sinhala Phrasebook

Glossary

ambalama – wayside shelter for pilgrims
Aurudu – Sinhalese and Tamil New Year, celebrated on 14 April
Avalokitesvara – the *Bodhisattva* of compassion
Ayurveda – traditional system of medicine that uses herbs and oils to heal and rejuvenate

bailas – folk tunes (often love songs) based on Portuguese, African and local music styles
baobab – water-storing tree *(Adansonia digitata)*, probably introduced to Mannar Island and the Vanni in northern Sri Lanka by Arab traders
bed tea – early morning cuppa served to you in bed
bodhi tree – large spreading tree *(Ficus religiosa)*; the tree under which the Buddha sat when he attained enlightment, and the many descendants grown from cuttings of this tree
Bodhisattva – divine being who, although capable of attaining *nirvana*, chooses to reside on the human plane to help ordinary people attain salvation
boutique – naturalised Portuguese word for a street stall or small shop
Brahmi – early Indian script used from the 5th century BC
bund – built-up bank or dyke surrounding a *tank*
Burgher – Sri Lankan Eurasian, generally descended from Portuguese-Sinhalese or Dutch-Sinhalese intermarriage

cadjan – coconut fronds woven into mats and used as building material
Ceylon – British-colonial name for Sri Lanka
chetiya – Buddhist shrine
Chola – powerful ancient South Indian kingdom that invaded Sri Lanka on several occasions
coir – mat or rope made from coconut fibres
copra – dried coconut kernel used to make cooking oil and also exported for use in the manufacture of confectionery
crore – 10 million of anything, but most often rupees
CTB – Central (formerly Ceylon) Transport Board, the state bus network
Culavamsa – 'Minor Chronicle', which continues the history commenced in the *Mahavamsa* up to 1758

dagoba – Buddhist monument composed of a solid hemisphere containing relics of the Buddha or a Buddhist saint; a *stupa*
devale – complex designed for worshipping a Hindu or Sri Lankan deity; the deities are also faithful servants of the Buddha
dharma – the word used by both Hindus and Buddhists to refer to their respective moral codes of behaviour

eelam – Tamil word for precious land
EPDP – Eelam People's Democratic Party

gala – rock
ganga – river
gedige – hollow temple with extremely thick walls and a corbelled roof
geta bera – Kandyan double-ended drum
gopuram – soaring pyramidal gateway of a Hindu temple; part of a style of architecture found principally in South India
guardstones – carved ornamental stones that flank doorways or entrances to temples
gurulu – legendary bird that preys on snakes, used as an image in carved *raksha* masks

Hanuman – the monkey king from the *Ramayana*

illama – a gravel-bearing stratum likely to hold gemstones
IPKF – Indian Peace Keeping Force; the Indian Army contingent present in northern Sri Lanka from 1987 to 1990

Jataka – stories of the previous lives of the Buddha
juggernaut – huge, extravagantly decorated temple cart dragged through the streets during Hindu festivals (sometimes called a 'car')
JVP – Janatha Vimukthi Peramuna (People's Liberation Army); a Sinhalese Marxist revolutionary organisation that rose up in 1971 and again in the late 1980s

kachcheri – administrative office
kadé – Sinhalese word for *boutique*
Karava – fisherfolk of Indian descent
karma – Hindu-Buddhist principle of retributive justice for past deeds
Kataragama – see *Murugan*
kiri bath – dessert of rice cooked in coconut milk; it also has ritual significance
kolam – meaning costume or guise, it refers to masked dance-drama; also the rice-flour designs that adorn thresholds of buildings in Tamil areas
kovil – Hindu temple; most Sri Lankan *kovils* are dedicated to the worship of Shiva
kulam – Tamil word for *tank*

lakh – 100,000; a standard unit of measurement in Sri Lanka and India
lingam – phallic symbol; symbol of Shiva
LTTE – Liberation Tigers of Tamil Eelam, also known as the Tamil Tigers; separatist group fighting for an independent Tamil Eelam in the north and east

Maha – northeast monsoon season

Mahavamsa – 'Great Chronicle', a written Sinhalese history running from the arrival of Prince Vijaya from India in the 6th century BC, through the meeting of King Devanampiyatissa with *Mahinda*, and on to the great kings of Anuradhapura

Mahaweli Ganga – Sri Lanka's longest river, which starts in the Hill Country near Adam's Peak, flows through Kandy and eventually reaches the sea near Trincomalee

Mahayana – later form of Buddhism prevalent in Korea, Japan and China, which literally means 'greater vehicle'. It emphasises the *Bodhisattva* ideal, which teaches the renunciation of *nirvana* to help other beings to reach enlightenment

Mahinda – son of the Indian Buddhist emperor Ashoka, credited with introducing Buddhism to Sri Lanka

mahout – elephant rider or master

Maitreya – future Buddha

makara – mythical beast that is a cross between a lion, a pig and an elephant, commonly carved in the balustrade of temple staircases

makara torana – ornamental archway

mandapaya – a raised platform with decorative pillars

masala – mix (often spices)

mawatha – avenue or street; abbreviated to 'Mw'

moonstone – semiprecious stone; also a carved stone 'doorstep' at temple entrances

mudra – symbolic hand position of a Buddha image

Murugan – Hindu god of war; also known as *Skanda* and *Kataragama*

naga – snake; also applies to snake deities and spirits

naga raksha – *raksha* mask featuring a 'coiffure' of writhing cobras

nirvana – ultimate aim of Buddhists, final release from the cycle of existence

nuwara – city

ola – leaves of the talipot palm; used in manuscripts and traditional books

oruva – outrigger canoe

oya – stream or small river

PA – People's Alliance; a coalition including the *SLFP* founded in 1994

paddy – unhusked rice; field where rice is grown

Pali – the language in which the Buddhist scriptures were originally recorded

palmyra – tall palm tree found in the dry northern region

perahera – procession, usually with dancers, drummers and elephants

pirivena – centre of learning attached to monastery

pokuna – artificial pond

poya – full-moon day; every *poya* is a holiday

puja – 'respect', offering or prayers

rajakariya – 'workers for the king', the tradition of feudal service

raksha – type of mask used in parades and festivals

Rakshasas – legendary rulers of Sri Lanka, who could also assume the form of demons; led by *Rawana*

Ramayana – ancient story of Rama and Sita and their conflict with *Rawana*

Rawana – 'demon king of Lanka' who abducts Rama's beautiful wife Sita in the Hindu epic the *Ramayana*

relic chamber – chamber in a *dagoba* housing a relic of the Buddha or a saint and representing the Buddhist concept of the cosmos

Ruhunu – ancient southern centre of Sinhalese power near Tissamaharama that survived even when Anuradhapura and Polonnaruwa fell to Indian invaders; also spelt Ruhuna

samudra – large *tank* or inland sea

Sangamitta – sister of *Mahinda*; she brought the sacred bodhi tree sapling from Bodhgaya in India

sanni – devil-dance mask

Sangha – the community of Buddhist monks; in Sri Lanka, an influential group divided into several Nikayas (orders)

Sanskrit – ancient Indian language, the oldest known member of the family of Indo-European languages

sari – traditional garment worn by women

school pen – ballpoint pen, often requested (or demanded!) from tourists by Sri Lankan children

sikhara – dome- or pyramid-shaped structure rising above the shrine room of a Hindu *kovil*

sinha – lion

Sinhala – language of the Sinhalese people

Sinhalese – majority population of Sri Lanka; principally Sinhala-speaking Buddhists

Skanda – see *Murugan*

SLFP – Sri Lanka Freedom Party

stupa – see *dagoba*

Tamils – a people of South Indian origin, comprising the largest minority population in Sri Lanka; principally Tamil-speaking Hindus

tank – artificial water-storage lake or reservoir; many of the tanks in Sri Lanka are very large and ancient

Theravada – orthodox form of Buddhism practised in Sri Lanka and Southeast Asia, which is characterised by its adherence to the *Pali* canon

unavakam – Tamil word for *boutique*

UNP – United National Party; the first political party to hold power in Sri Lanka after independence

vahalkada – solid panel of sculpture

vatadage – circular relic house consisting of a small central *dagoba* flanked by Buddha images and encircled by columns

Vedas – Hindu sacred books; a collection of sacred hymns composed in preclassical Sanskrit during the 2nd millennium BC and divided into four books: Rig-Veda, Yajur-Veda, Sama-Veda and Atharva-Veda

Veddahs – original inhabitants of Sri Lanka prior to the arrival of the Sinhalese from India; also called the *Wanniyala-aetto*

vel – trident; the god *Murugan* is often depicted carrying a *vel*

vihara, **viharaya** – Buddhist complex, including a shrine containing a statue of the Buddha, a congregational hall and a monks' house

Wanniyala-aetto – see *Veddahs*

wewa – see *tank*

yak bera – double-ended drum used in the South

Yala – southwest monsoon season

Behind the Scenes

THIS BOOK

This 10th edition of *Sri Lanka* was updated by Joe Cummings, Mark Elliott, Ryan Ver Berkmoes and Teresa Cannon. Tony Wheeler wrote and researched the first three editions of *Sri Lanka*, John Noble tackled the 4th edition, and, together with Susan Forsyth, updated the 5th edition. Christine Niven updated the 6th and 7th editions, the 8th edition was updated by Verity Campbell, and Richard Plunkett and Brigitte Ellemor updated the 9th edition. This guidebook was commissioned in Lonely Planet's Melbourne office, and produced by the following:

Commissioning Editors Janine Eberle, Lucy Monie, Marg Toohey
Coordinating Editor Laura Stansfeld
Coordinating Cartographer Joshua Geoghegan
Coordinating Layout Designer Jacqueline McLeod
Managing Cartographer Shahara Ahmed
Assisting Editors Brooke Clark, Emma Gilmour, Liz Heynes, Joanne Newell, Simon Williamson
Cover Designer Marika Kozak
Project Manager Fabrice Rocher
Language Content Coordinator Quentin Frayne

Thanks to Glenn Beanland, Jessa Boanas-Dewes, Sally Darmody, Ryan Evans, Martin Heng, Laura Jane, Kate McDonald, Trent Paton, Mick Ruff, Wibowo Rusli, Suzannah Shwer, Katie Thuy Bui, Gabbi Wilson, Celia Wood.

THANKS
JOE CUMMINGS

Among the many people who helped with my research in Sri Lanka, I'd like to especially thank the following: Sarojinie Ellawella, Sanjeev Gardner, Ethan Gelber, Druvi Gunasekara, Ruud Hulscher, R Jayaraj, Jeremy Rajiah, Faiesz Samad, Helga De Silva, Arun Tampoe, Andrew Taylor and Asela Wavita.

TERESA CANNON

Many people assisted in numerous ways in making my part of this project come together. Kulari Lokugé spoke enthusiastically of the life and customs of her homeland, while Mala and Rodney Arambewela weathered an absolutely drenching storm to provide information. Chandani Lokugé gave me many details, not just on her area of expertise – postcolonial literature – but also on legalities and architecture in Sri Lanka. Narvein Perera and his family were generous with hospitality, introductions and information. To Tilak Arachchi go many thanks for his guidance and thoughtfulness. While I conducted interviews, the staff at the Galle Face Hotel set a timely and reassuring pace as they delivered copious quantities of soda and lime.

At home, Peter and Aislinn kept suggestions and jokes flowing.

And at Lonely Planet, thanks to Janine and Lucy for their willing assistance, especially as I reacquainted myself with systems such as Freddie, Felix and FTP. To Joe, many thanks for his patience and coordination; thanks also to my fellow authors for their cooperation and suggestions. Finally, thanks to Laura, whose intelligent questions continued to make the writing process a fascinating and privileged one.

MARK ELLIOTT

It is impossible to thank all of the dozens of kind, helpful people who made my research so much easier. Nonetheless, special thanks are due to Ethan Gelber; Ramesh Thambalaringham in Batti; Wendy van den Beld and friends in Ampara; Seman, Raheem, Ranga and Santa in Arugam Bay; the Dissanayake family in Inginyagala, MC Manikkavasagar in Vavuniya; Richard Pereira at Namal Oya; Yolanda Foster in Mannar; Joseph, CMS Sriganandam and Brett Moore in Jaffna; Dorothea Schmidt for Mullaittivu insights; Soranya, Jo and James; Charlotte in the Vanni; Alan Woodburn and Lars Stuewe in Uppuveli; Esther Oh in Muttur; and Kathy Brown, Nimal, Rasika, Michael, Elaine, Mohammad Faiz, Sofia Macedo and Nuno Aramac.

Thanks also to my fellow authors and the whole team at Lonely Planet. Most of all a huge hug to my unbeatable parents and my long-suffering wife Dani for their love, inspiration and constant support. I owe them everything.

RYAN VER BERKMOES

Heartfelt thanks to the people in Sri Lanka who shared their stories of survival and loss with me during my visits. Seeing the devastation in January and then witnessing so many examples of resilience and rebirth nine months later was both moving and inspirational.

Individuals who helped me in my research include Chandima Hemakumara, who used the right side of his brain as he buzzed me around Galle. Sunil Abeyweera drove with precision and vital alacrity. Ajith Goonewardene provided welcome friendship and assistance. Christopher Ong and Karl Steinberg shared their passion for Galle with me – it is contagious. And of course Erin Corrigan gave me much to be thankful for when I returned to my own home.

At Lonely Planet, commissioning editor Janine Eberle knew all the poop and is a good friend to boot. And thanks to all the authors, editors, cartographers and more whose commitment and creativity can be found on every page of this book.

OUR READERS

Many thanks to the travellers who used the last edition and wrote to us with helpful hints, useful advice and interesting anecdotes:

A Andrew Adu-Boateng, Puck Akerman, Uwe Albertz, Michel Albregts, Maz Alldritt, Catherine Allen, Pauline Allen, Linzy & Stuart Allison, Juliette Amielle, Caroline Anderson, Mikael Andersson, Mr & Mrs Andlauer, Peter Andoetoe, Silvia Andrea, Sharon Andrews, Bala Anton, Alison Arnott, Maria & Theo Arp,

Lauren Ascroft, Catherine Austin, Nigel Austin, Elizabeth Ayarra **B** Tomer Bachar, Aloid Bajgar, Robert Bakker, Nathan Ball, Nicole Ball, Gal Barak, Anna Barnard, John Barnett, Brenda Barrett, Delano Barros, Kylie Barsdell, Carolyn Bartlett, RN Barton, Keith Bason, Simon Bather, Susanne Baumgartner, Kinta Beaver, Jon Beckley, Harry Beekman, Carola Beers, Thomas Benedikter, Lisa Bentham, Martina Beran, Matt Berry, Lauren Beswick, Steven-Shahid Bhatty, Pietro Blanchessi, Janit Bianic, Louisa Bienvenue, Debora Birio, Justin Blake, Bill Bliss, Rod Boakes, Manuela Boehm, Julia Boff, Lisbeth Bögli, Mary Bond, Laetitia Bonnet, Martinette Boonekamp, B Booth, Michael Borden, Helen Bowyer, Birgit Brandmeier, Silvia & Paul Brandt, Lisa Brennan, Susan Brennan, Adam Brett, Kathryn Brierley, Klaus Bronny, Angela & Grant Brown, Elspeth Brown, Mark & Cielito Brownbridge, Mark Browning, Andrea Brugnoli, Stefano Brunori, Michael Bucksmith, Veronica Budd, Greg Butler, Roger Bymolt **C** Lucy Campbell, Nick Campion, Dennis Candy, Elisa Cantoni, Francesca Cappitelli, Sheilagh Cardosa, Vicki Carmichael, Simone Carr, Sid Carter, George Casley, Heather Cassidy, Ed Chambers, Ian Chaplin, Anne Chevallier, Lenos Christidis, Michaela & Mark Christophers, Alice Clapp, Gillian Clark, Shelley Cockayne, Alan Colegrave, Marie Coleman, Donna Collins, Anna Cooper, Paul Copeland, Arja Copperwheat, F Corveleljn, Brian Cossey, Con Lotsios, Sarah Cotton, Harri Coyte, Helen Crisp, Sjaak Cuppen, Jenny Cutler **D** Jackie Dahaby, Maartje Dammers, Martin Dammrich, Brian Dandy, Jantje Daun, Ariëtte de Bruin, Cindy & Jill de Kok, Dane de Kretser, Rona de Loux, Aniek de Poorter, Bertrand de Saint Andre, Udaya de Silva, Joke de Vlas, Will de Wolf, Andrea Dye, Chantal Demaire, John Demshar, Barry den Reijer, Skye Dengate, Duncan Denley, Anne Densham, Mark Desrochers, Ange Devitt, Nihal Dharmarth, Klaus Diefenbeck, Paul Diggins, Kevin Dillow, Bernhard Doerr, Del Doucette, Albert Downs, Randell Drum, Craig Dugan **E** Juliet Eardley, Gabrielle Earl, Oliver Eichelberg, Jan Eisenring, Carly Eldridge, Sophia Elek, Mark Ellis, Gemma Emiowicz, Logan Envitesse, Arlanda Erzen, Huw Evans **F** Paul Falworth, Robert Fay, Carl Fell, Alberto Fernandez, Farncisco Fernandez, Marta Fernández Olmos, Carolina Ferrandis, Nuno Ferreira, Lesley Fidler, JA Finch, Victoria Findlay, Eliot Fineberg, Georg Fink, FJ Firmstone, Daryn Fletcher, Jo Fletcher-Lee, Carmelo Flores, Brigitte Foeller, Andrew Forsyth, Lawrence Foster, Angela Fox, Ruth & Derek Foxman, Gerard Franci, Suzanne Franks, J A Fraser, Mark Frick, Kate Frucher, Tim Fudge, John Fullbrook, Robert Fullerton, Louise Furniss, Saul Fust **G** Narash Gajendran, Carol Gallagher, Mark Gallon, Barbara Gamage, David Gardiner, Andrew Gardner, Tommy Gelbman, Judith Gibbs, Fionn Gill, Louisa & Caroline Gill, Tom Gillhespy, Judy Gilmour, Victor Gimenez Morote, Joerg Glag, Victoria Glendinning, Magdalena Gniot, Luisa Goergen, Morgan Goff, Florian Goger, YH Goh, Emily Goodall, Primož Goršic, DJ Graham, Dave Gray, Mike & Christabel Grimmer, Adam Gross, Martha Grove **H** Mariella Habring, Jennifer Haire, Beccy Hall, Clare Hampton, K Hansen, John Hardiman, Franny Hardy, Kathrine Hartvigsen, Rita, Cynthia & John Hawes, James Hawkins, Brenda Hayes, Chris Hayward, Pieter & Emily Heesterbeek, Paul Heinrich, Cathy Hembry, Jan Hennings, Brenda Herbert, Ivo & Lucia Hettelaar, Michiel Hillenius, Geoff Hiller, Angela Hodgson, Ketil

Hofslett, Leigh Holding, Bill Holdsworth, Ursula Holman, Kate & Will Holme, Jan Horak, David & Alicia Horemans, Geraldine Horner, Howard Houck, Anna Hruba, Claude Hubert, Alex Hughes, Barbara Hunziker, Alex Hutchings, Petronella Hutchinson **I** Ili Ilonka, Ruwan Indika, Lindesay Irvine, Dave Irwin, Daryl & Sally Isaac, Debbie Isbell, Taishi Ito **J** Simon & Sharon Jackson, Philip Jacobs, Susan James, Simon Janssen, Marie Javins, Dushara Jayasinghe, Erik Jelinek, Kate Jenkinson, Peter Jensen, Ramya Jirasinghe Hewavitharne, Alexandra Johnson, Anna Johnson, Andrew Jones, Richard Jones **K** Kann Kalies, Ajay Kamalakaran, Haemish Kane, Martina Karli, Shlomi Kaztin, David Kerkhoff, Gavin Kerns, Amanda Kerr, Deb Kesterson, C Kim, Janis Kirpitis, Thomas Knapp, Birgit Knopse, Eric Knopse, Peter Koehler, George Kokar, Tibor Kramer, Iflal Kuddoos, Lam Kuo, Jane Kyme **L** Hans Landskroon, David Lane, Maureen Larter, Fiona Latham, Justin Lau Chon Lam, Irina Lauke, Anne Lavandon, Paul Lawrance, Stanley Lawson, Sang-Ho Lee, Anthony Leenknegt, Nicole Lehn, Cindy-Marie Leicester, Tore Lein-Mathisen, Debbie Letchford, Sally Lewis, Mei Petrie Lind, William Lindfors, Susan Lindner, Tom Linhart, Dai Liyanage, Jeanne Lodge, Lulu Lunn, Kelly Lynch **M** Joanna MacDonald, Lucy Maclaren, Jan Magnusson, Gareth & Emma Maguire, Martin Mallin, Oliver Mandetzky, Tom Mangan, Warren Mansell, Pauline Marett, Kevin Marino, Jennifer Marsh, Alan Martin, Catherine Martin, Silke & Raynald Martin, Chris Martinus, Tina Mary, Daniel Masny, Andrea Mason, Ben Masters, Catriona Matheson, Zehr Matthias, Stephanie Maurer, Leonard May, Vincent Mayot, Eisel Mazard, Bob Mcausland, Sian McClure, Alison McCormack, Bobby McCormack, Irene McCullough, Sarah McCully, Lauren McFarlane, Gerald McGrath, Kyla McGrath, Laura McGuiness, Elizabeth McIlwaine, Kip McKay, Sandra McKenzie, Kevin Meadowcroft, John Meers, Nik Mehta, Suzie Meiklejohn, Marek Mengel, David Menhinick, David Merhinich, Silvia Merli, Helen Merriman, Jan Mertens, Alex Meyrick, Georgina Middleton, Tara Middlewood, Silvi Mielke, Robert Miller, Sarah Milner, Carmen Monasterio, Manoja & John Monro, Angela Moore, Josephine Moran, Nicolas Moroz, Margaret Morrison, Tony Moss, Koli Mukhopadhyay, Veronique Muller, Anne Munks, Sonja Munnix, Alan Murphy, Terry Murphy, Tony Murphy, Alysha Murray, Patrick Mussel, Abi Myles **N** Jochem Nagtegaal, Jimmy Nakajima, Angela Neub, Jodi Newsome, Judy Newton, Guy Nicholson, Elisabeth Nicolson, Christian & Anita Niederer, Alexandre Noel, Sam North, Rosemary Northcote, Jamie Norwell, Roy Nye **O** Caroline Oberndorfer, Monika Olischar, Jonas Olsson, Barbara Oppelaar, Karen O'Reilly, Martin O'Reilly, Vanessa Osbourne, Jay O'Shea, R Oswald **P** Mary Palmer, Joy Palmer-Cooper, Melvin Palmiano, Karen Parker, Allan Parkinson, Nikesh Patel, Benjamin Pereira, Nihal Perera, Snezhana Peretyagina, Per Persson, Robert Petty, Peter Phillips, Inka Pibilova, Bettina Pieri, Nilanka Pieris, Claudine Pinel, Maresa & Valter Piucco, Elliot Podwill, Nigel Pogmore, Kirsty Pontifex, Adrian Porter, Beate Prellwitz, Jim Price, Janine Prudhoe, R E Purnell, Bernard Puttaert **R** Venkata Ramana, Diana Rayfield, Chris & Wanda Redfern, Ceri Reed, Jon Rees, Miles Reid, Clementine Reijrink, Kathrin Reinke, Kay Renius, Jordan Revah, Duncan Reynolds, Mandy Rhodes, Sarah Richards, James Riley, Gillian Rimington, Katrina Roads, Terry Robert, David Roberts, Alan Robertson, Charlie Robinson, Tara Robinson, Katy Rochester, Beverley Rogers, Olesya Romanyuk, Karen & Tom Rops, Gregory Rose, Nils Rosmuller, Jens Roth, Jay Ruchamkin, Saitov Ruslan, Rowena Russell, Wies Rutten, Wolfgang Ruttkowski, Jon Ryan **S** Willem Saher, Matsui Saiko, Thomas Sainsbury, Ben Salter, Sue Samad, Alex Saro, Sebastian Scanlain, Thomas Schaller, Christian Schmidt, Markus Schmidt, Georg Schmolzer, Gil Schneider, Georg Schober, Marian Schokker, Ulric Schollaert, Nanja Schoonheim, Astrid Schrocker, Olly Scott, Robyn Secomb, Christian Sedelmayer, Johann Selvarajah, Parakrama Seneviratne, Rajvi & Ash Shah, Rhea Shah, David Sharman, Tony Shaw, Sam Shepherd, Tsur Shezaf, Val Shingleton, Yariv Ben Shooshan, David Simpson, Ashok Singh, Rajinderpal Singh, Nathan Sinnott, Kirsten Skriver, Angelika Skrubel, Irene Slegt, Preston Smith, Sandie Smith, Eddie Soulier, Eric Spanjaard, James Spratt, Maire & Mark Spurrier, Tony Stabile, Jonny Stevenson, Claire Stewart, Renske Stichbury, Rosie Stowell, Rainer & Ellen Strassfeld, Maja Strünkelnberg, Tim Sturrock, Yair Suari, Maggie Suggett, Sheeja Sukumaran, Steve Swallow, Christian Szeglat **T** Emily Taylor, Ian Taylor, Paul Taylor, Derek Teeley, Fritz Thier, Matthew Thomas, Paul Thomas, Sheila Thomas, Nicola Thompson, Carsten Thomsen, Craig Thomson, Craig & Wendy Thomson, Gene Thune, Gabor Tiroler, Jimmy Tornestrand, Laura Towers, Reinhard Troeger, Deborah Tweedy **U** Viviane

SEND US YOUR FEEDBACK

We love to hear from travellers – your comments keep us on our toes and help make our books better. Our well-travelled team reads every word on what you loved or loathed about this book. Although we cannot reply individually to postal submissions, we always guarantee that your feedback goes straight to the appropriate authors, in time for the next edition. Each person who sends us information is thanked in the next edition – and the most useful submissions are rewarded with a free book. See the Behind the Scenes section.

To send us your updates – and find out about Lonely Planet events, newsletters and travel news – visit our award-winning website: **www.lonelyplanet.com/feedback**.

Note: We may edit, reproduce and incorporate your comments in Lonely Planet products such as guidebooks, websites and digital products, so let us know if you don't want your comments reproduced or your name acknowledged. For a copy of our privacy policy, go to www.lonelyplanet .com/privacy.

Uhlmann, Alex Unsworth, Jakub Urbanski **V** Willemijn van Asselt, Monique van Bokkum, Sandra van Cadsand, Cocky van Dam, Bert van den Broeck, Margaret van der Eeze, Philip van der Klift, Suzian van der Maas, Jan van der Zaan, Jan & Brigitte van Kessel, RHJ Egeter van Kuyk, Angelique van Lieshout, Diana van Oort, Trudy van Schie, Peter van Spall, Evert van Wageningen, Fam van Wesemael, Ludmila Vankova, Carl-Johan Vincentzen, Charlotte Visser, Torsten & Patricia von Bartenwerffer, Maike Voorhuis, Sonja Voss **W** Axel Wabenhorst, Jonathan Wager, Juergen Wagner, Smurf Walker, Sue Wall, Caroline Walsh, Erin Walters, Henry Warren, Andy Waterman, Kelly Watts, Sarah Webb, YAS Weenathungur, Alison Weller, Peter Weller, SW & JD Weller, Sylvia Wetherell, Louise Wheeler, Captain White, Gary White, Joanna White, Amanda Whitehead, Dan Wigmore, Thanula Wijewardane, Stephen Williams, Sylvia Jean Wilson, Alison Wittenberg, Polly Woinwright, Ron Wong, Mark Woodard, Sandra Woplatek, Alison Wren **Y** Alice Young, Louise Ysart **Z** Orville Zander, Anna Zarebska, Michael Zimmermann

ACKNOWLEDGMENTS

Many thanks to the following for the use of their content:

Globe on back cover ©Mountain High Maps 1993 Digital Wisdom, Inc.

Index

000 Map pages
000 Photograph pages

INDEX

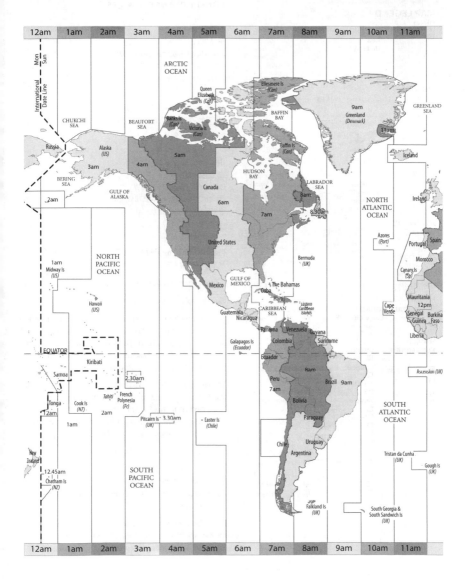

MAP LEGEND

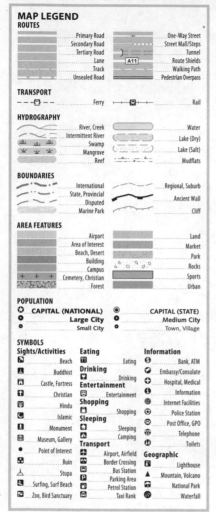

ROUTES

	Primary Road		One-Way Street
	Secondary Road		Street Mall/Steps
	Tertiary Road		Tunnel
	Lane	A11	Route Shields
	Track		Walking Path
	Unsealed Road		Pedestrian Overpass

TRANSPORT

	Ferry		Rail

HYDROGRAPHY

	River, Creek		Water
	Intermittent River		Lake (Dry)
	Swamp		Lake (Salt)
	Mangrove		Mudflats
	Reef		

BOUNDARIES

	International		Regional, Suburb
	State, Provincial		Ancient Wall
	Disputed		Cliff
	Marine Park		

AREA FEATURES

	Airport		Land
	Area of Interest		Market
	Beach, Desert		Park
	Building		Rocks
	Campus		Sports
+ + +	Cemetery, Christian		Urban
	Forest		

POPULATION

○	**CAPITAL (NATIONAL)**	◉	**CAPITAL (STATE)**
●	**Large City**	●	**Medium City**
●	Small City	○	Town, Village

SYMBOLS

Sights/Activities
- Beach
- Buddhist
- Castle, Fortress
- Christian
- Hindu
- Islamic
- Monument
- Museum, Gallery
- Point of Interest
- Ruin
- Stupa
- Surfing, Surf Beach
- Zoo, Bird Sanctuary

Eating
- Eating

Drinking
- Drinking

Entertainment
- Entertainment

Shopping
- Shopping

Sleeping
- Sleeping
- Camping

Transport
- Airport, Airfield
- Border Crossing
- Bus Station
- Parking Area
- Petrol Station
- Taxi Rank

Information
- Bank, ATM
- Embassy/Consulate
- Hospital, Medical
- Information
- Internet Facilities
- Police Station
- Post Office, GPO
- Telephone
- Toilets

Geographic
- Lighthouse
- Mountain, Volcano
- National Park
- Waterfall

LONELY PLANET OFFICES

Australia
Head Office
Locked Bag 1, Footscray, Victoria 3011
☎ 03 8379 8000, fax 03 8379 8111
talk2us@lonelyplanet.com.au

USA
150 Linden St, Oakland, CA 94607
☎ 510 893 8555, toll free 800 275 8555
fax 510 893 8572
info@lonelyplanet.com

UK
72–82 Rosebery Ave,
Clerkenwell, London EC1R 4RW
☎ 020 7841 9000, fax 020 7841 9001
go@lonelyplanet.co.uk

Published by Lonely Planet Publications Pty Ltd
ABN 36 005 607 983